VIRGINIA

SCIENCE
FUSiON

fusion [FYOO • zhuhn] a combination of two
or more things that releases energy

This **Interactive Student Edition** belongs to

_____

Teacher/Room

_____

HOLT McDOUGAL

 HOUGHTON MIFFLIN HARCOURT

Consulting Authors

Michael A. DiSpezio

Global Educator
North Falmouth, Massachusetts

Michael DiSpezio is a Renaissance educator who moved from the research laboratory of a Nobel Prize winner to the K–12 science classroom. He has authored or co-authored numerous textbooks and written more than 25 trade books. For nearly a decade he worked with the JASON Project, under the auspices of the National Geographic Society, where he designed curriculum, wrote lessons, and hosted dozens of studio and location broadcasts. Over the past two decades, he has developed supplementary material for organizations and shows that include PBS *Scientific American Frontiers, Discover* magazine, and the Discovery Channel. He has extended his reach outside the United States and into topics of crucial importance today. To all his projects, he brings his extensive background in science and his expertise in classroom teaching at the elementary, middle, and high school levels.

Marjorie Frank

Science Writer and Content-Area Reading Specialist
Brooklyn, New York

An educator and linguist by training, a writer and poet by nature, Marjorie Frank has authored and designed a generation of instructional materials in all subject areas, including past HMH Science programs. Her other credits include authoring science issues of an award-winning children's magazine; writing game-based digital assessments in math, reading, and language arts; and serving as instructional designer and co-author of pioneering school-to-work software for Classroom, Inc., a nonprofit organization dedicated to improving reading and math skills for middle and high school learners. She wrote lyrics and music for *Science Songs,* which was an American Library Association nominee for notable recording. In addition, she has served on the adjunct faculty of Hunter, Manhattan, and Brooklyn Colleges, teaching courses in science methods, literacy, and writing.

Acknowledgments for Covers

Front cover: *satellite dish* ©Robert Glusic/Getty Images; *lava* ©Bruce Omori/epa/Corbis; *mountain biker* ©Jerome Prevost/TempSport/Corbis; *mushroom rock* ©John Elk III/Alamy; *water droplet* ©L. Clarke/Corbis.

Back cover: *fossil* ©Yoshishi Tanaka/amana images/Getty Images; *Aurora Borealis* ©Wayne R. Bilenduke/Photographer's Choice/Getty Images; *racecar* ©David Madison/Corbis; *x-ray* ©Lester Lefkowitz/Getty Images.

Printed in the U.S.A.

ISBN 978-0-547-79837-0

9 10 0877 20 19 18 17 16 15 14

4500480986   BCDEFG

Michael R. Heithaus

Director, School of Environment and Society
Associate Professor, Department of Biological Sciences
Florida International University
North Miami, Florida

Mike Heithaus joined the Florida International University Biology Department in 2003. He has served as Director of the Marine Sciences Program and is now Director of the School of Environment and Society, which brings together the natural and social sciences and humanities to develop solutions to today's environmental challenges. While earning his doctorate, he began the research that grew into the Shark Bay Ecosystem Project in Western Australia, with which he still works. Back in the United States, he served as a Research Fellow with National Geographic, using remote imaging in his research and hosting a 13-part *Crittercam* television series on the National Geographic Channel. His current research centers on predator-prey interactions among vertebrates, such as tiger sharks, dolphins, dugongs, sea turtles, and cormorants.

Donna M. Ogle

Professor of Reading and Language
National-Louis University
Chicago, Illinois

Creator of the well-known KWL strategy, Donna Ogle has directed many staff development projects translating theory and research into school practice in middle and secondary schools throughout the United States. She is a past president of the International Reading Association and has served as a consultant on literacy projects worldwide. Her extensive international experience includes coordinating the Reading and Writing for Critical Thinking Project in Eastern Europe, developing an integrated curriculum for a USAID Afghan Education Project, and speaking and consulting on projects in several Latin American countries and in Asia. Her books include *Coming Together as Readers; Reading Comprehension: Strategies for Independent Learners; All Children Read;* and *Literacy for a Democratic Society.*

Program Advisors/Reviewers

Content Reviewers

Paul D. Asimow, PhD
Professor of Geology and Geochemistry
Division of Geological and Planetary Sciences
California Institute of Technology
Pasadena, CA

Laura K. Baumgartner, PhD
Postdoctoral Researcher
Molecular, Cellular, and Developmental Biology
University of Colorado
Boulder, CO

Eileen Cashman, PhD
Professor
Department of Environmental Resources Engineering
Humboldt State University
Arcata, CA

Hilary Clement Olson, PhD
Research Scientist Associate V
Institute for Geophysics, Jackson School of Geosciences
The University of Texas at Austin
Austin, TX

Joe W. Crim, PhD
Professor Emeritus
Department of Cellular Biology
The University of Georgia
Athens, GA

Elizabeth A. De Stasio, PhD
Raymond H. Herzog Professor of Science
Professor of Biology
Department of Biology
Lawrence University
Appleton, WI

Dan Franck, PhD
Botany Education Consultant
Chatham, NY

Julia R. Greer, PhD
Assistant Professor of Materials Science and Mechanics
Division of Engineering and Applied Science
California Institute of Technology
Pasadena, CA

John E. Hoover, PhD
Professor
Department of Biology
Millersville University
Millersville, PA

William H. Ingham, PhD
Professor (Emeritus)
Department of Physics and Astronomy
James Madison University
Harrisonburg, VA

Charles W. Johnson, PhD
Chairman, Division of Natural Sciences, Mathematics and Physical Education
Associate Professor of Physics
South Georgia College
Douglas, GA

Program Advisors/Reviewers *(continued)*

Tatiana A. Krivosheev, PhD
Associate Professor of Physics
Department of Natural Sciences
Clayton State University
Morrow, GA

Joseph A. McClure, PhD
Associate Professor Emeritus
Department of Physics
Georgetown University
Washington, DC

Mark Moldwin, PhD
Professor of Space Sciences
Atmospheric, Oceanic and
Space Sciences
University of Michigan
Ann Arbor, MI

Russell Patrick, PhD
Professor of Physics
Department of Biology,
Chemistry, and Physics
Southern Polytechnic State
University
Marietta, GA

Patricia M. Pauley, PhD
*Meteorologist, Data Assimilation
Group*
Naval Research Laboratory
Monterey, CA

Stephen F. Pavkovic, PhD
Professor Emeritus
Department of Chemistry
Loyola University of Chicago
Chicago, IL

L. Jeanne Perry, PhD
Director (Retired)
Protein Expression Technology
Center
Institute for Genomics and
Proteomics
University of California, Los
Angeles
Los Angeles, CA

Kenneth H. Rubin, PhD
Professor
Department of Geology and
Geophysics
University of Hawaii
Honolulu, HI

Brandon E. Schwab, PhD
Associate Professor
Department of Geology
Humboldt State University
Arcata, CA

Marllin L. Simon, PhD
Associate Professor
Department of Physics
Auburn University
Auburn, AL

Larry Stookey, PE
Upper Iowa University
Wausau, WI

Kim Withers, PhD
Associate Research Scientist
Center for Coastal Studies
Texas A&M University-Corpus
Christi
Corpus Christi, TX

Matthew A. Wood, PhD
Professor
Department of Physics & Space
Sciences
Florida Institute of Technology
Melbourne, FL

Adam D. Woods, PhD
Associate Professor
Department of Geological
Sciences
California State University,
Fullerton
Fullerton, CA

Natalie Zayas, MS, EdD
Lecturer
Division of Science and
Environmental Policy
California State University,
Monterey Bay
Seaside, CA

Teacher Reviewers

Deanne Barnett
Colonial Heights Middle School
Colonial Heights, VA

Ann Barrette, MST
Whitman Middle School
Wauwatosa, WI

Barbara Brege
Crestwood Middle School
Kentwood, MI

**Katherine Eaton Campbell,
M Ed**
Chicago Public Schools-Area 2
Office
Chicago, IL

**Karen Cavalluzzi, M Ed,
NBCT**
Sunny Vale Middle School
Blue Springs, MO

Katie Demorest, MA Ed Tech
Marshall Middle School
Marshall, MI

Jennifer Eddy, M Ed
Lindale Middle School
Linthicum, MD

Tully Fenner
George Fox Middle School
Pasadena, MD

Dave Grabski, MS Ed
P. J. Jacobs Junior High School
Stevens Point, WI

Amelia C. Holm, M Ed
McKinley Middle School
Kenosha, WI

Ben Hondorp
Creekside Middle School
Zeeland, MI

George E. Hunkele, M Ed
Harborside Middle School
Milford, CT

Jude Kesl
Science Teaching Specialist 6-8
Milwaukee Public Schools
Milwaukee, WI

Joe Kubasta, M Ed
Rockwood Valley Middle School
St. Louis, MO

Mary Larsen
Science Instructional Coach
Helena Public Schools
Helena, MT

Angie Larson
Bernard Campbell Middle School
Lee's Summit, MO

Dat Le, PhD, NBCT
Arlington Public Schools,
Science Office
Arlington, VA

Christy Leier
Horizon Middle School
Moorhead, MN

Michele K. Lombard, M Ed
Swanson Middle School
Arlington, VA

Helen Mihm, NBCT
Crofton Middle School
Crofton, MD

Jeff Moravec, Sr., MS Ed
Teaching Specialist
Milwaukee Public Schools
Milwaukee, WI

**Nancy Kawecki Nega, MST,
NBCT, PAESMT**
Churchville Middle School
Elmhurst, IL

Mark E. Poggensee, MS Ed
Elkhorn Middle School
Elkhorn, WI

Sherry Rich
Bernard Campbell Middle School
Lee's Summit, MO

Mike Szydlowski, M Ed
Science Coordinator
Columbia Public Schools
Columbia, MO

Nichole Trzasko, M Ed
Clarkston Junior High School
Clarkston, MI

Heather Wares, M Ed
Traverse City West Middle School
Traverse City, MI

**Alexandra Workman, M Ed,
NBCT**
Thomas Jefferson Middle School
Arlington, VA

Contents in Brief

Contents

Assignments:

_____

_____

_____

_____

_____

_____

_____

_____

These trees use a chemical reaction to make food just as single-celled organisms did over 3 billion years ago.

Assignments:

_____

_____

_____

_____

_____

_____

_____

Contents (continued)

Although most of Earth's water is found in the oceans, on land, and in ice, a large amount of water is also part of the atmosphere.

What happens when solar wind particles reach the upper atmosphere over the Arctic? The aurora borealis!

Assignments:

_____
_____
_____
_____
_____
_____

Contents *(continued)*

Although humans don't have thick fur or the ability to survive without drinking water for months, we have found other ways to live in extreme climates.

These rafters are on a wild ride downriver! They are using the river currents that form as water flows from higher elevations to lower elevations.

Assignments:
_____
_____
_____
_____
_____
_____
_____

Contents *(continued)*

Careful management of renewable resources, such as trees and fish, will help maintain their populations for the future.

© Houghton Mifflin Harcourt Publishing Company • Image Credits: (l) ©David R. Frazier/Photo Researchers, Inc.; (r) ©Jeff Rotman/The Image Bank/Getty Images

Protecting our resources helps us and all of the other organisms that rely on the same resources.

Contents *(continued)*

Imagine living where the sun never sets! That's what summer is like north of the Arctic Circle.

Assignments:

_____

_____

_____

_____

_____

Earth orbits the sun in the "Goldilocks Zone," where it's not too hot and not too cold. It's just right for liquid water and life!

Contents (continued)

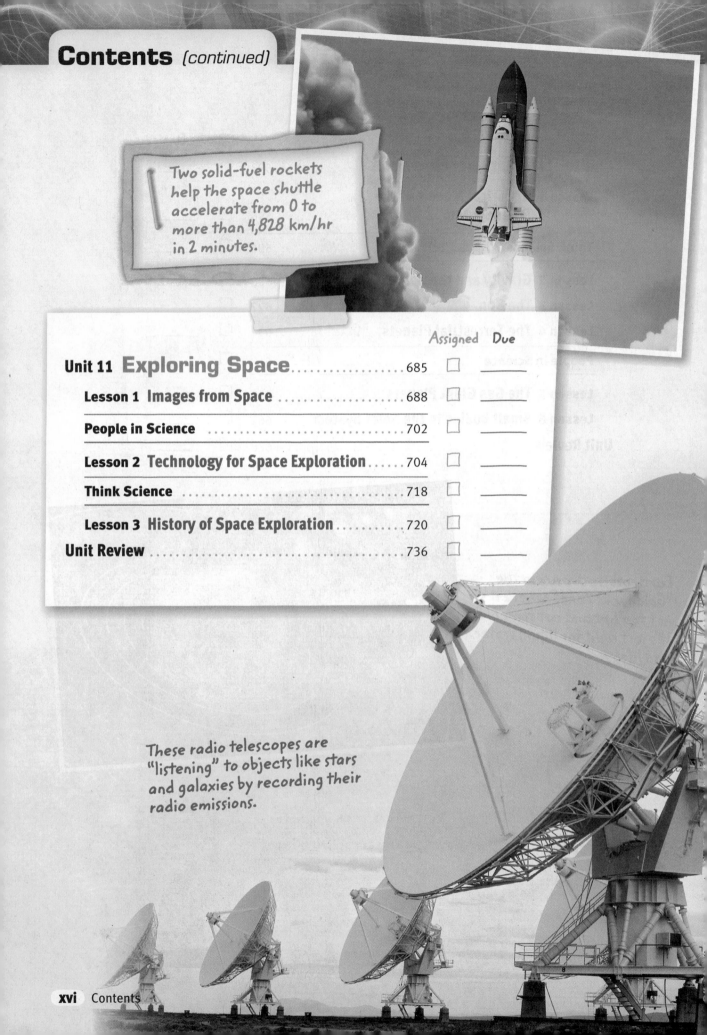

Two solid-fuel rockets help the space shuttle accelerate from 0 to more than 4,828 km/hr in 2 minutes.

These radio telescopes are "listening" to objects like stars and galaxies by recording their radio emissions.

Assignments:

Power up with Science Fusion!

Your program fuses . . .

e-Learning and Virtual Labs

Labs and Activities

Write-In Student Edition

. . . *to generate energy for today's science learner — you.*

S.T.E.M. Engineering & Technology

S.T.E.M. activities throughout the program!

Write-In Student Edition

Be an active reader, and make this book your own!

You can answer questions, ask questions, create graphs, make notes, write your own ideas, and highlight information right in your book.

Learn science concepts and skills by interacting with every page.

Labs and Activities

ScienceFusion includes lots of exciting hands-on inquiry labs and activities, each one designed to bring science skills and concepts to life and get you involved.

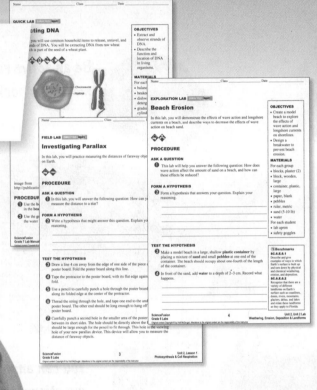

By asking questions, testing your ideas, organizing and analyzing data, drawing conclusions, and sharing what you learn...

You are the scientist!

e-Learning and Virtual Labs

Digital lessons and virtual labs provide e-learning options for every lesson of ScienceFusion.

SCIENCE FUSION | Video-Based Projects

The Sea Turtles of Shark Bay

English / Spanish

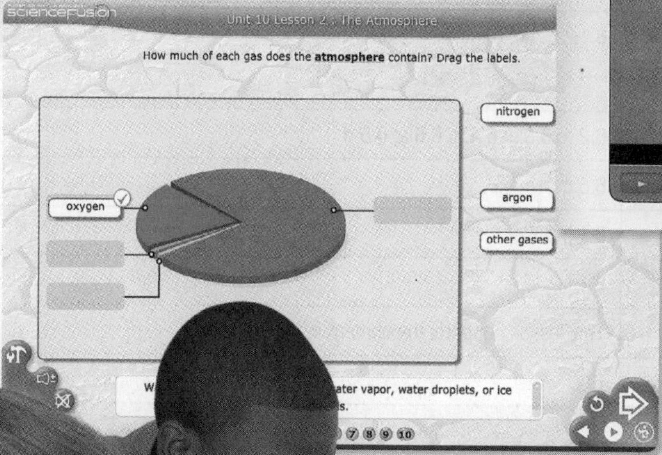

sciencefusion

Unit 10 Lesson 2 · The Atmosphere

How much of each gas does the **atmosphere** contain? Drag the labels.

nitrogen

oxygen ✓

argon

other gases

w...ater vapor, water droplets, or ice

7 8 9 10

On your own or with a group, explore science concepts in a digital world.

360° of Inquiry

Standards

HOLT MCDOUGAL SCIENCE FUSION CORRELATION TO

Virginia Science Standards of Learning

Units and Lessons	Standards
Unit 1: The Nature of Science	
1 Scientific Knowledge	This lesson supports the content in this Unit.
People in Science: Dijanna Figueroa	6.1.j
2 Scientific Investigations	6.1.a; 6.1.d; 6.1.e; 6.1.f
3 Representing Data	6.1.h; 6.1.i; 6.1.j
Unit 2: Matter	
1 Atoms and Elements	6.4.a; 6.4.b; 6.4.c; 6.4.g; 6.6.a
2 Chemical Bonding	6.4.d
People in Science: Shirley Ann Jackson	6.1.j
3 Chemical Reactions	6.1.i; 6.4.c; 6.4.d; 6.4.e; 6.4.f
Unit 3: Earth's Surface	
1 Earth's Spheres	6.2.e; 6.3.a; 6.4.g; 6.6.a; 6.6.d
2 Weathering	6.5.c
3 Erosion and Deposition by Water	6.1.j; 6.7.c
Think Science: Searching the Internet	6.1.j
4 Erosion and Deposition by Wind, Ice, and Gravity	This lesson supports the content in this Unit.
5 Soil Formation	6.1.i
Unit 4: Earth's Atmosphere	
1 The Atmosphere	6.6.a; 6.6.b; 6.6.c
2 Energy Transfer	6.3.b; 6.3.c; 6.5.d
S.T.E.M. Engineering and Technology: Building a Wind Turbine	6.1.i; 6.1.j
3 Wind in the Atmosphere	6.3.c; 6.6.e
Unit 5: Weather and Climate	
1 Elements of Weather	6.1.a; 6.6.b
2 Clouds and Cloud Formation	6.3.d
S.T.E.M. Engineering and Technology: Using Data in Systems	6.1.j; 6.6.f
3 What Influences Weather?	6.3.c; 6.3.d; 6.3.e; 6.5.d; 6.6.b; 6.6.e
4 Severe Weather and Weather Safety	6.3.e; 6.6.e
5 Weather Maps and Weather Prediction	6.1.i; 6.1.j; 6.6.f

Units and Lessons	Standards
People in Science: J. Marshall Shepherd	This feature supports the content in this Unit.
6 Climate	6.3.c; 6.3.d; 6.5.d
7 Climate Change	6.1.h; 6.6.d
Unit 6: Water on Earth	
1 Water and Its Properties	6.5.a; 6.5.b; 6.5.e
2 Ocean Currents	6.3.b; 6.3.c; 6.5.d
Think Science: Bathymetric Maps	6.1.c; 6.1.g; 6.1.h; 6.1.j
3 Surface Water and Groundwater	6.5.e; 6.7.c
S.T.E.M. Engineering and Technology: Analyzing Water Power	6.1.i; 6.1.i.j; 6.5.e
4 Virginia's Watersheds	6.7.a; 6.7.b; 6.7.c; 6.7.d; 6.7.e; 6.7.f; 6.7.g
Unit 7: Earth's Resources	
1 Earth's Support of Life	6.3.b; 6.6.a; 6.8.f
2 Natural Resources	6.2.a; 6.2.b; 6.2.c; 6.2.d; 6.2.e
3 Energy and Energy Resources	6.2.a; 6.2.b; 6.2.e
4 Nonrenewable Energy Resources	6.1.j; 6.2.b; 6.2.c; 6.9.d
5 Renewable Energy Resources	6.1.j; 6.2.b; 6.2.d; 6.9.d
S.T.E.M. Engineering and Technology: Analyzing the Life Cycle of a Paper Cup	6.9.d
6 Managing Resources	6.9.a; 6.9.b; 6.9.c; 6.9.d
Unit 8: Human Impact on the Environment	
1 Human Impact on Water	6.5.e; 6.5.f; 6.9.c
People in Science: Angel Montoya	This feature supports the content in this Unit.
2 Human Impact on Land	6.9.c
3 Human Impact on the Atmosphere	6.6.a; 6.6.d
4 Protecting Earth's Water, Land, and Air	6.5.f; 6.6.d; 6.9.c
Unit 9: The Earth-Moon-Sun System	
1 Earth's Days, Years, and Seasons	6.8.d; 6.8.e; 6.8.g
Think Science: Analyzing Scientific Explanations	6.1.a; 6.1.e; 6.1.j
2 Moon Phases and Eclipses	6.8.c; 6.8.d; 6.8.e
S.T.E.M. Engineering and Technology: Harnessing Tidal Power	6.1.i; 6.1.j
3 Earth's Tides	6.8.h

Units and Lessons	Standards
Unit 10: The Solar System	
1 Historical Models of the Solar System	6.8.i
Think Science: Mean, Median, Mode, and Range	This feature supports the content in this Unit.
2 Gravity and the Solar System	6.8.c
3 The Sun	6.3.b; 6.8.a
4 The Terrestrial Planets	6.8.a; 6.8.b; 6.8.f
People in Science: A. Wesley Ward	6.8.i
5 The Gas Giant Planets	6.8.a; 6.8.b
6 Small Bodies in the Solar System	6.1.j; 6.8.a
Unit 11: Exploring Space	
1 Images from Space	6.1.j
People in Science: Sandra Faber	This feature supports the content in this Unit.
2 Technology for Space Exploration	6.1.j; 6.8.i
Think Science: Testing and Modifying Theories	This feature supports the content in this Unit.
3 History of Space Exploration	6.8.i

Assignments:

The Nature of Science

Special power drills that can be used in low-gravity environments were developed to drill for moon samples. Today, astronauts use these drills for space-station repairs.

Scientists use careful observations and clear reasoning to understand processes and patterns in nature.

What do you think?

Technology helps people perform different tasks, from the everyday to the amazing. How might technology need to be modified for use in space?

Power drills are often used in homes.

Unit 1
The Nature of Science

Launching Humanity into Space

The idea of exploring space was first popularized by science fiction writers of the late 19th and early 20th centuries. It took until the 1940s and 1950s for advances in rocket technology to make the idea of launching humans into space even seem possible. As of today, 12 astronauts have landed on the moon, and teams of astronauts have lived on space stations. What is the next step for space exploration?

1926
Robert Goddard was inspired by turn-of-the-century science fiction to develop his theories about rockets that could travel to the moon. In 1926, he launched the world's first liquid-propellant rocket—but the media thought the idea of going to the moon was just too wild.

Robert Goddard and his liquid-propellant rocket.

The space shuttle *Columbia*

Sputnik 1

Buzz Aldrin

1957

It took several decades to perfect the rocket technology that allowed the Soviet Union to launch the first man-made object into orbit. The Sputnik 1, which weighed only 84 kg, took 96 minutes to orbit Earth.

1969

It only took another 12 years before humans were walking on the moon. Neil Armstrong and Buzz Aldrin became the first humans to set foot on the lunar surface. Back home on Earth, millions of people watched on television.

1981–2011

The new challenge for humans became getting to space as safely and as cost-efficiently as possible. *Columbia* was the first space shuttle NASA developed as a reusable vehicle that could protect astronauts from launch to re-entry.

Take It Home — Closer to Home

① Think About It

In 2011, the space shuttle program entered retirement. NASA has explored many different options for future launches. Are you familiar with any of the replacement programs? What are they called?

_____

_____

_____

_____

_____

- Have new, more stable materials been developed that could be used in construction?
- Have our goals for space exploration changed?
- Are there any new fuels that are more efficient for use in space travel?
- What lessons have we learned from the shuttle program about space travel?

③ Make a Plan

Identify two vehicles designed to replace the space shuttle and transport astronauts. Design a brochure that describes each option, its features, and its design history. Be sure to include the following information:

- Cost information
- Safety features

② Ask Some Questions

Do some Internet research to learn more about the plans NASA has for updating the technology we use for space travel.

Scientific Knowledge

ESSENTIAL QUESTION

What are the types of scientific knowledge?

By the end of this lesson, you should be able to differentiate the methods that scientists use to gain empirical evidence in a variety of scientific fields and explain how this leads to scientific change.

Underwater may seem like an odd place to conduct a science experiment. But scientists often go to faraway places to gather data.

✋ Lesson Labs

Quick Labs
• Pluto on Trial
• Theory of Claim?

Exploration Lab
• Science-Based Commercials

Engage Your Brain

1 Predict Check T or F to show whether you think each statement is true or false.

T   F

☐   ☐   All branches of science have scientific theories.

☐   ☐   A scientist can use only one method to investigate.

☐   ☐   Theories are scientific ideas that have not yet been tested.

☐   ☐   Scientific laws describe what happens in the world.

2 Synthesize An aeolipile is a device powered by steam. When heated, water in the bulb produces steam. The bulb rotates as the steam escapes from the nozzles. People were making these devices as long as 2,000 years ago. How do you think they came up with the idea even though they did not have our modern understanding of science?

_____

_____

_____

aeolipile

Active Reading

3 Infer The word *empirical* comes from the Greek word *empeirikos*, meaning "experienced." Based on this information, infer how scientists get empirical evidence.

_____

_____

_____

_____

Vocabulary Terms

• empirical evidence
• theory
• law

4 Apply As you learn the definition of each vocabulary term in this lesson, create your own definition or sketch to help you remember the meaning of the term.

...From the **Beginning**

What is science?

Think Outside the Book Inquiry

5 Define Before you begin reading the lesson, write down what you think science and scientific knowledge are. Reread your definition at the end of the lesson. Has your definition changed?

Science is the study of the natural world. Scientists study everything from the deepest parts of the ocean to the objects in outer space. Some scientists study living things. Others study forces such as gravity and magnetism. Name anything you see around you. Chances are, there is a scientist who studies it.

The natural sciences are divided into three areas: biology or life science, geology or Earth science, and physics or physical science. The three areas differ in the subjects they study and the methods they use. Biology is the study of living things. Biologists study everything from the tiniest organisms to human beings. Geology is the study of Earth: what it's made of and the processes that shape it. Physical science is the study of nonliving matter and energy. Chemistry often is included under physical science. A scientist's work sometimes may overlap two or more areas. For example, a biologist often must know chemistry to understand the processes in living things.

Each of the photographs below relates to one of the areas of science in some way. From the captions, can you identify to which area each belongs?

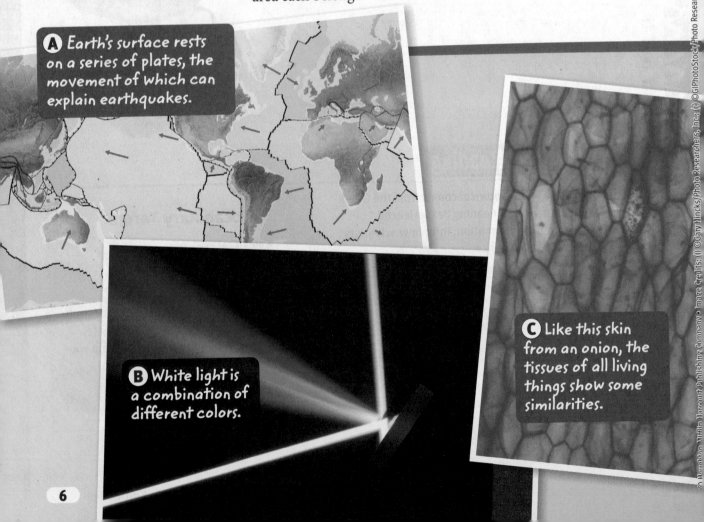

A Earth's surface rests on a series of plates, the movement of which can explain earthquakes.

B White light is a combination of different colors.

C Like this skin from an onion, the tissues of all living things show some similarities.

What does science tell us?

Active Reading **6 Identify** Underline what a theory is in science.

You may think that what you read in a science book is accepted by everyone and is unchanging. That is not always the case. The "facts" of science are simply the most widely accepted explanations. Scientific knowledge is and probably always will be changing.

What we learn when we study science are what most scientists agree are the best explanations about how things happen. They are *theories* scientists have about the world. Commonly, we think of a theory as a kind of guess or "hunch." In science, a theory is much more. A scientific theory is an explanation supported by a large amount of evidence. Theories are what most scientists agree to be the best explanations based upon what we now know.

The table below lists three important scientific theories. Each theory relates to one of the areas of science described before. Each also corresponds to a photograph on the previous page. Can you think of what kinds of evidence would support each theory?

Visualize It!

7 Identify For each of the three theories listed in the table below, write the letter of the corresponding photograph at the left. On the lines provided, describe what might be some evidence that would support the theory.

Scientific Theories

	What scientists think	What is some evidence?
Biology	__Cell theory: Living things are made up of cells that perform the basic functions of life.	
Geology	__Plate tectonics: Earth's surface is made up of plates that move.	
Physics	__Wave theory of light: Each color of visible light has a wave of a specific wavelength.	

Not a Theory—

How do scientific theories differ from laws?

Active Reading **8 Identify** As you read, underline a real-world example of Boyle's law.

To understand the nature of scientific knowledge, you must understand how scientists use certain words. Often, the meanings are very specialized. *Law* and *theory* are two familiar words that have very special scientific meanings.

Laws Describe Principles of Nature

A scientific **law** is a description of a specific relationship under given conditions in the natural world. In short, scientific laws describe the way the world works. They hold anywhere in the universe. You can't escape them.

Boyle's law is one scientific law. According to Boyle's law, at a constant temperature, as the pressure on a gas increases, its volume decreases. To get an appreciation of Boyle's law, think of how it would feel to squeeze a partially deflated beach ball. If you apply pressure by squeezing, the volume, or size, of the ball gets smaller.

You can feel the effects of Boyle's law. A membrane or *eardrum* separates your middle ear from outer ear. Normally, the air spaces on either side are at equal pressure. But sometimes, the pressure on the outer ear can change. For example, the scuba diver in the photo feels an increase in pressure on her eardrum as she descends in the water. By holding her nose and blowing gently, she can force more air into her middle ear. The action momentarily opens the *eustachian tube* connecting the middle ear to the throat. This allows more air from the mouth to rush into the middle ear and equalize the pressure between the two spaces.

Divers need to be aware of Boyle's law and equalize the pressure in their ears.

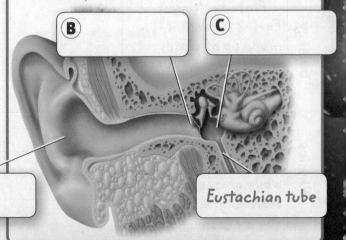

Visualize It!

9 Label Label the middle ear, the outer ear, and eardrum in the illustration.

Air pressure is equalized in the ear by momentarily opening the eustachian tube. You may feel this as a "pop" in your ear.

B

C

A

Eustachian tube

It's a Law!

Theories Describe How Things Happen

While laws describe what happens, scientific theories attempt to explain how things happen. A scientific **theory** is a well-supported explanation of nature. Theories help us understand the laws we observe.

For example, the kinetic theory of gases can explain Boyle's law. The kinetic theory describes a gas as being composed of quickly-moving particles. The particles of gas constantly bounce off of the walls of the container they occupy. The pressure of the gas increases the more frequently the particles bounce off the sides of the container.

Two factors increase how frequently the particles of a gas will bounce off the walls of their container: temperature and volume. If the temperature of a gas increases, the particles move more quickly. The particles, therefore, come into contact with the container's walls more often. Decreasing volume also increases the encounters because the particles have less distance to travel before hitting the wall. The container walls can be anything: a metal cylinder, a beach ball, or your eardrum. The illustration below will give you some of idea of how this works.

Visualize It!

10 Compare In the table below, circle the signs that show the relationships between the volumes, pressures, and temperatures of the gases in the two cylinders. The first is done for you.

Cylinder 1	Relationship	Cylinder 2
Volume	<　　=　　(>)	Volume
Pressure	<　　=　　>	Pressure
Temperature	<　　=　　>	Temperature

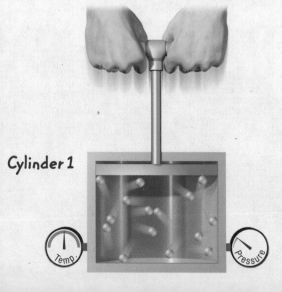

Cylinder 1

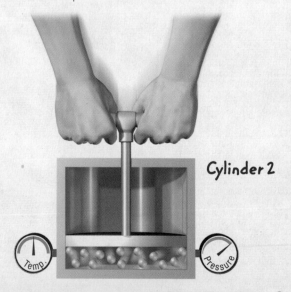

Cylinder 2

What's Your Evidence?

Where do scientists get their evidence?

Scientists are curious. They look at everything going on around them and ask questions. They collect any information that might help them answer these questions.

Scientific knowledge is based on *empirical evidence*. **Empirical evidence** is all the measurements and data scientists gather in support of a scientific explanation. Scientists get empirical evidence in many different places. Generally, scientific work is categorized as field or laboratory work.

12 Analyze What empirical evidence might the scientist in the photograph be trying to gather?

_____

_____

_____

_____

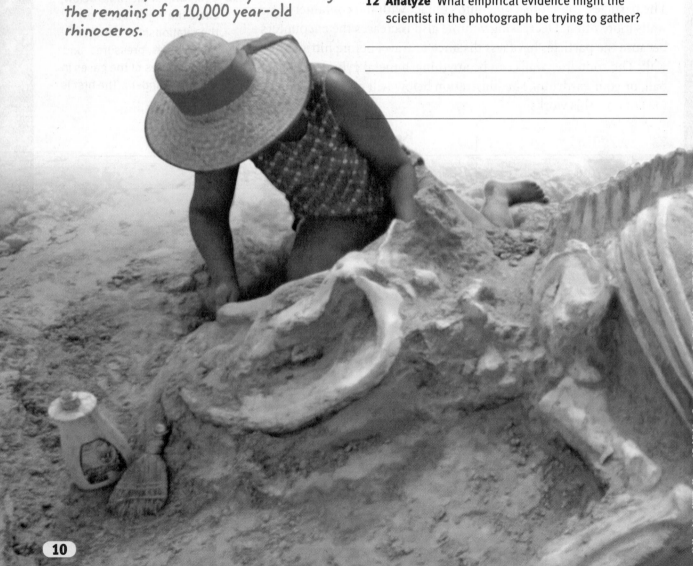

This scientist is a paleontologist. A paleontologist looks for fossilized bones. Here, she is carefully excavating the remains of a 10,000 year-old rhinoceros.

In the Field

Generally, gathering empirical evidence outdoors or where conditions cannot be controlled is known as working in the field or *fieldwork*. Fieldwork gives scientists the opportunity to collect data in an original setting. Biologists and geologists do fieldwork.

A biologist might observe how animals behave in their natural environment. They may look at how the animals gather food or interact with other animals. A geologist may be interested in the minerals in rocks found in a certain area. They may be trying to determine how the rocks formed.

In the Laboratory

In a laboratory, scientists have the opportunity to collect data in a controlled environment. Unlike in the field, the laboratory allows scientists to control conditions like temperature, lighting, and even what is in the surrounding air. A laboratory is where scientists usually do experiments. In an experiment, scientists try to see what happens under certain conditions. A chemist might be trying to see how two substances react with each other. A physicist might study the energy of a new laser. Even scientists who mainly work in the field, like paleontologists and geologists, may wish to look at a bone or rock in the laboratory.

Laboratories come in many varieties. They can be in the ocean or in the sky. Robotic laboratories even have been sent to Mars!

Image Credits: (inset) ©Pierre-Phillipe Marcou/AFP/Getty Images

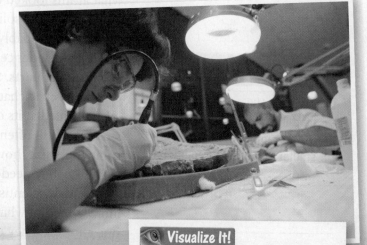

13 Predict What might a scientist look for to collect evidence about the formation of a volcano?

_____

_____

_____

Visualize It!

14 Infer The paleontologists in the photo above have taken a specimen back to the laboratory. What might they be looking for?

_____

_____

The **Debate** Continues

How do scientific ideas change?

Recall that scientific knowledge is agreed-upon knowledge. It is what scientists think are the most-likely explanations for what we see. Over time, these most-likely explanations can change. Sometimes, these changes are very large. More often, they are very small. Why do scientific ideas and explanations change? It's usually because new evidence was found or someone found a better way of explaining the old evidence.

Active Reading

15 Identify Underline an example of a scientific idea that was modified after it was first introduced.

By New Evidence

The theory of atoms is a good example of how new evidence can modify an established theory. By the mid-1800s, most scientists agreed matter was made of atoms. However, they were not sure what atoms looked like. At first, they thought atoms probably looked like tiny, solid marbles. They assumed atoms of different substances probably differed by their masses.

Later evidence suggested that atoms most likely contained even smaller parts. Scientists observed that these smaller parts carried electric charges and that most of an atom's mass was concentrated at its center. Scientists still saw atoms as extremely small and still often treated them like they were tiny marbles. They came to realize, however, that to explain how atoms interact in the best way, they needed a more complex picture of them.

Today, scientists are still trying to refine the picture of the atom. Much of what they do involves literally smashing atoms into one another. They examine the patterns made by the crashes. It is almost like an atomic game of marbles.

Visualize It!

16 Analyze How does the early model of the atom differ from the current model? What is similar about the two models?

_____

_____

_____

_____

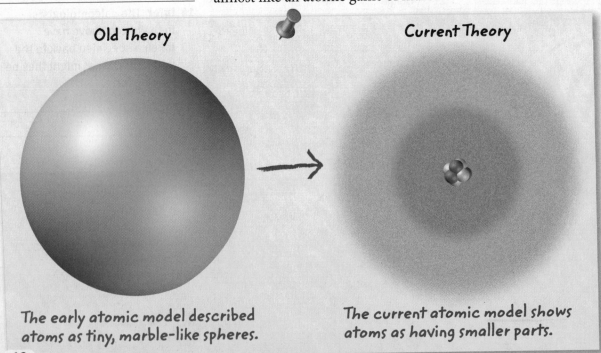

Old Theory → **Current Theory**

The early atomic model described atoms as tiny, marble-like spheres.

The current atomic model shows atoms as having smaller parts.

By Collaboration and Debate

Most scientists do not work in isolation. They collaborate and share ideas. In a way, all scientists are trying to solve a puzzle. Often, many brains are better than one when solving a puzzle.

Scientists regularly gather at meetings to discuss and debate ideas. This helps them to come to an agreement on their ideas. Many ideas are not accepted at first. It is the nature of science to question every idea. Many times, challenges are even welcomed. This rigorous evaluation ensures that scientific knowledge is solidly supported.

Think Outside the Book Inquiry

17 Evaluate Describe a time when you had to ask someone's help in solving a problem. Why did you ask for help?

To the left is an example of how scientists study atoms today. The "streaks" show the paths of subatomic particles after two atoms collide. The scientists below study and discuss images like these in a group in hopes to better understand atoms.

Visual Summary

To complete this summary, fill in the blanks with the correct word or phrase. Then, use the key below to check your answers. You can use this page to review the main concepts of the lesson.

The facts we may think of as science are simply the most widely accepted explanations.

18 A scientific_____ describes what happens, but a scientific _____ describes for what reasons it happens.

Scientific Knowledge

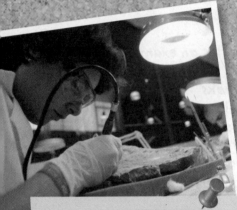

Empirical evidence is all the measurements and data scientists gather in support of a scientific explanation.

19 Empirical evidence about rocks might be collected by a _____ doing _____

20 Empirical evidence about how substances combine might be collected by a _____ doing work in the _____

Scientific knowledge often changes with new evidence or new interpretations.

21 Scientists often_____ and _____ to help them interpret complex ideas.

22 **Justify** Could a scientific theory be thought of as a scientific law that doesn't have as much evidence supporting it? Explain your answer.

Lesson Review

Vocabulary

Circle the term that best completes each of the following sentences.

1 A scientific *law / theory* is an explanation for how something occurs. It is supported by a great deal of evidence.

2 Scientists look for *empirical evidence / law* either in the field or in the laboratory.

3 A basic principle that applies everywhere and in all situations is best described as a scientific *law / theory*.

Key Concepts

4 List Into what three areas are the natural sciences commonly divided?

_____

_____

5 Distinguish How is the use of the word *theory* in science different from its more common use?

_____

_____

_____

6 Differentiate How would you distinguish a scientific theory from a scientific law?

_____

_____

_____

7 Identify Name two methods scientists use to obtain empirical evidence.

_____

_____

8 Apply What is a difference between research in the field and in the laboratory?

_____

_____

_____

_____

Critical Thinking

Use this picture to answer the following question.

9 Interpret As the flames heat the gases in the balloon, the volume of the gases increases. At constant pressure, the volume of all gases increases with increasing temperature. Is this statement a scientific theory or law? Explain.

_____

_____

_____

10 Defend Someone tells you that scientific knowledge cannot be changed or modified. How would you answer this statement?

_____

_____

_____

11 Conclude Each year, the American Chemical Society holds a national meeting and many regional meetings for chemists. Reports of these meetings are then circulated all over the world. Why do you think this has become standard practice?

_____

_____

_____

_____

My Notes

Dijanna Figueroa

MARINE BIOLOGIST

Dijanna Figueroa has wanted to be a marine biologist for as long as she can remember. Like many scientists, she now wears a lab coat and safety glasses most days. She spends up to 12 hours a day in the lab. There, she studies the metabolisms of creatures that live in extreme environments. These creatures live more than two kilometers below the ocean's surface, in a habitat that sunlight never reaches. The water pressure is so great that it would crush a human being. Creatures living in these conditions must therefore produce foods in ways that were unknown until only recently. In order to get specimens of these animals for her lab, Dr. Figueroa had to go down to where they live.

Dr. Figueroa's job has taken her onto the big screen, too. She appeared in the IMAX film *Aliens of the Deep*, with other scientists. The film shows footage of expeditions down to the deep-sea ocean vents. These vents may be one of the harshest environments on the planet. The scientists traveled in *Alvin*, a deep-sea submarine.

Dr. Figueroa currently works as a project scientist at the Marine Science Institute in California. She also works to get young people interested in real-life science through fun and exciting hands-on activities.

Dr. Figueroa in *Alvin*—2,400 m deep!

Language Arts Connection

Think of a science-related job that you would like to know more about. Research the job and write a plan for a documentary film that teaches what you have learned about the job.

JOB BOARD

Museum Educational Interpreter

What You'll Do: Tell students and groups visiting a museum about what they are looking at. You might create educational programs, give tours, and answer questions.

Where You Might Work: Likely places are a science museum or a museum of technology.

Education: Educational interpreters usually need a bachelor's degree in science, and may need extra training in museums or in teaching.

Other Job Requirements: You need to enjoy working with people, be good at public speaking, and be able to answer questions clearly.

Pyrotechnician

What You'll Do: Work with explosives to create explosions and fireworks for special effects. Blow things up in the safest way possible, using a lot of safety measures to keep things from getting out of hand.

Where You Might Work: A company that designs special effects or that creates and performs fireworks shows is a possibility. A pyrotechnician spends time in the workshop and on-site, so you may find yourself on a film set blowing up cars, or on a hillside setting off fireworks.

Education: You need a high-school diploma with additional training in pyrotechnics and safety.

Other Job Requirements: Strong math skills, ability to concentrate, and careful attention to detail are required.

PEOPLE IN SCIENCE NEWS

Jon BOHMER

Cooking with Sunlight

Jon Bohmer isn't the first person to invent an oven that uses sunlight to heat food and water. He's one of many people to use cardboard, foil, and sunlight to build an oven. In some countries, people use firewood for most of their cooking, and must boil all of their water before they drink it. Jon's Kyoto Box oven uses two cardboard boxes painted black on the inside and coated with foil on the outside. It costs only about $5 to make, but it gets hot enough to boil water and cook food.

Lesson (2)

Scientific Investigations

ESSENTIAL QUESTION

How do scientists work?

By the end of this lesson, you should be able to summarize the processes and characteristics of different kinds of scientific investigations.

Virginia Science Standards of Learning

6.1 The student will demonstrate an understanding of scientific reasoning, logic, and the nature of science by planning and conducting investigations in which:

6.1.a observations are made involving fine discrimination between similar objects and organisms;

6.1.d hypotheses are stated in ways that identify the independent and dependent variables;

6.1.e a method is devised to test the validity of predictions and inferences; and

6.1.f one variable is manipulated over time, using many repeated trials.

Geologists are able to create artificial earthquakes on this model of a portion of Earth's crust. They can investigate the rock types through which seismic waves travel, all from a computer!

 **Lesson Labs**

Quick Labs
• Identifying Minerals
• Soil Texture and Water Flow

Exploration Lab
• Predicting and Inferring Outcomes

Engage Your Brain

1 Predict Check T or F to show whether you think each statement is true or false.

T F

☐ ☐ There is only one correct way to carry out a scientific investigation.

☐ ☐ A hypothesis is a conclusion you draw after you carry out a scientific experiment.

☐ ☐ In a controlled experiment, scientists try to control all but one variable.

☐ ☐ Scientists may come up with different interpretations of the same data.

2 Explain Observe the hills shown in the picture. Write some questions you would like to investigate about the sedimentary rock layers.

_____

_____

_____

_____

Active Reading

3 Synthesize You can often define an unknown word if you know the meaning of its word parts. Use the word part and sentence below to make an educated guess about the meaning of the term _independent variable_.

Word part	Meaning
in-	not

Example Sentence
In an experiment about how light affects plant growth, the <u>independent variable</u> is the number of hours that a plant is exposed to light.

Independent variable:

_____

_____

_____

Vocabulary Terms

• **experiment**
• **observation**
• **hypothesis**
• **independent variable**
• **dependent variable**
• **data**

4 Identify This list contains the vocabulary terms you'll learn in this lesson. As you read, underline the definition of each term.

Detective Story

What are some types of scientific investigations?

The two basic types of scientific investigations are *experiments* and field *observations*. Most scientists carry out both experiments and observations. Experiments are often based on observations of the world. Experiments also produce observations when they are carried out. But observations do not always lead to experiments.

Active Reading

5 Identify As you read these two pages, underline characteristics of the different types of scientific investigations discussed.

Scientific Investigations

Experiments

An **experiment** is an organized procedure to study something under controlled conditions. Scientists often conduct experiments to find out the cause of something they have observed.

In 1928, Alexander Fleming found a fungus growing on a nutrient plate that was coated with bacteria. He noticed that there were no bacterial colonies growing close to the fungal colony. He thought that the fungus produced something that killed the bacteria.

Fleming conducted experiments showing that the fungus produced a chemical that kills bacteria. He named the chemical penicillin after the fungus that made it. Based on this work, scientists developed the first antibiotic drugs.

Experiments such as Fleming's are done in a laboratory. Most conditions that might affect the results of an experiment can be controlled in a laboratory. Experiments can also be done in the field, which means outside of a laboratory. Fewer conditions can be controlled in the field. However, field experiments may be needed to show that something found in a laboratory also occurs in nature.

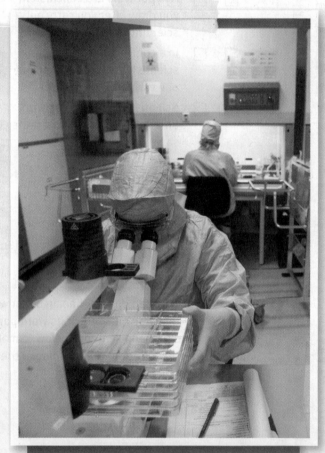

These scientists work in a laboratory called a clean room. A clean room must be free of all possible contaminants.

6 Infer Why is it harder to control conditions in the field than in a laboratory?

_____

_____

_____

Observations and Models

Scientists can also study the natural world without carrying out experiments. **Observation** is the process of gathering information by using the senses. The term can also mean the information gathered by using the senses or special tools.

For example, an archaeologist observes a bone at a prehistoric site. The bone is small and does not look like other bones collected there. Based on its size and shape, the scientist wonders if it came from a small animal. She compares the bone to those from various other small animals. After making these observations, she concludes that people once kept pets at the site.

Another type of investigation is the building of models. Models are representations of an object or system. Models are useful for studying things that are very small, large, or too complex to observe directly. For example, computer models of Earth's atmosphere help scientists forecast the weather.

This scientist is observing flies in their natural habitat.

 **Visualize It!**

7 Observe The fruit flies shown here are members of the same species. Carefully observe the flies, paying close attention to detail. You may want to use a hand lens and ruler to better observe details. In the space below, describe differences you observe between the flies.

_____
_____
_____
_____
_____
_____
_____
_____
_____
_____
_____
_____
_____

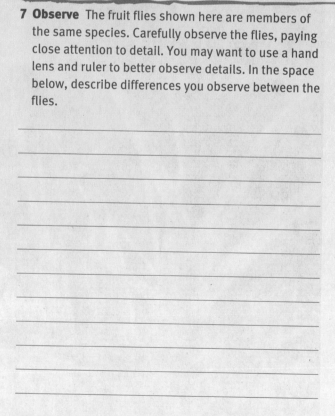

A

B

Parts of a Whole

What are some parts of scientific investigations?

Scientists study all aspects of the natural world. The work they do varies, but their investigations have some basic elements in common.

Hypothesis

A **hypothesis** (hy•PAHTH•ih•sis) is a testable idea or explanation that leads to scientific investigation. A scientist may make a hypothesis after making observations or after reading about other scientists' investigations. The hypothesis can be tested by experiment or observation.

Hypotheses must be carefully constructed so they can be tested in a meaningful way. The hypothesis must be specific and identify the relationship between factors, or variables.

Prediction

When making a hypothesis, scientists often predict the outcome of an investigation. A prediction is a statement about a cause-and-effect relationship that will occur under specific conditions. Predictions are based on prior knowledge, observations, and reasoning. If you hear thunder, you might predict it will rain.

Predictions and hypotheses are sometimes confused. It may be helpful to remember that a prediction states what may happen next under certain conditions. In contrast, a hypothesis is a testable statement that describes relationships among factors in an investigation.

👁 **Visualize It!**

8 Develop Write a hypothesis that could be tested on the plants shown in this photo. Identify the variables.

_____
_____
_____
_____
_____

These plants are being grown in a laboratory and tested under carefully controlled conditions. A scientist could conduct a variety of experiments with these plants.

Independent Variables

Variables are factors that can change in a scientific investigation. An **independent variable** is the factor that is deliberately adjusted in an investigation. The hypothesis identifies the independent variable. For example, Fleming hypothesized that something made by the penicillin fungus stopped the growth of bacteria. The independent variable was the penicillin fungus. The fungus was the factor that caused the change in bacterial growth.

Most experiments have only one independent variable. Other variables are kept constant, or unchanged, so they do not affect the results. Scientists can then conclude that any changes observed are due to the variable that was changed. It is not always possible to control all other variables, however, particularly for investigations in the field.

Dependent Variables

A **dependent variable** is the factor that changes as a result of adjusting the independent variable. In Fleming's experiments with bacteria, the dependent variable was the survival of the bacteria. The bacteria either lived or died. Both the independent variable and the dependent variable should be identified in the hypothesis for an experiment.

Dependent variables can be measured outside of experiments. Consider the hypothesis that crickets chirp faster at higher temperatures. The independent variable would be the temperature. The dependent variable would be the cricket chirps. If this study is carried out in the field rather than in a lab, it might not be possible to control all variables. Factors such as the presence of females or male competitors must be taken into account.

---

9 Apply Complete the missing parts of the table below, which describes three experiments.

Investigation	Independent Variable	Dependent Variable
How is plant height affected by amount of sunlight it receives?	Hours of sunlight per day	
	Altitude of water	Boiling temperature
How does a person's heart rate change as speed of movement increases?		Heart rate

---

Observations and Data

Active Reading

10 Identify As you read, underline the types of data that scientists record.

Data are information gathered by observation or experimentation that can be used in calculating or reasoning. Everything a scientist observes must be recorded. The setup and procedures of an experiment also need to be recorded. By carefully recording this data, scientists will not forget important information.

Scientists analyze data to determine the relationship between the independent and dependent variables. Then they conclude whether or not the data support an investigation's hypothesis.

Many Methods

What are some scientific methods?

Conducting experiments and other scientific investigations is not like following a cookbook recipe. Scientists do not always use the same steps in every investigation or use steps in the same order. They may even repeat some of the steps. The following graphic shows one path a scientist might follow while conducting an experiment.

 **Visualize It!**

11 Diagram Using a different color, draw arrows showing another path a scientist might follow if the data from an experiment did not support the hypothesis.

Defining a Problem

After making observations or reading scientific reports, a scientist might be curious about some unexplained aspect of a topic. A scientific problem is a specific question that a scientist wants to answer. The problem must be well-defined, or precisely stated, so that it can be investigated.

Planning an Investigation

A scientific investigation must be carefully planned so that it tests a hypothesis in a meaningful way. Scientists need to decide whether an investigation should be done in the field or in a laboratory. They must also determine what equipment and technology are needed and how to get materials for the investigation.

Forming a Hypothesis and Making Predictions

A hypothesis describes possible relationships between variables. A hypothesis must be tested to see if results of the test support the hypothesis or not. Before testing a hypothesis, scientists make predictions about what might happen. These predictions are based on prior knowledge, reasoning, and observations.

Identifying Variables

The independent and dependent variables of an experiment are identified in the hypothesis. But scientists need to decide how the independent variable will change. They also must identify other variables that will be controlled and decide how they will measure the results of the experiment. The dependent variable often can be measured in more than one way. For example, if the dependent variable is plant growth, a scientist could measure height, weight, or even flower or fruit production.

Collecting and Organizing Data

The data collected in an investigation must be recorded and properly organized so that they can be analyzed. Data such as measurements and numbers are often organized into tables, spreadsheets, or graphs. Data from multiple trials are often compared using tables.

A **B**

12 Compare What are the similarities and differences between these two microscopic organisms?

_____

_____

_____

Interpreting Data and Analyzing Information

After they finish collecting data, scientists must analyze this information. Their analysis will help them draw conclusions about the results. Scientists may have different interpretations of the same data because they analyze the data using different methods.

A Journey from

Puppy to Guide

Drawing Conclusions

Scientists conclude whether the results of their investigation support the hypothesis. If the hypothesis is not supported, scientists may think about the problem some more and try to come up with a new hypothesis to test. Or they may repeat an experiment to see if any mistakes were made. When they publish the results of their investigation, scientists must be prepared to defend their conclusions if they are challenged by other scientists.

Drawing Conclusions

What are predictions and inferences?

Scientists use both predictions and inferences when they conduct scientific investigations. While a prediction is a statement about a possible outcome, an inference is an explanation. Both predictions and inferences are based on existing knowledge. Developing predictions and making inferences involve critical thinking skills. Both can help support theories or lead to new hypotheses.

Predictions Show Possible Cause-and-Effect Relationships

A prediction is a statement that shows a cause-and-effect relationship that may occur under specific conditions. A scientific prediction is based on logic and prior knowledge. For example, you likely know from experience that plants need water to live. In an experiment investigating the effect of water on plants, you might predict that a plant will die if not given water for two weeks.

Inferences are Explanations Based on Known Facts

An inference is an explanation that is based on prior knowledge. For example, you know that plants absorb water, so you may infer that plants absorb water through their roots. Inference also explains events that cannot be directly observed. For example, the orbit of planets around the sun and movement of electrons around the nucleus are based on inferences.

How do scientists form conclusions?

Scientists interpret the data, or results, from an experiment to form a conclusion. Data must be interpreted in a valid, or correct, way, to arrive at a correct conclusion. The actual data must also be correct and thorough. Incorrect or incomplete data, as well as faulty reasoning, can lead to incorrect conclusions.

For example, imagine that a scientist observed a butterfly in a large field. The butterfly landed only on purple flowers. It would it be incorrect, however, to conclude that all butterflies prefer purple flowers. That conclusion is incorrect because it is based on incomplete data and faulty reasoning. It is not logical to draw conclusions about all butterflies after observing just one. Also, other factors such as flower shape, size, and amount of nectar, were not considered. The scientist could, however, design investigations to find out what factor or factors cause butterflies to visit certain flowers.

Logical reasoning is important in all parts of an investigation, not just to form conclusions. Scientists must decide if data support their predictions and inferences or if the data show they are false.

13 Reason Leo's garden is full of spicy pepper plants. He read that birds cannot taste spiciness. He also knows that some birds are attracted to the color red. He predicts that birds will eat the red peppers in his garden but not the green ones. How could Leo see if his prediction is correct?

_____

_____

_____

_____

_____

How are inferences and conclusions related?

14 Identify As you read, underline an example of an inference.

An inference is not a fact. Inferences often lead to further investigation or to valid conclusions. For example, you may infer that water moves up the stems of plants. You cannot directly observe this action, but you can carry out an experiment to see if your inference is valid. You could put a stalk of celery in a cup with a small amount of dyed water. After a certain amount of time, you could cut open the celery to see if the dyed water moved up the stalk. If it did, you could make the conclusion that your inference is correct—water does move up the stems of plants.

Visualize It!

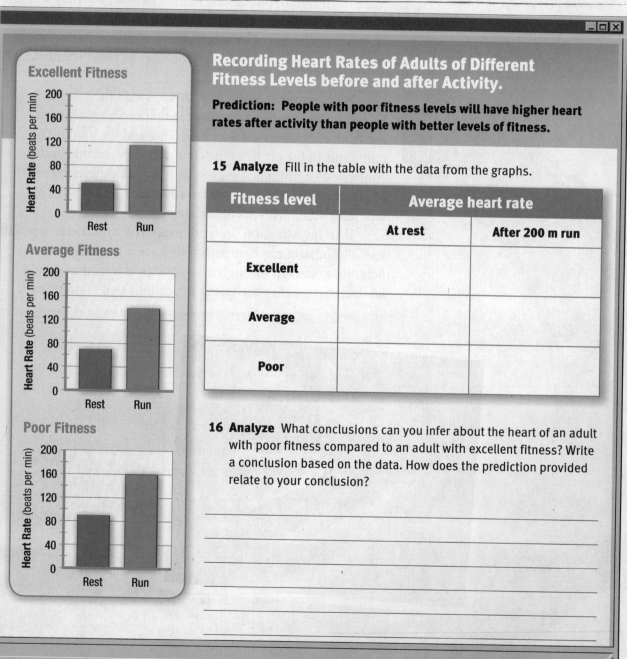

Recording Heart Rates of Adults of Different Fitness Levels before and after Activity.

Prediction: People with poor fitness levels will have higher heart rates after activity than people with better levels of fitness.

15 Analyze Fill in the table with the data from the graphs.

Fitness level	Average heart rate	
	At rest	**After 200 m run**
Excellent		
Average		
Poor		

Excellent Fitness — Heart Rate (beats per min): Rest, Run

Average Fitness — Heart Rate (beats per min): Rest, Run

Poor Fitness — Heart Rate (beats per min): Rest, Run

16 Analyze What conclusions can you infer about the heart of an adult with poor fitness compared to an adult with excellent fitness? Write a conclusion based on the data. How does the prediction provided relate to your conclusion?

_____

_____

_____

_____

_____

Make It Work

Think Outside the Book Inquiry

17 **Compose** Choose a plant or animal you would like to study. How would you learn about what it needs to live, grow, and reproduce? Write a paragraph describing the kinds of investigations you would conduct to learn more about this organism.

How are scientific methods used?

Scientific methods are used in physical, life, and earth sciences. The findings of scientific investigations support previous work and add new knowledge.

Different Situations Require Different Methods

After forming a hypothesis, scientists decide how they will test it. Some hypotheses can only be tested through observation. Others must be tested in experiments. However, observation and experiments are often used together to build scientific knowledge.

For example, a biologist wants to study the effects of air pollution on a plant species. He makes observations in the field. He gathers data on the plants and the amount of pollutants in the air. Then he conducts experiments under controlled conditions. He exposes plants to different levels of pollution to test how they are affected. He compares his laboratory data with his field data.

If an investigation does not support a hypothesis, it is still useful. The data can help scientists form a better hypothesis. Scientists often go through many cycles of testing and data analysis before they arrive at a hypothesis that is supported.

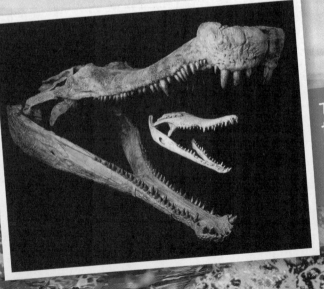

This photo shows the large jaws of SuperCroc and the smaller jaws of a modern crocodile.

Scientific Methods Are Used in the Different Sciences

Earth science includes the study of fossils, which are the remains of organisms that lived long ago. Scientific methods allow scientists to learn about species that died out millions of years ago.

One team of scientists found dinosaur fossils in the Sahara. They found a set of jaws 1.8 meters (6 feet) long. They could tell from the shape of the jaws and teeth that it was not from a dinosaur. They also knew that rivers once flowed through this now extremely dry region. The team hypothesized that the jaws belonged to a giant crocodile that lived in rivers.

To support their hypothesis, the scientists needed more data. They later found skulls, vertebrae, and limb bones. They assembled about half of a complete crocodile skeleton. The scientists measured the fossils and compared them with the bones of modern crocodiles. Their analysis showed that the crocodile grew to a length of 12 meters (40 feet) and weighed as much as 10 tons.

The scientists concluded that the fossils supported their original hypothesis. They published their findings about the large crocodile called *Sarcosuchus* and nicknamed it "SuperCroc."

After scientists find fossils, scientific artists draw what they determine the animals looked like. SuperCroc was large enough to snack on T. rex dinosaurs.

© Houghton Mifflin Harcourt Publishing Company

Quality Control

What makes a good scientific investigation?

The standards for scientific investigations are high. Possible sources of errors, such as poor experimental design or errors in measurements, should be identified and corrected. Experiments should be carried out enough times so that results are reliable. Data and procedures must be carefully recorded. Together, these checks help ensure that good scientific practices are followed.

📖 **Active Reading**

19 Identify As you read this page and the next, underline the meanings of *repetition* and *replication*.

Repetition occurs when an activity is repeated by the same person. When a person bakes a cake multiple times using the same recipe, it is repetition, and the cake should turn out the same. When a scientist repeats her experiment, she should achieve similar results each time.

Repetition and Replication

There are two ways that scientific investigations can be carried out again. First, the scientist who conducted the original investigation can repeat the study. Repetition with similar results provides support for the conclusions. Second, other scientists can replicate the investigation. Replication of the findings by other scientists in other locations also provides support to the results and conclusion.

Open Communication

Scientists may share their research with each other by publishing reports and papers. Scientific papers must include all parts of the investigation so other scientists may replicate the investigation. Before an investigation can be published in a journal, it is reviewed by scientists who are not involved in the investigation. Open communication between scientists helps decrease the possibility of errors and unethical behavior.

Where is there reliable scientific information?

The most reliable scientific information is found in peer-reviewed scientific journals. Peer review is the review of investigations by other scientists. But, scientific journals are often difficult to understand for people who are not scientists. Sometimes, reliable summaries of investigations are published in newspapers or on the Internet. Many scientists write books for the public. People who are not scientists but who are knowledgeable about a particular field or topic may also write reliable books and articles.

The most reliable Internet sources are government or academic webpages. Commercial webpages are often unreliable because they are trying to sell something. As a result, the information on these sites may be biased. Information is biased if it has a particular slant that changes how the information is presented.

Replication occurs when an activity is repeated by a different person. When a person bakes a cake using a recipe from someone else, it should be the same as the first person's cake. When a scientist replicates another scientist's experiment, he or she should achieve the same results.

20 Classify Read each of the scenarios below. Check one of the boxes next to each statement to classify each scenario as an example of repetition, replication, or both.

Scenario 1:
You go to a neighborhood park five times. Each time, you take notes on the birds you see and hear.
- ☐ Replication
- ☐ Repetition
- ☐ Both

Scenario 2:
You go to the same neighborhood park with a friend. You give your friend a copy of the notes you took when you went to the park on your own. You and your friend both take notes on the birds you see and hear.
- ☐ Replication
- ☐ Repetition
- ☐ Both

Scenario 3:
Your friend goes by himself to the same neighborhood park. Your friend takes notes on the birds he sees and hears.
- ☐ Replication
- ☐ Repetition
- ☐ Both

Visual Summary

To complete this summary, fill in the blanks with the correct word or phrase. Then use the key below to check your answers. You can use this page to review the main concepts of the lesson.

Scientific Investigations

Scientific investigations may involve observations, experiments, and models.

Scientific methods include making observations, planning experiments, collecting data, and drawing conclusions.

21 Scientific investigations can be conducted in a(n) _____ or in the field.

22 The _____ of an experiment must be testable.

23 In an experiment, the variable that a scientist plans to change is the _____ variable.

24 The results of an experiment are the _____ collected.

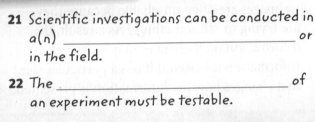

Characteristics of good scientific investigations include using controls, identifying variables, and having reproducible results.

25 If your classmate repeats an experiment that you have already conducted, that is an example of _____

26 One way that the quality of scientific information is evaluated is that it is reviewed by _____

Answers: 21 laboratory; 22 hypothesis; 23 independent; 24 data; 25 replication; 26 peers

27 Identify Suppose that you soak ten seeds in water and ten seeds in a mixture of water and vinegar to see how acidity affects the sprouting of seeds. You observe them for two weeks. What are the independent and dependent variables of this experiment?

Lesson Review

Vocabulary

Circle the term that best completes each of the following sentences.

1 A(n) *hypothesis/observation* is tested in an experiment.

2 In an experiment, the *independent/dependent* variable is the one that scientists manipulate on purpose.

3 The *data/hypothesis* is/are the result(s) obtained from an experiment.

Key Concepts

4 Explain What is a basic requirement that a scientific hypothesis must have?

_____

_____

5 Identify A group of students wants to see how temperature affects the time it takes for spilled water to dry up. In their investigation, what will be the dependent and independent variables?

_____

_____

_____

_____

6 Assess What is the difference between repetition and replication of an investigation?

_____

_____

_____

_____

_____

7 List Write a list of at least five scientific methods.

_____

_____

_____

_____

Critical Thinking

Use this photograph to answer the following questions.

8 Compile Record your observations about the fossil in the photograph. Be sure to include as much detail as you can observe.

_____

_____

_____

_____

_____

9 Produce Write a hypothesis about this fossil that you could test in an investigation.

_____

_____

_____

10 Formulate Describe how you would test your hypothesis. You don't need to identify specific tests or instruments. Rather, describe the kinds of information you would want to collect.

_____

_____

_____

_____

My Notes

Representing Data

ESSENTIAL QUESTION

In what ways can you make sense of data?

By the end of this lesson, you should be able to use models, simulations, tables, and graphs to display and analyze scientific data.

Virginia Science Standards of Learning

6.1 The student will demonstrate an understanding of scientific reasoning, logic, and the nature of science by planning and conducting investigations in which:

6.1.h data are analyzed and communicated through graphical representation;

6.1.i models and simulations are designed and used to illustrate and explain phenomena and systems; and

6.1.j current applications are used to reinforce science concepts.

Scientists depend on tools called seismographs to record the motion of earthquakes. The graph produced by a seismograph is called a seismogram. This seismogram shows the ground motion of an earthquake that hit the United Kingdom in 2007.

🧠 Engage Your Brain

1 Predict Check T or F to show whether you think each statement is true or false.

T	F	
☐	☐	Scientific models have been used to show results of scientific experiments.
☐	☐	Certain types of graphs are better than others for displaying specific types of data.
☐	☐	Most graphs are confusing and unnecessary.
☐	☐	If something can be shown in a table, then it should not be shown in a graph.

2 Evaluate Name two things about the model shown that are similar to the object that the model represents. Then name two things about the model that are different.

_____

_____

_____

_____

_____

_____

_____

_____

_____

_____

✏️ Active Reading

3 Apply Many words, such as *model*, have multiple meanings. Use context clues to write your own definition for each meaning of the word *model*.

Example sentence
After getting an *A* on another test, Julio's teacher told him he was a <u>model</u> student.

model:

_____

_____

Example sentence
For her science project, Samantha created a <u>model</u> of the solar system.

model:

_____

_____

Vocabulary Terms

• model   • simulation

4 Identify As you read this lesson, underline examples of models.

Crunching Data!

How do scientists make sense of data?

Before scientists begin an experiment, they often create a data table for recording their data. *Data* are the facts, figures, and other evidence gathered through observations and experimentation. The more data a scientist collects, the greater is the need for the data to be organized in some way. Data tables are one helpful way to organize a lot of scientific data.

Scientists Organize the Data

A data table provides an organized way for scientists to record the data that they collect. Information types that might be recorded in data tables are times, amounts, and *frequencies,* or the number of times something happens.

When creating a data table, scientists must decide how to organize the table into columns and rows. Any units of measurement, such as seconds or degrees, should be included in the column headings and not in the individual cells. Finally, a title must always be added to describe the data in the table.

The data table below shows the number of movie tickets sold each month at a small theater.

Movie Tickets Sold Monthly

Month	Number of tickets
January	15,487
February	12,654
March	15,721
April	10,597
May	10,916
June	11,797
July	18,687
August	18,302
September	16,978
October	10,460
November	11,807
December	17,497

 **Do the Math** You Try It

5 Extend Circle the row in the table that shows the month when the greatest number of tickets were sold. Then circle the row that shows the month when the least number of tickets were sold. Finally, subtract the least number from the greatest number to find the range of the number of tickets sold.

$$\underset{\substack{\text{Greatest} \\ \text{number of} \\ \text{tickets}}}{\underline{\hspace{3cm}}} - \underset{\substack{\text{Least} \\ \text{number of} \\ \text{tickets}}}{\underline{\hspace{3cm}}} = \underset{\text{Range}}{\underline{\hspace{3cm}}}$$

Scientists Graph and Analyze the Data

In order to analyze their collected data for patterns, it is often helpful for scientists to construct a graph of their data. The type of graph they use depends upon the data they collect and what they want to show.

A *bar graph* is used to display and compare data in a number of separate categories. The length, or height, of each bar represents the number in each category. For example, for the movie theater data, the months are the categories. The lengths of the bars represent the number of tickets sold each month.

Other types of graphs include line graphs and circle graphs. A *line graph* is often used to show continuous change over time. A *circle graph,* or pie chart, is used to show how each group of data relates to all of the data. For example, you could use a circle graph to show the percentages of boys and girls in your class.

Active Reading

6 Interpret What kind of data would you display in a bar graph?

Visualize It!

7 Analyze The data in the graph below are the same as the data in the table at the left. During what three months are the most movie theater tickets sold?

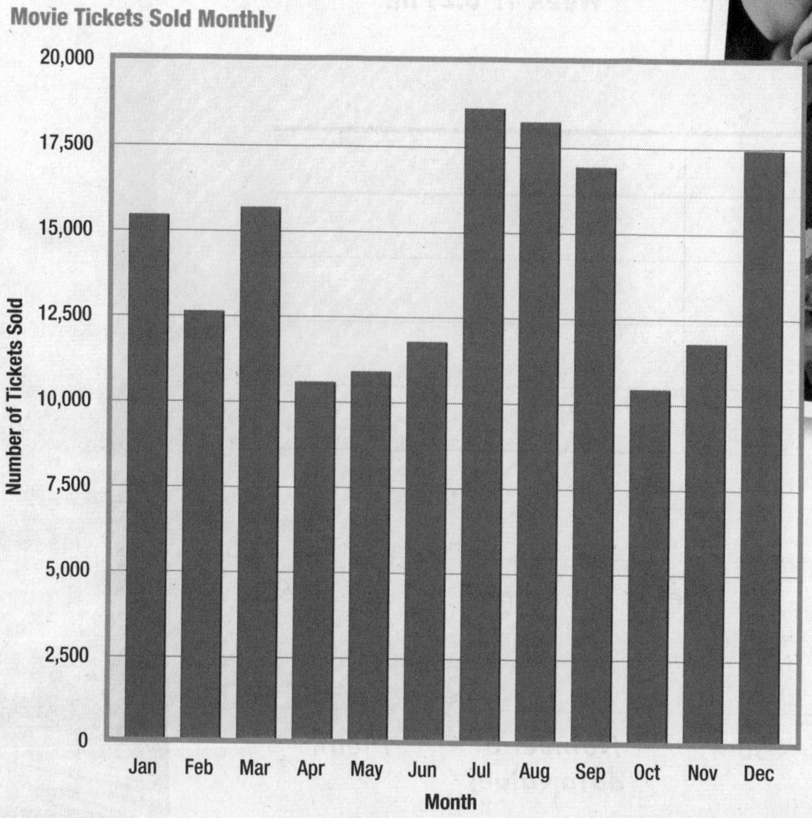

Movie Tickets Sold Monthly

Bar graph titled "Movie Tickets Sold Monthly" with y-axis "Number of Tickets Sold" ranging from 0 to 20,000 and x-axis "Month" showing Jan through Dec.

8 Extend What other kind of data could you collect at home that might show differences over the course of a year?

Graph It!

What do graphs show?

Graphs are visual representations of data. They show information in a way that is often easier to understand than data shown in tables are.

Graphs can help you compare data. They can be used to identify trends and patterns. They can also be used to group data. A bar graph of the total rainfall each month might show increasing and decreasing trends. Months could be easily grouped into low or high rainfall months.

Repeated trials are used in many experiments. The more trials there are, the clearer trends usually become. Scientists often use graphs to help them analyze the data from repeated trials. The data can also be summarized by calculating the mean. The *mean* is the average of the data. Scientists may report the mean of the data from several trials.

Visualize It!

9 Complete The data at the right show the amount of rain, in inches, that fell in each of four weeks at a school. Use the empty table below to organize the data. Include a title for the table, the column headings, and all of the data.

Week 1: 0.62 in.
Week 2: 0.40 in.
Week 3: 1.12 in.
Week 4: 0.23 in.

Title

Headings

Data

Do the Math You Try It

10 Extend The average, or mean, of the rainfall data is the sum of the data values divided by the number of data values. Calculate the mean of the rainfall data. Round your answer to the nearest hundredth.

_____ + _____ + _____ + _____ = _____

Weeks 1 through 4 .... Sum

_____ ÷ _____ ≈ _____

Sum   Number of   Mean
data values

How are graphs constructed?

11 Identify As you read, number the steps used to construct a graph. You may want to rely on signal words that indicate a new step, such as *then* or *next*.

To make a bar graph of the rainfall data at the left, first draw a horizontal axis and a vertical axis. Next, write the names of the categories to be graphed along the horizontal axis. Include an overall label for the axis as well. Next, label the vertical axis with the name of the dependent variable. Be sure to include the units of measurement. Then create a scale along the axis by marking off equally spaced numbers that cover the range of the data collected. For each category, draw a solid bar using the scale on the vertical axis to determine the height. Make all the bars the same width. Finally, add a title that describes the graph.

12 Graph Construct a bar graph of the rainfall data at the left. On the lines provided, include a title for the graph and axis labels. Use a scale of 0.20 in. for the horizontal axis, and label the bars on the vertical axis.

Visualize It!

13 Analyze During which week was the rainfall amount approximately twice what it was during week 4? Use your graph to explain.

Title: _____

Amount of Rainfall (in.)

0.0

Week 1 ____ ____ ____ ____

_____

This rain gauge is used to gather and measure liquid precipitation.

Model It!

What types of models can be used to represent data?

A crash-test dummy, a mathematical equation, and a road map are all models that represent real things. A **model** is a representation of an object or a process that allows scientists to study something in greater detail. A model uses something familiar to help you understand something that is not familiar.

Models can represent things that are too small to see, such as atoms. They can also represent things that are too large to see fully, such as Earth. Models can be used to explain the past and the present. They can even be used to predict future events. Kinds of scientific models include physical models, conceptual models, mathematical models, and simulations.

 Active Reading

14 Apply As you read, underline different ways that scientists use models.

Physical and Conceptual Models

Physical models are models that you can touch. Toy cars, models of buildings, maps, and globes are all physical models. *Conceptual models* are representations of how parts are related or organized. A diagram is an example of a conceptual model. For example, this model of Earth shows that Earth is divided into three layers—the crust, the mantle, and the core. The table shows the estimated densities of each of Earth's layers.

Density of Earth's Layers

Layer	Density (g/cm³)
crust	2.6–2.9
mantle	3.4–5.6
core	9.9–13.1

Visualize It!

15 Apply Explain how a peach could be used as a physical model of the Earth's layers.

_____

_____

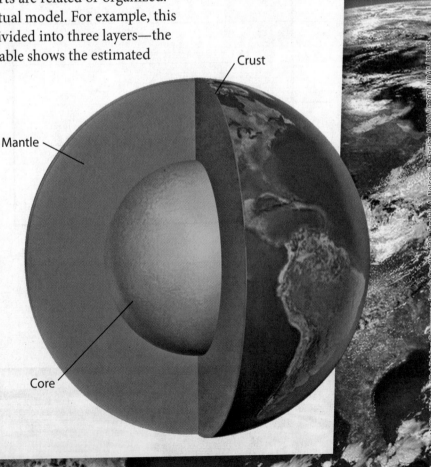

Crust

Mantle

Core

Mathematical Models

Every day, people try to predict the weather. One way to predict the weather is to use *mathematical models*. A mathematical model is made up of mathematical equations and data. Some mathematical models are simple. These models allow you to calculate things such as how far a car will travel in an hour or how much you would weigh on the moon. A chemical equation is another example of a mathematical model.

Other mathematical models are very complex. Computers are often used to process them. Some of these very complex models, such as population growth models, have many variables. Sometimes, certain variables that no one thought of exist in the model. A change in any variable could cause the model to fail.

What are some benefits and limitations of models?

Models are used to represent things that are too small or too large to see. Models also benefit scientists in other ways. They allow scientists to do experiments without affecting or harming the subject of the study. For example, crash-test dummies simulate how car accidents affect people.

All models are limited because they are simpler versions of the systems that they try to explain. The simpler model is easier to understand and use. However, information is left out when a model is made.

The size and scale of a model can differ from the real thing. Models have different properties. They are often made of different materials than the real thing. These factors influence how models behave. This means that models do not function exactly like the object or system they represent.

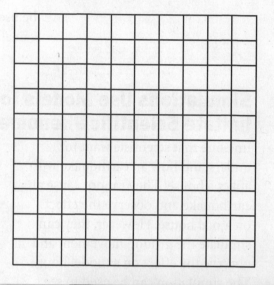

Do the Math You Try It

16 Calculate The air we breathe is made up of 78% nitrogen, 21% oxygen, and 1% other gases. Use three different colored pencils to color the appropriate number of squares in the grid for each of these percentages.

Think Outside the Book Inquiry

17 Apply With a classmate, discuss the benefits and limitations of globes and maps as physical models.

How do simulations represent data?

A **simulation** uses a model to copy the function, behavior, or process of the thing it represents. The model used in a simulation can be a physical model. Computer simulations are also common. Simulations are often used to study systems that are large or complex, such as weather systems. They can also imitate processes that are difficult to study directly. For example, they could be used to study earthquakes or the melting of the polar ice caps.

Scientists observe and collect data from the simulation. It can be used to explain events in the past and the present. Simulations can also be used to make predictions.

Simulations Use Models to Imitate Scientific Phenomena

Imagine that scientists want to understand how an earthquake will affect a house. They cannot cause an earthquake and observe the effect on a real house. However, they can simulate the ground movement and observe the effect on a model house. The simulation can be used to see how the house moves, what damage occurs, or how the materials react. The simulation is not exactly the same as the real thing; there are always some variables that differ. However, it is a practical way to learn more about real events.

Scientists can simulate how the movement of an earthquake affects different types of structures.

Simulations Help Explain Scientific Phenomena

An earthquake simulation may show that a house has been damaged. This information is not useful on its own. Scientists also need to understand why the damage occurred.

A simulation can be used to analyze events in detail. Scientists can then understand the causes of events. The information gained from earthquake simulations can be used in design. Houses can be designed with features that help reduce damage. More simulations could be used to test the features to see if they work. If they do not work, scientists would again ask why.

Visualize It!

Special metal connectors secure one part of the house to another.

Wood walls are secured to the foundation using special anchors and bolts.

Walls are reinforced with strong materials.

19 Infer The features shown were added to the house because an earthquake simulation suggested they would reduce damage. Describe what might have happened during the simulation.

_____

_____

_____

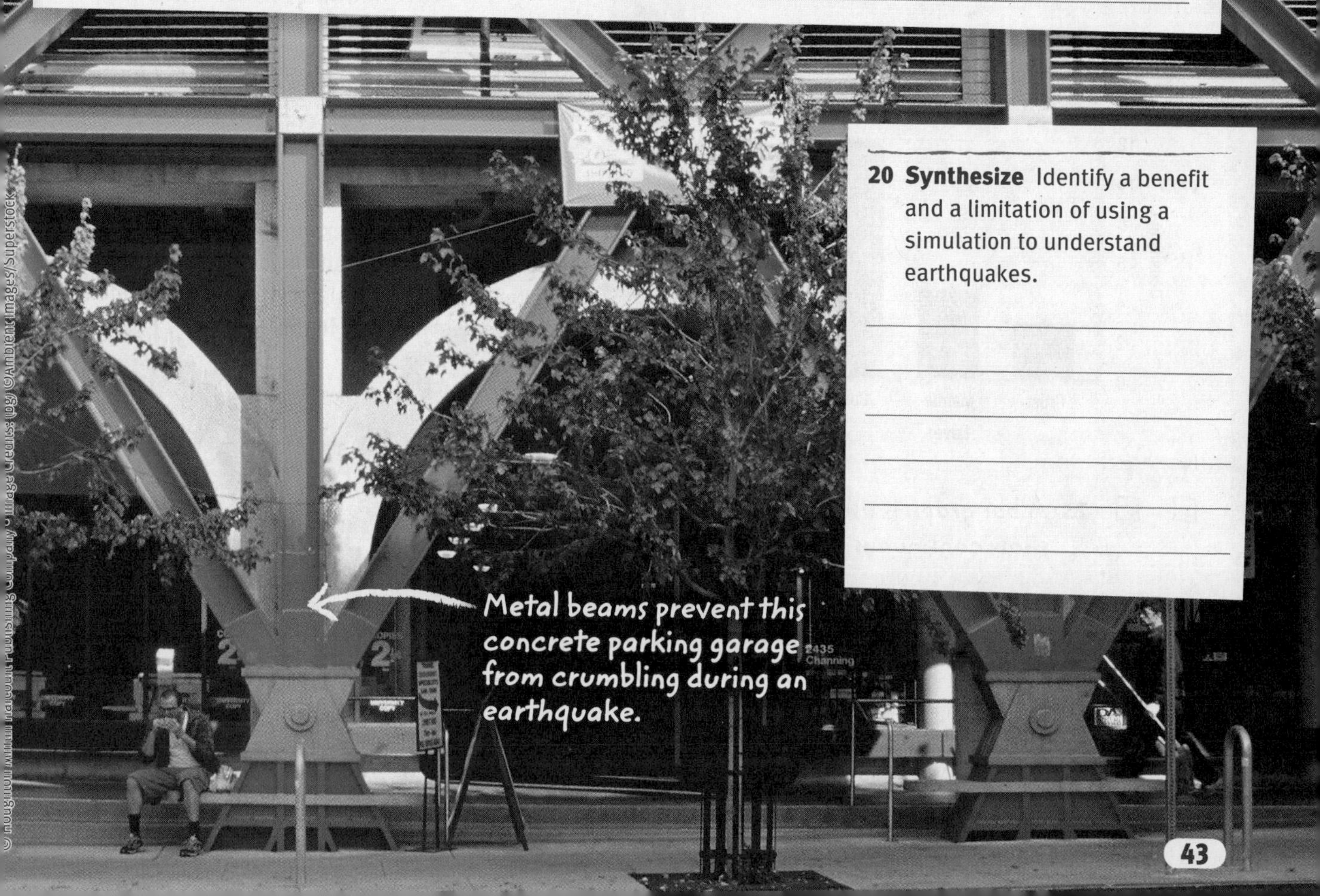

20 Synthesize Identify a benefit and a limitation of using a simulation to understand earthquakes.

_____

_____

_____

_____

_____

_____

Metal beams prevent this concrete parking garage from crumbling during an earthquake.

Visual Summary

To complete this summary, check the box that indicates true or false. Then, use the key below to check your answers. You can use this page to review the main concepts of the lesson.

Representing Data

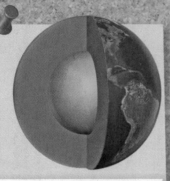

Scientists use models and simulations to learn about objects, systems, and concepts.

T F
☐ ☐ **21** The equation for density is a physical model.

A table can be used to record and organize data as it is being collected.

Density of Earth's Layers	
Layer	Density (g/cm³)
crust	2.7–3.3
mantle	3.3–5.7
core	9.9–13.1

T F
☐ ☐ **22** Units of measurement should be placed with the column or row headings in tables.

A graph is a visual display of data that shows relationships between the data.

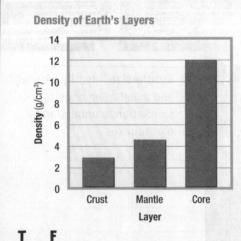

Density of Earth's Layers

T F
☐ ☐ **23** A bar graph is used to show continuous data.

24 Synthesize Provide an example of something in the natural world that could be depicted in each of the following ways: a table, a graph, and a model. (Use examples not given in this lesson.)

Lesson Review

Vocabulary

Fill in the blank with the term that best completes the following sentences.

1 A(n) _____ can be a visual or mathematical representation of an object, system, or concept.

2 A(n) _____ imitates the function, behavior, or process of the thing it represents.

3 Data can be arranged in visual displays called _____ to make identifying trends easier.

Key Concepts

4 Differentiate How is a diagram different from a simulation?

_____
_____
_____
_____

5 Predict A data table shows the height of a person on his birthday each year from age 2 to 12. What trend would you expect to see in a line graph of the data?

_____
_____
_____
_____

6 Judge Which kind of graph would be best for depicting data collected on the weight of a baby every month for six months?

_____
_____
_____
_____

7 Apply What kind of model would you use to represent the human heart?

_____
_____

Critical Thinking

Use this graph to answer the following questions.

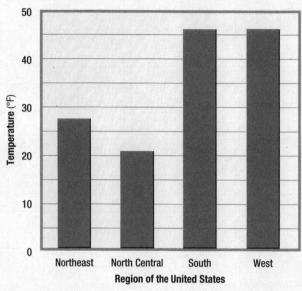

Average January Temperatures

8 Identify Which region of the country has the coldest January temperatures?

_____

9 Estimate What was the average temperature of the South in January? How did you arrive upon your answer?

_____
_____
_____
_____
_____

10 Apply Give an example of a physical model, and explain one limitation of the model. Then give an example of a mathematical model, and explain one limitation.

_____
_____
_____
_____
_____

My Notes

Unit 1   Big Idea

Scientists use careful observations and clear reasoning to understand processes and patterns in nature.

Lesson 1
ESSENTIAL QUESTION
What are the types of scientific knowledge?

Differentiate the methods that scientists use to gain empirical evidence in a variety of scientific fields, and explain how this leads to scientific change.

Lesson 2
ESSENTIAL QUESTION
How do scientists work?

Summarize the processes and characteristics of different kinds of scientific investigations.

Lesson 3
ESSENTIAL QUESTION
In what ways can you organize data to fully understand them?

Use tables, graphs, models, and simulations to display and analyze scientific data.

Connect ESSENTIAL QUESTIONS
Lessons 1 and 2

1 Compare Explain the difference between scientific investigations and scientific knowledge.

_____

_____

_____

_____

_____

_____

Think Outside the Book

2 Synthesize Choose one of these activities to help synthesize what you have learned in this unit.

☐ Using what you learned in lessons 2 and 3, demonstrate how scientists communicate results by graphing data. Use library or Internet resources to find an investigation with data that you can display as a graph.

☐ Using what you learned in lessons 1 and 2, plan an investigation that could be conducted by experimentation or by observation. Write a procedure for both types of investigation, and explain the advantages and disadvantages of each.

Vocabulary

Fill in each blank with the term that best completes the following sentences.

1 The cumulative body of observations on which scientific explanations are based is called _____.

2 The _____ variable is the factor that is changed in order to test the effect of the change.

3 A(n) _____ uses a model to test the function, behavior, or process of the thing the model represents.

4 A testable idea or explanation that leads to scientific investigations is called a(n) _____.

5 A scientific _____ is a description of a specific relationship under given conditions in the natural world.

Key Concepts

Read each question below, and circle the best answer.

6 Which statement describes how a scientist makes scientific explanations?

A A scientist bases scientific explanations on a large body of observations of the world.

B A scientist bases scientific explanations only on other scientists' opinions.

C A scientist bases scientific explanations on personal experience and opinions.

D A scientist suggests scientific explanations and makes up evidence to make them true.

7 Which of these answers describes a scientific law?

A an interesting idea based on the opinions of scientists

B a well-supported and widely accepted explanation of nature

C a specific relationship under given conditions in the natural world

D an explanation of how particular events happen in the natural world

8 The figure below illustrates Boyle's law, which describes the effect of pressure on the volume of a gas that is kept at constant temperature.

Boyle's Law

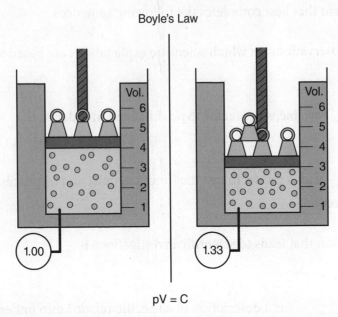

$pV = C$

Based on the figure, which statement is an accurate explanation of Boyle's law?

A Boyle's law explains why the volume of a gas gets smaller when the pressure on a gas is increases.

B Boyle's law explains what happens to a gas if the temperature of the gas is changed.

C Boyle's law identifies the relationships among temperature, pressure, and volume for gases in a closed system.

D Boyle's law states that, at a constant temperature, as the pressure on a certain amount of gas increases, its volume decreases.

9 Which of these scientists would most likely engage in fieldwork to observe organisms?

A chemist   **C** physicist

B biologist   **D** mathematician

10 Which sequence of events is a logical order for a scientific investigation?

A experiment → hypothesis → analysis of data → conclusion

B hypothesis → experiment → conclusion → analysis of data

C analysis of data → conclusion → experiment → hypothesis

D hypothesis → experiment → analysis of data → conclusion

11 The following graph shows how the speed of an object changes over time.

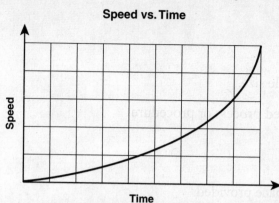

Speed vs. Time

Based on this graph, four different lab groups came to the following conclusions. Which group's conclusion best describes the result shown in the graph?

A Group 1: The speed of the object increases as time passes.

B Group 2: The speed of the object decreases as time passes.

C Group 3: The speed of the object does not change as time passes.

D Group 4: The speed of the object decreases then increases as time passes.

12 The graph shows the results of an experiment done by four groups. Each group used rubber bands of the same size and recorded how far the rubber bands stretched as weight was added to them.

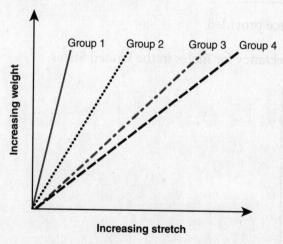

Which of the following best explains why the four groups got different results?

A They all used metric rulers to measure.

B There were differences in the rubber bands.

C They performed the test at different times.

D They tested the rubber bands with the same weights.

13 Which of the following characteristics is part of a good scientific experiment?

A Results can be reproduced.

B Results are not reviewed by peers.

C Results are based on a small sample size.

D Results are based on an undisclosed process or procedure.

Critical Thinking

Answer the following questions in the space provided.

14 Why is it important for experimental procedures and results to be reproducible?

_____

_____

15 What are the differences between a three-dimensional model and a simulation?

_____

_____

_____

Connect **ESSENTIAL QUESTIONS**
Lessons 2 and 3

Answer the following question in the space provided.

16 This table shows the average life expectancy for males in the United States.

Year of birth	Average life expectancy (y)
1900	48
1920	56
1940	62
1960	67
1980	70
2000	74

What is one inference you can make based on the data in the table? What is one prediction you can make based on the data in the table?

_____

_____

_____

_____

Matter

Chitin is a polymer that makes up the shells of animals like this crawfish. The chemical and physical properties of the chitin molecule allow it to function as a hard exoskeleton.

Big Idea

Atoms join together and break apart to form the variety of substances found on Earth.

What do you think?

Chitin is made up of atoms of carbon, oxygen, nitrogen, and hydrogen. Many other substances also contain these atoms. How do these and other kinds of atoms combine to form all the matter around us?

Unit 2

Matter

CITIZEN SCIENCE

Making and Using Models

Models are useful tools for analyzing information. There are different kinds of models. Physical models are useful when trying to examine something that is too large or too small to see completely. A physical model can be a molecule, a planet, or a skyscraper.

1 Think About It

In this activity, you will build a model of an atom. Because an atom is much too small to see, you will want to scale your model much larger than the atom. Below, indicate which atom you would like to model and what the normal size of that atom is. You can find the size of your atom on the Internet. Next, determine which particles you need to account for in your model. Also, as you are modeling your atom, determine how large the electron cloud will be.

____

____

____

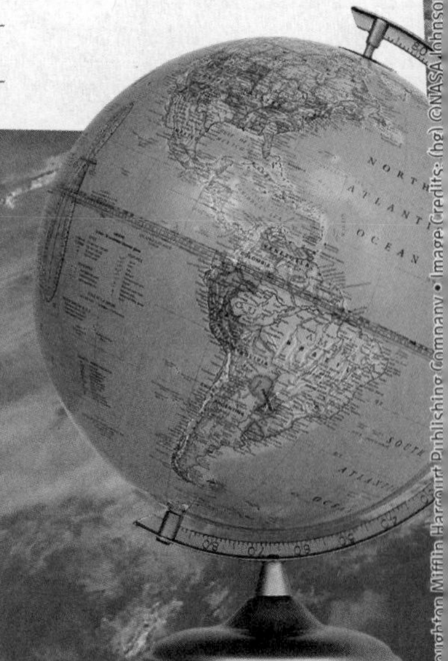

A globe is a physical model of Earth. A globe can show countries and sometimes data such as the height of mountains or the depth of the ocean floor.

What materials will you use?

Decide what type of materials you need to construct your model atom. Use household materials from grocery or hardware stores. Below, list your materials and the particles those materials will be modeling.

_____
_____
_____
_____
_____
_____

This paper snowflake is a physical model of a real snowflake. Each snowflake is unique, and almost all have six sides.

③ **Make A Plan**

Calculate how large the particles need to be based on your estimate of how large your model will be compared to a real atom. In the space below, record what materials you will use for the protons, neutrons, and electrons. Next, record the actual size of these particles in an atom and the size of these particles in your atom. Then, gather up the materials you will use to make your model.

Particle or structure	Actual size	Size in model
neutron		
proton		
electron		
diameter of electron cloud		

After you have constructed your model of your chosen atom, present the model to another class at your school. You could also present the model to the school with other students in your class.

It is difficult to see all of the individual snowflakes in this image. A model of a snowflake can help us understand just how many snowflakes make up a large amount of snow such as this.

Take It Home

With an adult, use the skills from this activity to make a model of something that is very large. Scale your model smaller than the item, and plan what materials you will use to make the model. Present your model to your classroom.

Atoms and Elements

ESSENTIAL QUESTION

What particles make up matter?

By the end of this lesson, you should be able to describe atoms and how the atoms of an element are alike.

Virginia Science Standards of Learning

6.4 The student will investigate and understand that all matter is made up of atoms. Key concepts include:

6.4.a atoms consist of particles, including electrons, protons, and neutrons;

6.4.b atoms of a particular element are alike but are different from atoms of other elements;

6.4.c elements may be represented by chemical symbols; and

6.4.g a limited number of elements comprise the largest portion of the solid Earth, living matter, the oceans, and the atmosphere.

6.6 The student will investigate and understand the properties of air and the structure and dynamics of Earth's atmosphere. Key concepts include:

6.6.a air as a mixture of gaseous elements and compounds;

Earth is made of many elements. The fantastic formations in this cave contain atoms of calcium, carbon, and oxygen.

🧠 Engage Your Brain

1 Predict Check T or F to show whether you think each statement is true or false.

T	F	
☐	☒	Nothing is smaller than an atom.
☒	☐	Single atoms can be seen with a powerful light microscope.
☒	☐	There are more than 100 elements on the periodic table of elements.

2 Infer Why do the two elements silver and iron have different properties?

Because they are found in a cliff areas and they were formed differenrly

✏️ Active Reading

3 Synthesize Many English words have their roots in other languages. Use the Greek word below to make an educated guess about the meaning of the word *atom*.

Greek word	Meaning
atomos	indivisible

Example sentence
All matter is made up of particles called <u>atoms</u>.

atom:

an indivisable part of a molecule

Vocabulary Terms

- atom
- proton
- neutron
- electron
- element
- atomic number
- chemical symbol

4 Identify As you read, create a reference card for each vocabulary term. On one side of the card, write the term and its meaning. On the other side, draw an image that illustrates or makes a connection to the term. These cards can be used as bookmarks in the text so that you can refer to them while studying.

A Small World

These dots of ink, like all matter, are made up of much smaller particles called atoms.

What are atoms?

When you magnify printed letters like the ones on this page, you can see that they are made up of small dots of different colors of ink. A fixed ratio of magenta and cyan ink dots make a light purple color. In a similar way, all matter is made up arrangements of very small particles called atoms. **Atoms** are the basic building blocks of matter. Different types of atoms can be combined in different ways to form all of the substances we encounter every day. Atoms are so small that they cannot be observed using a light microscope.

What are the parts of an atom?

Atoms contain even smaller particles known as subatomic particles. **Protons** are particles that have a positive electric charge. Protons are found at the center, or *nucleus,* of the atom. The nucleus also contains another type of subatomic particle called **neutrons.** Neutrons have no charge. The nucleus makes up most of the mass of an atom. Outside of the nucleus is a region called the *electron cloud.* The electron cloud contains a third type of particle called electrons. **Electrons** are very small, negatively charged particles that move around the nucleus. Atoms are electrically neutral overall because they have the same number of protons as electrons. The positive charges of the protons balance out the negative charges of the electrons. The image below is a model of an atom and its subatomic parts.

Think Outside the Book · Inquiry

5 **Model** Create a model of an atom using materials of your choice. Include protons, neutrons, and the electron cloud in your model. Show your atom to the class, and explain how it models the structure or behavior of atoms.

Visualize It!

6 **Apply** Fill in the blanks with words that describe the parts of the model atom shown at the right.

The _____nucleus_____ at the center

of the atom contains two types of particles:

protons and _____neutrons._____

Electrons are found in a region called the

_____electron cloud_____,

represented by the light blue color.

Carbon Fiber Composites

Carbon fiber composites (CFCs) are a combination of a polymer coating, such as polyester or nylon, reinforced with extremely thin carbon fibers. The fibers are very strong, and the polymer bonds them together tightly. The composite they make is light, strong, and tough.

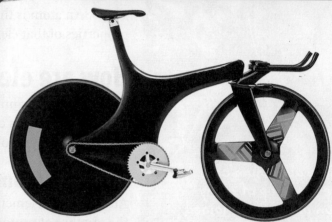

Strong and Light!

CFCs work very well when durable yet lightweight materials are required. Racing cars and fighter jets use parts made from CFCs. Many sporting goods use CFCs, too. Racquets, canoes, skis, and bicycles made of CFCs are strong and light.

An Expensive Choice

CFCs are relatively expensive, so using them requires making a trade-off. People must either be willing to pay the high price for the strongest and lightest material or switch to a less expensive material that is not quite as light or strong. For example, making the body of this car from aluminum would have cost less, but an aluminum-bodied car would be heavier.

Extend

Inquiry

7 Identify Which category of materials do CFCs belong to?

Composites

8 Research Investigate an application of carbon fiber composites and explain why CFCs are important for this application.

money

9 Create Illustrate three ways that carbon fiber composites could be used in your home or community. Why do you think they are not already used this way?

The Element of Surprise

These aluminum cans are made up of many aluminum atoms joined together.

What is an element?

An **element** is a substance that is made up of one type of atom. For example, the metal aluminum is an element made up of aluminum atoms. An atom is the smallest unit of an element that has the properties of that element.

How are elements described?

Each element has unique properties that differ from those of other elements. Elements can be distinguished by their atomic numbers and chemical symbols.

By Their Atomic Numbers

Atoms of one element differ from atoms of another element by the number of protons they have. The **atomic number** of an element is the number of protons in the nucleus of one of its atoms. Every atom of a given element has the same atomic number. For example, the atomic number of aluminum is 13. Each atom of aluminum contains 13 protons. While the number of protons in the nucleus is constant for a given element, the number of neutrons can vary. Most atoms have about as many neutrons as protons.

The atomic number of each element is listed on the periodic table of elements. On the periodic table on the next page, the atomic number appears at the top of each element square. The periodic table is organized in rows by increasing atomic number.

Visualize It!

10 **Apply** In the space below, draw a model of an atom of the element aluminum. Use information from this page to determine how many protons and neutrons to include in your model.

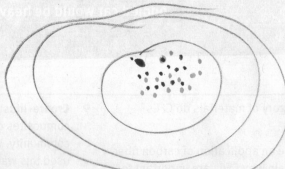

Protons. Blue
Nuetrons. P...

By Their Chemical Symbols

Active Reading 11 **Identify** As you read, underline chemical symbols of elements.

Elements can also be described by their chemical symbols. A **chemical symbol** is an abbreviation that represents an element. The first letter is always capitalized, and the remaining letters are always lowercase. Most elements have a one- or two-letter chemical symbol. These symbols allow chemists to write chemical names in a shorter form. The last few elements on the periodic table have three-letter chemical symbols, such as Uuq. These symbols are placeholders for elements that have not yet been discovered or that do not have official names. After an element has been approved by an international committee of scientists, it will be given a permanent name and a one- or two-letter chemical symbol.

For many elements, the chemical symbol contains one or more letters from the element's name. For example, hydrogen is represented by H, and zinc is represented by Zn. Some chemical symbols come from the names of the elements in other languages. The chemical symbol of gold is Au, from the Latin word for gold—*aurum*. The symbol for tungsten, W, comes from its German name—*wolfram*.

Visualize It!

12 Describe Helium appears in the uppermost right corner of the periodic table. What are the atomic number and chemical symbol for helium?

2, 4.00

13
Al
Aluminum
26.98

Each square on the periodic table shows the atomic number, chemical symbol, name, and average atomic mass of an element.

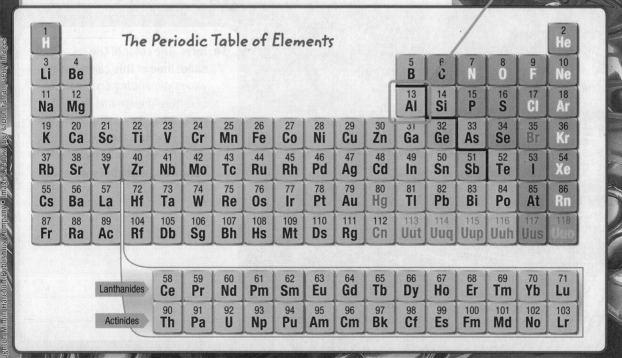

The Periodic Table of Elements

Elements in Our World

What elements make up Earth?

Nine elements account for almost all of the matter that makes up our planet. These elements are oxygen, silicon, aluminum, calcium, sodium, potassium, magnesium, nickel, and iron. Iron makes up about one third of Earth's mass.

Earth has three layers: the crust, the mantle, and the core. Each layer has a different mix of elements. The continents and the ocean floor are parts of the crust. The main elements in the crust are oxygen, silicon, and aluminum. Along with smaller amounts of other elements, they form the minerals found in rocks and soil. Earth's mantle is made of rock that is hot enough to slowly flow. Most of this rock is made of silicon, oxygen, iron, and magnesium. The main components of Earth's core are the metals iron and nickel.

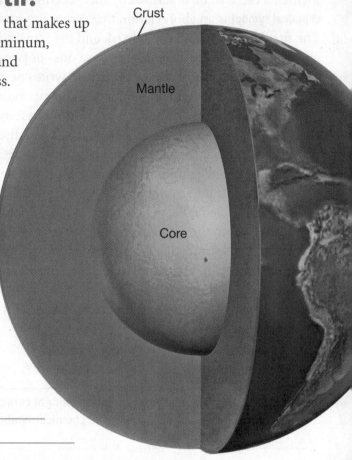

Crust

Mantle

Core

Active Reading 13 **Identify** What elements are abundant in both the crust and the mantle?

Silicon

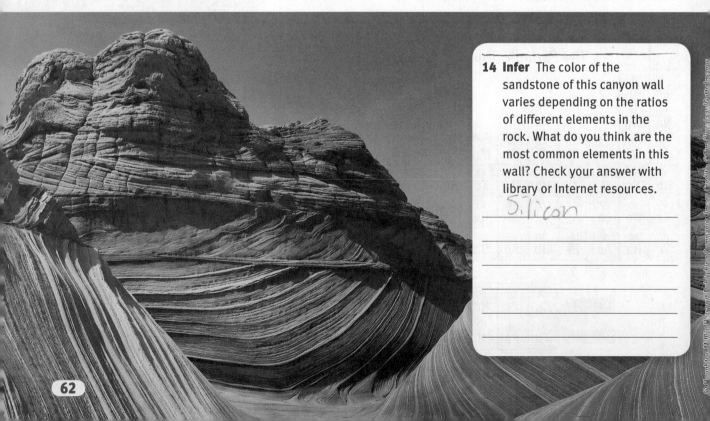

14 **Infer** The color of the sandstone of this canyon wall varies depending on the ratios of different elements in the rock. What do you think are the most common elements in this wall? Check your answer with library or Internet resources.

Silicon

What elements make up the atmosphere and ocean?

The atmosphere and ocean are above Earth's crust. The atmosphere is a layer of gases that surrounds Earth. The elements nitrogen and oxygen account for almost all of the atmosphere. The atmosphere contains 78% nitrogen and 21% oxygen. The atmosphere also contains small amounts of argon, helium, neon, and gases that are composed of hydrogen or carbon atoms.

The ocean is mainly water. Water molecules are made of hydrogen and oxygen atoms joined together, so these two elements are the most abundant in Earth's oceans. If you have ever tasted ocean water, you know that it is salty. Salt compounds make up several percent of the ocean. In all, ocean water contains about 30 elements. The salts in the ocean include the elements sodium, chlorine, sulfur, magnesium, calcium, and potassium.

What elements make up living things?

All living things and things that were once alive contain the element carbon. This includes fossil fuels, such as coal and petroleum, that come from the remains of organisms that lived millions of years ago. Other elements that are abundant in living things include hydrogen, oxygen, nitrogen, phosphorus, and calcium. Living things need a variety of other elements, such as iron, in small amounts. Some of these elements may be obtained from a balanced diet. Eating a variety of healthy foods will help you to get all the elements your body needs.

This sea lion, as well as the water and air that it needs to survive, is composed of just a few elements joined in different ways.

---

15 Compare In the table below, write the names and chemical symbols of elements found in Earth, the atmosphere, the oceans, and living things. Use the periodic table to look up unfamiliar chemical symbols.

Earth	Earth's Atmosphere	Earth's Oceans	Living Things
Oxygen, silicon, aluminum, calcium, sodium, potassium, magnesium, nickel,	Nitrogen, oxygen, helium, neon, hydrogen, and carbon	hydrogen, oxygen, sodium, chlorine, sulfur, magnesium, calcium, potassium	iron, hydrogen, oxygen, nitrogen, phosphorus, calcium

Visual Summary

To complete this summary, fill in the blanks with the correct word or phrase. Then use the key below to check your answers. You can use this page to review the main concepts of the lesson.

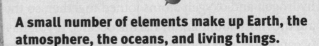

Atoms and Elements

Atoms are the basic building blocks of matter.

16 Atoms are made up of protons, neutrons, and _electrons_

A small number of elements make up Earth, the atmosphere, the oceans, and living things.

18 The most common elements in the atmosphere are _nitrogen_ and _oxygen_

19 The most common elements in the ocean are _hydrogen_ and _oxygen_, which make up water.

13
Al
Aluminum
26.98

Elements can be described by their atomic number and chemical symbol.

17 The atomic number of an element is the number of _protons_ in an atom's nucleus.

Answers: 16 electrons; 17 protons; 18 nitrogen, oxygen; 19 hydrogen, oxygen

20 **Synthesize** An unknown mineral sample contains the element calcium. What information could you learn about calcium from the periodic table?

The number of protons and neutrons

Lesson Review

Vocabulary

Draw a line to connect the following terms to their definitions.

1 nucleus

2 element

3 chemical symbol

A a substance made up of atoms of the same type

B letters that represent an element

C the central region of an atom

Key Concepts

4 Relate Explain how the terms *atom* and *element* are related.

Atoms are in the elements and elements are made up of atoms

5 Infer The atomic number of barium is 56. What do you know about the subatomic particles in an atom of this element? BA

there will be 56 protons in barium.

6 Compare Water is found in the atmosphere, the oceans, and living things. What elements make up water?

h2o   hydrogen and oxygen

7 Explain Atoms contain positively charged protons and negatively charged electrons. Why does an ordinary atom have no charge?

because positives and negatives cancel each other out

Critical Thinking

Use this diagram to answer the following questions.

Elements in Amazonite

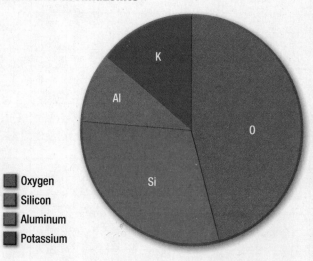

- Oxygen
- Silicon
- Aluminum
- Potassium

8 Analyze The chart shows the abundance of elements in amazonite by mass. Which element is most abundant in amazonite?

Oxygen

9 Identify List the chemical symbols of the elements that make up the mineral amazonite.

16.0
28.1
27.0
39.1

10 Synthesize Based on its chemical makeup, where do you think amazonite is found? Explain.

with the gases because 3/4 of it is chemicals are placed there

© Houghton Mifflin Harcourt Publishing Company

My Notes

Chemical Bonding

ESSENTIAL QUESTION

How do chemical bonds form?

By the end of this lesson, you should be able to describe and compare different types of chemical bonds.

This large framework is held together by links between individual components. In a similar way, atoms in substances are connected by chemical bonds.

Virginia Science Standards of Learning
6.4 The student will investigate and understand that all matter is made up of atoms. Key concepts include:
6.4.d two or more atoms interact to form new substances, which are held together by electrical forces (bonds).

Image Credits: (b) ©Pinto/Corbis / ©Houghton Mifflin Harcourt Publishing Company

🧠 Engage Your Brain

1 Predict Check T or F to show whether you think each statement is true or false.

T	F	
☐	☐	Chemical bonds can be broken.
☐	☐	Chemical bonds form due to interactions between protons and neutrons.
☐	☐	Chemical changes destroy atoms.

2 Identify Unscramble the letters below to find elements that have metallic bonds. Write your words on the blank lines. (**Hint:** Use the periodic table of elements if you get stuck.)

DOLG _____

TABCOL _____

RISLEV _____

DALE _____

ELKCIN _____

✏️ Active Reading

3 Apply Many scientific words, such as *bond*, also have everyday meanings. Use context clues to write your own definition for each meaning of the word *bond*.

Example sentence
A <u>bond</u> can form between two carbon atoms and start the building of a long carbon chain.

bond:

_____

_____

_____

Example sentence
Zach and Leroy first became friends when they formed a <u>bond</u> over their love of basketball.

bond:

_____

_____

_____

Vocabulary Terms

- chemical bond
- ionic bond
- covalent bond
- metallic bond

4 Apply As you learn the definition of each vocabulary term in this lesson, create your own definition or sketch to help you remember the meaning of the term.

Hold It Together!

What is a chemical bond?

All matter is made up of atoms. There are about 100 types of atoms that combine in different ways to form millions of substances. A **chemical bond** is an interaction that joins atoms together. Recall that atoms are made up of a nucleus surrounded by electrons. A chemical bond is an electrical force that holds two atoms together. This force acts between the positively charged nuclei and negatively charged electrons.

In some chemical bonds, electrons are transferred from one atom to another. An *ion* is formed when an atom gains or loses electrons. Sodium chloride, or table salt, is made up of ions. In sodium chloride, each sodium atom donates one electron to a chlorine atom. The result is positively charged sodium ions and negatively charged chloride ions. Each ion is chemically bonded to other ions that have an opposite charge.

In other types of chemical bonds, electrons can be shared between atoms. In a water molecule, each oxygen atom shares electrons with two hydrogen atoms. The sharing of electrons forms bonds that hold the individual water molecules together.

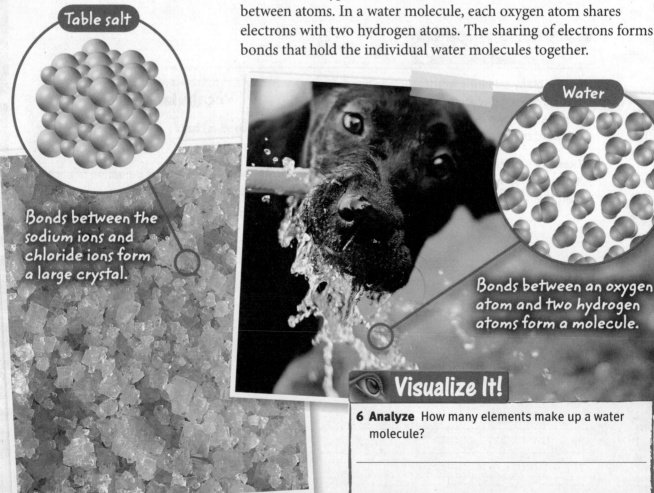

Table salt

Bonds between the sodium ions and chloride ions form a large crystal.

Water

Bonds between an oxygen atom and two hydrogen atoms form a molecule.

Visualize It!

6 Analyze How many elements make up a water molecule?

_____

_____

What happens to chemical bonds during a chemical change?

A brand new penny is bright and shiny. Over time, it becomes darker. This change occurs as copper atoms on the surface interact with oxygen atoms. The oxygen comes from the air and substances on people's hands. New substances called copper oxides are formed on the surface of the penny.

The formation of copper oxides is an example of a *chemical change*. A chemical change occurs when one or more substances react to form new substances. During a chemical change, existing bonds can break, and new chemical bonds can form. After the change, atoms are arranged in a different way. The new substances that form have different physical and chemical properties. For example, copper oxides are made up of copper atoms bonded to oxygen atoms. The color of these compounds is not the same as the color of copper.

During a chemical change, atoms themselves do not change. The same number and types of atoms exist in the new substances. This is why the mass stays constant during a chemical change. Only the arrangement of atoms changes.

👁 Visualize It!

7 Analyze The models below represent chemical changes that occur in Earth's atmosphere. In the second model, draw the molecule that forms when these substances are joined by a chemical bond.

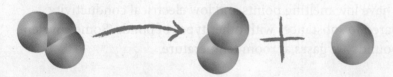

Ozone is made up of three oxygen atoms bonded together. When chemical bonds in the ozone molecule break, two new substances are formed.

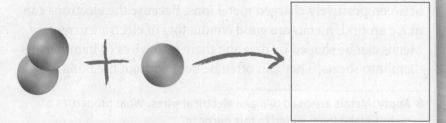

Chemical bonds can form between an oxygen molecule and an oxygen atom. A molecule of ozone is formed.

Ozone molecules in the atmosphere can undergo chemical changes.

Bonding Time

What are three types of chemical bonds?

The electrons of atoms interact in different ways to form different types of bonds. The properties of a substance depend on what type of chemical bonds it has.

Ionic

An **ionic bond** is an attractive force between ions with opposite charges. This bond forms when electrons are transferred from one atom to another. In many compounds, electrons are transferred from metal atoms to nonmetal atoms. Solid ionic compounds form a repeating three-dimensional pattern called a crystal lattice. Most ionic compounds have high melting points. They are often brittle. Solutions of ionic compounds in water conduct electric current.

Covalent

A different type of bond forms between two nonmetal atoms. A **covalent bond** forms when two atoms share electrons. For example, a water molecule is made up of two hydrogen atoms joined by covalent bonds to an oxygen atom. Substances with covalent bonds often have low melting points and low electrical conductivity compared to substances with other types of bonds. Some covalent compounds are gases at room temperature.

Metallic

Metals are held together by a third type of chemical bond. A **metallic bond** forms due to the attraction between metal ions and the free electrons around them. Negatively charged electrons move between positively charged metal ions. Because the electrons can move around, metals are good conductors of electric current. Metals can be shaped by drawing them into wires or hammering them into sheets. They can often be bent without breaking.

---

8 Apply Metals are used to make electrical wires. What properties of metals make them suited to this purpose?

_____

_____

Metals are easily bent and shaped because of the type of bond that holds the atoms together.

In Harcourt Publishing Company • Image Credits: (bg) ©Jack Sullivan/Alamy Images

9 Compare Draw a line to connect each substance to the type of bonding found in that substance.

Fluorite
Calcium ions and fluoride ions form regular crystals in fluorite. Fluorite has a high melting point and is brittle.

Copper
Copper is a good conductor of electric current. Copper can be formed into shapes such as wires and sheets.

Palmitic acid
Palmitic acid is a compound derived from beeswax. It has a fairly low melting point.

Ionic

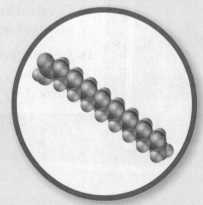

Covalent

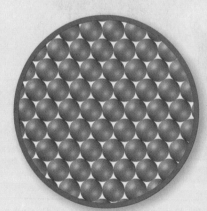

Metallic

Visual Summary

To complete this summary, circle the correct word. Then use the key below to check your answers. You can use this page to review the main concepts of the lesson.

Chemical Bonding

Chemical bonds are electrical forces that hold atoms together.

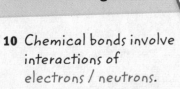

10 Chemical bonds involve interactions of electrons / neutrons.

11 The products and original substances in a chemical change have similar / different properties.

12 A chemical change involves a change in the quantity / arrangement of atoms.

Three types of chemical bonds are ionic bonds, covalent bonds, and metallic bonds.

13 Compounds with ionic bonds usually have low / high melting points.

14 Covalent bonds usually form between the atoms of metals / nonmetals.

15 Substances with covalent / metallic bonds are usually good conductors of electric current.

Answers: 10 electrons; 11 different; 12 arrangement; 13 high; 14 nonmetals; 15 metallic

16 **Design** A scientist is analyzing a yellow powder. Describe a test that could help determine whether the substance contains covalent or ionic bonds.

Lesson Review

Vocabulary

Draw a line to connect the following terms to their definitions.

1 ionic bond

2 covalent bond

3 metallic bond

A A bond formed between positive ions and free electrons

B A bond formed by the transfer of electrons

C A bond formed by the sharing of electrons

Key Concepts

4 Define What is a chemical bond?

_____

_____

_____

_____

_____

5 Compare How is an ionic bond different from a covalent bond?

_____

_____

_____

_____

_____

6 Identify What types of elements are generally involved in an ionic bond?

_____

_____

_____

_____

Critical Thinking

7 Evaluate Can a chemical change alter the total number of atoms? Explain.

_____

_____

_____

8 Infer Why does the formation of a chemical bond indicate a chemical change?

_____

_____

_____

_____

Use this diagram to answer the following questions.

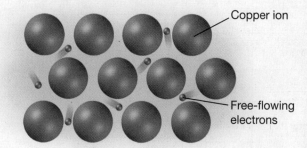

Copper ion

Free-flowing electrons

9 Describe Identify and describe the type of bonding shown.

_____

_____

_____

_____

10 Predict What are some of the likely properties of this substance?

_____

_____

_____

_____

My Notes

Shirley Ann Jackson

PHYSICIST AND EDUCATOR

How can you make contributions to many areas of science all at once? One way is to promote the study of science by others. This is precisely what physicist Dr. Shirley Ann Jackson does as the president of Rensselaer Polytechnic Institute in Troy, New York.

Earlier in her career, she was a research scientist, investigating the electrical and optical properties of matter. Engineers used her research to help develop products for the telecommunications industry. She later became a professor of physics at Rutgers University in New Jersey.

In 1995, President Bill Clinton appointed Dr. Jackson to chair the U.S. Nuclear Regulatory Commission (NRC). The NRC is responsible for promoting the safe use of nuclear energy. At the NRC, Dr. Jackson used her knowledge of how the particles that make up matter interact and can generate energy. She also used her leadership skills. She helped to start the International Nuclear Regulators Association. This group made it easier for officials from many nations to discuss issues of nuclear safety.

Dr. Jackson's interest in science started when she observed bees in her backyard. She is still studying the world around her, making careful observations, and taking actions based on what she learns. These steps for learning were the foundation for all her later contributions to science. As a student, Dr. Jackson learned the same things about matter and energy that you are learning.

Nuclear power plant

Language Arts Connection

Research how nuclear energy is generated, what it can be used for, and what concerns surround it. Write a summary report to the government outlining the risks and benefits of using nuclear energy.

JOB BOARD

Chemical Technician

What You'll Do: Help chemists and chemical engineers in laboratory tests, observe solids, liquids, and gases for research or development of new products. You might handle hazardous chemicals or toxic materials.

Where You Might Work: Mostly indoors in laboratories or manufacturing plants, but may do some research outdoors.

Education: An associate's degree in applied science or science-related technology, specialized technical training, or a bachelor's degree in chemistry, biology, or forensic science is needed.

Other Job Requirements: You need to follow written steps of procedures and to accurately record measurements and observations. You need to understand the proper handling of hazardous materials.

Chef

What You'll Do: Prepare, season, and cook food, keep a clean kitchen, supervise kitchen staff, and buy supplies and equipment.

Where You Might Work: Restaurants, hotels, the military, schools, and in your own kitchen as a private caterer.

Education: Many chefs gain on-the-job training without formal culinary school training. However, you can also learn cooking skills at culinary institutes and earn a two-year or four-year degree.

Other Job Requirements: Your job will require you to be on your feet for many hours and lift heavy equipment and boxes of food.

PEOPLE IN SCIENCE NEWS

Andy Goldsworthy

Changing Matter Is Art

Andy Goldsworthy is interested in how matter changes over time. He is inspired by the changes that occur in nature. As a sculptor, he uses materials found in nature, like snow, ice, twigs, and leaves. Many of his sculptures do not last for very long, but these materials show the changing state of matter. For example, for one of his art projects, he made 13 large snowballs in the winter and placed them in cold storage. In the middle of summer, he placed the snowballs around London. It took five days for the snowballs to melt. During that time they were reminders of a wider world of nature. Movement, change, light, growth, and decay are factors that affect his pieces. Because his work is constantly changing, Goldsworthy takes photographs of his sculptures.

Chemical Reactions

ESSENTIAL QUESTION

How are chemical reactions modeled?

By the end of this lesson, you should be able to use balanced chemical equations to model chemical reactions.

A chemical reaction that releases light energy occurs inside lightning bugs.

Virginia Science Standards of Learning

6.1 The student will demonstrate an understanding of scientific reasoning, logic, and the nature of science by planning and conducting investigations in which:

6.1.i models and simulations are designed and used to illustrate and explain phenomena and systems.

6.4 The student will investigate and understand that all matter is made up of atoms. Key concepts include:

6.4.c elements may be represented by chemical symbols;

6.4.d two or more atoms interact to form new substances, which are held together by electrical forces (bonds);

6.4.e compounds may be represented by chemical formulas; and

6.4.f chemical equations can be used to model chemical changes.

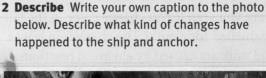

Lesson Labs

Quick Labs
- Breaking Bonds in a Chemical Reaction
- Catalysts and Chemical Reactions

Exploration Lab
- Change of Pace

Engage Your Brain

1 Identify Unscramble the letters below to find two types of energy that can be released when chemical reactions occur. Write your words on the blank lines.

GLITH _____

DSNUO _____

2 Describe Write your own caption to the photo below. Describe what kind of changes have happened to the ship and anchor.

_____

_____

_____

_____

Active Reading

3 Synthesize You can often define an unknown word if you know the meaning of its word parts. Use the word parts and sentence below to make an educated guess about the meaning of the word *exothermic*.

Word part	Meaning
exo-	go out, exit
therm-	heat

Example sentence
Exothermic reactions can sometimes quickly release so much heat that they can melt iron.

exothermic:

_____

_____

_____

Vocabulary Terms

- **chemical reaction**
- **chemical formula**
- **chemical equation**
- **reactant**
- **product**
- **law of conservation of mass**
- **endothermic reaction**
- **exothermic reaction**
- **law of conservation of energy**

4 Identify This list contains the vocabulary terms you'll learn in this lesson. As you read, circle the definition of each term.

Change It Up!

What are the signs of a chemical reaction?

Have you seen leaves change color in the fall or smelled sour milk? The changes in leaves and milk are caused by chemical reactions. A **chemical reaction** is the process in which atoms are rearranged to produce new substances. During a chemical reaction, the bonds that hold atoms together may be formed or broken. The properties of the substances produced in a chemical reaction are different than the properties of the original substances. So, a change in properties is a sign that a chemical reaction may have happened. For example, a solid substance called a *precipitate* may form in a solution. A color change, a change in odor, precipitate formation, and the appearance of gas bubbles are all evidence of a chemical reaction.

👁 Visualize It!

5 Identify In each blank box, identify the evidence that a chemical reaction has taken place.

B The change in Color

A black column forms when sugar reacts with sulfuric acid.

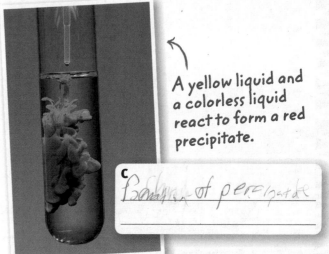

A yellow liquid and a colorless liquid react to form a red precipitate.

C Benation of percipitate

New substances that smell bad are produced when milk turns sour.

A The Change in Odor

Gas bubbles form when baking soda and vinegar react.

D formation of gass bubbles

© Houghton Mifflin Harcourt Publishing Company • Image Credits: (t) ©Charles D. Winters/Photo Researchers, Inc.; (c) ©Charles D. Winters/Photo Researchers, Inc.; (b) ©HMH; (b) ©Charles D. Winters/Photo Researchers, Inc.

How are chemical reactions modeled?

You can describe the substances before and after a reaction by their properties. You can also use symbols to identify the substances. Each element has its own chemical symbol. For example, H is the symbol for hydrogen, and O is the symbol for oxygen. You can use the periodic table to find the chemical symbol for any element. A **chemical formula** uses chemical symbols and numbers to represent a given substance. The chemical symbols in a chemical formula tell you what elements make up a substance. The numbers written below and to the right of chemical symbols are called *subscripts*. Subscripts tell you how many of each type of atom are in a molecule. For example, the chemical formula for water is H_2O. The subscript 2 tells you that there are two atoms of hydrogen in each water molecule. There is no subscript on O, so each molecule of water contains only one oxygen atom.

6 Identify Circle the subscript in the chemical formula below.

H₂O

A water molecule has two hydrogen (H) atoms and one oxygen (O) atom.

With Chemical Equations

To model reactions, chemical formulas can be joined together in an equation. A **chemical equation** is an expression that uses symbols to show the relationship between the starting substances and the substances that are produced by a chemical reaction. The chemical equation below shows that carbon and oxygen react to form carbon dioxide. The chemical formulas of carbon and oxygen are written to the left of the arrow. The chemical formula of carbon dioxide is written to the right of the arrow. Plus signs separate the chemical formulas of multiple products or reactants.

Visualize It!

Reactants are the substances that participate in a chemical reaction. Their chemical formulas are written on the left.

Products are the substances formed in a reaction. Their chemical formulas are written on the right.

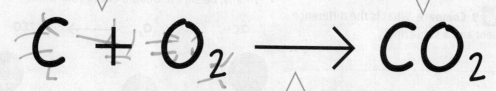

An arrow known as a *yields sign* points from reactants to products.

7 Analyze Atoms of which elements are involved in this reaction?

Carbon And Oxygen

8 Apply How many atoms of each element are in one molecule of the product?

1 carbon atom 2 Oxygen atom

A Balancing Act

How do chemical equations show the law of conservation of mass?

The **law of conservation of mass** states that matter is neither created nor destroyed in ordinary physical and chemical changes. This law means that a chemical equation must show the same numbers and kinds of atoms on both sides of the arrow. When writing a chemical equation, you must be sure that the reactants and products contain the same number of atoms of each element. This is called *balancing the equation*.

You use coefficients to balance an equation. A *coefficient* is a number that is placed in front of a chemical formula. For example, $3H_2O$ represents three water molecules. The number 3 is the coefficient. For an equation to be balanced, all atoms must be counted. So, you must multiply the subscript of each element in a formula by the formula's coefficient. There are a total of six hydrogen atoms and three oxygen atoms in $3H_2O$. Only coefficients—not subscripts—can be changed when balancing equations. Changing the subscripts in the chemical formula of a compound would change the identity of that compound. For example, H_2O_2 represents the compound hydrogen peroxide, not water.

Active Reading **9 Compare** What is the difference between a coefficient and a subscript?

Subscript tell you how many atoms each element and the coefficient tells you how many molecules there are

---

Do the Math Sample Problem

Follow these steps to write a balanced chemical equation.

Identify

A Count the atoms of each element in the reactants and in the product. You can see that there are more oxygen atoms in the reactants than in the product.

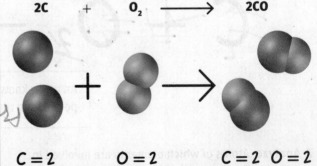

$$C \quad + \quad O_2 \quad \longrightarrow \quad CO$$

$C = 1 \qquad O = 2 \qquad\qquad C = 1 \quad O = 1$

Solve

B To balance the number of oxygen atoms, place the coefficient 2 in front of CO. Now the number of oxygen atoms in the reactants is the same as in the product. Next, the number of carbon atoms needs to be balanced. Place the coefficient 2 in front of C. Finally, be sure to double-check your work!

$$2C \quad + \quad O_2 \quad \longrightarrow \quad 2CO$$

$C = 2 \qquad O = 2 \qquad\qquad C = 2 \quad O = 2$

Do the Math You Try It

10 Calculate Fill in the blanks below to balance this chemical equation. Sketch the products and reactants to show that the number of each type of atom is the same.

Identify

A Count the atoms of each element in the reactants and product in the unbalanced equation.

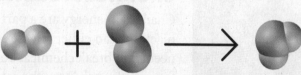

H_2 + O_2 ⟶ H_2O

H = _____   O = _____   H = _____   O = _____

Solve

B To balance the number of each type of atom, place coefficients in front of the appropriate chemical formulas. Sketch the products and reactants, showing the correct number of molecules of each.

_____ H_2 +   _____ O_2 ⟶   _____ H_2O

+   ⟶

H = _____   O = _____   H = _____   O = _____

Hydrogen and oxygen release energy when they react to form water, which forms the cloud shown. The released energy helped to propel this space shuttle.

Think Outside the Book Inquiry

11 Apply Research hydrogen-powered vehicles. Create a poster that describes the advantages and disadvantages of vehicles that use hydrogen as a fuel. Be sure to include a balanced chemical equation to represent the use of hydrogen fuel.

Energy, Energy

Plants absorb energy when they carry out photosynthesis.

Burning a candle releases energy as heat and light.

What happens to energy during chemical reactions?

Changes in energy are a part of all chemical reactions. Chemical reactions can either release energy or absorb energy. Energy is needed to break chemical bonds in the reactants. As new bonds form in the products, the reactants release energy. Reactions are described by the overall change in energy between the products and reactants.

Energy Can Be Absorbed

A chemical reaction that requires an input of energy is called an **endothermic reaction**. The energy taken in during an endothermic reaction is absorbed from the surroundings, usually as heat. This is why endothermic reaction mixtures often feel cold.

Photosynthesis is an example of an endothermic process that absorbs light energy. In photosynthesis, plants use energy from the sun to change carbon dioxide and water to oxygen and the sugar glucose. Overall, more energy is absorbed during photosynthesis than is released to the surroundings. Some of the absorbed energy is stored in the products: oxygen and glucose.

Energy Can Be Released

A chemical reaction in which energy is released to the surroundings is called an **exothermic reaction**. Exothermic reactions can give off energy in several forms. For example, you feel warmth and see a glow when a candle burns. Burning is an exothermic reaction. The products of the reaction are lower in energy than the reactants. Some of the energy in the bonds of the reactants changes to energy as heat and light. Exothermic reaction mixtures often feel warm when heat is released to the surroundings.

12 List Name three everyday exothermic chemical reactions.

Candle fire Sun

© Houghton Mifflin Harcourt Publishing Company • Image Credits: (t) ©Martin Ruegner/Photographer's Choice RF/Getty Images; (b) ©S. Solum/PhotoLink/Getty Images

Energy Is Always Conserved

The **law of conservation of energy** states that energy cannot be created or destroyed. However, energy can change form. The total amount of energy does not change in endothermic or exothermic reactions. For example, light energy from the sun changes into energy stored in chemical bonds during photosynthesis.

Methane (CH_4) burns when it reacts with oxygen (O_2). This reaction produces carbon dioxide (CO_2) and water (H_2O), as shown below. The reaction of methane and oxygen is exothermic. Burning methane releases energy as heat and light into the surroundings. This energy was first stored in the chemical bonds of the reactants. The energy that was stored in the bonds of the reactants is equal to the energy released plus the energy stored in the bonds of the products. The total amount of all of the types of energy is the same before and after every chemical reaction.

Active Reading

13 Describe What happens to the energy absorbed during an endothermic reaction?

The energy is bonds store

Exothermic Reaction of Methane and Oxygen

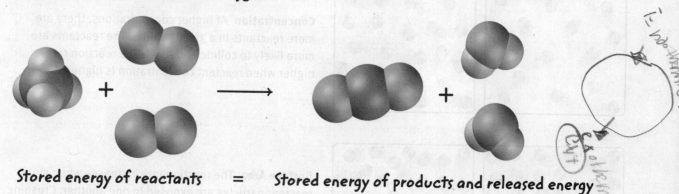

Stored energy of reactants = Stored energy of products and released energy

14 Compare Complete the Venn diagram to compare endothermic and exothermic reactions.

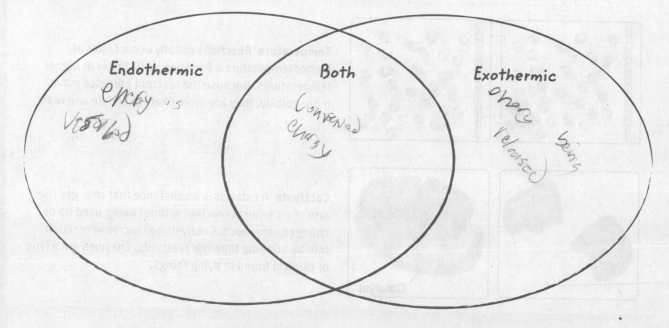

Endothermic — energy absorbed

Both — conserved energy

Exothermic — energy being released

The Need for Speed

Active Reading

15 Identify As you read, underline factors that affect reaction rate.

What affects the rates of reactions?

Some chemical reactions occur in less than a second. Others may take days. The rate of a reaction describes how fast the reaction occurs. For a reaction to occur, particles of the reactants must collide. Reaction rates are affected by how often the particles collide. Factors that affect reaction rates include concentration, surface area, temperature, and the presence of a catalyst.

Changing the Rate of Reaction

Decreased Rate	Increased Rate	Factors That Affect Reaction Rates

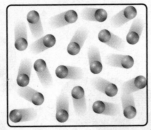

Concentration At higher concentrations, there are more reactants in a given volume. The reactants are more likely to collide and react. The reaction rate is higher when reactant concentration is higher.

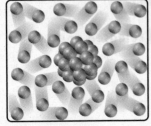 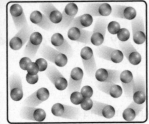

Surface Area The reaction rate increases when more reactant particles are exposed to one another. Crushing or grinding solids increases their surface area and the reaction rate.

 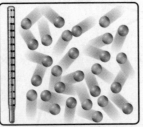

Temperature Reactions usually occur faster at higher temperatures. Particles move faster at higher temperatures. Because the reactant particles move more quickly, they are more likely to collide and react.

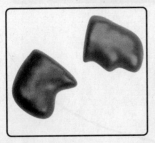 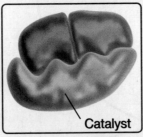

Catalyst

Catalysts A catalyst is a substance that changes the rate of a chemical reaction without being used up or changed very much. Catalysts can increase reaction rate by bringing together reactants. Enzymes are a type of catalyst found in living things.

Why It Matters

Enzymes

Enzymes that increase the rates of reactions keep your body going. They help digest food so your body has the energy it needs. They also help build the molecules your body needs to grow.

Energy

All living things need energy to function. This energy is released when food molecules break down. Enzymes speed up reactions so energy is readily available.

Medical Conditions

Problems with enzymes can cause medical conditions or changes in the body. Albinism, a lack of pigment, occurs when a certain enzyme in animals does not work the way it should work.

Cleaners

Enzymes are not only found in living things. They can be used outside of the body, too. The enzymes in some cleaners help break down substances such as grease.

Extend

Inquiry

16 Describe Explain how enzymes affect reactions.

17 Research Lactose intolerance is a condition that occurs when people are unable to digest milk products. Investigate the cause of lactose intolerance. Write a summary of your findings.

18 Design Create a project that explains how lactose intolerance affects people and why it occurs. Present your project as a written report, a poster, or an oral report.

Visual Summary

To complete this summary, fill in the blanks with the correct word or phrase. Then, use the key below to check your answers. You can use this page to review the main concepts of the lesson.

Bonds are broken and formed during chemical reactions to produce new substances.

19 One sign of a chemical reaction is the formation of a solid _precipitate_

A chemical equation uses symbols to show the relationship between the products and the reactants.

$$C + O_2 \longrightarrow CO_2$$

20 A balanced chemical equation shows that chemical reactions follow the law of conservation of _Mass_

Chemical Reactions

Exothermic reactions release energy to the surroundings, and endothermic reactions absorb energy from the surroundings.

21 The total amount of energy before and after a chemical reaction is _the same_

Reaction rate is affected by reactant concentration, temperature, surface area, and catalysts.

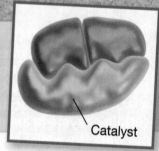

Catalyst

22 A _Catalyst_ is not changed much by a chemical reaction.

23 The rate of reaction is _faster_ at higher temperatures because particles collide more often.

Answers: 19 precipitate; 20 mass; 21 the same; 22 catalyst; 23 faster

24 Design Write a procedure for how you would measure the effect of reactant concentration on the reaction rate.

Lesson Review

Vocabulary

Draw a line to connect the following terms to their definitions.

1 reactant

2 product

A a substance that is produced by a chemical reaction

B a substance that participates in a chemical reaction

Key Concepts

3 Describe What happens to the atoms in the reactants during a chemical reaction?

_____

_____

_____

4 Explain How does a balanced chemical equation show that mass is never lost or gained in a chemical reaction?

_____

_____

_____

_____

_____

5 Relate Describe four ways you could increase the rate of a chemical reaction.

_____

_____

_____

_____

6 Compare How do exothermic and endothermic reactions differ?

_____

_____

_____

_____

Critical Thinking

Use this diagram to answer the following questions.

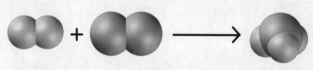

7 Model The reactants in the above reaction are hydrogen (H_2) and nitrogen (N_2). The product is ammonia (NH_3). In the space below, write a balanced chemical equation that represents the reaction.

8 Analyze This reaction releases energy as heat. Explain whether the reaction is exothermic or endothermic and whether it obeys the law of conservation of energy.

_____

_____

_____

_____

_____

9 Evaluate Two colorless solutions are mixed together. Bubbles form as the solution is stirred. Give two possible explanations for this result.

_____

_____

_____

_____

_____

10 Apply The chemical formula of glucose is $C_6H_{12}O_6$. What are the names of the elements in glucose, and how many atoms of each element are present in a glucose molecule?

_____

My Notes

Unit 2 〈 Big Idea 〈 Atoms join together and break apart to form the variety of substances found on Earth.

Lesson 1
ESSENTIAL QUESTION
What particles make up matter?

Describe atoms and how the atoms of an element are alike.

Lesson 2
ESSENTIAL QUESTION
How do chemical bonds form?

Describe how chemical bonding accounts for the variety of substances that make up our world.

Lesson 3
ESSENTIAL QUESTION
How are chemical reactions modeled?

Use balanced chemical equations to model chemical reactions.

Connect ESSENTIAL QUESTIONS
Lessons 2 and 3

1 Synthesize Identify two physical changes that indicate a chemical reaction has occurred. What role does bonding play in chemical reactions?

_____

_____

_____

_____

_____

Think Outside the Book

2 Synthesize Choose one of these activities to help synthesize what you have learned in this unit.

☐ Using what you have learned in lessons 1 and 2, describe a specific element in terms of atoms. Draw a diagram or create a model of your chosen element. Describe how and when the element was discovered or first scientifically described, and provide the origin of the element's name.

☐ Using what you learned in lessons 2 and 3, explain how chemical bonding differs in ionic, covalent, and metallic bonding. Include models to show how atoms are connected together.

Unit 2 Review

Vocabulary

Check the box to show whether each statement is true or false.

T	F	
☐	☐	**1** In a <u>chemical reaction</u>, atoms are rearranged and bonds can be broken or formed.
☐	☐	**2** An <u>endothermic reaction</u> releases energy.
☐	☐	**3** A <u>chemical bond</u> is an interaction that holds two atoms together.
☐	☐	**4** A <u>metallic bond</u> is the attractive force between oppositely charged ions.
☐	☐	**5** A <u>proton</u> is a negatively charged subatomic particle.

Key Concepts

Read each question below, and circle the best answer.

6 Chemical bonding accounts for many of the the properties of substances. Which of the following is a property of metals?

A low melting point

B good electrical conductor

C good thermal insulator

D cannot bend without breaking

7 Which of the following can speed up the rate of a chemical reaction?

A removing a catalyst

B lowering the reactant concentration

C lowering the temperature

D breaking up a reactant into smaller pieces

8 Every atom has a nucleus and an electron cloud. The diagram below is a model of an atom.

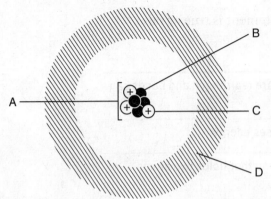

Which label points to a neutron?

A A

C C

B B

D D

9 In a neutral atom, the number of electrons equals the number of what other part?

A protons

C nuclei

B neutrons

D energy levels

10 Which of the following statements describe what happens during a chemical change?

A The number of atoms in the substances changes.

B Atoms break and form bonds with other atoms.

C Atoms remain attached to each other throughout the change.

D The identity of the atoms in the substances changes.

11 A chemical reaction is shown below.

$$3Fe + 4H_2O \rightarrow Fe_3O_4 + 4H_2$$

What are the products in the equation?

A Fe_3O_4 only

C Fe and H_2O

B Fe only

D Fe_3O_4 and H_2

© Houghton Mifflin Harcourt Publishing Company

12 What must happen for an ion to form?

A An atom must gain or lose an electron.

B An atom must gain or lose a proton.

C An atom must gain or lose a neutron.

D An atom must gain or lose a nucleus.

13 Which of the following groups of elements are most commonly found together in living things?

A iron, oxygen, silicon, aluminum

B carbon, titanium, magnesium, potassium

C hydrogen, carbon, oxygen, nitrogen

D sodium, iron, silicon, aluminum

14 Which of the following is an example of an exothermic chemical reaction?

A photosynthesis

B burning wood

C melting ice cubes

D boiling water

15 The diagram below shows a common molecule that is made up of two elements.

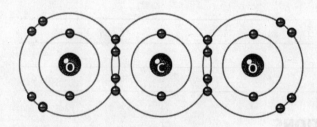

What elements is this molecule composed of?

A calcium and carbon

B argon and oxygen

C oxygen and nitrogen

D carbon and oxygen

Critical Thinking

Answer the following questions in the space provided.

16 Although they both contain the same element, the metal copper (Cu) and the compound copper sulphate ($CuSO_4$) are very different substances. Why can substances that contain the same element have very different properties?

_____

_____

17 The diagram below represents a model of an element.

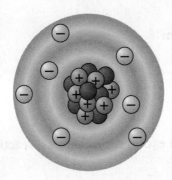

Assuming you can see every particle that makes up this model of an atom, what

is the atomic number of this atom? _____

This element is very common in the atmosphere, and is also found in living things. Hypothesize how this element might make its way from the atmosphere into the bodies of living organisms.

_____

_____

_____

_____

Connect **ESSENTIAL QUESTIONS**
Lessons 2 and 3

Answer the following question in the space provided.

18 Balance the following equation of the violent reaction between potassium and water. Fill in the missing product, and identify that product by name.

$$2K + 2H_2O \rightarrow 2KOH + \text{_____}$$

Earth's Surface

© Houghton Mifflin Harcourt Publishing Company • Image Credits: (bkgd) ©M. Timothy O'Keefe/Alamy; (b) AP Photo/The Florida Times-Union, Jon M. Fletcher

Big Idea

Continuous processes on Earth's surface result in the formation and destruction of landforms and the formation of soil.

Most of Florida's underground caves are also under water, which makes them ideal for diving.

What do you think?

Florida has many caves underground. If a cave is close to Earth's surface and its roof is weak, the roof may fall in, forming a sinkhole. How might these caves have formed?

Sinkholes often form suddenly.

Save a Beach

Like many other features on land, beaches can also change over time. But what could be powerful enough to wash away a beach? Waves and currents.

① Define The Problem

People love to visit the beach. Many businesses along the beach survive because of the tourists that visit the area. But in many places, the beach is being washed away by ocean waves and currents.

Beaches draw lots of tourists.

② Think About It

When waves from the ocean hit the beach at an angle, the waves will often pull some of the sand back into the ocean with them. This sand may then be carried away by the current. In this way, a beach can be washed away. What could you do to prevent a sandy beach from washing away? Looking at the photo below, design a way to prevent the beach from washing away. Then, conduct an experiment to test your design.

Check off the questions below as you use them to design your experiment.

✔ How will you create waves?

✔ At what angle should the waves hit the beach?

✔ Will people still be able to use the beach if your method were used?

Waves carry the sand back into the ocean with them.

③ Make A Plan

A Make a list of the materials you will need for your experiment in the space below.

_____

_____

_____

B Draw a sketch of the setup of your experiment in the space below.

C Conduct your experiment. Briefly state your findings.

_____

_____

_____

Take It Home

Find an area, such as the banks of a pond or a road, which may be eroding in your neighborhood. Study the area. Then, prepare a short presentation for your class on how to prevent erosion in this area.

Earth's Spheres

ESSENTIAL QUESTION

How do matter and energy move through Earth's spheres?

By the end of this lesson, you should be able to describe Earth's spheres, give examples of their interactions, and explain the flow of energy that makes up Earth's energy budget.

Virginia Science Standards of Learning

6.2 The student will investigate and understand basic sources of energy, their origins, transformations, and uses. Key concepts include:

6.2.e energy transformations.

6.3 The student will investigate and understand the role of solar energy in driving most natural processes within the atmosphere, the hydrosphere, and on Earth's surface. Key concepts include:

6.3.a Earth's energy budget.

6.4 The student will investigate and understand that all matter is made up of atoms. Key concepts include:

6.4.g a limited number of elements comprise the largest portion of the solid Earth, living matter, the oceans, and the atmosphere.

6.6 The student will investigate and understand the properties of air and the structure and dynamics of Earth's atmosphere. Key concepts include:

6.6.a air as a mixture of gaseous elements and compounds; and

6.6.d natural and human-caused changes to the atmosphere and the importance of protecting and maintaining air quality.

Emperor penguins spend time on land and need to breathe in oxygen from the air.

These penguins also swim and hold their breath for about 18 minutes as they hunt for fish. What do you have in common with these penguins?

Lesson Labs

Quick Labs
- Explaining Earth's Systems
- Model Earth's Spheres

S.T.E.M. Lab
- Change and Balance Between Spheres

Engage Your Brain

1 Predict Check T or F to show whether you think each statement is true or false.

T	F	
☐	☐	Earth is made up completely of solid rocks.
☐	☐	Animals live only on land.
☐	☐	Water in rivers often flows into the ocean.
☐	☐	Air in the atmosphere can move all over the world.

2 Analyze Think about your daily activities, and list some of the ways in which you interact with Earth.

_____
_____
_____
_____
_____

Active Reading

3 Synthesize You can often define an unknown word if you know the meaning of its word parts. Use the word parts and sentence below to make an educated guess about the meaning of the word *geosphere*.

Word part	Meaning
geo-	earth
-sphere	ball

Example sentence
Water flows across the surface of the geosphere.

geosphere:

_____
_____
_____

Vocabulary Terms

- Earth system
- geosphere
- hydrosphere
- cryosphere
- atmosphere
- biosphere
- energy budget

4 Apply As you learn the definition of each vocabulary term in this lesson, create your own notecards to help you remember the meaning of the term.

What on Earth?

What is the Earth system?

A system is a group of related objects or parts that work together to form a whole. From the center of the planet to the outer edge of the atmosphere, Earth is a system. The **Earth system** is all of the matter, energy, and processes within Earth's boundary. Earth is a complex system made up of many smaller systems. The Earth system is made of nonliving things, such as rocks, air, and water. It also contains living things, such as trees, animals, and people. Matter and energy continuously cycle through the smaller systems that make up the Earth system. The Earth system can be divided into five main parts—the geosphere (JEE•oh•sfir), the hydrosphere (HY•druh•sfir), the cryosphere (KRY•uh•sfir), the atmosphere, and the biosphere.

atmosphere
_____
_____

cryosphere
_____
_____

 Visualize It!

5 Identify In each box, list an example of that sphere that appears in the photo. Write whether the example is a living thing or a nonliving thing.

geosphere
_____
_____

biosphere
_____
_____

hydrosphere
_____
_____

What is the geosphere?

Active Reading 6 **Identify** As you read, underline what each of the three different compositional layers of the geosphere is made up of.

The **geosphere** is the mostly solid, rocky part of Earth. It extends from the center of Earth to the surface of Earth. The geosphere is divided into three layers based on chemical composition: the crust, the mantle, and the core.

The thin, outermost layer of the geosphere is called the crust. It is made mostly of silicate minerals. The crust beneath the oceans is called oceanic crust and is only 5 to 10 km thick. The continents are made of continental crust and range in thickness from about 35 to 70 km. Continental crust is thickest beneath mountain ranges.

The mantle lies below the crust. The mantle is made of hot, very slow-flowing, solid rock. The mantle is about 2,900 km thick. It is made of silicate minerals that are denser than the silicates in the crust.

The central part of Earth is the core, which has a radius of about 3,500 km. It is made of iron and nickel and is the densest layer. The core is actually composed of a solid inner core and a liquid outer core.

Crust
The crust is the thin, rigid outermost layer of Earth.

Mantle
The mantle is the hot layer of rock between Earth's crust and core. The mantle is denser than Earth's crust.

Core
The core is Earth's center. The core is about twice as dense as the mantle.

7 **Summarize** Fill in the table below with the characteristics of each of the geosphere's compositional layers.

Compositional layer	Thickness	Relative density
crust	5–10 km (oceanic) 35–70 km (continental)	least dense

Got Water?

What is the hydrosphere?

The **hydrosphere** is the part of Earth that is liquid water. Ninety-seven percent of all of the water on Earth is the saltwater found in the oceans. Oceans cover 71% of Earth's surface. The hydrosphere also includes the freshwater in lakes, rivers, and marshes. Rain and the water droplets in clouds are also parts of the hydrosphere. Even water that is underground is part of the hydrosphere.

The water on Earth is constantly moving. It moves through the ocean in currents because of wind and differences in the density of ocean waters. Water also moves from Earth's surface to the air by evaporation. It falls back to Earth as rain. It flows in rivers and through rocks under the ground. It even moves into and out of living things.

© Houghton Mifflin Harcourt Publishing Company • Image Credits: (l) ©Tim Hawley/Photographer's Choice RF/Getty Images; (r) ©Mike Briner/Alamy

Active Reading

8 Identify What are two things through which water moves?

_____

_____

Visualize It!

9 Identify After you read, write whether the example of water in each photo is part of the hydrosphere or the cryosphere.

Water droplets form clouds.

A

Water flows over Earth's surface.

B

What is the cryosphere?

Earth's **cryosphere** is made up of all of the frozen water on Earth. Therefore, all of the ice, sea ice, glaciers, ice shelves, and icebergs are a part of the cryosphere. So is permafrost, the frozen ground found at high latitudes. Most of the frozen water on Earth is found in the ice caps in Antarctica and in the Arctic. However, glaciers are found in mountains and at high latitudes all over the world. The amount of frozen water in most of these areas often changes with the seasons. These changes, in turn, play an important role in Earth's climate and in the survival of many species.

10 Compare Fill in the Venn diagram to compare and contrast the hydrosphere and the cryosphere.

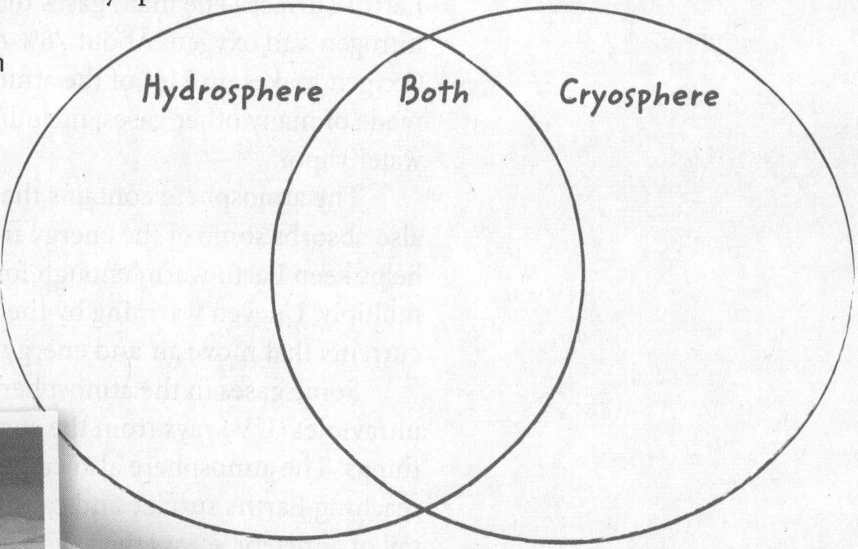

Hydrosphere   Both   Cryosphere

Ships can get stuck in sea ice.

C

D

Water moves in ocean currents across huge distances.

What a Gas!

What is the atmosphere?

The **atmosphere** is mostly made of invisible gases that surround Earth. The atmosphere extends outward about 500 to 600 km from the surface of Earth. But most of the gases lie within 8 to 50 km of Earth's surface. The main gases that make up the atmosphere are nitrogen and oxygen. About 78% of the atmosphere is nitrogen. Oxygen makes up 21% of the atmosphere. The remaining 1% is made of many other gases, including argon, carbon dioxide, and water vapor.

The atmosphere contains the air we breathe. The atmosphere also absorbs some of the energy from the sun's rays. This energy helps keep Earth warm enough for living things to survive and multiply. Uneven warming by the sun gives rise to winds and air currents that move air and energy around the world.

Some gases in the atmosphere absorb and reflect harmful ultraviolet (UV) rays from the sun, protecting Earth and its living things. The atmosphere also causes space debris to burn up before reaching Earth's surface and causing harm. Have you ever seen the tail of a meteor across the sky? Then you have seen a meteoroid burning up as it moves through the atmosphere!

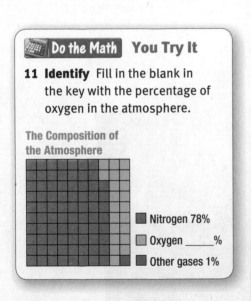

Do the Math · You Try It

11 Identify Fill in the blank in the key with the percentage of oxygen in the atmosphere.

The Composition of the Atmosphere

- ■ Nitrogen 78%
- □ Oxygen _____%
- ■ Other gases 1%

The atmosphere is a very thin layer around Earth. It is made up of a mixture of gases.

Think Outside the Book

12 Apply Design a magazine ad for the atmosphere to show what it does for Earth.

What is the biosphere?

The **biosphere** is made up of living things and the areas of Earth where they are found. The rocks, soil, oceans, lakes, rivers, and lower atmosphere all support life. Organisms have even been found deep in Earth's crust and high in clouds. But no matter where they live, all organisms need certain factors to survive.

Many organisms need oxygen or carbon dioxide to carry out life processes. Liquid water is also important for most living things. Many organisms also need moderate temperatures. You will not find a polar bear living in the Sahara, because it is too hot for the bear. However, some organisms do live in extreme environments, such as in ice at the poles and at volcanic vents on the sea floor.

A stable source of energy is also important for life. For example, plants and algae use the energy from sunlight to make their food. Other organisms get their energy by eating these plants or algae.

 **Active Reading**

13 Identify What factors are needed for life?

_____

_____

These crabs and clams live on the deep ocean floor where it is pitch dark. They rely on special bacteria for their food. Why are these bacteria special? They eat crude oil.

The hair on the sloth looks green because it has algae in it. The green color helps the sloth hide from predators. This is very useful because the sloth moves very, very slowly.

© Houghton Mifflin Harcourt Publishing Company • Image Credits: (bkgd) ©Blaine Harrington III/Corbis; (sloth) ©Gardner/Alamy; (crabs) ©OAR/National Undersea Research Program (NURP); Texas A&M Univ.

Visualize It! (Inquiry)

14 Predict What would happen if the biosphere in this picture stopped interacting with the atmosphere?

_____

_____

_____

_____

_____

What's the Matter?

How do Earth's spheres interact?

Earth's spheres interact as matter and energy change and cycle between the five different spheres. A result of these interactions is that they make life on Earth possible. Remember that the Earth system includes all of the matter, energy, and processes within Earth's boundary.

If matter or energy never changed from one form to another, life on Earth would not be possible. Imagine what would happen if there were no more rain and all of the freshwater drained into the oceans. Most of the life on land would quickly die. But how do these different spheres interact? An example of an interaction is when water cycles between land, ocean, air, and living things. To move between these different spheres, water absorbs, releases, and transports energy all over the world in its different forms.

© Houghton Mifflin Harcourt Publishing Company • Image Credits: (l) ©Orland Group/The Image Bank/Getty Images; (t) ©Nature Source/Photo Researchers, Inc.

Visualize It!

15 Analyze Fill in the boxes below each photo with the names of two spheres that are interacting in that photo.

Rain provides water for living things.

A

Decomposing organisms release nutrients into the soil.

B

By Exchanging Matter

Earth's spheres interact as matter moves between spheres. For example, the atmosphere interacts with the hydrosphere or cryosphere when water vapor condenses to form clouds. An interaction also happens as water from the hydrosphere or cryosphere evaporates to enter the atmosphere.

In some processes, matter moves through several spheres. For example, some bacteria in the biosphere remove nitrogen gas from the atmosphere. These bacteria then release a different form of nitrogen into the soil, or geosphere. Plants in the biosphere use this nitrogen to grow. When the plant dies and decays, the nitrogen is released in several forms. One of these forms returns to the atmosphere.

Active Reading **16 Identify** What is the relationship between Earth's spheres and matter?

_____

By Exchanging Energy

Earth's spheres also interact as energy moves between them. For example, plants use solar energy to make their food. Some of this energy is passed on to animals that eat plants. Some of the energy is released into the atmosphere as heat as the animals move. Some energy is released into the geosphere when organisms die and decay. In this case, energy has entered the biosphere and moved into the atmosphere and geosphere.

Energy also moves back and forth between spheres. For example, solar energy re-emitted by Earth's surface warms up the atmosphere, creating winds. Winds create waves and surface ocean currents that travel across Earth's oceans. When warm winds and ocean currents reach colder areas, thermal energy is transferred to the colder air and water, and warms them up. In this case, the energy has cycled between the atmosphere and the hydrosphere.

Icebergs melt in the sun.

(D)

Waves break where the sea floor is shallow.

(C)

Balancing the Budget

What is the source of Earth's energy?

Active Reading **17 Identify** As you read, underline the sources of Earth's energy.

Almost all of Earth's energy comes from the sun. Part of this solar energy is reflected into space. The rest is absorbed by Earth's surface. A tiny fraction of Earth's energy comes from ocean tides and geothermal sources such as lava and magma.

Energy on Earth moves through and between the five Earth spheres. These spheres are open systems that constantly exchange energy with each other. Energy is transferred between spheres, but it is not created anew or destroyed. It simply moves between spheres or changes into other forms of energy.

In any system, input must equal output in order to keep the system balanced. The same is true for the flow of energy through Earth's spheres. In Earth's energy system, any addition in energy must be balanced by an equal subtraction of energy. For example, energy taken away from the atmosphere may be added to the oceans or to the geosphere. Earth's **energy budget** is a way to keep track of energy transfers into and out of the Earth system.

The chart on the next page shows the net flow of energy that forms Earth's energy budget. Energy from the sun may be reflected back to space or absorbed by Earth's surface. Earth radiates energy into space in the form of heat.

When Earth's energy flow is balanced, global temperatures stay relatively stable over long periods of time. But sometimes changes in the system cause Earth's energy budget to become unbalanced.

The sun is Earth's main source of energy.

Think Outside the Book **Inquiry**

18 Apply With your classmates, discuss the idea that energy can never be created or destroyed. Think of an example from your daily life in which energy is changed from one form to another.

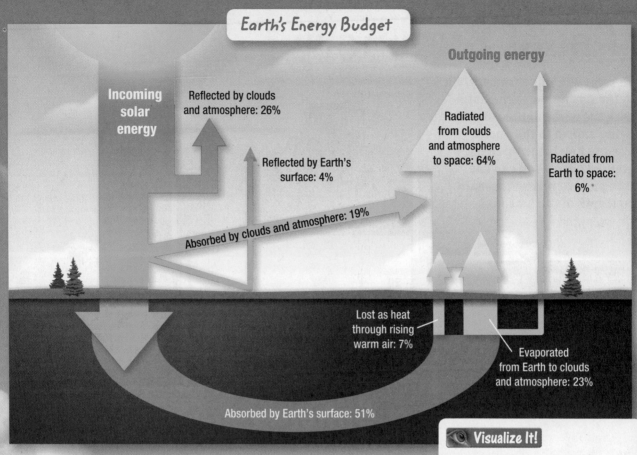

Earth's Energy Budget

Incoming solar energy

Reflected by clouds and atmosphere: 26%

Reflected by Earth's surface: 4%

Outgoing energy

Radiated from clouds and atmosphere to space: 64%

Radiated from Earth to space: 6%

Absorbed by clouds and atmosphere: 19%

Lost as heat through rising warm air: 7%

Evaporated from Earth to clouds and atmosphere: 23%

Absorbed by Earth's surface: 51%

What can disturb Earth's energy budget?

An unbalanced energy budget can increase or decrease global temperatures and disrupt the balance of energy in Earth's system. Two things that can disturb Earth's energy budget are an increase in greenhouse gases and a decrease in polar ice caps.

Greenhouse Gases

Greenhouse gases, such as carbon dioxide and water vapor, absorb energy from Earth's surface and keep that energy in the atmosphere. An increase in greenhouse gases decreases the amount of energy radiated out to space. Earth's temperatures then rise over time, which may lead to climate changes.

Melting Polar Ice

Bright white areas such as the snow-covered polar regions and glaciers reflect sunlight. In contrast, bodies of water and bare rock appear dark. They tend to absorb solar radiation. When snow and ice melt, the exposed water and land absorb and then radiate more energy than the snow or ice did. Earth's atmosphere becomes warmer, leading to increased global temperatures and climate changes.

> **Visualize It!**
>
> **19 Describe** Describe what happens to solar energy as it enters Earth's atmosphere.
>
> _____
>
> _____
>
> _____

Visual Summary

To complete this summary, fill in the box below each photo with the name of the sphere being shown in the photo. Then use the key below to check your answers. You can use this page to review the main concepts of the lesson.

20 _____

Earth's Spheres

21 _____

24 _____

22 _____

23 _____

Answers: 20 geosphere; 21 biosphere; 22 cryosphere; 23 hydrosphere; 24 atmosphere

25 Synthesize Diagram an interaction between any two of Earth's spheres.

Lesson Review

Vocabulary

Underline the term that best completes each of the following sentences.

1 The ice caps in the Antarctic and the Arctic are a part of the *geosphere/cryosphere/biosphere*.

2 Most of the water on Earth can be found in the *biosphere/hydrosphere/geosphere*.

3 The *hydrosphere/geosphere/atmosphere* protects organisms that live on Earth by blocking out harmful UV rays from the sun.

Key Concepts

Location	Sphere
4 Identify Forms a thin layer of gases around Earth	
5 Identify Extends from Earth's core to Earth's surface	
6 Identify Extends from inside Earth's crust to the lower atmosphere	

7 Describe What does the Earth system include?

_____

_____

8 Analyze Which spheres are interacting when a volcano erupts and releases gases into the air?

_____

_____

9 Identify What are the two most abundant gases in the atmosphere?

_____

10 Describe How do Earth's spheres interact?

_____

_____

Critical Thinking

Use this graph to answer the following question.

Earth's Solar Energy Balance

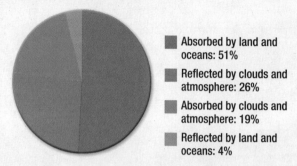

- Absorbed by land and oceans: 51%
- Reflected by clouds and atmosphere: 26%
- Absorbed by clouds and atmosphere: 19%
- Reflected by land and oceans: 4%

11 Infer Which parts of the graph would increase if all of Earth's polar ice melts? Which parts would decrease?

_____

_____

_____

12 Identify Name two ways in which the Earth system relies on energy from the sun.

_____

_____

_____

_____

13 Analyze How does the biosphere rely on the other spheres for survival?

_____

_____

_____

_____

14 Infer Where is most of Earth's liquid water? What must be done so humans can drink it?

_____

_____

_____

_____

My Notes

Weathering

ESSENTIAL QUESTION

How does weathering change Earth's surface?

By the end of this lesson, you should be able to analyze the effects of physical and chemical weathering on Earth's surface, including examples of each kind of weathering.

Virginia Science Standards of Learning
6.5 The student will investigate and understand the unique properties and characteristics of water and its roles in the natural and human-made environment. Key concepts include:
6.5.c the action of water in physical and chemical weathering.

Wave Rock in Australia may look like an ocean wave, but it was actually formed when the rock in the middle of this formation weathered faster than the rock at the top.

👋 **Lesson Labs**

Quick Labs
- Mechanical Weathering
- Weathering Chalk
- How Can Materials on Earth's Surface Change?

Engage Your Brain

1 Predict Check T or F to show whether you think each statement is true or false.

T	F	
☐	☐	Rocks can change shape and composition over time.
☐	☐	Rocks cannot be weathered by wind and chemicals in the air.
☐	☐	A rusty car is an example of weathering.
☐	☐	Plants and animals can cause weathering of rocks.

2 Describe Your class has taken a field trip to a local stream. You notice that the rocks in the water are rounded and smooth. Write a brief description of how you think the rocks changed over time.

_____

_____

_____

_____

_____

_____

Active Reading

3 Synthesize You can often find clues to the meaning of a word by examining the use of that word in a sentence. Read the following sentences and write your own definition for the word *abrasion*.

Example sentences
Bobby fell on the sidewalk and scraped his knee. The abrasion on his knee was painful because of the loss of several layers of skin.

Vocabulary Terms
- weathering
- physical weathering
- abrasion
- chemical weathering
- oxidation
- acid precipitation

4 Apply As you learn the definition of each vocabulary term in this lesson, create your own definition or sketch to help you remember the meaning of the term.

abrasion:

_____

_____

_____

_____

BreakItDown

What is weathering?

Did you know that sand on a beach may have once been a part of a large boulder? Over millions of years, a boulder can break down into many smaller pieces. The breakdown of rock material by physical and chemical processes is called **weathering**. Two kinds of weathering are *physical weathering* and *chemical weathering*.

What causes physical weathering?

Rocks can get smaller and smaller without a change in the composition of the rock. This is an example of a physical change. The process by which rock is broken down into smaller pieces by physical changes is **physical weathering**. Temperature changes, pressure changes, plant and animal actions, water, wind, and gravity are all agents of physical weathering.

As materials break apart, they can become even more exposed to physical changes. For instance, a large boulder can be broken apart by ice and water over time. Eventually, the boulder can split in two. Now there are two rocks exposed to the agents of physical weathering. In other words, the amount of surface area exposed to the agents of physical weathering increases. The large boulder can become thousands of tiny rocks over time as each new rock increases the amount of surface area able to be weathered.

Active Reading

5 Identify As you read, place the names of some common agents of physical weathering in the graphic organizer below.

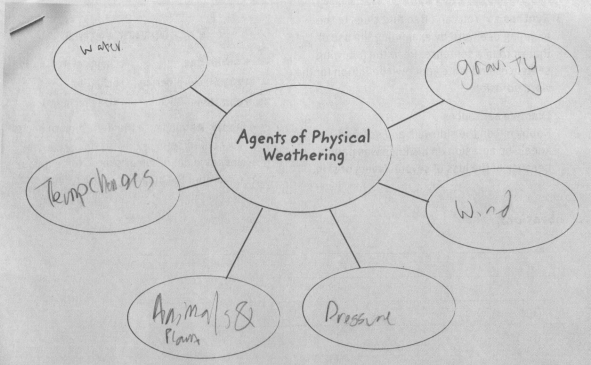

6 Describe Write a caption for each of the images to describe the process of ice wedging

Ice Wedging

Water

Water flows
through the crack.

Ice

The ice is causing
the crack to expand.

Water

The ice melts
and moveinto
of some in

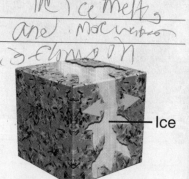

Ice

the water freezes
when meives it
expand

Temperature Change

Changes in temperatures can cause a rock to break apart. A rise in temperature will cause a rock to expand. A decrease in temperature will cause a rock to contract. Repeated temperature changes can weaken the structure of a rock, causing the rock to crumble. Even changes in temperature between day and night can cause rocks to expand and contract. In desert regions differences in day and night temperatures can be significant. Rocks can weaken and crumble from the stress caused by these temperature changes.

Ice wedging, sometimes known as *frost wedging*, can also cause rocks to physically break apart, as shown in the image below. Ice wedging causes cracks in rocks to expand as water seeps in and freezes. When water collects in cracks in rock and the temperature drops, the water may freeze. Water expands as it freezes to become ice. As the ice expands, the crack will widen. As more water enters the crack, it can expand to an even larger size. Eventually, a small crack in a rock can cause even the largest of rocks to split apart.

7 Hypothesize Where on Earth would physical weathering from temperature changes be most common? Least common? Explain.

desert regions b/c it get hot
in the day earth it gets really cold
where the glaers

These cracks, which were caused by ice wedging, will continue to expand over time.

Enchanted Rock was once buried deep inside Earth.

Pressure Change

Physical weathering can be caused by pressure changes. Rocks formed under pressure deep within Earth can become exposed at the surface. As overlying materials are removed above the rock, the pressure decreases. As a result, the rock expands, causing the outermost layers of rock to separate from the underlying layers, as shown to the left. *Exfoliation* (ex•foh•lee•AY•shun) is the process by which the outer layers of rock slowly peel away due to pressure changes. Enchanted Rock in Texas is a 130 m–high dome of granite that is slowly losing the outermost layers of rock due to exfoliation and other processes.

Animal Action

Animals can cause physical weathering. Many animals dig burrows into the ground, allowing more rock to be exposed. Common burrowing animals include ground squirrels, prairie dogs, ants, and earthworms. These animals move soils and allow new rocks, soils, and other materials to be exposed at the surface, as shown below. Materials can undergo weathering below the surface, but are more likely to be weathered once exposed at the surface.

Visualize It!

8 Describe Write a caption for each animal describing how it might cause physical weathering.

Prairie dog

A They dig in the ground so the rocks come up

Some pocket gophers can dig burrows up to 240 m in length.

C It digs in the ground and brings rocks out

Earthworm

B They dig down digging

Wind, Water, and Gravity

Rock can be broken down by the action of other rocks over time. **Abrasion** (uh•BRAY•zhuhn) is the breaking down and wearing away of rock material by the mechanical action of other rock. Three agents of physical weathering that can cause abrasion are moving water, wind, and gravity. Also, rocks suspended in the ice of a glacier can cause abrasion of other rocks on Earth's surface.

In moving water, rock can become rounded and smooth. Abrasion occurs as rocks are tumbled in water, hitting other rocks. Wind abrasion occurs when wind lifts and carries small particles in the air. The small particles can blast away at surfaces and slowly wear them away. During a landslide, large rocks can fall from higher up a slope and break more rocks below, causing abrasion.

 **Active Reading**

9 Identify As you read, underline the agents of weathering that cause abrasion.

Rocks are tumbled in water, causing abrasion.

Wind-blown sand can blast small particles away.

Rocks can be broken down in a landslide.

Plant Growth

You have probably noticed that just one crack in a sidewalk can be the opening for a tiny bit of grass to grow. Over time, a neglected sidewalk can become crumbly from a combination of several agents of physical weathering, including plant growth. Why?

Roots of plants do not start out large. Roots start as tiny strands of plant matter that can grow inside small cracks in rocks. As the plant gets bigger, so do the roots. The larger a root grows, the more pressure it puts on rock. More pressure causes the rock to expand, as seen to the right. Eventually, the rock can break apart.

Think Outside the Book Inquiry

10 Summarize Imagine you are a rock. Write a short biography of your life as a rock, describing the changes you have gone through over time.

This tree started as a tiny seedling and eventually grew to split the rock in half.

© Houghton Mifflin Harcourt Publishing Company • Image Credits: (tl) ©Comstock/Getty Images; (tc) ©Galen Rowell/Corbis; (tr) ©Kevin R. Morris/Corbis; (br) ©geogphotos/Alamy

Reaction

What causes chemical weathering?

Chemical weathering changes both the composition and appearance of rocks. **Chemical weathering** is the breakdown of rocks by chemical reactions. Agents of chemical weathering include oxygen in the air and acids.

Reactions with Oxygen

Oxygen in the air or in water can cause chemical weathering. Oxygen reacts with the compounds that make up rock, causing chemical reactions. The process by which other chemicals combine with oxygen is called **oxidation** (ahk•si•DAY•shun).

Rock surfaces sometimes change color. A color change can mean that a chemical reaction has taken place. Rocks containing iron can easily undergo chemical weathering. Iron in rocks and soils combines quickly with oxygen that is dissolved in water. The result is a rock that turns reddish orange. This is rust! The red color of much of the soil in the southeastern United States and of rock formations in the southwestern United States is due to the presence of rust, as seen in the image below.

Reactions with Acid Precipitation

Acids break down most minerals faster than water alone. Increased amounts of acid from various sources can cause chemical weathering of rock. Acids in the atmosphere are created when chemicals combine with water in the air. Rain is normally slightly acidic. When fossil fuels are burned, other chemicals combine with water in the atmosphere to produce even stronger acids. When these stronger acids fall to Earth, they are called **acid precipitation** (AS•id prih•sip•ih•TAY•shun). Acid precipitation is recognized as a problem all around the world and causes rocks to break down and change composition.

Active Reading

11 Identify As you read, underline examples of chemical weathering.

These rocks in Arizona are red because of oxidation.

Active Reading **12 Describe** How does acid precipitation cause rocks to weather faster?

B/c som of the rocks can be dissolve faster from acid

© Houghton Mifflin Harcourt Publishing Company • Image Credits: ©Craig Lovell/Corbis

Reactions with Acids in Groundwater

Water in the ground, or groundwater, can cause chemical weathering. As groundwater moves through spaces or cracks in rock, acids in the water can cause rocks to dissolve. A small crack in a rock can result in the formation of extensive cave systems that are carved out over time under Earth's surface, as shown to the right. The dissolved rock material is carried in water until it is later deposited. Stalactites (stuh•LAHK•tyt) and stalagmites (stuh•LAHG•myt) are common features in cave systems as dissolved chemicals are deposited by dripping water underground.

Reactions with Acids in Living Things

Acids are produced naturally by certain living organisms. For instance, lichens (LY•kuhns) and mosses often grow on rocks and trees. As they grow on rocks, they produce weak acids that can weather the rock's surface. As the acids move through tiny spaces in the rocks, chemical reactions can occur. The acids will eventually break down the rocks. As the acids seep deeper into the rocks, cracks can form. The rock can eventually break apart when the cracks get too large.

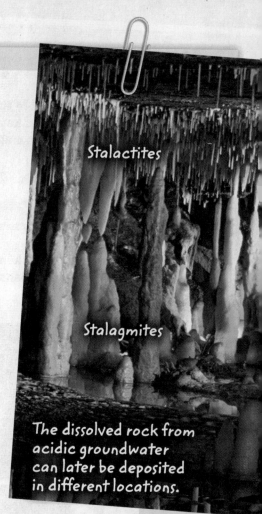

Stalactites

Stalagmites

The dissolved rock from acidic groundwater can later be deposited in different locations.

This gear is rusted, which indicates that a chemical reaction has taken place.

Think Outside the Book

13 Apply Think of an item made by humans that could be broken down by the agents of physical and chemical weathering. Describe to your classmates all of the ways the item could change over time.

Visual Summary

To complete this summary, fill in the blanks with the correct word or phrase. Then use the answer key to check your answers. You can use this page to review the main concepts of the lesson.

Weathering

Physical weathering breaks rock into smaller pieces by physical means.

Chemical weathering breaks down rock by chemical reactions.

14 Label the images with the type of physical weathering shown.

A _Plant growth_

B _animal action_

C _ice wedging_

15 Label the images with the type of chemical weathering shown.

A _Oxcidation_

B _reactions_

Answers: 14 A, plant growth; B, animal action; C, ice wedging; 15 A, oxidation; B, reactions with acids

16 Relate Why are some rocks more easily weathered than other rocks?

© Houghton Mifflin Harcourt Publishing Company • Image Credits: (tree) ©geophotos/Alamy; (worm) ©Dr. Jeremy Burgess/Photo Researchers, Inc.; (rocks) ©Peter Mc Cabe/Alamy; (mountains) ©Craig Lovell/Corbis; (cave) ©Hans Strand/Stone/Getty Images

Erosion and Deposition by Water

ESSENTIAL QUESTION

How does water change Earth's surface?

By the end of this lesson, you should be able to relate the processes of erosion and deposition by water to the landforms that result from these processes.

Rivers aren't only found on Earth's surface. They also flow underground! Underground rivers can carve out caves full of channels, waterfalls, and even lakes.

Virginia Science Standards of Learning

6.1 The student will demonstrate an understanding of scientific reasoning, logic, and the nature of science by planning and conducting investigations in which:

6.1.j current applications are used to reinforce science concepts.

6.7 The student will investigate and understand the natural processes and human interactions that affect watershed systems. Key concepts include:

6.7.c divides, tributaries, river systems, and river and stream processes.

Lesson Labs

Quick Labs
- Wave Action on the Shoreline
- Moving Sediment
- Modeling Stalactites and Stalagmites

Exploration Lab
- Exploring Stream Erosion and Deposition

Engage Your Brain

1 Predict Check T or F to show whether you think each statement is true or false.

T	F	
☐	☐	Water is able to move rocks as big as boulders.
☐	☐	Rivers can help to break down mountains.
☐	☐	Water cannot change rock underneath Earth's surface.
☐	☐	Waves and currents help to form beaches.

2 Explain Write a caption that explains how you think this canyon formed.

_____

_____

_____

Active Reading

3 Synthesize Several of the vocabulary terms in this lesson are compound words, or two separate words combined to form a new word that has a new meaning. Use the meanings of the two separate words to make an educated guess about the meaning of the compound terms shown below.

flood + plain = floodplain

_____

_____

ground + water = groundwater

_____

_____

shore + line = shoreline

_____

_____

sand + bar = sandbar

_____

_____

Vocabulary Terms

- erosion
- deposition
- floodplain
- delta
- alluvial fan
- groundwater
- shoreline
- beach
- sandbar
- barrier island

4 Apply As you learn the definition of each vocabulary term in this lesson, create your own definition or sketch to help you remember the meaning of the term.

Go with the Flow

How does flowing water change Earth's surface?

If your job was to carry millions of tons of rock and soil across the United States, how would you do it? You might use a bulldozer or a dump truck, but your job would still take a long time. Did you know that rivers and other bodies of flowing water do this job every day? Flowing water, as well as wind and ice, can move large amounts of material, such as soil and rock. Gravity also has a role to play. Gravity causes water to flow and rocks to fall downhill.

By Erosion

Acting as liquid conveyor belts, rivers and streams erode soil, rock, and sediment. *Sediment* is tiny grains of broken-down rock. **Erosion** is the process by which sediment and other materials are moved from one place to another. Eroded materials in streams may come from the stream's own bed and banks or from materials carried to the stream by rainwater runoff. Over time, erosion causes streams to widen and deepen.

By Deposition

After streams erode rock and soil, they eventually drop, or deposit, their load downstream. **Deposition** is the process by which eroded material is dropped. Deposition occurs when gravity's downward pull on sediment is greater than the push of flowing water or wind. This usually happens when the water or wind slows down. A stream deposits materials along its bed, banks, and mouth, which can form different landforms.

5 Compare Fill in the Venn diagram to compare and contrast erosion and deposition.

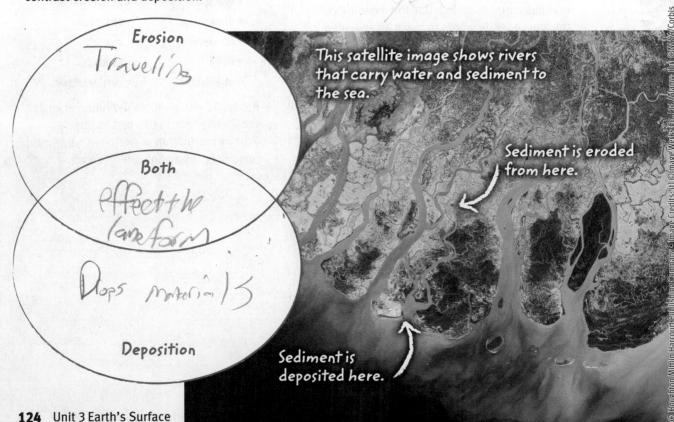

Erosion

Traveling

Both

effect the lanform

Drops materials

Deposition

This satellite image shows rivers that carry water and sediment to the sea.

Sediment is eroded from here.

Sediment is deposited here.

What factors relate to a stream's ability to erode material?

Some streams are able to erode large rocks, while others can erode only very fine sediment. Some streams move many tons of material each day, while others move very little sediment. So what determines how much material a stream can erode? A stream's gradient, discharge, and load are the three main factors that control what sediment a stream can carry.

Gradient

Gradient is the measure of the change in elevation over a certain distance. You can think of gradient as the steepness of a slope. The water in a stream that has a high gradient—or steep slope—moves very rapidly because of the downward pull of gravity. This rapid water flow gives the stream a lot of energy to erode rock and soil. A river or stream that has a low gradient has less energy for erosion, or erosive energy.

Load

Materials carried by a stream are called the stream's *load*. The size of the particles in a stream's load is affected by the stream's speed. Fast-moving streams can carry large particles. The large particles bounce and scrape along the bottom and sides of the streambed. Thus, a stream that has a load of large particles has a high erosion rate. Slow-moving streams carry smaller particles and have less erosive energy.

Discharge

The amount of water that a stream carries in a given amount of time is called *discharge*. The discharge of a stream increases when a major storm occurs or when warm weather rapidly melts snow. As the stream's discharge increases, its erosive energy, speed, and load increase.

Active Reading

6 Explain Why do some streams and rivers cause more erosion and deposition than others?

B/c somehow higher
gradient or they are a little
Steeper.

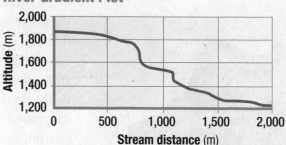

Do the Math

River Gradient Plot

A river gradient plot shows how quickly the elevation of a river falls along its course. The slope of the line is the river's gradient. The line has a steep slope at points along the river where the gradient is steep. The line has a nearly level slope where the river gradient is shallow.

Identify

7 Along this river, at which two approximate altitude ranges are the gradients the steepest?

_1,750m to 1,550m_
alt 1,600, to 1,400m

8 At which altitude ranges would you expect the highest streambed erosion rate?

9 At which altitude ranges would you expect the slowest streambed erosion rate?

What landforms can streams create?

A stream forms as water erodes soil and rock to make a channel. A *channel* is the path that a stream follows. As the stream continues to erode rock and soil, the channel gets wider and deeper. Over time, canyons and valleys can form.

Canyons and Valleys by Erosion

The processes that changed Earth's surface in the past continue to be at work today. For example, erosion and deposition have taken place throughout Earth's history. Six million years ago, Earth's surface in the area now known as the Grand Canyon was flat. The Colorado River cut down into the rock and formed the Grand Canyon over millions of years. Landforms, such as canyons and valleys, are created by the flow of water through streams and rivers. As the water moves, it erodes rock and sediment from the streambed. The flowing water can cut through rock, forming steep canyons and valleys.

Think Outside the Book

10 Apply Discuss with your classmates some landforms near your town that were likely made by flowing water.

Visualize It!

11 Apply On the lines below, label where erosion and deposition are occurring.

Canyon

A _____

B _____

Meander

Floodplains by Deposition

When a stream floods, a layer of sediment is deposited over the flooded land. Many layers of deposited sediment can form a flat area called a **floodplain**. Sediment often contains nutrients needed for plant growth. Because of this, floodplains are often very fertile.

As a stream flows through an area, its channel may run straight in some parts and curve in other parts. Curves and bends that form a twisting, looping pattern in a stream channel are called *meanders*. The moving water erodes the outside banks and deposits sediment along the inside banks. Over many years, meanders shift position. During a flood, a stream may cut a new channel that bypasses a meander. The cut-off meander forms a crescent-shaped lake, which is called an *oxbow lake*.

Deltas and Alluvial Fans by Deposition

When a stream empties into a body of water, such as a lake or an ocean, its current slows and it deposits its load. Streams often deposit their loads in a fan-shaped pattern called a **delta**. Over time, sediment builds up in a delta, forming new land. Sometimes the new land can extend far into the lake or ocean. A similar process occurs when a stream flows onto a flat land surface from mountains or hills. On land, the sediment forms an alluvial fan. An **alluvial fan** is a fan-shaped deposit that forms on dry land.

Active Reading

12 Identify As you read, underline the definitions of *delta* and *alluvial fan*.

13 Compare Compare and contrast alluvial fans and deltas.

_____

_____

_____

_____

_____

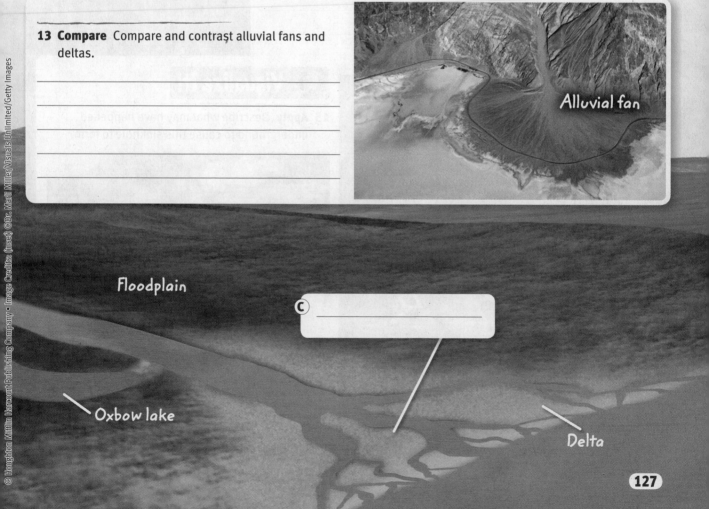

Alluvial fan

Floodplain

C _____

Oxbow lake

Delta

More Waterworks

What landforms are made by groundwater erosion?

As you have learned, rivers cause erosion when water picks up and moves rock and soil. The movement of water underground can also cause erosion. **Groundwater** is the water located within the rocks below Earth's surface. Slightly acidic groundwater can cause erosion by dissolving rock. When underground erosion happens, caves can form. Most of the world's caves formed over thousands of years as groundwater dissolved limestone underground. Although caves are formed by erosion, they also show signs of deposition. Water that drips from cracks in a cave's ceiling leaves behind icicle-shaped deposits known as *stalactites* and *stalagmites*. When the groundwater level is lower than the level of a cave, the cave roof may no longer be supported by the water underneath. If the roof of a cave collapses, it may leave a circular depression called a *sinkhole*.

Active Reading 14 **Explain** How does groundwater cause caves to form?

_____

_____

Stalactites are caused by deposition.

Groundwater can erode rock, causing caves to form.

Visualize It!

15 **Apply** Describe what may have happened underground to cause this sinkhole to form.

_____

_____

_____

_____

What forces shape a shoreline?

A **shoreline** is the place where land and a body of water meet. Ocean water along a shoreline moves differently than river water moves. Ocean waves crashing against the shoreline have a great deal of energy. Strong waves may erode material. Gentle waves may deposit materials. In addition to waves, ocean water has *currents,* or streamlike movements of water. Like waves, currents can also erode and deposit materials.

Waves

Waves play a major part in building up and breaking down a shoreline. Waves slow down as they approach a shoreline. The first parts of the shoreline that waves meet are the *headlands,* or pieces of land that project into the water. The slowing waves bend toward the headlands, which concentrates the waves' energy. A huge amount of energy is released when waves crash into headlands, causing the land to erode. The waves striking the areas between headlands have less energy. Therefore, these waves are more likely to deposit materials rather than erode materials.

Currents

When water travels almost parallel to the shoreline very near shore, the current is called a *longshore current*. Longshore currents are caused by waves hitting the shore at an angle. Waves that break at angles move sediment along the coast. The waves push the sand in the same angled direction in which they break. But the return water flow moves sand directly away from the beach. The end result is a zigzag movement of the sand. As sand moves down a beach, the upcurrent end of the beach is eroded away while the downcurrent end of the beach is built up.

As waves approach a shoreline, they bend toward the headlands and crash against them. The energy in the waves between the headlands is spread out, so they have less erosive power.

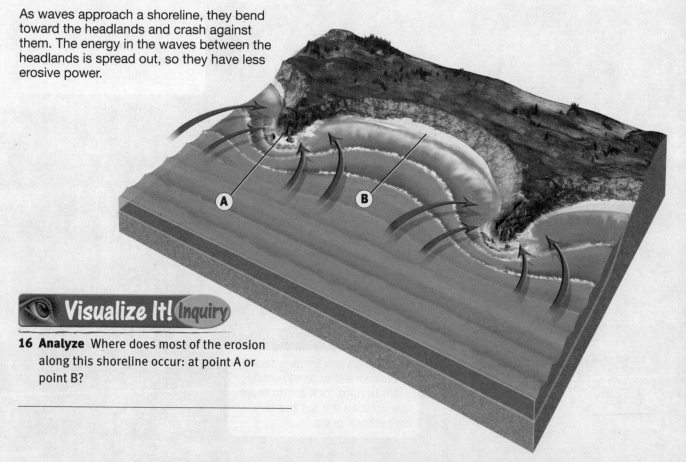

Visualize It! Inquiry

16 Analyze Where does most of the erosion along this shoreline occur: at point A or point B?

_____

Surf Versus Turf

What coastal landforms are made by erosion?

Active Reading

17 Identify As you read, underline the sentence that summarizes the factors that determine how fast a shoreline erodes.

Wave erosion produces a variety of features along a shoreline. The rate at which rock erodes depends on the hardness of the rock and the energy of the waves. Gentle waves cause very little erosion. Strong waves from heavy storms can increase the rate of erosion. During storms, huge blocks of rock can be broken off and eroded away. In fact, a severe storm can noticeably change the appearance of a shoreline in a single day.

In addition to wave energy, the hardness of the rock making up the coastline affects how quickly the coastline is eroded. Very hard rock can slow the rate of erosion because it takes a great deal of wave energy to break up hard rock. Soft rock erodes more rapidly. Many shoreline features are caused by differences in rock hardness. Over time, a large area of softer rock can be eroded by strong waves. As a result, part of the shoreline is carved out and forms a bay.

Sea caves form when waves cut large holes into fractured or weak rock along the base of sea cliffs.

Wave-cut platforms form when a sea cliff is worn back from shore, producing a nearly level platform beneath the water at the base of the cliff.

Headlands are finger-shaped projections that form when cliffs of hard rock erode more slowly than the surrounding softer rock does.

Sea Cliffs and Wave-cut Platforms

A *sea cliff* forms when waves erode and undercut rock to make steep slopes. Waves strike the cliff's base, wearing away the rock. This process makes the cliff steeper. As a sea cliff erodes above the waterline, a bench of rock usually remains beneath the water at the cliff's base. This bench is called a *wave-cut platform*. Wave-cut platforms are almost flat because the rocks eroded from the cliff often scrape away at the platform.

Sea Caves, Arches, and Stacks

Sea cliffs seldom erode evenly. Often, headlands form as some parts of a cliff are cut back faster than other parts. As the rock making up sea cliffs and headlands erodes, it breaks and cracks. Waves can cut deeply into the cracks and form large holes. As the holes continue to erode, they become *sea caves*. A sea cave may erode even further and eventually become a *sea arch*. When the top of a sea arch collapses, its sides become *sea stacks*.

18 Summarize Complete the chart by filling in descriptions of each coastal landform.

Coastal Landform	Description
Headland	
Sea cave	
Sea arch	
Sea stack	
Wave-cut platform	

Sea arches form when wave action erodes sea caves until a hole cuts through a headland.

Sea stacks form when the tops of sea arches collapse and leave behind isolated columns of rock.

19 Analyze Which of these features do you think took longer to form: the sea stack, sea arch, or sea cave? Explain.

Shifting Sands

What coastal landforms are made by deposition?

Waves and currents carry a variety of materials, including sand, rock, dead coral, and shells. Often, these materials are deposited on a shoreline, where they form a beach. A **beach** is an area of shoreline that is made up of material deposited by waves and currents. A great deal of beach material is also deposited by rivers and then is moved down the shoreline by currents.

Beaches

You may think of beaches as sandy places. However, not all beaches are made of sand. The size and shape of beach material depend on how far the material has traveled from its source. Size and shape also depend on the type of material and how it is eroded. For example, in areas with stormy seas, beaches may be made of pebbles and boulders deposited by powerful waves. These waves erode smaller particles such as sand.

Visualize It!

20 Infer Would it take more wave energy to deposit sand or the rocks shown on this beach? Explain.

_____

_____

_____

Barrier islands lie nearly parallel to the shore.

Barrier islands are ridges of sand.

Sandbars and Barrier Islands

When waves erode material from the shoreline, longshore currents can transport and deposit this material offshore. This process creates landforms in open water.

A **sandbar** is an underwater or exposed ridge of sand, gravel, or shell material. A **barrier island** is a long, narrow island, usually made of sand, that forms parallel to the shoreline a short distance offshore.

Living on the Edge

Barrier islands are dynamic landforms that are constantly changing shape. What's here today may be gone tomorrow!

Barrier islands

Landform in Limbo

Barrier islands are found all over the world, including the United States. They can be eroded away by tides and large storms. The barrier island at the left was eroded by a hurricane. Because of erosion, the shape of a barrier island is always changing.

Building on Barriers

Barrier islands are popular spots to build vacation homes and hotels. Residents of barrier islands often use anti-erosion strategies to protect their property from erosion by tides and storms. Short-term solutions include using sand bags, like those shown on the right, to slow down erosion.

Extend

Inquiry

21 Explain Give a step-by-step description of how a barrier island could form.

22 Identify Research different technologies and strategies people can use to slow the erosion of a barrier island.

23 Model Choose one of the anti-erosion methods identified in your research and design an experiment to test how well the technology or strategy slows down the process of erosion.

Visual Summary

To complete this summary, fill in the blanks. Then use the key below to check your answers. You can use this page to review the main concepts of the lesson.

Erosion and Deposition by Water

Streams alter the shape of Earth's surface.

24 Caused by erosion: canyons, valleys

Caused by deposition: floodplains, deltas, _____

Groundwater erodes and deposits materials.

25 Caused by erosion: caves,

_____

Caused by deposition: stalactites, stalagmites

Waves and currents change the shape of the shoreline.

26 Caused by erosion: bays, inlets, headlands, wave-cut platforms, sea cliffs, sea caves, sea stacks,

_____

Caused by deposition: beaches, sandbars, barrier islands

Answers: 24 alluvial fans; 25 sinkholes; 26 sea arches

27 Explain How do erosion and deposition work together to form a delta?

_____

_____

Lesson Review

Vocabulary

Circle the term that best completes the following sentences.

1 *Erosion/Deposition* occurs when materials drop out of wind or water.

2 When a river flows into an ocean, it slows down and deposits materials in its *alluvial fan/delta*.

3 When a river periodically floods and deposits its sediments, a flat area known as a *floodplain/shoreline* forms over time.

Key Concepts

Complete the table below.

Landform	How It Forms
Canyon	**4 Explain**
Sinkhole	**5 Explain**
Sea cave	**6 Explain**

7 Synthesize How does gravity relate to a stream's ability to erode and deposit materials?

_____

_____

_____

8 Identify What are the two main factors that affect how quickly a coastline erodes?

_____

_____

9 Describe How does a longshore current change a beach?

_____

_____

Critical Thinking

Use this graph, which shows erosion and deposition on a beach, to answer questions 10–11.

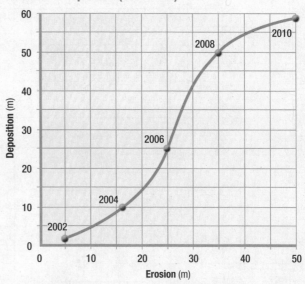

Erosion and Deposition (2002-2010)

10 Analyze In 2004, was there more erosion or deposition taking place?

_____

11 Evaluate Explain how waves and currents are affecting this beach over time.

_____

_____

_____

_____

_____

12 Hypothesize Many communities pump groundwater to irrigate crops and supply homes with water. How do you think overpumping groundwater is related to the formation of sinkholes?

_____

_____

_____

_____

_____

My Notes

Searching the Internet

The Internet can be a great tool for finding scientific information and reference material. But, because the Internet contains so much information, finding useful information on it may be difficult. Or, you may find information that is unreliable or not suitable.

Tutorial

The procedure below can help you retrieve useful, reliable information from the Internet.

Choose a search engine There are many search engines available for finding information. Evaluate different search engines using the following criteria:

- number of relevant sites listed in search results;
- how easy the search engine is to use;
- how fast the search is; and
- how easy the documents on the site are to access, and what type of documents they are.

Choose and enter keywords Identify specific keywords for the topic of interest. You can make lists or draw concept maps to help you think of keywords or key phrases. Enter your keyword(s) into the search engine. You can enter one keyword at a time, or you can enter multiple keywords. You can put the word *and* or *+* between two keywords to find both words on the site. Use the word *or* between two keywords to find at least one of the keywords on the site. Use quotations ("like this") around keywords to find exact matches.

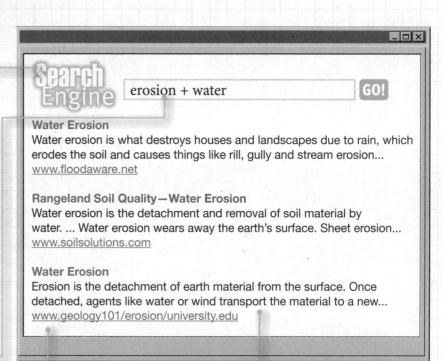

Search Engine erosion + water **GO!**

Water Erosion
Water erosion is what destroys houses and landscapes due to rain, which erodes the soil and causes things like rill, gully and stream erosion...
www.floodaware.net

Rangeland Soil Quality—Water Erosion
Water erosion is the detachment and removal of soil material by water. ... Water erosion wears away the earth's surface. Sheet erosion...
www.soilsolutions.com

Water Erosion
Erosion is the detachment of earth material from the surface. Once detached, agents like water or wind transport the material to a new...
www.geology101/erosion/university.edu

Look at the URL Examine the address in the search results list. Ask yourself if a reliable organization is behind the webpage such as government agencies (.gov or .mil), educational institutions (.edu), and non-profit organizations (.org). Avoid personal sites and biased sources, which may tell only one side of a story. These types of sources may lead to inaccurate information or a false impression.

Look at the content of the webpage Decide whether the webpage contains useful information. Read the page's title and headings. Read the first sentences of several paragraphs. Look at tables and diagrams. Ask yourself: How current is the webpage?; Are the sources documented?; and Are there links to more information? Decide whether the webpage contains the kind of information that you need.

You Try It!

Weathering is the physical and chemical alteration of rock.

Weathering processes have led to the formations you see here in Bryce Canyon. Study the photo and then do some research on the Internet to find out more about weathering processes.

Morning light on Thor's Hammer in Bryce Canyon National Park in Utah

1 Choosing Keywords Think about what you want to learn about mechanical weathering. You may want to focus on one topic, such as frost wedging, exfoliation, or thermal expansion. Choose relevant keyword(s) or phrases for the topic that you are researching.

_____

_____

_____

_____

_____

2 Searching the Internet Enter the keywords in a search engine. Which keywords or phrases prompted the most relevant and reliable sites?

_____

_____

_____

_____

_____

3 Evaluating Websites Use the table below to evaluate websites on how useful they are and on the quality of the information. As you visit different websites for your research, make notes about each site's relevance and suitability.

Webpage	Comments

Erosion and Deposition by Wind, Ice, and Gravity

ESSENTIAL QUESTION

How do wind, ice, and gravity change Earth's surface?

By the end of this lesson, you should be able to describe erosion and deposition by wind, ice, and gravity as well as identify the landforms that result from these processes.

In this desert, wind has sculpted hills of sand, spreading them out like fingers.

Engage Your Brain

1 Predict How do you think wind can erode materials?

_____

_____

_____

_____

2 Infer The dark bands you see in the photo on the right are dirt and rocks frozen in the ice. What do you think will happen to the dirt and rocks when the ice melts?

_____

_____

_____

_____

_____

Active Reading

3 Define In this lesson, you will be learning about how different agents of erosion can abrade rock. Use a dictionary to look up the meaning of the word *abrade*. Record the definition:

_____

_____

Now use the word *abrade* in your own sentence:

_____

_____

As you read this lesson, circle the word *abrade* whenever you come across it. Compare the sentences that include this word with the sentence you wrote above.

Vocabulary Terms

- • **dune**
- • **loess**
- • **glacier**
- • **glacial drift**
- • **creep**
- • **rockfall**
- • **landslide**
- • **mudflow**

4 Apply As you learn the definition of each vocabulary term in this lesson, create your own definition or sketch to help you remember the meaning of the term.

How can wind shape Earth?

Have you ever been outside and had a gust of wind blow a stack of papers all over the place? If so, you have seen how wind erosion works. In the same way that wind moved your papers, wind moves soil, sand, and rock particles. When wind moves soil, sand, and rock particles, it acts as an agent of erosion.

Abraded Rock

When wind blows sand and other particles against a surface, it can wear down the surface over time. The grinding and wearing down of rock surfaces by other rock or by sand particles is called *abrasion*. Abrasion happens in areas where there are strong winds, loose sand, and soft rocks. The blowing of millions of grains of sand causes a sandblasting effect. The sandblasting effect slowly erodes the rock by stripping away its surface. Over time, the rock can become smooth and polished.

Desert Pavement

The removal of fine sediment by wind is called *deflation*. This process is shown in the diagram below. During deflation, wind removes the top layer of fine sediment or soil. Deflation leaves behind rock fragments that are too heavy to be lifted by the wind. After a while, these rocks may be the only materials left on the surface. The resulting landscape is known as desert pavement. As you can see in the photo below, desert pavement is a surface made up mostly of pebbles and small, broken rocks.

Wind Direction

Desert Pavement

👁 Visualize It!

5 Describe How did the desert pavement in this photo most likely form?

_____

_____

_____

Wind

Dunes

Wind carries sediment in much the same way that rivers do. Just as rivers deposit their loads, winds eventually drop the materials that they are carrying. For example, when wind hits an obstacle, it slows and drops materials on top of the obstacle. As the material builds up, the obstacle gets larger. This obstacle causes the wind to slow more and deposit more material, which forms a mound. Eventually, the original obstacle is buried. Mounds of wind-deposited sand are called **dunes**. Dunes are common in deserts and along the shores of lakes and oceans.

Generally, dunes move in the same direction the wind is blowing. Usually, a dune's gently sloped side faces the wind. Wind constantly moves material up this side of the dune. As sand moves over the crest of the dune, the sand slides down the slip face and makes a steep slope.

Loess

Wind can carry extremely fine material long distances. Thick deposits of this windblown, fine-grained sediment are known as **loess** (LOH•uhs). Loess can feel like the talcum powder a person may use after a shower. Because wind carries fine-grained material much higher and farther than it carries sand, loess deposits are sometimes found far away from their source. Loess deposits can build up over thousands and even millions of years. Loess is a valuable resource because it forms good soil for growing crops.

6 Infer Why do you think loess can be carried further than sand?

_____

_____

_____

Visualize It!

Wind direction ⟶

Windward slope

Slip face

Direction of dune movement ⟶

7 Determine Look at the photo above the illustration. Which direction does the wind blow across the photographed dune: from left to right or right to left?

_____

8 Identify Which side of the dune in the photograph is the slip face: A or B?

_____

Groovy Glaciers

What kinds of ice shape Earth?

Have you ever made a snowball from a scoop of fluffy snow? If so, you know that when the snow is pressed against itself, it becomes harder and more compact. The same idea explains how a glacier forms. A **glacier** is a large mass of moving ice that forms by the compacting of snow by natural forces.

Flowing Ice

Glaciers can be found anywhere on land where it is cold enough for ice to stay frozen year round. Gravity causes glaciers to move. When enough ice builds up on a slope, the ice begins to move downhill. The steeper the slope is, the faster the glacier moves.

As glaciers move, they pick up materials. These materials become embedded in the ice. As the glacier moves forward, the materials scratch and abrade the rock and soil underneath the glacier. This abrasion causes more erosion. Glaciers are also agents of deposition. As a glacier melts, it drops the materials that it carried. **Glacial drift** is the general term for all of the materials carried and deposited by a glacier.

Active Reading **10 Infer** Where in North America would you expect to find glaciers?

_____

_____

_____

Think Outside the Book

9 Apply Find out whether glaciers have ever covered your state. If so, what landforms did they leave behind?

As a glacier flowed over this rock, it scratched out these grooves.

This glacier is moving down the valley like a river of ice.

Alpine Glaciers

An alpine glacier is a glacier that forms in a mountainous area. Alpine glaciers flow down the sides of mountains and create rugged landscapes. Glaciers may form in valleys originally created by stream erosion. The flow of water in a stream forms a V-shaped valley. As a glacier slowly flows through a V-shaped valley, it scrapes away the valley floor and walls. The glacier widens and straightens the valley into a broad U-shape. An alpine glacier can also carve out bowl-shaped depressions, called *cirques* (surks), at the head of a valley. A sharp ridge called an *arête* (uh•RAYT) forms between two cirques that are next to each other. When three or more arêtes join, they form a sharp peak called a *horn*.

Visualize It!

11 Summarize Use the illustration below to write a description for each of the following landforms.

Landforms made by alpine glaciers	Description
Arête	
Cirque	
Horn	
U-shaped valley	

Horns are sharp, pyramid-shaped peaks that form when several arêtes join at the top of a mountain.

Arêtes are jagged ridges that form between two or more cirques that cut into the same mountain.

Hanging valleys are small glacial valleys that join the deeper, main valley. Many hanging valleys form waterfalls after the ice is gone.

Cirques are bowl-shaped depressions where glacial ice cuts back into the mountain walls.

U-shaped valleys form when a glacier erodes a river valley. The valley changes from its original V-shape to a U-shape.

Continental Glaciers

Continental glaciers are thick sheets of ice that may spread over large areas, including across entire continents. These glaciers are huge, continuous masses of ice. Continental glaciers create very different landforms than alpine glaciers do. Alpine glaciers form sharp and rugged features, whereas continental glaciers flatten and smooth the landscape. Continental glaciers erode and remove features that existed before the ice appeared. These glaciers smooth and round exposed rock surfaces in a way similar to the way that bulldozers can flatten landscapes.

Erosion and deposition by continental glaciers result in specific, recognizable landforms. Some of the landforms are shown below. Similar landforms can be found in the northern United States, which was once covered by continental glaciers.

Visualize It!

12 Compare What does the formation of erratics and kettle lakes have in common?

_____

_____

_____

_____

_____

Erratics are large boulders that were transported and deposited by glaciers.

Kettle lakes form when chunks of ice are deposited by a glacier and glacial drift builds up around the ice blocks. When the ice melts, a lake forms.

Melting the Ice

A CHANGING WORLD

What would you do if an Ice Age glacial dam broke and let loose millions of gallons of water? Get out of the way and get ready for some erosion!

A Crack in the Ice
During the last Ice Age, a huge ice dam held back Glacial Lake Missoula, a 320-km-long body of water. Then one day, the dam burst. Water roared out, emptying the lake in less than 48 hours!

Giant ripple marks from the Missoula floods

Large-Scale Landforms
The erosion caused by the roaring water carved out a landscape of huge waterfalls, deep canyons, and three-story-high ripple marks. Many of these features are in an area called the Scablands.

History Repeats Itself
Lake Missoula eventually reformed behind another ice dam. The breaking of the dam and the floods repeated about 40 more times, ripping away topsoil and exposing and cracking the bedrock.

Extend

Inquiry

13 Relate Where have you seen ripple marks before and how do they compare to the ripple marks shown in the photo on this page?

14 Explain How do you think the three-story-high ripple marks shown here were formed?

15 Model Use sand, pebbles, and other materials to model how a severe flood can alter the landscape. Photograph or illustrate the results of your investigation. Present your results in the form of an animation, slide show, or illustrated report.

Slippery Slopes

The shape of this tree trunk indicates that creep has occurred along the slope.

How can gravity shape Earth?

Although you can't see it, the force of gravity, like water, wind, and ice, is an agent of erosion and deposition. Gravity not only influences the movement of water and ice, but it also causes rocks and soil to move downslope. This shifting of materials is called *mass movement*. Mass movement plays a major role in shaping Earth's surface.

Slow Mass Movement

Even though most slopes appear to be stable, they are actually undergoing slow mass movement. In fact, all the rocks and soil on a slope travel slowly downhill. The ground beneath the tree shown on the left is moving so slowly that the tree trunk curved as the tree grew. The extremely slow movement of material downslope is called **creep**. Many factors contribute to creep. Water loosens soil and allows the soil to move freely. In addition, plant roots act as wedges that force rocks and soil particles apart. Burrowing animals, such as gophers and groundhogs, also loosen rock and soil particles, making it easier for the particles to be pulled downward.

16 Analyze As the soil on this hill shifts, how is the tree changing so that it continues to grow upright?

_____

_____

_____

© Houghton Mifflin Harcourt Publishing Company • Image Credits: ©ThinkStock/age fotostock

Rapid Mass Movement

The most destructive mass movements happen suddenly and rapidly. Rapid mass movement can be very dangerous and can destroy everything in its path. Rapid mass movement tends to happen on steep slopes because materials are more likely to fall down a steep slope than a shallow slope.

While traveling along a mountain road, you may have noticed signs along the road that warn of falling rocks. A **rockfall** happens when loose rocks fall down a steep slope. Steep slopes are common in mountainous areas. Gravity causes loosened and exposed rocks to fall down steep slopes. The rocks in a rockfall can range in size from small fragments to large boulders.

Another kind of rapid mass movement is a landslide. A **landslide** is the sudden and rapid movement of a large amount of material downslope. As you can see in the photo on the right, landslides can carry away plants. They can also carry away animals, vehicles, and buildings. Heavy rains, deforestation, construction on unstable slopes, and earthquakes increase the chances of a landslide.

A rapid movement of a large mass of mud is a **mudflow**. Mudflows happen when a large amount of water mixes with soil and rock. The water causes the slippery mud to flow rapidly downslope. Mudflows happen in mountainous regions after deforestation has occurred or when a long dry season is followed by heavy rains. Volcanic eruptions or heavy rains on volcanic ash can produce some of the most dangerous mudflows. Mudflows of volcanic origin are called lahars. Lahars can travel at speeds greater than 80 km/h and can be as thick as wet cement.

17 Identify List five events that can trigger a mass movement.

_____

_____

_____

_____

_____

_____

This landslide in California was caused by heavy rains.

A

B

Visualize It!

18 Infer On which slope, A or B, would a landslide be more likely to occur? Explain.

_____

_____

© Houghton Mifflin Harcourt Publishing Company • Image Credits: (t) ©Randy Jibson, USGS

Visual Summary

To complete this summary, fill in the blanks with the correct word or phrase. Then, use the key below to check your answers. You can use this page to review the main concepts of the lesson.

Erosion and Deposition by Wind, Ice, and Gravity

Wind forms dunes and desert pavement.

19 Wind forms dunes through:

_____

20 Wind forms desert pavement through:

_____

Ice erodes and deposits rock.

21 Alpine glaciers make landforms such as:

_____

_____

_____

_____

_____

22 Continental glaciers make landforms such as:

_____

_____

_____

Gravity pulls materials downward.

23 Type of slow mass movement: _____

24 Three major types of rapid mass movement:

_____ _____ _____

25 Summarize Describe the role that gravity plays in almost all examples of erosion and deposition.

Lesson Review

Vocabulary

Use a term from the section to complete each sentence below.

1 When an obstacle causes wind to slow down and deposit materials, the materials pile up and eventually form a _____

2 Large masses of flowing ice called _____ are typically found near Earth's poles and in other cold regions.

3 Very fine sediments called _____ can be carried by wind over long distances.

4 As glaciers retreat, they leave behind deposits of _____

Key Concepts

5 Explain How can glaciers cause deposition?

_____

_____

_____

_____

6 Compare Compare and contrast how wind and glaciers abrade rock.

_____

_____

_____

_____

_____

_____

_____

7 Distinguish What is the difference between creep and a landslide?

_____

_____

_____

_____

_____

Critical Thinking

Use the diagram to answer the question below.

8 Synthesize Which of the four locations would be the best and worst places to build a house? Rank the four locations and explain your reasoning.

_____

_____

_____

_____

_____

_____

9 Integrate Wind erosion occurs at a faster rate in deserts than in places with a thick layer of vegetation covering the ground. Why do you think this is the case?

_____

_____

_____

_____

_____

_____

My Notes

Soil Formation

ESSENTIAL QUESTION

How does soil form?

By the end of this lesson, you should be able to describe the physical and chemical characteristics of soil layers and identify the factors that affect soil formation, including the action of living things.

Living things, such as this shelf fungus **(Laetiporus sulphureus)**, help to break down organic matter. The organic matter mixes with minerals, weathered sediment, water, and air to form soil.

Lesson Labs

Quick Labs
- Observing Life in Soil
- Modeling a Soil Profile
- Observing the Impact of Earthworms on Soil

Field Lab
- Comparing Soil Characteristics

Engage Your Brain

1 Predict Check T or F to show whether you think each statement is true or false.

T	F	
☐	☐	Soil contains air and water.
☐	☐	Soil does not contain living things.
☐	☐	Soils are the same from place to place.
☐	☐	Climate can affect how fertile soils are.

2 Explain How might the burrows formed by ants affect the soil?

_____

_____

_____

Active Reading

3 Apply Many scientific words, such as *weather*, have more than one meaning. Use context clues to write your own definition for each meaning of the word *weather*.

Example sentence
The <u>weather</u> outside is nice.

weather:

_____

_____

_____

Example sentence
Wind, water, and plant roots <u>weather</u> rock into sediment.

weather:

_____

_____

_____

Vocabulary Terms

- soil
- humus
- soil profile
- soil horizon

4 Apply As you learn the definition of each vocabulary term in this lesson, write your own definition or sketch to help you remember the meaning of the term.

The Dirt on Soil

What causes soil to form?

Soil is important to your life. You walk on grass that is rooted in soil. You eat foods that need soil in order to grow. But what exactly is soil? Where does it come from? How does it form?

A scientist might define **soil** as a loose mixture of small rock fragments, organic matter, water, and air that can support the growth of vegetation. The very first step in soil formation is the weathering of *parent rock*. Parent rock is the source of inorganic soil particles. Soil forms directly above the parent rock. Soil either develops here, or it is eroded and transported to another location.

Weathering of Parent Rock

Weathering breaks down parent rock into smaller and smaller pieces. These pieces of rock eventually become very small particles that are mixed in with organic matter to form soil. The process of soil formation can take a very long time. The amount of time it takes depends on many factors that you will learn about later in this lesson.

Soil formation begins when parent rock weathers into small fragments.

Plant roots grow and can break down sediment even further.

Burrowing animals increase the rate of weathering. They mix the soil, allowing more air to enter. They bring sediment to the surface where it is weathered more quickly by water, wind, and organisms.

© Houghton Mifflin Harcourt Publishing Company • Image Credits: (t) ©Premaphotos/Alamy

Decomposition and Mixing by Living Things

Some microorganisms, such as bacteria and fungi, are decomposers that live in soil. These tiny decomposers perform the important task of breaking down the remains of plants and animals. These remains are decayed organic matter called **humus**. Humus is found in the top layer of soils. It is important because it contains nutrients that plants need to grow. Plants take up these nutrients through their roots. When plants or animals die, they are broken down by decomposers, and the nutrients are returned to the soil.

Larger animals, such as earthworms and moles, also live in soil. They loosen and mix the soil as they burrow through it. The mixing increases the amount of air in soil and improves the ability of soil to drain water.

6 Apply How might a fallen leaf eventually become part of soil?

_____

_____

7 Summarize How do decomposers and plants cycle nutrients in soil?

_____

_____

_____

At least a million microorganisms can fit into one spoonful of soil! These tiny organisms have the big job of decomposing plant and animal remains.

Thick Tops, Rocky Bottoms

What factors determine how long it takes for soils to form?

Soil formation and development are processes that take place over a very long period of time. There are four main factors in determining exactly how long these processes take. They include the parent rock type, climate, topography, and plants and animals.

- Rock type: Certain rock types weather at different rates and in different ways. The rate of weathering depends on the structure of the rock and minerals that make up the rock.
- Climate: Soil usually develops more quickly in warm, wet areas than in cold, dry areas.
- Topography: Sediments on steep slopes are often eroded. Soils usually develop faster in flatter areas where sediments are not easily eroded.
- Plants and animals: Plant roots hold sediments in place, allowing soil to develop quickly. Areas teeming with life have higher rates of decomposition and mixing. Soils tend to develop more quickly in these areas. Without a lot of plants and animals, soil tends to develop slowly.

Active Reading

8 Identify As you read, underline the factors that affect how long it takes for soils to form and develop.

9 Compare List some possible characteristics of an area where soils would develop quickly. Then do the same for an area where soils would develop slowly.

Area where Soils Develop Quickly	*Area where Soils Develop Slowly*

What are the main soil horizons?

Picture the rich, dark soil in a garden. Now imagine what the soil looks like as you dig deeper beneath the surface. Does the soil look and feel the same as you dig deeper? A vertical section of soil that shows all of the different layers is a **soil profile**. Each layer in the soil profile that has different physical properties is called a **soil horizon**. The main horizons include the A horizon, B horizon, and C horizon. There are many other horizons as well.

A Horizon

The A horizon is at the top of the soil profile. It is often referred to as *topsoil*. Decomposers live in this horizon, so it has the most decayed organic matter. This humus gives it a dark color. Plant roots break up fragments and animals burrow and mix the the soil. These processes increase the rate of weathering, so the A horizon is usually the most developed. As you'll learn later in this lesson, rich soils generally have high amounts of humus. Dead leaves, branches, and other organic matter may cover the surface of the A horizon.

B Horizon

The B horizon lies below the A horizon. It is not as developed as the A horizon and has less humus. Following precipitation events, water seeps down through the A horizon. Water carries material, such as iron minerals and clay, from the A horizon down to the B horizon. This is known as *leaching*. The leached materials commonly give the B horizon a reddish or brownish color.

C Horizon

The C horizon lies below the B horizon. It is the least-developed soil horizon. It contains the largest rock fragments and usually has no organic matter. The C horizon lies directly above the parent rock. Recall that this is the weathered rock from which the soil was formed.

Visualize It!

10 Analyze Which soil horizon contains the largest rocks?

_____

A Horizon

B Horizon

C Horizon

All About Soil

What are some properties of soil?

Plants grow well in some soils and poorly in others. Soils look and feel different. They also contain different minerals and particles. Soil properties are used to classify different soils. These properties include soil texture, color, chemistry, pore space, and fertility.

Soil Texture

11 Identify As you read, underline the three kinds of soil particles.

The term *soil texture* is a property that describes the relative amounts of differently sized soil particles. Soil particles are classified as sand, silt, or clay. Most soils are a mixture of all three. Sand is the largest particle, ranging from 0.05 mm to 2 mm. Soils containing a lot of sand feel coarse. Silt particles are smaller than sand particles. They range from 0.002 mm to 0.05 mm. Silty soils have a smooth, silky feel. At less than 0.002 mm, clay particles are the smallest soil particles. Clayey soils feel very smooth and are usually sticky when they are wet.

Visualize It!

12 Distinguish The last space in each row contains three circles. Fill in the circle that shows the correct relative size of the particle shown in that row.

Particle	Size Range	Relative Size
sand	0.05 mm–2 mm	
silt	0.002 mm–0.05 mm	
clay	less than 0.002 mm	

Soil Color

Soils can be black, brown, red, orange, yellow, gray, and even white. Soil color is a clue to the types and amounts of minerals and organic matter in the soil. Iron minerals make soil orange or reddish. Soils that contain a lot of humus are black or brown. Color can also be a clue about the environmental conditions. Gray soil can indicate that an area is often wet and has poor drainage.

Soils are usually a mixture of colors, such as reddish brown. Scientists use the Munsell System of Color Notation to describe soil colors. The system uses a book of color chips, much like the paint chips found in a paint store. Scientists compare a soil to the color chips in the book to classify soils.

Think Outside the Book

13 Apply Find out about the qualities of your local soil. Describe its texture, color, chemistry, pore space, and fertility. Choose one of these activities to present your description: draw a poster or diagram, create a brochure, or write a poem.

Soil and Climate

Climate can affect how soil forms in different regions on Earth. Warm, rainy regions produce tropical soils and temperate soils. Dry regions produce desert soils and arctic soils.

Tropical Soils form in warm, wet regions. Heavy rains wash away and leach soils, leaving only a thin layer of humus. Soil development is fast in these regions. They are not suitable for growing most crops.

Desert Soils form in dry regions. These soils are shallow and contain little organic matter. Because of the low rainfall, chemical weathering and soil development is slow in desert regions.

Temperate Soils form in regions with moderate rainfall and temperatures. Some temperate soils are dark-colored, rich in organic matter and minerals, and good for growing crops.

Arctic Soils form in cold, dry regions where chemical weathering is slow. They typically do not have well-developed horizons. Arctic soils may contain many rock fragments.

© Houghton Mifflin Harcourt Publishing Company • Image Credits: (tl) ©L Heusinkveld/Alamy; (tr) ©Adam Jones/Digital Vision/Getty Images; (bl) ©BARNpix.com/Alamy; (br) ©Alan Kearney/Photographer's Choice RF/Getty Images

Soil Chemistry

Soil pH is determined by the combination of minerals, sediment, and organic matter found in soil. The pH of soil is a measure of how acidic or basic a soil is. The pH is based on a scale of 0 to 14. If pH is less than 7, the soil is acidic. If pH is above 7, the soil is basic. In the middle of the pH scale is 7, which means the soil is neither acidic nor basic; it is neutral. Scientists measure soil pH to determine whether the soil can support different plants. For example, soybeans grow best in a soil with a pH between 6.0 and 7.0. Peanuts thrive when the pH of soil is between 5.3 and 6.6.

Farmers can adjust the pH of soil to meet the needs of their plants. They can add lime to make acidic soils more basic. They can add acids to make basic soils more acidic.

Pore Space

Pore space describes the spaces between soil particles. Water and air are found in the pore spaces of soils. Water and air move easily through soils with many well-connected pore spaces. Soils with this property are well-drained and typically good for plant growth.

Plants need both water and air to grow. About 25 to 60 percent of the volume of most soils is pore space. The best soil for growing most plants has about 50 percent of its volume as pore space, with that volume equally divided between water and air.

The pH of a soil can be tested to make sure it will support the plants being grown.

Visualize It!

14 Describe Write a caption that describes the pore space for each diagram below.

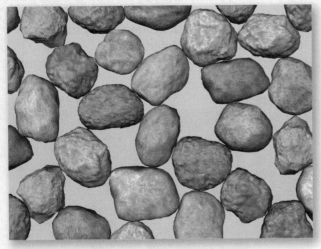

A _____
_____
_____

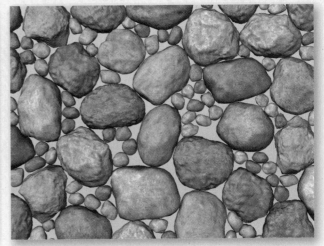

B _____
_____
_____

Soil Fertility

Soil fertility describes how well a soil can support plant growth. This quality is affected by factors that include the climate of the area; the amount of humus, minerals, and nutrients in the soil; and the topography of the area.

Fertile soils are often found in areas with moderate rainfall and temperatures. Soils with a lot of humus and the proper proportions of minerals and nutrients have high soil fertility. Soils found in dry areas or on steep hillsides often have low fertility. Farmers can add chemical fertilizers or organic material to soils to improve soil fertility. They also can grow crops, such as legumes, to restore certain nutrients to soil or leave cropland unplanted for a season to replenish its fertility.

Active Reading **15 Apply** What could you do to improve the fertility of the soil in your garden?

_____

_____

This meadow's bluebonnets thrive in well-drained soil. Bluebonnets also grow best in slightly basic soils.

Inquiry

16 Infer Use what you have learned to infer why Soils A and B have the following soils properties.

Soil Properties	Possible Reasons for Soil Properties
Soil A is black, well-drained, and good for growing plants.	
Soil B feels smooth and sticky and is gray in color.	

Visual Summary

To complete this summary, fill in the blanks with the correct word. Then use the key below to check your answers. You can use this page to review the main concepts of the lesson.

Soil Formation

Soil formation involves weathering of rock, addition of organic material, and actions by plants and animals that live in the soil.

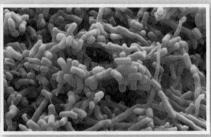

17 In general, soils in cold, dry areas will take _____ to develop than soils in warm, wet areas.

Characteristics of soil include texture, color, chemistry, pore space, and soil fertility.

19 _____ describes the spaces between soil particles.

A soil profile commonly has the A horizon, B horizon, and C horizon. They each have distinct physical characteristics.

18 The _____ contains the most organic matter; leaching carries minerals and humus down to the _____.

Answers: 17 longer; 18 A horizon, B horizon; 19 Pore space

20 Summarize Describe how living things can affect the different characteristics and development of soil.

Lesson Review

Vocabulary

Draw a line to connect the following terms to their definitions.

1 soil

2 humus

3 soil profile

4 soil horizon

A decomposed organic matter

B layer of soil with distinct physical properties in a soil profile

C vertical section showing the soil horizons

D mixture of weathered sediment, organic material, water, and air

Key Concepts

5 Identify What is the first step of soil formation?

_____
_____

6 Explain What are the main factors that determine how long it takes for a soil to form and develop?

_____
_____
_____

7 Describe How would a soil that developed in a warm, wet place be different than one that developed in a hot, dry place?

_____
_____
_____
_____
_____

8 Compare How might a dark colored, coarse soil differ from a reddish, smooth soil?

_____
_____
_____
_____

Critical Thinking

Use this table to answer the following question.

Climate Data for Locations A and B		
	Average Yearly Temperature (°C)	Average Yearly Precipitation (cm)
Location A	27	190
Location B	3	26

9 Analyze In which location would soils develop faster? Explain.

_____
_____
_____
_____

10 Infer Which soil would you expect to be better developed: the soil on a hillside or the soil on a valley floor? Why?

_____
_____
_____
_____
_____

11 Synthesize Describe the cycle that involves soil, decomposers, and other living things.

_____
_____
_____
_____
_____

My Notes

Unit 3 [Big Idea] ◄ Continuous processes on Earth's surface result in the formation and destruction of landforms and the formation of soil.

Lesson 1
ESSENTIAL QUESTION
How do matter and energy move through Earth's spheres?

Describe Earth's spheres, give examples of their interactions, and explain the flow of energy that makes up Earth's energy budget.

Lesson 4
ESSENTIAL QUESTION
How do wind, ice, and gravity change Earth's surface?

Describe erosion and deposition by wind, ice, and gravity as well as identify the landforms that result from these processes.

Lesson 2
ESSENTIAL QUESTION
How does weathering change Earth's surface?

Analyze the effects of physical and chemical weathering on Earth's surface, including examples of each kind of weathering.

Lesson 5
ESSENTIAL QUESTION
How does soil form?

Describe the physical and chemical characteristics of soil layers and identify the factors that affect soil formation, including the action of living things.

Lesson 3
ESSENTIAL QUESTION
How does water change Earth's surface?

Relate the processes of erosion and deposition by water to the landforms that result from these processes.

Think Outside the Book

2 Synthesize Choose one of these activities to help synthesize what you have learned in this unit.

☐ Using what you learned in lessons 2, 4, and 5, explain the role that physical weathering plays in soil formation by making a flipbook.

☐ Using what you learned in lessons 1 and 2, write a short essay explaining how different spheres of Earth interact with each other during the process of chemical weathering.

Connect **ESSENTIAL QUESTIONS**

Lessons 2 and 4

1 Synthesize Explain how gravity causes erosion.

_____

_____

_____

© Houghton Mifflin Harcourt Publishing Company • Image Credits: (tl) ©John Eastcott And Yva Momatiuk/National Geographic/Getty Images; (tr) ©George Steinmetz/Corbis;

Unit 3 Review

Name _____

Vocabulary

Fill in each blank with the term that best completes the following sentences.

1 _____ is the dark, organic-rich material formed as a top layer in soil from the decayed remains of plants and animals.

2 The process by which rocks break down as a result of chemical reactions is called _____.

3 The fan-shaped mass of sediment deposited by a stream into an ocean or a lake is called a _____.

4 The rock material deposited by glaciers as they melt and retreat is called _____.

5 The _____ is the part of Earth where life exists and extends from the deep ocean floors up into the lower atmosphere.

Key Concepts

Read each question below, and circle the best answer.

6 Which term describes the ability a soil has to support plant growth?

A chemistry

B fertility

C texture

D pore space

7 What are two processes that result in rocks being broken down into smaller pieces?

A sunlight and glacial melting

B chemical weathering and physical weathering

C chemical weathering and deposition

D physical weathering and humus

8 This diagram shows a landform called an alluvial fan.

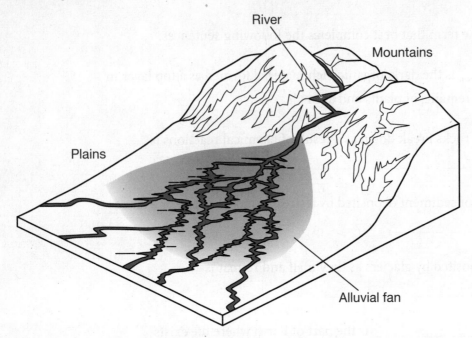

How does an alluvial fan form?

A It forms where a stream enters an ocean or lake, slows down, and deposits sediments there over time.

B It forms from a stream overflowing and depositing sediments.

C It forms where part of a meandering stream is cut off.

D It forms where a stream reaches a flat area of land, slows down, and deposits sediments there over time.

9 While walking along a seashore, Antonio determined that the shore has been affected by stormy seas and rough waves. What did Antonio observe?

A The beach was sandy.   **C** The beach was rocky.

B There were sandbars.   **D** There was a sea stack.

10 Landslides, rockfalls, and creep are examples of erosion and deposition by which erosion agent?

A gravity   **C** oxidation

B solar energy   **D** wind

11 The diagram below shows a landform called a sinkhole.

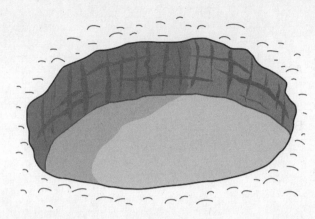

How does a sinkhole form?

A Stalactites erode the ceiling of a cavern.

B A flowing stream in the mountains erodes sediment and the ground caves in.

C Underground water erodes rock forming a cavern, and over time the cavern's roof collapses.

D A flowing stream erodes soil and rock making the stream deeper and wider.

12 A glacier is a large mass of moving ice. What conditions are necessary for a glacier to form?

A The weather must be below freezing and very dry.

B The weather must be below freezing, and more snow must fall than melt.

C The weather must be mild, and there must be a lot of precipitation.

D The weather must be below freezing, and more snow must melt than fall.

Critical Thinking

Answer the following questions in the space provided.

13 Explain whether water is a cause of either chemical weathering, physical weathering, or both.

_____

_____

_____

_____

_____

14 Below is a diagram of the soil profile of three layers of soil.

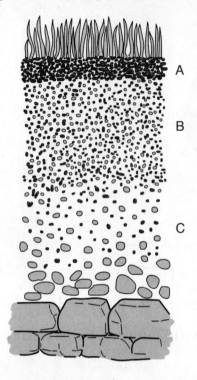

A

B

C

Describe the characteristics and properties of the three layers of soil.

_____

_____

_____

_____

_____

Connect **ESSENTIAL QUESTIONS**
Lessons 3 and 4

Answer the following question in the space provided.

15 How can water and gravity work together to erode soil, sediment, and rock?
Give two examples. _____

_____

_____

_____

Explain how water deposits soil, sediment, and rock. Give two examples. _____

_____

_____

_____

Earth's Atmosphere

© Houghton Mifflin Harcourt Publishing Company • Image Credits: (bkgd) ©Scott Smith/Corbis; (br) ©DLILLC/Corbis

Big Idea

Earth's atmosphere is a mixture of gases that interacts with solar energy.

Earth's atmosphere is divided into different layers. These clouds have formed in the troposphere, the lowest layer of the atmosphere where most weather occurs.

Wind is the movement of air caused by differences in air pressure.

What do you think?

Like other parts of the Earth system, energy is transferred through Earth's atmosphere. What are the three processes by which energy is transferred through the atmosphere?

Unit 4
Earth's Atmosphere

Clearing the Air

In some areas, there are many vehicles on the roads every day. Some of the gases from vehicle exhausts react with sunlight to form ozone. There are days when the concentration of ozone is so high that it becomes a health hazard. Those days are especially difficult for people who have problems breathing. What can you do to reduce gas emissions?

① Think About It

A How do you get to school every day?

_____

_____

_____

B How many of the students in your class come to school by car?

_____

Gas emissions are high during rush-hour traffic.

② Ask A Question

How can you reduce the number of vehicles students use to get to school one day each month?

With your teacher and classmates, brainstorm different ways in which you can reduce the number of vehicles students use to get to school.

Ride a bicycle to school.

Check off the points below as you use them to design your plan.

☐ how far a student lives from school

☐ the kinds of transportation students may have available to them

③ Make A Plan

A Write down different ways that you can reduce the number of vehicles that bring students to school.

_____
_____
_____
_____
_____
_____
_____

B Create a short presentation for your principal that outlines how the whole school could become involved in your vehicle-reduction plan. Write down the points of your presentation in the space below.

_____
_____
_____
_____
_____
_____
_____
_____
_____

C In the space below, design a sign-up sheet that your classmates will use to choose how they will come to school on the designated day.

Take It Home

Give your presentation to an adult. Then, have the adult brainstorm ways to reduce their daily gas emissions.

The Atmosphere

ESSENTIAL QUESTION

What is the atmosphere?

By the end of this lesson, you should be able to describe the composition and structure of the atmosphere and explain how the atmosphere protects life and insulates Earth.

The atmosphere is a very thin layer compared to the whole Earth. However, it is essential for life on our planet.

Virginia Science Standards of Learning
6.6 The student will investigate and understand the properties of air and the structure and dynamics of Earth's atmosphere. Key concepts include:
6.6.a air as a mixture of gaseous elements and compounds;
6.6.b pressure, temperature, and humidity; and
6.6.c atmospheric changes with altitude.

Lesson Labs

Quick Labs
• Modeling Air Pressure
• Modeling Air Pressure Changes with Altitude

Field Lab
• Measuring Oxygen in the Air

Engage Your Brain

1 Predict Check T or F to show whether you think each statement is true or false.

T	F	
☐	☐	Oxygen is in the air we breathe.
☐	☐	Pressure is not a property of air.
☐	☐	The air around you is part of the atmosphere.
☐	☐	As you climb up a mountain, the temperature usually gets warmer.

2 Explain Does the air in this balloon have mass? Why or why not?

_____

_____

_____

_____

_____

Active Reading

3 Synthesize Many English words have their roots in other languages. Use the ancient Greek words below to make an educated guess about the meanings of the words *atmosphere* and *mesosphere*.

Greek word	Meaning
atmos	vapor
mesos	middle
sphaira	ball

Vocabulary Terms

• atmosphere
• air pressure
• thermosphere
• mesosphere
• stratosphere
• troposphere
• ozone layer
• greenhouse effect

4 Apply As you learn the definition of each vocabulary term in this lesson, create your own definition or sketch to help you remember the meaning of the term.

atmosphere:

_____

_____

mesosphere:

_____

_____

Up and Away!

What is Earth's atmosphere?

The mixture of gases that surrounds Earth is the **atmosphere**. This mixture is most often referred to as air. The atmosphere has many important functions. It protects you from the sun's damaging rays and also helps to maintain the right temperature range for life on Earth. For example, the temperature range on Earth allows us to have an abundant amount of liquid water. Many of the components of the atmosphere are essential for life, such as the oxygen you breathe.

A Mixture of Gases and Small Particles

As shown below, the atmosphere is made mostly of nitrogen gas (78%) and oxygen gas (21%). The other 1% is other gases. The atmosphere also contains small particles such as dust, volcanic ash, sea salt, and smoke. There are even small pieces of skin, bacteria, and pollen floating in the atmosphere!

Water is also found in the atmosphere. Liquid water, as water droplets, and solid water, as snow and ice crystals, are found in clouds. But most water in the atmosphere exists as an invisible gas called water vapor. Under certain conditions, water vapor can change into solid or liquid water. Then, snow or rain might fall from the sky.

Visualize It!

5 Identify Fill in the missing percentage for oxygen.

Nitrogen is the most abundant gas in the atmosphere.

Oxygen is the second most abundant gas in the atmosphere.

The remaining 1% of the atmosphere is made up of argon, carbon dioxide, water vapor, and other gases.

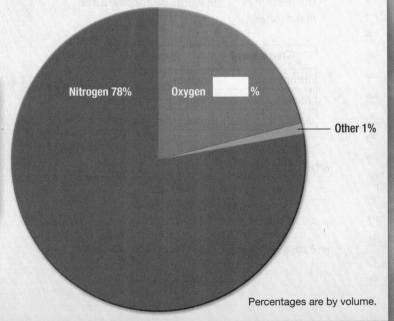

Composition of the Atmosphere

Nitrogen 78%

Oxygen ___ %

Other 1%

Percentages are by volume.

How do pressure and temperature change in the atmosphere?

Active Reading

6 Identify As you read, underline what happens to temperature and to pressure as altitude increases.

The atmosphere is held around Earth by gravity. Gravity pulls gas molecules in the atmosphere toward Earth's surface, causing air pressure. **Air pressure** is the measure of the force with which air molecules push on an area of a surface. At sea level, air pressure is over 1 lb for every square centimeter of your body. That is like carrying a 1-liter bottle of water on the tip of your finger!

However, air pressure is not the same throughout the atmosphere. Although there are many gas molecules that surround you on Earth, there are fewer and fewer gas molecules in the air as you move away from Earth's surface. So, as altitude increases, air pressure decreases.

As altitude increases, air temperature also changes. These changes are mainly due to the way solar energy is absorbed in the atmosphere. Some parts of the atmosphere are warmer because they contain a high percentage of gases that absorb solar energy. Other parts of the atmosphere contain less of these gases and are cooler.

Inquiry

7 Explain Why does a mountain climber need an oxygen supply at very high altitudes, even though the air still contains 21% oxygen?

_____

_____

_____

At high altitudes such as the top of Mount Everest, air pressure and temperature are lower than they are at sea level.

175

Look Way Up

What are the layers of the atmosphere?

Earth's atmosphere is divided into four layers, based on temperature and other properties. As shown at the right, these layers are the troposphere (TROH•puh•sfir), stratosphere (STRAT•uh•sfir), mesosphere (MEZ•uh•sfir), and thermosphere (THER•muh•sfir). Although these names sound complicated, they give you clues about the layers' features. *Tropo-* means "turning" or "change," and the troposphere is the layer where gases turn and mix. *Strato-* means "layer," and the stratosphere is where gases are layered and do not mix very much. *Meso-* means "middle," and the mesosphere is the middle layer. Finally, *thermo-* means "heat," and the thermosphere is the layer where temperatures are highest.

Think Outside the Book

8 Describe Research the part of the thermosphere called the ionosphere. Describe what the aurora borealis is.

The aurora borealis occurs in the thermosphere.

Thermosphere

The **thermosphere** is the uppermost layer of the atmosphere. The temperature increases as altitude increases because gases in the thermosphere absorb high-energy solar radiation. Temperatures in the thermosphere can be 1,500 °C or higher. However, the thermosphere feels cold. The density of particles in the thermosphere is very low. Too few gas particles collide with your body to transfer heat energy to your skin.

Mesosphere

The **mesosphere** is between the thermosphere and stratosphere. In this layer, the temperature decreases as altitude increases. Temperatures can be as low as −120 °C at the top of the mesosphere. Meteoroids begin to burn up in the mesosphere.

Stratosphere

The **stratosphere** is between the mesosphere and troposphere. In this layer, temperatures generally increase as altitude increases. Ozone in the stratosphere absorbs ultraviolet radiation from the sun, which warms the air. An ozone molecule is made of three atoms of oxygen. Gases in the stratosphere are layered and do not mix very much.

Troposphere

The **troposphere** is the lowest layer of the atmosphere. Although temperatures near Earth's surface vary greatly, generally, temperature decreases as altitude increases. This layer contains almost 80% of the atmosphere's total mass, making it the densest layer. Almost all of Earth's carbon dioxide, water vapor, clouds, air pollution, weather, and life forms are in the troposphere.

 **Visualize It!**

In the graph, the green line shows pressure change with altitude.
The red line shows temperature change with altitude.

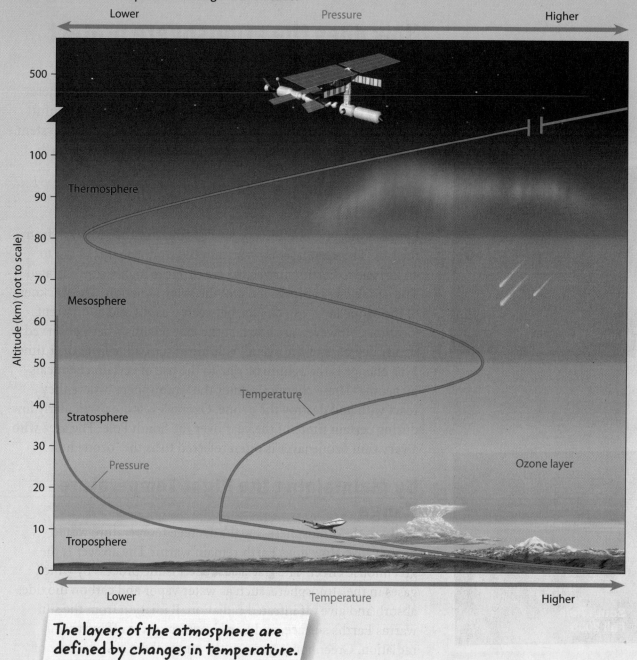

The layers of the atmosphere are defined by changes in temperature.

9 Analyze Using the graph and descriptions provided, indicate if air pressure and temperature increase or decrease with increased altitude in each layer of the atmosphere. One answer has been provided for you.

Layer	Air pressure	Temperature
Thermosphere	decreases	
Mesosphere		
Stratosphere		
Troposphere		

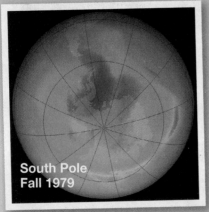

South Pole
Fall 1979

Less
ozone

More
ozone

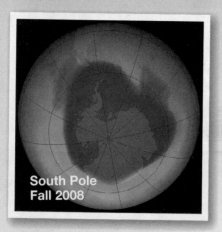

South Pole
Fall 2008

10 Compare How did the ozone layer over the South Pole change between 1979 and 2008?

_____

_____

_____

How does the atmosphere protect life on Earth?

The atmosphere surrounds and protects Earth. The atmosphere provides the air we breathe. It also protects Earth from harmful solar radiation and from space debris that enters the Earth system. In addition, the atmosphere controls the temperature on Earth.

By Absorbing or Reflecting Harmful Radiation

Earth's atmosphere reflects or absorbs most of the radiation from the sun. The **ozone layer** is an area in the stratosphere, 15 km to 40 km above Earth's surface, where ozone is highly concentrated. The ozone layer absorbs most of the solar radiation. The thickness of the ozone layer can change between seasons and at different locations. However, as shown at the left, scientists have observed a steady decrease in the overall volume of the ozone layer over time. This change is thought to be due to the use of certain chemicals by people. These chemicals enter the stratosphere, where they react with and destroy the ozone. Ozone levels are particularly low during certain times of the year over the South Pole. The area with a very thin ozone layer is often referred to as the "ozone hole."

By Maintaining the Right Temperature Range

Without the atmosphere, Earth's average temperature would be very low. How does Earth remain warm? The answer is the greenhouse effect. The **greenhouse effect** is the process by which gases in the atmosphere, such as water vapor and carbon dioxide, absorb and give off infrared radiation. Radiation from the sun warms Earth's surface, and Earth's surface gives off infrared radiation. Greenhouse gases in the atmosphere absorb some of this infrared radiation and then reradiate it. Some of this energy is absorbed again by Earth's surface, while some energy goes out into space. Because greenhouse gases keep energy in the Earth system longer, Earth's average surface temperature is kept at around 15°C (59°F). In time, all the energy ends up back in outer space.

Active Reading **11 List** Name two examples of greenhouse gases.

_____

_____

the Sun...

The Greenhouse Effect

Greenhouse gas molecules absorb and emit infrared radiation.

Atmosphere without Greenhouse Gases

Without greenhouse gases in Earth's atmosphere, radiation from Earth's surface is lost directly to space.
Average Temperature: -18°C

Atmosphere with Greenhouse Gases

With greenhouse gases in Earth's atmosphere, radiation from Earth's surface is lost to space more slowly, which makes Earth's surface warmer.
Average Temperature: 15°C

sunlight   infrared radiation

The atmosphere is much thinner than shown here.

Visualize It!

12 Illustrate Draw your own version of how greenhouse gases keep Earth warm.

Visual Summary

To complete this summary, fill in the blanks with the correct word or phrase. Then, use the key below to check your answers. You can use this page to review the main concepts of the lesson.

Both air pressure and temperature change within the atmosphere.

The atmosphere protects Earth from harmful radiation and helps to maintain a temperature range that supports life.

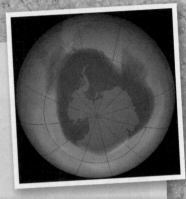

13 As altitude increases, air pressure
_____

14 Earth is protected from harmful solar radiation by the
_____

The Atmosphere

The atmosphere is divided into four layers, according to temperature and other properties.

15 The four layers of the atmosphere are the
_____
_____
_____
_____

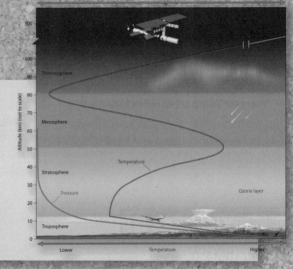

Answers: 13 decreases; 14 ozone layer; 15 troposphere, stratosphere, mesosphere, thermosphere

16 **Hypothesize** What do you think Earth's surface would be like if Earth did not have an atmosphere?

Lesson Review

Vocabulary

Fill in the blanks with the terms that best complete the following sentences.

1 The _____ is a mixture of gases that surrounds Earth.

2 The measure of the force with which air molecules push on a surface is called _____ .

3 The _____ is the process by which gases in the atmosphere absorb and reradiate heat.

Key Concepts

4 List Name three gases in the atmosphere.

_____

_____

5 Identify What layer of the atmosphere contains the ozone layer?

_____

6 Identify What layer of the atmosphere contains almost 80% of the atmosphere's total mass?

_____

7 Describe How and why does air pressure change with altitude in the atmosphere?

_____

_____

_____

8 Explain What is the name of the uppermost layer of the atmosphere? Why does it feel cold there, even though the temperature can be very high?

_____

_____

_____

_____

Critical Thinking

9 Hypothesize What would happen to life on Earth if the ozone layer was not present?

_____

_____

_____

10 Criticize A friend says that temperature increases as altitude increases because you're moving closer to the sun. Is this true? Explain.

_____

_____

_____

11 Predict Why would increased levels of greenhouse gases contribute to higher temperatures on Earth?

_____

_____

_____

Use this graph to answer the following questions.

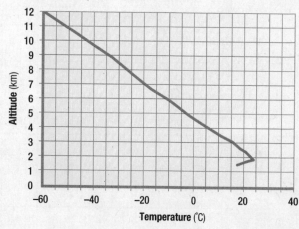

Changes in Temperature with Altitude

Source: National Weather Service. Data taken at Riverton, Wyoming, 2001

12 Analyze The top of Mount Everest is at about 8,850 m. What would the approximate air temperature be at that altitude? _____

13 Analyze What is the total temperature change between 3 km and 7 km above Earth's surface? _____

My Notes

Energy Transfer

ESSENTIAL QUESTION

How does energy move through Earth's system?

By the end of this lesson, you should be able to summarize the three mechanisms by which energy is transferred through Earth's system.

Ice absorbs energy from the sun. This can cause ice to melt—even these icicles in Antarctica.

Virginia Science Standards of Learning

6.3 The student will investigate and understand the role of solar energy in driving most natural processes within the atmosphere, the hydrosphere, and on Earth's surface. Key concepts include:

6.3.b the role of radiation and convection in the distribution of energy; and

6.3.c the role of radiation and convection in the distribution of energy.

6.5 The student will investigate and understand the unique properties and characteristics of water and its roles in the natural and human-made environment. Key concepts include:

6.5.d the ability of large bodies of water to store thermal energy and moderate climate.

 **Lesson Labs**

Quick Labs
- The Sun's Angle and Temperature
- How Does Color Affect Temperature?
- Modeling Convection

S.T.E.M. Lab
- Heat from the Sun

Engage Your Brain

1 Describe Fill in the blank with the word or phrase that you think correctly completes the following sentences.

An example of something hot is

_____

An example of something cold is

_____

The sun provides us with

_____

A thermometer is used to measure

_____

2 Explain If you placed your hands around this mug of hot chocolate, what would happen to the temperature of your hands? Why do you think this would happen?

_____

_____

_____

_____

_____

Active Reading

3 Apply Many scientific words, such as *heat*, are used to convey different meanings. Use context clues to write your own definition for each meaning of the word *heat*.

The student won the first <u>heat</u> of the race.

heat:

_____

_____

The man wondered if his rent included <u>heat</u>.

heat:

_____

_____

Energy in the form of <u>heat</u> was transferred from the hot pan to the cold counter.

heat:

_____

_____

Vocabulary Terms
- **temperature**
- **thermal energy**
- **thermal expansion**
- **heat**
- **radiation**
- **convection**
- **conduction**

4 Identify This list contains the vocabulary terms you'll learn in this lesson. As you read, circle the definition of each term.

Hot and Cold

How are energy and temperature related?

All matter is made up of moving particles, such as atoms or molecules. When particles are in motion, they have kinetic energy. Because particles move at different speeds, each has a different amount of kinetic energy.

Temperature (TEMM•per•uh•choor) is a measure of the average kinetic energy of particles. The faster a particle moves, the more kinetic energy it has. As shown below, the more kinetic energy the particles of an object have, the higher the temperature of the object. Temperature does not depend on the number of particles. A teapot holds more tea than a cup. If the particles of tea in both containers have the same average kinetic energy, the tea in both containers is at the same temperature.

Thermal energy is the total kinetic energy of particles. A teapot full of tea at a high temperature has more thermal energy than a teapot full of tea at a lower temperature. Thermal energy also depends on the number of particles. The more particles there are in an object, the greater the object's thermal energy. The tea in a teapot and a cup may be at the same temperature, but the tea in the pot has more thermal energy because there is more of it.

Visualize It!

5 Analyze Which container holds particles with the higher average kinetic energy?

_____

_____

What is thermal expansion?

When the temperature of a substance increases, the substance's particles have more kinetic energy. Therefore, the particles move faster and move apart. As the space between the particles increases, the substance expands. The increase in volume that results from an increase in temperature is called **thermal expansion**. Most substances on Earth expand when they become warmer and contract when they become cooler. Water is an exception. Cold water expands as it gets colder and then freezes to form ice.

Thermal expansion causes a change in the density of a substance. *Density* is the mass per unit volume of a substance. When a substance expands, its mass stays the same but its volume increases. As a result, density decreases. Differences in density that are caused by thermal expansion can cause movement of matter. For example, air inside a hot-air balloon is warmed, as shown below. The air expands as its particles move faster and farther apart. As the air expands, it becomes less dense than the air outside the balloon. The less-dense air inside the balloon is forced upward by the colder, denser air outside the balloon. This same principle affects air movement in the atmosphere, water movement in the oceans, and rock movement in the geosphere.

7 Apply Why would an increase in the temperature of the oceans contribute to a rise in sea level?

_____

_____

_____

6 Predict What might happen to the hot-air balloon if the air inside it cooled down?

_____

_____

When the air in this balloon becomes hotter, it becomes less dense than the surrounding air. So, the balloon goes up, up, and away!

Getting Warm

What is heat?

Active Reading

8 Identify As you read, underline the direction of energy transfer between objects that are at different temperatures.

You might think of the word *heat* when you imagine something that feels hot. But heat also has to do with things that feel cold. In fact, heat is what causes objects to feel hot or cold. You may often use the word *heat* to mean different things. However, in this lesson, the word *heat* has only one meaning. **Heat** is the energy that is transferred between objects that are at different temperatures.

Energy Transferred Between Objects

When objects that have different temperatures come into contact, energy will be transferred between them until both objects reach the same temperature. The direction of this energy transfer is always from the object with the higher temperature to the object with the lower temperature. When you touch something cold, energy is transferred from your body to that object. When you touch something hot, like the pan shown below, energy is transferred from that object to your body.

Visualize It!

9 Predict Draw an arrow to show the direction in which energy is transferred between the pan and the oven mitts.

This pan is being removed from the oven and is very hot.

Why can the temperatures of land, air, and water differ?

When the same amount of energy is being transferred, some materials will get warmer or cooler at a faster rate than other materials. Suppose you are walking along a beach on a sunny day. You may notice that the land feels warmer than the air and the water, even though they are all exposed to the same amount of energy from the sun. This is because the land warms up at a faster rate than the water and air do.

Specific Heat

The different rates at which materials become warmer or cooler are due to a property called *specific heat*. A substance that has a high specific heat requires a lot of energy to show an increase in temperature. A substance with a lower specific heat requires less energy to show the same increase in temperature. Water has a higher specific heat than land. So, water warms up more slowly than land does. Water also cools down more slowly than land does.

10 Predict Air has a lower specific heat than water. Once the sun goes down, will the air or the water cool off faster? Why?

_____

_____

_____

The temperatures of land, water, and air may differ— even when they are exposed to the same amount of energy from the sun.

Heat

How is energy transferred by radiation?

On a summer day, you can feel warmth from the sun on your skin. But how did that energy reach you from the sun? The sun transfers energy to Earth by radiation. **Radiation** is the transfer of energy as electromagnetic (ee•LEK•troh•mag•NEH•tik) waves. Radiation can transfer energy between objects that are not in direct contact with each other. Many objects other than the sun also radiate energy as light and heat. These include a hot burner on a stove and a campfire, shown below.

Electromagnetic Waves

Energy from the sun is called *electromagnetic radiation*. This energy travels in waves. You are probably familiar with one form of radiation called *visible light*. You can see the visible light that comes from the sun. Electromagnetic radiation includes other forms of energy, which you cannot see. Most of the warmth that you feel from the sun is infrared radiation. This energy has a longer wavelength and lower energy than visible light. Higher-energy radiation includes x-rays and ultraviolet light.

Visualize It!

11 Analyze Write a caption for the campfire photo on the right. Make sure the caption relates the image to radiation.

_____

_____

_____

Energy from this hot burner is being transferred by radiation.

Energy from the sun is transferred through space.

Where does radiation occur on Earth?

We live almost 150 million km from the sun. Yet almost all of the energy on Earth is transmitted from the sun by radiation. The sun is the major source of energy for processes at Earth's surface. Receiving that energy is absolutely vital for life on Earth. The electromagnetic waves from the sun also provide energy that drives the water cycle.

When solar radiation reaches Earth, some of the energy is reflected and scattered by Earth's atmosphere. But much of the energy passes through Earth's atmosphere and reaches Earth's surface. Some of the energy that Earth receives from the sun is absorbed by the atmosphere, geosphere, and hydrosphere. Then, the energy is changed into thermal energy. This thermal energy may be reradiated into the Earth system or into space. Much of the energy is transferred through Earth's systems by the two other ways—convection and conduction.

Think Outside the Book

13 Apply Research ultraviolet radiation from the sun and its role in causing sunburns.

12 Summarize Give two examples of what happens when energy from the sun reaches Earth.

_____

_____

_____

_____

Heating Up

How is energy transferred by convection?

Have you ever watched a pot of boiling water, such as the one below? If so, you have seen convection. **Convection** (kun•VECK•shuhn) is the transfer of energy due to the movement of matter. As water warms up at the bottom of the pot, some of the hot water rises. At the same time, cooler water from other parts of the pot sink and replace the rising water. This water is then warmed and the cycle continues.

Convection Currents

Convection involves the movement of matter due to differences in density. Convection occurs because most matter becomes less dense when it gets warmer. When most matter becomes warmer, it undergoes thermal expansion and a decrease in density. This less-dense matter is forced upward by the surrounding colder, denser matter that is sinking. As the hot matter rises, it cools and becomes more dense. This causes it to sink back down. This cycling of matter is called a *convection current*. Convection most often occurs in fluids, such as water and air. But convection can also happen in solids.

wax

convection current

energy sources

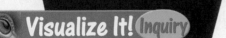

Visualize It! Inquiry

14 Apply How is convection related to the rise and fall of wax in lava lamps?

_____

_____

_____

_____

Where does convection occur on Earth?

If Earth's surface is warmer than the air, energy will be transferred from the ground to the air. As the air becomes warmer, it becomes less dense. This air is pushed upward and out of the way by cooler, denser air that is sinking. As the warm air rises, it cools and becomes denser and begins to sink back toward Earth's surface. This cycle moves energy through the atmosphere.

Convection currents also occur in the ocean because of differences in the density of ocean water. More dense water sinks to the ocean floor, and less dense water moves toward the surface. The density of ocean water is influenced by temperature and the amount of salt in the water. Cold water is denser than warmer water. Water that contains a lot of salt is more dense than less-salty water.

Energy produced deep inside Earth heats rock in the mantle. The heated rock becomes less dense and is pushed up toward Earth's surface by the cooler, denser surrounding rock. Once cooled near the surface, the rock sinks. These convection currents transfer energy from Earth's core toward Earth's surface. These currents also cause the movement of tectonic plates.

Active Reading **15 Name** What are three of Earth's spheres in which energy is transferred by convection?

_____

_____

Visualize It!

16 Apply Draw the convection current that could occur in the body of water in this image.

Convection currents occur throughout the Earth system.

191

Ouch!

How is energy transferred by conduction?

Have you ever touched an ice cube and wondered why it feels cold? An ice cube has only a small amount of energy, compared to your hand. Energy is transferred to the ice cube from your hand through the process of conduction. **Conduction** (kun•DUHK•shuhn) is the transfer of energy from one object to another object through direct contact.

Direct Contact

Remember that the atoms or molecules in a substance are constantly moving. Even a solid block of ice has particles in constant motion. When objects at different temperatures touch, their particles interact. Conduction involves the faster-moving particles of the warmer object transferring energy to the slower-moving particles in the cooler object. The greater the difference in energy of the particles, the faster the transfer of energy by conduction occurs.

Active Reading **17 Apply** Name two examples of conduction that you experience every day.

_____

_____

_____

_____

These desert sands would feel hot because of conduction.

Where does conduction occur on Earth?

Energy can be transferred between the geosphere and the atmosphere by conduction. When cooler air molecules come into direct contact with the warm ground, energy is passed to the air by conduction. Conduction between the ground and the air happens only within a few centimeters of Earth's surface.

Conduction also happens between particles of air and particles of water. For example, if air transfers enough energy to liquid water, the water may evaporate. If water vapor transfers energy to the air, the kinetic energy of the water decreases. As a result, the water vapor may condense to form liquid water droplets.

Inside Earth, energy transfers between rock particles by conduction. However, rock is a poor conductor of heat, so this process happens very slowly.

Visualize It!

18 Compare Does conduction also occur in a city like the one shown below? Explain.

_____

_____

_____

_____

_____

19 Summarize Complete the following spider map by describing the three types of energy transfer. One answer has been started for you.

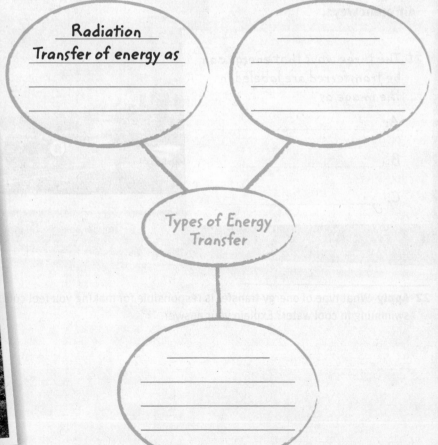

Radiation
Transfer of energy as
_____
_____

_____
_____
_____

Types of Energy Transfer

_____
_____
_____

Visual Summary

To complete this summary, fill in the blanks with the correct word or phrase. Then, use the key below to check your answers. You can use this page to review the main concepts of the lesson.

Energy Transfer

Heat is the energy that is transferred between objects that are at different temperatures.

20 The particles in a hot pan have _____ kinetic energy than the particles in a cool oven mitt.

Energy can be transferred in different ways.

21 The three ways that energy can be transferred are labeled in the image as

A: _____

B: _____

C: _____

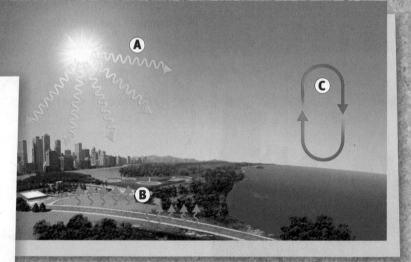

Answers: 20 more; 21 A: radiation, B: conduction, C: convection

22 Apply What type of energy transfer is responsible for making you feel cold when you are swimming in cool water? Explain your answer.

Engineering Design Process

Skills
Identify a need
Conduct research
✓ Brainstorm solutions
✓ Select a solution
Design a prototype
✓ Build a prototype
✓ Test and evaluate
✓ Redesign to improve
✓ Communicate results

Objectives

- Explain how a need for clean energy has driven a technological solution.
- Describe two examples of wind-powered generators.
- Design a technological solution to a problem.
- Test and modify a prototype to achieve the desired result.

Building a Wind Turbine

During the Industrial Revolution, machines began to replace human and animal power for doing work. From agriculture and manufacturing to transportation, machines made work faster and easier. However, these machines needed fuel. Fossil fuels, such as coal, oil, and gasoline, powered the Industrial Revolution and are still used today. But burning fossil fuels produces waste products that harm the environment. In addition, fossil fuels will eventually run out. As a result, we need to better understand alternative, renewable sources of energy.

Brainstorming Solutions

There are many sources of energy besides fossil fuels. One of the most abundant renewable sources is wind. A wind turbine is a device that uses energy from the wind to turn an axle. The turning axle can be attached to other equipment to do jobs such as pumping water, cutting lumber, or generating electricity. To generate electricity, the axle spins magnets around a coiled wire. This causes electrons to flow in the wire. Flowing electrons produce an electric current. Electric current is used to power homes and businesses or electrical energy can be stored in a battery.

1 Brainstorm What are other possible sources of renewable energy that could be used to power a generator?

_____

_____

_____

_____

_____

_____

_____

HAWTs must be pointed into the wind to work. A motor turns the turbine to keep it facing the wind. HAWT blades are angled so that wind strikes the front of the blades, and then pushes the blades as it flows over them. Because wind flows over the blades fairly evenly, there is little vibration. So HAWTs are relatively quiet, and the turbines last a long time.

Wind direction

Blade moves counterclockwise

The Modern Design

There are two general types of modern wind turbines. A horizontal-axis wind turbine (HAWT) has a main axle that is horizontal, and a generator at the top of a tall tower. A vertical-axis wind turbine (VAWT) has a main axle that is vertical, and a generator at ground level. The blades are often white or light gray, to blend with the clouds. Blades can be more than 40 meters (130 ft) long, supported by towers more than 90 meters (300 ft) tall. The blade tips can travel more than 320 kilometers (200 mi) per hour!

2 Infer What problems may have been encountered as prototypes for modern wind turbines were tested?

_____

_____

_____

VAWTs do not need to be pointed into the wind to work. The blades are made so that one blade is pushed by the wind while the other returns against the wind. But because each blade moves against the wind for part of its rotation, VAWTs are less efficient than HAWTs. They also tend to vibrate more and, as a result, make more noise.

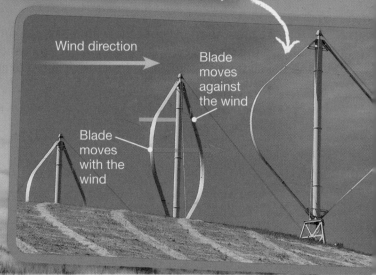

Wind direction

Blade moves against the wind

Blade moves with the wind

👋 You Try It! ⟶

Now it's turn to design a wind turbine that will generate electricity and light a small bulb.

 **You Try It!**

Now it's your turn to design an efficient wind turbine that will generate enough electricity to light a small bulb.

Materials

✓ assorted wind turbine parts
✓ fan
✓ gears
✓ small bulb
✓ small motor
✓ socket

1 Brainstorm solutions

Brainstorm ideas for a wind turbine that will turn an axle on a small motor. The blades must turn fast enough so that the motor generates enough electricity to light a small bulb. Fill in the table below with as many ideas as you can for each part of your wind turbine. Circle each idea you decide to try.

Type of axis	Shape of turbine	Attaching axis to motor	Control speed

2 Select a solution

From the table above, choose the features for the turbine you will build. In the space below, draw a model of your wind turbine idea. Include all the parts and show how they will be connected.

(3) Build a prototype

Now build your wind turbine. As you built your turbine, were there some parts of your design that could not be assembled as you had predicted? What parts did you have to revise as you were building the prototype?

_____

_____

_____

_____

(4) Test and evaluate

Point a fan at your wind turbine and see what happens. Did the bulb light? If not, what parts of your turbine could you revise?

_____

_____

_____

_____

(5) Redesign to improve

Choose one part to revise. Modify your design and then test again. Repeat this process until your turbine lights up the light bulb.

_____

_____

_____

_____

(6) Communicate results

Which part of the turbine seemed to have the greatest effect on the brightness of the light bulb?

_____

_____

_____

_____

_____

Wind in the Atmosphere

ESSENTIAL QUESTION

What is wind?

By the end of this lesson, you should be able to explain how energy provided by the sun causes atmospheric movement, called wind.

Virginia Science Standards of Learning

6.3 The student will investigate and understand the role of solar energy in driving most natural processes within the atmosphere, the hydrosphere, and on Earth's surface. Key concepts include:

6.3.c the motion of the atmosphere and the oceans.

6.6 The student will investigate and understand the properties of air and the structure and dynamics of Earth's atmosphere. Key concepts include:

6.6.e the relationship of atmospheric measures and weather conditions.

Although you cannot see wind, you can see how it affects things like these kites.

Engage Your Brain

1 Predict Check T or F to show whether you think each statement is true or false.

T	F	
☐	☐	The atmosphere is often referred to as air.
☐	☐	Wind does not have direction.
☐	☐	During the day, there is often a wind blowing toward shore from the ocean or a large lake.
☐	☐	Cold air rises and warm air sinks.

2 Explain if you opened the valve on this bicycle tire, what would happen to the air inside of the tire? Why do you think that would happen?

_____

_____

_____

Active Reading

3 Synthesize You can often define an unknown phrase if you know the meaning of its word parts. Use the word parts below to make an educated guess about the meanings of the phrases *local wind* and *global wind*.

Word part	Meaning
wind	movement of air due to differences in air pressure
local	involving a particular area
global	involving the entire Earth

Vocabulary Terms

• wind
• Coriolis effect
• global wind
• jet stream
• local wind

4 Identify This list contains the vocabulary terms you'll learn in this lesson. As you read, circle the definition of each term.

local wind: _____

_____

_____

global wind: _____

_____

_____

Blow It Out!

What causes wind?

The next time you feel the wind blowing, you can thank the sun! The sun does not warm the whole surface of the Earth in a uniform manner. This uneven heating causes the air above Earth's surface to be at different temperatures. Cold air is more dense than warmer air is. Colder, denser air sinks. When denser air sinks, it places greater pressure on the surface of Earth than warmer, less-dense air does. This results in areas of higher air pressure. Air moves from areas of higher pressure toward areas of lower pressure. The movement of air caused by differences in air pressure is called **wind**. The greater the differences in air pressure, the faster the air moves.

Areas of High and Low Pressure

Cold, dense air at the poles creates areas of high pressure at the poles. Warm, less-dense air at the equator forms an area of lower pressure. This pressure gradient results in global movement of air. However, instead of moving in one circle between the equator and the poles, air moves in smaller circular patterns called *convection cells,* shown below. As air moves from the equator, it cools and becomes more dense. At about 30°N and 30°S latitudes, a high-pressure belt results from the sinking of air. Near the poles, cold air warms as it moves away from the poles. At around 60°N and 60°S latitudes, a low-pressure belt forms as the warmed air is pushed upward.

Visualize It!

5 Identify In the white oval area on the map, draw the convection cell that was left out. Use a pencil to indicate warm air and a pen to indicate cool air.

The warming and cooling of air produces pressure belts every 30° of latitude.

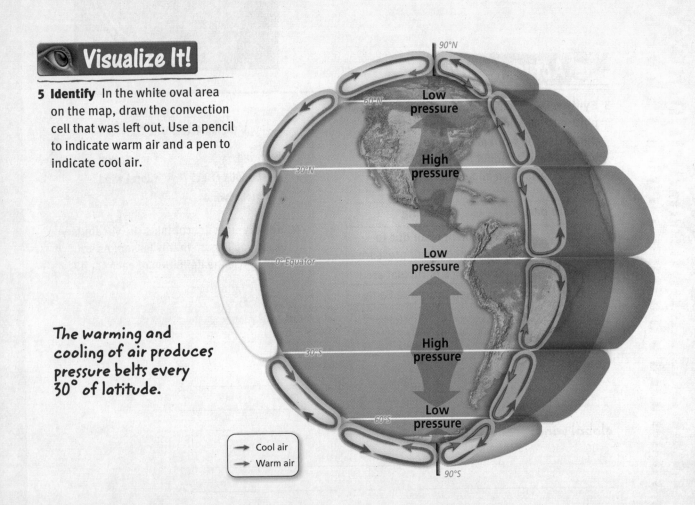

How does Earth's rotation affect wind?

Pressure differences cause air to move between the equator and the poles. If Earth was not rotating, winds would blow in a straight line. However, winds are deflected, or curved, due to Earth's rotation, as shown below. The apparent curving of the path of a moving object from an otherwise straight path due to Earth's rotation is called the **Coriolis effect** (kawr•ee•OH•lis ih•FEKT). This effect is most noticeable over long distances.

Because each point on Earth makes one complete rotation every day, points closer to the equator must travel farther and, therefore, faster than points closer to the poles do. When air moves from the equator toward the North Pole, it maintains its initial speed and direction. If the air travels far enough north, it will have traveled farther east than a point on the ground beneath it. As a result, the air appears to follow a curved path toward the east. Air moving from the North Pole to the equator appears to curve to the west because the air moves east more slowly than a point on the ground beneath it does. Therefore, in the Northern Hemisphere, air moving to the north curves to the east and air moving to the south curves to the west.

Active Reading

6 Identify As you read, underline how air movement in the Northern Hemisphere is influenced by the Coriolis effect.

Visualize It!

7 Label In the white ovals on the map, draw the direction and path of the winds that would occur at those locations on Earth.

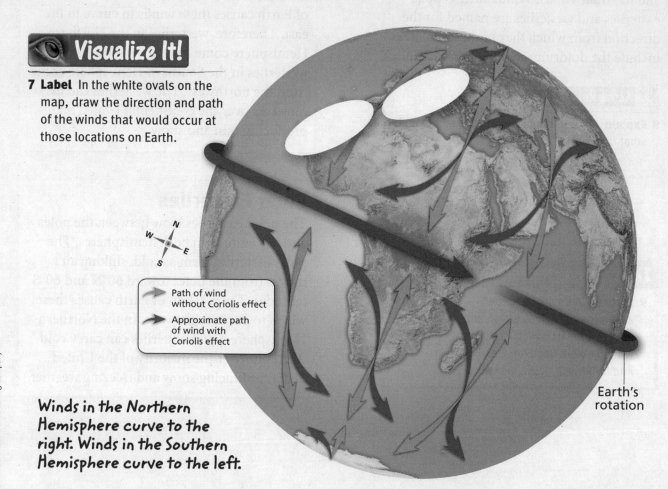

Path of wind without Coriolis effect

Approximate path of wind with Coriolis effect

Earth's rotation

Winds in the Northern Hemisphere curve to the right. Winds in the Southern Hemisphere curve to the left.

Blowin Around

What are examples of global winds?

Recall that air travels in circular patterns called convection cells that cover approximately 30° of latitude. Pressure belts at every 30° of latitude and the Coriolis effect produce patterns of calm areas and wind systems. These wind systems occur at or near Earth's surface and are called **global winds**. As shown at the right, the major global wind systems are the *polar easterlies* (EE•ster•leez), the *westerlies* (WES•ter•leez), and the *trade winds*. Winds such as polar easterlies and westerlies are named for the direction from which they blow. Calm areas include the doldrums and the horse latitudes.

Active Reading

8 Explain If something is being carried by westerlies, what direction is it moving toward?

_____

_____

Think Outside the Book Inquiry

9 Model Winds are described according to their direction and speed. Research wind vanes and what they are used for. Design and build your own wind vane.

Trade Winds

The trade winds blow between 30° latitude and the equator in both hemispheres. The rotation of Earth causes the trade winds to curve to the west. Therefore, trade winds in the Northern Hemisphere come from the northeast, and trade winds in the Southern Hemisphere come from the southeast. These winds became known as the trade winds because sailors relied on them to sail from Europe to the Americas.

Westerlies

The westerlies blow between 30° and 60° latitudes in both hemispheres. The rotation of Earth causes these winds to curve to the east. Therefore, westerlies in the Northern Hemisphere come from the southwest, and westerlies in the Southern Hemisphere come from the northwest. The westerlies can carry moist air over the continental United States, producing rain and snow.

Polar Easterlies

The polar easterlies blow between the poles and 60° latitude in both hemispheres. The polar easterlies form as cold, sinking air moves from the poles toward 60°N and 60°S latitudes. The rotation of Earth causes these winds to curve to the west. In the Northern Hemisphere, polar easterlies can carry cold Arctic air over the majority of the United States, producing snow and freezing weather.

The major global wind systems

10 Identify Label the polar easterlies, the westerlies, and the trade winds in the white boxes on the map.

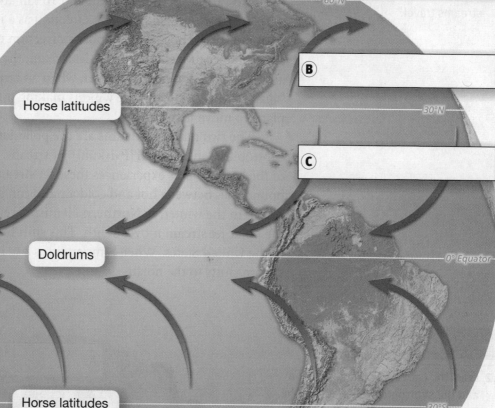

The Doldrums and Horse Latitudes

The trade winds of both hemispheres meet in a calm area around the equator called the *doldrums* (DOHL•druhmz). Very little wind blows in the doldrums because the warm, less-dense air results in an area of low pressure. The name doldrums means "dull" or "sluggish." At about 30° latitude in both hemispheres, air stops moving and sinks. This forms calm areas called the *horse latitudes*. This name was given to these areas when sailing ships carried horses from Europe to the Americas. When ships were stalled in these areas, horses were sometimes thrown overboard to save water.

The Jet Streams

A flight from Seattle to Boston can be 30 min faster than a flight from Boston to Seattle. Why? Pilots can take advantage of a jet stream. **Jet streams** are narrow belts of high-speed winds that blow from west to east, between 7 km and 16 km above Earth's surface. Airplanes traveling in the same direction as a jet stream go faster than those traveling in the opposite direction of a jet stream. When an airplane is traveling "with" a jet stream, the wind is helping the airplane move forward. However, when an airplane is traveling "against" the jet stream, the wind is making it more difficult for the plane to move forward.

The two main jet streams are the polar jet stream and the subtropical (suhb•TRAHP•i•kuhl) jet stream, shown below. Each of the hemispheres experiences these jet streams. Jet streams follow boundaries between hot and cold air and can shift north and south. In the winter, as Northern Hemisphere temperatures cool, the polar jet stream moves south. This shift brings cold Arctic air to the United States. When temperatures rise in the spring, this jet stream shifts to the north.

11 Identify As you read, underline the direction that the jet streams travel.

Visualize It!

12 Identify Label the polar jet stream and the subtropical jet stream in the Northern Hemisphere.

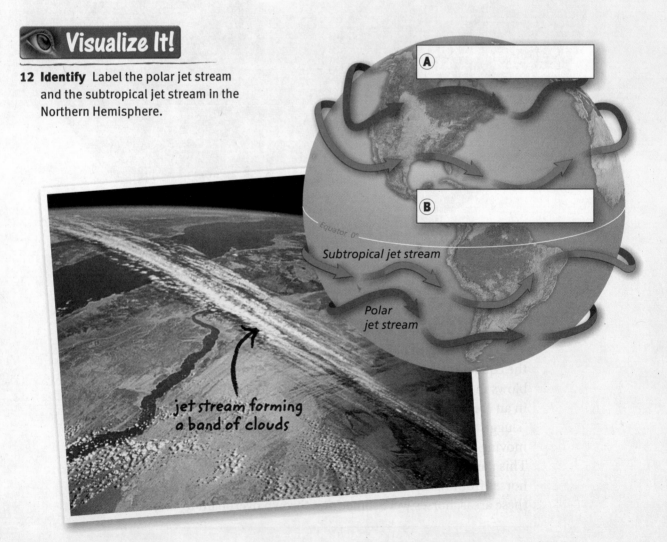

jet stream forming a band of clouds

A

B

Equator 0°

Subtropical jet stream

Polar jet stream

© Houghton Mifflin Harcourt Publishing Company • Image Credits: (bl) ©NASA/Science Source/Photo Researchers, Inc.

Desert Trades

How does some of the Sahara end up in the Americas?
Global winds carry it.

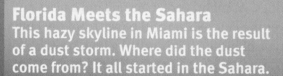

Trade Wind Carriers
Trade winds can carry
Saharan dust across the
Atlantic Ocean to Florida
and the Caribbean.

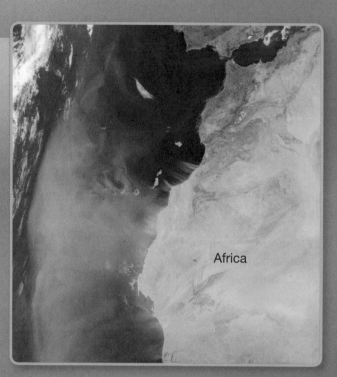

Africa

Florida Meets the Sahara
This hazy skyline in Miami is the result
of a dust storm. Where did the dust
come from? It all started in the Sahara.

The Sahara
The Sahara is the world's largest
hot desert. Sand and dust storms
that produce skies like this are
very common in this desert.

Extend

Inquiry

13 Explain Look at a map and explain how trade
winds carry dust from the Sahara to the Caribbean.

14 Relate Investigate the winds that blow in your
community. Where do they usually come from?
Identify the wind system that could be involved.

15 Apply Investigate how winds played a role in
distributing radioactive waste that was released
after an explosion at the Chernobyl Nuclear Power
Plant in Ukraine. Present your findings as a map
illustration or in a poster.

Feelin' Breezy

Active Reading

16 Identify As you read, underline two examples of geographic features that contribute to the formation of local winds.

Visualize It!

17 Analyze Label the areas of high pressure and low pressure.

What are examples of local winds?

Local geographic features, such as a body of water or a mountain, can produce temperature and pressure differences that cause local winds. Unlike global winds, **local winds** are the movement of air over short distances. They can blow from any direction, depending on the features of the area.

Sea and Land Breezes

Have you ever felt a cool breeze coming off the ocean or a lake? If so, you were experiencing a sea breeze. Large bodies of water take longer to warm up than land does. During the day, air above land becomes warmer than air above water. The colder, denser air over water flows toward the land and pushes the warm air on the land upward. While water takes longer to warm than land does, land cools faster than water does. At night, cooler air on land causes a higher-pressure zone over the land. So, a wind blows from the land toward the water. This type of local wind is called a land breeze.

sea breeze

Ⓑ _____ pressure

Ⓐ _____ pressure

land breeze

Ⓓ _____ pressure

Ⓒ _____ pressure

Valley and Mountain Breezes

Areas that have mountains and valleys experience local winds called mountain and valley breezes. During the day, the sun warms the air along the mountain slopes faster than the air in the valleys. This uneven heating results in areas of lower pressure near the mountain tops. This pressure difference causes a valley breeze, which flows from the valley up the slopes of the mountains. Many birds float on valley breezes to conserve energy. At nightfall, the air along the mountain slopes cools and moves down into the valley. This local wind is called a mountain breeze.

Visualize It!

18 Analyze Label the areas of high pressure and low pressure.

valley breeze

Ⓑ _____ pressure

Ⓐ _____ pressure

mountain breeze

Ⓓ _____ pressure

Ⓒ _____ pressure

© Houghton Mifflin Harcourt Publishing Company

Visual Summary

To complete this summary, circle the correct word or phrases. Then use the key below to check your answers. You can use this page to review the main concepts of the lesson.

Wind is the movement of air from areas of higher pressure to areas of lower pressure.

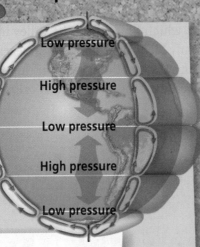

Low pressure

High pressure

Low pressure

High pressure

Low pressure

19 Cool air sinks, causing an area of high / low air pressure.

Global wind systems occur on Earth.

20 High-speed wind between 7 km and 16 km above Earth's surface is a jet stream / mountain breeze.

Wind in the Atmosphere

Geographic features can produce local winds.

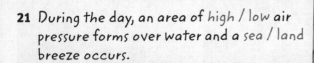

21 During the day, an area of high / low air pressure forms over water and a sea / land breeze occurs.

22 Explain Would there be winds if the air above Earth's surface was the same temperature everywhere? Explain your answer.

Lesson Review

Vocabulary

Fill in the blanks with the term that best completes the following sentences.

1 Another term for air movement caused by differences in air pressure is

_____

2 Pilots often take advantage of the
_____ , which are high-speed winds between 7 km and 16 km above Earth's surface.

3 The apparent curving of winds due to Earth's rotation is the _____

Key Concepts

4 Explain How does the sun cause wind?

_____
_____
_____
_____

5 Predict If Earth did not rotate, what would happen to the global winds? Why?

_____
_____
_____

6 Explain How do convection cells in Earth's atmosphere cause high- and low-pressure belts?

_____
_____
_____
_____

7 Describe What factors contribute to global winds? Identify areas where winds are weak.

_____
_____
_____
_____

8 Identify Name a latitude where each of the following occurs: polar easterlies, westerlies, and trade winds.

_____
_____

Critical Thinking

9 Predict How would local winds be affected if water and land absorbed and released heat at the same rate? Explain your answer.

_____
_____
_____
_____

10 Compare How is a land breeze similar to a sea breeze? How do they differ?

_____
_____
_____
_____

Use this image to answer the following questions.

11 Analyze What type of local wind would you experience if you were standing in the valley? Explain your answer.

_____
_____
_____

12 Infer Would the local wind change if it was nighttime? Explain.

_____
_____
_____

My Notes

Unit 4 Big Idea Earth's atmosphere is a mixture of gases that interacts with solar energy.

Lesson 1

ESSENTIAL QUESTION
What is the atmosphere?

Describe the composition and structure of the atmosphere and explain how the atmosphere protects life and insulates Earth.

Lesson 2

ESSENTIAL QUESTION
How does energy move through Earth's system?

Summarize the three mechanisms by which energy is transferred through Earth's system.

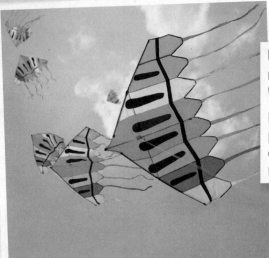

Lesson 3

ESSENTIAL QUESTION
What is wind?

Explain how energy provided by the sun causes atmospheric movement, called wind.

Think Outside the Book

2 Synthesize Choose one of these activities to help synthesize what you have learned in this unit.

☐ Using what you learned in lessons 2 and 3, make a poster presentation explaining the role that radiation, conduction, and convection play in the transfer of energy in Earth's atmosphere.

☐ Using what you learned in lessons 1 and 2, explain how solar radiation contributes to the greenhouse effect. Include the terms *radiation* and *reradiation* in your explanation.

Connect ESSENTIAL QUESTIONS
Lessons 2 and 3

1 Synthesize Explain how the uneven warming of Earth causes air to move.

_____

_____

_____

_____

Name _____

Vocabulary

Check the box to show whether each statement is true or false.

T	F	
☐	☐	**1** <u>Radiation</u> is a measure of the average kinetic energy of the particles in an object.
☐	☐	**2** <u>Thermal expansion</u> is the increase in volume that results from an increase in temperature.
☐	☐	**3** The <u>stratosphere</u> is the top layer of Earth's atmosphere.
☐	☐	**4** A <u>jet stream</u> is a wide band of low-speed winds that flow in the middle atmosphere.
☐	☐	**5** The curving of the path of a moving object as a result of Earth's rotation is called the <u>Coriolis effect</u>.

Key Concepts

Read each question below, and circle the best answer.

6 The picture below shows all three methods of energy transfer.

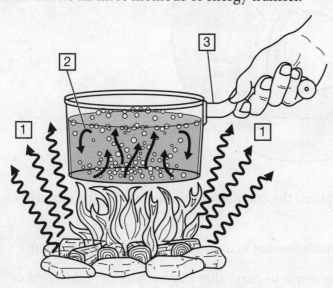

Which of these correctly identifies the three methods of energy transfer?

A 1: convection   2: radiation   3: conduction

B 1: radiation   2: conduction   3: convection

C 1: conduction   2: convection   3: radiation

D 1: radiation   2: convection   3: conduction

7 Which of these is not a way in which energy is transferred to Earth from the sun?

A conduction

C visible light

B infrared radiation

D x-rays

8 A plastic spoon that has a temperature of 78° F is placed into a bowl of soup that has a temperature of 84° F. Which of these correctly describes what will happen?

A Energy as heat moves from the spoon to the soup.

B Energy as heat does not move, because the spoon is plastic.

C Energy as heat moves from the soup to the spoon.

D Energy as heat does not move, because the temperature difference is too small.

9 Refer to the diagram of winds and currents below to answer the question.

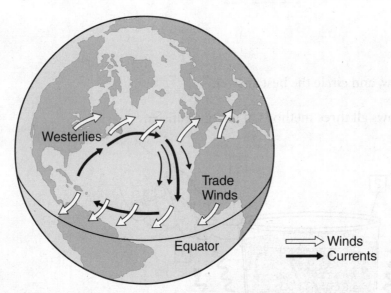

Which of the following best explains the curvature of the arrows for the westerlies and the trade winds?

A The ocean currents create winds flowing in a similar direction to the current.

B The Coriolis effect causes the winds to curve that way because the Earth rotates from left to right.

C The Coriolis effect causes the winds to curve that way because the Earth rotates from right to left.

D The sun is shining and warming the air from the right side of this diagram.

10 An astronomer studying planets outside our solar system has analyzed the atmospheres of four planets. Which of these planets' atmospheres would be most able to support a colony of humans?

A Planet A: 76% Nitrogen, 23% Oxygen, 1% Other

B Planet B: 82% Nitrogen, 11% Oxygen, 7% Other

C Planet C: 78% Nitrogen, 1% Oxygen, 21% Other

D Planet D: 27% Nitrogen, 3% Oxygen, 70% Other

11 Refer to the picture below to answer the question.

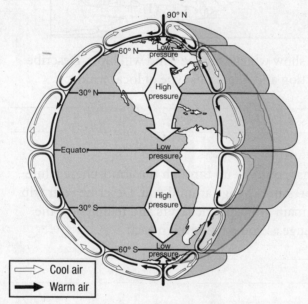

Which of the following is most responsible for the moving bands of air around Earth that are shown in the picture above?

A conduction   **C** Coriolis effect

B convection   **D** greenhouse effect

12 Which of the following describes the general pattern of winds near the equator?

A Winds are generally weak because the equator is a region where low and high air pressure atmospheric bands come together.

B Winds are generally strong because the equator is a region where low and high air pressure atmospheric bands come together.

C Winds are generally strong because the equator is a region of mostly high air pressure.

D Winds are generally weak because the equator is a region of mostly low air pressure.

Critical Thinking

Answer the following questions in the space provided.

13 The picture below shows a situation that causes local winds.

(B) Warm air

(A) Cool air

Draw an arrow on the picture to show which way the wind will blow. Describe why the wind blows in that direction and name this type of local wind.

_____

_____

14 Suppose you were a superhero that could fly up through the atmosphere while feeling the temperature and air pressure change around you. Describe your trip in a paragraph, naming the four main atmospheric layers and telling how the temperature and air pressure change as you pass through each.

_____

_____

_____

_____

Connect **ESSENTIAL QUESTIONS**
Lessons 1, 2, and 3

Answer the following question in the space provided.

15 Explain how Earth gets energy from the sun and what the atmosphere does with that energy to help life survive on Earth.

_____

_____

_____

_____

Weather and Climate

Strong winds create huge waves that crash on shore.

Big Idea

Air pressure, temperature, air movement, and humidity in the atmosphere affect both weather and climate.

What do you think?

The weather can change very quickly. In severe weather, people and pets can get hurt, and property can be damaged. Can you think of ways to keep people, pets, and property safe?

Warning flags are used to show how safe this beach is.

Unit 5
Weather and Climate

CITIZEN SCIENCE

Exit Strategy

When there is an emergency, knowing what to do helps keep people as safe as possible. So what's the plan?

1 Think About It

A Do you know what to do if there were a weather emergency while you were in school?

____

B What kinds of information might you need to stay safe? List them below.

____

____

____

____

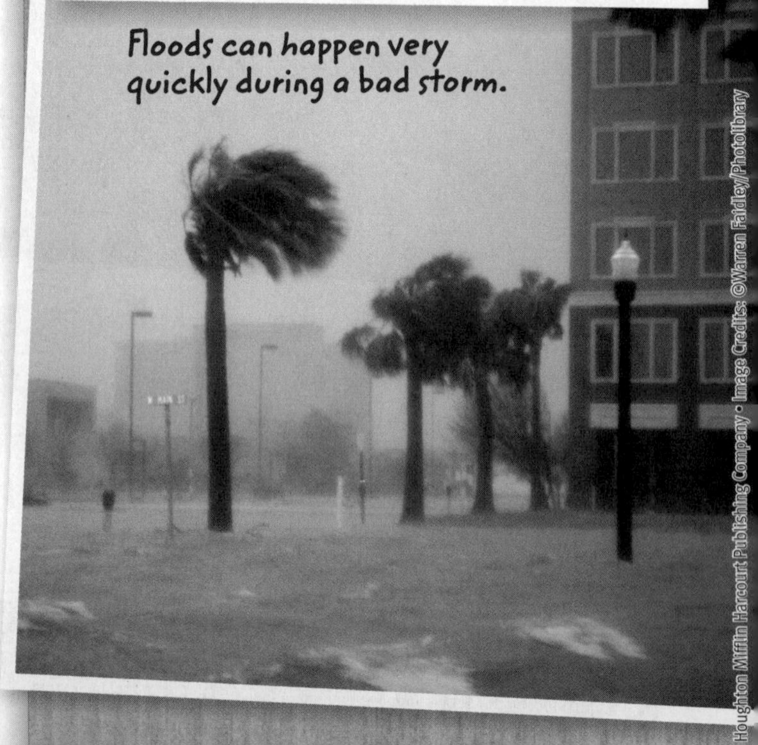

Floods can happen very quickly during a bad storm.

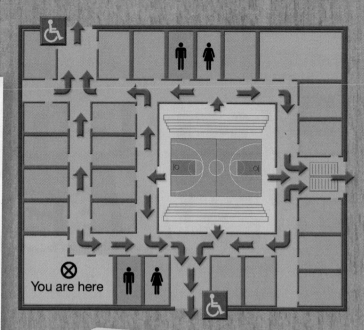

② Ask A Question

How well do you know your school's emergency evacuation plan? Obtain a copy of the school's emergency evacuation plan. Read through the plan and answer the following questions as a class.

A Is the emergency evacuation plan/map easy for students to understand?

_____

B How would you know which way to go?

_____

_____

C How often do you have practice drills?

_____

EMERGENCY EVACUATION ROUTE

⬅

③ Propose and Apply Improvements

A Using what you have learned about your school's emergency evacuation plan, list your ideas for improvements below.

_____

_____

_____

_____

_____

B Develop and give a short oral presentation to your principal about your proposal on ways to improve the school's emergency evacuation plan. Write the main points of your presentation below.

_____

_____

_____

_____

C As a class, practice the newly improved emergency evacuation plan. Describe how well the improved emergency evacuation plan worked.

_____

_____

_____

_____

_____

_____

_____

_____

Take It Home

With an adult, create an emergency evacuation plan for your family or evaluate your family's emergency evacuation plan and propose improvements.

Elements of Weather

© Houghton Mifflin Harcourt Publishing Company • Image Credits: (bkgd) ©British Antarctic Survey/Photo Researchers, Inc.

ESSENTIAL QUESTION

What is weather and how can we describe different types of weather conditions?

By the end of this lesson, you should be able to describe elements of weather and explain how they are measured.

Weather stations placed all around the world allow scientists to measure the elements, or separate parts, of weather.

A researcher checks an automatic weather station on Alexander Island, Antarctica.

Virginia Science Standards of Learning

6.1 The student will demonstrate an understanding of scientific reasoning, logic, and the nature of science by planning and conducting investigations in which:

6.1.a observations are made involving fine discrimination between similar objects and organisms.

6.6 The student will investigate and understand the properties of air and the structure and dynamics of Earth's atmosphere. Key concepts include:

6.6.b pressure, temperature, and humidity.

Lesson Labs

Quick Labs
- Investigate the Measurement of Rainfall
- Classifying Features of Different Types of Clouds

Field Lab
- Comparing Different Ways to Estimate Wind Speed

 ## Engage Your Brain

1 Predict Check T or F to show whether you think each statement is true or false.

T   F

☐ ☐ Weather can change every day.

☐ ☐ Temperature is measured by using a barometer.

☐ ☐ Air pressure increases as you move higher in the atmosphere.

☐ ☐ Visibility is a measurement of how far we can see.

2 Describe Use at least three words that might describe the weather on a day when the sky looks like the picture above.

_____

_____

_____

_____

 ## Active Reading

3 Distinguish The words *weather, whether,* and *wether* all sound alike but are spelled differently and mean entirely different things. You may have never heard of a wether—it is a neutered male sheep or ram.

Circle the correct use of the three words in the sentence below.

The farmer wondered *weather / whether / wether* the cold *weather / whether / wether* had affected his *weather / whether / wether*.

Vocabulary Terms

- weather
- humidity
- relative humidity
- dew point
- precipitation
- air pressure
- wind
- visibility

4 Apply As you learn the definition of each vocabulary term in this lesson, create your own definition or sketch to help you remember the meaning of the term.

Wonder about Weather?

What is weather?

Weather is the condition of Earth's atmosphere at a certain time and place. Different observations give you clues to the weather. If you see plants moving from side to side, you might infer that it is windy. If you see a gray sky and wet, shiny streets, you might decide to wear a raincoat. People talk about weather by describing factors such as temperature, humidity, precipitation, air pressure, wind, and *visibility* (viz•uh•BIL•i•tee).

What is temperature and how is it measured?

Temperature is a measure of how hot or cold something is. An instrument that measures and displays temperature is called a *thermometer*. A common type of thermometer uses a liquid such as alcohol or mercury to display the temperature. The liquid is sealed in a glass tube. When the air gets warmer, the liquid expands and rises in the tube. Cooler air causes the liquid to contract and fill less of the tube. A scale, often in Celsius (°C) or Fahrenheit (°F), is marked on the glass tube.

Another type of thermometer is an electrical thermometer. As the temperature becomes higher, electric current flow increases through the thermometer. The strength of the current is then translated into temperature readings.

Extreme Weather Facts

Earth's highest recorded temperature was in El Azizia, Libya, on September 1922 at 58 °C (136 °F).

Earth's lowest recorded temperature was in Vostok, Antarctica, on July 1983 at −89 °C (−128 °F).

Visualize It!

5 Identify Color in the liquid in the thermometer above to show Earth's average temperature in 2009 (58 °F). Write the Celsius temperature that equals 58 °F on the line below.

What is humidity and how is it measured?

As water evaporates from oceans, lakes, and ponds, it becomes water vapor, or a gas that is in the air. The amount of water vapor in the air is called **humidity**. As more water evaporates and becomes water vapor, the humidity of the air increases.

Humidity is often described through relative humidity. **Relative humidity** is the amount of water vapor in the air compared to the amount of water vapor needed to reach saturation. As shown below, when air is saturated, the rates of evaporation and condensation are equal. Saturated air has a relative humidity of 100%. A psychrometer (sy•KRAHM•i•ter) is an instrument that is used to measure relative humidity.

Air can become saturated when evaporation adds water vapor to the air. Air can also become saturated when it cools to its dew point. The **dew point** is the temperature at which more condensation than evaporation occurs. When air temperature drops below the dew point, condensation forms. This can cause dew on surfaces cooler than the dew point. It also can form fog and clouds.

Active Reading

6 Identify Underline the name of the instrument used to measure relative humidity.

Visualize It!

7 Sketch In the space provided, draw what happens in air that is below the dew point.

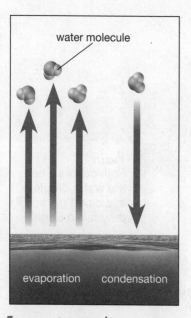

In unsaturated air, more water evaporates into the air than condenses back into the water.

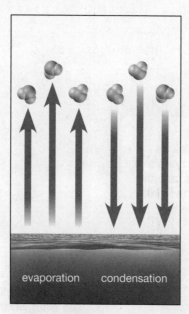

In saturated air, the amount of water that evaporates equals the amount that condenses.

When air cools below its dew point, more water vapor condenses into water than evaporates.

8 Explain Why does dew form on grass overnight?

_____

_____

What is precipitation and how is it measured?

Water vapor in the air condenses not only on Earth's surfaces, but also on tiny particles in the air to form clouds. When this water from the air returns to Earth's surface, it falls as precipitation. **Precipitation** is any form of water that falls to Earth's surface from the clouds. The four main forms of precipitation are rain, snow, hail, and sleet.

Rain is the most common form of precipitation. Inside a cloud, the droplets formed by condensation collide and form larger droplets. They finally become heavy enough to fall as raindrops. Rain is measured with a rain gauge, as shown in the picture below. A funnel or wide opening at the top of the gauge allows rain to flow into a cylinder that is marked in centimeters.

Snow forms when air temperatures are so low that water vapor turns into a solid. When a lot of snow has fallen, it is measured with a ruler or meterstick. When balls or lumps of ice fall from clouds during thunderstorms it is called *hail*. Sleet forms when rain falls through a layer of freezing air, producing falling ice.

Visualize It! Inquiry

9 Synthesize What are two ways in which all types of precipitation are alike?

_____

_____

_____

Snow
Snow can fall as single ice crystals or ice crystals can join to form snowflakes.

Rain
Rain occurs when the water droplets in a cloud get so big they fall to Earth.

Sleet
Small ice pellets fall as sleet when rain falls through cold air.

Hail
Hailstones are layered lumps of ice that fall from clouds.

10 Measure How much rain has this rain gauge collected?

_____

Watching Clouds

Cirrus Clouds

Cumulus Clouds

Stratus Clouds

As you can see above, cirrus (SIR•uhs) clouds appear feathery or wispy. Their name means "curl of hair." They are made of ice crystals. They form when the wind is strong.

Cumulus (KYOOM•yuh•luhs) means "heap" or "pile." Usually these clouds form in fair weather but if they keep growing taller, they can produce thunderstorms.

Stratus (STRAY•tuhs) means "spread out." Stratus clouds form in flat layers. Low, dark stratus clouds can block out the sun and produce steady drizzle or rain.

If you watch the sky over a period of time, you will probably observe different kinds of clouds. Clouds have different characteristics because they form under different conditions. The shapes and sizes of clouds are mainly determined by air movement. For example, puffy clouds form in air that rises sharply or moves straight up and down. Flat, smooth clouds covering large areas form in air that rises gradually.

Extend

Inquiry

11 Reflect Think about the last time you noticed the clouds. When are you most likely to notice what type of cloud is in the sky?

12 Research Word parts are used to tell more about clouds. Look up the word parts -*nimbus* and *alto*-. What are cumulonimbus and altostratus clouds?

227

The Air Out There

What is air pressure and how is it measured?

Scientists use an instrument called a *barometer* (buh•RAHM•i•ter) to measure air pressure. **Air pressure** is the force of air molecules pushing on an area. The air pressure at any area on Earth depends on the weight of the air above that area. Although air is pressing down on us, we don't feel the weight because air pushes in all directions. So, the pressure of air pushing down is balanced by the pressure of air pushing up.

Air pressure and density are related; they both decrease with altitude. Notice in the picture that the molecules at sea level are closer together than the molecules at the mountain peak. Because the molecules are closer together, the pressure is greater. The air at sea level is denser than air at high altitude.

Air pressure and density are lower at a high altitude.

Air pressure and density are higher at sea level.

© Houghton Mifflin Harcourt Publishing Company • Image Credits: (tl) ©Philippe Giraud/Sygma/Corbis; (bl) ©David Buffington/Photographer's Choice/Getty Images

13 Identify Look at the photos below and write whether wind direction or wind speed is being measured.

Anemometer

An anemometer measures:

_____

Wind vane

A wind vane measures:

_____

What is wind and how is it measured?

Wind is air that moves horizontally, or parallel to the ground. Uneven heating of Earth's surface causes pressure differences from place to place. These pressure differences set air in motion. Over a short distance, wind moves directly from higher pressure toward lower pressure.

An anemometer (an•uh•MAHM•i•ter) is used to measure wind speed. It has three or four cups attached to a pole. The wind causes the cups to rotate, sending an electric current to a meter that displays the wind speed.

Wind direction is measured by using a wind vane or a windsock. A wind vane has an arrow with a large tail that is attached to a pole. The wind pushes harder on the arrow tail due to its larger surface area. This causes the wind vane to spin so that the arrow points into the wind. A windsock is a cone-shaped cloth bag open at both ends. The wind enters the wide end and the narrow end points in the opposite direction, showing the direction the wind is blowing.

What is visibility and how is it measured?

Visibility is a measure of the transparency of the atmosphere. Visibility is the way we describe how far we can see, and it is measured by using three or four known landmarks at different distances. Sometimes not all of the landmarks will be visible. Poor visibility can be the result of air pollution or fog.

Poor visibility can be dangerous for all types of travel, whether by air, water, or land. When visibility is very low, roads may be closed to traffic. In areas where low visibility is common, signs are often posted to warn travelers.

 **Active Reading**

14 Explain What are two factors that can affect visibility?

_____

_____

Fog forms as land cools overnight, causing water vapor in the air above the land to condense.

What are some ways to collect weather data?

Many forms of technology are used to gather weather data. The illustration below shows some ways weather information can be collected. Instruments within the atmosphere can make measurements of local weather conditions. Satellites can collect data from above the atmosphere.

 **Visualize It! Inquiry**

15 Infer What are the benefits of stationary weather collection? Moving weather collection?

_____

_____

_____

_____

Satellite

Ground station

Airplane

Stationary
Some forms of technology provide measurements from set locations.

Moving
Some forms of technology report changing measurements along their paths.

Weather buoy

Ship

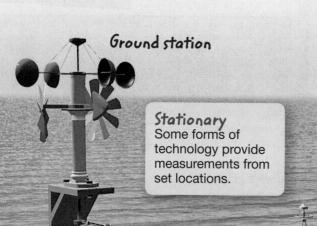

Visual Summary

To complete this summary, fill in the blanks with the correct word or phrase. Then use the key below to check your answers. You can use this page to review the main concepts of the lesson.

Elements of Weather

Weather is a condition of the atmosphere at a certain time and place.

16 Weather is often expressed by describing _____, humidity, precipitation, air pressure, wind, and visibility.

Uneven heating of Earth's surface causes air pressure differences and wind.

18 Wind moves from areas of _____ pressure to areas of _____ pressure.

Precipitation occurs when the water that condenses as clouds falls back to Earth in solid or liquid form.

20 The main types of precipitation are hail, snow, _____, and rain.

Humidity describes the amount of water vapor in the air.

17 The amount of moisture in the air is commonly expressed as _____ humidity.

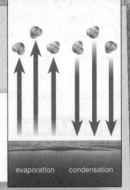

evaporation   condensation

Visibility describes how far into the distance objects can be seen.

19 Visibility can be affected by air pollution and _____

Answers: 16 temperature; 17 relative; 18 higher, lower; 19 fog; 20 sleet

21 **Synthesize** What instruments would you take along if you were going on a 3-month field study to measure how the weather on a mountaintop changes over the course of a season?

Lesson Review

Vocabulary

In your own words, define the following terms.

1 weather _____

_____

_____

2 humidity _____

_____

_____

3 air pressure _____

_____

_____

4 visibility _____

_____

_____

Key Concepts

Weather element	Instrument
5 Identify Measures temperature	
	6 Identify Is measured by using a barometer
7 Identify Measures relative humidity	
	8 Identify Is measured by using a rain gauge or meterstick
9 Identify Measures wind speed	

10 List What are four types of precipitation?

_____

_____

Critical Thinking

11 Apply Explain how wind is related to the uneven heating of Earth's surfaces by the sun.

_____

_____

_____

_____

12 Explain Why does air pressure decrease as altitude increases?

_____

_____

_____

13 Synthesize What is the relative humidity when the air temperature is at its dew point?

_____

The weather data below was recorded from 1989–2009 by an Antarctic weather station similar to the station in the photo at the beginning of this lesson. Use these data to answer the questions that follow.

	Jan.	Apr.	July	Oct.
Mean max. temp. (°C)	2.1	−7.4	−9.9	−8.1
Mean min. temp. (°C)	−2.6	−14.6	−18.1	−15.1
Mean precip. (mm)	9.0	18.04	28.5	16.5

14 Identify Which month had the lowest mean minimum and maximum temperatures?

15 Infer The precipitation that fell at this location was most likely in what form?

My Notes

Clouds and Cloud Formation

ESSENTIAL QUESTION

How do clouds form, and how are clouds classified?

By the end of this lesson, you should be able to describe the formation and classification of clouds.

These altocumulus clouds cover the sky like a bluish-gray blanket. Clouds take various shapes and appear at different altitudes in the lower atmosphere. Scientists classify clouds by both their shape and the altitude at which they form.

Virginia Science Standards of Learning
6.3 The student will investigate and understand the role of solar energy in driving most natural processes within the atmosphere, the hydrosphere, and on Earth's surface. Key concepts include:
6.3.d cloud formation.

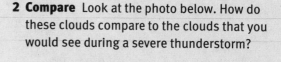

Engage Your Brain

1 Identify Read over the following vocabulary terms. In the spaces provided, place a + if you know the term well, a ~ if you have heard the term but are not sure what it means, and a ? if you are unfamiliar with the term. Then write a sentence that includes one of the words you are most familiar with.

_____ cloud
_____ dew point
_____ fog

Sentence using known word:

_____

_____

2 Compare Look at the photo below. How do these clouds compare to the clouds that you would see during a severe thunderstorm?

_____

_____

_____

_____

_____

Active Reading

3 Synthesize Many English words have their roots in other languages. Use the Latin words below to make an educated guess about the meaning of *cirrus cloud* and *cumulus cloud*.

Latin word	Meaning
cirrus	curl
cumulus	heap

Example sentence
Cirrus clouds are seen high in the sky.

cirrus cloud:

_____

_____

Example Sentence
Cumulus clouds change shape often.

cumulus cloud:

_____

_____

Vocabulary Terms

- cloud
- dew point
- stratus cloud
- cumulus cloud
- cirrus cloud
- fog

4 Apply As you learn the definition of each vocabulary term in this lesson, create your own definition or sketch to help you remember the meaning of the term.

Head in the Clouds

Storm clouds appear dark gray. They are so full of water droplets that little light can pass through them.

What are clouds?

When you look into the sky, you see the amazing shapes that clouds take and how quickly those shapes change. But, have you ever asked yourself what clouds are made of or how they form? And did you know that there are different types of clouds?

A **cloud** is a collection of small water droplets or ice crystals that are suspended in the air. Clouds are visible because water droplets and ice crystals reflect light. Clouds are most often associated with precipitation. However, the reality is that most cloud types do not produce precipitation.

How do clouds affect climate?

The precipitation that falls from clouds has a significant effect on local climate. In particular, the pattern of precipitation of an area will determine the climate of that area. For instance, a desert is an area that receives less than 25 cm of precipitation a year. But, a tropical rainforest may average 250 cm of precipitation a year.

Clouds also affect temperatures on Earth. About 25% of the sun's energy that reaches Earth is reflected back into space by clouds. Low-altitude clouds, which are thick and reflect more sunlight, help to cool Earth. On the other hand, thin, high-altitude clouds absorb some of the energy that radiates from Earth. Part of this energy is reradiated back to Earth's surface. This warms Earth, because this energy is not directly lost to space.

Active Reading **5 Describe** What are two ways in which clouds affect Earth's climate?

_____

_____

_____

6 Apply Sketch a cloud, and write a caption that relates the drawing to the content on this page.

_____

_____

_____

_____

How do clouds form?

Clouds form when water vapor condenses, or changes from a gas to a liquid. For water vapor to condense, two things must happen. Air must be cooled to its dew point, and there must be a solid surface on which water molecules can condense.

Air Cools to the Dew Point

As warm air rises in Earth's atmosphere, it expands and cools. If air rises high enough into the atmosphere, it cools to its dew point. **Dew point** is the temperature at which the rate of condensation equals the rate of evaporation. *Evaporation* is the change of state from a liquid to a gas that usually occurs at the surface of a liquid. Evaporation takes place at the surface of an ocean, lake, stream, or other body of water. Water vapor in the air can condense and form water droplets or ice crystals when the temperature is at or below the dew point.

Water Droplets or Ice Crystals Form on Nuclei

Water molecules condense much more rapidly when there is a solid surface on which to condense. In clouds, tiny solid particles called *cloud condensation nuclei* are the surfaces on which water droplets condense. Examples of cloud condensation nuclei include dust, salt, soil, and smoke.

Clouds are most commonly made of very large numbers of very small water droplets. However, at high altitudes, where temperatures are very cold, clouds are composed of ice crystals.

D Cloud formation takes place.

C Condensation takes place on nuclei.

condensation nucleus
0.0002 millimeter diameter

cloud droplet
0.05 millimeter diameter

B
_____
_____

A Warm air rises, expands, and cools.

7 Conclude Complete the flow chart by filling in the missing information.

235

What is the role of solar energy in cloud formation?

The water cycle is the movement of water between the atmosphere, land, and ocean. Solar energy drives the water cycle and, therefore, provides the energy for cloud formation.

About 50 percent of the sun's incoming energy is absorbed by land, by water on the land's surface, and by surface waters in the oceans. This absorbed energy causes liquid water at the water's surface to become water vapor, a gas. This process is called evaporation. The water vapor rises into the atmosphere with air that has been warmed near Earth's surface.

Solar energy does not warm the surface of Earth evenly. Unequal heating of Earth's surface causes areas of high pressure and low pressure to form in the atmosphere. Air flows horizontally from areas of high pressure to areas of low pressure. This horizontal movement of air is called *wind*. Wind causes clouds to move around Earth's surface. However, for air to be cooled to its dew point so that clouds can form, the air is pushed up, or is lifted, into the atmosphere.

What processes cool air enough to form clouds?

 **Active Reading** **8 Identify** As you read, underline the processes that can cool air enough to form clouds.

There are several ways in which air can be cooled to its dew point. These include frontal and orographic lifting (ohr•uh•GRAF•ik LIFT•ing). Frontal lifting can occur when a warm air mass rises over a cold air mass. Once the rising air cools to its dew point, condensation occurs and clouds form.

Frontal lifting can also occur when a mass of cold air slides under a mass of warm air, pushing the warm air upward. The rising air cools to the dew point. Clouds form that often develop into thunderstorms.

Orographic lifting occurs when an obstacle, such as a mountain range, forces a mass of air upward. Water vapor in the air cools to its dew point and condenses. The clouds that form release large amounts of precipitation as rain or snow as they rise up the mountain. The other side of the mountain receives little precipitation.

Visualize It!

9 Compare The images below show two processes by which clouds form when an air mass is lifted. In what ways are these two processes similar? In what ways are these two processes different?

_____

_____

_____

Frontal Lifting

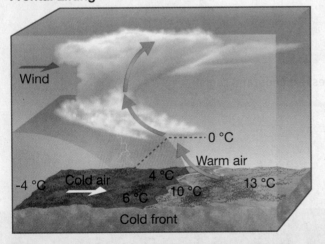

Wind

0 °C

Warm air

-4 °C   Cold air   4 °C   13 °C

6 °C   10 °C

Cold front

Orographic Lifting

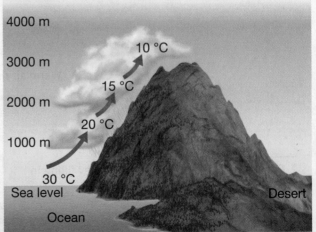

4000 m

3000 m   10 °C

2000 m   15 °C

1000 m   20 °C

30 °C

Sea level   Desert

Ocean

What are three cloud shapes?

You have probably noticed the different shapes that clouds take as they move through the sky. Some clouds are thick and puffy. Other clouds are thin and wispy. Scientists use shape as a way to classify clouds. The three classes of clouds based on shape are stratus (STRAT•uhs) clouds, cumulus (KYOOM•yuh•luhs) clouds, and cirrus (SIR•uhs) clouds.

Stratus Clouds

The lowest clouds in the atmosphere are stratus clouds. **Stratus clouds** are thin and flat, and their edges are not clearly defined. *Stratus* is a Latin word that means "layer." Stratus clouds often merge into one another and may look like a single layer that covers the entire sky. Stratus clouds are often gray. Light mist or drizzle may fall from these clouds. Fog is a type of stratus cloud that forms at or near the ground.

Cumulus Clouds

Cumulus is a Latin word that means "heap." **Cumulus clouds** are thick and puffy on top and generally flat on the bottom. These clouds have well-defined edges and can change shape rapidly. Some may tower high into the atmosphere, where the top of the cloud sometimes flattens.

Fair-weather cumulus clouds are bright and white. But cumulus clouds can become dark as more and more water droplets or ice crystals are added to the cloud. Cumulus clouds can produce severe weather. Thunder, lightning, and heavy precipitation are associated with cumulus clouds.

Cirrus Clouds

Cirrus is a Latin word that means "curl." **Cirrus clouds** look feathery, and their ends curl. Cirrus clouds are white.

Cirrus clouds form high in the atmosphere. At the altitudes where cirrus clouds form, there is little water vapor, and temperatures are very cold. As a result, cirrus clouds are made of ice crystals rather than liquid water droplets. They do not produce precipitation that reaches Earth's surface.

Visualize It!

10 Identify Name the three different clouds based on shape.

A _____

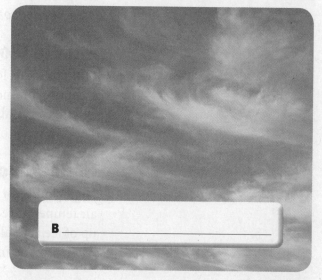

B _____

C _____

I've Looked at Clouds

Active Reading

11 Identify As you read the text, underline the prefixes associated with each class of cloud. If a class has no prefix, underline that information too.

What are the types of clouds based on altitude?

Scientists classify clouds by altitude as well as shape. The four classes of clouds based on altitude are low clouds, middle clouds, high clouds, and clouds of vertical development. These four classes are made up of 10 cloud types. Prefixes are used to name the clouds that belong to some of these classes.

Low Clouds

Low clouds form between Earth's surface and 2,000 m altitude. Water droplets commonly make up these clouds. The three types of low clouds are stratus, stratocumulus, and nimbostratus. There is no special prefix used to name low clouds. However, *nimbus* means "rain," so *nimbo*stratus clouds are rain clouds.

Middle Clouds

Middle clouds form between 2,000 m and 6,000 m altitude. They are most commonly made up of water droplets, but may be made up of ice crystals. The prefix *alto-* is used to name middle clouds. The two types of middle clouds are altocumulus and altostratus.

High Clouds

High clouds form above 6,000 m altitude. At these high altitudes, air temperature is below freezing. Therefore, high clouds are made up of ice crystals. The prefix *cirro-* is used to name high clouds. Cirrus, cirrocumulus, and cirrostratus are the types of high clouds.

Clouds of Vertical Development

Clouds of vertical development can rise high into the atmosphere. Although the cloud base is at low altitude, cloud tops can reach higher than 12,000 m. Clouds of vertical development are commonly formed by the rapid lifting of moist, warm air, which can result in strong vertical growth. There is no special prefix used to name clouds of vertical development. The two types of clouds of vertical development are cumulus and cumulonimbus.

Cumulonimbus clouds have the greatest vertical development of any cloud type. Air currents within these clouds can move upward at as much as 20 m/s. Cumulonimbus clouds are linked to severe weather and can produce rain, hail, lightning, tornadoes, and dangerous, rapidly sinking columns of air that strike Earth.

Think Outside the Book Inquiry

12 Apply Research cumulonimbus clouds. When you complete your research, consider different materials that might be used to create a model of a cumulonimbus cloud. Then, use your materials to build a model that shows the structure of a cumulonimbus cloud.

from Both Sides Now

© Houghton Mifflin Harcourt Publishing Company

cirrostratus

cirrus

cirrocumulus

A cumulo_____

High altitude

Medium altitude

B _____

altostratus

Medium altitude

Low altitude

stratocumulus

C _____

stratus

cumulus

Visualize It!

13 Identify Meteorologists recognize 10 cloud types based on the altitude at which the clouds form. Using the illustration above, identify the names of the cloud types on the write-on lines provided.

Word Bank

cirrocumulus	cirrostratus
stratus	cumulus
altostratus	cirrus
stratocumulus	cumulonimbus
altocumulus	nimbostratus

How does fog form?

Water vapor that condenses very near Earth's surface is called **fog**. Fog forms when moist air at or near Earth's surface cools to its dew point. Fog is simply a stratus cloud that forms at ground level.

Ground fog, which is also called *radiation fog*, generally forms in low-lying areas on clear, calm nights. As Earth's surface cools, moist air near the ground cools to its dew point. Water vapor in the air condenses into water droplets, which form fog.

Fog also forms when warm, moist air moves across cold water and is cooled to its dew point. This is how sea fog, or advection fog, forms. Unlike ground fog, sea fog occurs at all times of day.

Another type of fog forms when evaporation takes place into cold air that is lying over warmer water. Called *steam fog*, this fog appears as steam directly above bodies of water. It occurs most commonly on cold fall mornings.

Fog is a hazard because it reduces visibility. Very dense fog can reduce visibility to a few meters. Water droplets in fog scatter light. This makes objects difficult for people to see clearly. Without visible landmarks, it is also hard to judge distance and speed.

Active Reading

14 Identify As you read the text, underline ways in which fog forms.

Visualize It!

15 Describe Which type of fog is shown below, and why does it form above cold water?

_____

_____

_____

Ground fog forms at night when Earth's surface cools. Moist air near the ground cools to its dew point, which causes water vapor to condense.

Clouds
on Other Worlds

Like Earth, other bodies in the solar system have clouds in their atmosphere. There are clouds on Venus and Mars. Jupiter and Saturn both have deep atmospheres with clouds arranged in bands that circle the planet. Even Saturn's moon Titan has clouds in a thick, planet-like atmosphere.

Venus is surrounded by thick clouds of sulfur dioxide that reflect much of the sunlight that falls on them back into space.

Clouds and dust can be seen in the Martian atmosphere. Mars is covered in a red iron oxide dust. Dust particles act as condensation nuclei that can cause clouds to have a pinkish color.

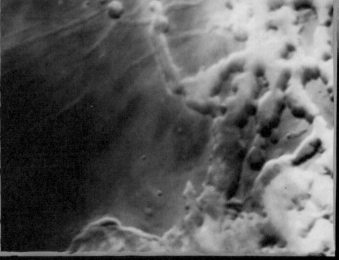

In 1976, *Viking Orbiter 1* took this photo of water-filled clouds that had formed over a large system of canyons just after the Martian sunrise.

Extend

Inquiry

16 Infer Can clouds form on all bodies in the solar system?

17 Apply Research clouds on another body in the solar system. Describe properties of clouds there.

18 Design Create a poster presentation or a slide presentation that examines the way in which clouds on the solar system body that you chose to research differ from clouds on Earth.

Visual Summary

To complete this summary, circle the correct word. Then, use the key below to check your answers. You can use this page to review the main concepts of the lesson.

Clouds and Cloud Formation

Clouds form when rising air cools to the dew point and condensation occurs.

19 Warm air that is forced upward by a cold front is an example of frontal/orographic lifting.

Clouds can be classified by altitude.

20 Clouds that are made up entirely of ice crystals are middle/high clouds.

Clouds can be classified by shape.

21 Thin, wispy clouds that do not produce precipitation are cirrus/cumulus clouds.

Fog is a cloud that has formed very near Earth's surface.

22 Ground/Sea fog generally forms in low-lying areas, such as valleys.

Answers: 19 frontal; 20 high; 21 cirrus; 22 Ground

23 **Synthesis** How can clouds be used to help predict the weather?

Lesson Review

Vocabulary

Fill in the blank with the term that best completes the following sentences.

1 A _____ cloud is thin, wispy, and made of ice crystals.

2 The temperature at which water vapor condenses is the _____

3 _____ is condensed water vapor that forms very close to Earth's surface.

Key Concepts

4 Compare What are two differences between stratus clouds and cirrus clouds?

_____

_____

_____

_____

5 List What are the four classes of clouds based on altitude?

_____

_____

_____

_____

6 Describe What are three ways in which clouds affect climate?

_____

_____

_____

_____

_____

7 Explain What part do tiny, solid particles in the atmosphere play in cloud formation?

_____

_____

_____

_____

Critical Thinking

Use this diagram to answer the following questions.

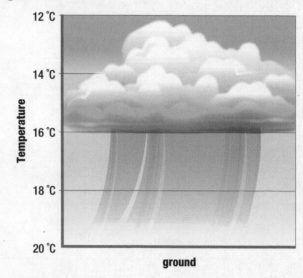

ground

8 Analyze What is the dew-point temperature at which cloud formation began?

_____

_____

9 Explain Why doesn't cloud formation take place until the dew-point temperature is reached?

_____

_____

_____

_____

_____

10 Apply What kind of clouds would you expect to form at the leading edge of a cold front, where warm air is gradually being pushed above cold air?

_____

_____

_____

_____

My Notes

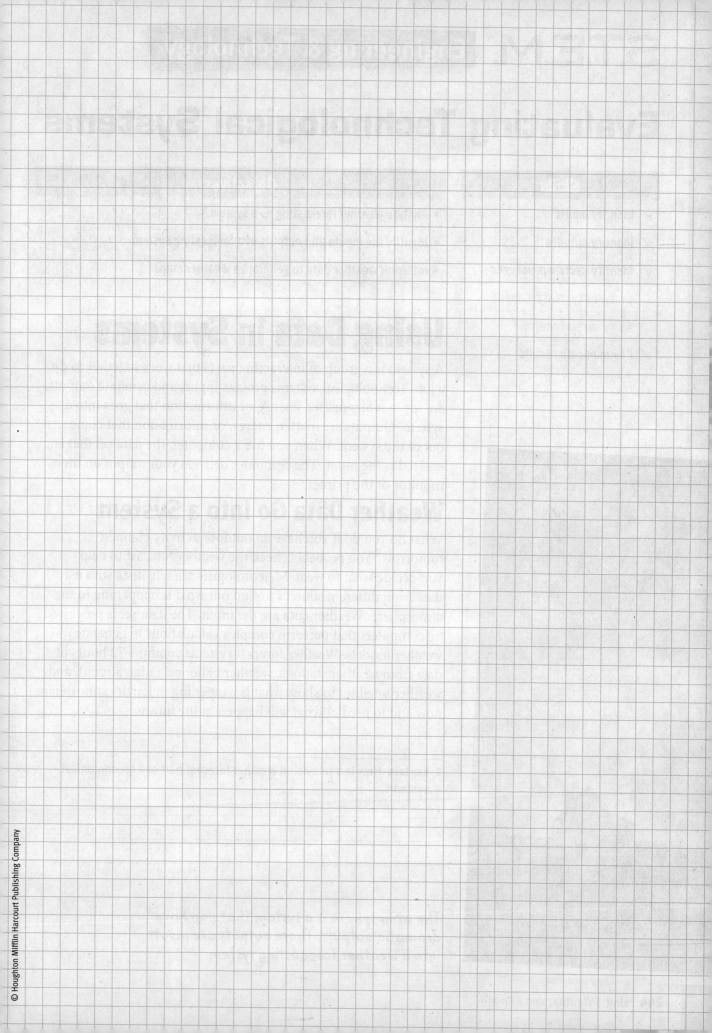

Evaluating Technological Systems

Skills
✓ Identify inputs
✓ Identify outputs
✓ Identify system processes
Evaluate system feedback
Apply system controls
✓ Communicate results

Objectives
• Analyze weather forecasting as a system.
• Identify the inputs and outputs of a forecasting system.
• Interpret weather data to generate a weather map.

Using Data in Systems

A system is a group of interacting parts that work together to do a job. Technological systems process inputs and generate outputs. An input is any matter, energy, or information that goes into a system. Outputs are matter, energy, or information that come out of the system. When you use a computer, the data set that is entered is the input. The computer delivers your output on the monitor or the printer.

Weather Data Go Into a System

What do you do if you have an outdoor activity planned tomorrow? You probably check the weather forecast to help you decide what to wear. Meteorologists are scientists who use data from different sources to find out what is happening in the atmosphere. Weather data are the input. The data set is processed by computers that perform complex calculations to generate weather models. Weather forecast systems combine 72 hours of data from weather stations, weather balloons, radar, aircraft, and weather satellites to show what is happening in Earth's atmosphere now and to predict what will happen in the future.

1 Explain How is a television weather forecast part of a technological system?

_____

_____

_____

The atmosphere is a system that can have dramatic outputs. Those outputs are inputs into a weather forecasting system.

Forecast Data Come Out of the System

Weather maps are one type of output from a weather forecasting system. On a weather map you can find information about atmospheric pressure, and about the direction and temperature of moving air. The numbered lines on a weather map are called *isobars*. Isobars connect areas that have the same atmospheric pressure. Isobars center around areas of high and low pressure. An area of high pressure (H) indicates a place where cool, dense air is falling. An area of low pressure (L) indicates a place where warm, less dense air is rising. Pressure differences cause air to move. The leading edge of a cool air mass is called a *cold front*. The leading edge of a warm air mass is called a *warm front*. On a weather map, blue lines with triangles show cold fronts and red lines with half circles show warm fronts.

The direction of the triangles or half circles on a map shows which way a front is moving. Wind direction is described in terms of the direction from which the wind is blowing. A west wind is blowing from west to east.

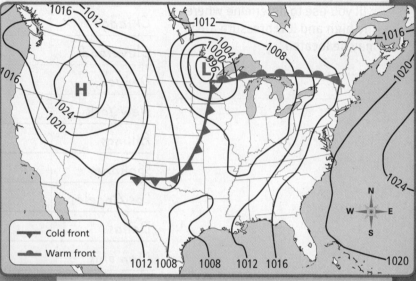

Cold front

Warm front

2 Analysis How would you describe the wind direction behind the warm and cold fronts shown on the map?

_____

_____

_____

Anemometer (wind speed)

Wind vane (wind direction)

Barometer (air pressure) & Rain gauge (precipitation)

Thermometer (temperature) & Hygrometer (humidity)

Weather instruments constantly measure conditions in the atmosphere and deliver data.

You Try It!

Now it's your turn to use weather data to make a forecast.

 You Try It!

Now it's your turn to become part of the weather forecasting system. The table and map on these pages show some weather data for several cities in the United States. You will use those data to analyze weather and make predictions.

1 Identify Inputs

Which information in the table will you use to determine where the high and low pressure areas may be located?

_____

_____

City	Barometric pressure (mbar)	Wind direction	Temperature (°F)
Atlanta	1009	S	63
Chicago	1012	W	36
Cleveland	1006	S	35
Denver	1021	S	34
New York	990	S	58
Billings	1012	SW	28
Spokane	1009	SW	27
Los Angeles	1009	W	68
Dallas	1012	NW	50
Memphis	1012	NW	45
Orlando	1006	S	78
Raleigh	998	S	60

2 Identify Outputs

What outputs from weather stations are included on a weather map?

_____

_____

3 Identify System Processes

How will you process the information in the table and on the map to make predictions? Describe how you will use the inputs to develop an output.

_____

_____

_____

_____

④ Communicate Results

Use data from the table and the map to answer the questions below.

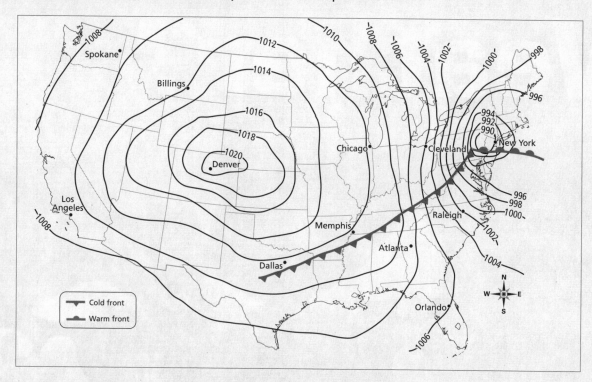

A According to the data in the table, where are the centers of the high and low pressure systems at this time? Mark them on the map using an H or an L.

B Add the temperature listed in the table for each city to the map.

C Imagine that you are a meteorologist in Atlanta and this is the current map. What temperature change would you predict over the next few hours, and why?

_____

_____

_____

_____

D What pressure change would you predict for Denver over the next few days, and why?

_____

_____

_____

_____

What Influences Weather?

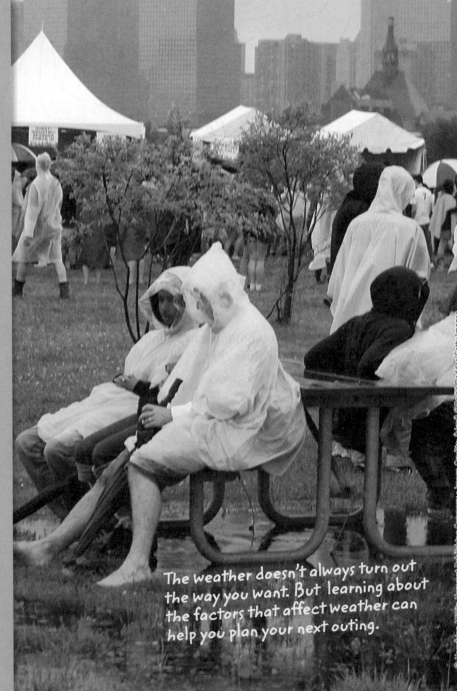

ESSENTIAL QUESTION

How do the water cycle and other global patterns affect local weather?

By the end of this lesson, you should be able to explain how global patterns in Earth's system influence weather.

Virginia Science Standards of Learning

6.3 The student will investigate and understand the role of solar energy in driving most natural processes within the atmosphere, the hydrosphere, and on Earth's surface. Key concepts include:

6.3.c the motion of the atmosphere and the oceans;

6.3.d cloud formation; and

6.3.e the role of thermal energy in weather-related phenomena including thunderstorms and hurricanes.

6.5 The student will investigate and understand the unique properties and characteristics of water and its roles in the natural and human-made environment. Key concepts include:

6.5.d the ability of large bodies of water to store thermal energy and moderate climate.

6.6 The student will investigate and understand the properties of air and the structure and dynamics of Earth's atmosphere. Key concepts include:

6.6.b pressure, temperature, and humidity; and

6.6.e the relationship of atmospheric measures and weather conditions.

The weather doesn't always turn out the way you want. But learning about the factors that affect weather can help you plan your next outing.

Lesson Labs

Quick Labs
- Analyze Weather Patterns
- Coastal Climate Model

Exploration Lab
- Modeling El Niño

 ## Engage Your Brain

1 Predict Check T or F to show whether you think each statement is true or false.

T   F

☐   ☐   The water cycle affects weather.

☐   ☐   Air can be warmed or cooled by the surface below it.

☐   ☐   Warm air sinks, cool air rises.

☐   ☐   Winds can bring different weather to a region.

2 Explain How can air temperatures along this coastline be affected by the large body of water that is nearby?

_____

_____

_____

 ## Active Reading

3 Infer A military front is a contested armed frontier between opposing forces. A *weather front* occurs between two air masses, or bodies of air. What kind of weather do you think usually happens at a weather front?

_____

_____

_____

_____

_____

_____

Vocabulary Terms

- air mass
- front
- jet stream

4 Apply As you learn the definition of each vocabulary term in this lesson, create your own definition or sketch to help you remember the meaning of the term.

Water, Water

How does the water cycle affect weather?

Weather is the short-term state of the atmosphere, including temperature, humidity, precipitation, air pressure, wind, and visibility. These elements are affected by the energy received from the sun and the amount of water in the air. To understand what influences weather, then, you need to understand the water cycle.

The *water cycle* is the continuous movement of water between the atmosphere, the land, the oceans, and living things. In the water cycle, shown to the right, water is constantly being recycled between liquid, solid, and gaseous states. The water cycle involves the processes of evaporation, condensation, and precipitation.

Evaporation occurs when liquid water changes into water vapor, which is a gas. Condensation occurs when water vapor cools and changes from a gas to a liquid. A change in the amount of water vapor in the air affects humidity. Clouds and fog form through condensation of water vapor, so condensation also affects visibility. Precipitation occurs when rain, snow, sleet, or hail falls from the clouds onto Earth's surface.

Active Reading

5 List Name at least 5 elements of weather.

_____

_____

_____

 **Visualize It!**

6 Summarize Describe how the water cycle influences weather by completing the sentences on the picture.

Ⓐ Evaporation **affects weather by** _____

_____

_____

Everywhere . . .

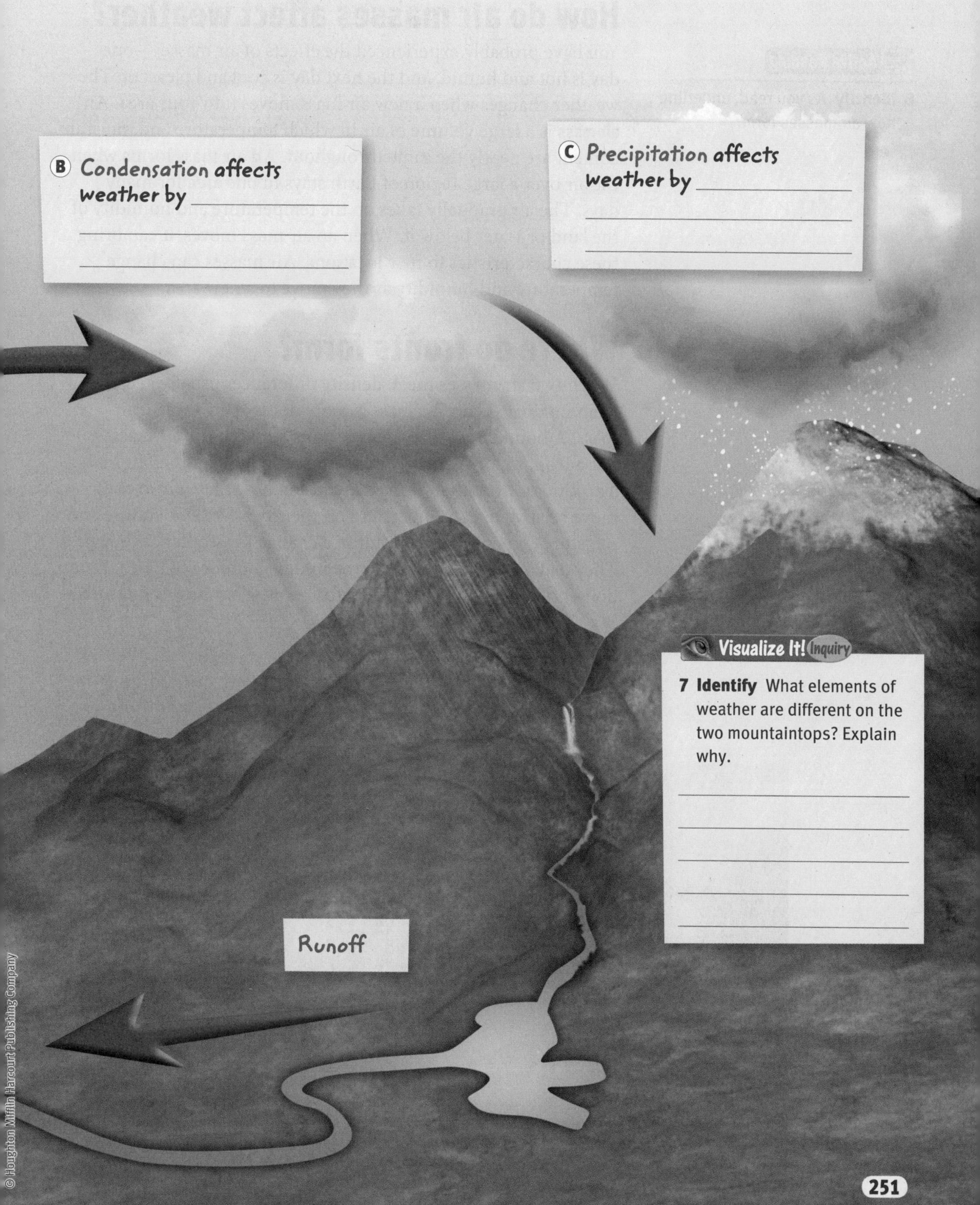

How do air masses affect weather?

B Condensation affects
weather by _____
_____
_____

C Precipitation affects
weather by _____
_____
_____

Runoff

👁 **Visualize It!** (Inquiry)

7 Identify What elements of
weather are different on the
two mountaintops? Explain
why.

_____
_____
_____
_____

Putting Up a **Front**

How do air masses affect weather?

Active Reading

8 Identify As you read, underline how air masses form.

You have probably experienced the effects of air masses—one day is hot and humid, and the next day is cool and pleasant. The weather changes when a new air mass moves into your area. An **air mass** is a large volume of air in which temperature and moisture content are nearly the same throughout. An air mass forms when the air over a large region of Earth stays in one area for many days. The air gradually takes on the temperature and humidity of the land or water below it. When an air mass moves, it can bring these characteristics to new locations. Air masses can change temperature and humidity as they move to a new area.

Where do fronts form?

When two air masses meet, density differences usually keep them from mixing. A cool air mass is more dense than a warm air mass. A boundary, called a **front**, forms between the air masses. For a front to form, one air mass must run into another air mass. The kind of front that forms depends on how these air masses move relative to each other, and on their relative temperature and moisture content. Fronts result in a change in weather as they pass. They usually affect weather in the middle latitudes of Earth. Fronts do not often occur near the equator because air masses there do not have big temperature differences.

The boundary between air masses, or front, cannot be seen, but is shown here to illustrate how air masses can take on the characteristics of the surface below them.

Air masses that form above water are moist.

Air masses that form above land are dry.

Cold Fronts Form Where Cold Air Moves under Warm Air

Warm air is less dense than cold air is. So, a cold air mass that is moving can quickly push up a warm air mass. If the warm air is moist, clouds will form. Storms that form along a cold front are usually short-lived but can move quickly and bring heavy rain or snow. Cooler weather follows a cold front.

9 Apply If you hear that a cold front is headed for your area, what type of weather might you expect?

_____

_____

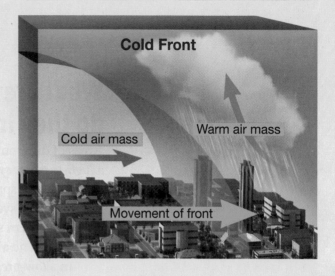

Cold Front

Warm air mass

Cold air mass

Movement of front

Warm Fronts Form Where Warm Air Moves over Cold Air

A warm front forms when a warm air mass follows a retreating cold air mass. The warm air rises over the cold air, and its moisture condenses into clouds. Warm fronts often bring drizzly rain and are followed by warm, clear weather.

10 Identify The rainy weather at the edge of a warm front is a result of

☐ the cold air mass that is leaving.

☐ the warm air rising over the cold air.

☐ the warm air mass following the front.

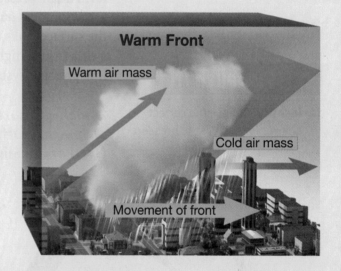

Warm Front

Warm air mass

Cold air mass

Movement of front

Stationary Fronts Form Where Cold and Warm Air Stop Moving

In a stationary front, there is not enough wind for either the cold air mass or the warm air mass to keep moving. So, the two air masses remain in one place. A stationary front can cause many days of unchanging weather, usually clear.

11 Infer When could a stationary front become a warm or cold front?

_____

_____

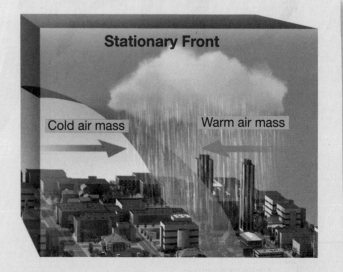

Stationary Front

Cold air mass

Warm air mass

Feeling the Pressure!

What are pressure systems, and how do they interact?

Areas of different air pressure cause changes in the weather. In a *high-pressure system*, air sinks slowly down. As the air nears the ground, it spreads out toward areas of lower pressure. Most high-pressure systems are large and change slowly. When a high-pressure system stays in one location for a long time, an air mass may form. The air mass can be warm or cold, humid or dry.

In a *low-pressure system*, air rises and so has a lower air pressure than the areas around it. As the air in the center of a low-pressure system rises, the air cools.

The diagram below shows how a high-pressure system can form a low-pressure system. Surface air, shown by the black arrows, moves out and away from high-pressure centers. Air above the surface sinks and warms. The green arrows show how air swirls from a high-pressure system into a low-pressure system. In a low-pressure system, the air rises and cools.

A high-pressure system can spiral into a low-pressure system, as illustrated by the green arrows below. In the Northern Hemisphere, air circles in the directions shown.

Visualize It!

12 Identify Choose the correct answer for each of the pressure systems shown below.

A In a high-pressure system, air

☐ rises and cools.

☐ sinks and warms.

B in a low-pressure system, air

☐ rises and cools.

☐ sinks and warms.

How do different pressure systems affect us?

When air pressure differences are small, air doesn't move very much. If the air remains in one place or moves slowly, the air takes on the temperature and humidity of the land or water beneath it. Each type of pressure system has it own unique weather pattern. By keeping track of high- and low-pressure systems, scientists can predict the weather.

High-Pressure Systems Produce Clear Weather

High-pressure systems are areas where air sinks and moves outward. The sinking air is denser than the surrounding air, and the pressure is higher. Cooler, denser air moves out of the center of these high-pressure areas toward areas of lower pressure. As the air sinks, it gets warmer and absorbs moisture. Water droplets evaporate, relative humidity decreases, and clouds often disappear. A high-pressure system generally brings clear skies and calm air or gentle breezes.

Low-Pressure Systems Produce Rainy Weather

Low-pressure systems have lower pressure than the surrounding areas. Air in a low-pressure system comes together, or converges, and rises. As the air in the center of a low-pressure system rises, it cools and forms clouds and rain. The rising air in a low-pressure system causes stormy weather.

A low-pressure system can develop wherever there is a center of low pressure. One place this often happens is along a boundary between a warm air mass and a cold air mass. Rain often occurs at these boundaries, or fronts.

Visualize It!

13 Match Label each picture as a result of a high- or low-pressure system. Then, draw a line from each photo to its matching air-pressure diagram.

A

B

Warm air rises

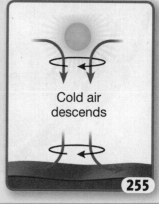

Cold air descends

Windy Weather

How do global wind patterns affect local weather?

Winds are caused by unequal heating of Earth's surface—which causes air pressure differences—and can occur on a global or on a local scale. On a local scale, air-pressure differences affect both wind speed and wind direction at a location. On a global level, there is an overall movement of surface air from the poles toward the equator. The heated air at the equator rises and forms a low-pressure belt. Cold air near the poles sinks and creates high-pressure centers. Because air moves from areas of high pressure to areas of low pressure, it moves from the poles to the equator. At high altitudes, the warmed air circles back toward the poles.

Temperature and pressure differences on Earth's surface also create regional wind belts. Winds in these belts curve to the east or the west as they blow, due to Earth's rotation. This curving of winds is called the *Coriolis effect* (kawr•ee•OH•lis eff•EKT). Winds would flow in straight lines if Earth did not rotate. Winds bring air masses of different temperatures and moisture content to a region.

Visualize It!

14 Apply Trade winds bring

☐ cool air to the warmer equatorial regions.

☐ warm air to the cooler, higher latitudes.

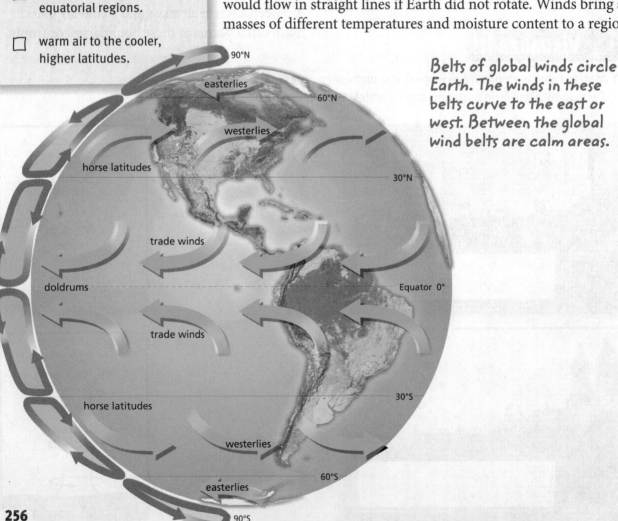

Belts of global winds circle Earth. The winds in these belts curve to the east or west. Between the global wind belts are calm areas.

90°N
easterlies
60°N
westerlies
horse latitudes
30°N
trade winds
doldrums
Equator 0°
trade winds
30°S
horse latitudes
westerlies
60°S
easterlies
90°S

How do jet streams affect weather?

Long-distance winds that travel above global winds for thousands of kilometers are called **jet streams**. Air moves in jet streams with speeds that are at least 92 kilometers per hour and are often greater than 180 kilometers per hour. Like global and local winds, jet streams form because Earth's surface is heated unevenly. They flow in a wavy pattern from west to east.

Each hemisphere usually has two main jet streams, a polar jet stream and a subtropical jet stream. The polar jet streams flow closer to the poles in summer than in winter. Jet streams can affect temperatures. For example, a polar jet stream can pull cold air down from Canada into the United States and pull warm air up toward Canada. Jet streams also affect precipitation patterns. Strong storms tend to form along jet streams. Scientists must know where a jet stream is flowing to make accurate weather predictions.

Active Reading **15 Identify** What are two ways jet streams affect weather?

_____

_____

_____

In winter months, the polar jet stream flows across much of the United States.

Polar jet stream

Subtropical jet streams

Polar jet stream

Visualize It!

16 Infer How does the polar jet stream influence the weather on the southern tip of South America?

_____

_____

_____

_____

© Houghton Mifflin Harcourt Publishing Company

Ocean Effects

How do ocean currents influence weather?

The same global winds that blow across the surface of Earth also push water across Earth's oceans, causing surface currents. Different winds cause currents to flow in different directions. The flow of surface currents moves energy as heat from one part of Earth to another. As the map below shows, both warm-water and cold-water currents flow from one ocean to another. Water near the equator carries energy from the sun to other parts of the ocean. The energy from the warm currents is transferred to colder water or to the atmosphere, changing local temperatures and humidity.

Oceans also have an effect on weather in the form of hurricanes and monsoons. Warm ocean water fuels hurricanes. Monsoons are winds that change direction with the seasons. During summer, the land becomes much warmer than the sea in some areas of the world. Moist wind flows inland, often bringing heavy rains.

Visualize It!

17 **Summarize** Describe how ocean currents help make temperatures at different places on Earth's surface more similar than they would be if there were no currents.

_____

_____

_____

_____

_____

Warm current
Cold current

Surface currents are caused by winds. They distribute energy across Earth's surface, changing local temperature and humidity.

Cool Ocean Currents Lower Coastal Air Temperatures

As currents flow, they warm or cool the atmosphere above, affecting local temperatures. The California current is a cold-water current that keeps the average summer high temperatures of coastal cities such as San Diego around 26 °C (78 °F). Cities that lie inland at the same latitude have warmer averages. The graph below shows average monthly temperatures for San Diego and El Centro, California.

👁 Visualize It!

18 Explain Why are temperatures in San Diego, California, usually cooler than they are in El Centro, California?

_____

_____

_____

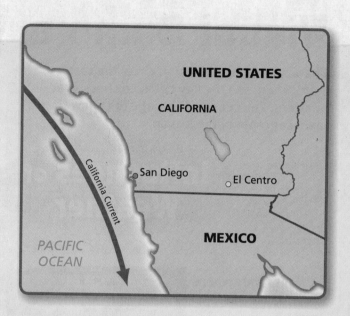

Average Monthly Temperatures

Source: weather.com

Warm Ocean Currents Raise Coastal Air Temperatures

In areas where warm ocean currents flow, coastal cities have warmer winter temperatures than inland cities at similar latitudes. For example, temperatures vary considerably from the coastal regions to the inland areas of Norway due to the warmth of the North Atlantic Current. Coastal cities such as Bergen have relatively mild winters. Inland cities such as Lillehammer have colder winters but temperatures similar to the coastal cities in summer.

👁 Visualize It!

19 Identify Circle the city that is represented by each color in the graph.

▬ Lillehammer/Bergen

▬ Lillehammer/Bergen

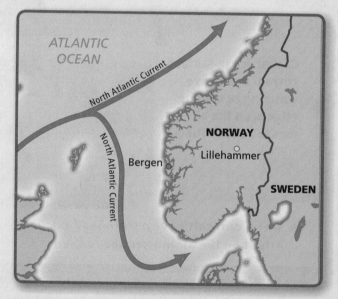

Average Monthly High Temperatures

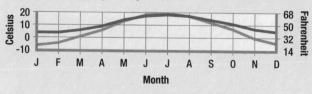

Source: worldweather.org

Visual Summary

To complete this summary, circle the correct word. Then, use the key below to check your answers. You can use this page to review the main concepts of the lesson.

Influences of Weather

Understanding the water cycle is key to understanding weather.

20 Weather is affected by the amount of oxygen / water in the air.

A front forms where two air masses meet.

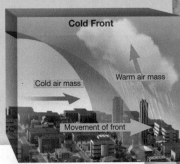

Cold Front

Cold air mass

Warm air mass

Movement of front

21 When a warm air mass and a cool air mass meet, the warm / cool air mass usually moves upward.

Low-pressure systems bring stormy weather, and high-pressure systems bring dry, clear weather.

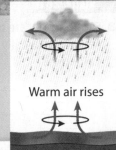

Warm air rises

22 In a low-pressure system, air moves upward / downward.

Pressure differences from the uneven heating of Earth's surface cause predictable patterns of wind.

23 Global wind patterns occur as, due to temperature differences, air rises / sinks at the poles and rises / sinks at the equator.

Global ocean surface currents can have warming or cooling effects on the air masses above them.

24 Warm currents have a warming / cooling effect on the air masses above them.

Answers: 20 water; 21 warm; 22 upward; 23 sinks, rises; 24 warming

25 Synthesize How do air masses cause weather changes?

Lesson Review

Vocabulary

For each pair of terms, explain how the meanings of the terms differ.

1 *front* and *air mass*

_____
_____
_____

2 *high-pressure system* and *low-pressure system*

_____
_____
_____

3 *jet streams* and *global wind belts*

_____
_____
_____

Key Concepts

4 Apply If the weather becomes stormy for a short time and then becomes colder, which type of front has most likely passed?

_____

5 Describe Explain how an ocean current can affect the temperature and the amount of moisture of the air mass above the current and above nearby coastlines.

_____
_____
_____
_____
_____

6 Synthesize How does the water cycle affect weather?

_____
_____
_____
_____
_____

Critical Thinking

Use the diagram below to answer the following question.

Cool air descends   Warm air rises

7 Interpret How does the movement of air affect the type of weather that forms from high-pressure and low-pressure systems?

_____
_____
_____
_____

8 Explain How does the polar jet stream affect temperature and precipitation in North America?

_____
_____
_____
_____

9 Describe Explain how changes in weather are caused by the interaction of air masses.

_____
_____
_____
_____
_____
_____

My Notes

Severe Weather and Weather Safety

ESSENTIAL QUESTION

How can humans protect themselves from hazardous weather?

By the end of this lesson, you should be able to describe the major types of hazardous weather and the ways human beings can protect themselves from hazardous weather and from sun exposure.

Lightning is often the most dangerous part of a thunderstorm. Thunderstorms are one type of severe weather that can cause a lot of damage.

Virginia Science Standards of Learning

6.3 The student will investigate and understand the role of solar energy in driving most natural processes within the atmosphere, the hydrosphere, and on Earth's surface. Key concepts include:

6.3.e the role of thermal energy in weather-related phenomena including thunderstorms and hurricanes.

6.6 The student will investigate and understand the properties of air and the structure and dynamics of Earth's atmosphere. Key concepts include:

6.6.e the relationship of atmospheric measures and weather conditions.

Lesson Labs

Quick Labs
- Create your Own Lightning
- Sun Protection

Exploration Lab
- Preparing for Severe Weather

Engage Your Brain

1 Describe Fill in the blanks with the word or phrase that you think correctly completes the following sentences.

A _____ forms a funnel cloud and has high winds.

A flash or bolt of light across the sky during a storm is called _____

_____ is the sound that follows lightning during a storm.

One way to protect yourself from the sun's rays is to wear _____

2 Identify Name the weather event that is occurring in the photo. What conditions can occur when this event happens in an area?

_____

_____

_____

_____

Active Reading

3 Synthesize Use the sentence below to help you make an educated guess about what the term *storm surge* means. Write the meaning below.

Example sentence
Flooding causes tremendous damage to property and lives when a <u>storm surge</u> moves onto shore.

storm surge:

_____

_____

_____

_____

Vocabulary Terms

- **thunderstorm**
- **lightning**
- **thunder**
- **hurricane**
- **storm surge**
- **tornado**

4 Apply As you learn the definition of each vocabulary term in this lesson, create your own definition or sketch to help you remember the meaning of the term.

☑ Take Cover!

What do we know about thunderstorms?

SPLAAAAAT! BOOOOM! The loud, sharp noise of thunder might surprise you, and maybe even make you jump. The thunder may have been joined by lightning, wind, and rain. A **thunderstorm** is an intense local storm that forms strong winds, heavy rain, lightning, thunder, and sometimes hail. A thunderstorm is an example of severe weather. Severe weather is weather that can cause property damage and sometimes death.

Thunderstorms Form from Rising Air

Thunderstorms get their energy from humid air. When warm, humid air near the ground mixes with cooler air above, the warm air creates an updraft that can build a thunderstorm quickly. Cold downdrafts bring precipitation and eventually end the storm by preventing more warm air from rising.

Step 1
In the first stage, warm air rises and forms a cumulus cloud. The water vapor releases energy when it condenses into cloud droplets. This energy increases the air motion. The cloud continues building up.

Step 2
Ice particles may form in the low temperatures near the top of the cloud. As the ice particles grow large, they begin to fall and pull cold air down with them. This strong downdraft brings heavy rain or hail.

Step 3
During the final stage, the downdraft can spread out and block more warm air from moving upward into the cloud. The storm slows down and ends.

5 Describe What role does warm air play in the formation of a thunderstorm?

Warm air rises and forms the storm.

© Houghton Mifflin Harcourt Publishing Company

Lightning is a Discharge of Electrical Energy

If you have ever shuffled your feet on a carpet, you may have felt a small shock when you touched a doorknob. If so, you have experienced how lightning forms. **Lightning** is an electric discharge that happens between a positively charged area and a negatively charged area. While you walk around, electrical charges can collect on your body. When you touch someone or something else, the charges jump to that person or object in a spark of electricity. In a similar way, electrical charges build up near the tops and bottoms of clouds as pellets of ice move up and down through the clouds. Suddenly, a flash of lightning will spark from one place to another.

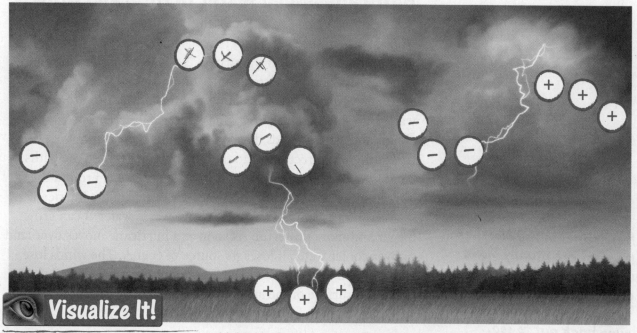

Visualize It!

6 Label Fill in the positive and negative charges in the appropriate spaces provided.

Lightning forms between positive and negative charges. The upper part of a cloud usually carries a positive electric charge. The lower part of the cloud carries mainly negative charges. Lightning is a big spark that jumps between parts of clouds, or between a cloud and Earth's surface.

Thunder Is a Result of Rapidly Expanding Air

Active Reading

7 Identify As you read, underline the explanation of what causes thunder during a storm.

When lightning strikes, the air along its path is heated to a high temperature. The superheated air quickly expands. The rapidly moving air causes the air to vibrate and release sound waves. The result is **thunder**, the sound created by the rapid expansion of air along a lightning strike.

You usually hear thunder a few seconds after you see a lightning strike, because light travels faster than sound. You can count the seconds between a lightning flash and the sound of thunder to figure out about how far away the lightning is. For every 3 seconds between lightning and its thunder, add about 1 km to the lightning strike's distance from you.

☑ Plan Ahead!

Active Reading

8 Identify As you read, underline the definition of *hurricane*.

What do we know about hurricanes?

A **hurricane** is a tropical low-pressure system with winds blowing at speeds of 119 km/h (74 mi/h) or more—strong enough to uproot trees. Hurricanes are called typhoons when they form over the western Pacific Ocean and cyclones when they form over the Indian Ocean.

Hurricanes Need Water to Form and Grow

A hurricane begins as a group of thunderstorms moving over tropical ocean waters. Thunderstorms form in areas of low pressure. Near the equator, warm ocean water provides the energy that can turn a low-pressure center into a violent storm. As water evaporates from the ocean, energy is transferred from the ocean water into the air. This energy makes warm air rise faster. Tall clouds and strong winds develop. As winds blow across the water from different directions into the low-pressure center, the paths bend into a spiral. The winds blow faster and faster around the low-pressure center, which becomes the center of the hurricane.

As long as a hurricane stays above warm water, it can grow bigger and more powerful. As soon as a hurricane moves over land or over cooler water, it loses its source of energy. The winds lose strength and the storm dies out. If a hurricane moves over land, the rough surface of the land reduces the winds even more.

Hurricanes in the Northern Hemisphere usually move westward with the trade winds. Near land, however, they will often move north or even back out to sea.

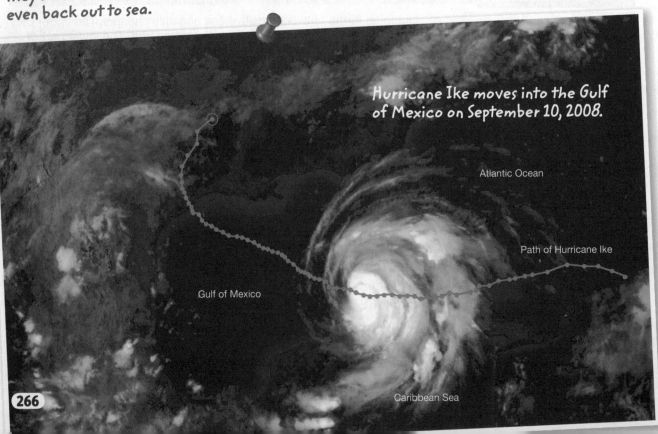

Hurricane Ike moves into the Gulf of Mexico on September 10, 2008.

Atlantic Ocean

Path of Hurricane Ike

Gulf of Mexico

Caribbean Sea

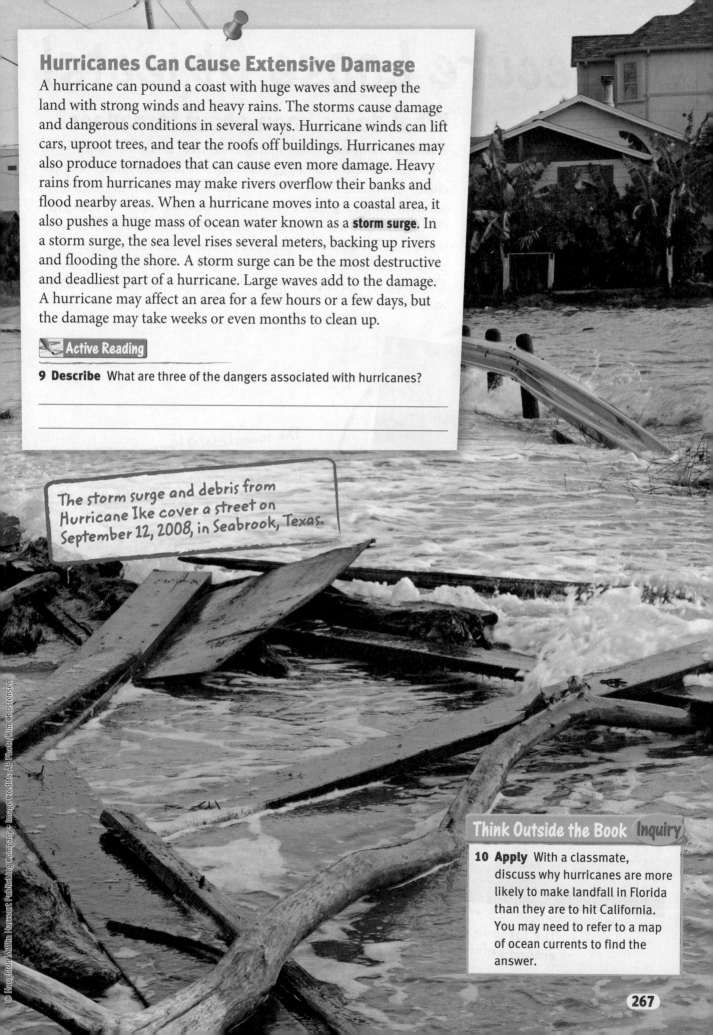

Hurricanes Can Cause Extensive Damage

A hurricane can pound a coast with huge waves and sweep the land with strong winds and heavy rains. The storms cause damage and dangerous conditions in several ways. Hurricane winds can lift cars, uproot trees, and tear the roofs off buildings. Hurricanes may also produce tornadoes that can cause even more damage. Heavy rains from hurricanes may make rivers overflow their banks and flood nearby areas. When a hurricane moves into a coastal area, it also pushes a huge mass of ocean water known as a **storm surge**. In a storm surge, the sea level rises several meters, backing up rivers and flooding the shore. A storm surge can be the most destructive and deadliest part of a hurricane. Large waves add to the damage. A hurricane may affect an area for a few hours or a few days, but the damage may take weeks or even months to clean up.

Active Reading

9 Describe What are three of the dangers associated with hurricanes?

_____

_____

The storm surge and debris from Hurricane Ike cover a street on September 12, 2008, in Seabrook, Texas.

Think Outside the Book Inquiry

10 Apply With a classmate, discuss why hurricanes are more likely to make landfall in Florida than they are to hit California. You may need to refer to a map of ocean currents to find the answer.

☑ Secure Loose Objects!

What do we know about tornadoes?

A **tornado** is a destructive, rotating column of air that has very high wind speeds and that is sometimes visible as a funnel-shaped cloud. A tornado forms when a thunderstorm meets horizontal winds at a high altitude. These winds cause the warm air rising in the thunderstorm to spin. A storm cloud may form a thin funnel shape that has a very low pressure center. As the funnel reaches the ground, the higher-pressure air rushes into the low-pressure area. The result is high-speed winds, which cause the damage associated with tornadoes.

Clouds begin to rotate, signaling that a tornado may form.

The funnel cloud becomes visible as the tornado picks up dust from the ground or particles from the air.

The tornado moves along the ground before it dies out.

Think Outside the Book

11 Illustrate Read the description of the weather conditions that cause tornadoes and draw a sketch of what those conditions might look like.

Most Tornadoes Happen in the Midwest

Tornadoes happen in many places, but they are most common in the United States in *Tornado Alley*. Tornado Alley reaches from Texas up through the midwestern United States, including Iowa, Kansas, Nebraska, and Ohio. Many tornadoes form in the spring and early summer, typically along a front between cool, dry air and warm, humid air.

Tornadoes Can Cause Extensive Damage

The danger of a tornado is mainly due to the high speed of its winds. Winds in a tornado's funnel may have speeds of more than 400 km/h. Most injuries and deaths caused by tornadoes happen when people are struck by objects blown by the winds or when they are trapped in buildings that collapse.

 **Active Reading**

12 Identify As you read, underline what makes a tornado so destructive.

13 Summarize In the overlapping sections of the Venn diagram, list the characteristics that are shared by the different types of storms. In the outer sections, list the characteristics that are specific to each type of storm.

Thunderstorms

Hurricanes

Tornadoes

14 Conclude Write a summary that describes the information in the Venn diagram.

_____

_____

_____

_____

☑ Be Prepared!

What can people do to prepare for severe weather?

Severe weather is weather that can cause property damage, injury, and sometimes death. Hail, lightning, high winds, tornadoes, hurricanes, and floods are all part of severe weather. Hailstorms can damage crops and cars and can break windows. Lightning starts many forest fires and kills or injures hundreds of people and animals each year. Winds and tornadoes can uproot trees and destroy homes. Flooding is also a leading cause of weather-related deaths. Most destruction from hurricanes results from flooding due to storm surges.

Plan Ahead

Have a storm supply kit that contains a battery-operated radio, batteries, flashlights, candles, rain jackets, tarps, blankets, bottled water, canned food, and medicines. Listen to weather announcements. Plan and practice a safety route. A safety route is a planned path to a safe place.

Listen for Storm Updates

During severe weather, it is important to listen to local radio or TV stations. Severe weather updates will let you know the location of a storm. They will also let you know if the storm is getting worse. A *watch* is given when the conditions are ideal for severe weather. A *warning* is given when severe weather has been spotted or is expected within 24 h. During most kinds of severe weather, it is best to stay indoors and away from windows. However, in some situations, you may need to evacuate.

Follow Flood Safety Rules

Sometimes, a place can get so much rain that it floods, especially if it is a low-lying area. So, like storms, floods have watches and warnings. However, little advance notice can usually be given that a flood is coming. A flash flood is a flood that rises and falls very quickly. The best thing to do during a flood is to find a high place to stay until it is over. You should always stay out of floodwaters. Even shallow water can be dangerous because it can move fast.

What can people do to stay safe during thunderstorms?

Stay alert when thunderstorms are predicted or when dark, tall clouds are visible. If you are outside and hear thunder, seek shelter immediately and stay there for 30 min after the thunder ends. Heavy rains can cause sudden, or flash, flooding, and hailstones can damage property and harm living things.

Lightning is one of the most dangerous parts of a thunderstorm. Because lightning is attracted to tall objects, it is important to stay away from trees if you are outside. If you are in an open area, stay close to the ground so that you are not the tallest object in the area. If you can, get into a car. Stay away from ponds, lakes, or other bodies of water. If lightning hits water while you are swimming or wading in it, you could be hurt or killed. If you are indoors during a thunderstorm, avoid using electrical appliances, running water, and phone lines.

How can people stay safe during a tornado?

Tornadoes are too fast and unpredictable for you to attempt to outrun, even if you are in a car. If you see or hear a tornado, go to a place without windows, such as basement, a storm cellar, or a closet or hallway. Stay away from areas that are likely to have flying objects or other dangers. If you are outside, lie in a ditch or low-lying area. Protect your head and neck by covering them with your arms and hands.

How can people stay safe during a hurricane?

If your family lives where hurricanes may strike, have a plan to leave the area, and gather emergency supplies. If a hurricane is approaching your area, listen to weather reports for storm updates. Secure loose objects outside, and cover windows with storm shutters or boards. During a storm, stay indoors and away from windows. If ordered to evacuate the area, do so immediately. After a storm, be aware of downed power lines, hanging branches, and flooded areas.

16 Apply What would you do in each of these scenarios?

Scenario	What would you do?
You are swimming at an outdoor pool when you hear thunder in the distance.	
You and your family are watching TV when you hear a tornado warning that says a tornado has been spotted in the area.	
You are listening to the radio when the announcer says that a hurricane is headed your way and may make landfall in 3 days.	

☑ Use Sun Sense!

How can people protect their skin from the sun?

Human skin contains melanin, which is the body's natural protection against ultraviolet (UV) radiation from the sun. The skin produces more melanin when it is exposed to the sun, but UV rays will still cause sunburn when you spend too much time outside. It is particularly important to protect your skin when the sun's rays are strongest, usually between 10 A.M and 4 P.M.

Active Reading

17 Identify As you read, underline when the sun's ray's are strongest during the day.

Have fun in the sun! Just be sure to protect your skin from harmful rays.

Know the Sun's Hazards

It's easy to notice the effects of a sunburn. Sunburn usually appears within a few hours after sun exposure. It causes red, painful skin that feels hot to the touch. Prolonged exposure to the sun will lead to sunburn in even the darkest-skinned people. Sunburn can lead to skin cancer and premature aging of the skin. The best way to prevent sunburn is to protect your skin from the sun, even on cloudy days. UV rays pass right through clouds and can give you a false feeling of protection from the sun.

Wear Sunscreen and Protective Clothing

Even if you tan easily, you should still use sunscreen. For most people, a sun protection factor (SPF) of 30 or more will prevent burning for about 1.5 h. Babies and people who have pale skin should use an SPF of 45 or more. In addition, you can protect your skin and eyes in different ways. Seek the shade, and wear hats, sunglasses, and perhaps even UV light-protective clothing.

How can people protect themselves from summer heat?

Heat exhaustion is a condition in which the body has been exposed to high temperatures for an extended period of time. Symptoms include cold, moist skin, normal or near-normal body temperature, headache, nausea, and extreme fatigue. *Heat stroke* is a condition in which the body loses its ability to cool itself by sweating because the victim has become dehydrated.

Limit Outdoor Activities

When outdoor temperatures are high, be cautious about exercising outdoors for long periods of time. Pay attention to how your body is feeling, and go inside or to a shady spot if you are starting to feel light-headed or too warm.

Drink Water

Heat exhaustion and heat stroke can best be prevented by drinking 6 to 8 oz of water at least 10 times a day when you are active in warm weather. If you are feeling overheated, dizzy, nauseous, or are sweating heavily, drink something cool (not cold). Drink about half a glass of cool water every 15 min until you feel like your normal self.

Drinking water is one of the best things you can do to keep yourself healthy in hot weather.

Visualize It!

18 Describe List all the ways the people in the photo of the beach may have protected themselves from overexposure to the sun.

_____
_____
_____
_____
_____
_____
_____
_____

Know the Signs of Heat Stroke

Active Reading **19 Identify** Underline signs of heat stroke in the paragraph below.

Heat stroke is life threatening, so it is important to know the signs and treatment for it. Symptoms of heat stroke include hot, dry skin; higher than normal body temperature; rapid pulse; rapid, shallow breathing; disorientation; and possible loss of consciousness.

What to Do In Case of Heat Stroke

☐ Seek emergency help immediately.

☐ If there are no emergency facilities nearby, move the person to a cool place.

☐ Cool the person's body by immersing it in a cool (not cold) bath or using wet towels.

☐ Do not give the person food or water if he or she is vomiting.

☐ Place ice packs under the person's armpits.

Lesson 4 Severe Weather and Weather Safety **273**

Visual Summary

To complete this summary, circle the correct word or phrase. Then use the key below to check your answers. You can use this page to review the main concepts of the lesson.

Severe Weather

Thunderstorms are intense weather systems that produce strong winds, heavy rain, lightning, and thunder.

20 One of the most dangerous parts of a thunderstorm is lightning / thunder.

A hurricane is a large, rotating tropical weather system with strong winds that can cause severe property damage.

21 An important step to plan for a hurricane is to buy raingear / stock a supply kit.

Tornadoes are rotating columns of air that touch the ground and can cause severe damage.

22 The damage from a tornado is mostly caused by associated thunderstorms / high-speed winds.

It is important to plan ahead and listen for weather updates in the event of severe weather.

23 One of the biggest dangers of storms that produce heavy rains or storm surges is flooding / low temperatures.

Prolonged exposure to the sun can cause sunburn, skin cancer, and heat-related health effects.

24 One of the best ways to avoid heat-related illnesses while in the sun is to stay active / drink water.

Answers: 20 lightning; 21 stock a supply kit; 22 high-speed winds; 23 flooding; 24 drink water

25 Synthesize What are three ways in which severe weather can be dangerous?

Lesson Review

Vocabulary

Draw a line that matches the term with the correct definition.

1 hurricane

2 tornado

3 severe weather

4 thunderstorm

5 storm surge

A a huge mass of ocean water that floods the shore

B a storm with lightning and thunder

C a violently rotating column of air stretching to the ground

D weather that can potentially destroy property or cause loss of life

E a tropical low-pressure system with winds of 119 km/h or more

Key Concepts

6 Thunder is caused by _____

7 An electrical discharge between parts of clouds or a cloud and the ground is called _____

8 The sun's ultraviolet rays can cause skin damage including sunburn and even skin _____

9 **Explain** How can a person prepare for hazardous weather well in advance?

_____
_____

10 **Describe** What can people do to stay safe before and during a storm with high winds and heavy rains?

_____
_____
_____

Critical Thinking

Use the map below to answer the following question.

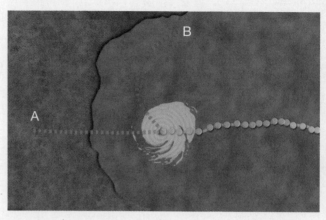

11 **Interpret** Would a hurricane be more likely to remain a hurricane if it reached point A or point B? Explain your answer.

_____
_____
_____

12 **Explain** Why do hurricanes form in tropical latitudes?

_____
_____

13 **Describe** What two weather conditions are needed for tornadoes to form?

_____
_____

14 **Explain** Why is hail sometimes dangerous?

_____
_____
_____

15 **Summarize** What can you do to avoid overexposure to the sun's rays?

_____
_____
_____

My Notes

Weather Maps and Weather Prediction

ESSENTIAL QUESTION

What tools do we use to predict weather?

By the end of this lesson, you should understand how meteorologists forecast the weather using weather maps and other data.

Weather forecasters use radar and satellite images to warn people of the approach of severe weather.

Virginia Science Standards of Learning

6.1 The student will demonstrate an understanding of scientific reasoning, logic, and the nature of science by planning and conducting investigations in which:

6.1.i models and simulations are designed and used to illustrate and explain phenomena and systems; and

6.1.j current applications are used to reinforce science concepts.

6.6 The student will investigate and understand the properties of air and the structure and dynamics of Earth's atmosphere. Key concepts include:

6.6.f basic information from weather maps, including fronts, systems, and basic measurements.

Engage Your Brain

1 Describe Fill in the blank with the word or phrase that you think correctly completes the following sentences.

The job of a _____ is to analyze scientific data to predict future weather conditions.

The location, movement, and intensity of precipitation can be found by using

_____

The elements of weather that are measured and analyzed to make accurate forecasts include

_____

2 Assess What industry is represented in the photo below? What other industries rely on accurate weather forecasts?

_____

_____

Active Reading

3 Synthesize You can often define an unknown word if you know the meaning of its word parts. Use the word parts and sentence below to make an educated guess about the meaning of the word *meteorology*.

Word part	Meaning
meteoron	phenomenon in the sky
-ology	the study of, science of

Example sentence
Studying <u>meteorology</u> helps you to understand weather events.

meteorology:

_____

_____

Vocabulary Terms

• weather forecasting
• meteorology
• station model

4 Identify This list contains the vocabulary terms you'll learn in this lesson. As you read, circle the definition of each term.

Cloudy with *a chance* of ...

What is weather forecasting?

Looking at the weather outdoors in the morning helps you to decide what clothes to wear that day. Different observations give clues to the current weather. The leaves in the trees may be moving if it is windy. If the sky is gray and the streets are shiny, it may be raining.

Checking the weather forecast also helps determine how the weather might change. **Weather forecasting** is the analysis of scientific data to predict future weather conditions.

What elements of weather are forecast?

Weather forecasters study the elements of weather to make detailed predictions. The study of weather and Earth's atmosphere is called **meteorology** [mee•tee•uh•RAHL•uh•jee]. Scientists who study meteorology are called *meteorologists*.

Eight elements of weather are observed around the clock. These elements are air temperature, humidity, wind direction, wind speed, clouds, precipitation, atmospheric pressure, and visibility. Using these eight elements to make accurate weather forecasts helps people stay safe and comfortable. To make the best predictions, meteorologists need accurate data.

5 Infer Forest firefighters need accurate and detailed weather forecasts. What weather elements would these firefighters be most interested in? Explain.

_____

_____

_____

_____

_____

_____

 **Visualize It!**

6 Apply Identify three elements of weather that appear in this beach scene.

A _____

B _____

C _____

Why It Matters

The Hurricane Hunters

Flying in stormy weather can be an uncomfortable and frightening experience. Yet, some pilots are trained to fly into the most intense storms. The Hurricane Hunters of the National Oceanic and Atmospheric Administration (NOAA) fly right into the eye of tropical storms and hurricanes to collect valuable data. Weather forecasters use the data to predict a storm's path and intensity.

Hurricane Hunter Planes

The weather-sensing equipment aboard NOAA's WP-3D Orion is quite advanced. The planes are equipped with radar in the nose, in the tail, and on the underside of the fuselage. Radiometers on the wings measure wind speed once every second. These and other data are sent immediately to the airplane's computer system.

UNITED STATES DEPT. OF COMM

Wind gust probe

Weather radar for 360-degree view

Sensors are released from the plane's belly.

Falling Dropsonde

A lightweight instrument package called a *dropsonde* [DRAHP•sahnd] is launched from the aircraft. As the dropsonde descends through the storm, it collects data twice every second. Data about temperature, humidity, wind speed, and air pressure are sent back to the plane.

Extend

Inquiry

7 Explain How do airplanes help weather forecasters make predictions about the movement and intensity of storms?

8 Research Find out about another technology that is used to gather weather data by sea or by air.

9 Assess Explain how this technology is used in an oral report, poster presentation, or slide show.

What's Going on *up There?*

How are weather data collected?

To predict the weather, meteorologists must look at data that come from different sources. Meteorologists use many kinds of advanced technologies to gather this data. These technologies are found at ground stations and in balloons, aircraft, and satellites.

By Ground Stations

Land-based ground stations, also called *automated surface stations*, collect weather data from the lower atmosphere 24 hours a day. A variety of weather-sensing instruments are found at these ground stations. These instruments measure pressure, temperature, humidity, precipitation, wind speed, visibility, and cloud cover. Many ground stations are located near airports and transmit computer-generated voice observations to aircraft regularly.

By Radar

Weather radar is useful for finding the location, movement, and intensity of storms. Radar works by bouncing radio waves off precipitation. The stronger the signal that is returned to the radar, the heavier the precipitation is. Also, the longer it takes for the signal to return to the radar, the farther away the precipitation is.

Doppler radar, a type of weather radar, can detect precipitation and air motion within a storm. This technology is important for detecting and tracking severe storms and tornadoes.

Satellites, balloons, and aircraft can provide wide views of Earth's weather systems.

👁 Visualize It!

10 Apply Which town is experiencing the most severe weather?

_____

_____

11 Apply In which town is it raining lightly?

_____

_____

Colors represent the intensity of precipitation.

Radar Map of a Strong Storm

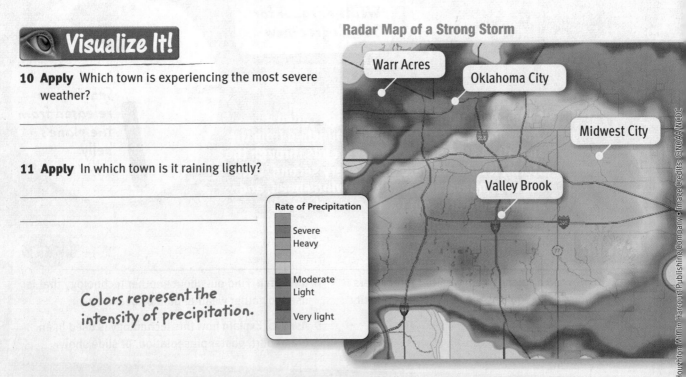

Warr Acres

Oklahoma City

Midwest City

Valley Brook

Rate of Precipitation

Severe
Heavy

Moderate
Light

Very light

By Balloons and Aircraft

Weather-sensing instruments carried by aircraft and balloons measure weather conditions in the middle to upper atmosphere. Aircraft can carry a variety of weather-sensing instruments and collect data in places far from ground stations, such as over oceans.

Weather balloons are released twice daily from stations around the world. These balloons collect weather information at different altitudes. Weather balloons carry a small instrument package called a radiosonde [RAY•dee•oh•sahnd]. Radiosondes measure atmospheric pressure, air temperature, and humidity up to about 32 km. They also measure wind speed and direction. Radiosondes send data by radio signal to ground stations.

Balloons such this one can gather weather data from high up in the atmosphere.

By Satellites

Orbiting weather satellites at high altitudes provide data on water vapor, cloud-top temperatures, and the movement of weather systems. Geostationary satellites and polar-orbiting satellites monitor Earth's weather. Geostationary weather satellites monitor Earth from a fixed position thousands of kilometers above Earth. Polar-orbiting satellites circle Earth and provide global information from hundreds of kilometers above Earth's surface. Cameras on satellites take images at regular intervals to track weather conditions on Earth. Digital images are sent back to ground stations. These images can be animated to show changes in weather over time.

Active Reading **12 Compare** What is the difference between geostationary and polar-orbiting satellites?

_____

_____

Think Outside the Book Inquiry

13 Describe Research ways that weather predictions were made before the use of aircraft, balloons, and satellites.

What kinds of symbols and maps are used to analyze the weather?

In the United States, meteorologists with the National Weather Service (NWS) collect and analyze weather data. The NWS prepares weather maps and station models to make weather data easy to use and understand.

Station Models

A **station model** is a set of meteorological symbols that represent the weather at a particular observing station. Station models are often shown on weather maps. Placing many station models on a map makes it possible to see large weather patterns, such as fronts.

A station model is a small circle that is surrounded by a set of symbols and numbers that represent current weather data at a specific location. Key weather elements shown on a station model are temperature, wind speed and direction, cloud cover, air pressure, and dew point. Note that the pointer, or wind barb, for wind direction points *into* the wind.

Active Reading

14 Identify What are the key weather elements shown by a station model?

_____

_____

_____

_____

 **Visualize It!**

15 Observe Where are the temperature and dew point recorded on a station model?

_____

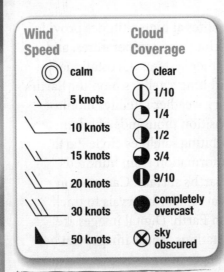

Wind Speed		Cloud Coverage	
⊚	calm	○	clear
	5 knots	◑	1/10
	10 knots	◕	1/4
	15 knots	◑	1/2
	20 knots	◕	3/4
	30 knots	◑	9/10
◤	50 knots	●	completely overcast
		⊗	sky obscured

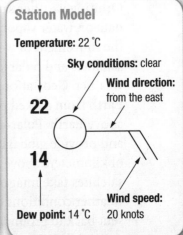

Station Model

Temperature: 22 °C

Sky conditions: clear

Wind direction: from the east

22

14

Dew point: 14 °C

Wind speed: 20 knots

16 Apply Draw a station model below to represent the following conditions: air temperature 8 °C; dew point 6 °C; sky 1/2 overcast; wind 15 knots from the south.

Surface Weather Maps

Meteorologists commonly use surface weather maps to show forecasts on television. A surface weather map displays air pressure and the locations of fronts. Precipitation may also be shown.

Air pressure is shown by using isobars. Isobars are lines that connect points of equal air pressure and are marked in units called *millibars*. Isobars form closed loops. The center of these loops is marked with either a capital H (high) or L (low). A capital H represents a center of high pressure, and a capital L represents a center of low pressure.

Fronts are also shown on surface weather maps. Blue lines with blue triangles are cold fronts. Red lines with red half circles are warm fronts. Stationary fronts alternate between blue and red.

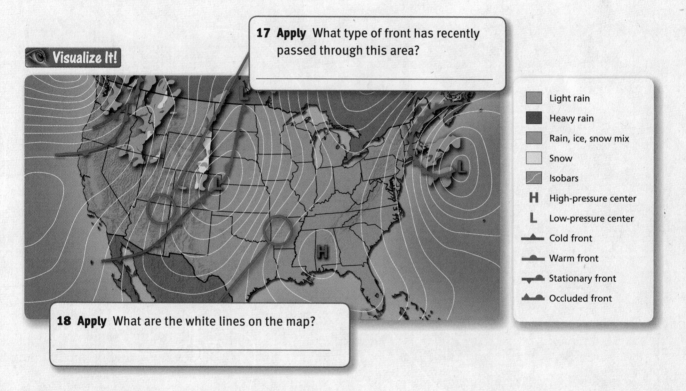

Visualize It!

17 Apply What type of front has recently passed through this area?

18 Apply What are the white lines on the map?

Legend:
- Light rain
- Heavy rain
- Rain, ice, snow mix
- Snow
- Isobars
- H High-pressure center
- L Low-pressure center
- Cold front
- Warm front
- Stationary front
- Occluded front

Upper-Air Charts

Another type of weather map used to analyze weather is the upper-air chart. Upper-air charts are based on data collected by instruments carried into the atmosphere by weather balloons.

Upper-air charts show wind and air pressure at middle and upper levels of Earth's atmosphere. Information from upper air charts indicates if and where weather systems will form, and if these systems will move, remain stationary, or fall apart. In addition, these charts are used to determine the position of jet streams. Airlines and airplane pilots use upper-air charts to determine flight paths and possible areas of turbulence.

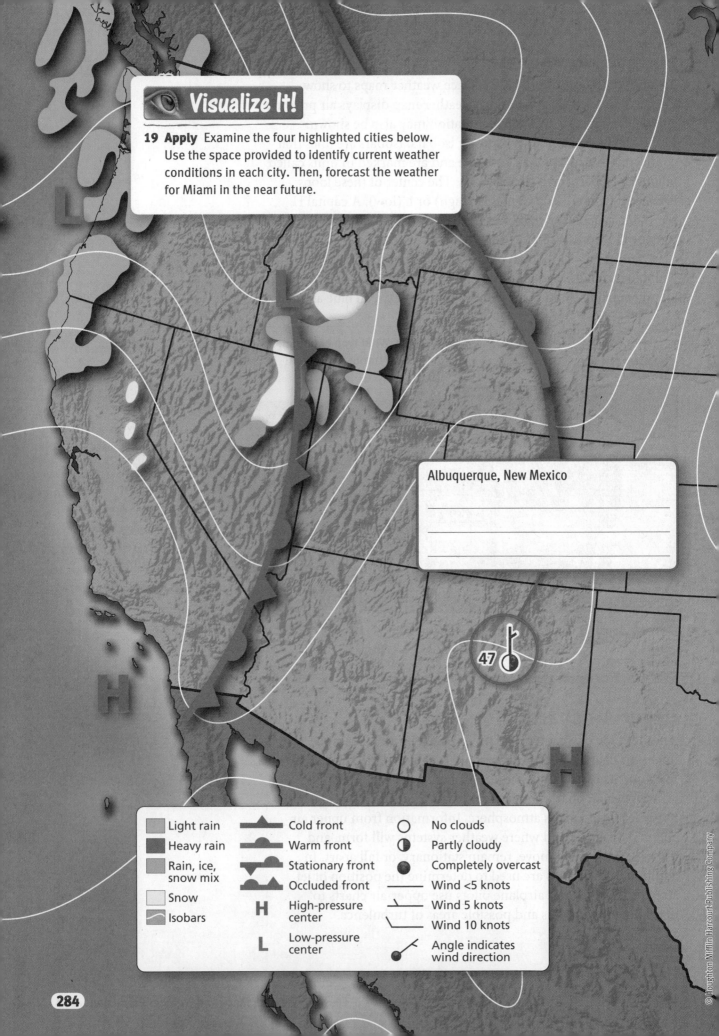

Visualize It!

19 Apply Examine the four highlighted cities below. Use the space provided to identify current weather conditions in each city. Then, forecast the weather for Miami in the near future.

Albuquerque, New Mexico

47

Light rain	Cold front	◯ No clouds	
Heavy rain	Warm front	◑ Partly cloudy	
Rain, ice, snow mix	Stationary front	● Completely overcast	
Snow	Occluded front	— Wind <5 knots	
Isobars	**H** High-pressure center	Wind 5 knots	
	L Low-pressure center	Wind 10 knots	
		Angle indicates wind direction	

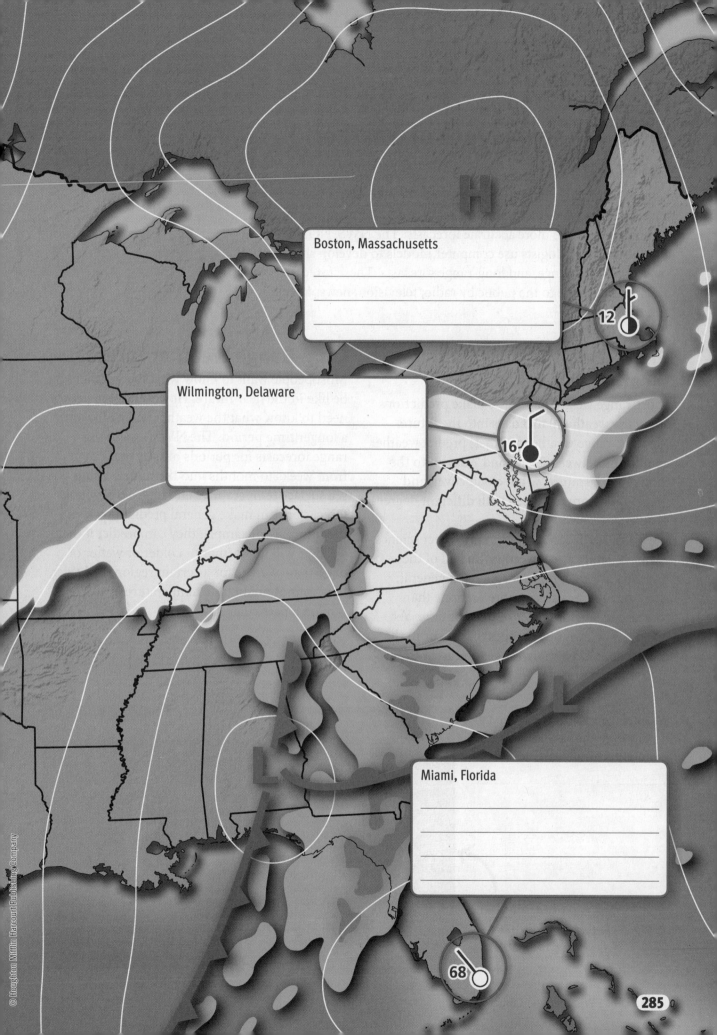

Boston, Massachusetts

_____

_____

_____

Wilmington, Delaware

_____

_____

_____

Miami, Florida

_____

_____

_____

_____

What are some types of weather forecasts?

As supercomputers have become faster in recent years, forecasts have also improved. Increasing amounts of weather data can be combined to create more accurate forecasts. The NWS, NOAA, and local meteorologists use computer models to develop short-range, medium-range, and long-range forecasts. These forecasts are made available to the public by radio, television, newspaper, and the Internet.

Short-Range and Medium-Range Weather Forecasts

Short-range weather forecasts make predictions about the weather 0 to 3 days into the future. Medium-range weather forecasts predict weather conditions between 3 days and 7 days into the future. Temperature, wind, cloud cover, and precipitation are predicted with different degrees of accuracy.

Weather forecasting is an imperfect science. Many variables affect weather, and all of these variables are changing constantly. In general, short-term forecasts are more accurate than forecasts made for longer periods of time. Yet, given the continuous changes that occur in the atmosphere, even short-range forecasts cannot always be accurate.

Long-Range Weather Forecasts

Most people want to know what the weather will be like in the near future. However, some people need to know what the weather will be like over a longer time period. The NWS issues long-range forecasts for periods of time that range from weeks to months into the future. Using sea surface temperatures and high-level winds, forecasters can make general predictions about the future. For example, they can predict if the weather will be warmer or colder or wetter or drier than average for a certain region. However, they cannot predict the temperature or if it will rain on a particular day.

20 Infer Why is it important for the farmer to know the long-range forecast?

_____

_____

_____

Some meteorologists prepare specialized forecasts for farmers.

Hazardous Weather Forecasts

An important job of meteorologists is to warn the public about severe weather. This information is shown as a weather "crawl" at the bottom of a television screen. The NWS issues three types of hazardous weather forecasts: weather advisories, weather watches, and weather warnings.

A weather advisory is issued when the expected weather conditions will not be a serious hazard but may cause inconvenience if caution is not used. When severe weather conditions are possible over a large geographic area, a weather watch is issued. People should prepare and have a plan of action in place in case a storm threatens. A weather warning is issued when weather conditions that pose a threat to life and property are happening or are about to happen. People who live in the path of the storm need to take immediate action.

Active Reading **21 Compare** What is the difference between a weather watch and a weather warning?

_____

_____

_____

_____

_____

_____

_____

The National Weather Service issues weather advisories, weather watches, and weather warnings to inform the public about hazardous weather.

Visualize It!

22 Compose Write a caption for the photo based on a hazardous weather forecast.

_____

Visual Summary

To complete this summary, check the box that indicates true or false. Then use the key below to check your answers. You can use this page to review the main concepts of the lesson.

Weather Maps and Weather Prediction

Weather forecasting is the analysis of scientific data to predict likely future weather conditions.

T F

23 ☐ ☐ In order to forecast the weather, meteorologists gather weather data for five important weather elements.

Different kinds of weather data can be shown together on station models and weather maps.

18

12

T F

24 ☐ ☐ Two types of weather maps that meteorologists use to show the weather are surface weather maps and upper-air charts.

Weather data come from many sources on land and in the air.

T F

25 ☐ ☐ Weather balloons and aircraft allow for surface weather observations.

Meteorologists use computer models to make short-range, medium-range, and long-range weather forecasts.

T F

26 ☐ ☐ Three types of hazardous weather forecasts are weather advisories, weather watches, and weather warnings.

Answers: 23 F; 24 T; 25 F; 26 T

27 Synthesis Describe the technologies used to gather data, prepare a forecast, and broadcast a forecast for a town in the path of a hurricane.

Vocabulary

Fill in the blank with the term that best completes the following sentences.

1 A _____ is a group of meteorological symbols that represents the weather at a particular observing station.

2 _____ is the analysis of scientific data to predict likely future weather conditions.

3 The scientific study of Earth's atmosphere and weather is called _____

Key Concepts

4 List What are the eight elements of weather that are observed for making weather forecasts?

_____

_____

_____

5 Identify What kinds of data do surface weather maps provide?

_____

_____

_____

6 Summarize Describe each of the three types of hazardous weather forecasts.

_____

_____

_____

_____

_____

_____

_____

_____

Critical Thinking

Use the diagram to answer the following questions.

Mon	Tue	Wed	Thu	Fri
74°	70°	56°	56°	66°
62°	64°	48°	54°	56°

7 Analyze On what day will there likely be severe weather?

_____

8 Infer Between which two days will a cold front arrive? Explain.

_____

_____

_____

9 Diagram Draw a station model based on the Thursday forecast, if winds are 15 knots from the northwest.

10 Assess Why do you think weather observations are made frequently at airports around the world?

_____

_____

_____

_____

My Notes

J. Marshall Shepherd

METEOROLOGIST AND CLIMATOLOGIST

J. Marshall Shepherd

Dr. Marshall Shepherd, who works at the University of Georgia, has been interested in weather since he made his own weather-collecting instruments for a school science project. Although the instruments he uses today, like computers and satellites, are much larger and much more powerful than the ones he made in school, they give him some of the same information.

In his work, Dr. Shepherd tries to understand weather events, such as hurricanes and thunderstorms, and relate them to current weather and climate change. He once led a team that used space-based radar to measure rainfall over urban areas. The measurements confirmed that the areas downwind of major cities experience more rainfall in summer than other areas in the same region. He explained that the excess heat retained by buildings and roads changes the way the air circulates, and this causes rain clouds to form.

While the most familiar field of meteorology is weather forecasting, research meteorology is also used in air pollution control, weather control, agricultural planning, climate change studies, and even criminal and civil investigations.

Social Studies Connection

An almanac is a type of calendar that contains various types of information, including weather forecasts and astronomical data, for every day of the year. Many people used almanacs before meteorologists started to forecast the weather. Use an almanac from the library or the Internet to find out what the weather was on the day that you were born.

© Houghton Mifflin Harcourt Publishing Company • Image Credits: (bkgd) ©Mike Theiss/National Geographic/Getty Images

JOB BOARD

Atmospheric Scientist

What You'll Do: Collect and analyze data on Earth's air pressure, humidity, and winds to make short-range and long-range weather forecasts. Work around the clock during weather emergencies like hurricanes and tornadoes.

Where You Might Work: Weather data collecting stations, radio and television stations, or private consulting firms.

Education: A bachelor's degree in meteorology, or in a closely related field with courses in meteorology, is required. A master's degree is necessary for some jobs.

Airplane Pilot

What You'll Do: Fly airplanes containing passengers or cargo, or for crop dusting, search and rescue, or fire-fighting. Before flights, check the plane's control equipment and weather conditions. Plan a safe route. Pilots communicate with air traffic control during flight to ensure a safe flight and fill out paperwork after the flight.

Where You Might Work: Flying planes for airlines, the military, radio and tv stations, freight companies, flight schools, farms, national parks, or other businesses that use airplanes.

Education: Most pilots will complete a four-year college degree before entering a pilot program. Before pilots become certified and take to the skies, they need a pilot license and many hours of flight time and training.

Snow Plow Operator

What You'll Do: In areas that receive snowfall, prepare the roads by spreading a mixture of sand and salt on the roads when snow is forecast. After a snowfall, drive snow plows to clear snow from roads and walkways.

Where You Might Work: For public organizations or private companies in cities and towns that receive snowfall.

Education: In most states, there is no special license needed, other than a driver's license.

Climate

ESSENTIAL QUESTION

How is climate affected by energy from the sun and variations on Earth's surface?

By the end of this lesson, you should be able to describe the main factors that affect climate and explain how scientists classify climates.

Earth has a wide variety of climates, including polar climates like the one shown here. What kind of climate do you live in?

Virginia Science Standards of Learning

6.3 The student will investigate and understand the role of solar energy in driving most natural processes within the atmosphere, the hydrosphere, and on Earth's surface. Key concepts include:

6.3.c the motion of the atmosphere and the oceans; and

6.3.d cloud formation.

6.5 The student will investigate and understand the unique properties and characteristics of water and its roles in the natural and human-made environment. Key concepts include:

6.5.d the ability of large bodies of water to store thermal energy and moderate climate.

Lesson Labs

Quick Labs
- Determining Climate
- Factors That Affect Climate
- The Angles of the Sun's Rays

Field Lab
- How Land Features Affect Climate

Engage Your Brain

1 Predict Check T or F to show whether you think each statement is true or false.

T   F

☐   ☐   Locations in Florida and Oregon receive the same amount of sunlight on any given day.

☐   ☐   Temperature is an important part of determining the climate of an area.

☐   ☐   The climate on even the tallest mountains near the equator is too warm for glaciers to form.

☐   ☐   Winds can move rain clouds from one location to another.

2 Infer Volcanic eruptions can send huge clouds of gas and dust into the air. These dust particles can block sunlight. How might the eruption of a large volcano affect weather for years to come?

_____

_____

_____

_____

_____

Active Reading

3 Synthesize You can often define an unknown word if you know the meaning of its word parts. Use the word parts and sentence below to make an educated guess about the meaning of the word *topography*.

Word part	Meaning
topos-	place
-graphy	writing

Example sentence
The <u>topography</u> of the area is varied, because there are hills, valleys, and flat plains all within a few square miles.

topography:

_____

_____

Vocabulary Terms

- weather
- climate
- latitude
- topography
- elevation
- surface currents

4 Apply As you learn the definition of each vocabulary term in this lesson, create your own definition or sketch to help you remember the meaning of the term.

How's the Climate?

What determines climate?

Weather conditions change from day to day. **Weather** is the condition of Earth's atmosphere at a particular time and place. **Climate**, on the other hand, describes the weather conditions in an area over a long period of time. For the most part, climate is determined by temperature and precipitation (pree•SIP•uh•tay•shuhn). But what factors affect the temperature and precipitation rates of an area? Those factors include latitude, wind patterns, elevation, locations of mountains and large bodies of water, and nearness to ocean currents.

Temperature

Temperature patterns are an important feature of climate. Although the average temperature of an area over a period of time is useful information, using only average temperatures to describe climate can be misleading. Areas that have similar average temperatures may have very different temperature ranges.

A temperature range includes all of the temperatures in an area, from the coldest temperature extreme to the warmest temperature extreme. Organisms that thrive in a region are those that can survive the temperature extremes in that region. Temperature ranges provide more information about an area and are unique to the area. Therefore, temperature ranges are a better indicator of climate than are temperature averages.

5 Identify As you read, underline two elements of weather that are important in determining climate.

Visualize It!

6 Infer How might the two different climates shown below affect the daily lives of the people who live there?

_____

_____

_____

_____

_____

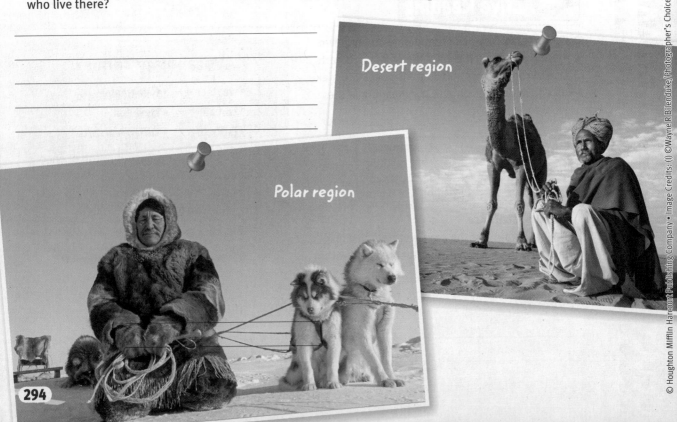

Desert region

Polar region

Precipitation

Precipitation, such as rain, snow, or hail, is also an important part of climate. As with temperature, the average yearly precipitation alone is not the best way to describe a climate. Two places that have the same average yearly precipitation may receive that precipitation in different patterns during the year. For example, one location may receive small amounts of precipitation throughout the year. This pattern would support plant life all year long. Another location may receive all of its precipitation in a few months of the year. These months may be the only time in which plants can grow. So, the pattern of precipitation in a region can determine the types of plants that grow there and the length of the growing season. Therefore, the pattern of precipitation is a better indicator of the local climate than the average precipitation alone.

Think Outside the Book Inquiry

8 Apply With a classmate, discuss what condition, other than precipitation, is likely related to better plant growth in the temperate area shown directly below than in the desert on the bottom right.

Visualize It!

7 Interpret Match the climates represented in the bar graph below to the photos by writing *A*, *B*, or *C* in the blank circles.

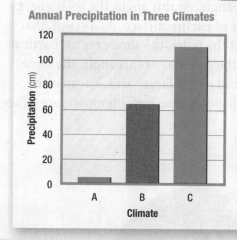

Annual Precipitation in Three Climates

○ There are enough resources in the area for plants to thickly cover the ground.

○ Some plants that grow in deserts have long roots to reach the water deep underground.

○ Conditions in a tropical forest allow lots of plants to grow quickly and closely together.

Here Comes the Sun!

How is the sun's energy related to Earth's climate?

The climate of an area is directly related to the amount of energy from the sun, or *solar energy*, that the area receives. This amount depends on the latitude (LAHT•ih•tood) of the area. **Latitude** is the angular distance in degrees north and south from the equator. Different latitudes receive different amounts of solar energy. The available solar energy powers the water cycle and winds, which affect the temperature, precipitation, and other factors that determine the local climate.

Latitude Affects the Amount of Solar Energy an Area Receives and that Area's Climate

Latitude helps determine the temperature of an area, because latitude affects the amount of solar energy an area receives. The figure below shows how the amount of solar energy reaching Earth's surface varies with latitude. Notice that the sun's rays travel in lines parallel to one another. Near the equator, the sun's rays hit Earth directly, at almost a 90° angle. At this angle, the solar energy is concentrated in a small area of Earth's surface. As a result, that area has high temperatures. At the poles, the sun's rays hit Earth at a lesser angle than they do at the equator. At this angle, the same amount of solar energy is spread over a larger area. Because the energy is less concentrated, the poles have lower temperatures than areas near the equator do.

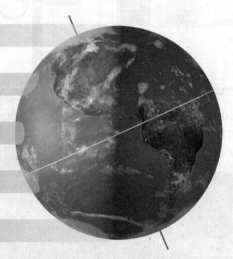

The amount of solar energy an area receives depends on latitude.

Drawing is not to scale.

The Sun Powers the Water Cycle

It is easy to see how the water cycle affects weather and climate. For example, when it rains or snows, you see precipitation. In the water cycle, energy from the sun warms the surface of the ocean or other body of water. Some of the liquid water evaporates, becoming invisible water vapor, a gas. When cooled, some of the vapor condenses, turning into droplets of liquid water and forming clouds. Some water droplets collide, becoming larger. Once large enough, they fall to Earth's surface as precipitation.

11 Apply Using the figure below, explain how the water cycle affects the climate of an area.

_____

_____

_____

_____

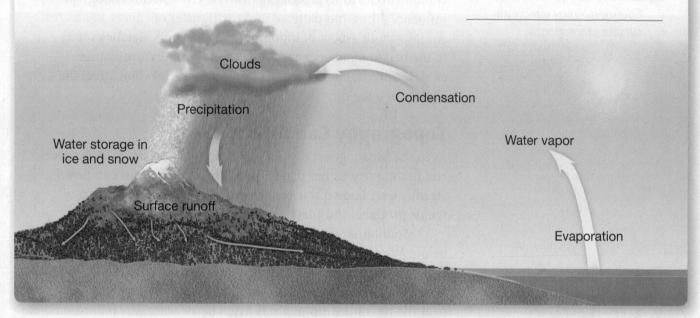

Clouds

Condensation

Precipitation

Water vapor

Water storage in ice and snow

Surface runoff

Evaporation

The Sun Powers Wind

The sun warms Earth's surface unevenly, creating areas of different air pressure. As air moves from areas of higher pressure to areas of lower pressure, it is felt as wind, as shown below. Global and local wind patterns transfer energy around Earth's surface, affecting global and local temperatures. Winds also carry water vapor from place to place. If the air cools enough, the water vapor will condense and fall as precipitation. The speed, direction, temperature, and moisture content of winds affect the climate and weather of the areas they move through.

Warm, less dense air rises, creating areas of low pressure.

Cold, more dense air sinks, creating areas of high pressure.

Wind forms when air moves from a high-pressure area to a low-pressure area.

Warm surface

Cool surface

Latitude Isn't Everything

How do Earth's features affect climate?

On land, winds have to flow around or over features on Earth's surface, such as mountains. The surface features of an area combine to form its **topography** (tuh•POG•ruh•fee). Topography influences the wind patterns and the transfer of energy in an area. An important aspect of topography is elevation. **Elevation** refers to the height of an area above sea level. Temperature changes as elevation changes. Thus, topography and elevation affect the climate of a region.

Topography Can Affect Winds

Even the broad, generally flat topography of the Great Plains gives rise to unique weather patterns. On the plains, winds can flow steadily over large distances before they merge. This mixing of winds produces thunderstorms and even tornadoes.

Mountains can also affect the climate of an area, as shown below. When moist air hits a mountain, it is forced to rise up the side of the mountain. The rising air cools and often releases rain, which supports plants on the mountainside. The air that moves over the top of the mountain is dry. The air warms as it descends, creating a dry climate, which supports desert formation. Such areas are said to be in a *rain shadow*, because the air has already released all of its water by the time that it reaches this side of the mountain.

Active Reading

12 Identify As you read, underline how topography affects the climate of a region.

Visualize It!

13 Apply Circle the rain gauge in each set that corresponds to how much rain each side of the mountain is likely to receive.

The Rain Shadow Effect

The Wet Side Air rises up the mountainside. The rising air cools and releases precipitation. The precipitation supports a lush plant community in this area.

The Dry Side Dry air flows over the mountain and warms as it sinks. The warm air absorbs moisture and creates conditions under which deserts may develop.

298

Elevation Influences Temperature

Elevation has a very strong effect on the temperature of an area. If you rode a cable car up a mountain, the temperature would decrease by about 6.5 °C (11.7 °F) for every kilometer you rose in elevation. Why does it get colder as you move higher up? Because the lower atmosphere is mainly warmed by Earth's surface that is directly below it. The warmed air lifts to higher elevations, where it expands and cools. Even close to the equator, temperatures at high elevations can be very cold. For example, Mount Kilimanjaro in Tanzania is close to the equator, but it is still cold enough at the peak to support a permanent glacier. The example below shows how one mountain can have several types of climates.

Visualize It!

14 Apply Circle the thermometer that shows the most likely temperature for each photo at different elevations.

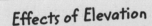
Effects of Elevation

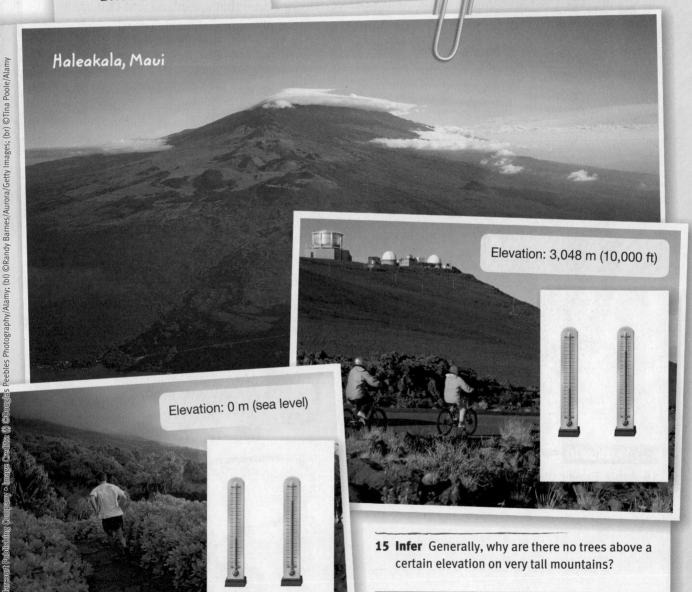
Haleakala, Maui

Elevation: 3,048 m (10,000 ft)

Elevation: 0 m (sea level)

15 Infer Generally, why are there no trees above a certain elevation on very tall mountains?

_____

_____

_____

Waterfront Property

How do large bodies of water affect climate?

Large bodies of water, such as the ocean, can influence an area's climate. Water absorbs and releases energy as heat more slowly than land does. So, water helps moderate the temperature of nearby land. Sudden or extreme temperature changes rarely take place on land near large bodies of water. The state of Michigan, which is nearly surrounded by the Great Lakes, has more moderate temperatures than places far from large bodies of water at the same latitude. California's coastal climate is also influenced by a large body of water—the ocean. Places that are inland, but that are at the same latitude as a given place on California's coast, experience wider ranges of temperature.

Crescent City, California
Temperature Range:
4 °C to 19 °C
Latitude 41.8°N

Council Bluffs, Iowa
Temperature Range:
-11 °C to 30.5 °C
Latitude 41.3°N

Cleveland, Ohio
Temperature Range:
-4 °C to 28 °C
Latitude 41.4°N

GULF STREAM

ANTILLES CURRENT

CARIBBEAN CURRENT

Visualize It!

16 Apply Explain the difference in temperature ranges between Crescent City, Council Bluffs, and Cleveland.

_____

_____

_____

_____

_____

_____

How do ocean currents affect climate?

An *ocean current* is the movement of water in a certain direction. There are many different currents in the oceans. Ocean currents move water and distribute energy and nutrients around the globe. The currents on the surface of the ocean are called **surface currents.** Surface currents are driven by winds and carry warm water away from the equator and carry cool water away from the poles.

Cold currents cool the air in coastal areas, while warm currents warm the air in coastal areas. Thus, currents moderate global temperatures. For example, the Gulf Stream is a surface current that moves warm water from the Gulf of Mexico northeastward, toward Great Britain and Europe. The British climate is mild because of the warm Gulf Stream waters. Polar bears do not wander the streets of Great Britain, as they might in Natashquan, Canada, which is at a similar latitude.

NORWAY CURRENT

Natashquan, Canada
Temperature Range:
-18 °C to 14 °C
Latitude: 50.2°N

LABRADOR CURRENT

London, England
Temperature Range:
2 °C to 22 °C
Latitude 51.5°N

NORTH ATLANTIC CURRENT

GULF STREAM

ATLANTIC OCEAN

17 Summarize How do currents distribute heat around the globe?

_____

_____

_____

 Visualize It!

18 Infer How do you think that the Canary current affects the temperature in the Canary Islands?

_____

_____

_____

CANARY CURRENT

Canary Islands, Spain
Temperature Range:
12 °C to 26 °C
Latitude: 28°N

NORTH EQUATORIAL CURRENT

Zoning Out

What are the three major climate zones?

Earth has three major types of climate zones: tropical, temperate, and polar. These zones are shown below. Each zone has a distinct temperature range that relates to its latitude. Each of these zones has several types of climates. These different climates result from differences in topography, winds, ocean currents, and geography.

Active Reading

19 Identify Underline the factor that determines the temperature ranges in each zone.

Temperate

Temperate climates have an average temperature below 18 °C (64 °F) in the coldest month and an average temperature above 10 °C (50 °F) in the warmest month. There are five temperate zone subclimates: marine west coast climates, steppe climates, humid continental climate, humid subtropical climate, and Mediterranean climate. The temperate zone is characterized by lower temperatures than the tropical zone. It is located between the tropical zone and the polar zone.

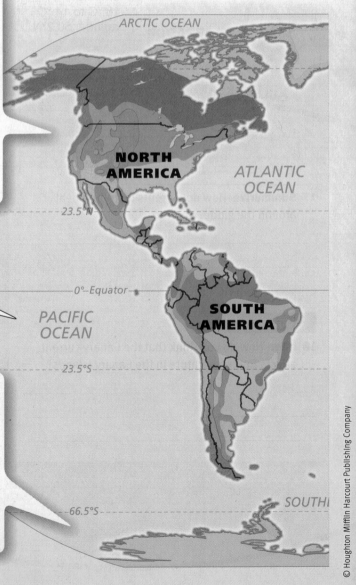

Visualize It!

20 Label What climate zone is this?

_____

Polar

The polar zone, at latitudes of 66.5° and higher, is the coldest climate zone. Temperatures rarely rise above 10 °C (50 °F) in the warmest month. The climates of the polar regions are referred to as the *polar climates*. There are three types of polar zone subclimates: subarctic climates, tundra climates, and polar ice cap climates.

21 Summarize Fill in the table for either the factor that affects climate or the effect on climate the given factor has.

Factor	Effect on climate
Latitude	
	Cooler temperatures as you travel up a tall mountain
Winds	
	Moderates weather so that highs and lows are less extreme
Surface ocean currents	
	Impacts wind patterns and the transfer of energy in an area

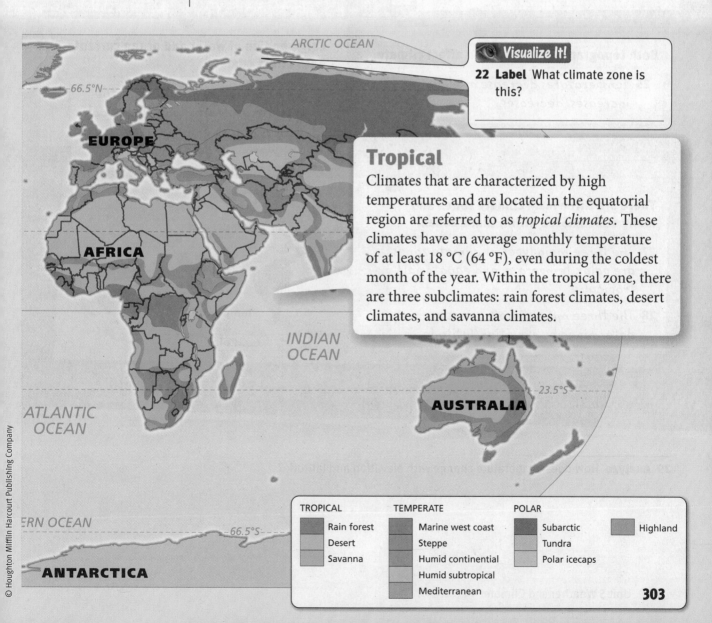

Visualize It!

22 Label What climate zone is this?

_____

Tropical

Climates that are characterized by high temperatures and are located in the equatorial region are referred to as *tropical climates*. These climates have an average monthly temperature of at least 18 °C (64 °F), even during the coldest month of the year. Within the tropical zone, there are three subclimates: rain forest climates, desert climates, and savanna climates.

ARCTIC OCEAN

66.5°N

EUROPE

AFRICA

INDIAN OCEAN

23.5°S

AUSTRALIA

ATLANTIC OCEAN

ERN OCEAN

66.5°S

ANTARCTICA

TROPICAL	TEMPERATE	POLAR	
Rain forest	Marine west coast	Subarctic	Highland
Desert	Steppe	Tundra	
Savanna	Humid continential	Polar icecaps	
	Humid subtropical		
	Mediterranean		

303

© Houghton Mifflin Harcourt Publishing Company

Visual Summary

To complete this summary, circle the correct word or phrase. Then, use the key below to check your answers. You can use this page to review the main concepts of the lesson.

Climate

Temperature and precipitation are used to describe climate.

23 Climate is the characteristic weather conditions in a place over a short/long period.

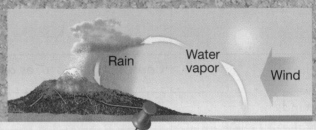

Rain   Water vapor   Wind

Winds transfer energy and moisture to new places.

24 Winds can affect the amount of precipitation in/elevation of an area.

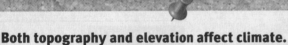

Both topography and elevation affect climate.

25 Temperatures decrease as elevation increases/decreases.

Large bodies of water and ocean currents both affect climate.

26 Large bodies of water affect the climate of nearby land when cool waters absorb energy as heat from the warm air/cold land.

There are three main climate zones and many subclimates within those zones.

27 The three main types of climate zones are polar, temperate, and equatorial/tropical.

28 The three main climate zones are determined by elevation/latitude.

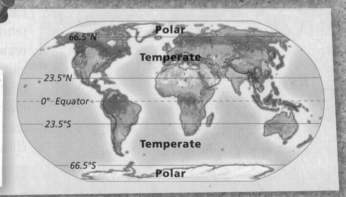

66.5°N   Polar
          Temperate
23.5°N
0° Equator
23.5°S
          Temperate
66.5°S   Polar

29 **Analyze** How does temperature change with elevation and latitude?

Lesson Review

Vocabulary

In your own words, define the following terms.

1 topography

_____

_____

2 climate

_____

_____

Key Concepts

Fill in the table below.

Factor	Effect on Climate
3 Identify Latitude	
4 Identify Elevation	
5 Identify Large bodies of water	
6 Identify Wind	

7 Explain What provides Great Britain with a moderate climate? How?

_____

_____

_____

8 Identify What are two characteristics used to describe the climate of an area?

Critical Thinking

Use the image below to answer the following question.

9 Explain Location A receives nearly 200 cm of rain each year, while Location B receives only 30 cm. Explain why Location A gets so much more rain. Use the words *rain shadow* and *precipitation* in your answer.

_____

_____

_____

_____

_____

_____

10 Analyze What climate zone are you in if the temperatures are always very warm? Where is this zone located on Earth?

_____

11 Analyze How does the sun's energy affect the climate of an area?

_____

_____

_____

_____

_____

My Notes

Climate Change

ESSENTIAL QUESTION

What are the causes and effects of climate change?

By the end of this lesson, you should be able to describe climate change and the causes and effects of climate change.

Temperatures are rising in the Arctic. Warmer temperatures cause the ice sheets to freeze later and melt sooner. With less time on the ice to hunt for seals, polar bears are struggling to survive.

Virginia Science Standards of Learning

6.1 The student will demonstrate an understanding of scientific reasoning, logic, and the nature of science by planning and conducting investigations in which:

6.1.h data are analyzed and communicated through graphical representation.

6.6 The student will investigate and understand the properties of air and the structure and dynamics of Earth's atmosphere. Key concepts include:

6.6.d natural and human-caused changes to the atmosphere and the importance of protecting and maintaining air quality.

Engage Your Brain

1 Predict Check T or F to show whether you think each statement is true or false.

T　**F**

☐　☐　There have been periods on Earth when the climate was colder than the climate is today.

☐　☐　The ocean does not play a role in climate.

☐　☐　Earth's climate is currently warming.

☐　☐　Humans are contributing to changes in climate.

2 Describe Write your own caption relating this photo to climate change.

_____

_____

_____

Active Reading

3 Apply Many scientific terms, such as *greenhouse effect,* also have everyday meanings. Use context clues to write your own definition for the words *greenhouse* and *effect*.

Example sentence
The <u>greenhouse</u> is filled with tropical plants that are found in Central America.

greenhouse:

_____

_____

Example sentence
What are some of the <u>effects</u> of staying up too late?

effect:

_____

_____

_____

Vocabulary Terms

- ice age
- greenhouse effect
- global warming

4 Identify As you read, create a reference card for each vocabulary term. On one side of the card, write the term and its meaning. On the other side, draw an image that illustrates or makes a connection to the term. These cards can be used as bookmarks in the text so that you can refer to them while studying.

The Temps are a–**Changin'**

What are some natural causes of climate change?

The weather conditions in an area over a long period of time are called *climate*. Natural factors have changed Earth's climate many times during our planet's history. Natural changes in climate can be long-term or short-term.

Movement of Tectonic Plates

Tectonic plate motion has contributed to long-term climate change over billions of years. And Earth's plates are still moving!

The present continents once fit together as a single landmass called *Pangaea* (pan•JEE•uh). Pangaea began to break up about 200 million years ago. By 20 million years ago, the continents had moved close to their current positions. Some continents grew warmer as they moved closer to the equator. Other continents, such as Antarctica, moved to colder, higher latitudes.

The eruption of Mt. Pinatubo sent ash and gases as high as 34 km into the atmosphere.

Visualize It!

5 Infer Today, Antarctica is the coldest desert on Earth. But fossils of trees and dinosaurs have been found on this harsh continent. Explain how life could thrive on ancient Antarctica.

When   Antarctica
was   part of Pangaea
it was warm but when
it broke apart the poills
got frozen over

EURASIA

NORTH
AMERICA

Tethys Sea

SOUTH
AMERICA

AFRICA

INDIA

AUSTRALIA

ANTARCTICA

Antarctica was part of the supercontinent Pangaea about 250 million years ago. Antarctica is located at the South Pole today.

EURASIA

NORTH
AMERICA

AFRICA

PACIFIC
OCEAN

SOUTH
AMERICA

ATLANTIC
OCEAN

INDIAN
OCEAN

AUSTRALIA

ANTARCTICA

If you look closely at the current shapes of the continents, you can see how they once fit together to form Pangaea.

Climate Change After Mt. Pinatubo Eruption

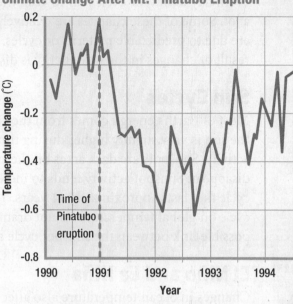

Source: Goddard Institute for Space Studies, NASA, 1997

This graph shows the *change* in average global temperature, not the actual temperature.

Particles in the Atmosphere

Short-term changes in climate can be due to natural events that send *particulates* into the atmosphere. Particulates are tiny, solid particles that are suspended in air or water. They absorb some of the sun's energy and reflect some of the sun's energy back into space. This process temporarily lowers temperatures on Earth.

Where do particulates come from? Asteroid impacts throw large amounts of dust into the atmosphere. Dust from the asteroid that struck near Mexico around 65 million years ago would have blocked the sun's rays. This reduction in sunlight may have limited photosynthesis in plants. The loss of plant life may have caused the food chain to collapse and led to dinosaur extinction.

Volcanic eruptions also release enormous clouds of ash and gases into the atmosphere. Particulates from large eruptions can circle Earth. The average global surface temperature fell by about 0.5 °C for several years after the 1991 eruption of Mt. Pinatubo in the Philippines. Twenty million tons of sulfur dioxide and 5 km³ of ash were blasted into the atmosphere. The sulfur-rich gases combined with water to form an Earth-cooling haze.

Active Reading **7 Describe** Give one example of a long-term and one example of a short-term change in climate caused by natural factors.

_____?_____

_____

_____

Visualize It!

6 Analyze What happened to global temperatures after the eruption of Mt. Pinatubo? How long did this effect last?

the temperatures fell about 0.5°C for several year

© Houghton Mifflin Harcourt Publishing Company • Image Credits:(t) ©StockTrek/Photodisc/Getty Images

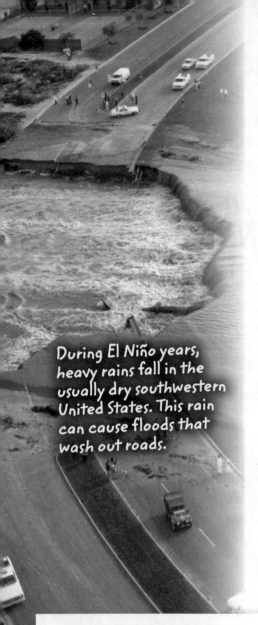

During El Niño years, heavy rains fall in the usually dry southwestern United States. This rain can cause floods that wash out roads.

What are some causes of repeating patterns of climate change?

From day to day, or even year to year, the weather can change quite a lot. Some of these changes are relatively unpredictable, but others are due to predictable patterns or cycles. These patterns are the result of changes in the way energy is distributed around Earth.

Sun Cycles

Most of Earth's energy comes from the sun. And the output from the sun is very slightly higher during times of higher sunspot activity. Sunspots are dark areas on the sun that appear and disappear. Sunspot activity tends to increase and decrease in a cycle that lasts approximately 11 years. The effect of this sunspot cycle on global temperatures is not dramatic. But studies show a possible link between the sunspot cycle and global rain patterns.

El Niño and La Niña

Changes in ocean temperature also affect climate. During El Niño years, ocean temperatures are higher than usual in the tropical Pacific Ocean. The warmer water causes changes in global weather patterns. Some areas are cooler and wetter than normal. Other areas are warmer and dryer than normal.

The opposite effect occurs during La Niña years. Ocean temperatures are cooler than normal in the equatorial eastern Pacific Ocean. El Niño and La Niña conditions usually alternate, and both can lead to conditions such as droughts and flooding.

Do the Math

8 Calculate About what percentage of years are El Niño years, with warmer than average ocean temperatures? About what percentage are La Niña years? About what percentage are neither El Niño or La Niña years?

El niño 50 %   La Niña   13

Cycles of El Niño and La Niña

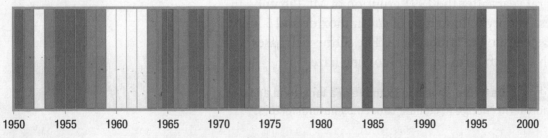

1950 1955 1960 1965 1970 1975 1980 1985 1990 1995 2000

- La Niña years
- El Niño years

Source: International Research Institute for Climate and Society, Columbia University, 2007

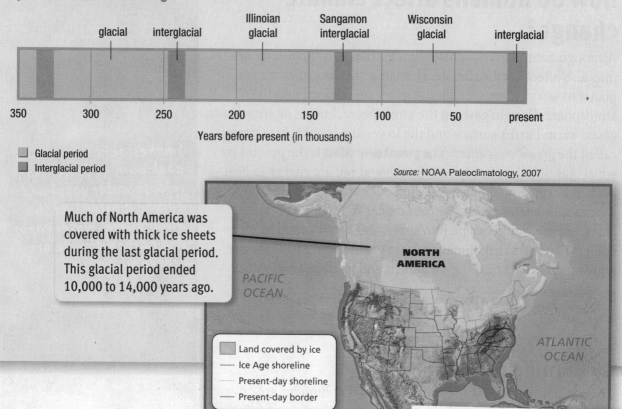

Visualize It!

During the last 2 million years, continental ice sheets have expanded far beyond the polar regions. There have been multiple advances of ice sheets (glacial periods) and retreats of ice sheets (interglacial periods). The timeline shows recent glacial and interglacial periods.

Cycles of the Recent Ice Age

Source: NOAA Paleoclimatology, 2007

Much of North America was covered with thick ice sheets during the last glacial period. This glacial period ended 10,000 to 14,000 years ago.

Ice Ages

The geological record shows that at different times Earth's climate has been both cooler *and* warmer than it is today. Earth's history contains multiple extremely cold periods when thick sheets of ice covered much of the continents. These periods are called *ice ages*. An **ice age** is a long period of cooling during which ice sheets spread beyond the polar regions. The exact cause of ice ages is not fully understood. Some hypotheses propose that ice ages include changes in Earth's orbit, shifts in the balance of incoming and outgoing solar radiation, and changes in heat exchange rates between the equator and the poles.

Geologic evidence indicates that ice ages occur over widely spaced intervals of time—approximately every 200 million years. Each ice age lasts for millions of years. The most recent ice age began about 2 million years ago, with its peak about 20,000 years ago. Large ice sheets still cover Greenland and Antarctica.

Active Reading **10 List** What are some possible causes of ice ages?

Global cooling

9 Infer Locate your home state on the map. Then, describe the climate your state likely experienced during the last glacial period.

It will mostly between 16 r20°F

© Houghton Mifflin Harcourt Publishing Company

Lesson 7 Climate Change **311**

Is It Getting HOTTER?

How do humans affect climate change?

Although natural events cause climate change, human activities may also affect Earth's climate. Human activities can cause the planet to warm when greenhouse gases are released into the atmosphere. Certain gases in the atmosphere, known as *greenhouse gases*, warm Earth's surface and the lower atmosphere by a process called the *greenhouse effect*. The **greenhouse effect** is the process by which gases in the atmosphere absorb and radiate energy as heat back to Earth. Greenhouse gases include carbon dioxide (CO_2), water vapor, methane, and nitrous oxide. Without greenhouse gases, energy would escape into space, and Earth would be colder. Two ways that humans release greenhouse gases into the atmosphere are by burning fossil fuels and by deforestation.

Active Reading 11 **List** What are four greenhouse gases?

Carbon dioxide water vapor methane nitrous oxicc

Smokestacks from a coal-burning power plant release water vapor and carbon dioxide into the atmosphere. Water vapor and carbon dioxide are greenhouse gases.

By Burning Fossil Fuels

There is now evidence to support the idea that humans are causing a rise in global CO_2 levels. Burning fossil fuels, such as gasoline and coal, adds greenhouse gases to the atmosphere. Since the 1950s, scientists have measured increasing levels of CO_2 and other greenhouse gases in the atmosphere. During this same period, the average global surface temperature has also been rising.

Correlation is when two sets of data show patterns that can be related. Both CO_2 level and average global surface temperature have been increasing over the same period of time, as shown by the graphs on the following page. So, there is a correlation between CO_2 levels in Earth's atmosphere and rising temperature. However, even though the two trends can be correlated, this does not show causation, or that one causes the other. In order to show causation, an explanation for how one change causes another has to be accepted. The explanation lies in the greenhouse effect. CO_2 is a greenhouse gas. An increase in greenhouse gases will warm Earth's surface and lower atmosphere. As greenhouse gas levels in the atmosphere have been rising, Earth's surface temperatures have been increasing, and so have temperatures in Earth's lower atmosphere. This shows that it is likely that rising CO_2 levels are causing global warming.

By Deforestation

Some processes, such as burning fossil fuels, add CO_2 and other carbon-based gases to the atmosphere. Processes that emit carbon into the atmosphere are called *carbon sources*. Processes such as the growth of plants and trees remove carbon from the atmosphere. Processes that remove carbon from the atmosphere are called *carbon sinks*. Deforestation is the mass removal of trees for farming, timber, and land development. The loss of trees represents the loss of an important carbon sink. Deforestation often includes the burning of trees, which is another source of carbon dioxide. So deforestation affects the amount of carbon in the atmosphere by converting a carbon sink into a carbon source.

Scientists think that the deforestation of rain forests plays a large role in greenhouse gas emissions. Tropical deforestation is thought to release 1.5 billion tons of carbon each year.

Active Reading **12 Describe** How does deforestation affect the amount of carbon dioxide that is in the atmosphere?

_____

_____

Deforestation is one of the leading sources of greenhouse gases.

Visualize It!

13 Apply Based on the trend shown in the graph, how do you expect CO_2 levels to change over the next 20 years?

_____

_____

14 Explain Describe the changes in average global temperature during the years represented by the CO_2 graph.

_____

_____

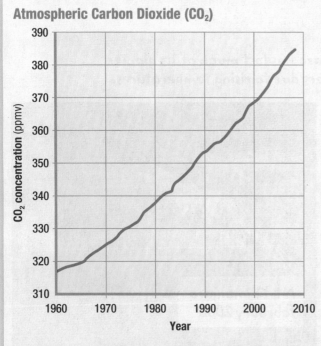

Atmospheric Carbon Dioxide (CO_2)

Source: Scripps Institution of Oceanography, UCSD, 2010

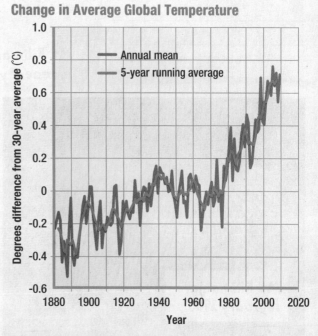

Change in Average Global Temperature

— Annual mean
— 5-year running average

Source: Goddard Institute for Space Studies, NASA, 2010

What are some predicted effects of climate change?

Data show that the world's climate has been warming in recent years. **Global warming** is a gradual increase in average global temperature. Global warming will affect global weather patterns, global sea level, and life on Earth.

Effects on the Atmosphere

Studies show that the average global surface temperature has increased by about 0.3 °C to 0.8 °C over the last 100 years. Even small changes in temperature can greatly affect weather and precipitation. Scientists predict that warming will generate more severe weather. Predictions suggest that storms will be more powerful and occur more frequently. It has also been predicted that as much as half of Earth's surface may be affected by drought.

Effects on the Hydrosphere and Cryosphere

Much of the ice on Earth occurs in glaciers in mountains, arctic sea ice, and ice sheets that cover Greenland and Antarctica. As temperatures increase, some of this ice will melt. A 2010 report observed record-setting hot temperatures, which resulted in record ice melt of the Greenland ice sheet.

When ice on land melts, global sea level rises because water flows into the ocean. Global sea level rose by 10 to 20 cm during the 1900s. Scientists project that sea level may rise 60 cm by 2100. Higher sea level is expected to increase flooding in coastal areas, some of which are highly populated. New York City; Shanghai, China; and Mumbai, India; are some cities that could be affected.

15 Infer How do melting ice caps and glaciers affect sea level?

_____

_____

_____

Mt. Kilimanjaro has lost much of its glacier in recent years due to rising temperatures.

Mt. Kilimanjaro
February 1993

Mt. Kilimanjaro
February 2000

A warmer climate may force some species northward, including sugar maples.

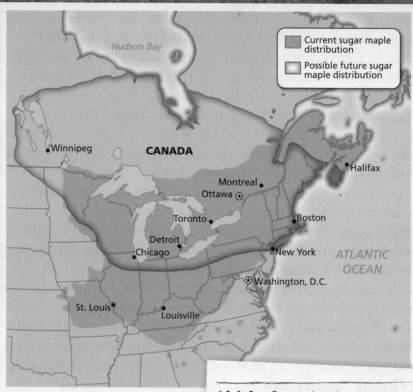

Current sugar maple distribution

Possible future sugar maple distribution

Hudson Bay

CANADA

Winnipeg

Halifax

Montreal
Ottawa ⊗

Toronto

Boston

Detroit
Chicago

New York

ATLANTIC
OCEAN

⊗ Washington, D.C.

St. Louis

Louisville

Effects on the Biosphere

Active Reading **17 Summarize** Underline some of the effects of predicted climate change on the biosphere.

Scientists predict that global warming will change ecosystems. These changes may threaten the survival of many plant and animal species. Some species may move to cooler areas or even go extinct. Some butterflies, foxes, and alpine plants have already moved north to cooler climates. In Antarctica, emperor penguin populations could be reduced by as much as 95 percent by the end of this century if sea ice loss continues at its current rate. On the other hand, some species may benefit from expanded habitats in a warmer world.

Changes in temperature and precipitation will affect crops and livestock. If Earth warms more than a few degrees Celsius, many of the world's farms could suffer. Higher temperatures, reduced rainfall, and severe flooding can reduce crop production. Changes in weather will especially affect developing countries with large rural areas, such as countries in South Asia. A less severe warming would actually help agriculture in some regions by lengthening the growing season.

Warmer temperatures could increase the number of heat-related deaths and deaths from certain diseases, such as malaria. However, deaths associated with extreme cold could decrease.

16 Infer Some plant home ranges are shifting northward due to regional warming. What might happen to plant populations that are unable to spread northward?

_____
_____
_____
_____

How are climate predictions made?

Instruments have been placed in the atmosphere, in the oceans, on land, and in space to collect climate data. NASA now has more than a dozen spacecraft in orbit that are providing continuous data on Earth's climate. These data are added to historical climate data that are made available to researchers at centers worldwide. The data are used to create climate models. *Climate models* use mathematical formulas to describe how different variables affect Earth's climate. Today, there are about a dozen climate models that can be used to simulate different parts of the Earth system and the interactions that take place between them.

When designing a model to predict future climate change, scientists first model Earth's current climate system. If the model does a good job describing current conditions, then the variables are changed to reflect future conditions. Scientists usually run the model multiple times using different variables.

Climate models are the means by which scientists predict the effects of an increase in greenhouse gases on future global climate. These models use the best data available about the ways in which Earth's systems interact. No climate model can perfectly reproduce the system that is being modeled. However, as our understanding of Earth's systems improves, models of climate change are becoming more accurate.

Visualize It!

18 Predict As Earth is warming, the oceans are rising. This is due to both melting ice and the expansion of water as it warms. Predict what the change in sea level will be by the year 2020 if the current trend continues. You may draw on the graph to extend the current trend.

_____

_____

Sea level has been rising steadily since the late 1800s. By the year 2000, global average sea level had risen 50 mm above mean sea level, represented by 0 on the graph.

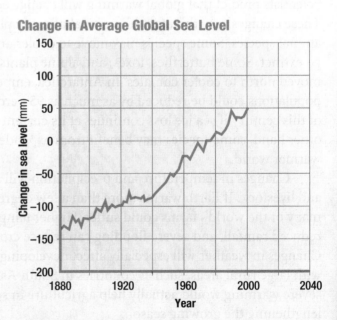

Change in Average Global Sea Level

Source: National Climatic Data Center, NOAA, 2007

Think Clean and Green

How can people reduce their impact on climate change?

People can take action to reduce climate change and its effects. Countries are working together to reduce their impact on Earth's climate. Communities and individuals are also doing their part to reduce greenhouse gas emissions.

Reduce Greenhouse Gas Emissions

The Kyoto Protocol, an international environmental agreement to reduce greenhouse gas emissions, was adopted in 1997. The Kyoto Protocol is the only existing international treaty in which nations have agreed to reduce CO_2 emissions. As of 2010, 191 countries had signed the protocol. At present, the Kyoto Protocol faces many complex challenges. One of the greatest challenges is that developing nations, which will be the largest future sources of CO_2 emissions, did not sign the protocol.

Individuals can reduce their impact on climate by conserving energy, increasing energy efficiency, and reducing the use of fossil fuels. Greenhouse gas emissions can be reduced by driving less and by switching to nonpolluting energy sources. Simple energy conservation solutions include turning off lights and replacing light bulbs. Recycling and reusing products also reduce energy use.

For most materials, recycling uses less energy than making products from scratch. That means less greenhouse gases are emitted.

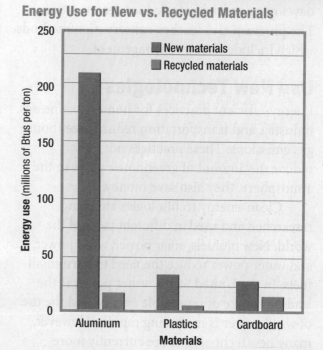

Do the Math | You Try It

19 Calculate How much energy is saved by using recycled aluminum to make new aluminum cans instead of making aluminum cans from raw materials?

_____

_____

20 Calculate By what percentage does recycling aluminum reduce energy use?

_____

_____

_____

Energy Use for New vs. Recycled Materials

Chart legend:
- ■ New materials
- ■ Recycled materials

Y-axis: Energy use (millions of Btus per ton), scale 0 to 250
X-axis: Materials — Aluminum, Plastics, Cardboard

Source: US EPA Solid Waste Management and Greenhouse Gases, 2002

- Reduce use of automobile.
- Use new, cleaner technologies.
- Plant a tree.

Reduce the Rate of Deforestation

Deforestation contributes up to 20 percent of greenhouse gases globally. Planting trees and supporting reforestation programs are ways that carbon sources can be balanced by carbon sinks. Another solution is to educate people about the importance of the carbon that is stored in forests for stabilizing climate. In 2008, the United Nations began a program called REDD, or *Reducing Emissions from Deforestation and Forest Degradation*. REDD offers incentives to developing countries to reduce deforestation. The program also teaches conservation methods, which include forestry management.

Use New Technologies

Energy-efficient practices for homes, businesses, industry, and transportation reduce greenhouse gas emissions. These practices not only reduce the amount of greenhouse gases in the atmosphere, they also save money.

Clean-energy technologies are being researched and used in different parts of the world. New biofuels, solar power, wind power, and water power reduce the need to burn fossil fuels. In the United States, water power is the leading source of renewable energy, and the use of wind power is increasing rapidly. However, many new technologies are currently more expensive than fossil fuels.

21 Summarize Use the table to summarize ways in which sources of greenhouse gases in the atmosphere can be reduced.

Sources of greenhouse gases	Ways to reduce greenhouse gases
cars	Walk or use bikes more often.

What are some economic and political issues related to climate change?

🔖 **Active Reading** **22 Identify** Underline some of the economic and political issues that are related to climate change.

Climate change affects the entire Earth, no matter where greenhouse gases are produced. This makes climate change a global issue. The scientific concerns that climate change poses are not the only issues that have to be taken into account. There are economic and political issues involving climate change that are equally important.

Climate change is an economic issue. The cost of climate change includes the costs of crop failure, storm damage, and human disease. However, developing countries may not be able to afford technologies needed to reduce human impact on climate.

Climate change is also a political issue. Political action can lead to regulations that reduce greenhouse gas emissions. However, these laws may be challenged by groups who disagree with the need for change or disagree about what needs to change. No matter what choices are made to handle the challenges of climate change, it will take groups of people working together to make a difference.

Think Outside the Book Inquiry

23 Apply Research a recent extreme weather event from anywhere in the world. How might this event be related to climate change? Present your findings to the class as a news report or poster.

Climate change may make unusual weather the new norm. Rome, Italy, was brought to a standstill by unusually cold and snowy weather in 2010.

In Australia, years of unusually dry and hot weather led to devastating forest fires in 2009. Australia also suffered damaging floods in 2010.

24 Predict What are the possible economic and social consequences of unusually warm weather in a cold climate or unusually cool weather in a warm climate?

_____

_____

_____

Visual Summary

To complete this summary, fill in the blanks with the missing word or phrase. Then, use the key below to check your answers. You can use this page to review the main concepts of the lesson.

Natural factors have changed Earth's climate many times during Earth's history.

25 _____ have moved across Earth's surface over time and once formed a supercontinent called Pangaea.

Global warming affects many of Earth's systems.

27 If average global surface temperature continues to rise, then severe storms may become more _____

Climate Change

Greenhouse gases have a warming effect on the surface of Earth.

26 Scientists think that there is a connection between rising levels of _____ and rising _____

There are steps that people can take to reduce their impact on climate change.

28 People can reduce their impact on climate change by reducing greenhouse emissions and deforestation, and by _____

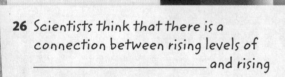

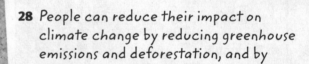

Sample answers: 25 Tectonic plates; 26 CO$_2$ (carbon dioxide); global temperatures; 27 frequent; 28 using new technologies

29 **Synthesize** How can burning fossil fuels cause global warming?

Lesson Review

Vocabulary

Fill in the blank with the term that best completes the following sentences.

1 _____ is a gradual increase in average global surface temperature.

2 A long period of climate cooling during which ice sheets spread beyond the polar regions is called a(n) _____

3 The warming of Earth's surface and lower atmosphere that occurs when greenhouse gases absorb and reradiate energy is called the _____

Key Concepts

4 Identify What are some natural events that have caused changes in Earth's climate?

_____
_____
_____
_____
_____
_____

5 Identify What are some predicted effects of climate change linked to global warming?

_____
_____
_____
_____
_____
_____
_____

6 Summarize List ways in which humans can reduce the rate of climate change.

_____
_____
_____
_____
_____
_____
_____

Critical Thinking

Use the graph to answer the following questions.

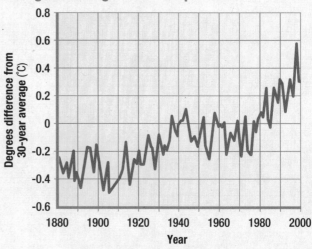

Change in Average Global Temperature

Source: Goddard Institute for Space Studies, NASA, 2010

7 Analyze Describe the trend shown in this graph. Why is it helpful to have many decades of data to make a graph such as this?

_____
_____
_____
_____

8 Infer What might cause average global surface temperature to rise and fall from year to year?

_____
_____
_____
_____

9 Infer Why might some countries be more reluctant than others to take steps to reduce levels of greenhouse gases?

_____
_____
_____
_____
_____
_____

My Notes

Unit 5 〉 Big Idea 〉 Air pressure, temperature, air movement, and humidity in the atmosphere affect both weather and climate.

Lesson 1
ESSENTIAL QUESTION
What is weather and how can we describe types of weather conditions?

Describe elements of weather and explain how they are measured.

Lesson 2
ESSENTIAL QUESTION
How do clouds form, and how are clouds classified?

Describe the formation and classification of clouds.

Lesson 3
ESSENTIAL QUESTION
How do the water cycle and other global patterns affect local weather?

Explain how global patterns in Earth's system influence weather.

Lesson 4
ESSENTIAL QUESTION
How can humans protect themselves from hazardous weather?

Describe the major types of hazardous weather and the ways human beings can protect themselves from hazardous weather and from sun exposure.

Lesson 5
ESSENTIAL QUESTION
What tools do we use to predict weather?

Understand how meteorologists forecast the weather using weather maps and other data.

Lesson 6
ESSENTIAL QUESTION
How is climate affected by energy from the sun and variations on Earth's surface?

Describe the main factors that affect climate and explain how scientists classify climates.

Lesson 7
ESSENTIAL QUESTION
What are the causes and effects of climate change?

Describe climate change and the causes and effects of climate change.

Think Outside the Book

2 Synthesize Choose one of these activities to help synthesize what you have learned in this unit.

☐ Using what you learned in lessons 1, 2, 3, and 4, present a poster about water vapor and the formation of severe weather.

☐ Using what you learned in lessons 5, 6, and 7, explain in a short essay how weather predictions might change if additional greenhouse gases in Earth's atmosphere caused Earth to warm by several degrees C.

Connect ESSENTIAL QUESTIONS
Lessons 3 and 5

1 Synthesize Explain how a change in air pressure can signal a change in weather.

_____

_____

Unit 5 Review

Name _____

Vocabulary

Fill in each blank with the term that best completes the following sentences.

1 _____ is the ratio of the amount of water vapor in the air to the amount of water vapor needed to reach saturation at a given temperature.

2 White, thin clouds with a feathery appearance are called _____.

3 A(n) _____ is a violently rotating column of air stretching from a cloud to the ground.

4 _____ is the characteristic weather conditions in an area over a long period of time.

5 A long period of climate cooling during which ice sheets spread beyond the polar regions is called a(n) _____.

Key Concepts

Read each question below, and circle the best answer.

6 The graph shows the temperatures recorded at school one day.

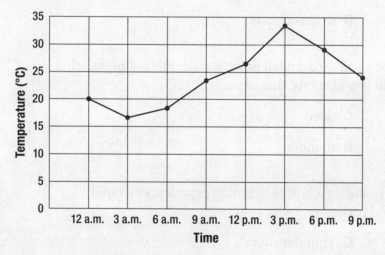

What can these temperature data tell us?

A The highest temperature of the day occurred at 6 p.m.

B The amount of water vapor in the air changed that day.

C The amount of energy as heat in the air changed during that day.

D The climate changed between 3 a.m. and 3 p.m.

7 Which of these types of weather data is measured using a barometer?

A air pressure

B precipitation

C relative humidity

D wind speed

8 The picture below shows the four parts of the water cycle labeled A, B, C, and D.

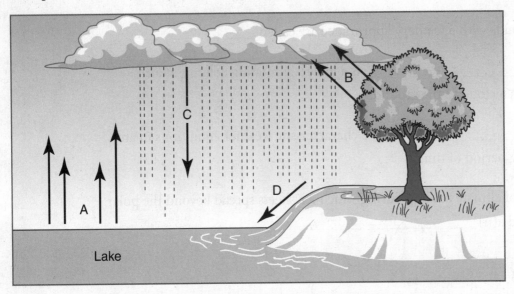

If rain (C) is falling as part of a thunderstorm, which type of clouds are shown?

A altostratus clouds

B cirrus clouds

C cumulonimbus clouds

D stratus clouds

9 If it rained all day but stopped and then cooled down considerably at night, what weather phenomenon would you likely see that night?

A fog

B hail

C sleet

D thunder

10 What results when air surrounding a bolt of lightning experiences a rapid increase in temperature and pressure?

A A tornado forms.

B Hail forms.

C Thunder sounds.

D Rain condenses.

11 Refer to the regions A, B, C, and D shown on the U.S. map below.

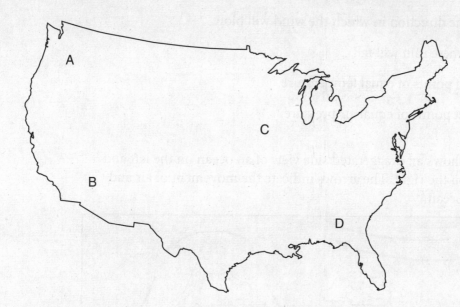

In which of these directions is the jet stream most likely to flow?

A from D to C   **C** from C to A

B from A to C   **D** from C to B

12 Which of the following should you do to escape a flood?

A Seek a high, safe point above the floodwaters and wait for assistance.

B Walk carefully into the floodwaters to get to safety.

C Swim through the floodwaters until you find a safer place.

D Use a lifejacket or flotation device to help you wade through the floodwaters.

13 What are the two main factors that determine climate?

A temperature and wind

B temperature and precipitation

C air pressure and humidity

D wind and precipitation

14 What do the curved concentric lines on weather forecast maps show?

   A The lines show the direction in which the wind will blow.

   B The lines show where rain will fall.

   C The lines connect points of equal temperature.

   D The lines connect points of equal air pressure.

15 The picture below shows an exaggerated side view of an ocean on the left and a mountain range on the right. The arrows indicate the movement of air and moisture from the ocean.

Which region is most likely to have a dry, desert-like climate?

   A region R   **C** region T

   B region S   **D** region W

16 Which of these is not a currently predicted effect of global climate change?

   A rising sea levels

   B increased precipitation everywhere on the globe

   C reduction in Arctic sea ice

   D more severe storms

17 The graph below shows the amount of carbon dioxide measured in the atmosphere between about 1960 and 2005.

Amount of Atmospheric Carbon Dioxide per Year

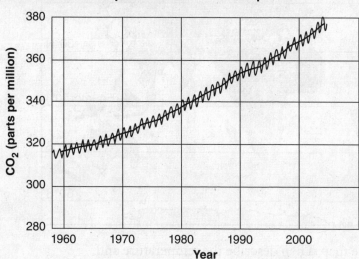

What conclusion can you make from the data displayed in the graph?

A The amount of carbon dioxide in the atmosphere more than doubled between 1960 and 2000.

B An increasing number of cars on the road between 1960 and 2000 caused an increase in carbon dioxide levels in the atmosphere.

C There was an overall increase in the level of carbon dioxide in the atmosphere between 1960 and 2000.

D Average global temperatures increased between 1960 and 2000 as a result of the increase in carbon dioxide in the atmosphere.

Critical Thinking

Answer the following questions in the space provided.

18 Explain generally what makes a cloud form.

_____

_____

Describe one specific situation in which a cloud can form.

_____

_____

19 Explain two ways in which forecasters collect weather data.

_____

_____

20 The map below shows the three different climate zones on Earth.

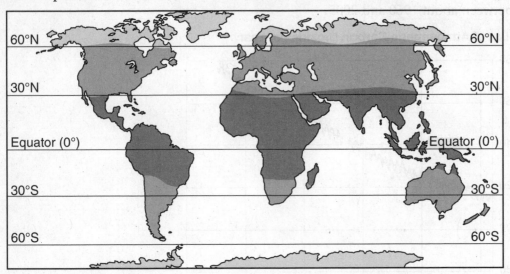

Label each climate zone on the map. Then describe the temperature and precipitation typical of each zone.

_____

_____

_____

Explain how latitude affects the climate of each zone.

_____

_____

_____

Connect ESSENTIAL QUESTIONS
Lessons 1, 2, 3, 4, and 6

Answer the following question in the space provided.

21 Even if you do not live on a coast, the movement of water in the oceans and water vapor in the atmosphere over the oceans does affect your weather. Using what you learned in lessons 1, 2, 3, 4, and 6, describe how the water cycle and the global movement of water through ocean currents and winds affect the climate of your local region.

_____

_____

_____

_____

_____

Water on Earth

Big Idea

Water moves through Earth's atmosphere, oceans, and land and is essential for life on Earth.

Waterfalls show the important role gravity plays in moving Earth's water.

What do you think?

Fresh water is found in ponds, lakes, streams, rivers, and underground aquifers. Where does the water in your school come from?

Humans rely on water to stay healthy.

Unit 6

Water on Earth

CITIZEN SCIENCE

Conserving Water

Fresh water evaporates into the air and then condenses to form clouds. It falls from the sky as precipitation and then flows over Earth's surface in streams and rivers. It seeps underground through soil and rocks. Fresh water makes up only a small fraction of Earth's water and is not evenly distributed.

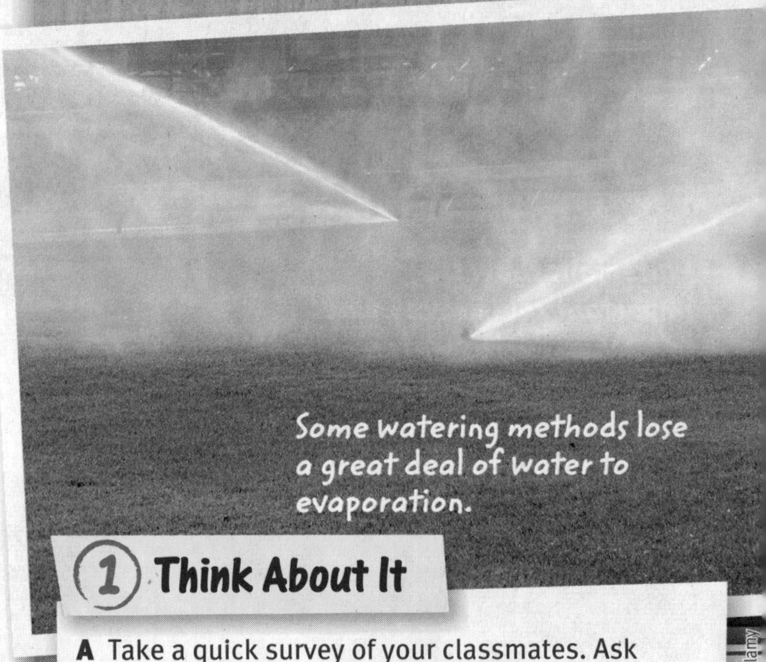

Some watering methods lose a great deal of water to evaporation.

1 Think About It

A Take a quick survey of your classmates. Ask them where the fresh water they use every day at home and at school comes from.

____

____

____

B Ask your classmates to identify different uses of water at your school.

____

____

____

② Ask a Question

How do you conserve water?

Water is an essential resource for everyone, but it is a limited resource. What are some ways that your school may be wasting water?

_____

_____

_____

_____

_____

_____

_____

_____

_____

Xeriscaping is a method of landscaping by using plants that require less water.

③ Make a Plan

A Make a list of five ways in which the school can conserve water.

_____

_____

_____

_____

_____

B In the space below, sketch out a design for a pamphlet or a poster that you can place in the hallways to promote water conservation at your school.

Take It Home

Take a pamphlet or a poster home. With an adult, talk about ways in which water can be conserved in and around your home.

Water and Its Properties

ESSENTIAL QUESTION

What makes water so important?

By the end of this lesson, you should be able to describe water's structure, its properties, and its importance to Earth's systems.

Not all liquids form round droplets, but water does. Water's unique properties have to do with the way water molecules interact.

Virginia Science Standards of Learning

6.5 The student will investigate and understand the unique properties and characteristics of water and its roles in the natural and human-made environment. Key concepts include:

6.5.a water as the universal solvent;

6.5.b the properties of water in all three phases; and

6.5.e the importance of water for agriculture, power generation, and public health.

Engage Your Brain

1 Predict Check T or F to show whether you think each statement is true or false.

    T   F

☐   ☐   Most of the water on Earth is fresh water.

☐   ☐   Water exists in three different states on Earth.

☐   ☐   Water can dissolve many different substances, such as salt.

☐   ☐   Flowing water can be used to generate electricity.

2 Identify The drawing below shows a water molecule. What do each of the three parts represent?

_____

_____

_____

 Active Reading

3 Synthesize You can often define an unknown word if you know the meaning of its word parts. Use the word parts and sentence below to make an educated guess about the meaning of the word *cohesion*.

Word part	Meaning
co-	with, together
-hesion	sticking, joined

Example sentence
When water forms droplets, it is displaying the property of <u>cohesion</u>.

Cohesion:

_____

_____

_____

Vocabulary Terms

- polarity
- cohesion
- adhesion
- specific heat
- solvent

4 Apply As you learn the definition of each vocabulary term in this lesson, create your own definition or sketch to help you remember the meaning of the term.

Watered Down

What are some of water's roles on Earth?

Water shapes Earth's surface and influences Earth's weather. Water is also vital for life. In fact, you are over 70% water. You depend on clean, fresh drinking water to maintain that 70% of you. But a limited amount of fresh water is available on Earth. Only 3% of Earth's water is drinkable. Of this 3% of water that is drinkable, over 75% is frozen in the polar icecaps and is not readily available for our use. Therefore, it is important that we protect our water resources.

Influencing Weather

 **6 Identify** As you read, underline four different forms of water that fall on Earth's surface.

All weather is related to water. Water constantly moves from Earth's surface to the atmosphere, where it may form clouds. Water falls back to Earth's surface again as <u>rain, snow, hail, or sleet</u>. Weather also depends on the amount of moisture in the air.

Shaping Earth's Surface

Over time, water can completely reshape a landscape. Water slowly wears away rock and carries away sediment and soil. Flowing rivers and pounding ocean waves are also examples of water shaping Earth's surface. Frozen water shapes Earth's surface, too. Glaciers, for example, scrape away rock and soil, depositing the sediment elsewhere when the glacier melts.

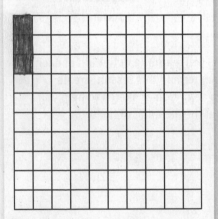

Do the Math

You Try It

5 Graph About 3% of water on Earth is fresh water. The rest is salt water. Fill out the percentage grid to show the percentage of fresh water on Earth.

© Houghton Mifflin Harcourt Publishing Company • Image Credits: ©Scott Barrow/Corbis

Supporting Life

Every living thing is largely made up of water, and nearly all biological processes use water. All of an organism's cellular chemistry depends on water. Water regulates temperature and helps transport substances. Without water, animals and plants would dry up and die.

For humans, clean water is vital for good health. People must have clean water to drink in order to survive. Contaminated water sources are a major public health problem in many countries. Contaminated water is also harmful to plants, animals, and can affect crops that provide food for humans.

Supporting Human Activities

Clean drinking water is necessary for all humans. Many humans use water at home for bathing, cleaning, and watering lawns and gardens.

More fresh water is used in industry than is used in homes. Over 20% of the fresh water used by humans is used for industrial purposes—to manufacture goods, cool power stations, clean industrial products, extract minerals, and generate energy by using hydroelectric dams.

More water is used for agriculture than industry. Most water used for agriculture is used to irrigate crops. It is also used to care for farm animals.

👁 Visualize It!

7 List List at least four roles of water in this scene.

Supporting life, baking
food, pushing sediments, shaping
earth's surface

Molecular Attraction

What is the structure of a water molecule?

Matter is made up of tiny particles called *atoms*. Atoms can join with other atoms to make molecules. A water molecule is made up of two hydrogen atoms and one oxygen atom—in other words, H_2O. Each hydrogen atom is linked to the oxygen atom, forming a shape like a cartoon mouse's ears sticking out from its head.

What makes water a polar molecule?

In a water molecule, the hydrogen atoms have a small positive charge. The oxygen atom has a small negative charge. So the water molecule has a partial positive charge at one end (mouse ears) and a partial negative charge at the other (mouse chin). Anything that has a positive charge at one end and negative charge at the other end is said to have **polarity**. A water molecule is therefore a polar molecule. In liquid water, the negative end of one water molecule is attracted to the positive end of another water molecule. Each water molecule interacts with the surrounding water molecules.

Visualize It!

8 Label Indicate the polarity of water by writing a + or − next to each atom that makes up the water molecule.

Because of polarity, the positive end of one water molecule interacts with the negative end of another molecule.

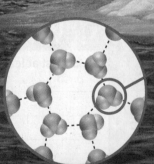

Water molecules have a positive end and a negative end.

What states of water occur on Earth?

📖 **Active Reading** **9 Identify** As you read, underline the three states of water that occur on Earth.

Most of Earth's water is in liquid form. Earth is the only planet in our solar system with abundant liquid water. Gravity causes liquid water to flow downhill and to rest in low-lying areas. As a result, Earth has rivers, lakes, and oceans. Like other liquids, liquid water takes the shape of whatever contains it.

Liquid water can change into an invisible gas called water vapor, or it can freeze into solid ice or snow. Like liquid water, water vapor and ice also have the chemical formula H_2O. So liquid water, water vapor, and ice are simply varieties, or states, of water. Conditions on Earth allow water to exist in these three different states. The three states of water can change into one another. When water changes state, it either takes up or releases energy.

Water vapor is a gas, so most water vapor is found in Earth's atmosphere. Water vapor cannot be seen. Clouds form when water vapor in the atmosphere condenses into liquid water droplets. Like all gases, water vapor expands or contracts to fill available space.

Unlike other liquids, water expands when it freezes. Molecules in liquid water, therefore, are closer together than are the molecules of solid water. In other words, there is more open space between the water molecules in ice. Due to this fact, solid water, or ice, is less dense than liquid water. So ice floats on liquid water.

Visualize It!

10 Describe Using your own words in the spaces provided, identify the state of water, and describe the properties of each state of water.

B

gas

A

Solid

C

liquid

The Universal Solvent

What are four properties of water?

The polarity of water molecules affects the properties of water. This is because water's polarity affects how water molecules interact with one another and with other types of molecules.

It Sticks to Itself

The property that holds molecules of a substance together is **cohesion**. Water molecules stick together tightly because of their polarity, so water has high cohesion. Because of cohesion, water forms droplets. And water poured gently into a glass can fill it above the rim because cohesion holds the water molecules together. Some insects can walk on still water because their weight does not break the cohesion of the water molecules.

It Sticks to Other Substances

The property that holds molecules of different substances together is **adhesion**. Polar substances other than water can attract water molecules more strongly than water molecules attract each other. These substances are called "wettable" because water adheres, or sticks, to them so tightly. Paper towels, for example, are wettable. Water drops roll off unwettable, or "waterproof," surfaces, which are made of non-polar molecules.

Visualize It!

11 **Label** Identify each photo as representing either adhesion or cohesion. Then write captions explaining the properties of water shown by each photo.

A

Cohesion

Because the water molecules are sticking together so that the animal can stick!

B

Adhesion

The water droplets are spread out over the web

These stalactites formed as water dripped down and left dissolved minerals behind.

It Can Absorb Large Amounts of Energy

The energy needed to heat a substance by a particular amount is called its **specific heat**. As water is warmed, its molecules are separated a little as the water expands. The attraction between polar water molecules means that separating them takes a great deal of energy, so the specific heat of water is very high. Because of its high specific heat, water can absorb more energy than many other substances can.

Warm water stores more energy than cold water does. And water vapor stores much more energy than liquid water does. The stored energy is released when warm water cools and when water vapor cools to form liquid. This ability of water to store and release heat is very important in weather and climate.

It Dissolves Many Things

A liquid that dissolves substances is called a **solvent**. Because of its polarity, water dissolves many substances. Therefore, water is often called the universal solvent. Salt, or NaCl, is a familiar substance that water dissolves.

Water as a solvent is very important to living things. Water transports vital dissolved substances through organisms. And most of the chemical reactions that take place inside organisms involve substances dissolved in water.

Only this one doesn't dissolve quickly in water.

12 Summarize What characteristic of water accounts for its properties of adhesion, cohesion, high specific heat, and nature as a solvent?

polarity

Think Outside the Book Inquiry

13 Apply Water dissolves a substance until the water becomes saturated and can dissolve no more of the substance. Starting with 100 ml water, determine how much salt or sugar can be dissolved before the solution is saturated.

Visual Summary

To complete this summary, fill in the blanks. Then use the key below to check your answers. You can use this page to review the main concepts of the lesson.

Water and Its Properties

Water plays many roles in Earth's systems.

14 Water has the following four major roles on Earth:

Influencing Weather

Shaping Earths surface

Supporting life

Use in human activity

Water has high cohesion, high adhesion to polar substances, high specific heat, and is a good solvent.

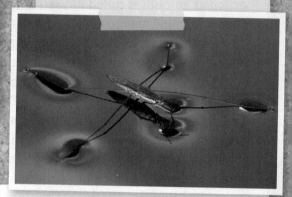

17 Water gets soaked up by a paper towel because of the property of

adhesion

18 Water is a commonly used solvent because it dissolves most substances.

Water is a polar molecule. On Earth, water may be found as a liquid, a solid, and a gas.

15 Water is made up of two hydrogen atoms and one oxygen atom.

16 Because water molecules have a negative end and a positive end, they have polarity

19 **Synthesize** Which properties of water make it useful for washing and cleaning? Explain your answer.

Lesson Review

Vocabulary

Fill in the blanks with the terms that best complete the following sentences.

1 Because a water molecule has a negative end and a positive end, it displays _Polarity_

2 Water's high _Spesific heat_ means that a large amount of energy is required to change the water's temperature.

3 When water molecules stick to the molecules of other substances, the molecules are displaying _adhesion_

Key Concepts

4 Summarize Why is water important to living things?

Because if we don't have water than fish one of our food sources would die

5 Describe Draw a water molecule in the space below. Label the atoms that make up the molecule, as well as their partial charges.

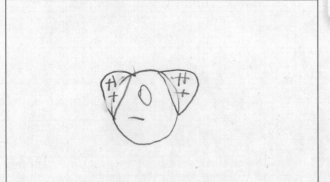

6 Explain Why does water have high cohesion?

because its polarity

Critical Thinking

Use the graph to answer the following questions.

Household Water Use in the United States

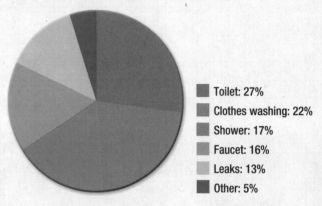

- Toilet: 27%
- Clothes washing: 22%
- Shower: 17%
- Faucet: 16%
- Leaks: 13%
- Other: 5%

Source: American Water Works Association Research Foundation, 1999

7 Identify In an average household, what is most water used for?

toilet

8 Infer What do you think are the three biggest changes a household could make to reduce its use of water?

turning off the the faucet stoping leaks and using the toilet less.

9 Explain Why do you think conserving fresh water might be important?

Because we don't have as much fresh water

10 Evaluate Which states of water can you find in your home? Explain.

Ice, tap water, steam

My Notes

3.1415926535936 45

Ocean Currents

© Houghton Mifflin Harcourt Publishing Company • Image Credits: ©Thomas Kitchin & Victoria Hurst/First Light/Getty Images

ESSENTIAL QUESTION

How does water move in the ocean?

By the end of this lesson, you should be able to describe the movement of ocean water, explain what factors influence this movement, and explain why ocean circulation is important in the Earth system.

This iceberg off the coast of Newfoundland broke off an Arctic ice sheet and drifted south on ocean surface currents.

Virginia Science Standards of Learning

6.3 The student will investigate and understand the role of solar energy in driving most natural processes within the atmosphere, the hydrosphere, and on Earth's surface. Key concepts include:

6.3.b the role of radiation and convection in the distribution of energy; and

6.3.c the motion of the atmosphere and the oceans.

6.5 The student will investigate and understand the unique properties and characteristics of water and its roles in the natural and human-made environment. Key concepts include:

6.5.d the ability of large bodies of water to store thermal energy and moderate climate.

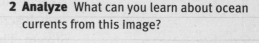

Lesson Labs

Quick Labs
- Modeling the Coriolis Effect
- The Formation of Deep Currents
- Can Messages Travel on Ocean Water?

Engage Your Brain

1 Predict Check T or F to show whether you think each statement is true or false.

T	F	
☐	☐	Ocean currents are always cold.
☐	☐	Continents affect the directions of currents.
☐	☐	Currents only flow near the surface of the ocean.
☐	☐	Wind affects currents.
☐	☐	The sun affects currents near the surface of the ocean.

This image shows sea ice caught in ocean currents.

2 Analyze What can you learn about ocean currents from this image?

_____

_____

_____

_____

Active Reading

3 Synthesize You can often define an unknown word if you know the meaning of its word parts. Use the word parts and sentence below to make an educated guess about the meaning of the word *upwelling*.

Word part	Meaning
up-	from beneath the ground or water
well	to rise

Example Sentence
In areas where <u>upwelling</u> occurs, plankton feed on nutrients from deep in the ocean.

upwelling:

_____

_____

Vocabulary Terms

- ocean current
- surface current
- Coriolis effect
- deep current
- convection current
- upwelling

4 Apply As you learn the definition of each vocabulary term in this lesson, create your own definition or sketch to help you remember the meaning of the term.

Going with the Flow

What are ocean currents?

The oceans contain streamlike movements of water called **ocean currents**. Ocean currents that occur at or near the surface of the ocean, caused by wind, are called **surface currents**. Most surface currents reach depths of about 100 m, but some go deeper. Surface currents also reach lengths of several thousand kilometers and can stretch across oceans. An example of a surface current is the Gulf Stream. The Gulf Stream is one of the strongest surface currents on Earth. The Gulf Stream transports, or moves, more water each year than is transported by all the rivers in the world combined.

Infrared cameras on satellites provide images that show differences in temperature. Scientists add color to the images afterward to highlight the different temperatures, as shown below.

What affects surface currents?

Surface currents are affected by three factors: continental deflections, the Coriolis effect, and global winds. These factors keep surface currents flowing in distinct patterns around Earth.

Active Reading

5 Identify As you read, underline three factors that affect surface currents.

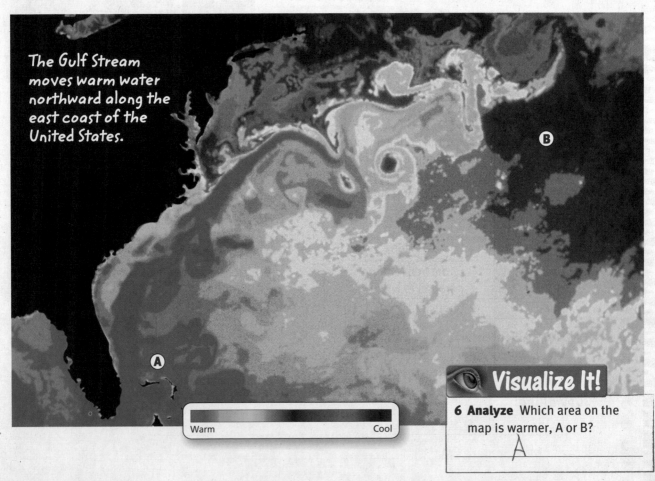

The Gulf Stream moves warm water northward along the east coast of the United States.

Warm — Cool

A

B

Visualize It!

6 Analyze Which area on the map is warmer, A or B?

A

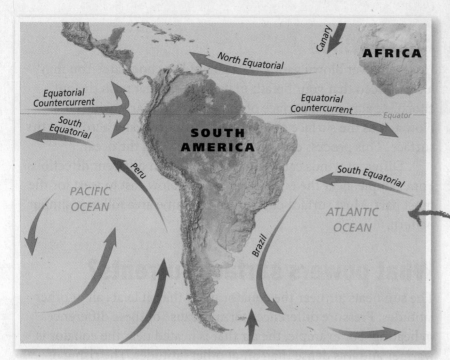

7 Identify Circle areas on the map where ocean currents have been deflected by a land mass.

Currents change direction when they meet continents.

Continental Deflections

If Earth's surface were covered only with water, surface currents would simply travel continually in one direction. However, water does not cover the entire surface of Earth. Continents rise above sea level over about one-third of Earth's surface. When surface currents meet continents, the currents are deflected and change direction. For example, the South Equatorial Current turns southward as it meets the coast of South America.

The Coriolis Effect

Earth's rotation causes all wind and ocean currents, except on the equator, to be deflected from the paths they would take if Earth did not rotate. The deflection of moving objects from a straight path due to Earth's rotation is called the **Coriolis effect** (kawr•ee•OH•lis ih•FEKT). Earth is spherical, so Earth's circumference at latitudes above and below the equator is shorter than the circumference at the equator. But the period of rotation is always 24 hours. Therefore, points on Earth near the equator travel faster than points closer to the poles.

The difference in speed of rotation causes the Coriolis effect. For example, wind and water traveling south from the North Pole actually go toward the southwest instead of straight south. Wind and water deflect to the right because the wind and water move east more slowly than Earth rotates beneath them. In the Northern Hemisphere, currents are deflected to the right. In the Southern Hemisphere, currents are deflected to the left.

The Coriolis effect is most noticeable for objects that travel over long distances, without any interruptions. Over short distances, the difference in Earth's rotational speed from one point to another point is not great enough to cause noticeable deflection.

In the Northern Hemisphere, currents are deflected to the right.

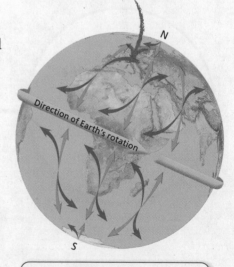

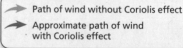
→ Path of wind without Coriolis effect
→ Approximate path of wind with Coriolis effect

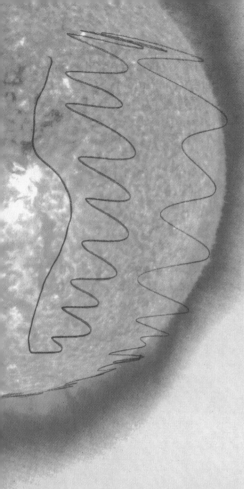

Global Winds

Have you ever blown gently on a cup of hot chocolate? You may have noticed that your breath makes ripples that push the hot chocolate across the surface of the liquid. Similarly, winds that blow across the surface of Earth's oceans push water across Earth's surface. This process causes surface currents in the ocean.

Different winds cause currents to flow in different directions. For example, near the equator, the winds blow east to west for the most part. Most surface currents in the same area follow a similar pattern.

What powers surface currents?

The sun heats air near the equator more than it heats air at other latitudes. Pressure differences form because of these differences in heating. For example, the air that is heated near the equator is warmer and less dense than air at other latitudes. The rising of warm air creates an area of low pressure near the equator. Pressure differences in the atmosphere cause the wind to form. So, the sun causes winds to form, and winds cause surface currents to form. Therefore, the major source of the energy that powers surface currents is the sun.

8 Analyze Fill in the cause-and-effect chart to show how the sun's energy powers surface ocean currents.

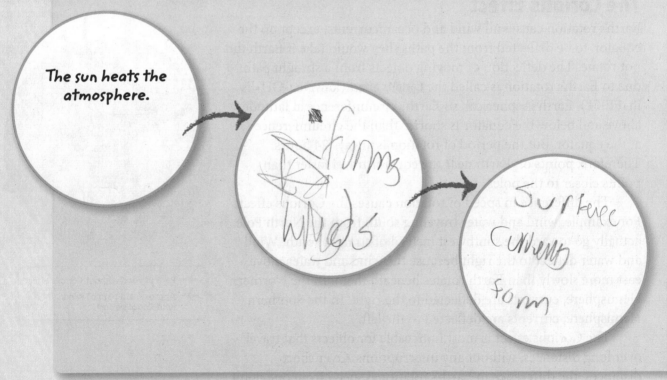

The sun heats the atmosphere. → forms winds → surface currents form

© Houghton Mifflin Harcourt Publishing Company • Image Credits: ©NASA/Photo Researchers, Inc.

Global Surface Winds

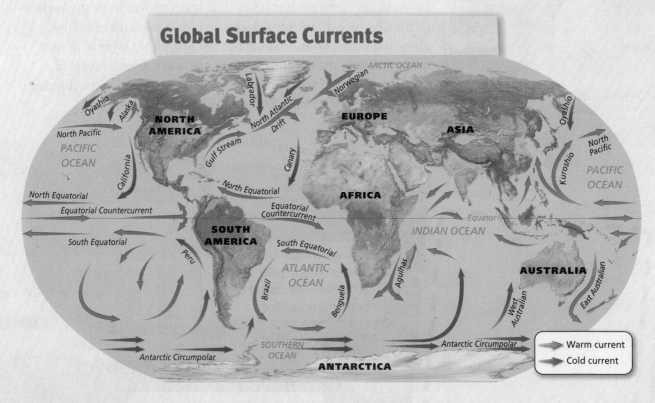

Global Surface Winds

NORTH AMERICA

EUROPE

ASIA

PACIFIC OCEAN

PACIFIC OCEAN

AFRICA

Equator

SOUTH AMERICA

INDIAN OCEAN

AUSTRALIA

ATLANTIC OCEAN

SOUTHERN OCEAN

ANTARCTICA

→ Ocean surface wind

Global Surface Currents

ARCTIC OCEAN

Oyashio

Alaska

Labrador

Norwegian

NORTH AMERICA

North Pacific

North Atlantic Drift

EUROPE

ASIA

Oyashio

PACIFIC OCEAN

Gulf Stream

Kuroshio

North Pacific

California

Canary

PACIFIC OCEAN

North Equatorial

North Equatorial

AFRICA

Equatorial Countercurrent

Equatorial Countercurrent

Equator

SOUTH AMERICA

INDIAN OCEAN

South Equatorial

South Equatorial

Peru

Brazil

ATLANTIC OCEAN

Agulhas

AUSTRALIA

Benguela

West Australian

East Australian

Antarctic Circumpolar

SOUTHERN OCEAN

Antarctic Circumpolar

Antarctic Circumpolar

ANTARCTICA

→ Warm current
→ Cold current

Visualize It!

9 Analyze Circle the same area on each map. Describe what you observe about these two areas.

_____

_____

_____

Current Events

How do deep currents form?

Active Reading

10 Identify As you read, underline the cause of deep currents.

Movements of ocean water far below the surface are called **deep currents**. Deep currents are caused by differences in water density. *Density* is the amount of matter in a given space or volume. The density of ocean water is affected by salinity (suh•LIN•ih•tee) and temperature. *Salinity* is a measure of the amount of dissolved salts or solids in a liquid. Water with high salinity is denser than water with low salinity. And cold water is denser than warm water. When water cools, it contracts and the water molecules move closer together. This contraction makes the water denser. When water warms, it expands and the water molecules move farther apart. The warm water is less dense, so it rises above the cold water.

When ocean water at the surface becomes denser than water below it, the denser water sinks. The water moves from the surface to the deep ocean, forming deep currents. Deep currents flow along the ocean floor or along the top of another layer of denser water. Because the ocean is so deep, there are several layers of water at any location in the ocean. The deepest and densest water in the ocean is Antarctic Bottom Water, near Antarctica.

Polar region

Convection current

B — Warm water from surface currents cools in polar regions, becomes denser, and sinks toward the ocean floor.

C — Deep currents carry colder, denser water in the deep ocean from polar regions to other parts of Earth.

Visualize It!

11 Illustrate Complete the drawing at part B on the diagram.

What are convection currents?

As you read about convection currents, refer to the illustration below. Surface currents and deep currents are linked in the ocean. Together they form convection currents. In the ocean, a **convection current** is a movement of water that results from density differences. Convection currents can be vertical, circular, or cyclical. Think of convection currents in the ocean as a conveyor belt. Surface currents make up the top part of the belt. Deep currents make up the bottom part of the belt. Water from a surface current may become a deep current in areas where water density increases. Deep current water then rises up to the surface in areas where the surface current is carrying low-density water away.

How do convection currents transfer energy?

Convection currents transfer energy. Water at the ocean's surface absorbs energy from the sun. Surface currents carry this energy to colder regions. The warm water loses energy to its surroundings and cools. As the water cools, it becomes denser and it sinks. The cold water travels along the ocean bottom. Then, the cold water rises to the surface as warm surface water moves away. The cold water absorbs energy from the sun, and the cycle continues.

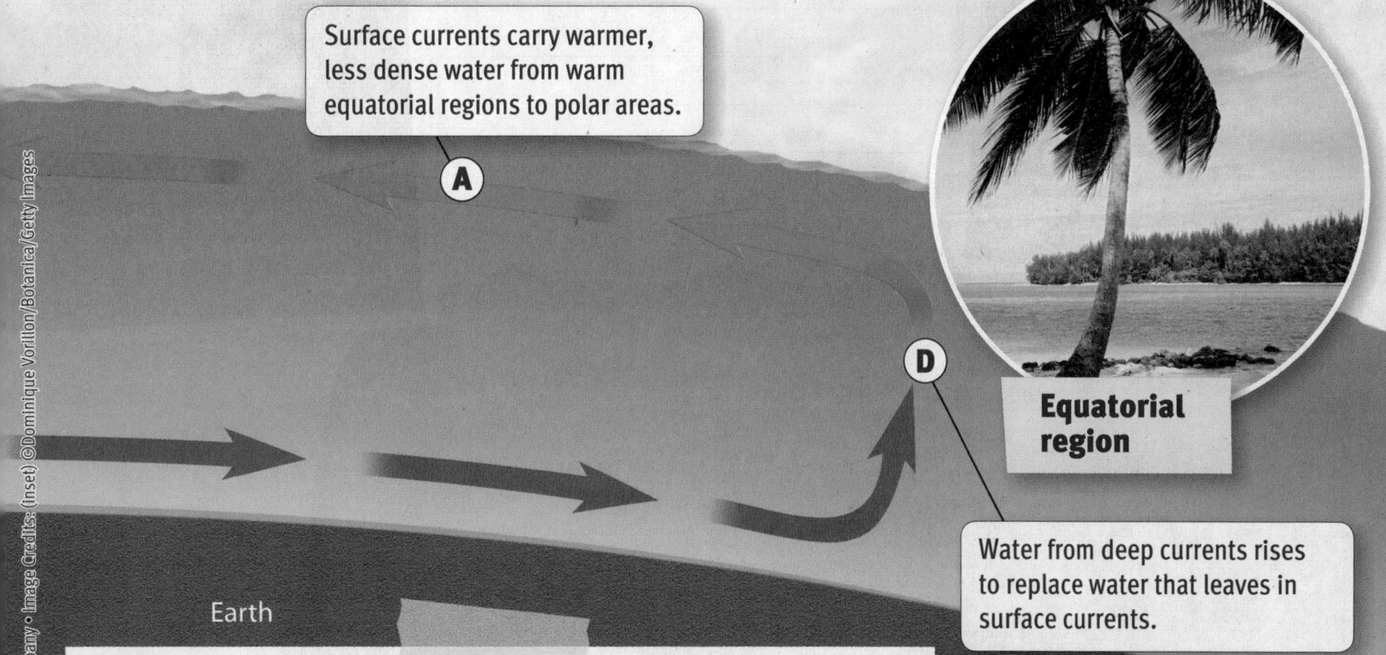

Surface currents carry warmer, less dense water from warm equatorial regions to polar areas.

A

D

Equatorial region

Water from deep currents rises to replace water that leaves in surface currents.

Earth

Note: Drawing is not to scale.

Think Outside the Book Inquiry

12 **Apply** Write an interview with a water molecule following a convection current. Be sure to include questions and answers. Can you imagine the temperature changes the molecule would experience?

Inquiry

13 **Inquire** How are convection currents important in the Earth system?

Energy

That's Swell!

Active Reading

14 Identify As you read, underline the steps that occur in upwelling.

What is upwelling?

At times, winds blow toward the equator along the northwest coast of South America and the west coast of North America. These winds cause surface currents to move away from the shore. The warm surface water is then replaced by cold, nutrient-rich water from the deep ocean in a process called **upwelling**. The deep water contains nutrients, such as iron and nitrate.

Upwelling is extremely important to ocean life. The nutrients that are brought to the surface of the ocean support the growth of phytoplankton (fy•toh•PLANGK•tuhn) and zooplankton. These tiny plants and animals are food for other organisms, such as fish and seabirds. Many fisheries are located in areas of upwelling because ocean animals thrive there. Some weather conditions can interrupt the process of upwelling. When upwelling is reduced, the richness of the ocean life at the surface is also reduced.

15 Predict What might happen to the fisheries if upwelling stopped?

they will go dave hill

The livelihood of these Peruvian fishermen depends on upwelling.

On the coast of California, upwelling sustains large kelp forests.

Wind

Warm surface water

During upwelling, cold, nutrient-rich water from the deep ocean rises to the surface.

Why It Matters

Hitching a Ride!

What do coconuts, plankton, and sea turtles have in common? They get free rides on ocean currents.

Sprouting Coconuts!
This sprouting coconut may be transported by ocean currents to a beach. This transport explains why coconut trees can grow in several areas.

World Travel
When baby sea turtles are hatched on a beach, they head for the ocean. They can then pick up ocean currents to travel. Some travel from Australia to South America on currents.

Fast Food
Diatoms are a kind of phytoplankton. They are tiny, one-celled plants that form the basis of the food chain. Diatoms ride surface currents throughout the world.

Extend

Inquiry

16 Identify List three organisms transported by ocean currents.

17 Research Investigate the Sargasso Sea. State why a lot of plastic collects in this sea. Find out whether any plastic collects on the shoreline nearest you.

18 Explain Describe how plastic and other debris can collect in the ocean by doing one of the following:
- make a poster
- write a song
- write a poem
- write a short story

Traveling the World

What do ocean currents transport?

Ocean water circulates through all of Earth's ocean basins. The paths are like the main highway on which ocean water flows. If you could follow a water molecule on this path, you would find that the molecule takes more than 1,000 years to return to its starting point! Along with water, ocean currents also transport dissolved solids, dissolved gases, and energy around Earth.

19 Identify As you read, underline the description of how energy reaches the poles.

20 Describe Choose a location on the map. Using your finger, follow the route you would take if you could ride a current. Describe your route. Include the direction you go and the landmasses you pass.

_____

_____

_____

_____

_____

Antarctica is not shown on this map, but the currents at the bottom of the map circulate around Antarctica.

Ocean Currents Transport Energy

Global ocean circulation is very important in the transport of energy in the form of heat. Remember that ocean currents flow in huge convection currents that can be thousands of kilometers long. These convection currents carry about 40% of the energy that is transported around Earth's surface.

Near the equator, the ocean absorbs a large amount of solar energy. The ocean also absorbs energy from the atmosphere. Ocean currents carry this energy from the equator toward the poles. When the warm water travels to cooler areas, the energy is released back into the atmosphere. Therefore, ocean circulation has an important influence on Earth's climate.

In the Pacific Ocean, surface currents transport energy from the tropics to latitudes above and below the equator.

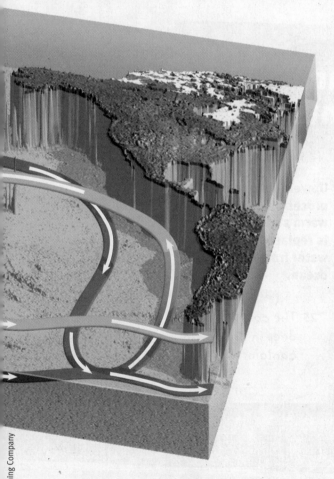

Ocean Currents Transport Matter

Besides water, ocean currents transport whatever is in the water. The most familiar dissolved solid in ocean water is sodium chloride, or table salt. Other dissolved solids are important to marine life. Ocean water contains many nutrients—such as nitrogen and phosphorus—that are important for plant and animal growth.

Ocean water also transports gases. Gases in the atmosphere are absorbed by ocean water at the ocean surface. As a result, the most abundant gases in the atmosphere—nitrogen, oxygen, argon, and carbon dioxide—are also abundant in the ocean. Dissolved oxygen and carbon dioxide are necessary for the survival of many marine organisms.

21 List Write three examples of matter besides water that are transported by ocean currents.

nitrogen

carbon d

Visual Summary

To complete this summary, draw an arrow to show each type of ocean current. Fill in the blanks with the correct word. Then use the key below to check your answers. You can use this page to review the main concepts of the lesson.

Surface currents are streamlike movements of water at or near the surface of the ocean.

22 The direction of a surface current is affected by ~~continental defelction that diseffects~~, and global minds

Deep currents are streamlike movements of ocean water located far below the surface.

23 Deep currents form where the density of ocean water increases.

Ocean Currents

A convection current in the ocean is any movement of matter that results from differences in density.

24 A convection current in the ocean transports matter and ~~enagy~~

Upwelling is the process in which warm surface water is replaced by cold water from the deep ocean.

25 The cold water from deep in the ocean contains ~~nutrients~~

Answers: 22 continental deflections, the Coriolis effect, global winds; 23 density; 24 energy; 25 nutrients

26 Describe State the two general patterns of global ocean circulation.

Lesson Review

Vocabulary

Fill in the blanks with the terms that best complete the following sentences.

1 _Ocean currents_ are streamlike movements of water in the ocean.

2 The _Coriolis_ causes currents in open water to move in a curved path rather than a straight path.

3 _upwelling_ causes cold, nutrient-rich waters to move up to the ocean's surface.

Key Concepts

4 Explain List the steps that show how the sun provides the energy for surface ocean currents.

_____

_____

_____

_____

_____

5 Explain State how a deep current forms.

_____

_____

_____

_____

_____

6 Describe Explain how a convection current transports energy around the globe.

_____

_____

_____

_____

7 List Write the three factors that affect surface ocean currents.

_____

_____

_____

Critical Thinking

Use this diagram to answer the following questions.

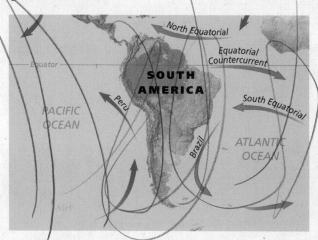

8 Apply Explain why the direction of the South Equatorial current changes.

_____

_____

_____

_____

9 Apply If South America were not there, explain how the direction of the South Equatorial current would be different.

_____

_____

_____

_____

_____

10 Apply Describe how surface currents would be affected if Earth did not rotate.

_____

_____

_____

_____

_____

_____

My Notes

Understanding a Bathymetric Map

Topographic maps are contour maps that illustrate the mountains, valleys, and hills on land. Bathymetric maps are contour maps that illustrate similar features on the ocean floor.

Tutorial

A bathymetric map uses curved contour lines that each represent a specific depth. Colors are also often used to show different depths. Because sea level is at 0 meters, increasing depths are shown by negative numbers. The bathymetric map below shows a part of the Mariana Trench, the deepest known part of the world's ocean.

Bathymetric Map

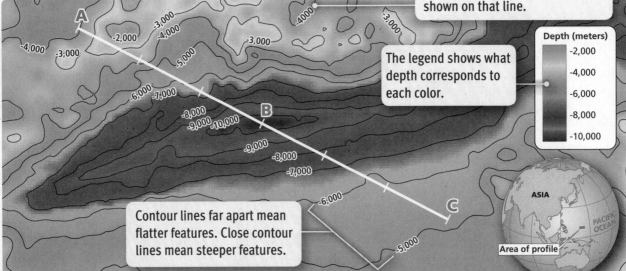

Every point along a contour line is at the same depth, the number shown on that line.

The legend shows what depth corresponds to each color.

Contour lines far apart mean flatter features. Close contour lines mean steeper features.

ASIA

PACIFIC OCEAN

Area of profile

Depth (meters)
-2,000
-4,000
-6,000
-8,000
-10,000

Bathymetric Profile

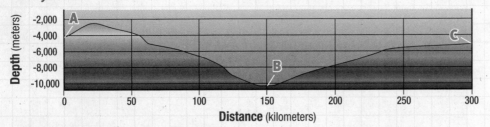

A bathymetric profile shows the change in depth across any chosen reference line on a bathymetric map. This profile details the change in depth across the line ABC shown on the map above. To see how the profile was made, move your finger along the line ABC on the map. Every time you cross a contour line, check that the profile crosses the same depth line on the grid.

You Try It!

Now follow the steps below to draw the profile for this bathymetric map of a region near Monterey Bay, California.

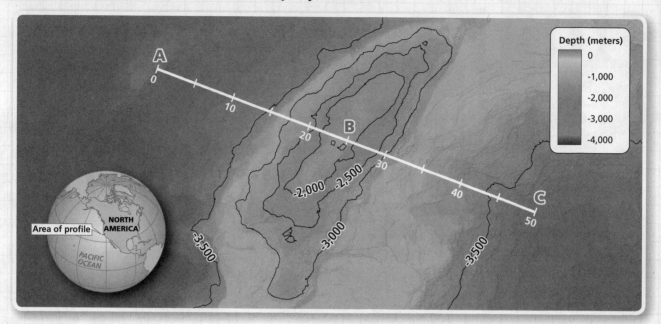

Profile Grid

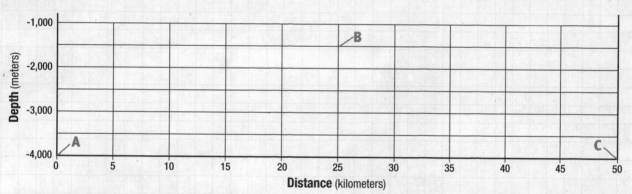

1 List Use the color legend to estimate the depths at points A, B, and C. Record this data in the table below.

Point	Color	Depth
A		
B		
C		

2 Distinguish For each tick mark on the line ABC, place a dot on the corresponding profile grid line at the correct depth.

3 Graph Move your finger along the ABC line on the map and place a dot on the profile grid at the correct depth for each contour line you cross.

4 Draw To complete the profile, connect the dots you plotted.

5 Evaluate Describe the ocean floor feature that you just plotted.

_____

_____

_____

_____

_____

_____

Surface Water and Groundwater

ESSENTIAL QUESTION

How does fresh water flow on Earth?

By the end of this lesson, you should be able to explain the processes involved in the flow of water, both above and below the ground.

Virginia Science Standards of Learning

6.5 The student will investigate and understand the unique properties and characteristics of water and its roles in the natural and human-made environment. Key concepts include:

6.5.e the importance of water for agriculture, power generation, and public health.

6.7 The student will investigate and understand the natural processes and human interactions that affect watershed systems. Key concepts include:

6.7.c divides, tributaries, river systems, and river and stream processes.

Fresh water flows on Earth's surface, sometimes tumbling over waterfalls like these.

Lesson Labs

Quick Labs
• Modeling Groundwater
• Model a Stream
Exploration Lab
• Aquifers and Development

Engage Your Brain

1 Identify Read over the following vocabulary terms. In the spaces provided, place a + if you know the term well, a ~ if you have heard of the term but are not sure what it means, and a ? if you are unfamiliar with the term. Then write a sentence that includes one of the words you are most familiar with.

_____ tributary
_____ surface water
_____ aquifer

Sentence using known word:

_____

_____

_____

2 Describe Write your own caption for this photo.

_____

_____

_____

_____

Active Reading

3 Apply Many scientific words, such as *channel*, also have everyday meanings. Use context clues to write your own definition for each meaning of the word *channel*.

Example sentence
She didn't like the TV show, so she changed the <u>channel</u>.

channel: _____

_____

_____

Example sentence
The <u>channel</u> of the river was broad and deep.

channel: _____

_____

_____

Vocabulary Terms

• surface water	• tributary
• groundwater	• watershed
• water table	• divide
• channel	• aquifer

4 Identify As you read, create a reference card for each vocabulary term. On one side of the card, write the term and its meaning. On the other side, draw an image that illustrates or makes a connection to the term. These cards can be used as bookmarks in the text so that you can refer to them while studying.

Getting Your Feet Wet

Where on Earth is fresh water found?

About 97% of Earth's water is salty, which leaves only 3% as fresh water. Most of that small amount of fresh water is frozen as ice and snow, so only about 1% of Earth's water is fresh liquid water. This fresh liquid water is found both on and below Earth's surface.

This tiny percentage of Earth's water must meet the large demand that all living things have for fresh, clean water. In addition to providing drinking water, fresh water is used for agriculture, industry, transportation, and recreation. It also provides a place to live for many plants and animals.

On Earth's Surface

Active Reading **5 Identify** As you read, underline three examples of surface water.

Water above Earth's surface is called **surface water**. Surface water is found in streams, rivers, and lakes. It either comes from precipitation, such as rain, or from water that comes up from the ground to Earth's surface. Springs are an example of underground water coming up to the surface. Surface water flows from higher ground to lower ground. Water that flows across Earth's surface is called *runoff*. Eventually, runoff can enter bodies of water.

Beneath Earth's Surface

Active Reading **6 Identify** As you read, underline how surface water becomes groundwater.

Not all runoff becomes surface water. Some runoff and surface water seep down into the ground. Water drains through the soil and filters down into underground rock, collecting in spaces between rock particles. The water found in the spaces between rock particles below Earth's surface is called **groundwater**.

Most drinking water in the United States comes from groundwater supplies. To use these supplies, people drill down to the water table to reach reservoirs of groundwater. The **water table** is the upper boundary, or surface, of groundwater.

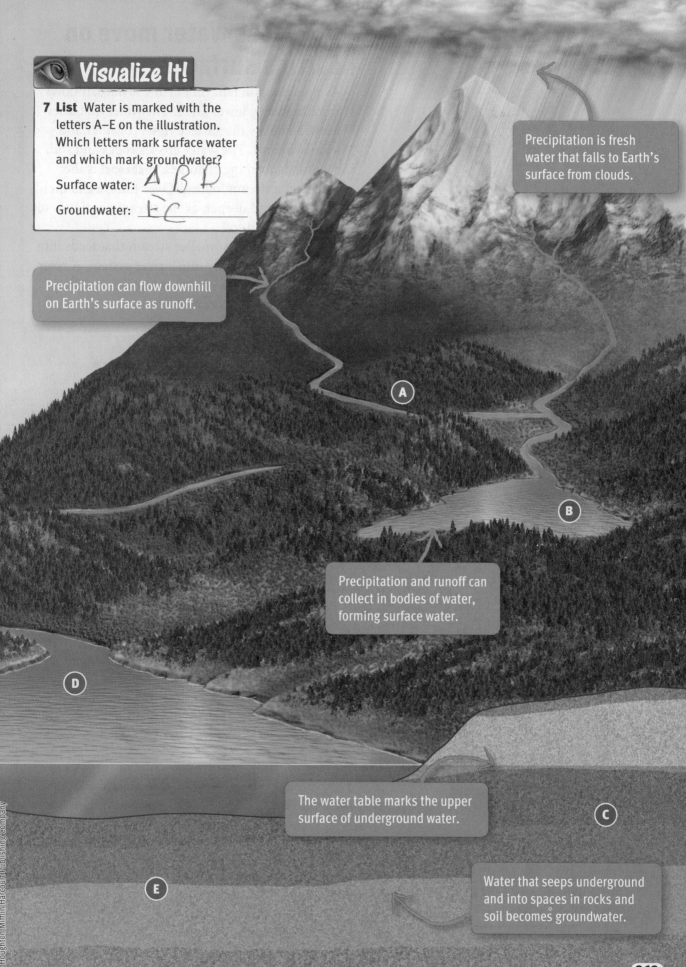

Visualize It!

7 List Water is marked with the letters A–E on the illustration. Which letters mark surface water and which mark groundwater?

Surface water: _A B D_

Groundwater: _E C_

Precipitation is fresh water that falls to Earth's surface from clouds.

Precipitation can flow downhill on Earth's surface as runoff.

A

B

Precipitation and runoff can collect in bodies of water, forming surface water.

D

The water table marks the upper surface of underground water.

C

E

Water that seeps underground and into spaces in rocks and soil becomes groundwater.

Cry Me a River

How does water move on Earth's surface?

As precipitation falls on Earth's surface, it flows from higher to lower areas. The water that does not seep below the surface flows together and forms streams. The water erodes rocks and soil, eventually forming channels. A **channel** is the path that a stream follows. Over time, a channel gets wider and deeper, as the stream continues to erode rock and soil.

A **tributary** is a smaller stream that feeds into a river and eventually into a river system. A river system is a network of streams and rivers that drains an area of its runoff.

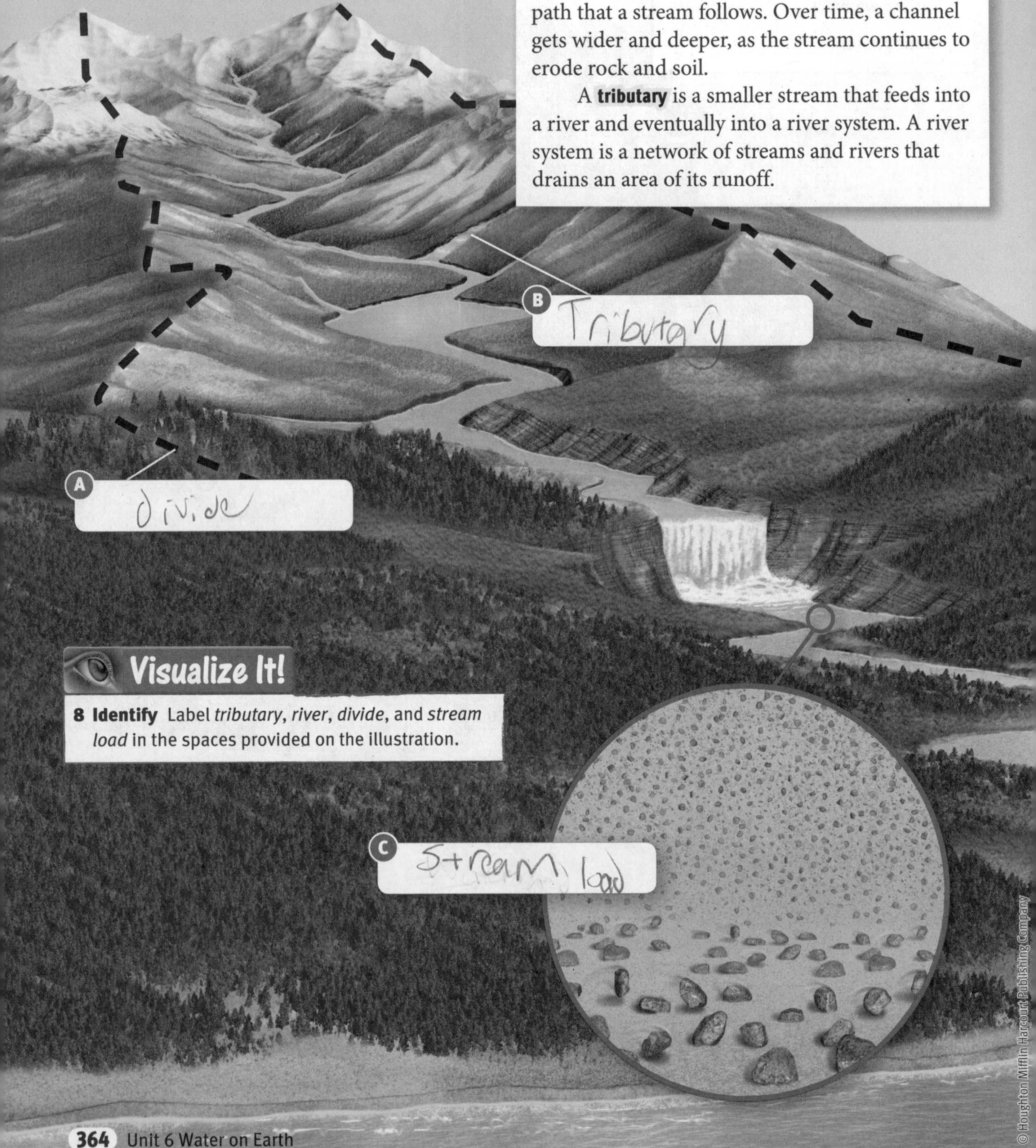

B Tributary

A Divide

Visualize It!

8 Identify Label *tributary*, *river*, *divide*, and *stream load* in the spaces provided on the illustration.

C Stream load

Within Watersheds

A **watershed** is the area of land that is drained by a river system. Streams, rivers, flood plains, lakes, ponds, wetlands, and groundwater all contribute water to a watershed. Watersheds are separated from one other by a ridge or an area of higher ground called a **divide**. Precipitation that falls on one side of a divide enters one watershed while the precipitation that falls on the other side of a divide enters another watershed.

The largest watershed in the United States is the Mississippi River watershed. It has hundreds of tributaries. It extends from the Rocky Mountains, in the west, to the Appalachian Mountains, in the east, and down the length of the United States, from north to south.

Many factors affect the flow of water in a watershed. For example, plants slow runoff and reduce erosion. The porosity and permeability of rocks and sediment determine how much water can seep down into the ground. The steepness of land affects how fast water flows over a watershed.

Active Reading 9 **State** Which land feature separates watersheds?

divides

In Rivers and Streams

Gradient is a measure of the change in elevation over a certain distance. In other words, gradient describes the steepness, or slope, of the land. The higher the gradient of a river or stream, the faster the water moves. The faster the water moves, the more energy it has to erode rock and soil.

A river's *flow* is the amount of water that moves through the river channel in a given amount of time. Flow increases during a major storm or when warm weather rapidly melts snow. An increase in flow causes an increase in a river's speed.

Materials carried by a stream are called *stream load*. Streams with a high flow carry a larger stream load. The size of the particles depends on water speed. Faster streams can carry larger particles. Streams eventually deposit their stream loads where the speed of the water decreases. This commonly happens as streams enter lakes and oceans.

Active Reading 10 **Summarize** How would an increase in gradient affect the speed of water?

go faster

D river

How does groundwater flow?

Although you can see some of Earth's fresh water in streams and lakes, you cannot see the large amount of water that flows underground as groundwater. Earth has much more fresh groundwater than fresh surface water.

It Trickles Down from Earth's Surface

Water from precipitation or streams may seep below the surface and become groundwater. Groundwater is either stored or it flows underground. It can enter back into streams and lakes, becoming surface water again. An **aquifer** is a body of rock or sediment that stores groundwater and allows it to flow.

Recall that the water table is the upper surface of underground water. The water table can rise or fall depending on the amount of water in the aquifer. In wet regions, the water table can be at or just beneath the soil's surface. In wetland areas, the water table is above the soil's surface.

It Fills Tiny Spaces Underground

An aquifer stores water in open spaces, or *pores*, between particles of rock or sediment. The storage space in an aquifer is measured by *porosity*, the percentage of the rock that is composed of pore space. The greater the pore space is, the higher the porosity is. A cup of gravel, for example, has higher porosity than a cup of sand does.

Permeability is a measure of how easily water can flow through an aquifer. High permeability means that many pores in the aquifer are connected, so water can flow easily. Aquifers with both high porosity and high permeability are useful as a water resource.

Visualize It!

11 Label Draw an arrow, ↑ (high) or ↓ (low), to indicate the porosity and permeability of each rock sample. One is already completed as an example.

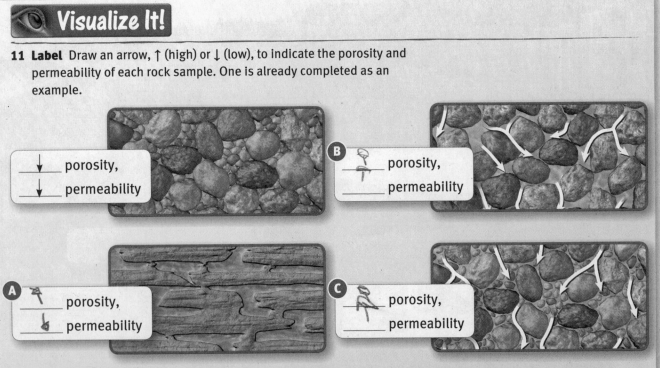

____ ↓ porosity, ____ ↓ permeability

B ____ porosity, ____ permeability

A ____ porosity, ____ permeability

C ____ porosity, ____ permeability

It Is Recharged and Discharged

Surface water that trickles down into the ground can reach the water table and enter an aquifer. This process is called *recharge*, and occurs in an area called the *recharge zone*.

Where the water table meets the surface, water may pool to form a wetland or may flow out as a spring. The process by which groundwater becomes surface water is called *discharge* and happens in *discharge zones*. Discharge can feed rivers, streams, and lakes. Groundwater is also discharged where water is extracted from wells that are drilled down into the water table. Through discharge and recharge, the same water circulates between surface water and groundwater.

13 Debate During times of little or no rainfall, many communities have regulations limiting water use. Imagine that you live in a community with a depleted aquifer. As a class, develop a set of regulations that you think residents should follow. Start by brainstorming as many uses of water as you can. Then decide which uses should be regulated and to what extent.

Visualize It!

12 Label On the illustration below, write a caption for *discharge zone* and for *aquifer*.

Water enters an aquifer in recharge zones.

Discharge

Save water by turning off the hose

Making a Splash

How do people use surface water and groundwater?

About 75% of all the fresh water used in the United States comes from surface water. The other 25% comes from groundwater. But surface water and groundwater are connected. In human terms, they are one resource. People use this freshwater resource in many different ways.

Active Reading

14 Identify As you read this page, underline how water is used in a typical home.

For Drinking and Use at Home

Groundwater is an important source of drinking water. Surface water is used for drinking, too. Fresh water is also used in many other ways in homes. In a typical home, about 50% of all water used is for washing clothes, bathing, washing dishes, and flushing toilets. About 33% is used to water lawns and gardens. The rest is used for drinking, cooking, and washing hands.

For Agriculture

Activities like growing crops and raising livestock use about 40% of fresh water used in the United States. These activities account for about 70% of all groundwater use. A little over half the water used in agriculture comes from surface water. A little less than half comes from groundwater.

For Industry

Almost half of the fresh water used in the United States is used for industry. Only about 20% of this water comes from groundwater. The rest is surface water. About 40% of water used in industry helps cool elements in power plants.

For Transportation and Recreation

Surface water is also used to transport products and people from place to place. In addition, people use rivers, streams, and lakes for swimming, sailing, kayaking, water skiing, and other types of recreation.

These rafters enjoy the exhilaration of river rapids.

Troubled Waters

Each hour, about 15,114 babies are born around the world. The human population has skyrocketed over the last few hundred years. But the amount of fresh water on Earth has remained roughly the same. The limited supply of fresh water is an important resource that must be managed so that it can meet the demands of a growing population.

Scientists are developing technologies for obtaining clean, fresh water to meet global needs. Here, a boy uses a water purifier straw that filters disease-causing microbes and certain other contaminants from surface water. The straw is inexpensive and can filter 700 L of water before it needs to be replaced—that's about how much water the average person drinks in one year.

Like many places on Earth, Zimbabwe is experiencing severe water shortages. The country has been plagued by droughts since the 1980s. Scientists estimate that about 1 billion people around the world do not have an adequate supply of clean, fresh water.

Extend

Inquiry

15 Infer Most of Earth is covered by water. How can we be experiencing shortages of drinking water?

16 Research Find out which diseases are caused by microbes found in untreated surface water. How might the water purifier straw reduce the number of people getting these diseases?

17 Recommend Conserving water is one way to ensure adequate supplies of drinking water. Work with a group to develop a plan to reduce water use at school. Present your plan to the class. As a class, select the best aspects of each group's plan. Combine the best suggestions into a document to present to the school administration.

Visual Summary

To complete this summary, fill in the blank with the correct word or phrase. Then, use the key below to check your answers. You can use this page to review the main concepts of the lesson.

Surface Water and Groundwater

Fresh surface water is found in streams, rivers, and lakes.

18 Smaller streams, or _trinties_, flow into the main river channel.

People use fresh water in homes, agriculture, and industry, for transportation, and for recreation.

20 Most industrial fresh water comes from rivers and other sources of _Surface Water_

Groundwater is found in pore spaces in rocks and sediment below Earth's surface.

19 The surface area where water enters an aquifer is called the _recharge_ zone.

Answers: 18 tributaries; 19 recharge; 20 surface water

21 **Relate** Describe how a raindrop could become surface water, then groundwater, and then end up back on Earth's surface again.

A gany

far more Different than
yars

Lesson Review

Vocabulary

In your own words, define the following terms.

1 surface water

Water above earth's surface

2 watershed

Area of land that is drined by a river system

3 groundwater

The water found in spaces between rock particles below Earth's surface

4 water table

The upper boundary or surface of groundwater

5 aquifer

A body of Rock or sediment that stores ground water and allows it to flow

Key Concepts

6 Identify What three factors describe the movement of surface water in streams and rivers?

Gradient, stream bude flow

7 Explain How does the gradient of a river affect its flow?

It makes it go faster

8 Describe How quickly would groundwater flow through rock with high porosity and high permeability? Explain your answer.

It would go fast because it could flow easily and has a lot of spaces

Critical Thinking

9 Conclude An area's rate of groundwater recharge exceeds its rate of groundwater discharge. What can you conclude about the area's groundwater supply?

The same water circulates between surface and groundwater

Use this graph to answer the following questions.

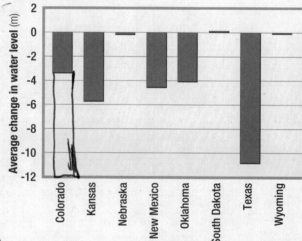

Average Water-Level Changes in the High Plains Aquifer by State (1950-2005)

10 Analyze What has happened to the amount of water in the High Plains Aquifer over time?

It had mostly low levels

11 Infer What might account for the changes described in question 10?

Us using water in differents things such as activity in our household

My Notes

Agony

Evaluating Technological Systems

Skills
✓ Identify inputs
✓ Identify outputs
Identify system processes
✓ Evaluate system feedback
✓ Apply system controls
✓ Communicate results

Objectives
• Analyze a hydroelectric power plant as a system.
• Identify the inputs and outputs of a system.
• Identify and evaluate feedback in a system.
• Examine how controls are used to regulate a system.

Analyzing Water Power

A system is a group of interacting parts that work together to do a job. Technological systems process inputs and generate outputs. An input is any matter, energy, or information that goes into a system. Outputs are matter, energy, or information that come out of the system. Most systems also generate some waste as an output.

Inputs and Outputs

Most renewable energy produced in the United States is generated using the energy of moving water. A hydroelectric dam is a system that changes the mechanical energy in moving water into electrical energy. Water is the input to a hydroelectric dam. Huge tunnels, called *penstocks,* carry water into the dam to fan-like turbines. Water flowing past the blades of the turbines causes the turbines to spin. This causes wire coils in the generator to spin. Spinning coiled wire in a magnetic field produces an electric current. Electric current is one output of the hydroelectric dam system. Water flowing out of the dam is another output. In a hydroelectric dam, some of the energy from the flowing water is wasted in the form of heat from the friction of the spinning turbines and coils.

---

1 Identify What are the inputs and outputs of a hydroelectric dam?

"Workers use bicycles or tricycles to travel from one turbine to the next over the length of the dam because the turbines are so large."

Feedback and Control

Feedback is information from one step in a process that affects a previous step in the process. Feedback can be used to regulate a system by applying controls. In a hydroelectric dam system, information about how much electricity is produced is sent back into the system. This information is used to regulate the amount of electricity that is produced. When more electricity is needed, giant gates, called *sluice gates,* are opened to allow water to flow. When less electricity is required, some gates are closed. The sluice gates act as the control in this system.

2 Analyze In the image below, place the terms *input, output,* and *control* in the boxes that correspond to the correct part of the hydroelectric dam system.

Reservoir

Sluice gates

Dam

Generator

Power plant

Transformer

A

Penstock

Turbine

Power transmission cables

B

Downstream outlet

C

Water flowing through a dam spins a turbine. This spins a generator, which produces electric current. Transformers convert the current so that it can be used in homes, businesses, and factories.

🖐 You Try It!

Now it's your turn to identify inputs, outputs, feedback, and controls. →

✋ You Try It!

Now it's your turn to identify inputs, outputs, feedback and controls in a system that uses water power. Working with a partner, think of another way that you could use moving water to do a job. For example, flowing water in water mills has been used to spin large cutting blades in saw mills or to grind grain in flour mills. You can use one of these systems or use your imagination to create your own system that uses moving water to do a job.

① Identify Inputs

In the oval below, enter a name for your system. Recall that inputs can be matter, energy, or information. List the inputs into your system on the lines above the arrows. If there are more than three inputs, you can add more arrows.

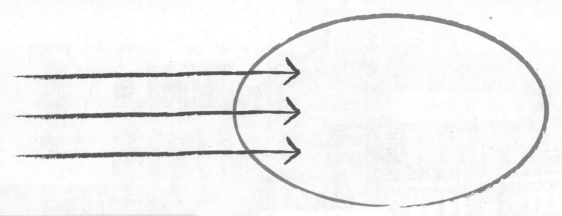

② Identify Outputs

As with the inputs, the outputs of a system can be matter, energy, or information. Keep in mind that most systems also generate some waste as an output. In the oval, write the name of your system. Use the arrows below to list the outputs of your system. If there are more than three outputs, you can add more arrows.

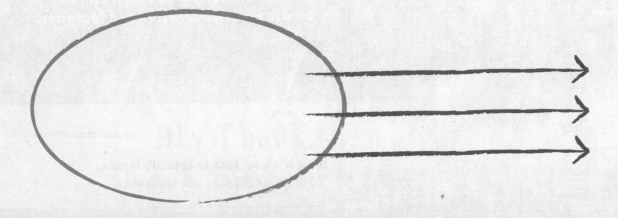

(3) Evaluate System Feedback

Now, consider which steps in your system could be used as feedback to regulate the system. Which outputs need to be monitored and why?

_____

_____

_____

_____

(4) Apply System Controls

Using the feedback you identified in the last step, propose one or more controls for your system that will keep the system working properly.

_____

_____

_____

_____

(5) Communicate Results

In the space below, draw a sketch of the system you developed. Label the inputs, outputs, feedback and controls.

Virginia's Watersheds

ESSENTIAL QUESTION

What are watershed systems?

By the end of this lesson, you should be able to explain the natural processes and human interactions that affect watershed systems.

This satellite view shows Chesapeake Bay and the rivers that flow into the bay from Virginia and Maryland.

Washington D.C.

Norfolk

Virginia Science Standards of Learning

6.7 The student will investigate and understand the natural processes and human interactions that affect watershed systems. Key concepts include:

6.7.a the health of ecosystems and the abiotic factors of a watershed;

6.7.b the location and structure of Virginia's regional watershed systems;

6.7.c divides, tributaries, river systems, and river and stream processes;

6.7.d wetlands;

6.7.e estuaries;

6.7.f major conservation, health, and safety issues associated with watersheds; and

6.7.g water monitoring and analysis using field equipment including hand-held technology.

Lesson Labs

Quick Labs
• Watersheds
• Wetland Filters

Field Lab
• How Healthy Is Our Watershed?

Engage Your Brain

1 Predict Check T or F to show whether you think each statement is true or false.

T	F	
☑	☐	Water flows from areas of low land to areas of high land.
☐	☑	Wetlands collect and filter water.
☐	☐	Weather conditions affect watersheds.

2 Describe Write your own caption to this photo.

_____

_____

Active Reading

3 Apply Use context clues to write your own definition for the words *monitor* and *restore*.

Example sentence
Amy kept a chart of her quiz scores so she could underline{monitor} her progress.

monitor:

_____

_____

Example sentence
The team of volunteers worked to restore the wetland to the way it once was.

restore:

_____

_____

Vocabulary Terms

• watershed
• wetland
• estuary
• abiotic factor

4 Identify As you read, create a reference card for each vocabulary term. On one side of the card, write the term and its meaning. On the other side, draw an image that illustrates or makes a connection to the term. These cards can be used as bookmarks in the text so that you can refer to them while studying.

Water, Water Everywhere!

What is a watershed?

An area of land drained by a river system is called a **watershed**. Watersheds can cover large areas. For example, the Chesapeake Bay watershed covers parts of six states, including much of Virginia.

Watersheds are made up of different parts. A watershed begins at the headwaters, which are found at the highest elevations in a watershed. Rainwater and runoff flow from these higher elevations to lower elevations due to the force of gravity. Small streams, called *tributaries,* flow into larger streams that flow into rivers. Watersheds are separated from one another by an area of higher ground called a *divide.* Divides are commonly ridges. Water flows down each side of a ridge into separate watersheds. Other important parts of watersheds are wetlands and estuaries.

Active Reading

5 Identify As you read, underline the different parts of a watershed.

Visualize It!

6 Identify Place *tributaries, headwaters,* or *divide* next to the correct letter in the illustration.

A ___Head Waters___

B ___Tributaries___

C ___divid___

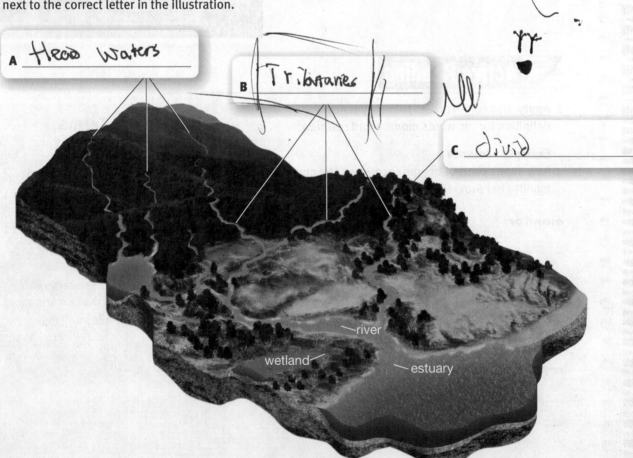

river

wetland

estuary

What is a wetland?

An area of land that is soaked with water for at least part of the year is a **wetland**. Bogs, marshes, and swamps are types of wetlands.

An ecosystem is a community of interacting organisms. Wetland ecosystems are home to many different animals and plants. Mammals, birds, fish, reptiles, crustaceans, insects, and mollusks all make wetlands their home. Mosses, grasses, vines, and trees also live in wetlands. Fish and birds rely on wetlands for food. They also breed and raise their young in wetlands.

Wetlands play important ecological roles. As water collects and slowly filters through wetlands, some pollutants are removed. During storms, wetlands absorb some wave energy so that large waves do not reach the shore. They also soak up rising waters, to prevent flooding. In addition, wetlands increase groundwater levels and fill underground spaces with clean, filtered water.

Active Reading

Identify What are some important ecological roles that are played by wetlands?

It, filter the water
it prevents the
dance

Visualize It!

8 Describe List at least one way each organism that is circled uses a wetland to survive.

Hello, I'm a bald eagle.
I feed on fish and mammals that live in the wetland.

Hello, I'm a deer.
I feed on grass and other plants and I drink the water

Hello, I'm a turtle.
I g. eat the alge in the water grows in the water

Hello, I'm a blue crab.
I live in the water

What is an estuary?

Within a watershed, all rivers flow into an ocean or bay. The partially enclosed area where <u>fresh water from the river mixes with salt water from the ocean is an</u> **estuary**. The Chesapeake Bay is the largest estuary in the United States.

Because estuaries have a mixture of fresh water and salt water, they support ecosystems that have a diverse community of organisms. Estuaries are a home, or habitat, for marine mammals, birds, fish, crustaceans, mollusks, and aquatic plants. They are also nurseries for many species of fish and amphibians.

Estuaries absorb wave energy and rising waters during storms. In this way, like wetlands, they act as a storm buffer. An estuary is also a recycling center for organic waste. The waste is broken down by the plants, animals, and bacteria in the estuary. This makes a supply of nutrients available for the organisms that live in the estuary.

 **Active Reading**

9 Identify As you read, underline the types of water that are found in estuaries.

 **Visualize It!**

10 Describe List at least one way each organism that is circled uses an estuary to survive.

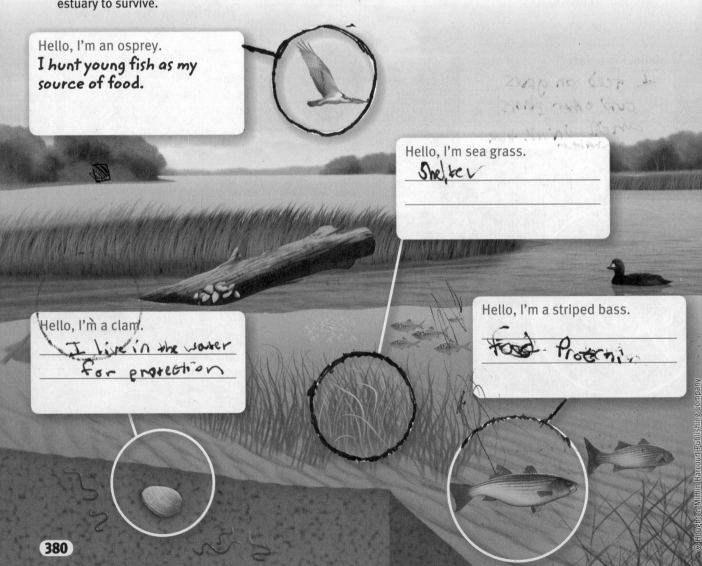

Hello, I'm an osprey.
I hunt young fish as my source of food.

Hello, I'm sea grass.
Shelter

Hello, I'm a clam.
I live in the water for protection

Hello, I'm a striped bass.
Food. Protein

Visualize It!

11 Identify List all of the Virginia watersheds that have rivers that flow into Chesapeake Bay.

Rappahannock, York
Richmond
Potomac → Shenandoah
James
Coastal Chesapeake Bay

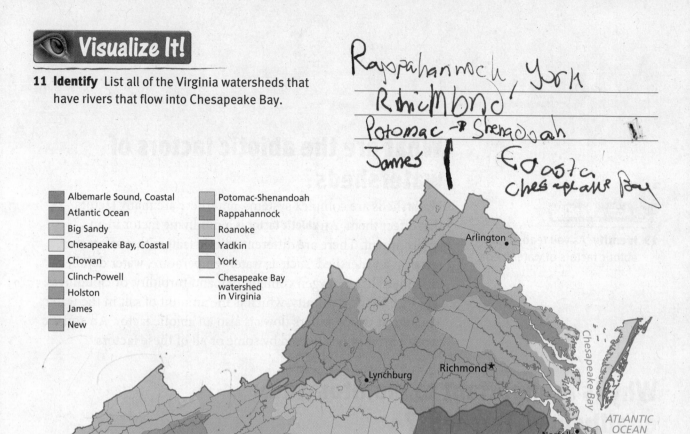

Key:
- Albemarle Sound, Coastal
- Atlantic Ocean
- Big Sandy
- Chesapeake Bay, Coastal
- Chowan
- Clinch-Powell
- Holston
- James
- New
- Potomac-Shenandoah
- Rappahannock
- Roanoke
- Yadkin
- York
- — Chesapeake Bay watershed in Virginia

Arlington • Lynchburg • Richmond ★ • Norfolk • Danville • Chesapeake Bay • ATLANTIC OCEAN

Virginia Department of Conservation and Recreation Stormwater Management

Where are Virginia's watersheds?

The Chesapeake Bay watershed covers more than 165,000 km². It includes all of the District of Columbia and parts of West Virginia, Maryland, Delaware, Pennsylvania, and New York. It also covers the northern part of Virginia. Water from the Chesapeake Bay watershed drains into Chesapeake Bay.

Several smaller watersheds can make up one large watershed. As long as all the watersheds drain into the same large body of water, they are included as part of a larger watershed system. For example, five watersheds in northern Virginia are included in the Chesapeake Bay watershed. The largest is the James watershed. It includes the James River, Appomattox River, Maury River, Jackson River, Rivanna River, and Chickahominy River. Other Virginia rivers that are part of the Chesapeake Bay watershed include the Shenandoah River, Potomac River, Rappahannock River, and York River. All of these rivers flow into Chesapeake Bay, but they are also part of one of the five smaller watersheds that are shown in the map above.

The watersheds in the southern portion of Virginia are not part of the Chesapeake Bay watershed. These include the Albemarle Sound, Coastal; Big Sandy; Chowan; Clinch-Powell; Holston; New; Roanoke; and Yadkin.

Think Outside the Book

12 Research With a partner, identify the watershed in which you live. Research the location and geography of the watershed. Present your findings as an oral or written report or a poster.

Measuring Up

What are the abiotic factors of watersheds?

Active Reading

13 Identify As you read, underline abiotic factors of watersheds.

Watersheds are complex systems, and there are many factors that affect them. An **abiotic factor** is a nonliving factor in an environment. There are different abiotic factors that affect the water in a watershed, such as water temperature, water depth, amount of light, oxygen content, pH, and turbidity, or cloudiness. Another factor is salinity, which is the amount of salt in the water. The rate at which waters flows is also an abiotic factor. An aquatic ecosystem may be affected by some or all of these factors.

Why is it important to monitor water quality in watersheds?

Many plants and animals live in watersheds. They can become unhealthy if the water quality is not good. Watersheds are also a source of drinking water for people. Monitoring water quality helps keep the water healthy for plants, animals, and people.

Water-quality monitoring programs are used to find chemical and biological imbalances in water. Finding these imbalances can help scientists to correct problems in an unhealthy watershed. Water quality can be measured using instruments that are lowered into the water from a boat. Special instruments that are mounted aboard aircraft and satellites can also monitor water quality.

Scientists take samples to check water quality.

What are some properties of water that are monitored in watersheds?

There are several properties of water that scientists monitor, or check, to determine the health of a watershed. Some chemical properties that are measured are pH, oxygen content, and salinity. Some physical properties that are measured are water temperature and *turbidity*, or the amount of undissolved particles in water.

Some properties are checked because they affect the quality of drinking water. Others are checked because they affect organisms that live in or near the water. Water may also be checked if scientists think that there is a problem with the water.

pH

The pH of water is a measure of how acidic or alkaline it is. Water with a pH of 7 is neutral. Water with a pH less than 7 is acidic. Water with a pH greater than 7 is alkaline, or basic. Most aquatic organisms survive best in water with a pH that is between 6 and 8. If the pH is lower or higher than this, many organisms will not get the nutrients necessary for their survival. If plant and animal species cannot survive in the water, this can also affect land animals that eat aquatic plants and animals.

Active Reading **14 Decide** How do changes in pH affect organisms that live in a wetland environment?

It can kill animals if it is not safe

Inquiry

15 Analyze How might an algal bloom such as the one shown below affect organisms that live in an estuary?

Animals are not able to get oxygen

The rapid growth of algae uses up a lot of the oxygen dissolved in water.

Oxygen Content

Water has oxygen dissolved in it. Fish and other aquatic organisms use the oxygen to breathe. Dissolved oxygen, or DO, is a measure of how much oxygen is dissolved in the water. Most aquatic organisms live best with a DO value between 5 and 15 parts per million. If the DO is lower than this, organisms may become stressed or even die. Pollutants such as sewage, fertilizer runoff, and animal waste can decrease DO levels. When there are too many nutrients in water, rapid growth of algae, known as an algal bloom, can decrease the oxygen dissolved in the water.

Water Temperature

Changes in water temperature affect the ability of aquatic organisms to survive. As water temperature increases, less oxygen stays dissolved in water. Aquatic organisms need this dissolved oxygen to live. A sudden increase in water temperature can cause the death of large numbers of fish. A sudden decrease in water temperature can also cause large numbers of fish to die.

Turbidity

Some water bodies look clear, while others do not. Water that is not clear contains a lot of suspended solids, which increase turbidity. For example, algal blooms and sediment increase turbidity. High water turbidity blocks sunlight from reaching plants that live underwater. Without sunlight, there is no photosynthesis, which means plants may not grow. Then other organisms cannot rely on them as a food source.

Salinity

The water in estuaries contains salt. Salinity is a measure of the amount of salt in water. Plants and animals in estuaries find places to live based on the level of salinity in which they can survive. If the salinity of the water in an estuary changes, the places where plants and animals can live in it may also change.

16 Explain In your own words, write a caption for this image of a fish die-off.

The sulinity was low

17 Summarize Fill in the table for either the factor that affects an ecosystem in a watershed or the effect on a watershed that the given factor has.

Factor	Effect
Low dissolved oxygen content	Stress or death of organisms
Change in pH	death
Turbidity	Reduces photosynthesis.
Increase in water temperature	Oxygon goes down
Salinity	Affects the distribution of organisms

What equipment is used to monitor water quality?

Scientists use special instruments to measure water quality. A pH meter is a hand-held tool. A probe is placed in the water, and the pH value of the water is displayed on a screen. Similar instruments are used to measure oxygen content and water temperature. Some tools can take all three of these measurements. Test kits that include special solutions or indicator strips can also be used to measure pH and oxygen content.

Turbidity can be measured with a Secchi disk. This is a black-and-white disk attached to a chain. The chain is lowered into the water until the disk can no longer be seen. The depth the disk reaches is read on the chain. This depth is called the *Secchi depth*. Turbidity can also be measured with an instrument called a *turbidimeter*. A turbidimeter measures the amount of light that is scattered in a water sample and displays a turbidity value.

 **Visualize It!**

18 Describe What role do Secchi disks and turbidimeters play in monitoring water quality?

Checking the
amount of
un dissolved str of

The Secchi disk reaches the Secchi depth just as it goes out of sight.

Changing Times

What are some factors that affect watersheds?

Changes within watersheds may take days, years, or even decades to occur. These changes can be caused by natural or human factors. Several factors can combine to affect a watershed at any one time.

Natural Factors

Extreme weather conditions have the greatest effect on watersheds. Strong storms that cause flooding can hurt water quality and habitats. Large amounts of rainfall increase the flow of fresh water in streams and rivers. This increased water flow causes more sediment to move through a watershed. This increases the turbidity of the water. An increase in water flow also adds more oxygen to the water. In addition, as fresh water flows from streams and rivers into wetlands and estuaries, it causes salinity levels to decrease.

An invasive species is a non-native plant or animal that can have a negative effect on the ecosystem it invades. Invasive species are generally introduced by humans, but some are introduced naturally. At least 46 invasive species have been introduced into the Chesapeake Bay watershed. Among the invaders are the mute swan, zebra mussel, and water chestnut.

Active Reading

19 Identify As you read, underline two types of natural factors that affect watersheds.

The softball player of the year goes to... Arianna Prymak

After periods of heavy rain and flooding, sediment causes the water to become brown and turbid.

Water in the Chesapeake Bay is usually blue with relatively low turbidity.

© Houghton Mifflin Harcourt Publishing Company • Image Credits: ©Jane Thomas, IAN Image Library (ian.umces.edu/imagelibrary/); (inset) ©David Trozzo/Alamy

Human Factors

As populations grow, more land is needed for human use. Land development can threaten watersheds. Erosion caused by land development introduces sediment into watersheds. Sediment increases turbidity in streams, rivers, and the bodies of water into which they flow. More sediment can increase the amount of nutrients in water, which causes the growth of algal blooms.

Land development also changes the surface of the land. An increase in paved surfaces causes more water to run off into streams and rivers. Runoff carries pollutants, such as mercury and pesticides, that can flow into streams and rivers. These chemicals are toxic to birds and to fish and other aquatic life.

Vehicle emissions are another source of pollutants. When these air pollutants eventually enter a watershed, they decrease water pH.

Think Outside the Book Inquiry

20 Apply Research ways that people can help reduce storm-water pollution. Make a list of steps you could take to reduce storm-water pollution.

Land development can harm watersheds. You can help protect them.

Inquiry

21 Analyze How might an introduced species such as the one shown in the photo affect other organisms in a watershed?

Change the way they live

The mute swan is an invasive species in the Chesapeake Bay watershed.

Taking Care of Business

Why is it important to protect watersheds?

Watersheds are complex systems that have many parts. Like a machine, if one part is broken, the other parts can be affected. All of the water resources in a watershed are connected. Any change to water in one part of a watershed can directly or indirectly affect water in another part of the same watershed. For example, the overuse of water resources in one part of a watershed can reduce the availability of water in other areas of a watershed. Also, contamination of water in one part of a watershed can contaminate water in other areas of a watershed. That is why it is important to protect all parts of a watershed.

Damage to watersheds can harm ecosystems and human health. Toxic chemicals that reach a watershed in runoff may be transferred from small aquatic organisms to fish and eventually to humans. Land development can change the way in which water flows through a watershed. This can increase the danger of flooding or reduce the amount of water that is available for use.

Today, storm water is the most important source of water pollution in the Chesapeake Bay watershed.

Visualize It!

22 Describe According to the map, which areas of the Chesapeake Bay watershed were in the poorest health as of 2010?

low eastern shore

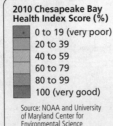

2010 Chesapeake Bay Health Index Score (%)

- 0 to 19 (very poor)
- 20 to 39
- 40 to 59
- 60 to 79
- 80 to 99
- 100 (very good)

Source: NOAA and University of Maryland Center for Environmental Science

How can watersheds be protected?

23 Identify As you read, underline how forests can help protect watersheds.

There are several ways in which people can protect watersheds. Decreasing the level of nutrients in the water can help protect watersheds. Nutrient levels in water can be lowered by improving wastewater-treatment plants. Releasing cleaner wastewater into watersheds will keep watersheds healthier. Reducing the nitrogen pollution levels in air can decrease the amount of nitrogen that enters watersheds. A decrease in nitrogen will help to prevent the growth of algal blooms that lower DO levels and decrease the amount of sunlight that reaches underwater plants.

Problems caused by turbidity are reduced when less sediment enters watersheds. Sediment enters watersheds when there is erosion caused by land development and agriculture. Land can be developed in ways that reduce erosion. Certain farming practices also reduce erosion.

Forests play an important role in the health of watersheds. They capture and filter air pollutants. Forests can be protected from harm and restored so that they are better able to filter air pollutants.

Watersheds include important habitats for plants and animals. Habitats that have been lost or damaged can be restored. This can be as simple as planting native vegetation in wetlands. Native organisms will then have sources of food, shelter, and places to breed and nest. Over time, the natural balance in a watershed may be restored.

describe

24 Describe In your own words, write a caption for this image of watershed restoration.

Volunteers are planting new plants that are native to the wet land

Visual Summary

To complete this summary, fill in the blanks with the correct word. Then, use the key below to check your answers. You can use this page to review the main concepts of the lesson.

Virginia's Watersheds

A watershed is an area of land that is drained by a river system.

25 Parts of a watershed include headwaters, divides, rivers, tributaries, _Wetlands_, and _estuaries_.

Properties of water that are often monitored include temperature, pH, turbidity, oxygen content, and salinity.

26 _Turbidity_ is the amount of particles undissolved in water.

Watersheds are affected by natural factors and human factors.

27 A species that is not native to a habitat is an _invasive_ species.

28 Pollutants, such as mercury and pesticides, are carried into rivers and streams by _runoff_.

Protecting watersheds benefits ecosystems and human health.

29 _Sediment_ enters watersheds when soil erosion takes place.

Answers: 25 wetlands, estuaries; 26 turbidity; 27 invasive; 28 runoff; 29 sediment.

30 Evaluate Ben says that water pollution in an area of a watershed far from people is not harmful. Do you agree? Explain.

Lesson Review

Vocabulary

Draw a line to connect the following terms to their definitions.

1 estuary

2 wetland

3 watershed

A an area of land drained by a river system

B an area where fresh water meets salt water

C an area of land that is soaked with water for part of the year

Key Concepts

4 Describe What are some ecological roles that wetlands and estuaries play?

Homes for animals and plants

5 Identify What are five abiotic factors that can affect water in a watershed?

Water one Turbidity, Salinity, Ph Oxygen content

6 Explain How can land development threaten watersheds?

It can cause turbidity

7 Identify What are four ways in which the health of watersheds can be protected?

No pollution less erosos soil, watch the salt levels Make sure their an plants

Critical Thinking

8 Evaluate Why do you think that storm-water runoff is the greatest current health threat to the Chesapeake Bay watershed?

It can cause major turbidity

Use this graph to answer the following questions.

Chesapeake Bay Oyster Harvest

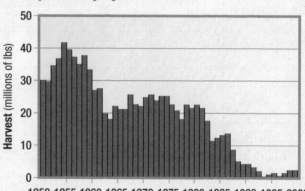

Source: *Chesapeake Bay Program and the National Marine Fisheries Service*

9 Apply During which year do you think it likely that an invasive species or disease affecting oysters was introduced into Chesapeake Bay? Explain your answer.

1955 because io bar the highest

10 Predict At which time do think the water conditions were the best for oyster growth? Explain your answer.

My Notes

Unit 6 〈 Big Idea 〈 Water moves through Earth's atmosphere, oceans, and land and is essential for life on Earth.

Lesson 1

ESSENTIAL QUESTION
What makes water so important?

Describe water's structure, its properties, and its importance to Earth's system.

Lesson 3

ESSENTIAL QUESTION
How does fresh water flow on Earth?

Explain the processes involved in the flow of water, both above and below the ground.

Lesson 2

ESSENTIAL QUESTION
How does water move in the ocean?

Describe the movement of ocean water, explain what factors influence this movement, and explain why ocean circulation is important in Earth's system.

Lesson 4

ESSENTIAL QUESTION
What are watershed systems?

Explain the natural processes and human interactions that affect watershed systems.

Connect ESSENTIAL QUESTIONS
Lessons 1 and 2

1 Synthesize Explain the factors that contribute to the density of ocean water.

_____

_____

_____

_____

Think Outside the Book

2 Synthesize Choose one of these activities to help synthesize what you have learned in this unit.

☐ Using what you have learned in lessons 3 and 4, create a poster or electronic presentation to show the prominent physical features of a local watershed. Identify the watershed from which your drinking water is extracted.

☐ Using what you have learned in lesson 3, create a model that distinguishes between porosity and permeability of soils.

Unit 6 Review

Name _____

Vocabulary

Fill in each blank with the term that best completes each sentence.

1 Water is a _____ molecule because its hydrogen atoms have a small positive charge and its oxygen atom has a small negative charge.

2 Water is called the universal _____ because it dissolves a large number of substances.

3 A(n) _____ is a partially enclosed body of water that forms when a river flows into an ocean.

4 The deflection of moving objects from a straight path due to Earth's rotation is called the _____ .

5 A(n) _____ is the area of land that is drained by a river system.

Key Concepts

Read each question below, and circle the best answer.

6 A glass of ice water is shown below before and after it reaches room temperature.

Which of the following correctly explains what occurred in the time that passed between these two images?

A The ice cubes expanded in volume as they melted into liquid water.

B As water vapor condensed on the glass, it absorbed energy.

C The water droplets outside the glass absorbed energy as they evaporated.

D Some liquid water inside the glass sublimated into water vapor in the air.

7 Which of these circle graphs most correctly shows the approximate proportions of fresh water and salt water on the surface of Earth?

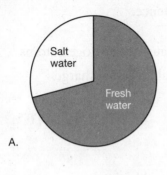

A.

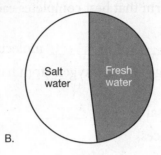

B.

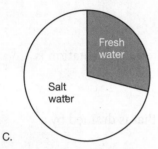

C.

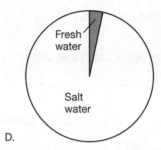

D.

8 Which of the following correctly shows the chain of energy transfers that create surface currents on the ocean?

A solar energy → wind energy → surface currents

B wind energy → solar energy → surface currents

C tidal energy → wind energy → surface currents

D geothermal energy → wind energy → surface currents

9 Which of the following is an incorrect statement about the flow of water through watersheds?

A A watershed can be fed by groundwater.

B The boundary separating two watersheds is called a divide.

C Plant life often alters the flow of water in a watershed by causing erosion.

D In a watershed, water flows from areas of high elevation to low elevation.

10 Which of the following is the name for all the materials carried by a stream other than the water itself?

A discharge

B flow

C gradient

D stream load

11 Which of the following is an example of an abiotic factor within a watershed?

A wading birds   **C** water temperature

B freshwater fishes   **D** seagrass

12 A large watershed is outlined in the map of Virginia shown below.

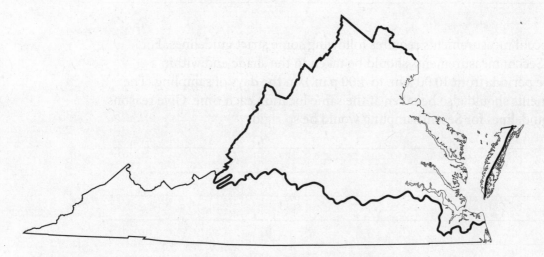

Fourteen major watersheds are located in Virginia. Five of these watersheds are a part of a larger watershed that is outlined on this map. What is the name of this large watershed?

A York watershed

B Chesapeake Bay watershed

C James watershed

D Potomac-Shenandoah watershed

Critical Thinking

Answer the following questions in the space provided.

13 Give two examples of the importance of water to human activities, explaining how the water is used.

_____

_____

_____

_____

_____

14 Explain what an upwelling is and why it is important to ocean life.

_____

_____

_____

_____

15 Taking Secchi measurements requires following some strict guidelines. For example, Secchi measurements should be taken in the shade and within a given time period (from 10:00 a.m. to 4:00 p.m.) on the days of sampling. The measurements should also be taken at the same location each time. Give reasons why the guidelines for Secchi sampling would be so rigid.

_____

_____

_____

_____

_____

_____

Connect **ESSENTIAL QUESTIONS**
Lessons 1, 2, and 3

Answer the following question in the space provided.

16 Describe what happens to a molecule of water as it moves from the precipitation that falls on Earth to becoming groundwater. Be sure to mention any changes of state, the absorption or release of energy, and the movement of the molecule through different parts of Earth's surface.

_____

_____

_____

_____

_____

_____

_____

Earth's Resources

Common building materials such as lumber, bricks, and glass are all made from natural resources.

Big Idea

Humans depend on natural resources for materials and for energy.

Wood for buildings comes from forests that have to be managed wisely.

What do you think?

The resources that humans need to live are found on Earth or come from the sun. What would happen if one or more of these resources were used up?

CITIZEN SCIENCE

Energy Sources

The world is filled with valuable resources. How we use, reuse, or use up those resources is important to this and future generations.

1 Think About It

Every time you walk into school on a normal school day, the lights are on, the rooms are comfortable, and there are material resources available for teacher and student use. Where does your school get its energy? Is it from a renewable or nonrenewable resource? Could the energy be used more efficiently?

_____

_____

_____

_____

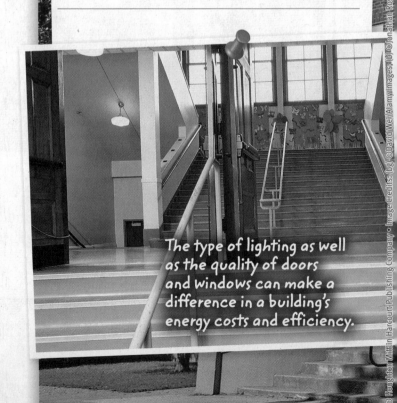

The type of lighting as well as the quality of doors and windows can make a difference in a building's energy costs and efficiency.

② Ask a Question

What is the energy source for your school's heating and cooling system?

With a partner or as a class, learn more about the source of energy for your school's heating and cooling system and the energy efficiency of your school building. As you talk about it, consider the items below.

Things to Consider

☐ Does your school have more than one energy source?

☐ Is your school building energy efficient?

③ Make a Plan

Once you have learned about your school building's energy efficiency, develop a proposal for your principal. Propose an alternative energy source for the heating and cooling system and ways to improve the building's energy efficiency.

A Describe the current energy source for your school's heating and cooling system.

_____

_____

B Describe one alternative energy source your school could use.

_____

_____

C List any noted energy inefficiencies and suggestions for improvements.

_____

_____

_____

Many older schools have been modified with new windows, doors, and insulation. These changes were made to save on heating and cooling costs and to provide a more comfortable learning environment.

Ideas for saving resources can help schools save money.

Take It Home

What energy sources supply your home? With an adult, talk about possible ways to improve energy efficiency where you live.

Earth's Support of Life

Earth's land, water, and atmosphere help to support life on the planet's surface and in its oceans.

ESSENTIAL QUESTION

How can Earth support life?

By the end of this lesson, you should be able to explain how the unique properties of Earth make it possible for life to exist.

Virginia Science Standards of Learning

6.3 The student will investigate and understand the role of solar energy in driving most natural processes within the atmosphere, the hydrosphere, and on Earth's surface. Key concepts include:

6.3.b the role of radiation and convection in the distribution of energy.

6.6 The student will investigate and understand the properties of air and the structure and dynamics of Earth's atmosphere. Key concepts include:

6.6.a air as a mixture of gaseous elements and compounds.

6.8 The student will investigate and understand the organization of the solar system and the interactions among the various bodies that comprise it. Key concepts include:

6.8.f the unique properties of Earth as a planet.

Lesson Labs

Quick Labs
- How Water Forms on Earth's Surface
- Temperature Variations on Earth

Exploration Lab
- Modeling the Greenhouse Effect

Engage Your Brain

1 Describe What kind of life is found on Earth?

_____

_____

_____

2 Compare Look at the differences between the pictures of Earth and Mars. Why do you think that Mars does not support the kind of life found on Earth?

_____

_____

_____

_____

_____

Mars

Active Reading

3 Synthesize You can often define an unknown word if you know the meaning of its word parts. Use the word parts and sentence below to make an educated guess about the meaning of the word *atmosphere*.

Word part	Meaning
atmo-	vapor, steam
-sphere	globe, ball

Example sentence
Earth's <u>atmosphere</u> is made of different layers of gases.

atmosphere:

_____

_____

Vocabulary Terms
- photosynthesis
- atmosphere
- ultraviolet radiation
- ozone

4 Identify As you read, place a question mark next to any words that you don't understand. When you finish reading the lesson, go back and review the text that you marked. If the information is still confusing, consult a classmate or teacher.

Living it Up

This poison dart frog lives in a bromeliad in the rain forest canopy.

What do living things need to survive?

Earth is covered in living things. Plants, animals, and other organisms live in oceans, rivers, forests, and any other place that you can think of. What do these organisms need to survive? Animals like the poison dart frog in the picture need to breathe air, drink water, and eat food. They need a place to live where they have protection from things that can harm them and where they can dispose of wastes. What do plants need to stay alive? Plants like the bromeliad in the picture need many of the same basic things that animals do. The basic necessities of life are air, water, a source of energy, and a habitat to live in.

How do Earth and the sun interact to support life on Earth?

The sun is a star, so it radiates energy out into space. Some of this energy reaches Earth's surface. Plants on Earth use the sun's energy to make food through the process of photosynthesis. During **photosynthesis**, plants convert carbon dioxide and water to oxygen and glucose. Glucose is a sugar that can be stored in cells. When plants need energy, they break down and use the glucose they have stored. Plant life on Earth forms the foundation of many food chains. Some animals eat plants to gain energy. Other animals eat these animals. In this way, energy from the sun is passed from plants to other organisms.

Plants use energy from sunlight to perform photosynthesis.

6 Identify Underline the food that is produced during photosynthesis.

$$\text{carbon dioxide} + \text{water} \xrightarrow{\text{solar energy}} \text{oxygen} + \text{glucose}$$

Earth's Rotation Distributes Solar Energy

Earth rotates continuously on its axis, spinning around completely every 24 hours. Earth's rotation allows most regions of Earth to receive sunlight regularly. Regular sunlight allows plants to grow in almost all places on Earth. Earth's rotation also protects areas on Earth from temperature extremes. Imagine how hot it would be if your town always faced the sun. And imagine how cold it would be if your town never faced the sun!

Earth Has a Unique Temperature Range

Earth's distance from the sun also protects it from temperature extremes. If Earth were closer to the sun, it might be like Venus. Venus has extremely high temperatures because it is closer to the sun, and because it has a very thick atmosphere. These factors make it is too hot to support life. If Earth were farther away from the sun, it might be like Mars. Mars has extremely low temperatures, so it is too cold to support life as we know it. Earth has an average temperature of 15° C (59° F). Regions of Earth range from freezing temperatures below 0° C (32° F) to hot temperatures above 38° C (100° F). This temperature range allows life to survive in even the coldest and hottest places on Earth.

Earth's rotation allows all parts of Earth to receive energy from the sun.

Think Outside the Book Inquiry

7 Apply Write a news story about what would happen to life on Earth if Earth stopped rotating.

 **Visualize It!**

8 Identify Write whether each planet in the drawing is too hot, too cold, or just right to support life.

464° C (867° F)

Venus   Earth   Mars

15° C (59° F)

-63° C (-81° F)

Water, Water Everywhere

What is unique about Earth's water?

When you look at a picture of Earth, you see lots and lots of water. How did Earth get so much water? Early Earth formed from molten materials, such as iron, nickel, and silica. These materials separated into layers and began to cool. As Earth cooled, it released steam and other gases into the air around its surface. The steam formed clouds, and water fell to Earth as rain. This was the beginning of Earth's oceans. Some of Earth's water also came from space. Icy comets and meteors impacted Earth and added water to Earth's oceans.

Only Earth Has Liquid Water to Support Life

Earth is unique in the solar system because it contains water in three states: solid, liquid, and gas. Most of Earth's water is in liquid form. In fact, Earth is the only known planet with a large supply of liquid water on its surface. About 71% of Earth's surface is now covered with water. Liquid water is essential to life because cells need liquid water in order to perform life processes. Water remains a liquid on Earth because surface temperatures generally stay above the freezing point of water. Temperatures also stay far below water's boiling point.

Visualize It!

10 Summarize The pictures below show how Earth's oceans formed. Write a caption for the last two pictures in your own words.

Earth's Formation

As Earth cooled, it released steam. The steam cooled to form clouds. Rain fell and began to form oceans.

Objects from Space

Modern Earth

Extremophiles

Extremophiles are organisms that live in extreme environments. Most extremophiles are unicellular, but some are multicellular. Extremophiles live in some of the coldest, hottest, driest, and saltiest places on Earth.

Living in the Cold
The Antarctic is home to ice-covered lakes and cold, dry valleys. Surprisingly, life can still be found in these harsh conditions.

Extreme Adaptations
A type of worm called a nematode survives in the cold by producing antifreeze in its cells. The nematode can also dry itself out when groundwater is not available. The nematode can then become active when water flows again underground.

Life on Other Planets?
The cold, dry Antarctic has some similarities to the cold, dry surface of Mars. The presence of organisms in extreme environments on Earth makes it seem more possible that some kind of life could exist in the extreme conditions on other planets.

Extend

Inquiry

11 **Explain** What is an extremophile?

12 **Describe** What are some adaptations that an extremophile might have in order to survive in a very salty environment?

13 **Extend** How could a greater knowledge of extremophiles help scientists to search for life on other planets?

407

Security Blanket

How does Earth's atmosphere support life?

Take a deep breath. The air you are breathing is part of Earth's atmosphere. An **atmosphere** is a mixture of gases that surround a planet, moon, or other space object.

Some space objects have atmospheres, and some do not. It often depends on the object's gravity. Earth and Venus have atmospheres because their gravity is strong enough to hold gases in place. Mercury and the Moon each have weaker gravity, so they do not have atmospheres.

Gases Fuel Life Processes

Earth's atmosphere is composed mainly of nitrogen and oxygen. It also has traces of other gases like carbon dioxide. Carbon dioxide and oxygen support most forms of life. Plants and some single-celled organisms use carbon dioxide for photosynthesis. Plants, animals, and most other organisms use oxygen to perform cell processes. Anaerobic bacteria are some forms of life that do not need oxygen to survive.

Earth's atmosphere has not always contained nitrogen, oxygen, and carbon dioxide. It was originally just hydrogen and helium. These gases were too light for Earth's gravity to hold, so they escaped into space. Volcanoes released water vapor, carbon dioxide, and ammonia into Earth's early atmosphere. Solar energy broke ammonia apart to add nitrogen and hydrogen to the atmosphere. Hydrogen escaped into space, but the nitrogen stayed in the atmosphere. Bacteria used carbon dioxide to perform photosynthesis, which released oxygen into the atmosphere.

Planet	% Gravity Compared to Earth
Mercury	38%
Venus	91%
Earth	100%

14 Infer Why doesn't Mercury have an atmosphere?

_____

_____

_____

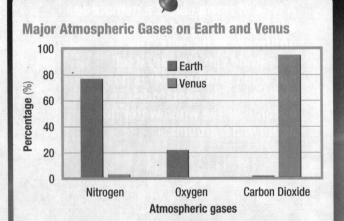

Major Atmospheric Gases on Earth and Venus

15 Infer If Venus has an atmosphere, why doesn't it support the kind of life that is now found on Earth?

_____

_____

Gases Insulate Earth

The gases in Earth's atmosphere support life in other ways. As radiation from the sun reaches Earth's atmosphere, some of it is reflected back into space. Some is absorbed by water vapor, carbon dioxide, and other gases in the atmosphere. Some solar radiation passes through the atmosphere and is absorbed by Earth's surface. Radiation from Earth's surface then moves into the atmosphere. This energy is absorbed and re-radiated by atmospheric gases, through a process called the greenhouse effect. The greenhouse effect keeps Earth warmer than it would be if Earth had no atmosphere.

The Ozone Layer Protects Earth

One type of solar radiation that can harm life is **ultraviolet radiation**. Ultraviolet radiation is harmful because it can damage the genetic material in organisms. Earth has a protective ozone layer that blocks most ultraviolet radiation before it reaches Earth's surface. The ozone layer contains ozone gas in addition to the other atmospheric gases. **Ozone** is a molecule that is made up of three oxygen atoms. Some human-made chemicals have damaged the ozone layer by breaking apart ozone molecules. International laws have banned the use of these ozone-destroying chemicals.

Solar Radiation

Visible Light and Infrared Radiation

Ultraviolet Radiation

Earth's ozone layer blocks most ultraviolet radiation.

Atmospheric gases absorb and re-radiate energy through a process called the greenhouse effect.

Ozone Layer

Infrared Radiation

◎ **Visualize It!**

16 Explain How does the ozone layer protect life on Earth?

_____

_____

_____

Visual Summary

To complete this summary, answer each question in the space provided. Then use the key below to check your answers. You can use this page to review the main concepts of the lesson.

Organisms need certain things to survive.

17 What do animals need to survive?

_____

_____

Earth's rotation and distance from the sun allow it to support life.

19 How does the sun support life on Earth?

_____

_____

Liquid water supports life on Earth.

18 Why is liquid water important to life?

_____

_____

Earth's atmosphere protects life on Earth.

20 What is an atmosphere?

_____

_____

Sample answers: **17** air, water, food, and a place to live; **18** Cells need liquid water to perform life processes; **19** It provides energy that warms Earth and allows plants to make food; **20** a blanket of gases around a space object

21 **Describe** How does Earth's position in space affect water on Earth?

Lesson Review

Vocabulary

Fill in the blank with the term that best completes the following sentences.

1 Plants produce glucose and oxygen during the process of _____

2 Earth's _____ absorbs solar radiation and re-radiates it to Earth's surface.

Key Concepts

3 Describe How does Earth's rotation affect life on Earth?

_____

_____

_____

4 List What are three ways that Earth is different from other planets?

_____

_____

_____

_____

5 Describe How did Earth's oceans form?

_____

_____

_____

_____

_____

_____

_____

6 Explain How does the carbon dioxide in Earth's atmosphere allow Earth to support life?

_____

_____

_____

_____

Critical Thinking

Use the image to answer the following questions.

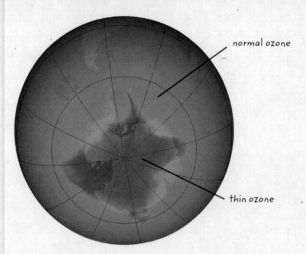

normal ozone

thin ozone

7 Describe The image shows the ozone layer. Why do you think it looks this way?

_____

_____

_____

8 Explain Why is it important to protect the ozone layer?

_____

_____

_____

_____

9 Apply What conditions would you look for if you were looking for life on moons or other planets besides Earth?

_____

_____

_____

_____

_____

My Notes

Natural Resources

ESSENTIAL QUESTION

What are Earth's natural resources?

By the end of this lesson, you should be able to understand the types and uses of Earth's natural resources.

Light produced from electrical energy helps people see at night. Natural resources are needed to produce electrical energy.

Virginia Science Standards of Learning

6.2 The student will investigate and understand basic sources of energy, their origins, transformations, and uses. Key concepts include:

6.2.a potential and kinetic energy;

6.2.b the role of the sun in the formation of most energy sources on Earth;

6.2.c nonrenewable energy sources;

6.2.d renewable energy sources; and

6.2.e energy transformations.

Lesson Labs

Quick Labs
• Renewable or Not?
• Production Impacts

Field Lab
• Natural Resources Used at Lunch

Engage Your Brain

1 Predict Check T or F to show whether you think each statement is true or false.

T F

☐ ☐ Energy from the sun can be used to make electrical energy.

☐ ☐ All of Earth's resources will last forever.

☐ ☐ Food, cloth, rope, lumber, paper, and rubber come from plants.

☐ ☐ Human activity can negatively affect Earth's resources.

2 Describe Name one item that you use every day. Describe how you think that item is made.

_____

_____

_____

_____

_____

_____

_____

_____

Active Reading

3 Apply Many scientific words, such as *natural* and *resource*, also have everyday meanings. Use context clues to write your own definition for each underlined word.

Oranges are a <u>natural</u> source of vitamin C.

natural:

_____

_____

His curly hair is <u>natural</u>.

natural:

_____

_____

A dictionary is a useful <u>resource</u> for learning words.

resource:

_____

_____

In the desert, water is a limited <u>resource</u>.

resource:

_____

_____

Vocabulary Terms

• natural resource
• renewable resource
• nonrenewable resource
• fossil fuel
• material resource
• energy resource

4 Identify This list contains the key terms you'll learn in this lesson. As you read, circle the definition of each term.

It's Only Natural

What are natural resources?

What do the water you drink, the paper you write on, the gasoline used in cars, and the air you breathe all have in common? They all come from Earth's natural resources. A **natural resource** is any natural material that is used by humans. Natural resources include air, soil, minerals, water, oil, plants, and animals.

Earth's natural resources provide everything needed for life. The atmosphere contains the air we breathe and produces rain as part of the water cycle. Rainfall from the atmosphere renews the water in oceans, rivers, lakes, streams, and underground. In turn, these water sources provide water for drinking, cleaning, and other uses. Earth's soil provides nutrients and a place for plants to grow. Plants provide food for some animals and humans. Animals provide food as well. Many of Earth's resources, such as oil and wind, provide energy for human use. The energy in these resources comes from the sun's energy. Earth's resources are also used to make products that make people's lives more convenient.

Active Reading

5 Identify List four examples of natural resources.

Visualize It!

6 Illustrate Draw or label the missing natural resources.

A

Bauxite is a rock that is used to make aluminum.

How can we categorize natural resources?

There are many different types of natural resources. Some can be replaced more quickly than others. A natural resource may be categorized as a renewable resource or a nonrenewable resource.

Think Outside the Book Inquiry

7 Debate Research why water or soil can be a renewable or nonrenewable resource. Discuss your points with a classmate.

Renewable Resources

Some natural resources can be replaced in a relatively short time. A natural resource that can be replaced at the same rate at which it is consumed is a **renewable resource**. Solar energy, water, and air are all renewable resources. Some renewable resources are considered to be *inexhaustible resources* [in•ig•ZAW•stuh•buhl REE•sohrs•iz] because the resources can never be used up. Solar energy and wind energy, which is powered by the sun, are examples of inexhaustible resources. Other renewable resources are not inexhaustible. Trees and crops that are used for food must be replanted and regrown. Water must be managed so that it does not become scarce.

Nonrenewable Resources

A resource that forms much more slowly than it is consumed is a **nonrenewable resource**. Some natural resources, such as minerals, form very slowly. Iron ore and copper are important minerals. A **fossil fuel** is a nonrenewable resource formed from the buried remains of plants and animals that lived long ago. Coal, oil, and natural gas are examples of fossil fuels. Coal and oil take millions of years to form. Once these resources are used up, humans will have to find other resources to use instead. Some renewable resources, such as water and wood, may become nonrenewable if they are not used wisely.

8 Compare List some examples of renewable and nonrenewable resources.

Renewable resources	Nonrenewable resources

Natural fibers from cotton plants are processed to make fabric.

B

A Material World

How do we use material resources?

Look around your classroom. The walls, windows, desks, pencils, books, and even the clothing you see are made of material resources. Natural resources that are used to make objects, food, or drink are called **material resources**. Material resources can be either renewable or nonrenewable. The cotton used in T-shirts is an example of a renewable resource. The metal used in your desk is an example of a nonrenewable resource.

To Make Food or Drink

Material resources come from Earth's atmosphere, crust, and waters. They also come from organisms that live on Earth. Think about what you eat and drink every day. All foods and beverages are made from material resources. Some foods come from plants, such as the wheat in bread or the corn in tortillas. These resources are renewable, since farmers can grow more. Other foods, such as milk, cheese, eggs, and meat, come from animals. Juices, sodas, and sport drinks contain water, which is a renewable resource.

Active Reading

9 Identify As you read, underline examples of material resources.

Visualize It!

10 List List two types of food or drink that are made from the material resources in each picture.

B
_____
_____

A
_____
_____

C
_____
_____

© Houghton Mifflin Harcourt Publishing Company • Image Credits: (l) ©Nir Miller/Alamy; (tr) ©Alvis Upitis/AgStock Images/Corbis; (br) ©Frank Krahmer/Corbis

To Make Objects

Any object you see is made from material resources. For example, cars are made of steel, plastic, rubber, glass, and leather. Steel comes from iron, which is mined from rock. Plastic is made from oil, which must be drilled from areas underground. Natural rubber comes from tropical trees. Glass is made from minerals found in sand. Leather comes from the hides of animals.

Iron, oil, and sand are nonrenewable. If these materials are used too quickly, they can run out. Rubber, leather, and wood are renewable resources. The plants and animals that produce these resources can be managed so that these resources do not run out.

👁 Visualize It!

11 Label Write the name of each material resource that is used to make objects in this house.

A house is made from many material resources.

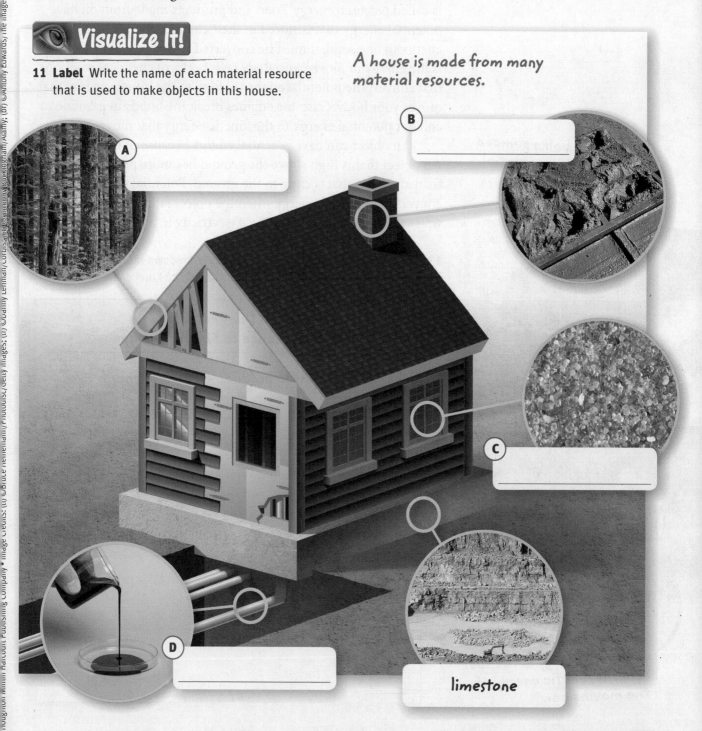

A

B

C

D

limestone

Change It Up!

Active Reading

12 Identify As you read, underline the different forms of energy.

How do we use energy resources?

Many objects need energy in order to be useful. For example, a bus needs energy so that it can move people around. Natural resources used to generate energy are called **energy resources**.

Energy is often stored in objects or substances. Stored energy is called *potential energy*. Food and products made from oil have potential energy that is stored in their chemical bonds. For this energy to be useful, it must be converted to *kinetic energy*, which is the energy of movement. Body cells perform chemical reactions that convert the potential energy in food to the kinetic energy that moves your body. Gasoline engines break the bonds in gasoline to convert potential energy to the kinetic energy that moves a car.

An object can have potential energy because of its position. An object that is high above the ground has more potential energy than an object that is close to the ground. Potential energy is converted to kinetic energy when the object falls, such as when water falls over a dam to produce electricity in a power plant.

13 List Look at the examples in the table. Write down three more situations in which potential energy changes to kinetic energy.

The gasoline being pumped into this car has potential energy in its chemical bonds.

This car's engine burns gasoline, converting the potential energy in the fuel into the kinetic energy of the moving car.

When Does Potential Energy Change to Kinetic Energy?
when coal burns to produce electrical energy in a power plant
when your body digests food to give you energy to move

How do everyday objects convert energy?

Energy cannot be created or destroyed, and energy must be converted to be useful. Energy conversions happen around us every day. Think about the appliances in your home. An electric oven warms food by converting electrical energy to energy as heat. A television converts electrical energy to light energy and sound energy, which is a type of kinetic energy. A fan moves by converting electrical energy to kinetic energy. Your body converts the chemical energy in food to kinetic energy as well as thermal energy. When you talk on the phone, the sound energy from your voice is converted to electrical energy. The phone on the other end of the conversation changes the electrical energy back to sound.

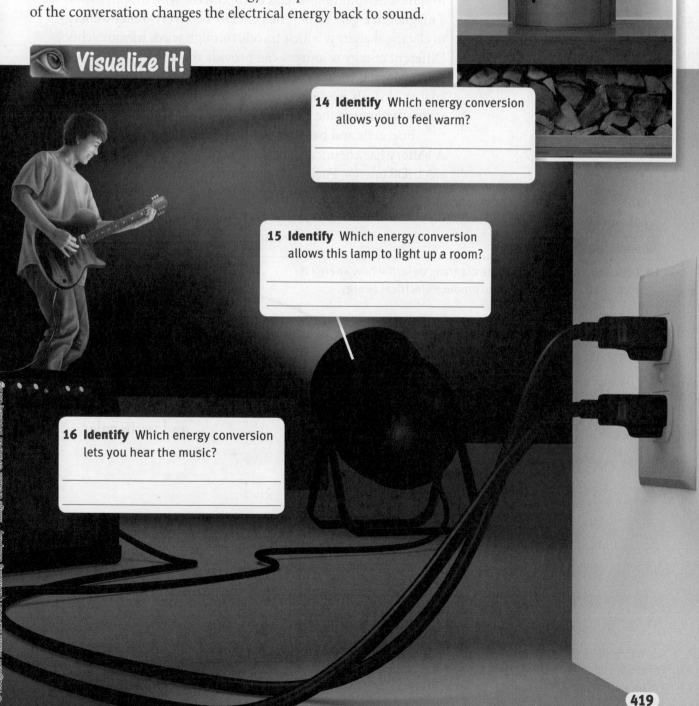

Visualize It!

14 Identify Which energy conversion allows you to feel warm?

15 Identify Which energy conversion allows this lamp to light up a room?

16 Identify Which energy conversion lets you hear the music?

Power Trip

How is electrical energy produced?

Computers and appliances need electrical energy to work. Electrical energy is available from outlets, but how does this energy get to the outlets?

In most electrical power plants, an energy source converts potential energy to kinetic energy, causing wheels in a turbine to spin. The spinning wheels cause coils of wire to spin inside a magnet in a generator. The generator converts kinetic energy to electrical energy, which travels through wires to your school. Different energy resources can provide the energy for a power plant. Moving wind or water can turn wheels in a turbine. Burning coal or biofuels made from crop plants can warm water, producing steam that moves the turbine.

Fuel cells and batteries are other sources of electrical energy. A battery has chemicals inside that convert chemical energy to electrical energy. Fuel cells convert chemical energy from hydrogen to produce electrical energy.

Active Reading

17 Identify As you read, underline the resources that can provide energy for a power plant.

Visualize It!

18 Describe After looking at the diagram, describe how energy is converted in a power plant to produce electrical energy.

Turbine

Generator

Powerlines

Energy source

Steam

Electrical energy is generated when coils of wire are turned inside a large magnet. This magnet might look different from bar magnets you have seen, but it still has north and south poles.

Clean Machines

Many car companies are introducing vehicles with hydrogen fuel cells. Hydrogen fuel cells use chemical reactions to produce electrical energy. These reactions produce no pollutants. If hydrogen fuel is made using renewable energy sources, these cars could truly be clean machines.

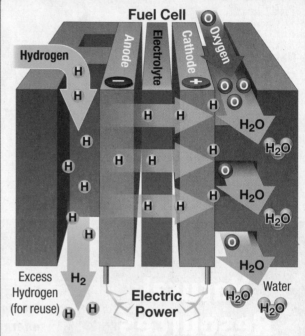

Fuel Cell

Hydrogen
Anode
Electrolyte
Cathode
Oxygen

Excess Hydrogen (for reuse) H_2

Electric Power

Water

H_2O

Small Packages
The hydrogen fuel cell in a car is about the size of a microwave oven.

HYDROGEN FUEL CELL ELECTRIC

Cell Technology
The fuel cell removes electrons from hydrogen atoms. Electron movement generates electrical energy. Hydrogen then combines with oxygen to form water. Water and excess hydrogen are the products of this reaction. No carbon dioxide or other pollutants are produced.

Extend

Inquiry

19 **Explain** What kind of energy conversion happens in a hydrogen fuel cell?

20 **Compare** How is the process of energy conversion different between a fuel-cell vehicle and a gasoline vehicle?

21 **Infer** Hydrogen fuel must be produced by splitting water into hydrogen and oxygen. This process requires energy. Does it matter if nonrenewable energy is used to produce hydrogen fuel? Support your answer.

Visual Summary

To complete this summary, answer the questions using the lines provided. Then, use the key below to check your answers. You can use this page to review the main concepts of the lesson.

Natural resources can be renewable or nonrenewable.

22 What makes a resource renewable?

_____

_____

Material resources are used to make objects, food, and drink.

23 What are two material resources in this picture?

_____

_____

Natural Resources

Energy can be converted from one form to another. Potential energy in energy resources can be converted to kinetic energy.

24 What are all the energy conversions that happen when wood burns?

_____

_____

_____

Answers: 22 Renewable resources are used more slowly than they are replaced; 23 cattle for food, trees for wood; 24 Chemical energy in the wood is converted to light energy, energy as heat, and sound energy

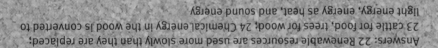

25 Illustrate Think of a natural resource that can be used as both a material resource and as an energy resource. Draw two pictures to illustrate each use of the resource.

Lesson Review

Vocabulary

Draw a line to connect the following terms to their definitions.

1 fossil fuel

2 material resource

3 natural resource

A resource used to make objects, food, or drink

B any natural material used by people

C a nonrenewable resource formed by buried remains of plants and animals

Key Concepts

4 List Name two material resources and give an example of how each is used.

_____

_____

_____

_____

5 Describe What makes a resource nonrenewable?

_____

_____

_____

_____

6 Explain How can the conversion from potential energy to kinetic energy provide energy that is useful to people.

_____

_____

_____

_____

_____

Critical Thinking

7 Apply What could people do in order to make nonrenewable resources last longer?

_____

_____

_____

_____

Use the drawing to answer the following questions.

8 Analyze What energy conversions are occurring in the illustration?

_____

_____

_____

9 Infer What form of energy that is not useful is being released from the flashlight when it is on?

_____

_____

10 Relate Assume that the batteries in the flashlight are rechargeable. What energy conversion would have to take place in order to recharge the batteries?

_____

_____

_____

My Notes

Energy and Energy Resources

At this wind farm, energy from the wind is transformed into electrical energy.

ESSENTIAL QUESTION

How is energy transformed when energy resources are used?

By the end of this lesson, you should be able to describe how different forms of energy are transformed when humans use energy resources.

Virginia Science Standards of Learning

6.2 The student will investigate and understand basic sources of energy, their origins, transformations, and uses. Key concepts include:

6.2.a potential and kinetic energy;

6.2.b the role of the sun in the formation of most energy sources on Earth; and

6.2.e energy transformations.

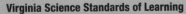

🤚 **Lesson Labs**

Quick Labs
- The Energy We Use
- Transforming Energy

Exploration Lab
- Comparing Energy Use

 **Engage Your Brain**

1 Predict Check T or F to show whether you think each statement is true or false.

T	F	
☐	☐	A moving car has kinetic energy.
☐	☐	Objects can have either potential energy or kinetic energy, but they cannot have both.
☐	☐	An energy transformation takes place when wood is burned.
☐	☐	The sun is the original source of energy in resources such as coal and wind.

2 Describe Write your own caption to this photo.

_____

_____

 **Active Reading**

3 Apply Use context clues to write your own definition for the words *process* and *extract*.

Example sentence
During the <u>process</u> of nuclear fission, a reaction occurs when the nuclei of atoms are split.

process:

_____

_____

Example sentence
Machines are used to <u>extract</u> coal from the ground.

extract:

_____

_____

Vocabulary Terms
- energy
- kinetic energy
- potential energy
- energy transformation
- energy resource

4 Identify As you read, place a question mark next to any words that you don't understand. When you finish reading the lesson, go back and review the text that you marked. If the information is still confusing, consult a classmate or a teacher.

Energize Me!

What are two types of energy?

It takes energy to open this book, turn the pages, and scan each page with your eyes. But what exactly is energy? **Energy** is the ability to cause change. There are many forms of energy, but they can all be classified into two major types. **Kinetic energy** is energy due to an object's motion. A moving car, for example, has kinetic energy. **Potential energy** is the energy an object has because of its position, shape, or condition. A ball that you hold over your head has potential energy. If the ball is released, it has the potential to fall to the ground.

Kinetic Energy

Some forms of energy are classified as kinetic energy. All moving objects have kinetic energy. Particles that are moving have kinetic energy. And a leopard in motion has kinetic energy.

Thermal energy is the total kinetic energy of a substance's particles. Particles in a substance move faster as thermal energy increases. Sound energy is caused by vibrations in a medium, such as air. When the particles in the medium vibrate, they have kinetic energy.

5 Identify Why does a running leopard have kinetic energy?

_____

A leopard sitting in a tree has potential energy.

A running leopard has kinetic energy.

Potential Energy

What did you eat for breakfast this morning? The food that you eat contains a type of potential energy called chemical potential energy. Chemical potential energy is found in foods and fuels. There are other types of potential energy, too. Gravitational potential energy is the potential energy of an object that is acted upon by gravity. Elastic potential energy is the potential energy stored in a stretched rubber band or spring. Potential energy can be thought of as "stored energy," which makes it useful to harness as an energy resource. Electrical energy and nuclear energy are two forms of potential energy that serve as energy resources.

6 Identify As you read this paragraph, underline different forms of potential energy.

Can objects have kinetic energy and potential energy at the same time?

Often, objects have both kinetic energy and potential energy. Mechanical energy is the amount of work an object can do because of both its kinetic and potential energies. A ball has potential energy when you hold it above your head and kinetic energy when you release it and it falls to the floor. Its total mechanical energy is the sum of its kinetic and potential energies.

Objects can have different forms of kinetic and potential energy at the same time. A computer, for example, uses electrical energy. As the computer runs, it gives off heat, light, and sound energy. Light energy, also known as *radiant energy,* is the energy of electromagnetic waves. It includes familiar visible light as well as invisible forms of light such as microwave and ultraviolet waves.

7 Summarize Fill in the table with an example of an object that has each form of energy.

Form of Energy	Example
Chemical	Food
Electrical	
Mechanical	
Radiant	
Sound	
Thermal	

© Houghton Mifflin Harcourt Publishing Company

Ch-Ch-Ch-Changes

What is an energy transformation?

When you eat lunch, some chemical energy from the food is stored in your body. When you head outside for recess after lunch, your body uses some of the stored chemical energy to move. Chemical energy is transformed to mechanical energy. This is an example of an energy transformation. An **energy transformation** is the change of one form of energy to another form of energy.

When you drop a ball to the ground, some of a ball's potential energy is converted to kinetic energy, the energy of motion. When the same ball bounces upward, kinetic energy is converted to potential energy.

What happens during an energy transformation?

According to *the law of conservation of energy*, energy is never created or destroyed, it only changes form. The energy of a bouncing ball converts from potential energy to kinetic energy and from kinetic energy back to potential energy. The total amount of energy stays the same. But not all of the kinetic energy converts to potential energy. When the ball bounces on the ground, some of the kinetic energy converts to energy as heat and sound energy.

Every time energy changes form, some energy converts to energy as heat. For example, when you run, chemical energy converts to mechanical energy. Your body temperature rises slightly as you run, and some energy from your body is released into the environment as heat.

Also, what do you hear as your feet strike the ground? *Thump, thump, thump.* Some energy can change to sound energy during an energy transformation.

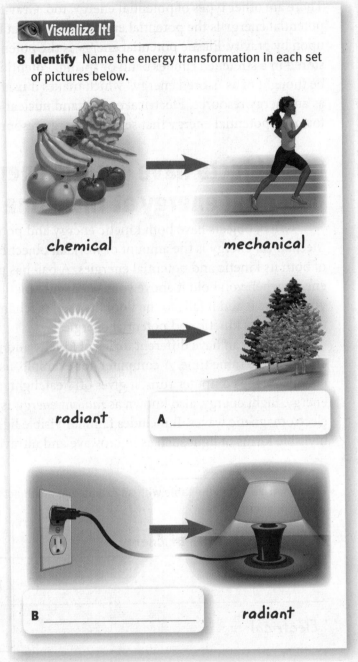

Visualize It!

8 Identify Name the energy transformation in each set of pictures below.

chemical → mechanical

radiant → A _____

B _____ → radiant

Active Reading

9 Explain How does a bouncing ball obey the law of conservation of energy?

_____

_____

_____

_____

What are some examples of energy transformations?

You have learned about simple energy transformations that involve one form of energy changing into another. However, energy may be transformed several times during some common processes. To see how this works, examine the diagram of the hybrid car below.

Some hybrid cars use both gasoline and batteries as energy sources. The fuel in the gas tank contains chemical energy. When the fuel burns in the engine, the chemical energy in the fuel transforms to energy as heat. Then, energy as heat is converted to mechanical energy, which turns the axles and wheels of the car. Chemical energy is also stored in the battery. This chemical energy changes to electrical energy, which runs the motor. Electrical energy converts to mechanical energy, which turns the axles.

A cell phone is another good example of multiple energy transformations. Cell phones run on batteries that store chemical energy. When you turn on the phone, the chemical energy in the batteries transforms to electrical energy. When you dial a number, some electrical energy changes to other forms of energy, such as light and sound.

Visualize It!

10 List On the lines provided, write the energy transformation that is taking place.

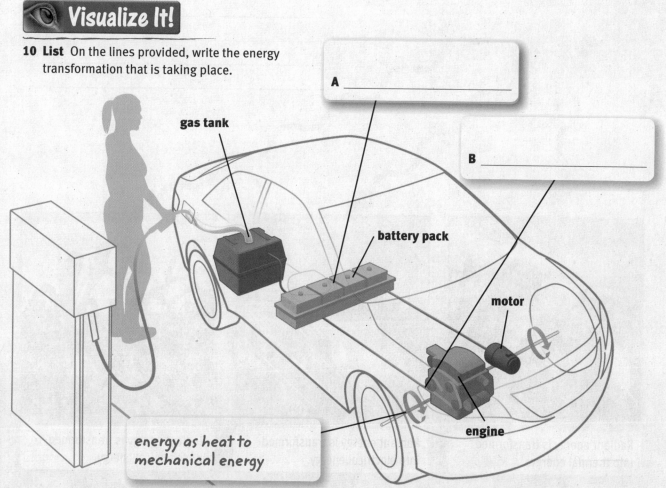

A _____

B _____

gas tank

battery pack

motor

engine

energy as heat to mechanical energy

How does the sun's energy change into other forms of energy on Earth?

Energy from the sun that reaches Earth is a form of radiant energy. Radiant energy from the sun is Earth's main source of energy.

Some radiant energy changes to thermal energy on Earth. This transformation warms Earth's atmosphere, surface, and oceans. It powers the water cycle and is the driving force behind weather.

Radiant energy can be transformed to electrical energy. Solar power plants convert radiant energy to electrical energy and provide electricity to homes on a large-scale basis.

Some radiant energy is also converted to chemical energy by plants during the process of photosynthesis. Plants use some of this energy as food and store some as chemical energy. Other organisms obtain chemical energy when they eat plants.

Active Reading

11 Identify As you read, underline ways in which radiant energy from the sun changes into other forms of energy on Earth.

Visualize It! Inquiry

12 Explain In what ways is the sun the energy source for most of the energy on Earth?

_____

_____

_____

_____

_____

Radiant energy is transformed into thermal energy.

Radiant energy is transformed into electrical energy.

Radiant energy is transformed into chemical energy.

How does energy change form when it is used to power technology?

Humans use energy to power technology. Where does this energy come from? **Energy resources** are natural resources humans use to generate energy. Energy resources include coal, natural gas, oil, sunlight, wind, water, atomic nuclei, and heat within Earth.

Energy from energy resources often changes form many times before it becomes the electricity that lights your home. Most power plants in the United States use the chemical energy stored in coal to generate electrical energy. The chemical energy in coal was once radiant energy from the sun. In a coal-burning power plant, such as the one shown in the diagram below, chemical energy is transformed to energy as heat when the coal is burned. This energy is used to make steam. The steam turns a turbine, which transforms energy as heat to mechanical energy. The turbine is connected to a generator that transforms mechanical energy to electrical energy that is sent to homes and businesses.

Visualize It!

13 List On the lines provided, write the energy transformation that is taking place.

A _____

B _____

C _energy as heat to mechanical energy_

D _____

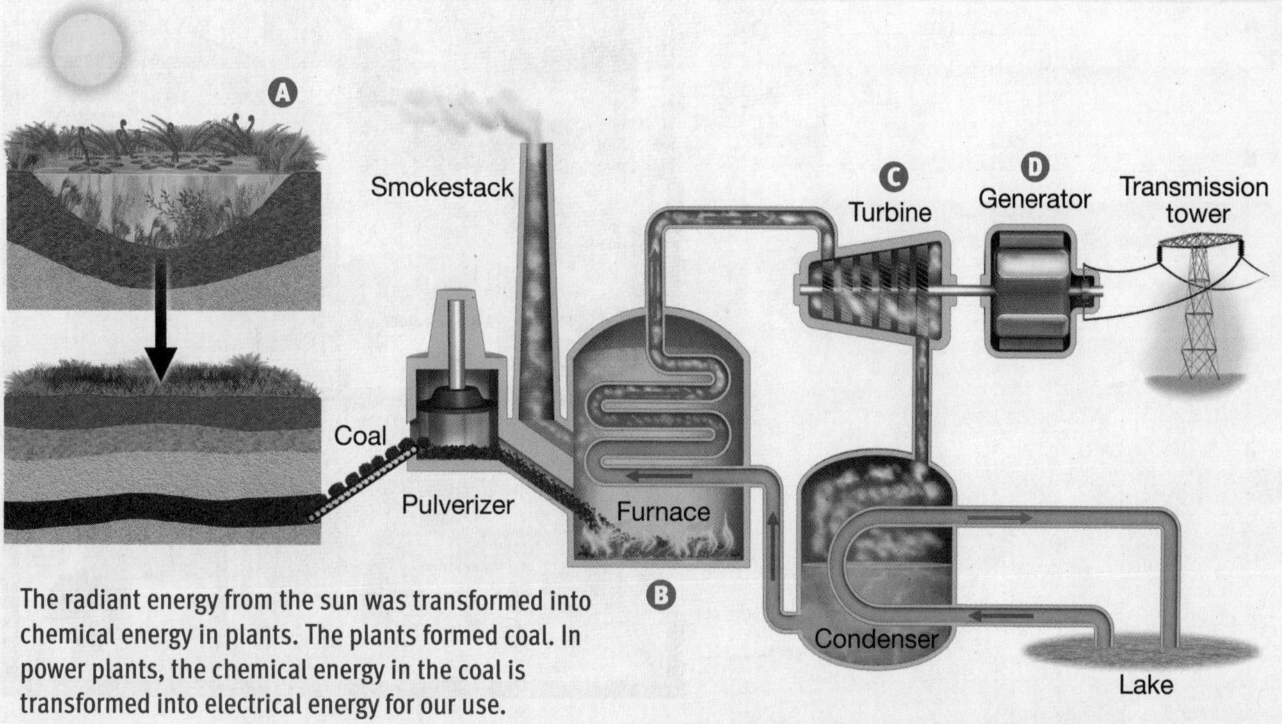

The radiant energy from the sun was transformed into chemical energy in plants. The plants formed coal. In power plants, the chemical energy in the coal is transformed into electrical energy for our use.

What are some ways in which humans use energy resources?

People use energy resources to heat and cool their homes. They also use energy resources to run lights and appliances, to cool and store food, and to fuel vehicles.

In the United States, a lot of the electricity produced comes from coal. Coal is relatively inexpensive to extract from the ground and to transport, but it does have drawbacks. Burning coal causes air pollution, and mining coal causes land and water pollution. Coal will likely continue to be a major energy resource until the nation transitions to cleaner, renewable resources in the future.

Although coal was once widely used to heat homes, other natural resources are more commonly used today. Most homes in the United States use oil or natural gas as a heating source.

Oil is by far the most widely used energy resource. It provides 40 percent of our total energy and nearly all the energy needed to power vehicles. Jet fuel, gasoline, and diesel fuel all come from oil.

Think Outside the Book

14 Identify Natural gas, electricity, fuel oil, propane, wood, and solar power are different energy resources that people use in their homes. Find out which energy resources are used in your home. Share and compare your findings with the class.

Visualize It!

15 Identify What is the energy resource required to run each object marked on the diagram? In some cases, more than one energy resource is possible.

A _____

B _____

C _____

The Northeast Blackout of 2003

One of the largest power outages in history took place on August 14, 2003, at 4:11 p.m. EDT. It occurred during a scorching-hot summer day when temperatures reached 90 °F plus. The cause of the failure: a high-voltage power line in Ohio brushed against overgrown trees and shut down, leaving places as far away as New York City (shown) in the dark.

CANADA

Ottawa

Toronto

Detroit

Cleveland

New York City

UNITED STATES

U.S. Department of Transportation

The North Goes Dark

The loss of electrical power affected about 50 million people in a 240 million–km^2 area that stretched across northeastern Canada and the northeastern United States. The areas that were without power are shown in purple.

At a Standstill

The power loss grounded passenger flights at airports, stopped subway traffic, knocked out traffic lights, and stopped all trains. In an attempt to return home, thousands of people in New York City walked across the Brooklyn Bridge.

Extend

Inquiry

16 Describe What are possible health risks associated with blackouts?

17 Infer What might be the benefit of a rolling blackout or an intentional blackout?

18 Research Find out how scientists, engineers, and government officials are working together to prevent future mass blackouts. Present your findings in an oral report, a written report, or a poster presentation.

Visual Summary

To complete this summary, fill in the blanks with the correct word or phrase. Then, use the key below to check your answers. You can use this page to review the main concepts of the lesson.

Energy and Energy Resources

Energy can change form, but it cannot be created or destroyed.

20 You eat breakfast, and then go for a run. Your body transforms _____ energy to _____ energy.

All forms of energy can be classified into two major types, kinetic or potential.

19 Radiant energy and thermal energy are forms of _____ energy.

People use energy to power technology.

21 Most electrical energy in the United States comes from _____.

Answers: 19 kinetic; 20 chemical; mechanical or kinetic; 21 coal

---

22 **Apply** Identify three specific energy transformations that you see occurring around you right now.

Lesson Review

Vocabulary

Fill in the blank with the word that best completes the following sentences.

1 _____ is the ability to cause change.

2 Moving objects have _____ energy.

3 Coal, wind, and water are examples of _____ used to power technology.

4 A(n) _____ occurs when energy changes from one form to another.

Key Concepts

5 Compare How are kinetic energy and potential energy alike? How are they different?

_____

_____

_____

_____

6 Explain How does the law of conservation of energy relate to energy transformation?

_____

_____

_____

_____

7 Describe What energy resources are used to provide electricity and heat for homes and fuel for vehicles in the United States?

_____

_____

_____

_____

Critical Thinking

Use this photo to answer the following question.

8 Identify What energy transformation is taking place?

_____

_____

_____

_____

_____

9 Evaluate Decide if this statement is true or false: The energy you get for life functions comes from the sun. Explain your reasoning.

_____

_____

_____

_____

10 Determine A child on a swing has both kinetic energy and potential energy. The child's position changes as she swings forward, reaches her greatest height, and then swings backward. At which point is the potential energy of the child on the swing the greatest?

_____

_____

_____

_____

My Notes

Nonrenewable Energy Resources

ESSENTIAL QUESTION

How do we use nonrenewable energy resources?

By the end of this lesson, you should be able to describe how humans use energy resources and the role of nonrenewable energy resources in society.

The energy that lights up this city and powers the vehicles comes from energy resources. Most of our energy resources are being used up faster than natural processes can replace them.

Virginia Science Standards of Learning

6.1 The student will demonstrate an understanding of scientific reasoning, logic, and the nature of science by planning and conducting investigations in which:

6.1.j current applications are used to reinforce science concepts.

6.2 The student will investigate and understand basic sources of energy, their origins, transformations, and uses. Key concepts include:

6.2.b the role of the sun in the formation of most energy sources on Earth; and

6.2.c nonrenewable energy sources.

6.9 The student will investigate and understand public policy decisions relating to the environment. Key concepts include:

6.9.d cost/benefit tradeoffs in conservation policies.

Engage Your Brain

1 Identify Unscramble the letters below to find substances that are nonrenewable resources.

ALCO _____

AUNTRLA SGA _____

NUUIMAR _____

MLPEOUTRE _____

2 Describe Write your own caption for this photo.

_____

_____

_____

 Active Reading

3 Synthesize Many English words have their roots in other languages. Use the Latin word below to make an educated guess about the meaning of the word *fission*.

Latin word	Meaning
fissus	to split

Example sentence
An atomic nucleus can undergo <u>fission</u>.

fission:

_____

_____

Vocabulary Terms
- energy resource
- nuclear energy
- fossil fuel
- fission

4 Identify This list contains the vocabulary terms you'll learn in this lesson. As you read, circle the definition of each term.

Be Resourceful!

What are the two main types of nonrenewable energy resources?

An **energy resource** is a natural resource that humans use to generate energy and can be renewable or nonrenewable. *Renewable resources* are replaced by natural processes at least as quickly as they are used. *Nonrenewable resources* are used up faster than they can be replaced. Most of the energy used in the United States comes from nonrenewable resources.

Fossil Fuels

A **fossil fuel** is a nonrenewable energy resource that forms from the remains of organisms that lived long ago. Fossil fuels release energy when they are burned. This energy can be converted to electricity or used to power engines. Fossil fuels are the most commonly used energy resource because they are relatively inexpensive to locate and process.

Nuclear Fuel

The energy released when the nuclei of atoms are split or combined is called **nuclear energy**. This energy can be obtained by two kinds of nuclear reactions—fusion and fission. Today's nuclear power plants use fission, because the technology for fusion power plants does not currently exist. The most common nuclear fuel is uranium. Uranium is obtained by mining and processing uranium ore, which is a nonrenewable resource.

Do the Math

You Try It

Nonrenewable Energy Resources Consumed in the U.S. in 2009

■ Fossil Fuels 90.37%
■ Nuclear Fuel 9.63%

5 Calculate In 2009, 86.8 quadrillion BTUs of the energy used in the United States was produced from nonrenewable energy resources. Using the graph above, calculate how much of this energy was produced from nuclear fuel.

6 Compare Fill in the Venn diagram to compare and contrast fossil fuels and nuclear fuel.

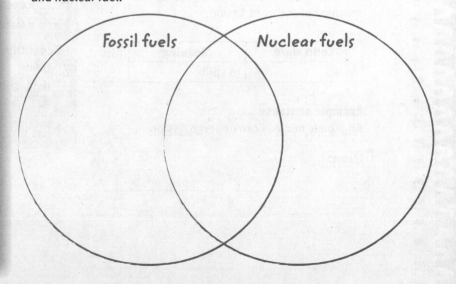

Fossil fuels   Nuclear fuels

What are the three main types of fossil fuels?

All living things contain the element carbon. Fossil fuels form from the remains of living things, so they also contain carbon. Most of this carbon is in the form of hydrocarbons, which are compounds made of hydrogen and carbon. Fossil fuels can be liquids, gases, or solids. Fossil fuels include petroleum, natural gas, and coal.

Active Reading **7 Identify** As you read, underline the state of matter for each fossil fuel.

Petroleum

Petroleum, or *crude oil,* is a liquid mixture of complex hydrocarbon compounds. Crude oil is extracted from the ground by drilling then processed for use. This process, called *refining,* separates the crude oil into different products such as gasoline, kerosene, and diesel fuel. More than 35 percent of the world's energy comes from crude oil products. Crude oil is also used to make products such as ink, bubble gum, and plastics.

This crude oil will be refined into gasoline, diesel fuel, heating oil, kerosene, and other products.

Natural Gas

Natural gas is a mixture of gaseous hydrocarbons. Most natural gas is used for heating and cooking, but some is used to generate electricity. Also, some vehicles use natural gas as fuel.

Methane is the main component of natural gas. Butane and propane can also be separated from natural gas. Butane and propane are used as fuel for camp stoves and outdoor grills. Some rural homes also use propane as a heating fuel.

Natural gas is a popular fuel for cooking because it is inexpensive.

Coal

The fossil fuel most widely used for generating electrical power is a solid called coal. Coal was once used to heat homes and for transportation. In fact, many trains in the 1800s and early 1900s were pulled by coal-burning steam locomotives. Now, most people use gasoline for transportation fuel. But more than half of our nation's electricity comes from coal-burning power plants.

Coal is a fossil fuel often used to generate electricity.

How do fossil fuels form?

How might a sunny day 200 million years ago relate to your life today? If you traveled to school by bus or car, you likely used energy from sunlight that warmed Earth that long ago.

Fossil fuels form over millions of years from the buried remains of ancient organisms. Fossil fuels differ in the kinds of organisms from which they form and in how they form. This process is continuing, too. The fossil fuels forming today will be available for use in a few million years!

Petroleum and Natural Gas Form from Marine Organisms

Petroleum and natural gas form mainly from the remains of microscopic sea organisms. When these organisms die, their remains sink and settle on the ocean floor. There, the dead organisms are gradually buried by sediment. The sediment is compacted by more layers of dead organisms and sediment. Over time the sediment layers become layers of rock.

Over millions of years, heat and pressure turn the remains of the organisms into petroleum and natural gas. The petroleum and natural gas, along with groundwater, flow into pores in the rock. A rock with pores is a *permeable rock*. Permeable rocks become reservoirs where the petroleum and natural gas are trapped and concentrated over time. Humans can extract the fuels from these reservoirs.

Petroleum and Natural Gas Formation

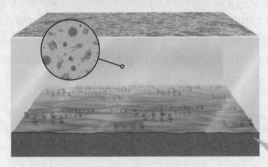

1 Microscopic marine organisms die and settle to the bottom of the sea.

2 Layers of sediment slowly bury the dead marine organisms.

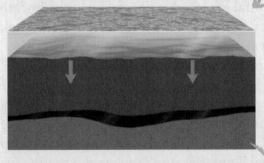

3 Heat and pressure on these layers slowly turn the remains of these organisms into petroleum and natural gas.

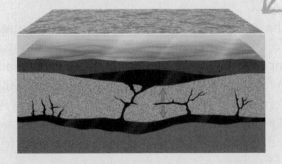

4 Petroleum and natural gas flow through permeable rocks, where they are trapped and become concentrated into reservoirs.

Think Outside the Book Inquiry

8 Apply With a classmate, discuss how the process of petroleum formation might affect oil availability in the future.

Coal Formation

1 **Peat** Partially decayed swamp plants sink and change into peat.

2 **Lignite** As sediment buries the peat, increases in temperature and pressure change peat to lignite.

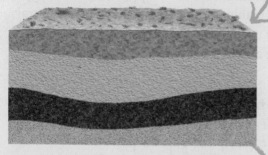

3 **Bituminous Coal** As sediment builds, increased temperature and pressure change lignite to bituminous coal.

4 **Anthracite** As sediments accumulate and temperature and pressure rise, bituminous coal changes to anthracite.

Coal Forms from Plant Remains

Active Reading **9 Identify** As you read, underline the factors that convert the buried plants into coal.

Coal is formed over millions of years from the remains of swamp plants. When the plants die, they sink to the swamp floor. Low oxygen levels in the water keep many plants from decaying and allow the process of coal formation to begin. Today's swamp plants may eventually turn into coal millions of years from now.

The first step of coal formation is plant matter changing into peat. Peat is made mostly of plant material and water. Peat is not coal. In some parts of the world, peat is dried and burned for warmth or used as fuel. Peat that is buried by layers of sediment can turn into coal after millions of years.

Over time, pressure and high temperature force water and gases out of the peat. The peat gradually becomes harder, and its carbon content increases. The amount of heat and pressure determines the type of coal that forms. Lignite forms first, followed by bituminous coal and, finally, anthracite. Anthracite is highly valued because it has the highest carbon content and gives off the most energy as heat when burned.

Today, all three types of coal are mined around the world. When burned, coal releases energy as heat and pollutes the air. The greater the carbon content of the coal, the fewer pollutants are released and the cleaner the coal burns.

Visualize It!

10 Compare What is similar about the way petroleum and coal form? What is different?

_____

_____

_____

_____

_____

_____

Power Trip

How are fossil fuels used as energy sources?

In the United States, petroleum fuels are mainly used for transportation and heating. Airplanes, trains, boats, and cars all use petroleum for energy. Some people also use petroleum as a heating fuel. There are some oil-fired power plants in the United States, but most are found in other parts of the world.

Natural gas can be used as transportation fuel but is mainly used for heating and cooking. The use of natural gas as a source of electrical power is increasing. The U.S. Department of Energy projects that most power plants in the near future will use natural gas. Today, coal is mainly used in the U.S. to generate electricity, which we use for lighting and to power appliances and technology.

Active Reading

11 Identify As you read, underline the uses of fossil fuels.

Visualize It!

Burning coal heats water to produce steam. The steam turns the turbines to generate electricity. Scrubbers and filters in the smokestack help reduce air pollution.

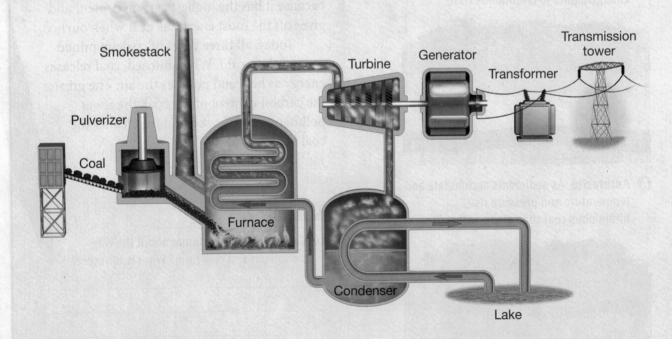

Coal-Fired Power Plant

How is energy produced from nuclear fuels?

During **fission**, the nuclei of radioactive atoms are split into two or more fragments. A small particle called a neutron hits and splits an atom. This process releases large amounts of energy as heat and radiation. Fission also releases more neutrons that bombard other atoms. The process repeats as a chain reaction. Fission takes place inside a reactor core. Fuel rods containing uranium, shown in green below, provide the material for the chain reaction. Control rods that absorb neutrons are used to regulate the chain reaction. The energy is released, which is used to generate electrical power. A closed reactor system contains the radioactivity. Nuclear wastes are contained separately for disposal.

During nuclear reactions, energy in the form of heat is released, which turns water into steam. Steam turns the turbines to generate electricity.

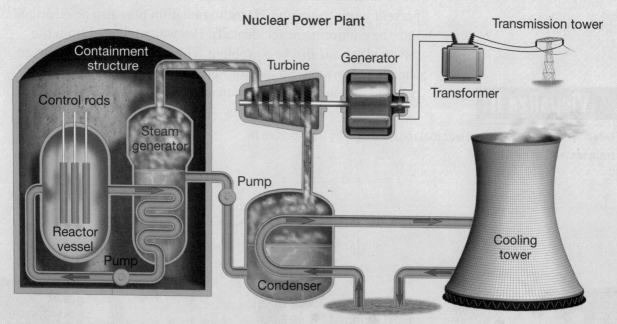

Nuclear Power Plant

12 Compare How are the two types of power plants similar? How are they different?

Similar

_____

_____

_____

_____

Different

_____

_____

_____

_____

The Pros and Cons

How can we evaluate nonrenewable energy resources?

There are advantages and disadvantages to using nonrenewable energy resources. Nonrenewable resources provide much of the energy that humans need to power transportation, warm homes, and produce electricity relatively cheaply. But the methods of obtaining and using these resources can have negative effects on the environment.

The Pros and Cons of Nuclear Fuel

Nuclear fission produces a large amount of energy and does not cause air pollution because no fuel is burned. Mining uranium also does not usually result in massive strip mines or large loss of habitats.

However, nuclear power does have drawbacks. Nuclear power plants produce dangerous wastes that remain radioactive for thousands of years. So the waste must be specially stored to prevent harm to anyone. Harmful radiation may also be released into the environment accidentally. Hot water released from the power plant can also be a problem. This heated water can disrupt aquatic ecosystems. So the hot water must be cooled before it is released into local bodies of water.

Active Reading

13 Identify As you read, underline the effects that nuclear power plants have on their surroundings.

Visualize It!

14 Infer Why do you think nuclear fuel rods are usually transported by train instead of by trucks?

_____

_____

Used nuclear fuel rods must be transported in specially built steel containers.

The Pros and Cons of Fossil Fuels

Fossil fuels are relatively inexpensive to obtain and use. However, there are problems associated with their use. Burning coal can release sulfur dioxide, which combines with moisture in the air to form acid rain. Acid rain causes damage to structures and the environment. Coal mining also disturbs habitats, lowers water tables, and pollutes water.

Environmental problems are also associated with using oil. In 2010, a blown oil well spilled an estimated 200 million gallons of crude oil in the Gulf of Mexico for 86 days. The environmental costs may continue for years.

Burning fossil fuels can cause smog, especially in cities with millions of vehicles. Smog is a brownish haze that can cause respiratory problems and contribute to acid rain. Burning fossil fuels also releases carbon dioxide into the atmosphere. Increases in atmospheric carbon dioxide can lead to global warming.

Some coal is mined by removing the tops of mountains to expose the coal. This damages habitats and can cause water pollution as well.

15 Evaluate In the chart below, list the advantages and disadvantages of using nuclear fuel and fossil fuels.

Type of fuel	Pros	Cons
nuclear fuel		
fossil fuels		

Visual Summary

To complete this summary, check the box that indicates true or false. Then use the key below to check your answers. You can use this page to review the main concepts of the lesson.

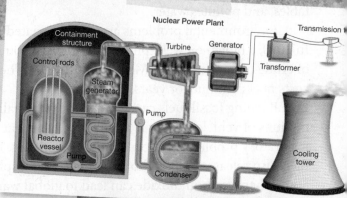

Nuclear Power Plant

Nuclear fuel is an energy resource that undergoes the process of fission to release energy for human use.

	T	F	
16	☐	☐	Uranium is often used as fuel in nuclear fission.
17	☐	☐	One disadvantage of nuclear fission is that it produces only a small amount of energy.

Nonrenewable Energy Resources

Most of the energy used today comes from fossil fuels, which include petroleum, natural gas, and coal.

	T	F	
18	☐	☐	Natural gas forms from microscopic marine organisms.
19	☐	☐	Most transportation fuels are products of coal.
20	☐	☐	Burning fossil fuels decreases the amount of carbon dioxide in the atmosphere.

Answers: 16 True; 17 False; 18 True; 19 False; 20 False

21 **Summarize** Identify the advantages and disadvantages for both fossil fuels and nuclear fuels.

Renewable Energy Resources

ESSENTIAL QUESTION

How do humans use renewable energy resources?

By the end of this lesson, you should be able to describe how humans use energy resources and the role of renewable energy resources in society.

Virginia Science Standards of Learning

6.1 The student will demonstrate an understanding of scientific reasoning, logic, and the nature of science by planning and conducting investigations in which:

6.1.j current applications are used to reinforce science concepts.

6.2 The student will investigate and understand basic sources of energy, their origins, transformations, and uses. Key concepts include:

6.2.b the role of the sun in the formation of most energy sources on Earth; and

6.2.d renewable energy sources.

6.9 The student will investigate and understand public policy decisions relating to the environment. Key concepts include:

6.9.d cost/benefit tradeoffs in conservation policies.

Panels such as these can turn an unused city roof into a miniature solar energy plant.

 **Lesson Labs**

Quick Labs
• Design a Turbine
• Understanding Solar Panels

S.T.E.M. Lab
• Modeling Geothermal Power

Engage Your Brain

1 Predict Check T or F to show whether you think each statement is true or false.

T	F	
☐	☐	Renewable energy resources can never run out.
☐	☐	Renewable energy resources do not cause any type of pollution.
☐	☐	Solar energy is the most widely used renewable energy resource in the United States.
☐	☐	Renewable energy resources include solar energy, wind energy, and geothermal energy.

2 Describe Write a caption to explain how the sun's energy is being used in this photo.

Active Reading

3 Synthesize You can often define an unknown word if you know the meaning of its word parts. Use the word parts and sentence below to make an educated guess about the meaning of the word *geothermal*.

Word part	Meaning
geo-	Earth
therm-	heat

Example sentence

A geothermal power plant uses steam produced deep in the ground to generate electricity.

geothermal:

_____

_____

_____

Vocabulary Terms

- energy resource
- wind energy
- hydroelectric energy
- solar energy
- biomass
- geothermal energy

4 Apply As you learn the definition of each vocabulary term in this lesson, create your own definition or sketch to help you remember the meaning of the term.

Energy *Déjà Vu*

What are the two main sources of renewable energy?

An **energy resource** is a natural resource used to generate electricity and other forms of energy. Most of the energy used by humans comes from *nonrenewable resources*. These resources are used more quickly than they can be replaced. But *renewable resources* can be replaced almost as quickly as they are used. Most renewable energy resources come from the sun and some from Earth itself.

The Sun

The sun's energy is a result of nuclear fusion. Fusion is the process by which two or more nuclei fuse together to form a larger nucleus. Fusion produces a large amount of energy, which is released into space as light and heat.

Solar energy warms Earth, causing the movement of air masses. Moving air masses form winds and some ocean currents. Solar energy also fuels plant growth. Animals get energy by eating plants. Humans can harness energy from wind, moving water, plant and animal materials, and directly from the light and heat that comes from the sun.

Earth

Energy from within Earth comes from two sources. One source is the decay of radioactive elements in Earth's mantle and crust, caused by nuclear fission. Fission is the splitting of the nuclei of radioactive atoms. The second source of energy within Earth is energy stored during Earth's formation. The heat produced from these sources radiates outward toward Earth's surface. Humans can harness this heat to use as an energy source.

---

5 Contrast Explain how energy production in the sun differs from energy production in Earth's interior.

_____

_____

_____

_____

_____

_____

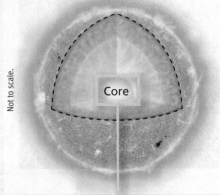

Not to scale.

Core

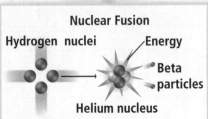

Nuclear Fusion

Hydrogen nuclei

Energy

Beta particles

Helium nucleus

When atomic nuclei fuse, energy is released.

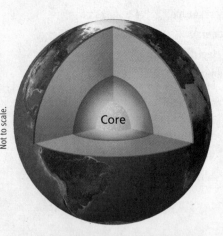

Not to scale.

Core

Earth's internal energy comes from the process of nuclear fission and the events that formed Earth.

How might a renewable energy resource become nonrenewable?

All of the energy resources you will learn about in this lesson are renewable. That doesn't mean that they can't become nonrenewable resources. Trees, for example, are a renewable resource. Some people burn wood from trees to heat their homes and cook food. However, some forests are being cut down but are not being replanted in a timely manner. Others are being cut down and replaced with buildings. If this process continues, eventually these forests will no longer be considered renewable resources.

6 Apply Read the caption below, then describe what might happen if the community uses too much of the water in the reservoir.

_____

_____

_____

_____

_____

7 Distinguish What is the difference between nonrenewable and renewable energy resources?

_____

_____

_____

_____

_____

Think Outside the Book

8 Apply Write an interview with a renewable resource that is afraid it might become nonrenewable. Be sure to include questions and answers.

A community uses this reservoir for water. The dam at the end of the reservoir uses moving water to produce electricity for the community.

Turn, Turn, Turn

How do humans use wind energy?

Wind is created by the sun's uneven heating of air masses in Earth's atmosphere. **Wind energy** uses the force of moving air to drive an electric generator or do other work. Wind energy is renewable because the wind will blow as long as the sun warms Earth. Wind energy is harnessed by machines called wind turbines. Electricity is generated when moving air turns turbine blades that drive an electric generator. Clusters of wind turbines, called wind farms, generate large amounts of electricity.

Although wind energy is a renewable energy resource, it has several disadvantages. Wind farms can be placed only in areas that receive large amounts of wind. The equipment required to collect and convert wind energy is also expensive to produce and maintain. And the production and maintenance of this equipment produces a small amount of pollution. The turbine blades can also be hazardous to birds.

Windmills such as these have been used for centuries to grind grain and pump surface water for irrigation.

A wind-powered water pump can pull water from deep underground when electricity is not available.

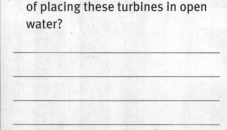

Wind farms are a form of clean energy, because they do not generate air pollution as they generate electricity.

9 Infer What is the main benefit of placing these turbines in open water?

_____

_____

_____

_____

_____

How do humans get energy from moving water?

Active Reading

10 Identify Underline the kind of energy that is found in moving water.

Like wind, moving water has kinetic energy. People have harnessed the energy of falling or flowing water to power machines since ancient times. Some grain and saw mills still use water to power their equipment. Electrical energy produced by moving water is called **hydroelectric energy**. Hydroelectric energy is renewable because the water cycle is driven by the sun. Water that evaporates from oceans and lakes falls on higher elevations and flows downhill in streams, rivers, and waterfalls. The energy in flowing water is converted to electrical energy when it spins turbines connected to electric generators inside the dam.

Hydroelectric energy is a good source of energy only in locations where there are large, reliable amounts of flowing water. Another disadvantage of hydroelectric energy is that hydroelectric dams and their technology are expensive to build. The dams also can block the movement of fish between the sea and their spawning grounds. Special fish ladders must be built to allow fish to swim around the dam.

Visualize It!

11 Explain What is the purpose of the lake that is located behind the dam of a hydroelectric plant?

_____

_____

_____

_____

_____

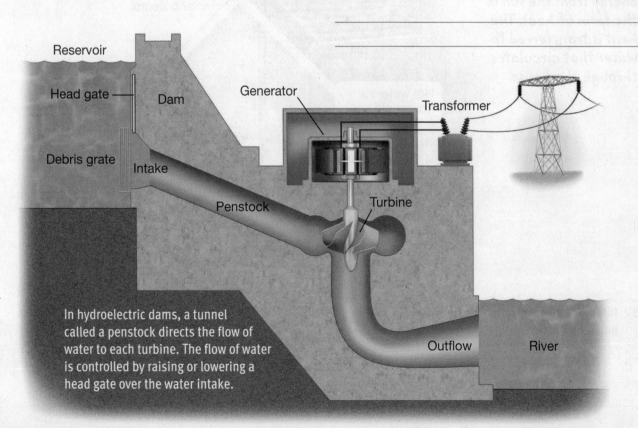

In hydroelectric dams, a tunnel called a penstock directs the flow of water to each turbine. The flow of water is controlled by raising or lowering a head gate over the water intake.

Let the Sunshine In

How do humans use solar energy?

Most forms of energy come from the sun—even fossil fuels begin with the sun as an energy resource. **Solar energy** is the energy received by Earth from the sun in the form of radiation. Solar energy can be used to warm buildings directly. Solar energy can also be converted into electricity by solar cells.

To Provide Energy as Heat

We can use liquids warmed by the sun to warm water and buildings. Some liquids, such as water, have a high capacity for absorbing and holding heat. When the heat is absorbed by the liquid in a solar collector, it can be transferred to water that circulates through a building. The hot water can be used for bathing or other household uses, or to warm the building. The only pollution generated by solar heating systems comes from the manufacture and maintenance of their equipment. Solar heating systems work best in areas with large amounts of sunlight.

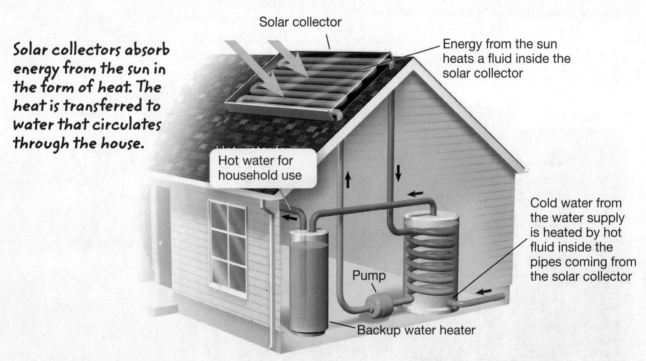

Solar collectors absorb energy from the sun in the form of heat. The heat is transferred to water that circulates through the house.

Solar collector

Energy from the sun heats a fluid inside the solar collector

Hot water for household use

Cold water from the water supply is heated by hot fluid inside the pipes coming from the solar collector

Pump

Backup water heater

12 Infer Not all solar collectors use water to absorb energy from the sun. Why might a solar heating system use a liquid other than water?

_____

_____

_____

To Produce Electricity

Solar collectors can also be used to generate electricity. First, heated fluid is used to produce steam. Then, the steam turns a turbine connected to an electric generator.

Electricity can also be generated when sunlight is absorbed by a photovoltaic cell. A single photovoltaic cell produces a small amount of electricity. The electricity from joined photovoltaic cells can power anything from calculators to entire communities. Many cells must be joined together to form each solar panel, as shown in the solar power plant below. Solar power plants must be built in places with adequate space and abundant sunshine year-round. These requirements increase the costs of solar power.

This calculator is powered by solar cells instead of a battery.

Visualize It! (Inquiry)

14 **Infer** Based on this image and your reading, what might be a disadvantage to using solar energy to supply electricity to a large community?

_____

_____

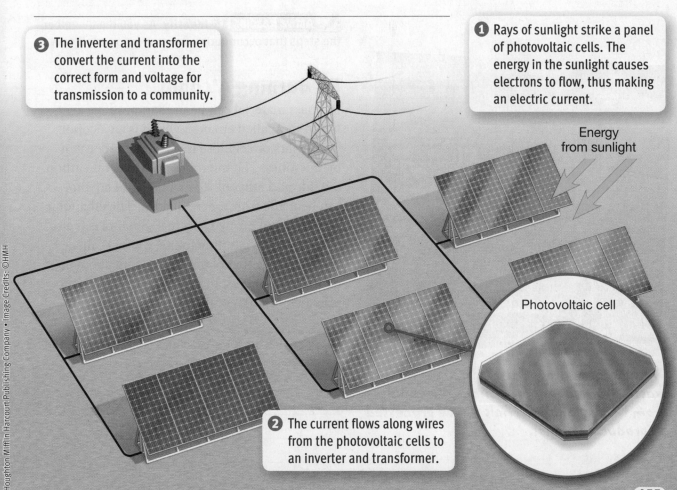

❸ The inverter and transformer convert the current into the correct form and voltage for transmission to a community.

❶ Rays of sunlight strike a panel of photovoltaic cells. The energy in the sunlight causes electrons to flow, thus making an electric current.

Energy from sunlight

Photovoltaic cell

❷ The current flows along wires from the photovoltaic cells to an inverter and transformer.

How do humans get energy from living things?

Plants absorb light energy from the sun and convert it to chemical energy through *photosynthesis*. This energy is stored in leaves, stems, and roots. Chemical energy is also present in the dung of animals. These sources of energy make up biomass.

By Burning Biomass

Biomass is organic matter from plants and from animal waste that contains chemical energy. Biomass can be burned to release energy. This energy can be used to cook food, provide warmth, or power an engine. Biomass sources include trees, crops, animal waste, and peat.

Biomass is inexpensive and can usually be replaced relatively quickly, so it is considered to be a renewable resource. Some types of biomass renew more slowly than others. Peat renews so slowly in areas where it is used heavily that it is treated as a nonrenewable resource. Like fossil fuels, biomass produces pollutants when it burns.

These peat pellets will be used to generate steam in the power plant in the background. The steam will generate electricity by turning turbines.

These wagons are loaded with sugar cane wastes from sugar production. The cellulose from these plant materials will be processed to produce ethanol.

Active Reading 15 **Identify** As you read, number the steps that occur during the production of ethanol.

By Burning Alcohol

Biomass material can be used to produce a liquid fuel called ethanol, which is an alcohol. The sugars or cellulose in the plants are eaten by microbes. The microbes then give off carbon dioxide and ethanol. Over 1,000 L of ethanol can be made from 1 acre of corn. The ethanol is collected and burned as a fuel. Ethanol can also be mixed with gasoline to make a fuel called gasohol. The ethanol produced from about 40% of one corn harvest in the United States would provide only 10% of the fuel used in our cars!

16 **List** What are three examples of how biomass can be used for energy?

_____

_____

_____

_____

How do humans use geothermal energy?

The water in the geyser at right is heated by geothermal energy. **Geothermal energy** is energy produced by heat from Earth's interior. Geothermal energy heats rock formations deep within the ground. Groundwater absorbs this heat and forms hot springs and geysers where the water reaches Earth's surface. Geothermal energy is used to produce energy as heat and electricity.

To Provide Energy as Heat

Geothermal energy can be used to warm and cool buildings. A closed loop system of pipes runs from underground into the heating system of a home or building. Water pumped through these pipes absorbs heat from the ground and is used to warm the building. Hot groundwater can also be pumped in and used in a similar way. In warmer months, the ground is cooler than the air, so this system can also be used for cooling.

To Produce Electricity

Geothermal energy is also used to produce electricity. Wells are drilled into areas of superheated groundwater, allowing steam and hot water to escape. Geothermal power plants pump the steam or hot water from underground to spin turbines that generate electricity, as shown at right. A disadvantage of geothermal energy is pollution that occurs during production of the technology needed to capture it. The technology is also expensive to make and maintain.

Because Earth's core will be very hot for billions of years, geothermal energy will be available for a long time.

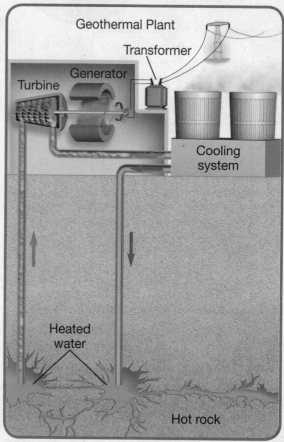

Geothermal Plant

Transformer

Generator

Turbine

Cooling system

Heated water

Hot rock

17 List What are some advantages and disadvantages to using geothermal energy?

Advantages	Disadvantages

Visual Summary

To complete this summary, fill in the blanks with the correct word or phrase. Then, use the key below to check your answers. You can use this page to review the main concepts of the lesson.

Renewable Energy Resources

The source of geothermal energy is energy from within Earth.

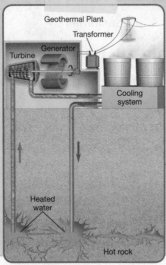

Geothermal Plant

Transformer

Generator

Turbine

Cooling system

Heated water

Hot rock

18 In geothermal power plants, hot water or _____ is pumped from within Earth's crust to produce electricity.

Most of the renewable energy resources that people use come from the sun.

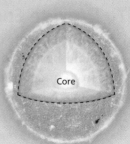

Core

19 Renewable resources that come from the sun include _____

_____

_____

Answers: 18 steam; 19 biomass, solar energy, wind energy, and hydroelectric energy

20 Synthesize Which type of renewable energy resource would be best to use to provide electricity for your town? Explain your answer.

Lesson Review

Vocabulary

Fill in the blanks with the term that best completes the following sentences.

1 Organic matter that contains stored energy is called _____

2 A resource that humans can use to produce energy is a(n) _____

3 _____ is an energy resource harnessed from flowing water.

Key Concepts

4 Describe Identify a major advantage and a major disadvantage of using renewable energy resources to produce electricity.

_____

_____

_____

_____

_____

_____

5 Explain If renewable energy resources can be replaced, why do we need to conserve them? Use an example to support your answer.

_____

_____

_____

_____

_____

_____

6 Describe What is the source of energy that powers wind and flowing water?

_____

_____

_____

_____

Critical Thinking

Use this graph to answer the following questions.

Total Renewable Energy Resources Consumed in 2009 in the United States

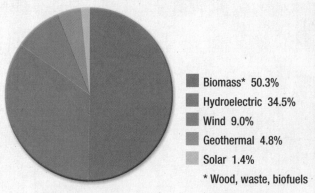

- Biomass* 50.3%
- Hydroelectric 34.5%
- Wind 9.0%
- Geothermal 4.8%
- Solar 1.4%

* Wood, waste, biofuels

Source: Annual Energy Review 2009, U.S. Energy Information Administration

7 Evaluate Which is the most used renewable energy resource in the United States? Why do you think this is the case?

_____

_____

_____

_____

_____

8 Evaluate Which is the least used renewable energy resource in the United States? Why do you think this is the case?

_____

_____

_____

_____

_____

_____

9 Relate How are biomass and alcohol production related to energy from the sun?

_____

_____

_____

_____

My Notes

Analyzing Technology

Skills
Identify risks
✓ Identify benefits
✓ Evaluate cost of technology
✓ Evaluate environmental impact
✓ Propose improvements
Propose risk reduction
Plan for technology failures
Compare technology
✓ Communicate results

Objectives
- Describe the effects of making paper cups on Earth's resources.
- Estimate the carbon dioxide saved by recycling paper cups.
- Propose improvements for the life cycle of a paper cup.

Analyzing the Life Cycle of a Paper Cup

A product's life cycle includes all of the phases in its "life," from getting raw materials to disposing of it once it has served its purpose. Most steps in the life cycle of a paper product affects the environment in some way.

Newspapers awaiting recycling

These paper cups probably will not be recycled.

Impact of a Paper Cup

A life cycle analysis of a paper cup shows that making it requires trees, water, ink, and plastic for a waterproof lining. The process also uses several different kinds of fuel, such as natural gas and diesel truck fuel for energy to make and transport the cups. The whole process releases about 110 grams (about ¼ pound) of carbon dioxide (KAR•buhn dy•AHK•syd) per cup into the atmosphere. This amount is 3 to 4 times the weight of a cup itself. And because of the plastic lining, paper cups are difficult to recycle.

1 Estimate Assume that a recycled paper cup is made up of only paper, and that paper could be recycled 5 times. About how much carbon dioxide would this prevent from being released into the atmosphere?

_____

_____

_____

Recycling Paper Products

Many paper products are more easily recycled than paper cups are. Over 70% of newspaper is recycled to make various products such as cereal boxes, egg cartons, and tissue paper. Many paper products can be recycled 5 to 7 times, after which the paper fibers are too short and no longer stick together well enough to make paper. Recycling paper products not only saves trees but also saves a lot of water, electricity, and gas and reduces air pollution.

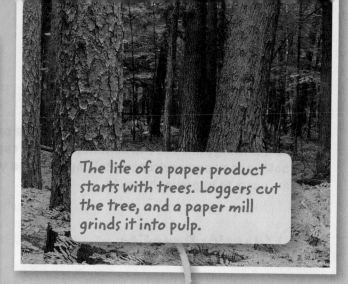

The life of a paper product starts with trees. Loggers cut the tree, and a paper mill grinds it into pulp.

Most newspapers are recycled, saving trees and energy used in logging.

The mill mixes the pulp with water and other chemicals to make paper, which is used to make paper products such as paper cups.

Most paper cups end up in a landfill.

2 Infer Most newspaper is recycled. Most paper cups are not. What is one difference in environmental impact between burial and incineration for used paper products?

_____

_____

_____

These products are used by all of us and then either recycled, incinerated, or buried in a landfill.

 **You Try It!** →

Now it's your turn to analyze the life cycle of a paper cup.

 # You Try It!

Now it's your turn to analyze the life cycle of a paper cup. You'll consider things such as the benefits of paper cups and their cost in both money and environmental impact. Then you can suggest some ways to improve the cycle.

① Identify Benefits

With your class, research the benefits of making and using paper cups. List those benefits below.

Benefits
_____

② Evaluate Cost of Technology

A A paper mill uses about 16,000 gallons of water and about 400 kWh of electricity to produce one ton of paper cups. Using the information shown here, what is the cost of the water and electricity that are used to make one ton of paper cups?

_____

_____

_____

B A modern paper mill costs around $1 billion to build. How many cups would a company need to sell to pay for the cost of the plant, the water, and the electricity?

_____

_____

_____

- Water costs about $0.0007 per gallon.

- Electricity costs about $0.072/kWh.

- 33,000 cups weighs about a ton.

- One ton of cups sells for $2,000.

③ Evaluate Environmental Impact

With a partner, discuss possible impacts of the life cycle of a paper cup on the environment. Consider things such as the harvesting of trees, the use of chlorine-based chemicals to bleach the pulp, the energy required by the paper mill, problems associated with disposal of paper cups after their use, etc.

_____

_____

_____

_____

_____

_____

④ Propose Improvements

With a partner, propose some improvements to the process of making or disposing of paper cups that might help make the life cycle of paper cups more environmentally friendly.

_____

_____

_____

_____

_____

⑤ Communicate Results

With your partner, tell the class the most important thing you have learned about the life cycle of a paper cup, and explain why you think it is important.

_____

_____

_____

_____

_____

_____

Managing Resources

ESSENTIAL QUESTION

Why should natural resources be managed?

By the end of this lesson, you should be able to explain the consequences of society's use of natural resources and the importance of managing these resources wisely.

Bauxite is a rock that is mined to make aluminum. The company that removed the bauxite from this hillside replanted the area with trees. Replanting restores habitat and helps to prevent erosion.

Virginia Science Standards of Learning

6.9 The student will investigate and understand public policy decisions relating to the environment. Key concepts include:

6.9.a management of renewable resources;

6.9.b management of nonrenewable resources;

6.9.c the mitigation of land-use and environmental hazards through preventive measures; and

6.9.d cost/benefit tradeoffs in conservation policies.

Engage Your Brain

1 Predict Check T or F to show whether you think each statement is true or false.

T F

☐ ☐ Renewable resources cannot be replaced at the same rate that they are used.

☐ ☐ Resource use always results in the pollution of natural areas.

☐ ☐ Placing limits on the amount of fish that can be caught can cause fish populations to increase.

☐ ☐ Recycling nonrenewable resources can cause them to be used up more quickly.

2 Describe What natural resources could be obtained from the areas in the picture?

_____

_____

_____

_____

_____

Active Reading

3 Apply Some words have similar meanings. Use context clues to write your own definitions for the words *conservation* and *stewardship*.

Example sentence
Hotels practice water <u>conservation</u> by installing water-saving showerheads.

conservation:

_____

_____

Example sentence
Fertilizers can run off into lakes and cause algae to bloom. People who live near lakes can practice good <u>stewardship</u> of the lake by not using lawn fertilizers.

stewardship:

_____

_____

Vocabulary Terms

- natural resource
- renewable resource
- nonrenewable resource
- stewardship
- conservation
- cost-benefit analysis

4 Identify This list shows vocabulary terms you'll learn in this lesson. As you read, underline the definition of each term.

Useful Stuff

What are the two main types of resources?

Any natural material that is used by people is a **natural resource**. Water, trees, minerals, air, and oil are just a few examples of Earth's resources. Resources can be divided into renewable and nonrenewable resources.

Renewable Resources

A natural resource that can be replaced as quickly as the resource is used is a **renewable resource**. Water, trees, and fish are examples of renewable resources. Renewable resources can become nonrenewable resources if they are used too quickly. For example, trees in a forest can become nonrenewable if they are cut down faster than new trees can grow to replace them.

Nonrenewable Resources

A natural resource that is used much faster than it can be replaced is a **nonrenewable resource**. Coal is an example of a nonrenewable resource. It takes millions of years for coal to form. Once coal is used up, it is no longer available. Minerals, oil, and natural gas are other examples of nonrenewable resources.

5 Compare How is a renewable resource different from a nonrenewable resource?

_____

_____

_____

_____

_____

_____

_____

6 Identify Label each picture as a renewable resource or nonrenewable resource.

salt mine

_____   _____   _____

What can happen when we use resources?

Natural resources can make people's lives easier. Natural resources allow us to heat and cool buildings, produce and use electricity, transport people and goods, and make products.

While natural resources are helpful, the way they are used can cause harm. Mining and oil spills can damage ecosystems. Oil spills can also harm local fishing or tourism industries. Burning coal or other fossil fuels can cause air and water pollution. Used products can fill landfills or litter beaches and other natural areas. Overuse of resources can make them hard to find. When resources are hard to find, they become more expensive.

Active Reading

7 Identify As you read, underline the possible harmful effects of resource use by people.

Visualize It!

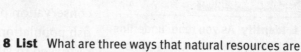

8 List What are three ways that natural resources are making life easier for this family?

_____

_____

_____

_____

_____

9 Explain How can the extraction of natural resources damage the environment?

_____

_____

_____

_____

_____

10 Describe How can human use of natural resources pollute the environment?

_____

_____

_____

_____

Best Practices

What are some effective ways to manage resources?

As human populations continue to grow, we will need more and more resources in order to survive. People can make sure that resources continue to be available by practicing stewardship and conservation. **Stewardship** is the careful and responsible management of resources. **Conservation** is the protection and wise use of natural resources.

Conserving Renewable Resources

Stewardship of renewable resources involves a variety of conservation practices. Limits on fishing or logging can increase fish populations and protect forest ecosystems. Fish can be restocked in lakes and rivers. Logged areas can be replanted with trees. Water conservation can reduce the amount of water used in an area so that rain can renew the water supply. Reducing the use of chemicals and energy resources can reduce the amount of pollution in air and water and on land.

Active Reading

11 Identify As you read, underline the ways that resources can be managed effectively.

Visualize It!

12 Identify Describe the ways that each activity in the picture shows stewardship of natural resources.

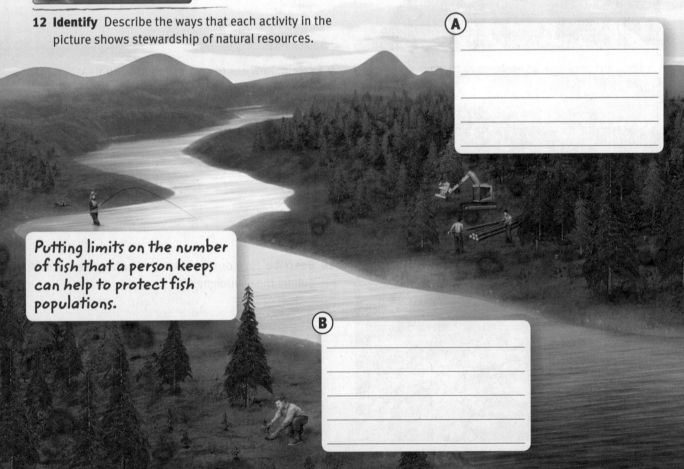

Ⓐ

Ⓑ

Putting limits on the number of fish that a person keeps can help to protect fish populations.

Conserving Nonrenewable Resources

You may have heard the phrase *reduce, reuse, and recycle*. These three practices can help conserve nonrenewable resources. For example, compact fluorescent light bulbs, or CFLs, use less energy to produce the same amount of light as incandescent light bulbs do. By using less electricity, less coal is needed to produce electricity. When we reuse products, we avoid using resources to make new products. But for things that can't be reused, recycling helps saves natural resources. Recycling aluminum means that we don't need to mine more aluminum from Earth. It also takes much less energy to recycle aluminum than it does to purify aluminum from ore.

You can reuse a plastic water bottle instead of buying bottled water. Reusing conserves water and oil.

13 Apply How can you reduce the use of nonrenewable resources? Write your ideas in the table below.

Resource	Is used to . . .	Ways to reduce
oil	Make plastic objects. Provide energy.	Use reusable containers. Recycle plastics. Drive less.
coal		
metal		

Compact fluorescent bulbs last longer than incandescent bulbs and use a lot less energy.

Cans, wires, and other objects made of metal can be collected and recycled into new objects.

Pluses and Minuses

What are the disadvantages and advantages of managing resources?

Managing and conserving resources does have some disadvantages. For example, developing technology that uses fewer resources is expensive. Buying this technology can also be expensive. Activities such as recycling can sometimes be difficult and inconvenient.

Managing resources also has many advantages. Management can reduce the loss of a valuable resource. It can also reduce waste. Less waste means less space is needed for landfills. Many resources produce pollution as they are gathered or used, so resource management can lead to less pollution.

Active Reading

14 Identify As you read, underline the advantages of managing resources.

Visualize It!

15 Place a (–) next to each property of the hybrid electric car that is a disadvantage. Place a (+) next to each property of the car that is an advantage.

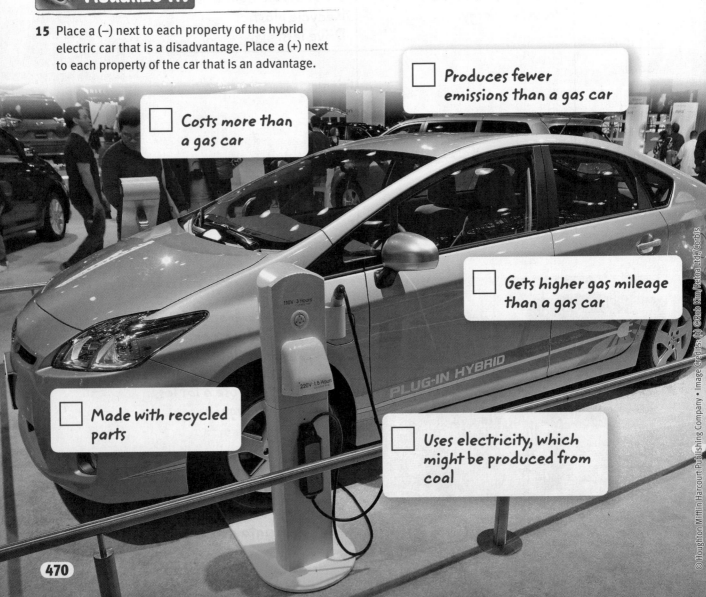

☐ Produces fewer emissions than a gas car

☐ Costs more than a gas car

☐ Gets higher gas mileage than a gas car

☐ Made with recycled parts

☐ Uses electricity, which might be produced from coal

How can we analyze the trade-offs of conservation decisions?

Conservation decisions are not simple. Most often, the outcome of the decision will involve trade-offs. A trade-off happens when something is given up to gain something else. A **cost-benefit analysis** is the process of determining whether the cost of doing something is worth the benefits. A cost-benefit analysis can help people evaluate the trade-offs that might result from a decision. This kind of analysis can include economic, environmental, social, and other factors.

Consider, for example, the construction of a new housing development. Should older trees on the property be saved? It would cost extra money and require changes in the placement of roads and buildings. But preserving the trees would increase home values and help maintain habitat for wildlife. Shade from the trees could help lower energy costs in the buildings. A cost-benefit analysis would include these and other factors.

16 Evaluate A city council wants to make it easier for people to travel by bike. Council members are trying to decide whether or not to build a bike trail that would go all over the city, including through some forested natural areas. Use the table below to evaluate the costs and benefits of building this trail.

Costs	Benefits

17 Evaluate Based on the costs and benefits, what do you think the city council should decide?

_____

_____

_____

What kinds of changes can we make to manage resources?

Managing natural resources takes place on global, national, state, local, and individual levels. On the global level, countries make agreements to help manage international resources. For example, countries agreed to stop using chemicals called CFCs after scientists discovered that CFCs were causing damage to the ozone layer. The ozone layer is a resource that protects Earth from harmful radiation. Ending the use of CFCs has slowed the breakdown of the ozone layer.

Change Laws

On the national level, countries pass laws to manage resources. For example, many nations have laws that determine where, when, and how many trees can be harvested for timber. Laws also govern how materials must be disposed of to prevent and reduce harm to land and water. States also pass laws and work to protect air, water, and land resources. Cities coordinate recycling programs and promote local conservation efforts. In addition, government funding helps researchers find new ways to conserve resources.

Change Habits

Think about all the things you do every day. Changing some of your habits can help to conserve resources. For example, at school, you can reuse lunch containers and recycle as much as possible. At home, you can conserve water by taking shorter showers and turning off the faucet while brushing your teeth. You and your family can save energy by turning off lights or TV sets when they are not being used. Families can buy energy-efficient appliances to save even more energy.

Think Outside the Book Inquiry

18 Apply With a partner, suggest laws that could be enacted in your community to protect resources.

Visualize It!

19 List What are some of the ways these students are conserving resources in their school lunchroom?

_____

_____

_____

_____

_____

_____

You can conserve resources in your school lunchroom.

ALUMINUM

MILK CARTONS

PLASTIC

© Houghton Mifflin Harcourt Publishing Company • Image Credits: ©HMH

It's a Dirty Job!

In many countries, ordinary household waste ends up in a *landfill*, a large, open pit in which trash is buried. Well-built landfills are inexpensive and safe ways to dispose of trash. Over time, the portion of the waste that is biodegradable breaks down and may form part of soil. Other materials, such as plastic, do not break down. Some trash can release harmful chemicals. Landfills must be carefully constructed and maintained to prevent chemicals from leaking out and polluting the surrounding ground and water supply.

Recycling
Some materials can be recycled instead of thrown away. Many cities pick up recycling at the curb. This makes recycling easy for families.

Toxic!
Some wastes pose serious environmental or health threats. These wastes require extra-careful handling and disposal. Depending on the type of waste, it may be burned to produce energy, poured into cement blocks, isolated in special landfills, or heated until it turns into carbon!

Extend

Inquiry

20 Analyze Make a cost-benefit analysis to evaluate the use of landfills for waste disposal.

21 Predict Describe what your home and city would be like if there were no waste management companies.

22 Research Use library or Internet sources to research plasma energy pyrolysis (PEPS). Write an educational brochure explaining the process and weighing the costs and benefits of using this method for hazardous waste disposal.

Visual Summary

To complete this summary, write the answer to each question.
Then use the key below to check your answers. You can use this
page to review the main concepts of the lesson.

Managing Resources

Humans use natural resources to carry out daily activities.

23 What is a negative impact of resource use?

_____

_____

Managing resources has advantages and disadvantages.

Managing resources can allow resources to be conserved.

24 List two ways that resources can be managed effectively.

_____

_____

25 What is one advantage of developing energy-efficient technologies?

_____

_____

26 Apply Fuels called biofuels can be made from plants such as sugar
cane and corn. What sorts of trade-offs might be involved in the use
of biofuels instead of fossil fuels?

_____

_____

_____

_____

Unit 7 ◀ Big Idea ◀ Humans depend on natural resources for materials and for energy.

Lesson 1
ESSENTIAL QUESTION
How can Earth support life?

Explain how the unique properties of Earth allow life to exist.

Lesson 4
ESSENTIAL QUESTION
How do we use nonrenewable energy resources?

Describe how humans use energy resources and the role of nonrenewable energy resources in society.

Lesson 2
ESSENTIAL QUESTION
What are Earth's natural resources?

Understand the types and uses of Earth's natural resources.

Lesson 5
ESSENTIAL QUESTION
How do humans use renewable energy resources?

Describe how humans use energy resources and the role of renewable energy resources in society.

Lesson 6
ESSENTIAL QUESTION
Why should natural resources be managed?

Explain the consequences of society's use of natural resources and the importance of managing these resources wisely.

Lesson 3
ESSENTIAL QUESTION
How is energy transformed when energy resources are used?

Describe how different forms of energy are transformed when humans use energy resources.

Think Outside the Book

2 Synthesize Choose one of these activities to help synthesize what you have learned in this unit.

☐ Using what you learned in lessons 2, 4, and 5, create a poster presentation that compares and contrasts one renewable resource and one nonrenewable resource. Include a discussion of at least one drawback for each resource type.

☐ Using what you learned in lessons 2 and 3, write a short story about a fossil fuel that follows the fuel from its formation to its use by humans. Identify the energy transformations that occur.

Connect ESSENTIAL QUESTIONS
Lessons 2, 3 and 6

1 Explain Why is it important to manage natural resources wisely?

_____

_____

_____

_____

Unit 7 Review

Vocabulary

Fill in each blank with the term that best completes each sentence.

1 The _____ layer helps insulate Earth.

2 _____ is the management of resources.

3 The process of energy changing from one form to another is called _____.

4 Organic matter, such as plant material and manure, that contains chemical energy is called _____.

5 Rocks, water, air, minerals, forests, wildlife, and soil are all examples of a _____.

Key Concepts

Read each question below, and circle the best answer.

6 The chemical bonds in fuel are changed when the fuel is burned to move a car. What type of energy conversion is taking place in this example?

A kinetic energy to mechanical energy

B chemical energy to potential energy

C potential energy to kinetic energy

D mechanical energy to electrical energy

7 Sometimes, a renewable resource can be considered nonrenewable because it is used up faster than it can be replaced. Which of the following choices is an example of this?

A Coal supply getting smaller because it takes millions of years to form.

B Forests being cut down at a quicker rate than they can grow.

C Solar energy being used to provide electricity to a home.

D Water in streams replaced by rainfall from the atmosphere.

8 The diagram below shows the process of photosynthesis.

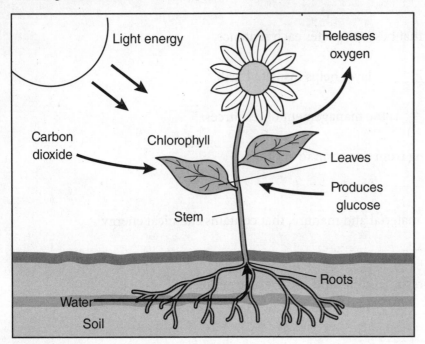

How is photosynthesis best summarized?

A The process by which oxygen enters a leaf and is converted into carbon dioxide.

B The process by which plants use the sun's energy to make chlorophyll.

C The process by which plants convert the sun's energy into energy stored as glucose.

D The process by which water enters through the roots and glucose is produced.

9 Which of the following is a disadvantage of managing resources?

A less of the natural resource is wasted

B reduction in pollution due to less manufacturing

C expense of recycling materials

D more resources extracted from Earth

10 What is a major reason solar energy is not used everywhere on a large scale?

A It is too difficult to purchase and install solar panels.

B Solar energy is not very effective at producing electricity.

C The manufacture of solar panels produces too much pollution.

D Solar panels are most efficient in places that receive lots of sunlight.

11 The chemicals released by burning petroleum in car engines contribute to what local and global effects?

A smog and climate change

B fog and radioactivity

C acid rain and fusion

D sulfur dioxide decrease and ozone buildup

12 What gas molecule found in Earth's atmosphere is made up of three oxygen atoms?

A ozone

B nitrogen

C sulfur dioxide

D carbon dioxide

13 Nuclear energy is best described as what type of energy resource?

A renewable

B nonrenewable

C renewable and inexhaustible

D nonrenewable because it is used up so rapidly

14 Which of the following is a form of potential energy?

A thermal energy

B radiant energy

C chemical energy

D kinetic energy

15 Plants and algae change the radiant energy of the sun into

A thermal energy.

B chemical energy.

C mechanical energy.

D electrical energy.

16 The diagram below shows the energy conversion that happens in flashlights.

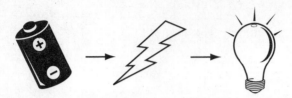

What type of energy transformation does the image show?

A electrical energy to chemical energy to light energy

B electrical energy to chemical energy to mechanical energy

C chemical energy to electrical energy to mechanical energy

D chemical energy to electrical energy to light energy

Critical Thinking

Answer the following questions in the space provided.

17 Below is an example of a technology used to harvest energy.

Is the type of energy harnessed by this equipment renewable or nonrenewable? Explain your answer.

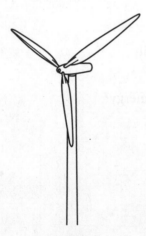

_____

_____

Name one advantage and one disadvantage of using this type of energy source.

_____

_____

_____

18 The unique properties of Earth make life possible. What are the five basic necessities that all living things need to survive on Earth?

_____

_____

_____

Why is the distance from Earth to the sun important for life on Earth?

_____

_____

_____

Why is the rotation of Earth important to conditions on Earth?

_____

_____

_____

19 Explain how the radiant energy from the sun supports life on Earth.

_____

_____

_____

20 To help cut down the amount of car traffic in the city, your city council is discussing creating a bus-only lane on some of the busiest streets. What topics might need to be discussed in a cost-benefit analysis of the situation?

_____

_____

_____

21 You read an article about a new type of engine. The developers of the engine say it is a "revolution in energy conservation" because it is 100 percent efficient. Do you believe this claim? Explain your answer.

_____

_____

_____

_____

Connect ESSENTIAL QUESTIONS
Lessons 4 and 6

Answer the following questions in the space provided.

22 Below is a graph of the production and use of petroleum in the United States in the past and present and of likely U.S. petroleum usage in the future.

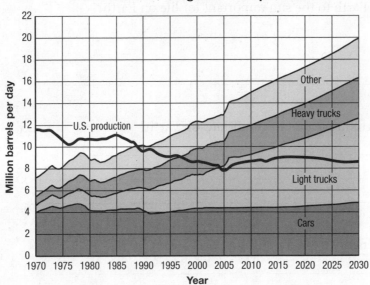

U.S. Petroleum Usage for Transportation

Summarize how current production and usage of petroleum compare.

_____

_____

_____

_____

Name two risks linked to offshore drilling and transporting petroleum.

_____

_____

_____

_____

Human Impact on the Environment

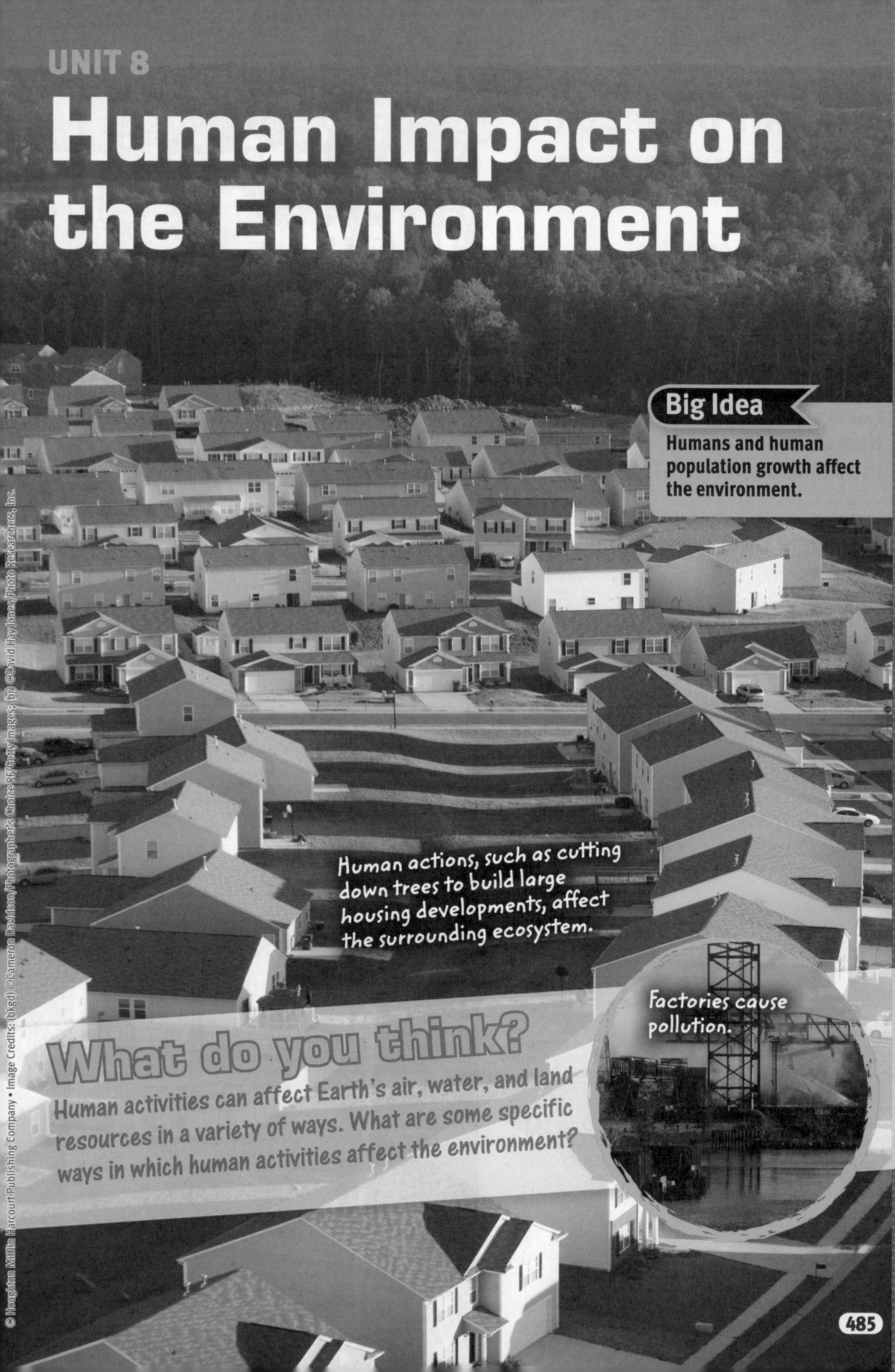

Big Idea

Humans and human population growth affect the environment.

Human actions, such as cutting down trees to build large housing developments, affect the surrounding ecosystem.

Factories cause pollution.

What do you think?

Human activities can affect Earth's air, water, and land resources in a variety of ways. What are some specific ways in which human activities affect the environment?

Unit 8
Human Impact on the Environment

CITIZEN SCIENCE
Investigating Water Resources

Fresh water is an important natural resource. It is found underground and on Earth's surface. People need fresh water for many things, including drinking and household uses.

① Think about It

A What makes fresh surface water and groundwater such valuable resources?

_____

_____

_____

B How does human activity affect the availability of fresh water?

_____

_____

_____

Rain barrels collect rainwater for home use.

② Ask A Question

Where does your water come from?

With a partner, research the source of the water used by your community. Consider contacting your local utility company for information.

Things to Consider

✔ How do our water supplies get replenished?

✔ What are the most common uses for water?

③ Make A Plan

A Describe the environment that surrounds your local water source.

_____

_____

B Describe threats to your local water supply and how your water supply can be protected.

Threats to Water Supply	Ways to Protect Water Supply

C Choose one of the ideas for protecting the water supply that you listed above. Describe how this method of protection might be implemented by your community.

_____

_____

_____

_____

Take It Home

Trace the water used in your home to its source. Use a map to determine the route by which the water you use must be transported from its source.

Lesson 1

Human Impact on Water

ESSENTIAL QUESTION

What impact can human activities have on water resources?

By the end of this lesson, you should be able to explain the impacts that humans can have on the quality and supply of fresh water.

Humans and other organisms depend on clean water to survive. More than half of the material inside humans is water.

Virginia Science Standards of Learning

6.5 The student will investigate and understand the unique properties and characteristics of water and its roles in the natural and human-made environment. Key concepts include:

6.5.e the importance of water for agriculture, power generation, and public health; and

6.5.f the importance of protecting and maintaining water resources.

6.9 The student will investigate and understand public policy decisions relating to the environment. Key concepts include:

6.9.c the mitigation of land-use and environmental hazards through preventative measures.

✋ **Lesson Labs**

Quick Labs
• Ocean Pollution From Land
• Turbidity and Water Temperature

Field Lab
• Investigating Water Quality

🐟 Engage Your Brain

1 Analyze Write a list of the reasons humans need water. Next to this list, write a list of reasons fish need water. Are there similarities between your two lists?

2 Identify Circle the word that correctly completes the following sentences.
The man in this photo is testing *water/air* quality.
The flowing body of water next to the man is a *river/lake*.

✏️ Active Reading

3 Synthesize You can often define an unknown word if you know the meaning of its word parts. Use the word parts and the sentence below to make an educated guess about the meaning of the word *nonrenewable*.

Word part	Meaning
renew	restore, make like new
-able	able to be
non-	not

Example sentence
Some of Earth's <u>nonrenewable</u> resources include coal and oil.

nonrenewable:

_____

_____

_____

_____

Vocabulary Terms

• water pollution
• point-source pollution
• nonpoint-source pollution
• thermal pollution
• eutrophication
• potable
• reservoir

4 Identify This list contains the key terms you'll learn in this lesson. As you read, circle the definition of each term.

Water, Water

Close up of a mayfly larva

Organisms need clean water for life and good health. For example, young mayflies live in water, humans drink water, and brown pelicans eat fish they catch in water.

Why is water important?

Earth is the only planet with large amounts of water. Water shapes Earth's surface and affects Earth's weather and climates. Most importantly, water is vital for life. Every living thing is made mostly of water. Most life processes use water. Water is an important natural resource. For humans and other organisms, access to clean water is important for good health.

There is lots of water, so what's the problem?

About 97% of Earth's water is salty, which leaves only 3% as fresh water. However, as you can see from the graph, over two-thirds of Earth's fresh water is frozen as ice and snow. But a lot of the liquid water seeps into the ground as groundwater. That leaves much less than 1% of Earth's fresh liquid water on the surface. Water is vital for people, so this small volume of fresh surface and groundwater is a limited resource.

Areas with high densities of people, such as cities, need lots of fresh water. Cities are getting bigger, and so the need for fresh water is increasing. *Urbanization* (ER•buh•ny•zhay•shuhn) is the growth of towns and cities that results from the movement of people from rural areas into the urban areas. The greater demand for fresh water in cities is threatening the availability of water for many people. Fresh water is becoming a natural resource that cannot be replaced at the same rate at which it is used.

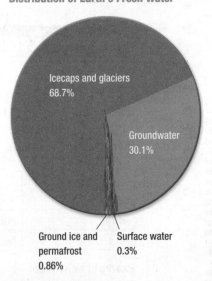

Distribution of Earth's Fresh Water

Icecaps and glaciers 68.7%

Groundwater 30.1%

Ground ice and permafrost 0.86%

Surface water 0.3%

👁 **Visualize It!**

5 Interpret What percentage of fresh water on Earth is frozen? What percentage of fresh water is liquid?

_____

_____

Everywhere...

Where do we get fresh water?

Fresh water may fall directly as precipitation, or may melt from ice and snow. Earth's fresh liquid water is found as surface water and groundwater. *Surface water* is any body of water above the ground. It includes liquid salt or fresh water, or solid water, like snow and ice. Water may seep below the surface to become *groundwater*. Groundwater is found under Earth's surface, in spaces in rocks or in soil, where it can be liquid or frozen.

Aquifers and Groundwater

Aquifers and ground ice are forms of groundwater. An *aquifer* is a body of rock or sediment that can store a lot of water, and that allows water to flow easily through it. Aquifers store water in spaces, called *pores,* between particles of rock or sediment. Wells are dug into aquifers to reach the water. In polar regions, water is often frozen in a layer of soil called *permafrost.*

Rivers, Streams, and Lakes

Rivers, streams, and most lakes are fresh surface waters. A stream or river may flow into a bowl-shaped area, which may fill up to form a lake. Many millions of people around the world depend on fresh water that is taken from rivers and fresh water lakes.

What are water quality and supply?

Water quality is a measure of how clean or polluted water is. Water quality is important because humans and other organisms depend on clean water to survive. It is vital for living things to not only have water, but also to have clean water. Dirty, contaminated water can make us sick or even kill us.

 Water supply is the availability of water. Water supply influences where and when farmers grow crops, and where people can build cities. *Water supply systems* carry water from groundwater or surface waters so people can use the water. The systems can be a network of underground pipes, or a bucket for scooping water from a well. A shortage of clean, fresh water reduces quality of life for people. Many people in developing countries do not have access to clean, fresh water.

Many people do not have a water supply to their homes. Instead, they have to go to a local stream, well, or pump to gather water for cooking, cleaning, and drinking.

Active Reading

6 List What are the different sources of fresh water?

Think Outside the Book Inquiry

7 Observe Keep a water diary for a day. Record every time you use water at school, at home, or elsewhere. At the end of the day, review your records. How could you reduce your water usage?

Under Threat

What threatens fresh water quality?

When waste or other material is added to water so that it is harmful to organisms that use it or live in it, **water pollution** (WAW•ter puh•LOO•shuhn) occurs. It is useful to divide pollution sources into two types. **Point-source pollution** comes from one specific site. For example, a major chemical spill is point-source pollution. Usually this type of pollution can be controlled once its source is found. **Nonpoint-source pollution** comes from many small sources and is more difficult to control. Most nonpoint-source pollution reaches water supplies by runoff or by seeping into groundwater. The main sources of nonpoint-source pollution are city streets, roads and drains, farms, and mines.

Active Reading

8 Identify As you read, underline the sources of water pollution.

Thermal Pollution

Any heating of natural water that results from human activity is called **thermal pollution**. For example, water that is used for cooling some power plants gets warmed up. When that water is returned to the river or lake it is at a higher temperature than the lake or river water. The warm water has less oxygen available for organisms that live in the water.

Chemical Pollution

Chemical pollution occurs when harmful chemicals are added to water supplies. Two major sources of chemical pollution are industry and agriculture. For example, refineries that process oil or metals and factories that make metal or plastic products or electronic items all produce toxic chemical waste. Chemicals used in agriculture include pesticides, herbicides, and fertilizers. These pollutants can reach water supplies by seeping into groundwater. Once in groundwater, the pollution can enter the water cycle and can be carried far from the pollution source. *Acid rain* is another form of chemical pollution. It forms when gases formed by burning fossil fuels mix with water in the air. Acid rain can harm both plants and animals. It can lower the pH of soil and water, and make them too acidic for life.

Biological Pollution

Many organisms naturally live in and around water, but they are not normally polluters. *Biological pollution* occurs when live or dead organisms are added to water supplies. Wastewater may contain disease-causing microbes from human or animal wastes. *Wastewater* is any water that has been used by people for such things as flushing toilets, showering, or washing dishes. Wastewater from feed lots and farms may also contain harmful microbes. These microbes can cause diseases such as dysentery, typhoid, or cholera.

Eutrophication

Fresh water often contains nutrients from decomposing organisms. An increase in the amount of nutrients in water is called **eutrophication** (yoo•TRAWF•ih•kay•shuhn). Eutrophication occurs naturally in water. However, *artificial eutrophication* occurs when human activity increases nutrient levels in water. Wastewater and fertilizer runoff that gets into waterways can add extra nutrients which upset the natural biology of the water. These extra nutrients cause the fast growth of algae over the water surface. An overgrowth of algae and aquatic plants can reduce oxygen levels and kill fish and other organisms in the water.

Visualize It!

Water can become polluted by human activities in many different ways.

Chemical Pollution
Sulfur in smoke and vehicle exhausts contributes to the acidification of rain, leading to acid rain. Acid rain can affect areas far from the point of pollution.

Biological pollution

Biological Pollution
Animal and human wastes can get washed into a water supply in runoff, or through leaking pipes.

Thermal pollution

Eutrophication

Chemical pollution

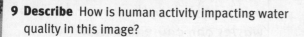

9 Describe How is human activity impacting water quality in this image?

_____

_____

_____

_____

10 Apply Identify one point-source and one nonpoint-source of pollution in this image.

_____

_____

_____

_____

How is water quality measured?

Before there were scientific methods of testing water, people could only look at water, taste it, and smell it to check its quality. Scientists can now test water with modern equipment, so the results are more reliable. Modern ways of testing water are especially important for finding small quantities of toxic chemicals or harmful organisms in water.

Water is a good solvent. So, water in nature usually contains dissolved solids, such as salt and other substances. Because most dissolved solids cannot be seen, it is important to measure them. Measurements of water quality include testing the levels of dissolved oxygen, pH, temperature, dissolved solids, and the number and types of microbes in the water. Quality standards depend on the intended use for the water. For example, drinking water needs to meet much stricter quality standards than environmental waters such as river or lake waters do.

Water Quality Measurement

Quality measurement	What is it?	How it relates to water quality
Dissolved solids	a measure of the amount of ions or microscopic suspended solids in water	Some dissolved solids could be harmful chemicals. Others such as calcium could cause scaling or build-up in water pipes.
pH	a measure of how acidic or alkaline water is	Aquatic organisms need a near neutral pH (approx. pH 7). Acid rain can drop the pH too low (acidic) for aquatic life to live.
Dissolved oxygen (DO)	the amount of oxygen gas that is dissolved in water	Aquatic organisms need oxygen. Animal waste and thermal pollution can decrease the amount of oxygen dissolved in water.
Turbidity	a measure of the cloudiness of water that is caused by suspended solids	High turbidity increases the chance that harmful microbes or chemicals are in the water.
Microbial load	the identification of harmful bacteria, viruses or protists in water	Microbes such as bacteria, viruses, and protists from human and animal wastes can cause diseases.

11 Predict Why might increased turbidity increase the chance of something harmful being in the water?

_____

_____

How is water treated for human use?

Active Reading 12 **Identify** As you read, number the basic steps in the water treatment process.

Natural water may be unsafe for humans to drink. So, water that is to be used as drinking water is treated to remove harmful chemicals and organisms. Screens take out large debris. Then chemicals are added that make suspended particles stick together. These particles drop out of the water in a process called *flocculation*. Flocculation also removes harmful bacteria and other microbes. Chlorine is often added to kill microbes left in the water. In some cities, fluoride is added to water supplies to help prevent tooth decay. Finally, air is bubbled through the water. Water that is suitable to drink is called **potable** water. Once water is used, it becomes wastewater. It enters the sewage system where pipes carry it to a wastewater treatment plant. There the wastewater is cleaned and filtered before being released back into the environment.

Drinking water is often mixed in large basins to help remove chemicals and harmful organisms. Paddles stir the water in the basins.

Who monitors and protects our water quality?

Active Reading 13 **Identify** As you read, underline the government agency that is responsible for enforcing water quality rules.

If a public water supply became contaminated, many people could get very sick. As a result, public water supplies are closely monitored so that any problems can be fixed quickly. The Safe Drinking Water Act is the main federal law that ensures safe drinking water for people in the United States. The act sets strict limits on the amount of heavy metals or certain types of bacteria that can be in drinking water, among other things. The Environmental Protection Agency (EPA) has the job of enforcing this law. It is responsible for setting the standards drinking water must meet before the water can be pumped into public water systems. Water quality tests can be done by trained workers or trained volunteers.

Samples of water are routinely taken to make sure the water quality meets the standards required by law.

Supply and Demand

How does water get to the faucet?

In earlier times, humans had to live near natural sources of fresh water. Over time, engineers developed ways to transport and store large amounts of water. So, humans can now live in places where fresh water is supplied by water pipes and other infrastructure. The ability to bring fresh water safely from its source to a large population has led to the urbanization of cities.

Creating Water Supply Systems

Freshwater supply is often limited, so we have found ways to store and transport water far from its source to where it is used. Surface water is collected and pumped to places where people need it. Groundwater can be found by digging wells into aquifers. Water can be lifted from a well by hand in buckets. It can be pumped into pipes that supply homes, farms, factories and cities. Piped water supply systems can deliver water over great distances to where humans need it. Water supply and storage systems are expensive to build and maintain.

👁 Visualize It!

A public water supply includes the water source, the treatment facilities, and the pipes and pumps that send it to homes, industries, businesses, and public facilities.

Water treatment and distribution

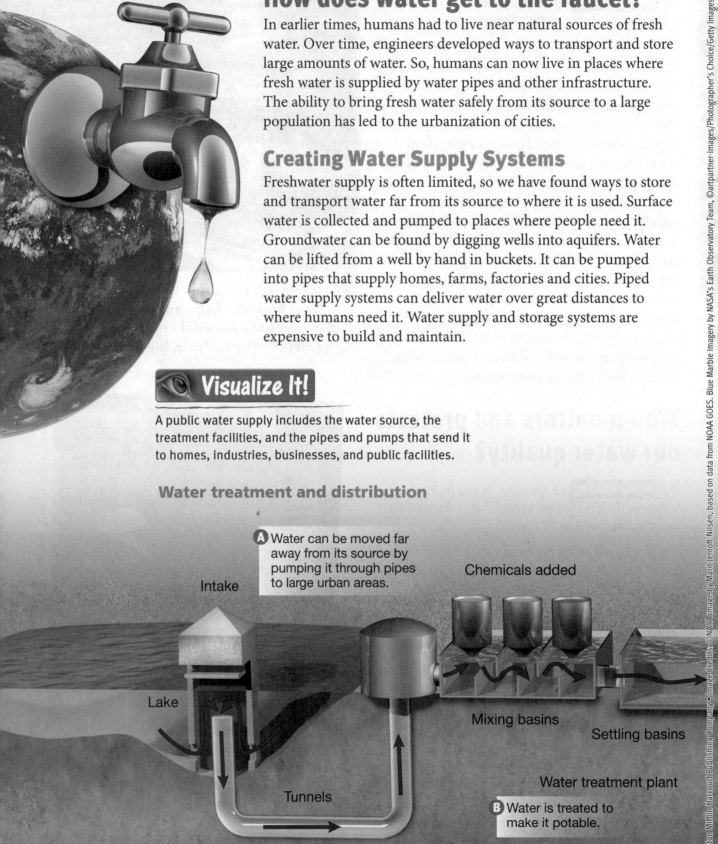

A Water can be moved far away from its source by pumping it through pipes to large urban areas.

Chemicals added

Intake

Lake

Tunnels

Mixing basins

Settling basins

Water treatment plant

B Water is treated to make it potable.

Changing the Flow of Water

Pumping and collecting groundwater and surface waters changes how water flows in natural systems. For example, a **reservoir** (REZ•uhr•vwohr) is a body of water that usually forms behind a dam. Dams stop river waters from flowing along their natural course. The water in a reservoir would naturally have flowed to the sea. Instead, the water can be diverted into a pipeline or into artificial channels called *canals* or *aqueducts*.

What threatens our water supply?

Active Reading **14 Identify** As you read, underline the things that are a threat to water supply.

As the human use of water has increased, the demand for fresh water has also increased. Demand is greater than supply in many areas of the world, including parts of the United States. The larger a population or a city gets, the greater the demand for fresh water. Increased demand for and use of water can cause water shortages. Droughts or leaking water pipes can also cause water shortages. Water is used to keep our bodies clean and healthy. It is also used to grow crops for food. Water shortages threaten these benefits.

15 Infer Why would a larger city have a larger demand for water?

C The infastructure shown here is used to supply clean water. Once water is used, it becomes wastewater. A different system, called a sewage system, carries wastewater away from urban areas to wastewater treatment plants.

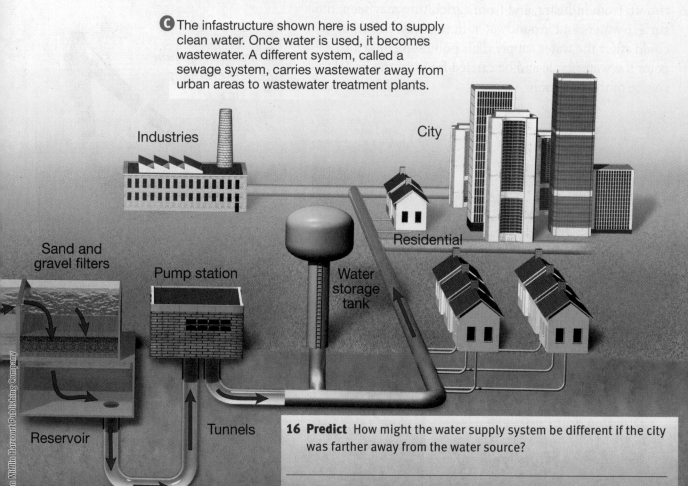

Industries

City

Residential

Sand and gravel filters

Pump station

Water storage tank

Reservoir

Tunnels

16 Predict How might the water supply system be different if the city was farther away from the water source?

© Houghton Mifflin Harcourt Publishing Company

How do efforts to supply water to humans affect the environment?

Growing urban populations place a greater demand on water supplies. Efforts to increase water supply can affect the environment. For example, building dams and irrigation canals changes the natural flow of water. The environment is physically changed by construction work. The local ecology changes too. Organisms that live in or depend on the water may lose their habitat and move away.

Aquifers are often used as freshwater sources for urban areas. When more water is taken from an aquifer than can be replaced by rain or snow, the water table can drop below the reach of existing wells. Rivers and streams may dry up and the soil that once held aquifer waters may collapse, or *subside*. In coastal areas, the overuse of groundwater can cause seawater to seep into the aquifer in a process called *saltwater intrusion*. In this way, water supplies can become contaminated with salt water.

Increasing population in an area can also affect water quality. The more people that use a water supply in one area, the greater the volume of wastewater that is produced in that area. Pollutants such as oil, pesticides, fertilizers, and heavy metals from city runoff, from industry, and from agriculture may seep into surface waters and groundwater. In this way, pollution could enter the water supply. This pollution could also enter the water cycle and be carried far from the initial source of the pollution.

Active Reading

17 Relate How can the increased demand on water affect water quality?

_____

_____

_____

_____

_____

_____

Digging irrigation canals changes the flow of rivers.

Building dams disrupts water flow and affects the ecology of the land and water.

Irrigating arid areas changes the ecology of those areas.

Why It Matters

Death of a Sea

The Aral Sea in Central Asia was once the world's fourth-largest inland salty lake. But it has been shrinking since the 1960s. In the 1940s, the courses of the rivers that fed the lake were changed to irrigate the desert, so that crops such as cotton and rice could be grown. By 2004, the lake had shrunk to 25% of its original size. The freshwater flow into the lake was reduced and evaporation caused the lake to become so salty that most of the plants and animals in it died or left the lake.

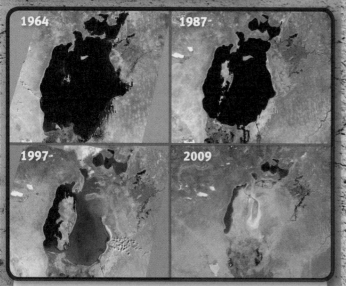

1964 1987 1997 2009

By 2007, the lake had shrunk to 10% of its original size and had split into three separate, smaller lakes.

Polluted Land

The Aral Sea is also heavily polluted by industrial wastes, pesticides, and fertilizer runoff. Salty dust that is blown from the dried seabed damages crops and pollutes drinking water. The salt- and dust-laden air cause serious public health problems in the Aral Sea region. One of the more bizarre reminders of how large the lake once was are the boats that lie abandoned on the exposed sea floor.

Extend

Inquiry

18 Identify What human activity has created the situation in the Aral Sea?

19 Apply Research the impact that of one of these two large water projects has had on people and on the environment: The Three Gorges Dam or the Columbia Basin Project.

20 Relate Research a current or past water project in the area where you live. What benefits will these projects have for people in the area? What risks might there be to the environment?

Visual Summary

To complete this summary, fill in the blanks with the correct word or phrase. Then use the key below to check your answers. You can use this page to review the main concepts of the lesson.

Human Impact on Water

Organisms need clean water for life and good health.

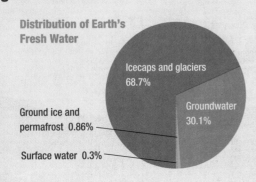

Distribution of Earth's Fresh Water

- Icecaps and glaciers 68.7%
- Groundwater 30.1%
- Ground ice and permafrost 0.86%
- Surface water 0.3%

21 Earth's fresh liquid water is found as surface water and _____

Water pollution can come from many different sources.

22 Runoff from farmland into a river is an example of _____ source pollution.

Federal laws set the standards for potable water quality. Water quality is constantly monitored.

23 Dissolved solids, pH, temperature, and dissolved oxygen are measures of _____.

Ensuring a constant supply of water for people can change the environment.

24 A _____ is a body of water that forms when a dam blocks a river.

Answers: 21 groundwater; 22 nonpoint; 23 water quality; 24 reservoir

25 Compare What is the difference between water quality and water supply?

Lesson Review

Vocabulary

Fill in the blank with the term that best completes the following sentences.

1 _____ water is a term used to describe water that is safe to drink.

2 The addition of nutrients to water by human activity is called artificial _____.

3 _____ pollution comes from many small sources.

Key Concepts

Complete the table below with the type of pollution described in each example.

Example	Type of pollution (chemical, thermal, or biological)
4 Identify A person empties an oil can into a storm drain.	
5 Identify A factory releases warm water into a local river.	
6 Identify Untreated sewage is washed into a lake during a rain storm.	

7 Describe Name two ways in which humans can affect the flow of fresh water.

_____

_____

_____

8 Explain Why does water quality need to be monitored?

_____

_____

Critical Thinking

Use this graph to answer the following questions.

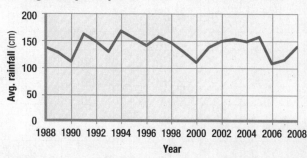

Average Yearly Precipitation in Florida from 1988 to 2008

Source: Florida State University Climate Center

9 Analyze Which year had the least precipitation?

_____

10 Infer What effect might many years of low precipitation have on water supply?

_____

_____

11 Explain Could a single person or animal be a cause of point-source pollution? Explain.

_____

_____

_____

_____

12 Apply In times of hot, dry, weather, some cities ban the use of garden sprinklers. Why do you think there is such a rule?

_____

_____

_____

_____

_____

My Notes

Angel Montoya

CONSERVATION BIOLOGIST

In 1990, Angel Montoya was a student intern working at Laguna Atascosa National Wildlife Refuge in Texas. He became interested in the Aplomado falcon, a bird of prey that disappeared from the southwestern United States during the first half of the 20th century. Montoya decided to go looking for the raptors. He found a previously unknown population of Aplomados in Chihuahua, Mexico. His work helped to make it possible for the falcons to be reintroduced to an area near El Paso, Texas.

Restoration of the Aplomado falcon became Angel's lifework. He has monitored and researched the falcon since 1992. He helps release falcons that have been raised in captivity back into the wild and monitors falcons that have already been released. It isn't easy to keep tabs on a falcon, however. "Their first year they are pretty vulnerable, because they haven't had parents," Montoya says. "Just like juveniles, they're always getting into trouble. But I think they will do just fine."

Angel Montoya releases an Aplomado falcon back into the wild.

JOB BOARD

Environmental Engineering Technician

What You'll Do: Work closely with environmental engineers and scientists to prevent or fix environmental damage. Take care of water and wastewater treatment systems, as well as equipment used for recycling. Test water and air quality and keep good records.

Where You Might Work: In a water treatment facility, or an environmental laboratory.

Education: an associate's degree in engineering technology.

Other Job Requirements: Good communication skills and the ability to work well with others.

Agronomist

What You'll Do: Study the best ways to grow crops and work with farmers to help them use their land better, and get better yields. Agronomists are scientists who study crops and soil.

Where You Might Work: On a farm, in an agricultural business, for the U.S. Department of Agriculture or state or local government agencies, or for seed companies. Agronomists may work both in fields and in laboratories.

Education: a four-year college degree in agronomy, agriculture, or soil conservation.

PEOPLE IN SCIENCE NEWS

YUMI Someya

Fueling the Family Business

Yumi Someya's family had worked in recycling for three generations, cleaning and recycling used cooking oil. In Japan, many people enjoy fried foods. They often throw out the used cooking oil. Yumi's family business collected used oil, cleaned it, and sold it for reuse.

When Yumi traveled to Nepal, she was caught in a landslide. She learned that deforestation was one cause of the landslide and began to think about environmental issues. When she returned home, she worked with her father to find new uses for the used cooking oil. They experimented with fertilizer and soap. Then, in 1992, they learned about biodiesel—fuel made from recycled soybean oil. They thought that used cooking oil might work to fuel cars, too. With a team of researchers, they created Vegetable Diesel Fuel (VDF).

Now, VDF fuels the company's oil-collecting trucks and some Tokyo buses. Yumi hopes to eventually recycle all of the cooking oil used in Japan.

Human Impact on Land

ESSENTIAL QUESTION

What impact can human activities have on land resources?

By the end of this lesson, you should be able to identify the impact that human activity has on Earth's land.

Human activities can carve up land features. A tunnel was cut into this mountain in Zion National Park, Utah, so that people may move around easily.

Virginia Science Standards of Learning
6.9 The student will investigate and understand public policy decisions relating to the environment. Key concepts include:
6.9.c the mitigation of land-use and environmental hazards through preventive measures.

Engage Your Brain

1 Predict Check T or F to show whether you think each statement is true or false.

T   F

☐ ☐ Urban areas have more open land than rural areas do.

☐ ☐ Many building materials are made from land resources.

☐ ☐ Soil provides habitat for plants but not animals.

☐ ☐ Soil can erode when trees are removed from an area.

2 Illustrate Draw a picture of an object or material that is taken from the land and that is commercially important.

 ## Active Reading

3 Synthesize You can often define an unknown word if you know the meaning of its word parts. Use the word parts to make an educated guess about the meaning of the words *land degradation* and *deforestation*.

Word part	Meaning
degrade	to damage something
deforest	to remove trees from an area
-ation	action or process

Vocabulary Terms

- urbanization
- land degradation
- desertification
- deforestation

4 Apply As you learn the definition of each vocabulary term in this lesson, create your own definition or sketch to help you remember the meaning of the term.

land degradation:

_____

_____

deforestation:

_____

_____

Land of Plenty

Why is land important?

It is hard to imagine human life without land. Land supplies a solid surface for buildings and roads. The soil in land provides nutrients for plants and hiding places for animals. Minerals below the land's surface can be used for construction materials. Fossil fuels underground can be burned to provide energy. Land and its resources affect every aspect of human life.

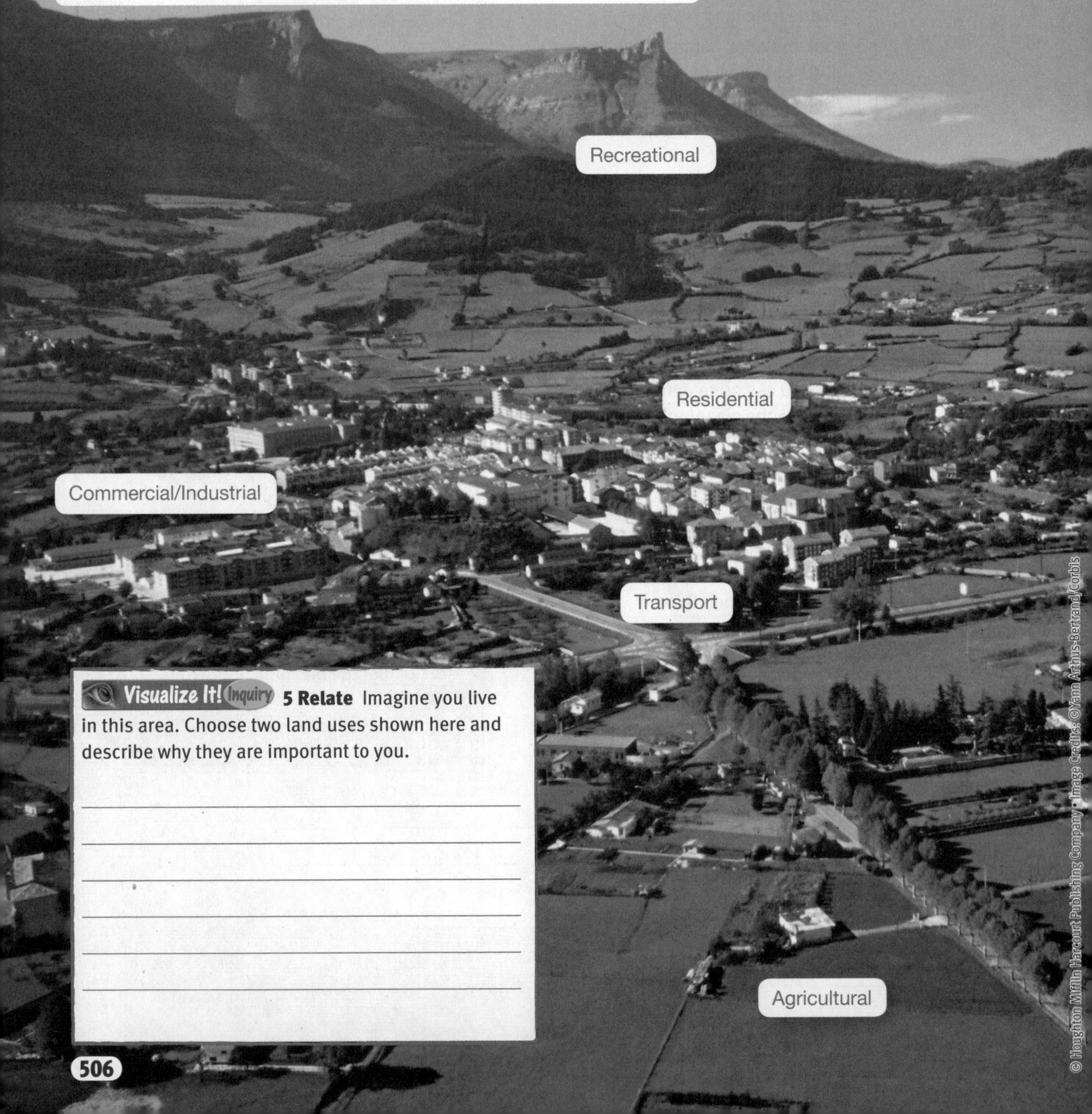

Recreational

Residential

Commercial/Industrial

Transport

Visualize It! Inquiry **5 Relate** Imagine you live in this area. Choose two land uses shown here and describe why they are important to you.

_____

_____

_____

_____

_____

Agricultural

What are the different types of land use?

We live on land in urban or rural areas. Cities and towns are urban areas. Rural areas are open lands that may be used for farming. Humans use land in many ways. We use natural areas for *recreation*. We use roads that are built on land for *transport*. We grow crops and raise livestock on *agricultural* land. We live in *residential* areas. We build *commercial* businesses on land and extract resources such as metals and water from the land.

Recreational

Natural areas are places that humans have left alone or restored to a natural state. These wild places include forests, grasslands, and desert areas. People use natural areas for hiking, bird-watching, mountain-biking, hunting, and other fun or recreational activities.

Transport

A large network of roads and train tracks connect urban and rural areas all across the country. Roads in the U.S. highway system cover 4 million miles of land. Trucks carry goods on these highways and smaller vehicles carry passengers. Railroads carrying freight or passengers use over 120,000 miles of land for tracks. Roads and train tracks are often highly concentrated in urban areas.

Agricultural

Much of the open land in rural areas is used for agriculture. Crops such as corn, soybeans, and wheat are grown on large, open areas of land. Land is also needed to raise and feed cattle and other livestock. Agricultural land is open, but very different from the natural areas that it has replaced. Farmland generally contains only one or two types of plants, such as corn or cotton. Natural grasslands, forests, and other natural areas contain many species of plants and animals.

Active Reading 6 **Identify** As you read, underline the ways rural areas differ from urban areas.

Residential

Where do you call home? People live in both rural and urban areas. Rural areas have large areas of open land and low densities of people. Urban areas have dense human populations and small areas of open land. This means that more people live in a square km of an urban area than live in a square km of a rural area. **Urbanization** is the growth of urban areas caused by people moving into cities. When cities increase in size, the population of rural areas near the city may decrease. When an area becomes urbanized, its natural land surface is replaced by buildings, parking lots, and roads. City parks, which contain natural surfaces, may also be built in urban areas.

Commercial and Industrial

As cities or towns expand, commercial businesses are built too, and replace rural or natural areas. Industrial businesses also use land resources. For example, paper companies and furniture manufacturers use wood from trees harvested on forest land. Cement companies, fertilizer manufacturers, and steel manufacturers use minerals that are mined from below the land's surface. Commercial and industrial development usually includes development of roads or railways. Transporting goods to market forms the basis of commerce.

Active Reading

7 **Identify** What effects does urbanization have on land?

_____

_____

_____

_____

_____

_____

Why is soil important?

Soil is a mixture of mineral fragments, organic material, water, and air. Soil forms when rocks break down and dead organisms decay. There are many reasons why soil is important. Soil provides habitat for organisms such as plants, earthworms, fungi, and bacteria. Many plants get the water and nutrients they need from the soil. Because plants form the base of food webs, healthy soil is important for most land ecosystems. Healthy soil is also important for agricultural land, which supplies humans with food.

It Is a Habitat for Organisms

Earthworms, moles, badgers, and other burrowing animals live in soil. These animals also find food underground. *Decomposers* are organisms that break down dead animal and plant material, releasing the nutrients into the soil. Decomposers such as fungi and bacteria live in soil. Soil holds plant roots in place, providing support for the plant. In turn, plants are food for herbivores and are habitats for organisms such as birds and insects. Many animals on Earth depend on soil for shelter or food.

It Stores Water and Nutrients

Falling rain soaks into soil and is stored between soil particles. Different types of soil can store different amounts of water. Wetland soils, for example, store large amounts of water and reduce flooding. Soils are also part of the nutrient cycle. Plants take up nutrients and water stored in soil. Plants and animals that eat them die and are broken down by decomposers such as bacteria and earthworms. Nutrients are released back into the soil and the cycle starts again.

Visualize It!

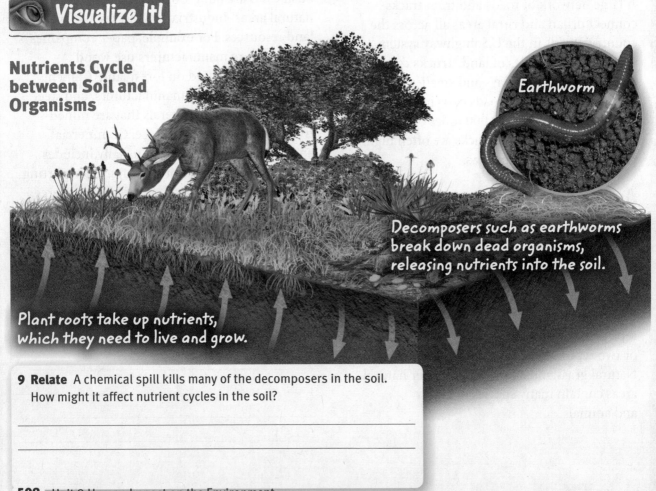

Nutrients Cycle between Soil and Organisms

Earthworm

Decomposers such as earthworms break down dead organisms, releasing nutrients into the soil.

Plant roots take up nutrients, which they need to live and grow.

9 Relate A chemical spill kills many of the decomposers in the soil. How might it affect nutrient cycles in the soil?

_____

_____

Dust Bowl

In the 1930s, huge clouds of dusty soil rolled across the southern Great Plains of the United States. Areas that were once farmlands and homesteads were wiped out. What caused the soil to blow away?

Drought and Overuse

Farmers who settled in the southern Great Plains overplowed and overgrazed their land. When severe drought hit in 1931, topsoil dried out. Winds lifted the soil and carried it across the plains in huge storms that farmers called "black blizzards." The drought and dust storms continued for years.

Modern Day Dust Bowl

Today in northwest China another dust bowl is forming. Large areas of farmland were made there by clearing the natural vegetation and plowing the soil. Herds of sheep and cattle are overgrazing the land, and large dust storms are common.

Extend

Inquiry

10 Identify What type of land use by people contributed to the Dust Bowl? Does it remain a common use of land today?

11 Compare Research another area under threat from overuse that differs from the feature. What type of land use is causing the problem?

12 Illustrate Do one of the following to show how the Dust Bowl or the area you researched affected society: make a poster, write a play, write a song, or draw a cartoon strip. Present your findings to the class.

Footprints

How can human activities affect land and soil?

Human activities can have positive and negative effects on land and soil. Some activities restore land to its natural state, or increase the amount of fertile soil on land. Other activities can degrade land. **Land degradation** is the process by which human activity and natural processes damage land to the point that it can no longer support the local ecosystem. Urbanization, deforestation, and poor farming practices can all lead to land degradation.

Think Outside the Book Inquiry

13 Apply With a classmate, discuss how you could help lessen the impact of urbanization on the land in the area where you live.

Active Reading

14 Identify As you read, underline the effects that urbanization can have on land.

Urban Sprawl

When urbanization occurs at the edge of a city or town, it is called *urban sprawl*. Urban sprawl replaces forests, fields, and grasslands with houses, roads, schools, and shopping areas. Urban sprawl decreases the amount of farmland that is available for growing crops. It decreases the amount of natural areas that surround cities. It increases the amount of asphalt and concrete that covers the land. Rainwater runs off hard surfaces and into storm drains instead of soaking into the ground and filling aquifers. Rainwater runoff from urban areas can increase the erosion of nearby soils.

Erosion

Erosion (ih•ROH•zhuhn) is the process by which wind, water, or gravity transports soil and sediment from one place to another. Some type of erosion occurs on most land. However, erosion can speed up when land is degraded. Roots of trees and plants act as anchors to the soil. When land is cleared for farming, the trees and plants are removed and the soil is no longer protected. This exposes soil to blowing wind and running water that can wash away the soil, as shown in this photo.

© Houghton Mifflin Harcourt Publishing Company • Image Credits: (bkgd) ©Martin Harvey/Photo Researchers, Inc.; (t) ©John Humble/Photographer's Choice/Getty Images

Nutrient Depletion and Land Pollution

Crops use soil nutrients to grow. If the same crops are planted year after year, the same soil nutrients get used up. Plants need the right balance of nutrients to grow. Farmers can plant a different crop each year to reduce nutrient loss. Pollution from industrial activities can damage land. Mining wastes, gas and petroleum leaks, and chemical wastes can kill organisms in the soil. U.S. government programs such as Superfund help to clean up polluted land.

Desertification

When too many livestock are kept in one area, they can overgraze the area. Overgrazing removes the plants and roots that hold topsoil together. Overgrazing and other poor farming methods can cause desertification. **Desertification** (dih•zer•tuh•fih•KAY•shuhn) is the process by which land becomes more desertlike and unable to support life. Without plants, soil becomes dusty and prone to wind erosion. Deforestation and urbanization can also lead to desertification.

Deforestation

The removal of trees and other vegetation from an area is called **deforestation**. Logging for wood can cause deforestation. Surface mining causes deforestation by removing vegetation and soil to get to the minerals below. Deforestation also occurs in rain forests, as shown in the photo, when farmers cut or burn down trees so they can grow crops. Urbanization can cause deforestation when forests are replaced with buildings. Deforestation leads to increased soil erosion.

👁 Visualize It!

15 Relate How has human activity affected the forest in this photo?

_____

_____

_____

_____

_____

Visual Summary

To complete this summary, circle the correct word or phrase.
Then use the key below to check your answers. You can use this
page to review the main concepts of the lesson.

Humans use land in different ways.

16 Crops are grown on recreational/agricultural land.

Soil is important to all organisms, including humans.

17 Decomposers/plants that live in soil break down dead matter in the soil.

Human Impact
on Land

Human activities can affect land and soil.

18 Poor farming practices and drought can lead to desertification/urbanization.

Answers: 16 agricultural; 17 decomposers; 18 desertification

19 Apply How could concentrating human populations in cities help to conserve agricultural and recreational lands?

Lesson Review

Vocabulary

Draw a line to connect the following terms to their definitions.

1 urbanization

2 deforestation

3 land degradation

4 desertification

A the removal of trees and other vegetation from an area

B the process by which land becomes more desertlike

C the process by which human activity can damage land

D the formation and growth of cities

Key Concepts

5 Contrast How are natural areas different from rural areas?

_____

_____

_____

_____

6 Relate How might deforestation lead to desertification?

_____

_____

_____

7 Relate Think of an animal that eats other animals. Why would soil be important to this animal?

_____

_____

_____

_____

Critical Thinking

Use this photo to answer the following questions.

8 Analyze What type of land degradation is occurring in this photo?

_____

9 Predict This type of soil damage can happen in urban areas too. Outline how urbanization could lead to this type of degradation.

_____

_____

_____

_____

_____

10 Apply What kinds of land uses are around your school? Write down each type of land use. Then describe how one of these land uses might affect natural systems.

_____

_____

_____

_____

_____

_____

My Notes

Human Impact on the Atmosphere

ESSENTIAL QUESTION

How do humans impact Earth's atmosphere?

By the end of this lesson, you should be able to identify the impact that humans have had on Earth's atmosphere.

Virginia Science Standards of Learning
6.6 The student will investigate and understand the properties of air and the structure and dynamics of Earth's atmosphere. Key concepts include:
6.6.a air as a mixture of gaseous elements and compounds; and
6.6.d natural and human-caused changes to the atmosphere and the importance of protecting and maintaining air quality.

Human activities that involve burning fuels, such as driving vehicles and keeping buildings cool, can cause air pollution.

Engage Your Brain

1 Identify Check T or F to show whether you think each statement is true or false.

T F

☐ ☐ Human activities can cause air pollution.

☐ ☐ Air pollution cannot affect you if you stay indoors.

☐ ☐ Air pollution does not affect places outside of cities.

☐ ☐ Air pollution can cause lung diseases.

2 Analyze The photo above shows the same city as the photo on the left, but on a different day. How are these photos different?

_____

_____

_____

_____

Active Reading

3 Apply Use context clues to write your own definitions for the words *contamination* and *quality*.

Example sentence
You can help prevent food <u>contamination</u> by washing your hands after touching raw meat.

contamination:

_____

_____

_____

Example sentence
The good sound <u>quality</u> coming from the stereo speakers indicated they were expensive.

quality:

_____

_____

_____

Vocabulary Terms

- greenhouse effect
- air pollution
- particulate
- smog
- acid precipitation
- air quality

4 Apply As you learn the definition of each vocabulary term in this lesson, create your own definition or sketch to help you remember the meaning of the term.

AIR
What Is It Good For?

Why is the atmosphere important?

If you were lost in a desert, you could survive a few days without food and water. But you wouldn't last more than a few minutes without air. Air is an important natural resource. The air you breathe forms part of Earth's atmosphere. The *atmosphere* (AT•muh•sfeer) is a mixture of gases that surrounds Earth. Most organisms on Earth have adapted to the natural balance of gases found in the atmosphere.

It Provides Gases That Organisms Need to Survive

Oxygen is one of the gases that make up Earth's atmosphere. It is used by most living cells to get energy from food. Every breath you take brings oxygen into your body. The atmosphere also contains carbon dioxide. Plants need carbon dioxide to make their own food through photosynthesis (foh•toh•SYN•thuh•sys).

It Absorbs Harmful Radiation

High-energy radiation from space would harm life on Earth if it were not blocked by the atmosphere. Fast-moving particles, called *cosmic rays,* enter the atmosphere every second. These particles collide with oxygen, nitrogen, and other gas molecules and are slowed down. A part of the atmosphere called the *stratosphere* contains ozone gas. The ozone layer absorbs most of the high-energy radiation from the sun, called *ultraviolet radiation* (UV), that reaches Earth.

It Keeps Earth Warm

Without the atmosphere, temperatures on Earth would not be stable. It would be too cold for life to exist. The **greenhouse effect** is the way by which certain gases in the atmosphere, such as water vapor and carbon dioxide, absorb and reradiate thermal energy. This slows the loss of energy from Earth into space. The atmosphere acts like a warm blanket that insulates the surface of Earth, preventing the sun's energy from being lost. For this reason, carbon dioxide and water vapor are called *greenhouse gases.*

Active Reading **5 Explain** How is Earth's atmosphere similar to a warm blanket?

_____

_____

What is air pollution?

The contamination of the atmosphere by pollutants from human and natural sources is called **air pollution**. Natural sources of air pollution include volcanic eruptions, wildfires, and dust storms. In cities and suburbs, most air pollution comes from the burning of fossil fuels such as oil, gasoline, and coal. Oil refineries, chemical manufacturing plants, dry-cleaning businesses, and auto repair shops are just some potential sources of air pollution. Scientists classify air pollutants as either gases or particulates.

6 Identify As you read, underline sources of air pollution.

Visualize It!

7 Analyze Which one of these images could be both a natural or a human source of air pollution? Give reasons for your answer.

_____

_____

_____

_____

_____

Forest fires and wildfires

Factory emissions

Vehicle exhaust

Gases

Gas pollutants include carbon monoxide, sulfur dioxide, nitrogen oxide, and ground-level ozone. Some of these gases occur naturally in the atmosphere. These gases are considered pollutants only when they are likely to cause harm. For example, ozone is important in the stratosphere, but at ground level it is harmful to breathe. Carbon monoxide, sulfur dioxide, and nitrogen dioxide are released from burning fossil fuels in vehicles, factories, and homes. They are a major source of air pollution.

Particulates

Particle pollutants can be easier to see than gas pollutants. A **particulate** (per•TIK•yuh•lit) is a tiny particle of solid that is suspended in air or water. Smoke contains ash, which is a particulate. The wind can pick up particulates such as dust, ash, pollen, and tiny bits of salt from the ocean and blow them far from their source. Ash, dust, and pollen are common forms of air pollution. Vehicle exhaust also contains particulates. The particulates in vehicle exhaust are a major cause of air pollution in cities.

It Stinks!

What pollutants can form from vehicle exhaust?

In urban areas, vehicle exhaust is a common source of air pollution. Gases such as carbon monoxide and particulates such as soot and ash are in exhaust fumes. Vehicle exhaust may also react with other substances in the air. When this happens, new pollutants can form. Ground-level ozone and smog are two types of pollutants that form from vehicle exhaust.

Active Reading

8 Identify As you read, underline how ground-level ozone and smog can form.

Ground-Level Ozone

Ozone in the ozone layer is necessary for life, but ground-level ozone is harmful. It is produced when sunlight reacts with vehicle exhaust and oxygen in the air. You may have heard of "Ozone Action Days" in your community. When such a warning is given, people should limit outdoor activities because ozone can damage their lungs.

Smog

Smog is another type of pollutant formed from vehicle exhaust. **Smog** forms when ground-level ozone and vehicle exhaust react in the presence of sunlight. Smog is a problem in large cities because there are more vehicles on the roads. It can cause lung damage and irritate the eyes and nose. In some cities, there can be enough smog to make a brownish haze over the city.

Visualize It!

Some compounds in smoke and exhaust are harmful by themselves. And some compounds in smoke and exhaust can react in the atmosphere to form other pollutants such as smog and acid precipitation.

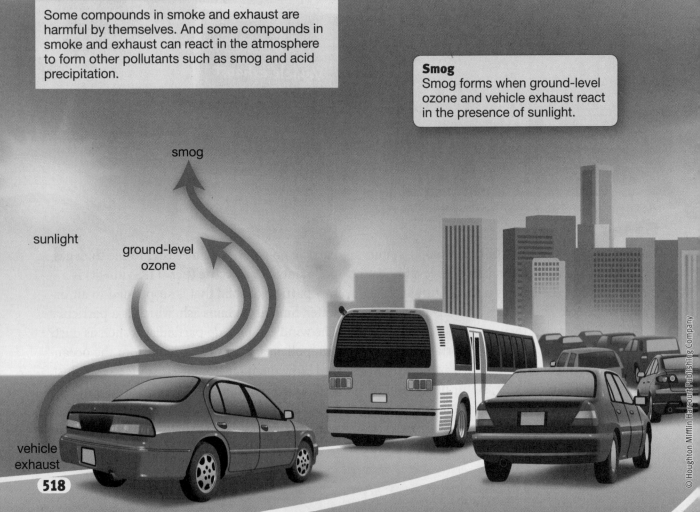

Smog
Smog forms when ground-level ozone and vehicle exhaust react in the presence of sunlight.

smog

sunlight

ground-level ozone

vehicle exhaust

How does pollution from human activities produce acid precipitation?

Active Reading **9 Identify** As you read, underline how acid precipitation forms.

Precipitation (prih•sip•ih•TAY•shuhn) such as rain, sleet, or snow that contains acids from air pollution is called **acid precipitation**. Burning fossil fuels releases sulfur dioxide and nitrogen oxides into the air. When these gases mix with water in the atmosphere, they form sulfuric acid and nitric acid. Precipitation is naturally slightly acidic. When carbon dioxide in the air and water mix, they form carbonic acid. Carbonic acid is a weak acid. Sulfuric acid and nitric acid are strong acids. They can make precipitation so acidic that it is harmful to the environment.

What are some effects of acid precipitation?

Acid precipitation can cause soil and water to become more acidic than normal. Plants have adapted over long periods of time to the natural acidity of the soils in which they live. When soil acidity rises, some nutrients that plants need are dissolved. These nutrients get washed away by rainwater. Bacteria and fungi that live in the soil are also harmed by acidic conditions.

Acid precipitation may increase the acidity of lakes or streams. It also releases toxic metals from soils. The increased acidity and high levels of metals in water can sicken or kill aquatic organisms. This can disrupt habitats and result in decreased biodiversity in an ecosystem. Acid precipitation can also erode the stonework on buildings and statues.

10 Analyze Explain how pollution from one location can affect the environment far away from the source of the pollution.

_____

_____

_____

_____

blowing winds

Smoke and fumes from factories and vehicles contain sulfur dioxide and nitrogen oxide gases, which can be blown long distances by winds.

Acid Precipitation
These gases dissolve in water vapor, and form sulfuric acids and nitric acids, which fall to Earth as acid precipitation.

How's the AIR?

What are measures of air quality?

Measuring how clean or polluted the air is tells us about **air quality**. Pollutants reduce air quality. Two major threats to air quality are vehicle exhausts and industrial pollutants. The air quality in cities can be poor. As more people move into cities, the cities get bigger. This leads to increased amounts of human-made pollution. Poor air circulation, such as a lack of wind, allows air pollution to stay in one area where it can build up. As pollution increases, air quality decreases.

Air Quality Index

The Air Quality Index (AQI) is a number used to describe the air quality of a location such as a city. The higher the AQI number, the more people are likely to have health problems that are linked to air pollution. Air quality is measured and given a value based on the level of pollution detected. The AQI values are divided into ranges. Each range is given a color code and a description. The Environmental Protection Agency (EPA) has AQIs for the pollutants that pose the greatest risk to public health, including ozone and particulates. The EPA can then issue advisories to avoid exposure to pollution that may harm health.

Indoor Air Pollution

The air inside a building can become more polluted than the air outside. This is because buildings are insulated to prevent outside air from entering the building. Some sources of indoor air pollution include chlorine and ammonia from household cleaners and formaldehyde from furniture. Harmful chemicals can be released from some paints and glues. Radon is a radioactive gas released when uranium decays. Radon can seep into buildings through gaps in their foundations. It can build up inside well-insulated buildings. *Ventilation,* or the mixing of indoor and outside air, can reduce indoor air pollution. Another way to reduce indoor air pollution is to limit the use of items that create the pollution.

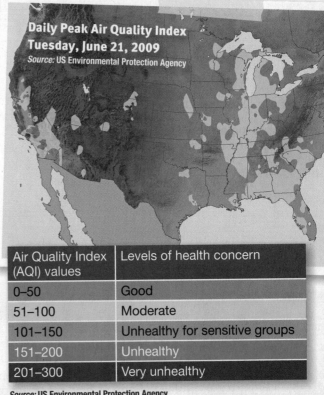

Daily Peak Air Quality Index
Tuesday, June 21, 2009
Source: US Environmental Protection Agency

Air Quality Index (AQI) values	Levels of health concern
0–50	Good
51–100	Moderate
101–150	Unhealthy for sensitive groups
151–200	Unhealthy
201–300	Very unhealthy

Source: US Environmental Protection Agency

Color codes based on the Air Quality Index show the air quality in different areas.

👁 Visualize It!

11 Recommend If you were a weather reporter using this map, what would you recommend for people living in areas that are colored orange?

_____

_____

_____

_____

12 Apply If this was your house, how might you decrease the sources of indoor air pollution?

Nitrogen oxides from unvented gas stove, wood stove, or kerosene heater

Chlorine and ammonia from household cleaners

Chemicals from dry cleaning

Formaldehyde from furniture, carpeting, particleboard, and foam insulation

Fungi and bacteria from dirty heating and air conditioning ducts

Chemicals from paint strippers and thinners

Gasoline from car and lawn mower

Carbon monoxide from car left running

How can air quality affect health?

Daily exposure to small amounts of air pollution can cause serious health problems. Children, elderly people, and people with asthma, allergies, lung problems, and heart problems are especially vulnerable to the effects of air pollution. The short-term effects of air pollution include coughing, headaches, and wheezing. Long-term effects, such as lung cancer and emphysema, are dangerous because they can cause death.

Think Outside the Book *Inquiry*

13 Evaluate Think about the community in which you live. What different things in your community and the surrounding areas might affect the air quality where you live?

Air Pollution and Your Health

Short-term effects	Long-term effects
coughing	asthma
headaches	emphysema
difficulty breathing	allergies
burning/itchy eyes	lung cancer
	chronic bronchitis

14 Identify Imagine you are walking next to a busy road where there are a lot of exhaust fumes. Circle the effects listed in the table that you are most likely to have while walking.

Things Are CHANGING

How might humans be changing Earth's climates?

The burning of fossil fuels releases greenhouse gases, such as carbon dioxide, into the atmosphere. The atmosphere today contains about 37% more carbon dioxide than it did in the mid-1700s, and that level continues to increase. Average global temperatures have also risen in recent decades.

Many people are concerned about how the greenhouse gases from human activities add to the observed trend of increasing global temperatures. Earth's atmosphere and other systems work together in complex ways, so it is hard to know exactly how much the extra greenhouse gases change the temperature. Climate scientists make computer models to understand the effects of climate change. Models predict that average global temperatures are likely to rise another 1.1 to 6.4 °C (2 to 11.5 °F) by the year 2100.

A Sunlight (radiant energy) passes through the windows of the car.

B Energy as heat is trapped inside by the windows.

C The temperature inside the car increases.

Visualize It!

15 Synthesize How is a car with closed windows a good analogy of the atmosphere's greenhouse effect?

_____

_____

_____

_____

What are some predicted effects of climate change?

Active Reading **16 Identify** As you read, underline some effects of an increasing average global temperature.

Scientists have already noticed many changes linked to warmer temperatures. For example, some glaciers and the Arctic sea ice are melting at the fastest rates ever recorded. A warmer Earth may lead to changes in rainfall patterns, rising sea levels, and more severe storms. These changes will have many negative impacts for life on Earth. Other predicted effects include drought in some regions and increased precipitation in others. Farming practices and the availability of food is also expected to be impacted by increased global temperatures. Such changes will likely have political and economic effects on the world, especially in developing countries.

Melt water pours from an iceberg that broke away from the Jakobshavn Glacier in West Greenland.

How is the ozone layer affected by air pollution?

In the 1980s, scientists reported an alarming discovery about Earth's protective ozone layer. Over the polar regions, the ozone layer was thinning. Chemicals called *chlorofluorocarbons* (klor•oh•flur•oh•kar•buhns) (CFCs) were causing ozone to break down into oxygen, which does not block harmful ultraviolet (UV) rays. The thinning of the ozone layer allows more UV radiation to reach Earth's surface. UV radiation is dangerous to organisms, including humans, as it causes sunburn, damages DNA (which can lead to cancer), and causes eye damage.

CFCs once had many industrial uses, such as coolants in refrigerators and air-conditioning units. CFC use has now been banned, but CFC molecules can stay in the atmosphere for about 100 years. So, CFCs released from a spray can 30 years ago are still harming the ozone layer today. However, recent studies show that breakdown of the ozone layer has slowed.

The dark blue area on this map shows the size of the ozone hole over the South Pole.

17 Infer How might these penguins near the South Pole be affected by the ozone hole?

_____

_____

_____

Satellite image of Arctic summer sea ice in September 1979.

Source: NASA

Satellite image of Arctic summer sea ice in September 2007.

Source: NASA

Inquiry

18 Relate What effect might melting sea ice have for people who live in coastal areas?

_____

_____

© Houghton Mifflin Harcourt Publishing Company • Image Credits: (bkgd) ©Paul Souders/Corbis; (tl) ©NASA/Goddard Space Flight Center Scientific Visualization Studio; (tr) Kyodo via AP Images; (bl) ©NASA/Goddard Space Flight Center Ozone Processing Team; Goddard Space Flight Center Scientific Visualization Studio. Thanks to Rob Gerston (GSFC) for providing the data.; (br) ©NASA/Goddard Space Flight Center Scientific Visualization Studio. Thanks to Rob Gerston (GSFC) for providing the data.

Visual Summary

To complete this summary, fill in the blanks with the correct word or phrase. Then use the key below to check your answers. You can use this page to review the main concepts of the lesson.

smog

Human activities are a major cause of air pollution.

19 Two types of air pollutants are gases and _____.

Car exhaust is a major source of air pollution in cities.

20 _____ is formed when exhausts and ozone react in the presence of sunlight.

Human Impact on the Atmosphere

Air quality and levels of pollution can be measured.

Air Quality Index (AQI) values	Levels of health concern
0–50	Good
51–100	Moderate
101–150	Unhealthy for sensitive groups
151–200	Unhealthy
201–300	Very unhealthy

21 As pollution increases, _____ decreases.

Climate change may lead to dramatic changes in global weather patterns.

22 The melting of polar ice is one effect of _____.

Answers: 19 particulates; 20 smog; 21 air quality; 22 global warming/climate change

23 Apply Explain in your own words what the following statement means: Each of your breaths, every tree that is planted, and every vehicle on the road affects the composition of the atmosphere.

Lesson Review

Vocabulary

Draw a line to connect the following terms to their definitions.

1 Air pollution

2 Greenhouse effect

3 Air quality

4 Particulate

5 Smog

A tiny particle of solid that is suspended in air or water

B the contamination of the atmosphere by the introduction of pollutants from human and natural sources

C pollutant that forms when ozone and vehicle exhaust react with sunlight

D a measure of how clean or polluted the air is

E the process by which gases in the atmosphere, such as water vapor and carbon dioxide, absorb and release energy as heat

Key Concepts

6 Identify List three effects that an increase in urbanization can have on air quality.

_____

_____

_____

7 Relate How are ground-level ozone and smog related?

_____

_____

_____

8 Explain How can human health be affected by changes in air quality?

_____

_____

Critical Thinking

Use this graph to answer the following questions.

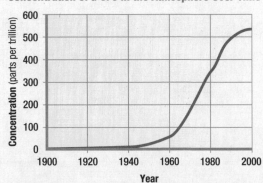

Concentration of a CFC in the Atmosphere Over Time

9 Analyze At what time in the graph did CFCs begin building up in the atmosphere?

_____

_____

10 Synthesize Since the late 1970s, the use of CFCs has been reduced, with a total ban in 2010. But CFCs can stay in the atmosphere for up to 100 years. In the space below, draw a graph showing the concentration of CFCs in the atmosphere over the next 100 years.

11 Apply Do you think it is important that humans control the amount of human-made pollution? Explain your reasoning.

_____

_____

_____

_____

_____

_____

My Notes

Protecting Earth's Water, Land, and Air

ESSENTIAL QUESTION

How can Earth's resources be used wisely?

By the end of this lesson, you should be able to summarize the value of conserving Earth's resources and the effect that wise stewardship has on land, water, and air resources.

Picking up litter to clean streams or rivers is one way we can help preserve Earth's natural resources.

Virginia Science Standards of Learning

6.5 The student will investigate and understand the unique properties and characteristics of water and its roles in the natural and human-made environment. Key concepts include:

6.5.f the importance of protecting and maintaining water resources.

6.6 The student will investigate and understand the properties of air and the structure and dynamics of Earth's atmosphere. Key concepts include:

6.6.d natural and human-caused changes to the atmosphere and the importance of protecting and maintaining air quality.

6.9 The student will investigate and understand public policy decisions relating to the environment. Key concepts include:

6.9.c the mitigation of land-use and environmental hazards through preventive measures.

👋 **Lesson Labs**

Quick Labs
• Soil Erosion
• Investigate the Value of Recycling

Exploration Lab
• Filtering Water

🧠 Engage Your Brain

1 Predict Check T or F to show whether you think each statement is true or false.

T	F	
☐	☐	Conservation is the overuse of natural resources.
☐	☐	It is everybody's job to be a good steward of the Earth's resources.
☐	☐	Reforestation is the planting of trees to repair degraded lands.
☐	☐	Alternative energy sources, like solar power, increase the amount of pollution released into the air.

2 Describe Have you ever done something to protect a natural resource? Draw a picture showing what you did. Include a caption.

✏️ Active Reading

3 Synthesize You can often guess the meaning of a word from its context, or how it is used in a sentence. Use the sentence below to guess the meaning of the word *stewardship*.

Example sentence
Stewardship of water resources will ensure that there is plenty of clean water for future generations.

stewardship:

_____

_____

Vocabulary Terms

• conservation   • stewardship

4 Apply As you learn the definition of each vocabulary term in this lesson, create your own definition or sketch to help remember the meaning of the term.

Keeping It Clean

What are conservation and stewardship?

Active Reading

5 Identify As you read, underline the definitions of *conservation* and *stewardship*.

In the past, some people have used Earth's resources however they wanted, without thinking about the consequences. They thought it didn't matter if they cut down hundreds of thousands of trees or caught millions of fish. They also thought it didn't matter if they dumped trash into bodies of water. Now we know that it does matter how we use resources. Humans greatly affect the land, water, and air. If we wish to keep using our resources in the future, we need to conserve and care for them.

Conservation: Wise Use of Resources

Conservation (kahn•sur•VAY•shuhn) is the wise use of natural resources. By practicing conservation, we can help make sure that resources will still be around for future generations. It is up to everybody to conserve and protect resources. When we use energy or create waste, we can harm the environment. If we conserve whenever we can, we reduce the harm we do to the environment. We can use less energy by turning off lights, computers, and appliances. We can reuse shopping bags, as in the picture below. We can recycle whenever possible, instead of just throwing things away. By doing these things, we take fewer resources from Earth and put less pollution into the water, land, and air.

Visualize It!

6 Identify How are the people in the picture below practicing conservation?

_____

_____

_____

This old tire is being used as a planter instead of being thrown away.

© Houghton Mifflin Harcourt Publishing Company • Image Credits: (l) ©Ariel Skelley/Blend Images/Getty Images; (r) ©Gunter Marx/Alamy

Stewardship: Managing Resources

Stewardship (stoo•urd•SHIP) is the careful and responsible management of a resource. If we are not good stewards, we will use up a resource or pollute it. Stewardship of Earth's resources will ensure that the environment stays clean enough to help keep people and other living things healthy. Stewardship is everybody's job. Governments pass laws that protect water, land, and air. These laws determine how resources can be used and what materials can be released into the environment. Individuals can also act as stewards. For example, you can plant trees or help clean up a habitat in your community. Any action that helps to maintain or improve the environment is an act of stewardship.

7 Compare Fill in the Venn diagram to compare and contrast conservation and stewardship.

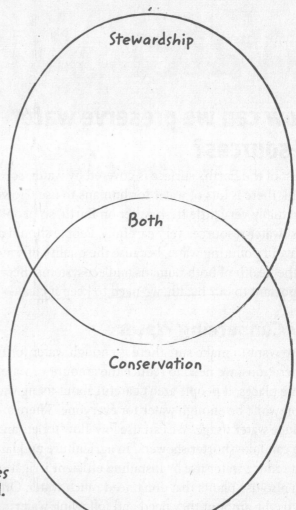

Stewardship

Both

Conservation

Turning empty lots into gardens improves the environment and provides people with healthy food.

Visualize It!

8 Identify How is the person in the picture to the right practicing stewardship?

_____

_____

_____

Sea turtles are endangered. Scientists help sea turtles that have just hatched find their way to the sea.

Water Wise!

How can we preserve water resources?

Most of the Earth's surface is covered by water, so you might think there is lots of water for humans to use. However, there is actually very little fresh water on Earth, so people should use freshwater resources very carefully. People should also be careful to avoid polluting water, because the quality of water is important to the health of both humans and ecosystems. Because water is so important to our health, we need to keep it clean!

By Conserving Water

If we want to make sure there is enough water for future generations, we need to reduce the amount of water we use. In some places, if people aren't careful about using water wisely, there soon won't be enough water for everyone. There are many ways to reduce water usage. We can use low-flow toilets and showerheads. We can take shorter showers. In agriculture and landscaping, we can reduce water use by installing efficient irrigation systems. We can also use plants that don't need much water. Only watering lawns the amount they need and following watering schedules saves water. The photo below shows a simple way to use less water—just turn off the tap while brushing your teeth!

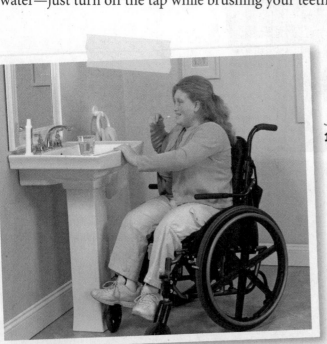

Do the Math

You Try It

9 Calculate How much fresh water is on Earth?

Solve

Each square on the grid equals 1%. Use the grid to fill in the percentage of each type of water found on Earth.

Earth's Water

- ☐ Salt water _____
- ☐ Ice (fresh water) _____
- ☐ Fresh liquid water _____

10 Identify What are some ways you can reduce the amount of water you use?

- Turn off the tap when brushing my teeth.
- _____
  _____
- _____
  _____
- _____

With Water Stewardship

Humans and ecosystems need clean water. The diagram below shows how a community keeps its drinking water clean. The main way to protect drinking water is to keep pollution from entering streams, lakes, and other water sources. Laws like the Clean Water Act and Safe Drinking Water Act were passed to protect water sources. These laws indicate how clean drinking water must be and limit the types of chemicals that businesses and private citizens can release into water. These laws also help finance water treatment facilities. We can help protect water by not throwing chemicals in the trash or dumping them down the drain. We can also use nontoxic chemicals whenever possible. Reducing the amount of fertilizer we use on our gardens also reduces water pollution.

For healthy ecosystems and safe drinking water, communities need to protect water sources. The first step to protecting water sources is keeping them from becoming polluted.

Protecting Water Resources

Water testing makes sure water is safe for people to drink. It also helps us find out if there is a pollution problem that needs to be fixed.

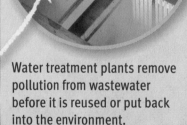

Water treatment plants remove pollution from wastewater before it is reused or put back into the environment.

Without clean water to drink, people can get sick. Clean water is also important for agriculture and natural ecosystems.

Visualize It!

11 Apply What steps should a community take to manage its water resources?

_____

_____

_____

_____

This Land Is Your Land

How can we preserve land resources?

People rely on land resources for recreation, agriculture, transportation, commerce, industry, and housing. If we manage land resources carefully, we can make sure that these resources will be around for generations and continue to provide resources for humans to use. We also need to make sure that there are habitats for wild animals. To do all these things, we must protect land resources from overuse and pollution. Sometimes we need to repair damage that is already done.

Through Preservation

Preservation of land resources is very important. *Preservation* means protecting land from being damaged or changed. Local, state, and national parks protect many natural areas. These parks help ensure that many species survive. Small parks can protect some species. Other species, such as predators, need larger areas. For example, wolves roam over hundreds of miles and would not be protected by small parks. By protecting areas big enough for large predators, we also protect habitats for many other species.

Active Reading

12 Identify As you read this page and the next, underline ways that we can protect land resources.

Yosemite National Park is one of the oldest national parks in the country. Like other national, state, and local parks, Yosemite was formed to preserve natural habitats.

Think Outside the Book

13 Apply Plant and animal species depend on land resources. Find out which endangered plant or animal species live in your area. Write a paragraph explaining how your community can help protect those species.

Through Reforestation

People use the wood from trees for many things. We use it to make paper and to build houses. We also use wood to heat homes and cook food. In many places, huge areas of forest were cut down to use the wood and nothing was done to replant the forests. Now when we cut trees down, they are often replanted, as in the picture at right. We also plant trees in areas where forests disappeared many years ago in order to help bring the forests back. The process of planting trees to reestablish forestland is called *reforestation*. Reforestation is important, but we can't cut down all forests and replant them. It is important to keep some old forests intact for the animals that need them to survive.

Through Reclamation

In order to use some resources, such as coal, metal, and minerals, the resources first have to be dug out of the ground. In the process, the land is damaged. Sometimes, large areas of land are cleared and pits are dug to reach the resource. Land can also be damaged in other ways, including by development and agriculture. *Reclamation* is the process by which a damaged land area is returned to nearly the condition it was in before people used it. Land reclamation, shown in the lower right photo, is required for mines in many states once the mines are no longer in use. Many national and state laws, such as the Surface Mining and Reclamation Act and the Resource Conservation and Recovery Act, guide land reclamation.

Reforestation

A mine being reclaimed

Visualize It!

14 Compare What are the similarities between reforestation and reclamation?

_____

_____

_____

_____

One way to reduce urban sprawl is to locate homes and businesses close together.

Through Reducing Urban Sprawl

Urban sprawl is the outward spread of suburban areas around cities. As we build more houses and businesses across a wider area, there is less land for native plants and animals. Reducing urban sprawl helps to protect land resources. One way to reduce sprawl is to locate more people and businesses in a smaller area. A good way to do this is with vertical development—that means constructing taller buildings. Homes, businesses, and even recreational facilities can be placed within high-rise buildings. We also can reduce sprawl using mixed-use development. This development creates communities with businesses and houses very close to one another. Mixed-use communities are also better for the environment, because people can walk to work instead of driving.

Through Recycling

Recycling is one of the most important things we can do to preserve land resources. *Recycling* is the process of recovering valuable materials from waste or scrap. We can recycle many of the materials that we use. By recycling materials like metal, plastic, paper, and glass, we use fewer raw materials. Recycling aluminum cans reduces the amount of bauxite that is mined. We use bauxite in aluminum smelting. Everyone can help protect land resources by recycling. Lots of people throw away materials that can be recycled. Find out what items you can recycle!

Bauxite mine

15 Apply Aluminum is mined from the ground. Recycling aluminum cans decreases the need for mining bauxite. Paper can also be recycled. How does recycling paper preserve trees?

_____

_____

Through Using Soil Conservation Methods

Soil conservation protects soil from erosion or degradation by overuse or pollution. For example, farmers change the way they plow in order to conserve soil. Contour plowing creates ridges of soil across slopes. The small ridges keep water from eroding soils. In strip cropping, two types of crops are planted in rows next to each other to reduce erosion. Terracing is used on steep hills to prevent erosion. Areas of the hill are flattened to grow crops. This creates steps down the side of the hill. *Crop rotation* means that crops with different needs are planted in alternating seasons. This reduces the prevalence of plant diseases and makes sure there are nutrients for each crop. It also ensures that plants are growing in the soil almost year-round. In no-till farming, soils are not plowed between crop plantings. Stalks and cover crops keep water in the soils and reduce erosion by stopping soil from being blown away.

 **Active Reading**

16 Identify As you read this page, underline five methods of soil conservation.

Visualize It!

Terracing involves building leveled areas, or steps, to grow crops on.

In contour plowing, crop rows are planted in curved lines along land's natural contours.

Strip cropping prevents erosion by creating natural dams that stop water from rushing over a field.

17 Analyze Which two soil conservation techniques would be best to use on gentle slopes?

- ☐ contour plowing
- ☐ crop terracing
- ☐ strip cropping

18 Analyze Which soil conservation technique would be best to use on very steep slopes?

- ☐ contour plowing
- ☐ crop terracing
- ☐ strip cropping

Into Thin Air

How can we reduce air pollution?

Polluted air can make people sick and harm organisms. Air pollution can cause the atmosphere to change in ways that are harmful to the environment and to people. There are many ways that we can reduce air pollution. We can use less energy. Also, we can develop new ways to get energy that produces less pollution. Everybody can help reduce air pollution in many different ways.

Through Energy Conservation

Energy conservation is one of the most important ways to reduce air pollution. Fossil fuels are currently the most commonly used energy resource. When they are burned, they release pollution into the air. If we use less energy, we burn fewer fossil fuels.

There are lots of ways to conserve energy. We can turn off lights when we don't need them. We can use energy-efficient lightbulbs and appliances. We can use air conditioners less in the summer and heaters less in the winter. We can unplug electronics when they are not in use. Instead of driving ourselves to places, we can use public transportation. We can also develop alternative energy sources that create less air pollution. Using wind, solar, and geothermal energy will help us burn less fossil fuel.

Houghton Mifflin Harcourt Publishing Company • Image Credits: (bkgd) ©Ulf Wallin/Stone/Getty Images; (t) ©Panoramic Images/Getty Images; (bl) ©Richard Levine/Alamy; (br) ©Chris Cooper-Smith/Alamy

Active Reading

19 **Identify** Underline the sentences that explain the relationship between burning fossil fuels and air pollution.

Using public transportation, riding a bike, sharing rides, and walking reduce the amount of air pollution produced by cars.

Many cities, such as Los Angeles, California, have air pollution problems.

Energy can be produced with very little pollution. These solar panels help us use energy from the sun and replace the use of fossil fuels.

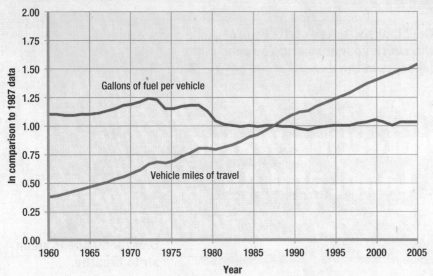

Vehicle Fuel Consumption and Miles Traveled, 1960–2005

Source: U.S. Department of Transportation

20 Analyze How has vehicle fuel consumption in comparison to miles traveled changed since 1960? What is the likely cause for this change?

Through Technology

There are lots of ways to generate energy without creating much air pollution. By developing these alternative energy sources, we can reduce the amount of pollution created by burning fossil fuels. Wind turbines generate clean power. So do solar panels that use energy from the sun. We also can use power created by water flowing through rivers or moving with the tides. Geothermal energy from heat in Earth's crust can be used to generate electricity. Hybrid cars get energy from their brakes and store it in batteries. They burn less gas and release less pollution. Driving smaller cars that can go farther on a gallon of gas also reduces air pollution.

New technologies, such as this compact fluorescent lightbulb (CFL), help limit air pollution. CFL bulbs use less energy to make the same amount of light.

Through Laws

Governments in many countries work independently and together to reduce air pollution. They monitor air quality and set limits on what can be released into the air. In the United States, the Clean Air Act limits the amount of toxic chemicals and other pollutants that can be released into the atmosphere by factories and vehicles. It is up to the Environmental Protection Agency to make sure that these limits are enforced. Because air isn't contained by borders, some solutions must be international. The Kyoto Protocol is a worldwide effort to limit the release of greenhouse gases—pollution that can warm the atmosphere.

21 Summarize List three ways air pollution can be reduced.

- _____

- _____

- _____

Visual Summary

To complete this summary, fill in the blanks with the correct word or phrase. Then use the key below to check your answers. You can use this page to review the main concepts of the lesson.

Protecting Water, Land, and Air

Water resources are important to our health.

22 A community's water supply can be protected by:

- conserving water
- preventing pollution
- _____
- treating wastewater

Land resources are used to grow food and make products.

23 Land resources can be protected by:

- preservation
- reclamation and reforestation
- reducing urban sprawl
- _____
- soil conservation

Everybody needs clean air to breathe.

24 The main way to reduce air pollution is to:

_____
_____
_____
_____
_____
_____

25 **Relate** How can you personally act as a steward of water, land, and air resources?

Lesson Review

Vocabulary

Fill in the blank with the term that best completes the following sentences.

1 _____ is the wise use of natural resources.

2 _____ is the careful and responsible management of a resource.

Key Concepts

3 Describe How can water pollution be prevented?

_____

_____

_____

_____

Fill in the table below.

Example	Type of land resource conservation
4 Identify A county creates a park to protect a forest.	
5 Identify A mining company puts soil back in the hole and plants grass seeds on top of it.	
6 Identify A logging company plants new trees after it has cut some down.	
7 Identify A plastic milk bottle is turned into planks for a boardwalk to the beach.	
8 Identify Instead of building lots of single houses, a city builds an apartment building with a grocery store.	

9 Determine How has technology helped decrease air pollution in recent years?

_____

_____

_____

_____

10 Explain Why is it important to protect Earth's water, land, and air resources?

_____

_____

_____

_____

_____

Critical Thinking

11 Explain Land reclamation can be expensive. Why might recycling materials lead to spending less money on reclamation?

_____

_____

_____

Use the graph to answer the following question.

Average Water Usage of U.S. Household

- Toilet flushes 29%
- Washing machine 21%
- Shower 21%
- Tap 12%
- Bath 9%
- Toilet leaks 5%
- Dish washing 3%

Source: U.S. Environmental Protection Agency

12 Analyze The graph above shows water use in the average U.S. household. Using the graph, identify three effective ways a household could conserve water.

_____

_____

My Notes

Unit 8 〈 Big Idea 〉 Humans and human population growth affect the environment.

Lesson 1
ESSENTIAL QUESTION
What impact can human activities have on water resources?

Explain the impact that humans can have on the quality and supply of fresh water.

Lesson 3
ESSENTIAL QUESTION
How do humans impact Earth's atmosphere?

Identify the impact that humans have had on Earth's atmosphere.

Lesson 2
ESSENTIAL QUESTION
What impact can human activities have on land resources?

Identify the impact that human activity has on Earth's land.

Lesson 4
ESSENTIAL QUESTION
How can Earth's resources be used wisely?

Summarize the value of conserving Earth's resources and the effect that wise stewardship has on land, water, and air resources.

Connect ESSENTIAL QUESTIONS
Lessons 1 and 2

1 Explain How does an increasing human population affect land and water resources?

_____

_____

_____

_____

Think Outside the Book

2 Synthesize Choose one of these activities to help synthesize what you have learned in this unit.

☐ Using what you learned in Lessons 1 through 4, create an informational poster that explains what steps humans can take to protect Earth's water, land, and air.

☐ Using what you learned in Lessons 1, 2, and 3, write a fable that explains how human activities can pollute water, land, or air resources. Provide a moral for your story that explains why pollution should be prevented.

© Houghton Mifflin Harcourt Publishing Company • Image Credits: (tl) ©Aurora Open/Justin Bailie/Getty Images; (tr) ©GIPhotoStock/Photo Researchers, Inc.; (bl) ©Nature Animals/Alamy; (br) ©Tim Pannell/Corbis

Unit 8 Review

Name _____

Vocabulary

Check the box to show whether each statement is true or false.

T	F	
☐	☐	**1** <u>Air quality</u> is a measure of how clean or polluted the air is.
☐	☐	**2** <u>Potable</u> water is suitable for drinking.
☐	☐	**3** <u>Conservation</u> is the wise use of natural resources.
☐	☐	**4** <u>Land degradation</u> is the process by which humans restore damaged land so that it can support the local ecosystem.
☐	☐	**5** <u>Stewardship</u> of Earth's resources helps make sure that the environment remains healthy.

Key Concepts

Read each question below, and circle the best answer.

6 Smog usually forms from ground-level ozone and what other human-made pollutant?

A acid precipitation

B volcanic gases

C vehicle exhaust

D smoke from cigarettes

7 Which of the following is true about the amount of water on Earth?

A There is an ever-increasing amount of water on Earth due to rain and snowfall.

B The amount of water on Earth is replaced much faster than it is being used up.

C There is a fixed amount of water on Earth that is continuously cycled.

D The water on Earth is more than enough for the growing population.

8 Which of the following is a source of indoor air pollution?

A greenhouse gases

B steam from a hot shower

C chemicals from certain cleaning products

D radiation from sunlight entering windows

9 The graph below shows how the amount of carbon dioxide (CO_2) in our atmosphere has changed since 1960.

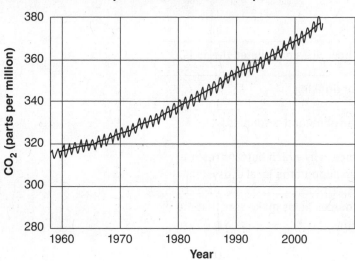

Amount of Atmospheric Carbon Dioxide per Year

Based on the information given in the graph, which of these phenomena has likely increased since 1960?

A land erosion

B coastal erosion

C ozone depletion

D greenhouse effect

10 A manufacturing plant is built on the bank of the Mississippi River. Water is diverted into the plant for use in the making of a product and is then piped back out into the river. If the water that is released back into the river is contaminated, what is this form of pollution called?

A thermal pollution

B biological pollution

C point-source pollution

D nonpoint-source pollution

11 What is the water from an artificial reservoir most likely to be reserved for?

A for future use by homes and businesses

B for recreational purposes such as swimming

C to provide a habitat for fish

D to cool hot industrial equipment

12 The picture below shows a common human activity.

FERTILIZER

What are examples of the effects this kind of pollution may cause?

A acid rain, which may cause diseases such as asthma

B global warming, which may cause diseases such as skin cancer

C respiratory diseases such as emphysema

D artificial eutrophication, harming aquatic animals

13 Humans use land in many ways. How is an area described if it contains few people, has large areas of open space, and is a mix of natural land, farmland, and parks?

A rural area   **C** natural area

B urban area   **D** industrial area

Critical Thinking

Answer the following questions in the space provided.

14 Can the atmosphere be considered a natural resource? Explain.

_____

_____

Give two examples of how the atmosphere is important to life on Earth.

_____

_____

_____

15 The picture below is of a dam built on a river.

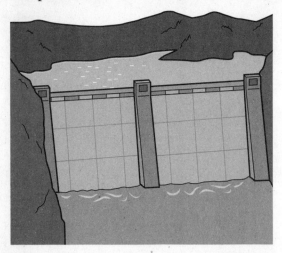

How does a dam affect the surrounding landscape behind and in front of the dam?

_____

_____

How does a dam affect the fish that live and breed in that river?

_____

Connect **ESSENTIAL QUESTIONS**
Lessons 1 and 2

Answer the following question in the space provided.

16 Urbanization has major effects on Earth's land and water. Natural vegetation is removed in order to make room for buildings, roads, and parking lots. How does removing vegetation affect the land?

_____

How do paved parking lots and roads with concrete or asphalt affect water flow on the land?

_____

What are three ways that urban populations can negatively affect water quality?

_____

_____

_____

How can urban populations affect a water supply?

_____

_____

The Earth-Moon-Sun System

Big Idea

Earth and the moon move in predictable ways and have predictable effects on each other as they orbit the sun.

What do you think?

Earth is affected by its sun and moon. The sun provides light and energy. The sun and moon regulate Earth's tides. How do tides affect life on Earth?

Tidal pool exposed by low tide

Measuring Shadows

One way to learn more about Earth's rotation and orbit is to study the shadows created by the sun throughout the year. Help students with an ongoing research project, called the Sun Shadows Project. The results are presented at the American Geophysical Union's Annual Conference every year.

(1) Think About It

Students at James Monroe Middle School in Albuquerque, New Mexico, asked the following questions: The seasons change, but do the length of shadows? How could this be measured? What do you think?

_____

_____

_____

Scientists in Antarctica measure shadows.

② Ask A Question

What effects do seasons have on the lengths of shadows in your area?

As a class, come up with a prediction. Then, research what students at James Monroe Middle School are doing to gather information.

Things to Consider

Some parts of the world participate in Daylight Savings Time. People move their clocks forward by an hour in the spring and back by an hour in the fall. Daylight Savings Time may affect the way that you will need to collect data in comparison to students at James Monroe Middle School. Make sure to take your measurements when shadows are shortest.

③ Apply Your Knowledge

A List the materials your class will need in order to make and record the measurements to gather the information needed by the students at James Monroe Middle School.

_____

_____

_____

_____

B Decide on a time frame for your class project. Will you participate for an entire season? What factors influence your decision?

_____

_____

_____

_____

_____

_____

C Track the information gathered by your class and draw your own preliminary conclusions.

_____

_____

_____

_____

Take It Home

Who else is participating in the Sun Shadows Project? Research the various national and international groups taking part, such as the U.S. Antarctic Program.

Earth's Days, Years, and Seasons

ESSENTIAL QUESTION

How are Earth's days, years, and seasons related to the way Earth moves in space?

By the end of this lesson, you should be able to relate Earth's days, years, and seasons to Earth's movement in space.

Virginia Science Standards of Learning

6.8 The student will investigate and understand the organization of the solar system and the interactions among the various bodies that comprise it. Key concepts include:

6.8.d revolution and rotation;

6.8.e the mechanics of day and night and the phases of the moon; and

6.8.g the relationship of Earth's tilt and the seasons.

In many parts of the world, blooming flowers are one of the first signs that spring has arrived. Spring flowers start blooming with the warmer temperatures of spring, even if there is still snow on the ground.

Lesson Labs

Quick Labs
• Earth's Rotation and Revolution
• Seasons Model

Field Lab
• Sunlight and Temperature

Engage Your Brain

1 Predict Check T or F to show whether you think each statement is true or false.

T	F	
☐	☐	A day is about 12 hours long.
☐	☐	A year is about 365 days long.
☐	☐	When it is summer in the Northern Hemisphere, it is summer all around the world.

2 Apply Write your own caption for this photo of leaves in the space below.

_____

_____

_____

_____

_____

Active Reading

3 Synthesize The term *rotation* can be tricky to remember because it is used somewhat differently in science than it is in everyday life. In baseball, a pitching *rotation* lists the order of a team's starting pitchers. The order starts over after the last pitcher on the list has played. On the lines below, write down any other examples you can think of that use the term *rotation*.

rotation:

_____

_____

_____

Vocabulary Terms

• rotation	• season
• day	• equinox
• revolution	• solstice
• year	

4 Apply As you learn the definition of each vocabulary term in this lesson, create your own definition or sketch to help you remember the meaning of the term.

Spinning in

What determines the length of a day?

Each planet spins on its axis. Earth's axis (ACK•sis) is an imaginary straight line that runs from the North Pole to the South Pole. The spinning of a body, such as a planet, on its axis is called **rotation**. The time it takes a planet to complete one full rotation on its axis is called a **day**.

Active Reading

5 Identify As you read, underline the places on Earth's surface at which the ends of Earth's axis would be.

The Time It Takes for Earth to Rotate Once

Earth rotates in a counterclockwise motion around its axis when viewed from above the North Pole. This means that as a location on Earth's equator rotates from west to east, the sun appears to rise in the east. The sun then appears to cross the sky and set in the west.

As Earth rotates, only one-half of Earth faces the sun at any given time. People on the half of Earth facing the sun experience daylight. This period of time in daylight is called *daytime*. People on the half of Earth that faces away from the sun experience darkness. This period of time in darkness is called *nighttime*.

Earth's rotation is used to measure time. Earth completes one rotation on its axis in 24 hours, or in one day. Most locations on Earth's surface move through daylight and darkness in that time.

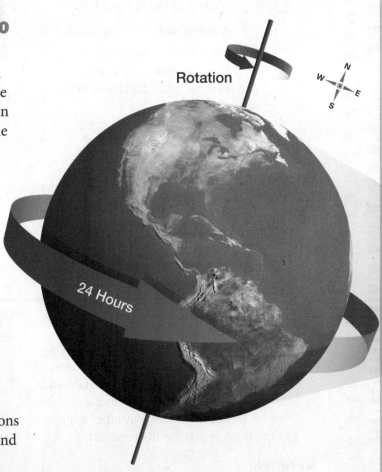

Rotation

24 Hours

Earth's motion is used to measure the length of an Earth day.

Circles

What determines the length of a year?

As Earth rotates on its axis, Earth also revolves around the sun. Although you cannot feel Earth moving, it is traveling around the sun at an average speed of nearly 30 km/s. The motion of a body that travels around another body in space is called **revolution** (reh•vuh•LOO•shun). Earth completes a full revolution around the sun in 365 ¼ days, or about one **year**. We have divided the year into 12 months, each month lasting from 28 to 31 days.

Earth's orbit is not quite a perfect circle. In January, Earth is about 2.5 million kilometers closer to the sun than it is in July. You may be surprised that this distance makes only a tiny difference in temperatures on Earth.

Think Outside the Book

6 Infer How is a leap year, in which a day is added to every fourth year, related to the time it takes Earth to revolve around the sun?

Visualize It!

7 Apply Imagine that Earth's current position is at point A below. Write the label B to show Earth's position 6 months from now in the same diagram.

This drawing is not to scale.

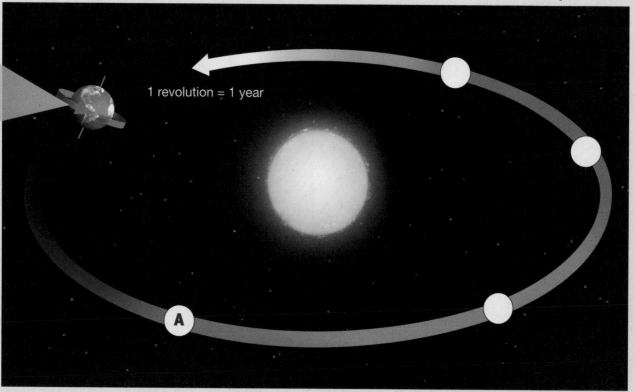

1 revolution = 1 year

A

Tilt-a-Whirl

What conditions are affected by the tilt of Earth's axis?

Earth's axis is tilted at 23.5°. Earth's axis always points toward the North Star as Earth revolves around the sun. Thus, during each revolution, the North Pole may be tilted toward the sun or away from the sun, as seen below. When the North Pole is tilted toward the sun, the Northern Hemisphere (HEHM•ih•sfeer) has longer periods of daylight than does the Southern Hemisphere. When the North Pole is tilted away from the sun, the opposite is true.

The direction of tilt of Earth's axis remains the same throughout Earth's orbit around the sun.

23.5°

23.5°

orbit

This drawing is not to scale.

Temperature

The angle at which the sun's rays strike each part of Earth's surface changes as Earth moves in its orbit. When the North Pole is tilted toward the sun, the sun's rays strike the Northern Hemisphere more directly. Thus, the region receives a higher concentration of solar energy and is warmer. When the North Pole is tilted away from the sun, the sun's rays strike the Northern Hemisphere less directly. When the sunlight is less direct, the solar energy is less concentrated and the region is cooler.

The spherical shape of Earth also affects how the sun warms up an area. Temperatures are high at point A in the diagram. This is because the sun's rays hit Earth's surface at a right angle and are focused in a small area. Toward the poles, the sun's rays hit Earth's surface at a lesser angle. Therefore, the rays are spread out over a larger area and the temperatures are cooler.

🔍 Visualize It!

8 Apply Which location on the illustration of Earth below receives more direct rays from the sun?
- ☐ A
- ☐ B
- ☐ They receive equal amounts.

9 Identify Which location is cooler? _____

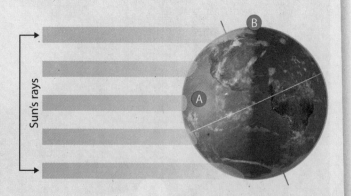

Sun's rays

B

A

Daylight Hours

All locations on Earth experience an *average* of 12 hours of light a day. However, the *actual* number of daylight hours on any given day of the year varies with location. Areas around Earth's equator receive about 12 hours of light a day. Areas on Earth's surface that are tilted toward the sun have more hours of daylight. These areas travel a longer path through the lit part of Earth than areas at the equator. Areas on Earth's surface that are tilted away from the sun have less than 12 hours of light a day. These areas travel a shorter path through the lit part of Earth, as shown below.

This drawing is not to scale.

Sun's Rays

During summer in the Northern Hemisphere, a person has already had many daylight hours by the time a person in the Southern Hemisphere reaches daylight.

About twelve hours later, the person in the Northern Hemisphere is close to daylight again, while the person in the Southern Hemisphere still has many hours of darkness left.

Midnight Sun

When it is summer in the Northern Hemisphere, the time in each day that it is light increases as you move north of the equator. Areas north of the Arctic Circle have 24 hours of daylight, called the "midnight sun," as seen in the photo. At the same time, areas south of the Antarctic Circle receive 24 hours of darkness, or "polar night." When it is winter in the Northern Hemisphere, conditions in the polar areas are reversed.

 **Visualize It!** Inquiry

10 Synthesize Why isn't the area in the photo very warm even though the sun is up all night long?

_____

_____

_____

This composite image shows that the sun never set on this Arctic summer day.

Seasons change...

What causes seasons?

Most locations on Earth experience seasons. Each **season** is characterized by a pattern of temperature and other weather trends. Near the equator, the temperatures are almost the same year-round. Near the poles, there are very large changes in temperatures from winter to summer. We experience seasons due to the changes in the intensity of sunlight and the number of daylight hours as Earth revolves around the sun. So, both the tilt of Earth's axis and Earth's spherical shape play a role in Earth's changing seasons.

As Earth travels around the sun, the area of sunlight in each hemisphere changes. At an **equinox** (EE•kwuh•nahks), sunlight shines equally on the Northern and Southern Hemispheres. Half of each hemisphere is lit, and half is in darkness. As Earth moves along its orbit, the sunlight reaches more of one hemisphere than the other. At a **solstice** (SAHL•stis), the area of sunlight is at a maximum in one hemisphere and at a minimum in the other hemisphere.

- **September Equinox** When Earth is in this position, sunlight shines equally on both poles.
- **December Solstice** About three months later, Earth has traveled a quarter of the way around the sun, but its axis still points in the same direction into space. The North Pole leans away from the sun and is in complete darkness. The South Pole is in complete sunlight.
- **March Equinox** After another quarter of its orbit, Earth reaches another equinox. Half of each hemisphere is lit, and the sunlight is centered on the equator.
- **June Solstice** This position is opposite to the December solstice. Now the North Pole leans toward the sun and is in complete sunlight, and the south pole is in complete darkness.

Visualize It!

The amount of sunlight an area on Earth receives changes during the year. These changes are due to Earth's tilt and position in its orbit around the sun. Equinoxes and solstices mark certain points in the range of sunlight each of Earth's hemispheres receives.

This drawing is not to scale.

March Equinox

April

May

June Solstice

11 Apply In what month does winter begin in the Southern Hemisphere?

_____

12 Infer During which solstice would the sun be at its highest point in the sky in the Northern Hemisphere?

_____

_____

Solstices

The seasons of summer and winter begin on days called _solstices_. Each year on June 21 or 22, the North Pole's tilt toward the sun is greatest. This day is called the _June solstice_. This solstice marks the beginning of summer in the Northern Hemisphere. By December 21 or 22, the North Pole is tilted to the farthest point away from the sun. This day is the December solstice.

February

January

December Solstice

November

October

July

August

September Equinox

13 Infer In which parts of the world is an equinox most different from other days of the year?

_____

_____

Equinoxes

The seasons fall and spring begin on days called _equinoxes_. The hours of daylight and darkness are approximately equal everywhere on Earth on these days. The _September equinox_ occurs on September 22 or 23 of each year. This equinox marks the beginning of fall in the Northern Hemisphere. The March equinox on March 20 or 21 of each year marks the beginning of spring.

Visual Summary

To complete this summary, circle the correct word. Then use the key below to check your answers. You can use this page to review the main concepts of the lesson.

The length of a day is determined by Earth's rotation.

14 It takes Earth 24 seconds/hours to make one rotation on its axis.

The length of a year is determined by Earth's revolution around the sun.

15 It takes Earth about 365 hours/days to revolve around the sun.

Earth's
Days, Years, and Seasons

Earth's tilt affects temperatures and daylight hours at different locations on Earth.

Sun's rays

16 Earth's temperatures and hours of daylight stay the most constant at the equator/poles.

This diagram shows how seasons change in the Northern Hemisphere as Earth orbits the sun.

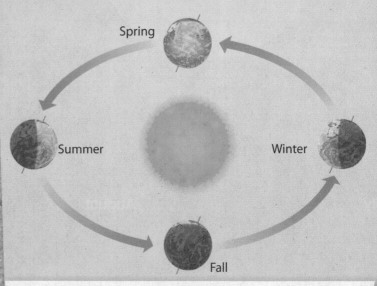

Spring

Summer

Winter

Fall

17 When it is summer in the Northern Hemisphere, it is summer/winter in the Southern Hemisphere.

Answers: 14 hours; 15 days; 16 equator; 17 winter

18 **Predict** How would conditions on Earth change if Earth stopped rotating on its axis?

Lesson Review

Vocabulary

In the space provided below, describe how each set of words are related.

1 revolution, year

_____

_____

2 rotation, day

_____

_____

3 season, equinox, solstice

_____

_____

_____

_____

_____

Key Concepts

4 Identify About how many days are in an Earth year? And how many hours in an Earth day?

_____

5 Describe How does the tilt of Earth's axis affect how the sun's rays strike Earth?

_____

_____

_____

_____

_____

6 Synthesize How does the tilt of Earth's axis affect the number of daylight hours and the temperature of a location on Earth?

_____

_____

_____

_____

_____

Critical Thinking

Use this image to answer the questions below.

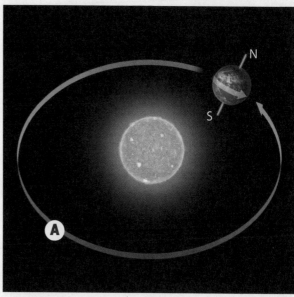

This drawing is not to scale.

7 Identify What season is the Northern Hemisphere experiencing in the image above?

_____

8 Explain How do the tilt of Earth's axis and Earth's movements around the sun cause seasons?

_____

_____

_____

_____

_____

_____

_____

_____

_____

9 Describe If the Earth moves to point A in the image above, what season will the Northern Hemisphere experience?

_____

_____

My Notes

Analyzing Scientific Explanations

Scientists use different methods to develop scientific explanations in different fields of study. Scientists base their explanations on data collected through observation and measurement. After scientists make observations and collect data, they analyze current explanations for what they observed. If a new observation doesn't fit an existing explanation, scientists might work to revise the explanation or to offer a new one.

Tutorial

The text below describes how Ptolemy, a Greek astronomer in the second century C.E., described the universe. Consider the following steps as you analyze scientific explanations.

As Aristotle put forth, Earth is at the center of the universe. All other planets and the Sun revolve around Earth, each on its own sphere. The spheres follow this order outward from Earth: Mercury, Venus, the Moon, the Sun, Mars, Jupiter, Saturn, and the Fixed Stars. Each sphere turns at its own steady pace. Bodies do appear to move backward during their wanderings, but that does not mean the spheres do not keep a steady pace. This is explained by the movement of the bodies along smaller spheres that turn along the edge of the larger spheres. My calculations and models agree with and predict the motions of the spheres. The constant turning of the spheres also moves the bodies closer to Earth and farther from Earth, which explains why the bodies appear brighter or darker at different times. Thus, the heavens remain perfect. This perfection leads to music in the heavens, created by the spheres.

Identify the evidence that supports the explanation. At least two different lines of evidence are needed to be considered valid.

Identify any evidence that does not support the explanation. A single line of evidence can disprove an explanation. Often, new evidence makes scientists reevaluate an explanation. By the 1500s, Ptolemy's model was not making accurate predictions. In 1543, Copernicus, a Polish astronomer, proposed a new explanation of how planets move.

Identify any additional lines of evidence that should be considered. They might point to additional investigations to further examine the explanation. The gravitational force between objects was not known in Ptolemy's time. However, it should be considered when explaining the motion of planets.

Decide whether the original explanation is supported by enough evidence. An alternative explanation might better explain the evidence or might explain a wider range of observations.

If possible, propose an alternative explanation that could fit the evidence. Often, a simpler explanation is better if it fits the evidence. Copernicus explained the apparent backward movement and changing brightness of planets by placing the sun at the center of the solar system with the planets revolving around it.

© Houghton Mifflin Harcourt Publishing Company

You Try It!

In 2006, an official definition of a planet was determined. Read and analyze the information below concerning the classification of the largest Main Belt asteroid, Ceres.

The members of the International Astronomical Union (IAU) voted for the official definition of a planet to be a celestial body that

1. orbits the sun,
2. has enough mass so that its gravity helps it to maintain a nearly round shape,
3. has cleared the neighborhood around its orbit.

A group suggests that Ceres be considered a planet under the new definition. As the largest Main Belt asteroid, Ceres orbits the sun along with thousands of smaller asteroids. Images of Ceres clearly show its nearly round shape. These points, says the group's leader, should qualify Ceres as a planet.

1 Making Observations Underline lines of evidence that support the explanation.

2 Evaluating Data Circle any lines of evidence that do not support the proposed explanation. Explain why this evidence does not support the classification.

_____

_____

_____

_____

3 Applying Concepts Identify any additional evidence that should be considered when evaluating the explanation.

_____

_____

_____

4 Communicating Ideas If possible, propose an alternative explanation that could fit the evidence.

_____

_____

_____

_____

_____

_____

_____

_____

Take It Home

Pluto was recently reclassified. What was it changed to and why? Identify the evidence that supported the decision. How does this compare to the proposed reclassification of Ceres? List similarities of the two explanations in a chart.

Moon Phases and Eclipses

ESSENTIAL QUESTION

How do Earth, the moon, and the sun affect each other?

By the end of this lesson, you should be able to describe the effects the sun and the moon have on Earth, including gravitational attraction, moon phases, and eclipses.

Why is part of the moon orange? Because Earth is moving between the moon and the sun, casting a shadow on the moon.

Virginia Science Standards of Learning

6.8 The student will investigate and understand the organization of the solar system and the interactions among the various bodies that comprise it. Key concepts include:

6.8.c the role of gravity;

6.8.e revolution and rotation; and

6.8.e the mechanics of day and night and the phases of the moon.

Lesson Labs

Quick Labs
• Moon Phases
• Lunar Eclipse

S.T.E.M. Lab
• What the Moon Orbits

 Engage Your Brain

1 Identify Fill in the blanks with the word or phrase you think correctly completes the following sentences.

We can see the moon because it _____ the light from the sun.

The moon's _____ affects the oceans' tides on Earth.

The impact craters on the moon were created by collisions with _____, meteorites, and asteroids.

2 Describe Write your own caption for this photo in the space below.

_____
_____
_____
_____
_____
_____

 Active Reading

3 Synthesize You can often define an unknown word if you know the meaning of its word parts. Use the word parts and sentence below to make an educated guess about the meaning of the word *penumbra*.

Word part	Meaning
umbra	shade or shadow
pen-, from the Latin *paene*	almost

Example sentence
An observer in the <u>penumbra</u> experiences only a partial eclipse.

Vocabulary Terms
• satellite   • eclipse
• gravity   • umbra
• lunar phases   • penumbra

4 Apply As you learn the definition of each vocabulary term in this lesson, create your own definition or sketch to help you remember the meaning of the term.

penumbra:
_____
_____
_____

'Round and 'Round They Go!

How are Earth, the moon, and the sun related in space?

Earth not only spins on its axis, but like the seven other planets in our solar system, Earth also orbits the sun. A body that orbits a larger body is called a **satellite** (SAT'l•yt). Six of the planets in our solar system have smaller bodies that orbit around each of them. These natural satellites are also called moons. Our moon is Earth's natural satellite.

Earth revolves around the sun as the moon revolves around Earth.

Drawing not to scale.

Active Reading

5 Identify As you read, underline the reason that the moon stays in orbit around Earth.

Earth and the Moon Orbit the Sun

All bodies that have mass exert a force that pulls other objects with mass toward themselves. This force is called **gravity.** The mass of Earth is much larger than the mass of the moon, and therefore Earth's gravity exerts a stronger pull on the moon than the moon does on Earth. It is Earth's gravitational pull that keeps the moon in orbit around Earth, forming the Earth–moon system.

The Earth–moon system is itself in orbit around the sun. Even though the sun is relatively far away, the mass of the sun exerts a large gravitational pull on the Earth–moon system. This gravitational pull keeps the Earth–moon system in orbit around the sun.

The Moon Orbits Earth

The pull of Earth's gravity keeps the moon, Earth's natural satellite, in orbit around Earth. Even though the moon is Earth's closest neighbor in space, it is far away compared to the sizes of Earth and the moon themselves.

The distance between Earth and the moon is roughly 383,000 km (238,000 mi)—about a hundred times the distance between New York and Los Angeles. If a jet airliner could travel in space, it would take about 20 days to cover a distance that huge. Astronauts, whose spaceships travel much faster than jets, need about 3 days to reach the moon.

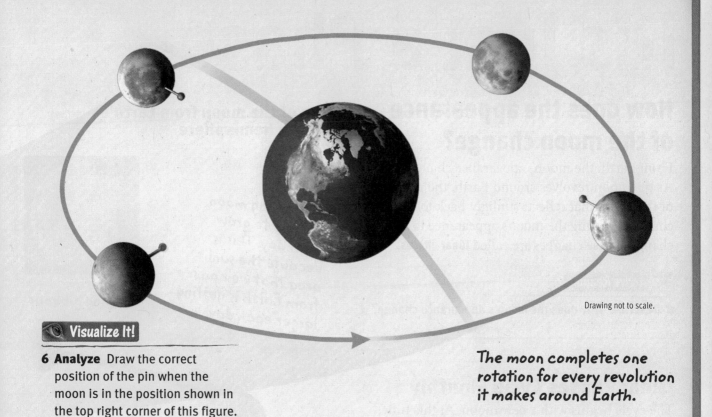

Drawing not to scale.

© Houghton Mifflin Harcourt Publishing Company

 Visualize It!

6 Analyze Draw the correct position of the pin when the moon is in the position shown in the top right corner of this figure.

The moon completes one rotation for every revolution it makes around Earth.

What does the moon look like from Earth?

The moon is only visible from Earth when it reflects the sunlight that reaches the moon. Although the moon is most easily seen at night, you have probably also seen it during daytime on some days. In the daytime, the moon may only be as bright as a thin cloud and can be easily missed. On some days you can see the moon during both the daytime and at night, whereas on other days, you may not see the moon at all.

When you can look at the moon, you may notice darker and lighter areas. Perhaps you have imagined them as features of a face or some other pattern. People around the world have told stories about the animals, people, and objects they have imagined while looking at the light and dark areas of the moon. The dark and light spots do not change over the course of a month because only one side of the moon faces Earth, often called the near side of the moon. This is because the moon rotates once on its own axis each time it orbits Earth. The moon takes 27.3 days or about a month to orbit Earth once.

Inquiry

7 Analyze How would the moon appear to an observer on Earth if the moon did not rotate?

_____

_____

_____

_____

It's Just a Phase!

How does the appearance of the moon change?

From Earth, the moon's appearance changes. As the moon revolves around Earth, the portion of the moon that reflects sunlight back to Earth changes, causing the moon's appearance to change. These changes are called **lunar phases.**

Active Reading

8 Describe Why does the moon's appearance change?

_____

_____

Lunar Phases Cycle Monthly

The cycle begins with a new moon. At this time, Earth, the moon, and the sun are lined up, such that the near side of the moon is unlit. And so there appears to be no moon in the sky.

As the moon moves along its orbit, you begin to see the sunlight on the near side as a thin crescent shape. The crescent becomes thicker as the moon waxes, or grows. When half of the near side of the moon is in the sunlight, the moon has completed one-quarter of its cycle. This phase is called the *first quarter.*

More of the moon is visible during the second week, or the *gibbous* (GIB•uhs) *phase.* This is when the near side is more than half lit but not fully lit. When the moon is halfway through its cycle, the whole near side of the moon is in sunlight, and we see a full moon.

During the third week, the amount of the moon's near side in the sunlight decreases and it seems to shrink, or wane. When the near side is again only half in sunlight, the moon is three-quarters of the way through its cycle. The phase is called the *third quarter.*

In the fourth week, the area of the near side of the moon in sunlight continues to shrink. The moon is seen as waning crescent shapes. Finally, the near side of the moon is unlit—*new moon.*

Views of the moon from Earth's northern hemisphere

The waxing moon appears to grow each day. This is because the sunlit area that we can see from Earth is getting larger each day.

Waxing gibbous

Full moon

Waning gibbous

Think Outside the Book

9 Apply Look at the night sky and keep a moon journal for a series of nights. What phase is the moon in now?

First quarter

Waxing crescent

10 Analyze What shape does the moon appear to be when it is closer to the sun than Earth is?

_____

_____

New moon

Drawing not to scale.

Waning crescent

Third quarter

The waning moon appears to shrink each day. When the moon is waning, the sunlit area is getting smaller. Notice above that even as the phases of the moon change, the total amount of sunlight that the moon gets remains the same. Half the moon is always in sunlight, just as half of Earth is always in sunlight. The moon phases have a period of 29.5 days.

Exploring Eclipses

How do lunar eclipses occur?

An **eclipse** (ih•KLIPS) is an event during which one object in space casts a shadow onto another. On Earth, a lunar eclipse occurs when the moon moves through Earth's shadow. There are two parts of Earth's shadow, as you can see in the diagram below. The **umbra** (UHM•bruh) is the darkest part of a shadow. Around it is a spreading cone of lighter shadow called the **penumbra** (pih•NUHM•bruh). Just before a lunar eclipse, sunlight streaming past Earth produces a full moon. Then the moon moves into Earth's penumbra and becomes slightly less bright. As the moon moves into the umbra, Earth's dark shadow seems to creep across and cover the moon. The entire moon can be in darkness because the moon is small enough to fit entirely within Earth's umbra. After an hour or more, the moon moves slowly back into the sunlight that is streaming past Earth. A total lunar eclipse occurs when the moon passes completely into Earth's umbra. If the moon misses part or all of the umbra, part of the moon stays light and the eclipse is called a partial lunar eclipse.

You may be wondering why you don't see solar and lunar eclipses every month. The reason is that the moon's orbit around Earth is tilted—by about 5°—relative to the orbit of Earth around the sun. This tilt is enough to place the moon out of Earth's shadow for most full moons and Earth out of the moon's shadow for most new moons.

This composite photo shows the partial and total phases of a lunar eclipse over several hours.

Lunar eclipse

👁 **Visualize It!**

11 Identify Fill in the boxes with the type of eclipse that would occur if the moon were in the areas being pointed to.

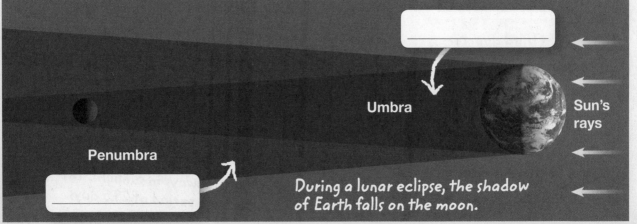

Penumbra

Umbra

Sun's rays

During a lunar eclipse, the shadow of Earth falls on the moon.

Drawing not to scale.

How do solar eclipses occur?

When the moon is directly between the sun and Earth, the shadow of the moon falls on a part of Earth and causes a solar eclipse. During a total solar eclipse, the sun's light is completely blocked by the moon, as seen in this photo. The umbra falls on the area of Earth that lies directly in line with the moon and the sun. Outside the umbra, but within the penumbra, people see a partial solar eclipse. The penumbra falls on the area that immediately surrounds the umbra.

The umbra of the moon is too small to make a large shadow on Earth's surface. The part of the umbra that hits Earth during an eclipse, is never more than a few hundred kilometers across, as shown below. So, a total eclipse of the sun covers only a small part of Earth and is seen only by people in particular parts of Earth along a narrow path. A total solar eclipse usually lasts between one to two minutes at any one location. A total eclipse will not be visible in the United States until 2017, even though there is a total eclipse somewhere on Earth about every one to two years.

Solar eclipse

During a solar eclipse, the moon passes between the sun and Earth so that the sun is partially or totally obscured.

Active Reading

12 Explain Why is it relatively rare to observe a solar eclipse?

_____

_____

_____

_____

Visualize It!

13 Describe Explain what happens during a solar eclipse.

_____

_____

_____

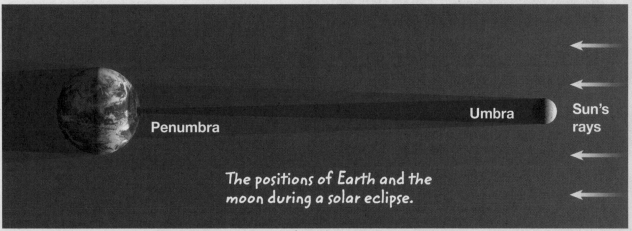

Penumbra

Umbra

Sun's rays

The positions of Earth and the moon during a solar eclipse.

Drawing not to scale.

Visual Summary

To complete this summary, circle the correct word. Then use the key below to check your answers. You can use this page to review the main concepts of the lesson.

Moon Phases and Eclipses

The appearance of the moon depends on the positions of the sun, the moon, and Earth.

The Earth–moon system orbits the sun.

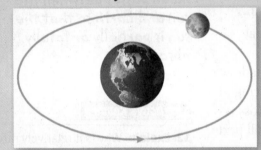

14 The moon takes about one day/month/year to orbit Earth.

Shadows in space cause eclipses.

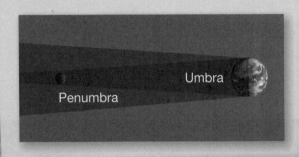

Umbra

Penumbra

15 When the moon is in Earth's umbra, a total solar/lunar eclipse is occurring.

16 The fraction of the moon that receives sunlight always/never changes.

17 Describe What causes the lunar phases that we see from Earth?

Lesson Review

Vocabulary

In your own words, define the following terms.

1 gravity

_____

_____

2 satellite

_____

_____

3 umbra

_____

_____

Key Concepts

4 Describe What are two phases of a waxing moon, and how do they appear?

_____

_____

_____

_____

_____

5 Identify Explain why the moon can be seen from Earth.

_____

_____

_____

6 Describe What is the relationship between Earth, the sun, and the moon in space?

_____

_____

_____

_____

Critical Thinking

Use the image below to answer the following question.

7 Identify What type of eclipse is shown in the diagram?

_____

_____

8 Describe Where is the moon in its orbit at the time of a solar eclipse?

_____

_____

9 Infer What phase is the moon in when there is a total solar eclipse?

_____

_____

10 Predict Which shape of the moon will you never see during the daytime, after sunrise and before sunset? *Hint:* Consider the directions of the sun and moon from Earth.

_____

_____

11 Synthesize If you were an astronaut in the middle of the near side of the moon during a full moon, how would the ground around you look? How would Earth, high in your sky look? Describe what is in sunlight and what is in darkness.

_____

_____

_____

_____

_____

_____

My Notes

Engineering Design Process

Skills

Identify a need

Conduct research

Brainstorm solutions

✓ Select a solution

✓ Design a prototype

✓ Build a prototype

✓ Test and evaluate

✓ Redesign to improve

✓ Communicate results

Objectives

- Explain several advantages of tidal energy over conventional energy sources.

- Design a technological solution to harnessing changing water levels.

- Test and modify a prototype to raise a mass as water levels change.

Harnessing Tidal Energy

Our society uses a lot of electrical energy. If the energy is generated by nuclear power plants or by burning fossil fuels, the waste products tend to harm the environment. However, in many places, these methods of obtaining energy are still used.

Scientists and engineers have been investigating alternative energy sources, such as solar, wind, and tidal energy. Tidal energy is energy from *tides,* the daily, predictable changes in the level of ocean water. The mechanical energy of the moving water can be transformed to other forms of energy that are useful in human activities. Tidal power facilities have less of an impact on nature and have low operating costs. And unlike fossil fuels or the uranium ore used in nuclear power plants, water is not used up in the generation of tidal energy. Generating electrical energy from tides and other alternative energy sources can be less harmful to the environment, but challenges must still be overcome.

Barrage tidal power facility at La Rance, France

1 Compare What are some advantages of generating electrical energy from tides instead of from fossil fuels?

© Houghton Mifflin Harcourt Publishing Company • Image Credits: (b) ©Robert Estall photo agency/Alamy Images

Types of Tidal Power Generators

There are three main types of tidal energy generators. One type is a system that uses a dam with turbines. The dam is called a *barrage*. The barrage allows water in during high tide and releases water during low tide. Barrage tidal power stations can affect marine life behind the barrage. Also, silt settles behind the barrage and must be dredged up and hauled out to sea. This is an older system of generating electrical energy from tides.

The other two types of tidal power generators are *horizontal-axis turbines* and *vertical-axis turbines*. These systems are like huge underwater fans turned by tidal currents instead of by wind. Because water is denser than air, slow-moving water can still produce a lot of power. These facilities have fewer effects on the environment.

2 Compare What is an advantage of using horizontal-axis turbines and vertical-axis turbines instead of barrage tidal power stations?

_____

_____

_____

_____

Four vertical-axis tidal power turbines are seen here. The blades rotate on an axis perpendicular to the ocean floor.

Two horizontal-axis tidal power turbines are seen here. The blades rotate on an axis parallel to the ocean floor.

✋ You Try It! ⟶

Now it's your turn to design and build a tidal power device.

Engineering Design Process

 # You Try It!

Now it's your turn to design and build a tidal power device that will lift two masses. You will lift the masses by harnessing energy from the changing water levels in a sink or tub. Adding water to the sink or tub will simulate a rising tide, and removing water will simulate a falling tide. One mass must be raised when the tide rises, and the other mass must be raised when the tide falls. Both masses must be outside the sink or tub.

 Select a Solution

A How will you use the falling tide to raise a mass?

_____

_____

_____

_____

B How will you use the rising tide to raise a mass?

_____

_____

_____

_____

 Design a Prototype

In the space below, draw and label a prototype of your tidal power device. You may have one idea for harnessing the falling tide and a different idea for harnessing the rising tide.

You Will Need

✔ block, wooden or foam

✔ bucket

✔ dowels, wooden

✔ duct tape

✔ masses, 50 g or 100 g (2)

✔ milk jug, 1 gallon, empty

✔ siphon hose

✔ string

✔ tub, plastic or sink

✔ water

③ Build a Prototype

Now build your tidal power device. As you built your device, were there some aspects of your design that could not be assembled as you had predicted? What aspects did you have to revise as you were building the prototype?

_____

_____

_____

_____

④ Test and Evaluate

Place your device in the tub. Add water to the tub to simulate a rising tide. Then drain water from the tub. Observe the motion of the masses as the tide rises and falls, and record your observations.

_____

_____

_____

_____

⑤ Redesign to Improve

Keep making revisions, one at a time, until your tidal power device can lift both masses. Describe the revisions you made.

_____

_____

_____

⑥ Communicate Results

Were you able to raise a mass more easily when the simulated tide was rising or falling? Why do you think that was? Record your ideas below. Then, compare your results with those of your classmates.

_____

_____

_____

_____

_____

Earth's Tides

ESSENTIAL QUESTION

What causes tides?

By the end of this lesson, you should be able to explain what tides are and what causes them in Earth's oceans and to describe variations in the tides.

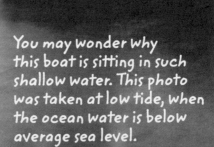

You may wonder why this boat is sitting in such shallow water. This photo was taken at low tide, when the ocean water is below average sea level.

Virginia Science Standards of Learning
6.8 The student will investigate and understand the organization of the solar system and the interactions among the various bodies that comprise it. Key concepts include:
6.8.h the cause of tides.

Engage Your Brain

1 Describe Fill in the blank with the word that you think correctly completes the following sentences.

The motion of the _____ around Earth is related to tides.

The daily rotation of _____ is also related to tides.

During a _____ tide, the water level is higher than the average sea level.

During a _____ tide, the water level is lower than the average sea level.

2 Label Draw an arrow to show where you think high tide might be.

Low tide ▶

Active Reading

3 Synthesize The word *spring* has different meanings. Use the meanings of the word *spring* and the sentence below to make an educated guess about the meaning of the term *spring tides*.

Meanings of *spring*
the season between winter and summer
a source of water from the ground
jump, or rise up
a coiled piece of metal

Example Sentence
During spring tides, the sun, the moon, and Earth are in a straight line, resulting in very high tides.

spring tides:

_____

_____

_____

Vocabulary Terms
• tide
• tidal range
• spring tide
• neap tide

4 Apply As you learn the definition of each vocabulary term in this lesson, create your own definition or sketch to help you remember the meaning of the term.

A Rising Tide of Interest

What causes tides?

![Active Reading]

5 Identify Underline the sentence that identifies which object is mainly responsible for tides on Earth.

The photographs below show the ocean at the same location at two different times. **Tides** are daily changes in the level of ocean water. Tides are caused by the difference in the gravitational force of the sun and the moon across Earth. This difference in gravitational force is called the *tidal force*. The tidal force exerted by the moon is stronger than the tidal force exerted by the sun because the moon is much closer to Earth than the sun is. So, the moon is mainly responsible for tides on Earth.

How often tides occur and how tidal levels vary depend on the position of the moon as it revolves around Earth. The gravity of the moon pulls on every particle of Earth. But because liquids move more easily than solids do, the pull on liquids is much more noticeable than the pull on solids is. The moon's gravitational pull on Earth decreases with the moon's distance from Earth. The part of Earth facing the moon is pulled toward the moon with the greatest force. So, water on that side of Earth bulges toward the moon. The solid Earth is pulled more strongly toward the moon than the ocean water on Earth's far side is. So, there is also a bulge of water on the side of Earth farthest from the moon.

At low tide, the water level is low, and the boats are far below the dock.

At high tide, the water level has risen, and the boats are close to the dock.

What are high tides and low tides?

The bulges that form in Earth's oceans are called high tides. *High tide* is a water level that is higher than the average sea level. Low tides form in the areas between the high tides. *Low tide* is a water level that is lower than the average sea level. At low tide, the water levels are lower because the water is in high-tide areas.

As the moon moves around Earth and Earth rotates, the tidal bulges move around Earth. The tidal bulges follow the motion of the moon. As a result, many places on Earth have two high tides and two low tides each day.

Visualize It!

6 Identify Label the areas where high tides form and the area where the other low tide forms.

Note: Drawing is not to scale.

Moon

A _____

B _____

Earth

Low tide

C _____

This grizzly bear in Alaska is taking advantage of low tide by digging for clams.

7 Predict What happens to the bear when high tide comes in?

_____

_____

Tide Me Over

What are two kinds of tidal ranges?

Active Reading

8 Identify As you read, underline the two kinds of tidal ranges.

Tides are due to the *tidal force,* the difference between the force of gravity on one side of Earth and the other side of Earth. Because the moon is so much closer to Earth than the sun is, the moon's tidal force is greater than the sun's tidal force. The moon's effect on tides is twice as strong as the sun's effect. The combined gravitational effects of the sun and the moon on Earth result in different tidal ranges. A **tidal range** is the difference between the levels of ocean water at high tide and low tide. Tidal range depends on the positions of the sun and the moon relative to Earth.

Spring Tides: The Largest Tidal Range

Tides that have the largest daily tidal range are **spring tides**. Spring tides happen when the sun, the moon, and Earth form a straight line. So, spring tides happen when the moon is between the sun and Earth and when the moon is on the opposite side of Earth, as shown in the illustrations below. In other words, spring tides happen during the new moon and full moon phases, or every 14 days. During these times, the gravitational effects of the sun and moon add together, causing one pair of very large tidal bulges. Spring tides have nothing to do with the season.

Note: Drawings are not to scale.

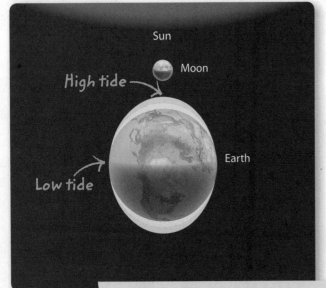

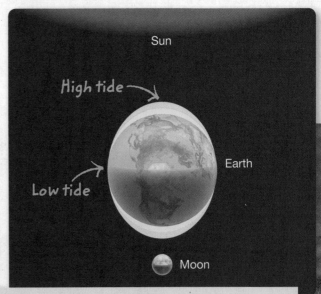

During spring tides, the tidal force of the sun on Earth adds to the tidal force of the moon. The tidal range increases.

Inquiry

9 Inquire Explain why spring tides happen twice a month.

_____

_____

_____

Neap Tides: The Smallest Tidal Range

Tides that have the smallest daily tidal range are **neap tides**. Neap tides happen when the sun, Earth, and the moon form a 90° angle, as shown in the illustrations below. During a neap tide, the gravitational effects of the sun and the moon on Earth do not add together as they do during spring tides. Neap tides occur halfway between spring tides, during the first quarter and third quarter phases of the moon. At these times, the sun and the moon cause two pairs of smaller tidal bulges.

Note: Drawings are not to scale.

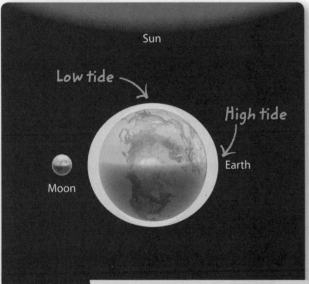

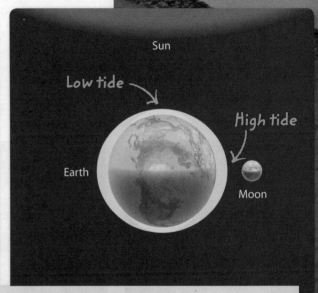

During neap tides, the gravitational effects of the sun and the moon on Earth do not add together. The tidal range decreases.

10 Compare Fill in the Venn diagram to compare and contrast spring tides and neap tides.

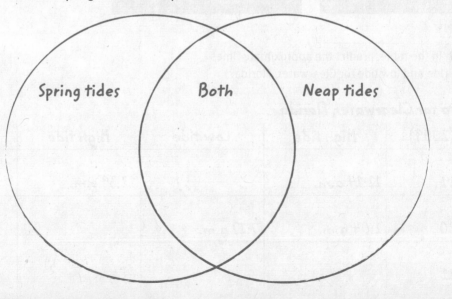

Spring tides   Both   Neap tides

What causes tidal cycles?

The rotation of Earth and the moon's revolution around Earth determine when tides occur. Imagine that Earth rotated at the same speed that the moon revolves around Earth. If this were true, the same side of Earth would always face the moon. And high tide would always be at the same places on Earth. But the moon revolves around Earth much more slowly than Earth rotates. A place on Earth that is facing the moon takes 24 h and 50 min to rotate to face the moon again. So, the cycle of high tides and low tides at that place happens 50 min later each day.

In many places there are two high tides and two low tides each day. Because the tide cycle occurs in 24 h and 50 min intervals, it takes about 6 h and 12.5 min (one-fourth the time of the total cycle) for water in an area to go from high tide to low tide. It takes about 12 h and 25 min (one-half the time of the total cycle) to go from one high tide to the next high tide.

Note: Drawings are not to scale.

Tuesday 11:00 a.m.

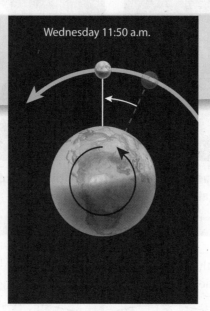

Wednesday 11:50 a.m.

The moon moves only a fraction of its orbit in the time that Earth rotates once.

Think Outside the Book Inquiry

11 Inquire Draw a diagram of Earth to show what Earth's tides would be like if the moon revolved around Earth at the same speed that Earth rotates.

12 Predict In the table, predict the approximate times of high tide and low tide for Clearwater, Florida.

Tide Data for Clearwater, Florida

Date (2009)	High tide	Low tide	High tide	Low tide
August 19	12:14 a.m.		12:39 p.m.	
August 20	1:04 a.m.	7:17 a.m.		
August 21				

Extreme Living Conditions

WEIRD SCIENCE

Some organisms living along ocean coastlines must be able to tolerate extreme living conditions. At high tide, much of the coast is under water. At low tide, much of the coast is dry. Some organisms must also survive the constant crashing of waves against the shore.

Barnacle Business

Barnacles must be able to live in water as well as out of water. They must also tolerate the air temperature, which may differ from the temperature of the water.

Ghostly Crabs

Ghost crabs live near the high tide line on sandy shores. They scurry along the sand to avoid being underwater when the tide comes in. Ghost crabs can also find cover between rocks.

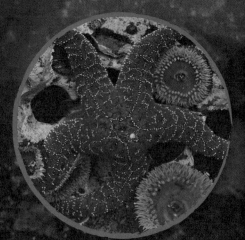

Stunning Starfish

Starfish live in tidal pools, which are areas along the shore where water remains at low tide. Starfish must be able to survive changes in water temperature and salinity.

Extend

Inquiry

13 Identify Describe how living conditions change for two tidal organisms.

14 Research and Record List the names of two organisms that live in the high tide zone or the low tide zone along a coastline of your choice.

15 Describe Imagine a day in the life of an organism you researched in question 14 by doing one of the following:
- make a poster
- write a play
- record an audio story
- make a cartoon

Visual Summary

To complete this summary, fill in the blanks with the correct word. Then use the key below to check your answers. You can use this page to review the main concepts of the lesson.

In many places, two high tides and two low tides occur every day.

16 The type of tide shown here is

_____

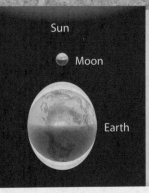

Tides on Earth

The gravitational effects of the moon and the sun cause tides.

17 Tides on Earth are caused mainly by the

_____

Moon

Earth

Note: Drawings are not to scale.

There are two kinds of tidal ranges: spring tides and neap tides.

Sun

Moon

Earth

Sun

Moon

Earth

18 During a spring tide, the sun, moon, and Earth are in a/an

_____

19 During a neap tide, the sun, moon, and Earth form a/an

_____

Answers: 16 low tide; 17 moon; 18 straight line; 19 90° angle

20 **Describe** State how the moon causes tides.

Lesson Review

Vocabulary

Answer the following questions in your own words.

1 Use *tide* and *tidal range* in the same sentence.

_____

_____

_____

2 Write an original definition for *neap tide* and for *spring tide*.

_____

_____

_____

_____

Key Concepts

3 Describe Explain what tides are. Include *high tide* and *low tide* in your answer.

_____

_____

_____

_____

_____

4 Explain State what causes tides on Earth.

_____

_____

_____

5 Identify Write the alignment of the moon, the sun, and Earth that causes a spring tide.

_____

_____

6 Describe Explain why tides happen 50 min later each day.

_____

_____

_____

Critical Thinking

Use this diagram to answer the next question.

Note: Drawing is not to scale.

Last quarter moon

7 Analyze What type of tidal range will Earth have when the moon is in this position?

_____

8 Apply How many days pass between the minimum and the maximum of the tidal range in any given area? Explain your answer.

_____

_____

_____

_____

_____

9 Apply How would the tides on Earth be different if the moon revolved around Earth in 15 days instead of 30 days?

_____

_____

_____

_____

_____

_____

_____

My Notes

Lesson 1
ESSENTIAL QUESTION
How are Earth's days, years, and seasons related to the way Earth moves in space?

Relate Earth's days, years, and seasons to Earth's movement in space.

Lesson 2
ESSENTIAL QUESTION
How do Earth, the moon, and the sun affect each other?

Describe the effects the sun and the moon have on Earth, including gravitational attraction, moon phases, and eclipses.

Lesson 3
ESSENTIAL QUESTION
What causes tides?

Explain what tides are and what causes them in Earth's oceans, and describe variations in the tides.

Think Outside the Book

2 Synthesize Choose one of these activities to help synthesize what you have learned in this unit.

☐ Using what you learned in lessons 2 and 3, make a flipbook showing the importance of the alignment of Earth, the moon, and the sun in the Earth-moon-sun system.

☐ Using what you learned in lessons 1, 2, and 3, describe the hierarchical relationship of gravitational attraction in the Earth-moon-sun system using a poster presentation.

Connect ESSENTIAL QUESTIONS
Lessons 1, 2, and 3

1 Synthesize Name the natural cycles that occur as a result of the Earth-moon-sun system.

_____

_____

_____

_____

Unit 9 Review

Vocabulary

Fill in each blank with the term that best completes the following sentences.

1 A _____ is the periodic rise and fall of the water level in the oceans and other large bodies of water.

2 A _____ is the motion of a body that travels around another body in space.

3 The force of _____ keeps Earth and other planets of the solar system in orbit around the sun and keeps the moon in orbit around Earth.

4 A natural or artificial body that revolves around a celestial body that is greater in mass is called a _____.

5 _____ is the counterclockwise spin of a planet or moon as seen from above a planet's north pole.

Key Concepts

Read each question below, and circle the best answer.

6 Look at the table of tide information.

Date	High tide time	High tide height (m)	Low tide time	Low tide height (m)
June 3	6:04 a.m.	6.11	12:01 a.m.	1.76
June 4	6:58 a.m.	5.92	12:54 a.m.	1.87
June 5	7:51 a.m.	5.80	1:47 a.m.	1.90
June 6	8:42 a.m.	5.75	2:38 a.m.	1.87
June 7	9:30 a.m.	5.79	3:27 a.m.	1.75
June 8	10:16 a.m.	5.90	4:13 a.m.	1.56
June 9	11:01 a.m.	6.08	4:59 a.m.	1.32
June 10	11:46 a.m.	6.28	5:44 a.m.	1.05
June 11	12:32 p.m.	6.47	6:30 a.m.	0.78

What was the tidal range on June 9?

A 4.76 m

C 6.08 m

B 7.40 m

D 4.76 ft

7 Aside from Earth's tilt, what other factor contributes to Earth's seasons?

  A the time of the day

  B the energy as heat from the moon

  C the angle of the sun's rays and the number of hours of daylight

  D cold or warm air blowing from the oceans

8 Ann is looking at the night sky. There is a first-quarter moon. What does she see?

  A a moon shaped like a crescent

  B a moon shaped like a half circle

  C a moon shaped like a circle, shining brightly

  D no moon in the sky

9 Which is a similarity between a neap tide and a spring tide?

  A Neap tides occur once a year in fall and spring tides once a year in spring.

  B Each occurs twice a year and relates to the phases of the moon.

  C A neap tide occurs at night, and a spring tide occurs during the day.

  D Each tide occurs twice a month, and is determined by the pull of gravity of the moon.

10 The diagram below shows the relative positions of the sun, the moon, and Earth.

  What does the diagram show?

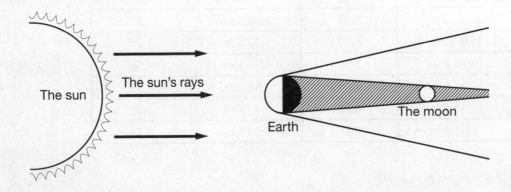

  A a solar eclipse   **C** a first-quarter moon

  B a lunar eclipse   **D** a third-quarter moon

11 During equinox, the sun's rays strike Earth at a 90-degree angle along the equator. What is the result of the equinox?

    A the hours of daylight and the hours of darkness are about the same

    B the hours of daylight are longer than the hours of darkness

    C the hours of darkness are longer than the hours of daylight

    D an unseasonably warm day in the midst of winter

12 Examine the diagram below.

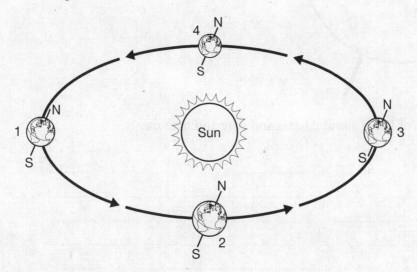

The position labeled "1" represents the season of summer in—

    A the Southern Hemisphere.   **C** the Eastern Hemisphere.

    B Antarctica.   **D** the Northern Hemisphere.

Critical Thinking

Answer the following questions in the space provided.

13 Janais lives near the ocean. How do Earth, the sun, and the moon interact to affect Janais's life?

_____
_____
_____
_____
_____
_____
_____

14 Look at the diagram of Earth.

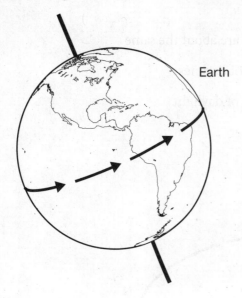

Earth

Describe the rotation of Earth about its axis and why an Earth day is 24 hours long.

_____

_____

_____

_____

_____

_____

Connect **ESSENTIAL QUESTIONS**
Lessons 2 and 3

Answer the following question in the space provided.

15 Explain what causes tides on Earth and why high and low tides occur.

_____

_____

_____

_____

_____

_____

_____

The Solar System

A brass orrery shows the rotation of planets around the sun.

Big Idea

Planets and a variety of other bodies form a system of objects orbiting the sun.

What do you think?

For thousands of years, scientists have created models to help us understand the solar system. What are some different ways in which scientists have modeled the solar system?

The Human Orrery models the solar system.

Unit 10
The Solar System

Solar System Discoveries

Today's knowledge of the solar system is the result of discoveries that have been made over the centuries. Discoveries will continue to change our view of the solar system.

Moons of Jupiter, 1610
On January 7, 1610, Galileo used a telescope he had improved and discovered the four largest moons of Jupiter. The moons are some of the largest objects in our solar system!

Ganymede is the largest of Jupiter's moons.

Comet Hyakutake

William Herschel

Comet Hyakutake, 1996

Amateur astronomer Yuji Hyakutake discovered Comet Hyakutake on January 31, 1996, using a pair of powerful binoculars. This comet will approach Earth only once every 100,000 years.

Uranus, 1781

British astronomer Sir William Herschel discovered Uranus on March 13, 1781. It was the first planet discovered with a telescope. Our knowledge of the solar system expanded in ways people had not expected.

Neptune, 1846

Mathematics helped scientists discover the planet Neptune. Astronomers predicted Neptune's existence based on irregularities in Uranus's orbit. On September 23, 1846, Neptune was discovered by telescope almost exactly where it was mathematically predicted to be.

Neptune

Take It Home | Future Explorations

① Think About It

What are some recent discoveries that have been made about the solar system?

_____

_____

_____

_____

B Will crewed missions to distant places in the solar system ever be possible? Justify your answer.

_____

_____

_____

_____

_____

② Ask Some Questions

Research efforts such as NASA's Stardust spacecraft to learn more about how space is being explored now.

A How is information being transmitted back to Earth?

_____

_____

③ Make A Plan

Design a poster to explain why humans are exploring the solar system. Be sure to include the following information:

- How we are using technology for exploration

- Why it benefits all of us to learn about the solar system

Historical Models
of the Solar System

ESSENTIAL QUESTION

How have people modeled the solar system?

By the end of this lesson, you should be able to compare various historical models of the solar system.

The Earth-centered model of the solar system was accepted for almost 1,400 years. It was replaced by the sun-centered model of the solar system, which is shown in this 17th-century illustration.

Virginia Science Standards of Learning
6.8 The student will investigate and understand the organization of the solar system and the interactions among the various bodies that comprise it. Key concepts include:
6.8.i the history and technology of space exploration.

Lesson Labs

Quick Labs
- The Geocentric Model of the Solar System
- The Heliocentric Model of the Solar System
- Orbital Ellipses

Field Lab
- Investigating Parallax

Engage Your Brain

1 Predict Check T or F to show whether you think each statement is true or false.

T	F	
☐	☐	The sun and planets circle Earth.
☐	☐	Most early astronomers placed the sun at the center of the solar system.
☐	☐	The planets orbit the sun in ellipses.
☐	☐	The telescope helped to improve our understanding of the solar system.

2 Evaluate What, if anything, is wrong with the model of the solar system shown below?

_____

_____

_____

_____

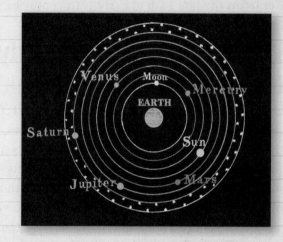

Active Reading

3 Synthesis You can often define an unknown word if you know the meaning of its word parts. Use the word parts and sentence below to make an educated guess about the meaning of the word *heliocentric*.

Word part	Meaning
helio-	sun
-centric	centered

Example sentence
The heliocentric model of the solar system was first proposed by Aristarchus.

heliocentric:

_____

_____

_____

Vocabulary Terms
- solar system
- heliocentric
- geocentric
- parallax

4 Apply As you learn the definition of each vocabulary term in this lesson, create your own definition or sketch to help you remember the meaning of the term.

What is the solar system?

The **solar system** is the sun and all of the bodies that orbit the sun. Our current model of the solar system is the *sun-centered* or *heliocentric* (hee•lee•oh•SEN•trik) model. In the **heliocentric** model, Earth and the other planets orbit the sun. The earliest models for the solar system assumed that the Earth was at the center of the solar system, with the sun, moon, and planets circling it. These models, which used Earth as the center, are called *Earth-centered* or **geocentric** (jee•oh•SEN•trik) models. The heliocentric model was not generally accepted until the work of Copernicus and Kepler in the late 16th to early 17th centuries.

Who proposed some early models of the solar system?

Until Galileo improved on the telescope in 1609, people observed the heavens with the naked eye. To observers, it appeared that the sun, the moon, the planets, and the stars moved around Earth each day. This caused them to conclude that Earth was not moving. If Earth was not moving, then Earth must be the center of the solar system and all other bodies revolved around it.

This geocentric model of the solar system became part of ancient Greek thought beginning in the 6th century BCE. Aristotle was among the first thinkers to propose this model.

Active Reading

5 Identify As you read the text, underline the definitions of geocentric and heliocentric.

Think Outside the Book

6 Research Use different sources to research a geocentric model of the solar system from either ancient Greece, ancient China, or Babylon. Write a short description of the model you choose.

Aristotle (384–322 BCE)

Aristotle

Aristotle (AIR•ih•staht'l) was a Greek philosopher. Aristotle thought Earth was the center of all things. His model placed the moon, sun, planets, and stars on a series of circles that surrounded Earth. He thought that if Earth went around the sun, then the relative positions of the stars would change as Earth moves. This apparent shift in the position of an object when viewed from different locations is known as **parallax** (PAIR•uh•laks). In fact, the stars are so far away that parallax cannot be seen with the naked eye.

of the Solar System?

Aristarchus

Aristarchus (air•i•STAHR•kuhs) was a Greek astronomer and mathematician. Aristarchus is reported to have proposed a heliocentric model of the solar system. His model, however, was not widely accepted at the time. Aristarchus attempted to measure the relative distances to the moon and sun. This was a major contribution to science. Aristarchus's ratio of distances was much too small but was important in the use of observation and geometry to solve a scientific problem.

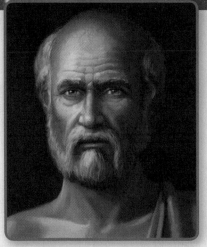

Aristarchus (about 310–230 BCE)

Aristotle thought that if Earth were moving, the positions of the stars should change as Earth moved. In fact, stars are so far away that shifts in their positions can only be observed by telescope.

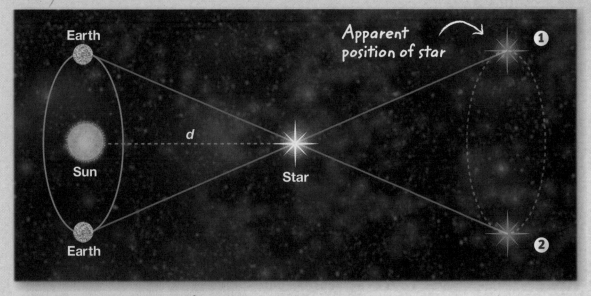

Diagram showing the shift in apparent position of a star at two different times of year seen from a telescope on Earth. A star first seen at point 1 will be seen at point 2 six months later.

 **Visualize It!**

7 Predict If a star appears at position 1 during the summer, during which season will it appear at position 2?

_____

_____

_____

Ptolemy (about 100–170 CE)

Ptolemy

Ptolemy (TOHL•uh•mee) was an astronomer, geographer, and mathematician who lived in Alexandria, Egypt, which was part of ancient Rome. His book, the *Almagest*, is one of the few books that we have from these early times. It was based on observations of the planets going back as much as 800 years. Ptolemy developed a detailed geocentric model that was used by astronomers for the next 14 centuries. He believed that a celestial body traveled at a constant speed in a perfect circle. In Ptolemy's model, the planets moved on small circles that in turn moved on larger circles. This "wheels-on-wheels" system fit observations better than any model that had come before. It allowed prediction of the motion of planets years into the future.

Visualize It!

8 Describe Use the diagram at the right to describe Ptolemy's geocentric model of the solar system.

_____

_____

_____

_____

_____

Ptolemaic Model

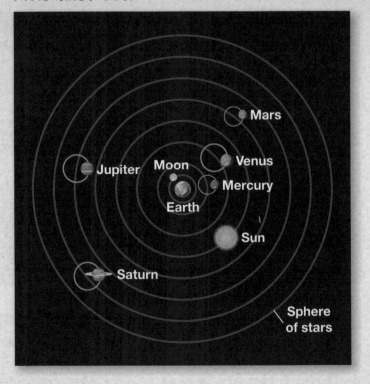

Think Outside the Book Inquiry

9 Defend As a class activity, defend Ptolemy's geocentric model of the solar system. Remember that during Ptolemy's time people were limited to what they could see with the naked eye.

Copernicus

The Polish astronomer Nicolaus Copernicus (nik•uh•LAY•uhs koh•PER•nuh•kuhs) felt that Ptolemy's model of the solar system was too complicated. He was aware of the heliocentric idea of Aristarchus when he developed the first detailed heliocentric model of the solar system. In Copernicus's time, data was still based on observations with the naked eye. Because data had changed little since the time of Ptolemy, Copernicus adopted Ptolemy's idea that planetary paths should be perfect circles. Like Ptolemy, he used a "wheels-on-wheels" system. Copernicus's model fit observations a little better than the geocentric model of Ptolemy. The heliocentric model of Copernicus is generally seen as the first step in the development of modern models of the solar system.

Nicolaus Copernicus (1473–1543)

Copernican Model

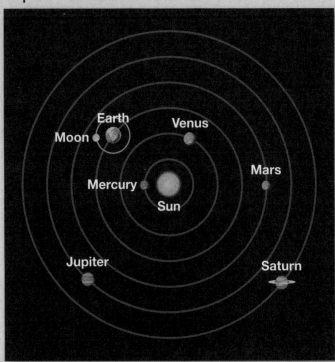

10 Compare How does Copernicus's model of the solar system differ from Ptolemy's model of the solar system?

Ptolemaic model	Copernican model

Active Reading

11 Identify Underline text that summarizes Kepler's three laws.

Kepler

Johannes Kepler (yoh•HAH•nuhs KEP•luhr) was a German mathematician and astronomer. After carefully analyzing observations of the planets, he realized that requiring planetary motions to be exactly circular did not fit the observations perfectly. Kepler then tried other types of paths and found that ellipses fit best.

Kepler formulated three principles, which today are known as Kepler's laws. The first law states that planetary orbits are ellipses with the sun at one focus. The second law states that planets move faster in their orbits when closer to the sun. The third law relates the distance of a planet from the sun to the time it takes to go once around its orbit.

Johannes Kepler (1571–1630)

12 Analyze How did Kepler's first law support the idea of a heliocentric solar system?

_____

_____

_____

_____

Kepler's First Law

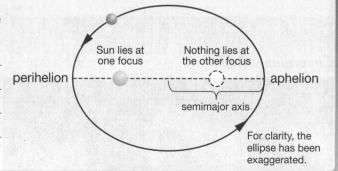

perihelion — Sun lies at one focus — Nothing lies at the other focus — aphelion

semimajor axis

For clarity, the ellipse has been exaggerated.

Galileo

Galileo Galilei (gahl•uh•LAY•oh gahl•uh•LAY) was a scientist who approached questions in the fashion that today we call *scientific methods*. Galileo made significant improvements to the newly invented telescope. He then used his more powerful telescope to view celestial objects. Galileo observed the moons Io, Europa, Callisto, and Ganymede orbiting Jupiter. Today, these moons are known as the Galilean satellites. His observations showed that Earth was not the only object that could be orbited. This gave support to the heliocentric model. He also observed that Venus went through phases similar to the phases of Earth's moon. These phases result from changes in the direction that sunlight strikes Venus as Venus orbits the sun.

Galileo Galilei (1564–1642)

Galileo

Galileo Galilei was an Italian mathematician, physicist, and astronomer who lived during the 16th and 17th centuries. Galileo demonstrated that all bodies, regardless of their mass, fall at the same rate. He also argued that moving objects retain their velocity unless an unbalanced force acts upon them. Galileo made improvements to telescope technology. He used his telescopes to observe sunspots, the phases of Venus, Earth's moon, the four Galilean moons of Jupiter, and a supernova.

Galileo's Telescopes

This reconstruction of one of Galileo's telescopes is on exhibit in Florence, Italy. Galileo's first telescopes magnified objects at 3 and then 20 times.

The *Galileo* Spacecraft

The *Galileo* spacecraft was launched from the space shuttle *Atlantis* in 1989. *Galileo* was the first spacecraft to orbit Jupiter. It studied the planet and its moons.

Extend

13 Identify What were Galileo's most important contributions to astronomy?

14 Research Galileo invented or improved upon many instruments and technologies, such as the compound microscope, the thermometer, and the geometric compass. Research one of Galileo's technological contributions.

15 Create Describe one of Galileo's experiments concerning the motion of bodies by doing one of the following:

- make a poster
- recreate the experiment
- draw a graphic novel of Galileo conducting an experiment

Visual Summary

To complete this summary, fill in the blanks with the correct word or phrase. Then use the key below to check your answers. You can use this page to review the main concepts of the lesson.

Models of the Solar System

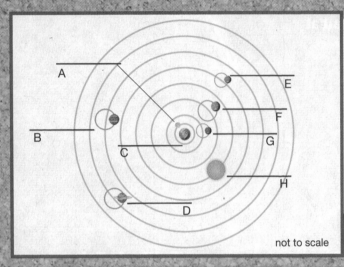

not to scale

Early astronomers proposed a geocentric solar system.

16 Label the solar system bodies as they appear in the geocentric model.

17 Which astronomers are associated with this model of the solar system?

_____

_____

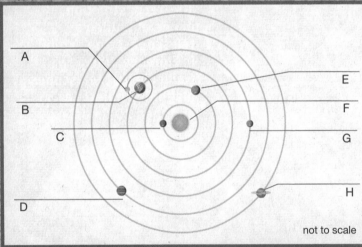

not to scale

The heliocentric solar system is the current model.

18 Label the solar system bodies as they appear in the heliocentric model.

19 Which astronomers are associated with this model of the solar system?

_____

_____

_____

Answers: 16 A. moon, B. Jupiter, C. Earth, D. Saturn, E. Mars, F. Venus, G. Mercury, H. sun; 17 Aristotle, Ptolemy; 18 A. moon, B. Earth, C. Mercury, D. Jupiter, E. Venus, F. sun, G. Mars, H. Saturn, Copernicus, Kepler, Galileo

20 **Compare** How does the geocentric model of the solar system differ from the heliocentric model of the solar system?

Lesson Review

Vocabulary

Fill in the blank with the term that best completes the following sentences.

1 The _____ is the sun and all of the planets and other bodies that travel around it.

2 Until the time of Copernicus, most scientists thought the _____ model of the solar system was correct.

3 An apparent shift in the position of an object when viewed from different locations is called _____.

Key Concepts

In the following table, write the name of the correct astronomer next to that astronomer's contribution.

Contribution	Astronomer
4 Identify Who first observed the phases of Venus?	
5 Identify Who attempted to measure the relative distances to the moon and the sun?	
6 Identify Who replaced circles with ellipses in a heliocentric model of the universe?	
7 Identify Whose geocentric model of the solar system was accepted for 1,400 years?	
8 Identify Whose heliocentric model is seen as the first step in the development of modern models of the solar system?	

Critical Thinking

Use the illustration to answer the following question.

9 Appraise How did data gathered using Galileo's early telescope support the heliocentric model?

_____

_____

_____

_____

10 Explain How did Aristotle's inability to detect parallax lead him to propose a geocentric model of the solar system?

_____

_____

_____

_____

_____

_____

My Notes

Mean, Median, Mode, and Range

You can analyze both the measures of central tendency and the variability of data using mean, median, mode, and range.

Tutorial

Orbit eccentricity measures how oval-shaped the elliptical orbit is. The closer a value is to 0, the closer the orbit is to a circle. Examine the eccentricity values below.

Orbit Eccentricities of Planets in the Solar System			
Mercury	0.205	**Jupiter**	0.049
Venus	0.007	**Saturn**	0.057
Earth	0.017	**Uranus**	0.046
Mars	0.094	**Neptune**	0.011

Mean The mean is the sum of all of the values in a data set divided by the total number of values in the data set. The mean is also called the *average*.	$$\frac{0.007 + 0.011 + 0.017 + 0.046 + 0.049 + 0.057 + 0.094 + 0.205}{8}$$ **1** Add up all of the values. **2** Divide the sum by the number of values. **mean** = 0.061
Median The median is the value of the middle item when data are arranged in numerical order. If there is an odd number of values, the median is the middle value. If there is an even number of values, the median is the mean of the two middle values.	0.007 0.011 0.017 0.046 0.049 0.057 0.094 0.205 **1** Order the values. **2** The median is the middle value if there is an odd number of values. If there is an even number of values, calculate the mean of the two middle values. **median** = 0.0475
Mode The mode is the value or values that occur most frequently in a data set. Order the values to find the mode. If all values occur with the same frequency, the data set is said to have no mode.	0.007 0.011 0.017 0.046 0.049 0.057 0.094 0.205 **1** Order the values. **2** Find the value or values that occur most frequently. **mode** = none
Range The range is the difference between the greatest value and the least value of a data set.	0.205 − 0.007 **1** Subtract the least value from the greatest value. **range** = 0.198

You Try It!

The data table below shows the masses and densities of the planets.

Mass and Density of the Planets		
	Mass (× 10²⁴ kg)	**Density (g/cm³)**
Mercury	0.33	5.43
Venus	4.87	5.24
Earth	5.97	5.52
Mars	0.64	3.34
Jupiter	1,899	1.33
Saturn	568	0.69
Uranus	87	1.27
Neptune	102	1.64

Using Formulas Find the mean, median, mode, and range for the mass of the planets.

Using Formulas Find the mean, median, mode, and range for the density of the planets.

③

Analyzing Data Find the mean density of the inner planets (Mercury through Mars). Find the mean density of the outer planets (Jupiter through Neptune). Compare these values.

Mean density of the inner planets: _____

Mean density of the outer planets: _____

Comparison:

_____

④

Evaluating Data The mean mass of the outer planets is 225 times greater than the mean mass of the inner planets. How does this comparison and the comparison of mean densities support the use of the term *gas giants* to describe the outer planets? Explain your reasoning.

_____

_____

Gravity and the Solar System

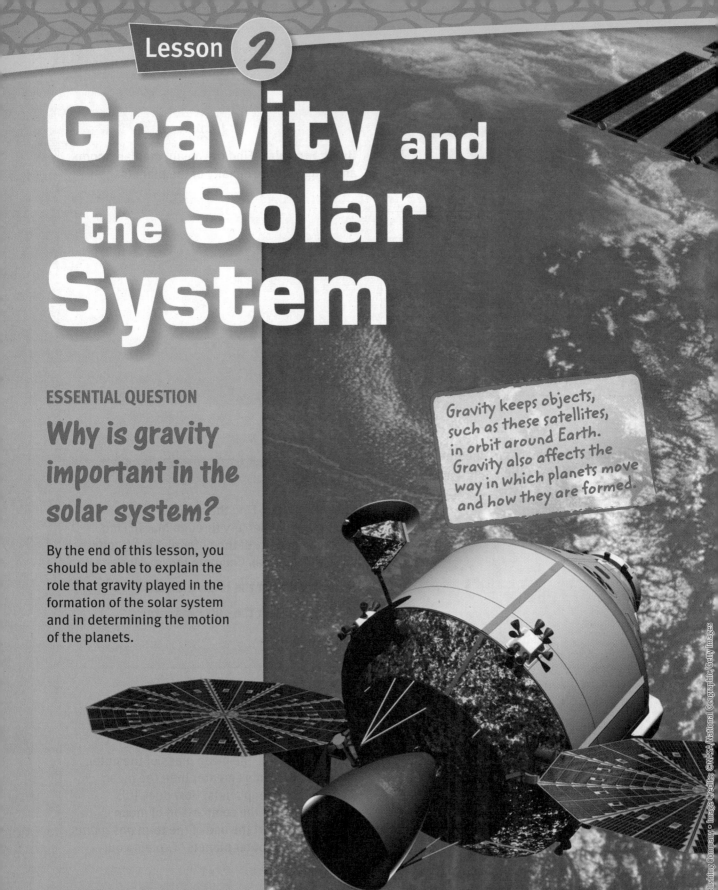

ESSENTIAL QUESTION

Why is gravity important in the solar system?

By the end of this lesson, you should be able to explain the role that gravity played in the formation of the solar system and in determining the motion of the planets.

Gravity keeps objects, such as these satellites, in orbit around Earth. Gravity also affects the way in which planets move and how they are formed.

Virginia Science Standards of Learning
6.8 The student will investigate and understand the organization of the solar system and the interactions among the various bodies that comprise it. Key concepts include:
6.8.c the role of gravity.

 **Lesson Labs**

Quick Labs
• Gravity's Effect
• Gravity and the Orbit of a Planet

Exploration Lab
• Weights on Different Celestial Bodies

Engage Your Brain

1 Predict Check T or F to show whether you think each statement is true or false.

T F

☐ ☐ Gravity keeps the planets in orbit around the sun.

☐ ☐ The planets follow circular paths around the sun.

☐ ☐ Sir Isaac Newton was the first scientist to describe how the force of gravity behaved.

☐ ☐ The sun formed in the center of the solar system.

☐ ☐ The terrestrial planets and the gas giant planets formed from the same material.

2 Draw In the space below, draw what you think the solar system looked like before the planets formed.

Active Reading

3 Synthesize You can often define an unknown word if you know the meaning of its word parts. Use the word parts and sentence below to make an educated guess about the meaning of the word *protostellar*.

Word part	Meaning
proto-	first
-stellar	of or having to do with a star or stars

Example sentence
The protostellar disk formed after the collapse of the solar nebula.

protostellar:

_____

_____

Vocabulary Terms

• gravity
• orbit
• aphelion
• perihelion
• centripetal force
• solar nebula
• planetesimal

4 Apply This list contains the key terms you'll learn in this section. As you read, circle the definition of each term.

Gravity

What is gravity?

Active Reading 5 **Identify** Underline the definition of and the effects of gravity.

Gravity is a force of attraction between objects that is due to their masses and the distances between them. Every object in the universe pulls on every other object. Objects with greater masses have a greater force of attraction than objects with lesser masses have. Objects that are close together have a greater force of attraction than objects that are far apart have.

Gravity is the weakest force in nature. A toy magnet can overcome the gravitational force acting on a paperclip by the entire mass of Earth. Yet, gravity is one of the most important forces in the universe. It accounts for the formation of planets, stars, and galaxies. It also keeps smaller bodies in orbit around larger bodies. An **orbit** is the path that a body follows as it travels around another body in space. For example, the moon orbits Earth, and Earth orbits the sun.

When astronauts are in orbit, Earth's gravity still pulls them downward toward the planet. However, they appear to be weightless and floating. They "float" because everything around them is falling at the same speed.

What are Kepler's laws?

The 16th-century Polish astronomer Nicolaus Copernicus (nik•uh•LAY•uhs koh•PER•nuh•kuhs) (1473–1543) changed our view of the solar system. He discovered that the motions of the planets could be best explained if the planets orbited the sun. But, like astronomers who came before him, Copernicus thought the planets followed circular paths around the sun.

Danish astronomer Tycho Brahe (TY•koh BRAH) (1546–1601) built what was at the time the world's largest observatory. Tycho used special instruments to measure the motions of the planets. His measurements were made over a period of 20 years and were very accurate. Using Tycho's data, Johannes Kepler (yoh•HAH•nuhs KEP•luhr) (1571–1630) made discoveries about the motions of the planets. We call these *Kepler's laws of planetary motion.*

Kepler found that objects that orbit the sun follow elliptical orbits. When an object follows an elliptical orbit around the sun, there is one point, called **aphelion** (uh•FEE•lee•uhn), where the object is farthest from the sun. There is also a point, called **perihelion** (perh•uh•HEE•lee•uhn), where the object is closest to the sun. Today, we know that the orbits of the planets are only slightly elliptical. However, the orbits of objects such as Pluto and comets are highly elliptical.

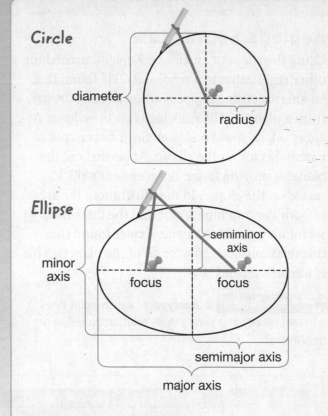

Circle

Ellipse

Visualize It!

6 Compare How is a circle different from an ellipse?

_____

_____

_____

_____

Kepler's First Law

Kepler's careful plotting of the orbit of Mars kept showing Mars's orbit to be a deformed circle. It took Kepler eight years to realize that this shape was an ellipse. This clue led Kepler to propose elliptical orbits for the planets. Kepler placed the sun at one of the foci of the ellipse. This is Kepler's first law.

Active Reading **7 Contrast** What is the difference between Copernicus's and Kepler's description of planetary orbits?

_____

_____

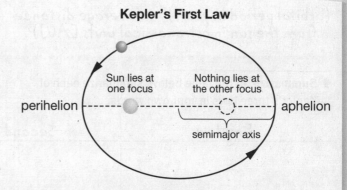

Kepler's First Law

Each planet orbits the sun in an ellipse with the sun at one focus. (For clarity, the ellipse is exaggerated here.)

Kepler's Second Law

Using the shape of an ellipse, Kepler searched for other regularities in Tycho's data. He found that an amazing thing happens when a line is drawn from a planet to the sun's focus on the ellipse. At aphelion, its speed is slower. So, it sweeps out a narrow sector on the ellipse. At perihelion, the planet is moving faster. It sweeps out a thick sector on the ellipse. In the illustration, the areas of both the thin blue sector and the thick blue sector are exactly the same. Kepler found that this relationship is true for all of the planets. This is Kepler's second law.

Active Reading **8 Analyze** At which point does a planet move most slowly in its orbit, at aphelion or perihelion?

As a planet moves around its orbit, it sweeps out equal areas in equal times.

Kepler's Second Law

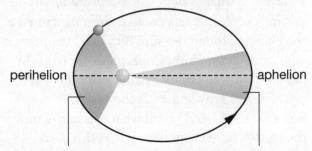

Near perihelion, a planet sweeps out an area that is short but wide.

Near aphelion, in an equal amount of time, a planet sweeps out an area that is long but narrow.

Kepler's Third Law

When Kepler looked at how long it took for the planets to orbit the sun and at the sizes of their orbits, he found another relationship. Kepler calculated the orbital period and the distance from the sun for the planets using Tycho's data. He discovered that the square of the orbital period was proportional to the cube of the planet's average distance from the sun. This law is true for each planet. This principle is Kepler's third law. When the units are years for the period and AU for the distance, the law can be written:

$(\text{orbital period in years})^2 = (\text{average distance from the sun in astronomical units [AU]})^3$

The square of the orbital period is proportional to the cube of the planet's average distance from the sun.

Kepler's Third Law

$p^2 \text{ yrs} = a^3 \text{ AU}$

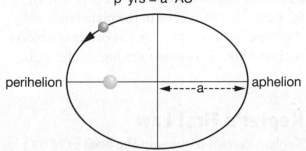

9 Summarize In the table below, summarize each of Kepler's three laws in your own words.

First law	Second law	Third law

© Houghton Mifflin Harcourt Publishing Company

What is the law of universal gravitation?

Using Kepler's laws, Sir Isaac Newton (EYE•zuhk NOOT'n) became the first scientist to mathematically describe how the force of gravity behaved. How could Newton do this in the 1600s before the force could be measured in a laboratory? He reasoned that gravity was the same force that accounted for both the fall of an apple from a tree and the movement of the moon around Earth.

In 1687, Newton formulated the *law of universal gravitation*. The law of universal gravitation states that all objects in the universe attract each other through gravitational force. The strength of this force depends on the product of the masses of the objects. Therefore, the gravity between objects increases as the masses of the objects increase. Gravitational force is also inversely proportional to the square of the distance between the objects. Stated another way this means that as the distance between two objects increases, the force of gravity decreases.

Sir Isaac Newton
(1642–1727)

 ## Do the Math

Newton's law of universal gravitation says that the force of gravity:
- increases as the masses of the objects increase and
- decreases as the distance between the objects increases

In these examples, M = mass, d = distance, and F = the force of gravity exerted by two bodies.

Sample Problems

A. In the example below, when two balls have masses of M and the distance between them is d, then the force of gravity is F. If the mass of each ball is increased to 2M (to the right) and the distance stays the same, then the force of gravity increases to 4F.

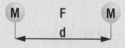 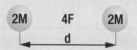

B. In this example, we start out again with a distance of d and masses of M, and the force of gravity is F. If the distance is decreased to ½ d, then the force of gravity increases to 4F.

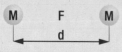

You Try It

Recall that M = mass, d = distance, and F = the force of gravity exerted by two bodies.

10 Calculate Compare the example below to the sample problems. What would the force of gravity be in the example below? Explain your answer.

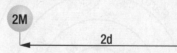

_____

_____

_____

_____

_____

How does gravity affect planetary motion?

The illustrations on this page will help you understand planetary motion. In the illustration at the right, a girl is swinging a ball around her head. The ball is attached to a string. The girl is exerting a force on the string that causes the ball to move in a circular path. The inward force that causes an object to move in a circular path is called **centripetal** (sehn•TRIP•ih•tuhl) **force**.

In the illustration at center, we see that if the string breaks, the ball will move off in a straight line. This fact indicates that when the string is intact, a force is pulling the ball inward. This force keeps the ball from flying off and moving in a straight line. This force is centripetal force.

In the illustration below, you see that the planets orbit the sun. A force must be preventing the planets from moving out of their orbits and into a straight line. The sun's gravity is the force that keeps the planets moving in orbit around the sun.

As the girl swings the ball, she is exerting a force on the string that causes the ball to move in a circular path.

Centripetal force pulls the ball inward, which causes the ball to move in a curved path.

direction ball would move if string broke

direction centripetal force pulls the ball

Center of rotation

String

path ball takes when moving around the center of rotation

Just as the string is pulling the ball inward, gravity is keeping the planets in orbit around the sun.

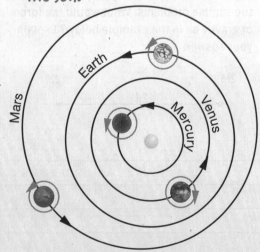

11 **Explain** In the illustration at the top of the page, what does the hand represent, the ball represent, and the string represent? (Hint: Think of the sun, a planet, and the force of gravity.)

_____

_____

_____

_____

Collapse

How did the solar system form?

The formation of the solar system is thought to have begun 4.6 billion years ago when a cloud of dust and gas collapsed. This cloud, from which the solar system formed, is called the **solar nebula** (SOH•ler NEB•yuh•luh). In a nebula, the inward pull of gravity is balanced by the outward push of gas pressure in the cloud. Scientists think that an outside force, perhaps the explosion of a nearby star, caused the solar nebula to compress and then to contract under its own gravity. It was in a single region of the nebula, which was perhaps several light-years across, that the solar system formed. The sun probably formed from a region that had a mass that was slightly greater than today's mass of the sun and planets.

Active Reading **12 Define** What is the solar nebula?

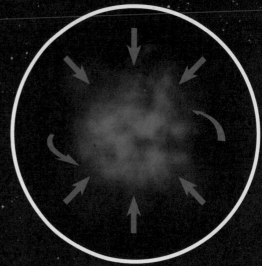

A cloud of dust and gas collapsed 4.6 billion years ago, then began to spin. It may have spun around its axis of rotation once every million years.

A Protostellar Disk Formed from the Collapsed Solar Nebula

As a region of the solar nebula collapsed, gravity pulled most of the mass toward the center of the nebula. As the nebula contracted, it began to rotate. As the rotation grew faster, the nebula flattened out into a disk. This disk, which is called a *protostellar disk* (PROH•toh•stehl•er DISK), is where the central star, our sun, formed.

As a region of the solar nebula collapsed, it formed a slowly rotating protostellar disk.

The Sun Formed at the Center of the Protostellar Disk

As the protostellar disk continued to contract, most of the matter ended up in the center of the disk. Friction from matter that fell into the disk heated up its center to millions of degrees, eventually reaching its current temperature of 15,000,000 °C. This intense heat in a densely packed space caused the fusion of hydrogen atoms into helium atoms. The process of fusion released large amounts of energy. This release of energy caused outward pressure that again balanced the inward pull of gravity. As the gas and dust stopped collapsing, a star was born. In the case of the solar system, this star was the sun.

Active Reading **13 Identify** How did the sun form?

_____

_____

_____

_____

_____

This is an artist's conception of what the protoplanetary disk in which the planets formed might have looked like.

Visualize It!

14 Describe Use the terms *planetesimal* and *protoplanetary disk* to describe the illustration above.

_____

_____

_____

_____

_____

_____

Planetesimals Formed in the Protoplanetary Disk

As the sun was forming, dust grains collided and stuck together. The resulting *dust granules* grew in size and increased in number. Over time, dust granules increased in size until they became roughly meter-sized bodies. Trillions of these bodies occurred in the protostellar disk. Collisions between these bodies formed larger bodies that were kilometers across. These larger bodies, from which planets formed, are called **planetesimals** (plan•ih•TES•ih•muhls). The protostellar disk had become the *protoplanetary disk*. The protoplanetary disk was the disk in which the planets formed.

Dust grains collided and stuck together.

Over time, dust granules grew to become meter-sized bodies.

Planetesimals formed from the collisions of meter-sized bodies.

Visualize It! Inquiry

15 Explain How can objects as small as dust grains become the building blocks of planets?

_____

_____

_____

_____

© Houghton Mifflin Harcourt Publishing Company • Image Credits: (bkgd) ©NASA/JPL-Caltech; (inset) ©Detlev van Ravenswaay/Photo Researchers, Inc.

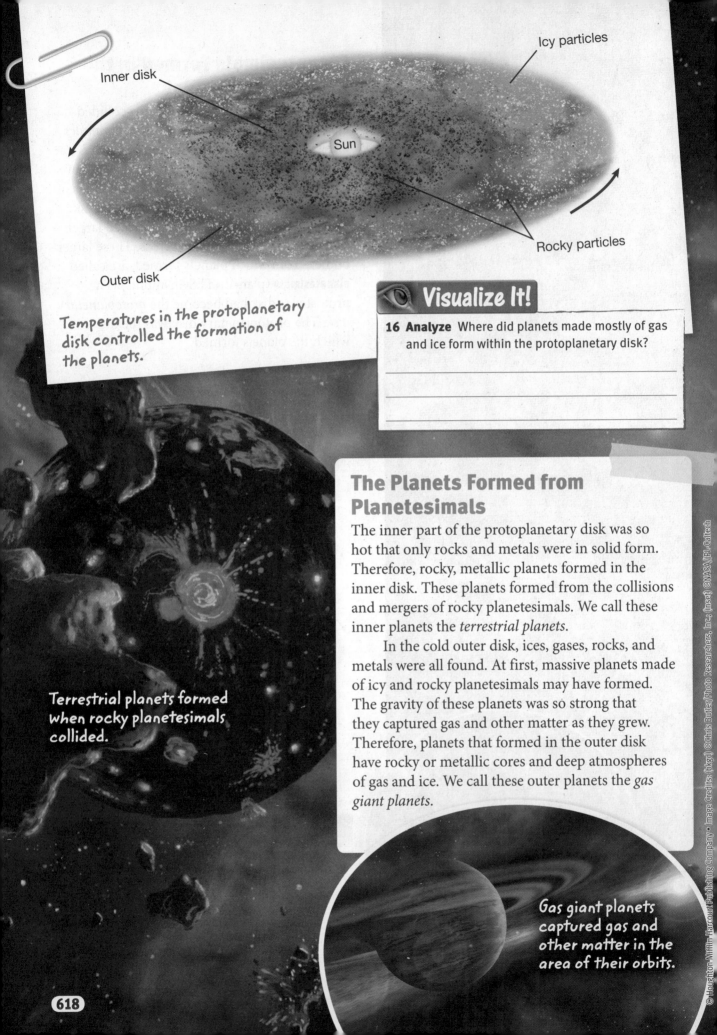

Icy particles

Inner disk

Sun

Outer disk

Rocky particles

Temperatures in the protoplanetary disk controlled the formation of the planets.

Visualize It!

16 Analyze Where did planets made mostly of gas and ice form within the protoplanetary disk?

_____

_____

_____

Terrestrial planets formed when rocky planetesimals collided.

The Planets Formed from Planetesimals

The inner part of the protoplanetary disk was so hot that only rocks and metals were in solid form. Therefore, rocky, metallic planets formed in the inner disk. These planets formed from the collisions and mergers of rocky planetesimals. We call these inner planets the _terrestrial planets_.

In the cold outer disk, ices, gases, rocks, and metals were all found. At first, massive planets made of icy and rocky planetesimals may have formed. The gravity of these planets was so strong that they captured gas and other matter as they grew. Therefore, planets that formed in the outer disk have rocky or metallic cores and deep atmospheres of gas and ice. We call these outer planets the _gas giant planets_.

Gas giant planets captured gas and other matter in the area of their orbits.

17 Describe In the spaces on the left, describe Steps 2 and 4 in the formation of the solar system. In the spaces on the right, draw the last two steps in the formation of the solar system.

Steps in the Formation of the Solar System

Step 1 The Solar Nebula Collapses

A cloud of dust and gas collapses. The balance between the inward pull of gravity and the outward push of pressure in the cloud is upset. The collapsing cloud forms a rotating protostellar disk.

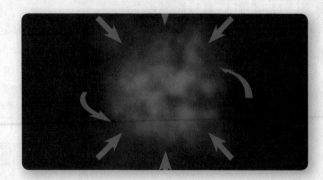

Step 2 The Sun Forms

_____
_____
_____
_____
_____

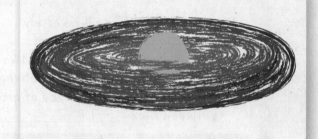

Step 3 Planetesimals Form

Dust grains stick together and form dust granules. Dust granules slowly increase in size until they become meter-sized objects. These meter-sized objects collide to form kilometer-sized objects called *planetesimals*.

Step 4 Planets Form

_____
_____
_____
_____
_____

Visual Summary

To complete this summary, fill in the blank with the correct word or phrase. Then use the key below to check your answers. You can use this page to review the main concepts of the lesson.

The Law of Universal Gravitation

Mass affects the force of gravity.

18 The strength of the force of gravity depends on the product of the _____ of two objects. Therefore, as the masses of two objects increase, the force that the objects exert on one another _____.

Distance affects the force of gravity.

19 Gravitational force is inversely proportional to the square of the _____ between two objects. Therefore, as the distance between two objects increases, the force of gravity between them _____.

Gravity affects planetary motion.

20 The sun exerts a _____, indicated by line B, on a planet so that at point C it is moving around the sun in orbit instead of moving off in a _____ as shown at line A.

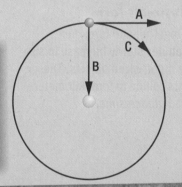

21 **Explain** In your own words, explain Newton's law of universal gravitation.

Lesson Review

Vocabulary

Fill in the blank with the term that best completes the following sentences.

1 Small bodies from which the planets formed are called _____

2 The path that a body follows as it travels around another body in space is its _____

3 The _____ is the cloud of gas and dust from which our solar system formed.

Key Concepts

4 Define In your own words, define the word *gravity*.

_____
_____

5 Describe How did the sun form?

_____
_____
_____
_____
_____
_____

6 Describe How did planetesimals form?

_____
_____
_____
_____
_____
_____
_____

Critical Thinking

Use the illustration below to answer the following question.

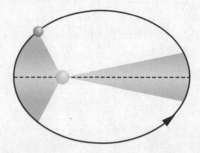

7 Identify What law is illustrated in this diagram?

_____

8 Analyze How does gravity keep the planets in orbit around the sun?

_____
_____
_____
_____
_____
_____

9 Explain How do temperature differences in the protoplanetary disk explain the arrangement of the planets in the solar system?

_____
_____
_____
_____
_____
_____

My Notes

The Sun

ESSENTIAL QUESTION

What are the properties of the sun?

By the end of this lesson, you should be able to describe the structure and rotation of the sun, energy production and energy transport in the sun, and solar activity on the sun.

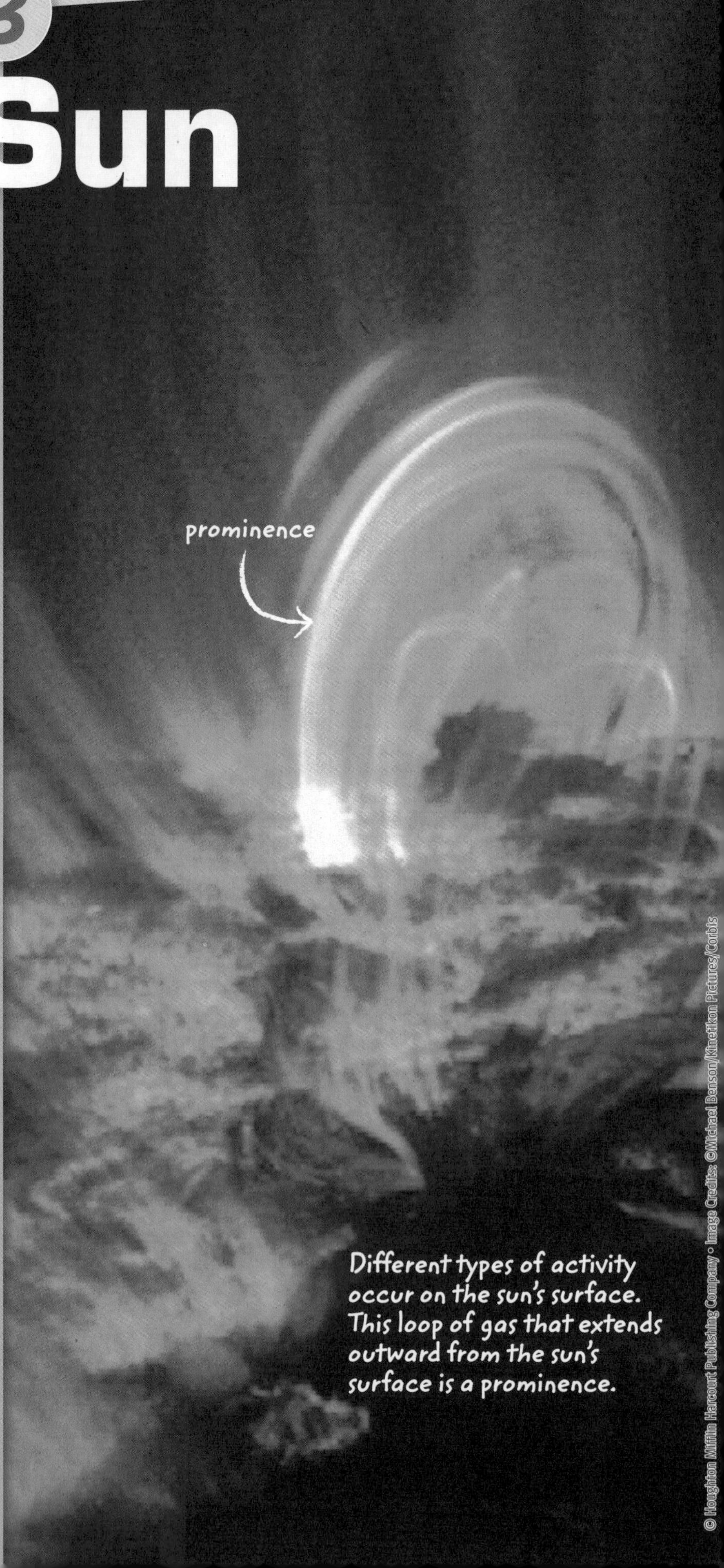

prominence

Different types of activity occur on the sun's surface. This loop of gas that extends outward from the sun's surface is a prominence.

Virginia Science Standards of Learning

6.3 The student will investigate and understand the role of solar energy in driving most natural processes within the atmosphere, the hydrosphere, and on Earth's surface. Key concepts include:

6.3.b the role of radiation and convection in the distribution of energy.

6.8 The student will investigate and understand the organization of the solar system and the interactions among the various bodies that comprise it. Key concepts include:

6.8.a the sun, moon, Earth, other planets and their moons, dwarf planets, meteors, asteroids, and comets.

 **Lesson Labs**

Quick Labs
• Model Solar Composition
• Model Solar Rotation

S.T.E.M. Lab
• Create a Model of the Sun

Engage Your Brain

1 Predict Check T or F to show whether you think each statement is true or false.

T	F	
☐	☐	The sun is composed mostly of hydrogen and helium.
☐	☐	Energy is produced in the sun's core.
☐	☐	The process by which energy is produced in the sun is known as *nuclear fission*.
☐	☐	Energy is transferred to the surface of the sun by the processes of radiation and conduction.
☐	☐	A dark area of the sun's surface that is cooler than the surrounding areas is called a *sunspot*.

2 Explain In your own words, explain the meaning of the word *sunlight*.

_____

_____

_____

_____

_____

_____

_____

_____

_____

Active Reading

3 Synthesize You can often define an unknown word if you know the meaning of its word parts. Use the word parts and sentence below to make an educated guess about the meaning of the word *photosphere*.

Word Part	Meaning
photo-	light
-sphere	ball

Example sentence
Energy is transferred to the sun's <u>photosphere</u> by convection cells.

photosphere:

_____

_____

_____

Vocabulary Terms

• **nuclear fusion**	• **solar flare**
• **sunspot**	• **prominence**

4 Apply This list contains the key terms you'll learn in this section. As you read, circle the definition of each term.

Here Comes the Sun

What do we know about the sun?

Since early in human history, people have marveled at the sun. Civilizations have referred to the sun by different names. Gods and goddesses who represented the sun were worshipped in different cultures. In addition, early astronomical observatories were established to track the sun's motion across the sky.

By the mid-19th century, astronomers had discovered that the sun was actually a hot ball of gas that is composed mostly of the elements hydrogen and helium. Scientists now know that the sun was born about 4.6 billion years ago. Every second, 4 million tons of solar matter is converted into energy. Of the light emitted from the sun, 41% is visible light, another 9% is ultraviolet light, and 50% is infrared radiation. And, perhaps most important of all, without the sun, there would be no life on Earth.

Sun Statistics	
Avg. dist. from Earth	149.6 million km
Diameter	1,390,000 km
Average density	1.41 g/cm³
Period of rotation	25 days (equator); 35 days (poles)
Avg. surface temp.	5,527 °C
Core temp.	15,000,000 °C
Composition	74% hydrogen, 25% helium, 1% other elements

Do the Math | You Try It

6 Calculate The diameter of Earth is 12,756 km. How many times greater is the sun's diameter than the diameter of Earth?

_____

_____

_____

A solar flare, which is shown in this image, is a sudden explosive release of energy in the sun's atmosphere.

What is the structure of the sun?

The composition of the sun and Earth are different. However, the two bodies are similar in structure. Both are spheres. And both have a layered atmosphere and an interior composed of layers.

In the middle of the sun is the core. This is where energy is produced. From the core, energy is transported to the sun's surface through the radiative zone and the convective zone.

The sun's atmosphere has three layers—the photosphere, the chromosphere, and the corona. The sun's surface is the photosphere. Energy escapes the sun from this layer. The chromosphere is the middle layer of the sun's atmosphere. The temperature of the chromosphere rises with distance from the photosphere. The sun's outer atmosphere is the corona. The corona extends millions of kilometers into space.

7 Analyze Why is the structure of the sun different from the structure of Earth?

_____
_____
_____
_____
_____
_____
_____

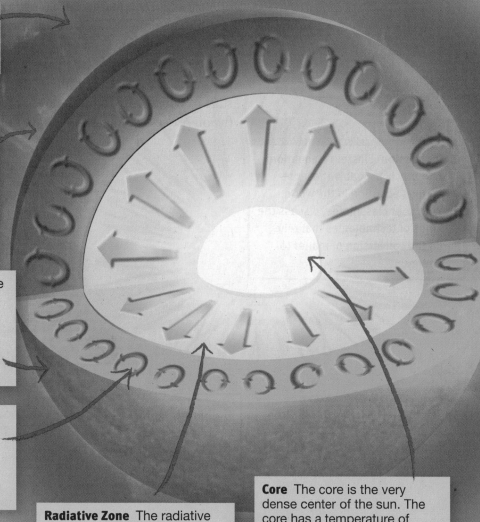

Corona The corona is the outer atmosphere of the sun. Temperatures in the corona may reach 2,000,000 °C.

Chromosphere The chromosphere is the middle layer of the sun's atmosphere. Temperatures in the chromosphere increase outward and reach a maximum of about 6,000 °C.

Photosphere The photosphere is the visible surface of the sun. It is the layer from which energy escapes into space. The photosphere has an average temperature of 5,527 °C.

Convective Zone The convective zone is the layer of the sun through which energy travels by convection from the radiative zone to the photosphere.

Radiative Zone The radiative zone is the layer of the sun through which energy is transferred away from the core by radiation.

Core The core is the very dense center of the sun. The core has a temperature of 15,000,000 °C, which is hot enough to cause the nuclear reactions that produce energy in the sun.

Let's Get Together

How does the sun produce energy?

Early in the 20th century, physicist Albert Einstein proposed that matter and energy are interchangeable. Matter can change into energy according to his famous equation $E = mc^2$. E is energy, m is mass, and c is the speed of light. Because c is such a large number, tiny amounts of matter can produce huge amounts of energy. Using Einstein's formula, scientists were able to explain the huge quantities of energy produced by the sun.

By Nuclear Fusion

Scientists know that the sun generates energy through the process of *nuclear fusion*. **Nuclear fusion** is the process by which two or more low-mass atomic nuclei fuse to form another, heavier nucleus. Nuclear fusion takes place in the core of stars. In stars that have core temperatures similar to the sun's, the fusion process that fuels the star starts with the fusion of two hydrogen nuclei. In older stars in which core temperatures are hotter than the sun's, the fusion process involves the fusion of helium into carbon.

Think Outside the Book

8 Discussion Einstein's equation $E = mc^2$ is probably the most famous equation in the world. With your classmates, discuss the kinds of technologies that rely on the conversion of matter to energy.

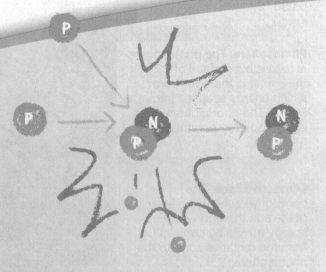

Visualize It!

9 Identify Fill in the circles to label the particles in the diagrams.

| P | Proton |
| N | Neutron |

Three Steps of Nuclear Fusion in the Sun

Step 1: Deuterium Two hydrogen nuclei (protons) collide. One proton emits particles and energy and then becomes a neutron. The proton and neutron combine to produce a heavy form of hydrogen called *deuterium*.

By the Fusion of Hydrogen into Helium

The most common elements in the sun are hydrogen and helium. Under the crushing force of gravity, these gases are compressed and heated in the sun's core, where temperatures reach 15,000,000 °C. In the sun's core, hydrogen nuclei sometimes fuse to form a helium nucleus. This process takes three steps to complete. This three-step process is illustrated below.

Most of the time, when protons are on a collision course with other protons, their positive charges instantly repel them. The protons do not collide. But sometimes one proton will encounter another proton and, at that exact moment, turn into a neutron and eject an electron. This collision forms a nucleus that contains one proton and one neutron. This nucleus is an isotope of hydrogen called *deuterium*. The deuterium nucleus collides with another proton and forms a variety of helium called *helium-3*. Then, two helium-3 nuclei collide and form a helium-4 nucleus that has two protons and two neutrons. The remaining two protons are released back into the sun's core.

The entire chain of fusion reactions requires six hydrogen nuclei and results in one helium nucleus and two hydrogen nuclei. There are approximately 10^{38} collisions between hydrogen nuclei taking place in the sun's core every second, which keeps the sun shining.

Active Reading

10 Identify As you read the text, underline the steps in the nuclear fusion process in the sun.

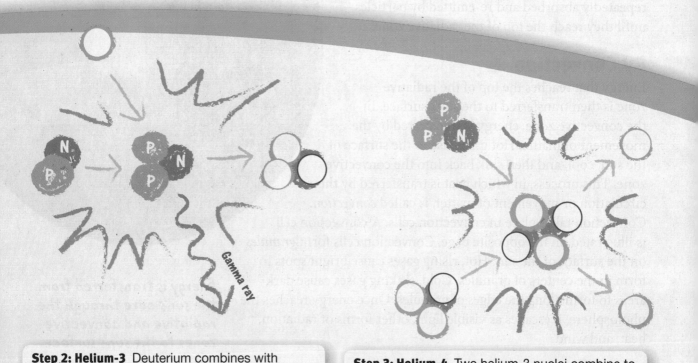

Step 2: Helium-3 Deuterium combines with another hydrogen nucleus to form a variety of helium called **helium-3**. More energy, including gamma rays, is released.

Step 3: Helium-4 Two helium-3 nuclei combine to form helium-4, which releases more energy and a pair of hydrogen nuclei (protons).

Mixing It Up

How is energy transferred to the sun's surface?

Energy is transferred to the surface of the sun by two different processes. Energy that is transferred from the sun's core through the radiative zone is transferred by the process of radiation. Energy that is transferred from the top of the radiative zone through the convective zone to the photosphere is transferred by the process of convection. Energy flow from the sun's core outward to the sun's surface by radiation and convection happens continuously.

By Radiation

When energy leaves the sun's core, it moves into the radiative zone. Energy travels through the radiative zone in the form of electromagnetic waves. The process by which energy is transferred as electromagnetic waves is called *radiation*. The radiative zone is densely packed with particles such as hydrogen, helium, and free electrons. Therefore, electromagnetic waves cannot travel directly through the radiative zone. Instead, they are repeatedly absorbed and re-emitted by particles until they reach the top of the radiative zone.

By Convection

Energy that reaches the top of the radiative zone is then transferred to the sun's surface. In the convective zone, energy is transferred by the movement of matter. Hot gases rise to the surface of the sun, cool, and then sink back into the convective zone. This process, in which heat is transferred by the circulation or movement of matter, is called *convection*. Convection takes place in convection cells. A convection cell is illustrated on the opposite page. Convection cells form *granules* on the surface of the sun. Hot, rising gases cause bright spots to form in the centers of granules. Cold, sinking gases cause dark areas to form along the edges of granules. Once energy reaches the photosphere, it escapes as visible light, other forms of radiation, heat, and wind.

Energy is transferred from the sun's core through the radiative and convective zones to the sun's surface.

© Houghton Mifflin Harcourt Publishing Company

The tops of convection cells form granules on the sun's surface.

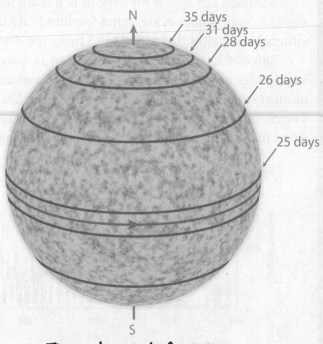

Hot, rising gases and colder, sinking gases form convection cells in the convective zone.

11 Compare How is energy transferred from the sun's core to the sun's surface in the radiative zone and in the convective zone?

Radiative zone	Convective zone

The sun's period of rotation varies with latitude.

N
35 days
31 days
28 days
26 days
25 days
S

How does the sun rotate?

The sun rotates on its axis like other large bodies in the solar system. However, because the sun is a giant ball of gas, it does not rotate in the same way as a solid body like Earth does. Instead, the sun rotates faster at its equator than it does at higher latitudes. This kind of rotation is known as differential rotation. *Differential rotation* is the rotation of a body in which different parts of a body have different periods of rotation. Near the equator, the sun rotates once in about 25 days. However, at the poles, the sun rotates once in about 35 days.

Even stranger is the fact that the sun's interior does not rotate in the same way as the sun's surface does. Scientists think that the sun's core and radiative zone rotate together, at the same speed. Therefore, the sun's radiative zone and core rotate like Earth.

12 Define In your own words, define the term *differential rotation*.

_____

_____

_____

_____

The Ring of Fire

What is solar activity?

Solar activity refers to variations in the appearance or energy output of the sun. Solar activity includes dark areas that occur on the sun's surface known as *sunspots*. Solar activity also includes sudden explosive events on the sun's surface, which are called *solar flares*. Prominences are another form of solar activity. *Prominences* are vast loops of gases that extend into the sun's outer atmosphere.

Sunspots

Dark areas that form on the surface of the sun are called **sunspots**. They are about 1,500 °C cooler than the areas that surround them. Sunspots are places where hot, convecting gases are prevented from reaching the sun's surface.

Sunspots can appear for periods of a few hours or a few months. Some sunspots are only a few hundred kilometers across. Others have widths that are 10 to 15 times the diameter of Earth.

Sunspot activity occurs on average in 11-year cycles. When a cycle begins, the number of sunspots is at a minimum. The number of sunspots then increases until it reaches a maximum. The number then begins to decrease. A new sunspot cycle begins when the sunspot number reaches a minimum again.

Sunspots, solar flares, and prominences are three kinds of solar activity that occur on the sun's surface.

↑ sunspot

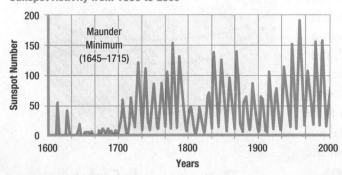

Sunspot Activity from 1600 to 2000

Maunder Minimum (1645–1715)

(Sunspot Number axis: 0, 50, 100, 150, 200)
(Years axis: 1600, 1700, 1800, 1900, 2000)

Do the Math You Try It

13 Analyze The sunspot range is the difference between the maximum number of sunspots and the minimum number of sunspots for a certain period of time. To find this range, subtract the minimum number of sunspots from the maximum number of sunspots. What is the range of sunspot activity between 1700 and 1800?

_____

_____

_____

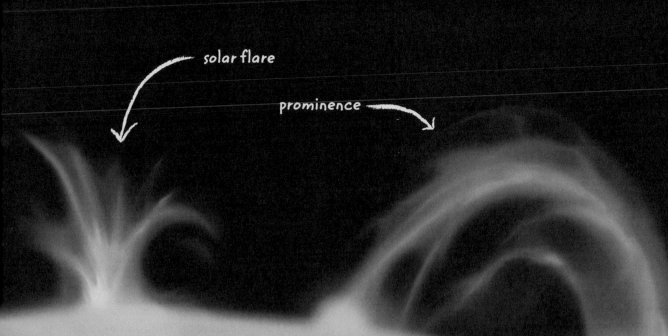

solar flare

prominence

Solar Flares

Solar flares appear as very bright spots on the sun's photosphere. A **solar flare** is an explosive release of energy that can extend outward as far as the sun's outer atmosphere. During a solar flare, enormous numbers of high-energy particles are ejected at near the speed of light. Radiation is released across the entire electromagnetic spectrum, from radio waves to x-rays and gamma rays. Temperatures within solar flares reach millions of degrees Celsius.

Prominences

Huge loops of relatively cool gas that extend outward from the photosphere thousands of kilometers into the outer atmosphere are called **prominences**. Several objects the size of Earth could fit inside a loop of a prominence. The gases in prominences are cooler than the surrounding atmosphere.

Prominences generally last from several hours to a day. However, some prominences can last for as long as several months.

14 Compare Use the Venn diagram below to compare solar flares and prominences.

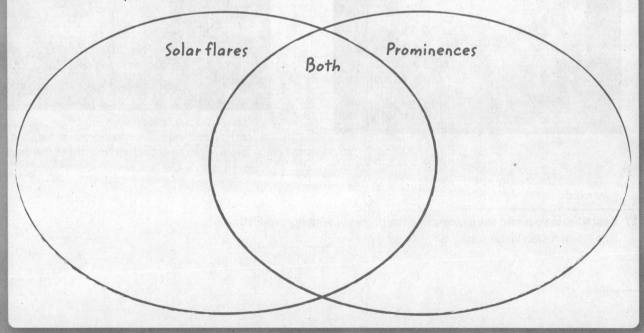

Solar flares   Both   Prominences

Visual Summary

To complete this summary, fill in the blanks with the correct word or phrase. Then use the key below to check your answers. You can use this page to review the main concepts of the lesson.

Properties of the Sun

The sun is composed of layers.

15 Identify the six layers of the sun, beginning with the innermost layer.

_____

_____

_____

_____

_____

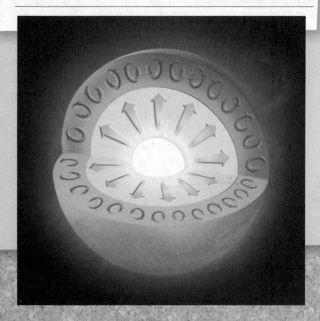

Energy is transferred from the sun's core to the photosphere.

16 By what process is the sun's energy transported in layer A?

_____

By what process is the sun's energy transported in layer B?

_____

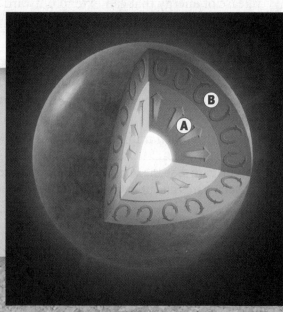

Answers: 15 the core, the radiative zone, the convective zone, the photosphere, the chromosphere, and the corona; 16 Layer A: radiation, Layer B: convection

17 **Describe** In your own words, describe the process of energy production by nuclear fusion in the sun.

Lesson Review

Vocabulary

Fill in the blank with the term that best completes the following sentences.

1 The process by which two or more low-mass atomic nuclei fuse to form another, heavier nucleus is called _____.

2 A _____ is a dark area on the surface of the sun that is cooler than the surrounding areas.

3 A _____ is a loop of relatively cool gas that extends above the photosphere.

Key Concepts

In the following table, write the name of the correct layer next to the definition.

Definition	Layer
4 Identify What is the layer of the sun from which energy escapes into space?	
5 Identify What is the layer of the sun in which energy is produced?	
6 Identify What is the layer of the sun through which energy is transferred away from the core by radiation?	

7 Identify What is the composition of the sun?

_____

_____

8 Explain What is the sunspot cycle?

_____

_____

_____

Critical Thinking

Use the illustration to answer the following questions.

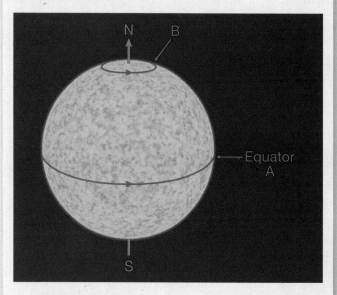

9 Determine How many days does it take for the sun to spin once on its axis at location A? How many days does it take for the sun to spin once on its axis at location B?

_____

_____

10 Compare How is the rotation of the sun different from the rotation of Earth?

_____

_____

_____

11 Explain In your own words, explain how energy is transported from the core to the surface of the sun by radiation and by convection.

_____

_____

_____

_____

My Notes

The Terrestrial Planets

Mars

Earth

Venus

Mercury

ESSENTIAL QUESTION

What is known about the terrestrial planets?

By the end of this lesson, you should be able to describe some of the properties of the terrestrial planets and how the properties of Mercury, Venus, and Mars differ from the properties of Earth.

The terrestrial planets are the four planets that are closest to the sun. Distances between the planets shown here are not to scale.

sun

Virginia Science Standards of Learning

6.8 The student will investigate and understand the organization of the solar system and the interactions among the various bodies that comprise it. Key concepts include:

6.8.a the sun, moon, Earth, other planets and their moons, dwarf planets, meteors, asteroids, and comets;

6.8.b relative size of and distance between planets; and

6.8.f the unique properties of Earth as a planet.

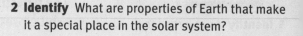

Engage Your Brain

1 Define Circle the term that best completes the following sentences.

Venus/Earth/Mars is the largest terrestrial planet.

Mercury/Venus/Mars has clouds that rain sulfuric acid on the planet.

Huge dust storms sweep across the surface of *Mercury/Venus/Mars*.

Venus/Earth/Mars is the most geologically active of the terrestrial planets.

Mercury/Venus/Earth has the thinnest atmosphere of the terrestrial planets.

2 Identify What are properties of Earth that make it a special place in the solar system?

_____

_____

_____

_____

Active Reading

3 Synthesize Many English words have their roots in other languages. Use the Latin words below to make an educated guess about the meaning of the word *astronomy*.

Latin word	Meaning
astrón	star
nomos	law

Example sentence
Some students who are interested in the night sky enter college to study <u>astronomy</u>.

astronomy:

_____

_____

Vocabulary Terms

- terrestrial planet
- astronomical unit

4 Apply As you learn the definition of each vocabulary term in this lesson, create your own definition or sketch to help you remember the meaning of the term.

Extreme to the Core

Active Reading

5 Identify As you read the text, underline important characteristics of the planet Mercury.

What are the terrestrial planets?

The **terrestrial planets** are the four small, dense, rocky planets that orbit closest to the sun. In order by distance from the sun, these planets are Mercury, Venus, Earth, and Mars. The terrestrial planets have similar compositions and consist of an outer crust, a central core, and a mantle that lies between the crust and core.

What is known about Mercury?

Mercury (MUR•kyuh•ree) is the planet about which we know the least. Until NASA's *Mariner 10* spacecraft flew by Mercury in 1974, the planet was seen as a blotchy, dark ball of rock. Today, scientists know that the planet's heavily cratered, moon-like surface is composed largely of volcanic rock and hides a massive iron core.

Mercury orbits only 0.39 AU from the sun. The letters *AU* stand for *astronomical unit*, which is the term astronomers use to measure distances in the solar system. One **astronomical unit** equals the average distance between the sun and Earth, or approximately 150 million km. Therefore, Mercury lies nearly halfway between the sun and Earth.

Statistics Table for Mercury	
Distance from the sun	0.39 AU
Period of rotation (length of Mercury day)	58 days 15.5 h
Period of revolution (length of Mercury year)	88 days
Tilt of axis	0°
Diameter	4,879 km
Density	5.44 g/cm³
Surface temperature	-184 °C to 427 °C
Surface gravity	38% of Earth's gravity
Number of satellites	0

Although this may look like the moon, it is actually the heavily cratered surface of the planet Mercury.

Mercury Has the Most Extreme Temperature Range in the Solar System

On Earth, a day lasts 24 h. On Mercury, a day lasts almost 59 Earth days. What does this fact have to do with temperatures on Mercury? It means that temperatures on that part of Mercury's surface that is receiving sunlight can build for more than 29 days. When it is day on Mercury, temperatures can rise to 427 °C, a temperature that is hot enough to melt certain metals. It also means that temperatures on the part of Mercury's surface that is in darkness can fall for more than 29 days. When it is night on Mercury, temperatures can drop to –184 °C. This means that surface temperatures on Mercury can change by as much as 600 °C between day and night. This is the greatest difference between high and low temperatures in the solar system.

Mercury Has a Large Iron Core

Mercury is the smallest planet in the solar system. It has a diameter of only 4,879 km at its equator. Amazingly, Mercury's central core is thought to be around 3,600 km in diameter, which accounts for most of the planet's interior. Scientists originally thought that Mercury had a core of solid iron. However, by observing changes in Mercury's spin as it orbits the sun, astronomers now think that the core is at least partially molten. Why is the core so large? Some scientists think that Mercury may have been struck by another object in the distant past and lost most of the rock that surrounded the core. Other scientists think that long ago the sun vaporized the planet's surface and blasted it away into space.

Think Outside the Book

6 Plan You are an astronaut who will be exploring Mercury. What equipment would you take to Mercury to help you survive?

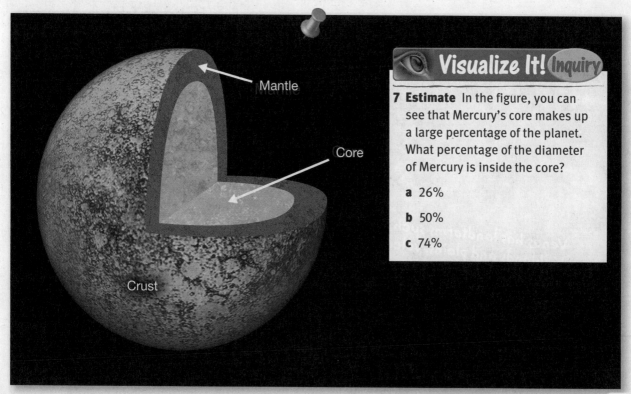

Mantle

Core

Crust

Visualize It! Inquiry

7 Estimate In the figure, you can see that Mercury's core makes up a large percentage of the planet. What percentage of the diameter of Mercury is inside the core?

a 26%

b 50%

c 74%

Harsh Planet

What is known about Venus?

Science-fiction writers once imagined Venus (VEE•nuhs) to be a humid planet with lush, tropical forests. Nothing could be further from the truth. On Venus, sulfuric acid rain falls on a surface that is not much different from the inside of an active volcano.

Venus Is Similar to Earth in Size and Mass

Venus has often been called "Earth's twin." At 12,104 km, the diameter of Venus is 95% the diameter of Earth. Venus's mass is around 80% of Earth's. And the gravity that you would experience on Venus is 89% of the gravity on Earth.

The rotation of Venus is different from the rotation of Earth. Earth has prograde rotation. *Prograde rotation* is the counterclockwise spin of a planet about its axis as seen from above the planet's north pole. Venus, however, has retrograde rotation. *Retrograde rotation* is the clockwise spin of a planet about its axis as seen from above its north pole.

Venus differs from Earth not only in the direction in which it spins on its axis. It takes more time for Venus to rotate once about its axis than it takes for the planet to revolve once around the sun. Venus has the slowest period of rotation in the solar system.

Active Reading

8 Identify Underline the definitions of the terms *prograde rotation* and *retrograde rotation* that appear in the text.

Venus has landforms such as highlands and plains, volcanoes, and impact craters.

Statistics Table for Venus

Distance from the sun	0.72 AU
Period of rotation	243 days (retrograde rotation)
Period of revolution	225 days
Tilt of axis	177.4°
Diameter	12,104 km
Density	5.20 g/cm³
Average surface temperature	465 °C
Surface gravity	89% of Earth's gravity
Number of satellites	0

© Houghton Mifflin Harcourt Publishing Company • Image Credits: ©NASA/Science Source/Photo Researchers Inc.

Gula Mons volcano is approximately 300 km wide and 3 km high.

Impact crater Cunitz, which is 48.5 km wide, was named after Maria Cunitz, a 17th-century European astronomer and mathematician.

Venus Has Craters and Volcanoes

In 1990, the powerful radar beams of NASA's *Magellan* spacecraft pierced the dense atmosphere of Venus. This gave us our most detailed look ever at the planet's surface. There are 168 volcanoes on Venus that are larger than 100 km in diameter. Thousands of volcanoes have smaller diameters. Venus's surface is also cratered. These craters are as much as 280 km in diameter. The sizes and locations of the craters on Venus suggest that around 500 million years ago something happened to erase all of the planet's older craters. Scientists are still puzzled about how this occurred. But volcanic activity could have covered the surface of the planet in one huge outpouring of magma.

The Atmosphere of Venus Is Toxic

Venus may have started out like Earth, with oceans and water running across its surface. However, after billions of years of solar heating, Venus has become a harsh world. Surface temperatures on Venus are hotter than those on Mercury. Temperatures average around 465 °C. Over time, carbon dioxide gas has built up in the atmosphere. Sunlight that strikes Venus's surface warms the ground. However, carbon dioxide in the atmosphere traps this energy, which causes temperatures near the surface to remain high.

Sulfuric acid rains down onto Venus's surface, and the pressure of the atmosphere is at least 90 times that of Earth's atmosphere. No human—or machine—could survive for long under these conditions. Venus is a world that is off limits to human explorers and perhaps all but the hardiest robotic probes.

9 **Contrast** How is the landscape of Venus different from the landscape of Earth?

_____
_____
_____
_____
_____
_____

Active Reading

10 **Identify** As you read the text, underline those factors that make Venus an unlikely place for life to exist.

No Place Like Home

What is special about Earth?

As far as scientists know, Earth is the only planet in the solar system that has the combination of factors needed to support life. Life as we know it requires liquid water and an energy source. Earth has both. Earth's atmosphere contains the oxygen that animals need to breathe. Matter is continuously cycled between the environment and living things. And a number of ecosystems exist on Earth that different organisms can inhabit.

Earth Has Abundant Water and Life

Earth's vast liquid-water oceans and moderate temperatures provided the ideal conditions for life to emerge and flourish. Around 3.5 billion years ago, organisms that produced food by photosynthesis appeared in Earth's oceans. During the process of making food, these organisms produced oxygen. By 560 million years ago, more complex life forms arose that could use oxygen to release energy from food. Today, the total number of species of organisms that inhabit Earth is thought to be anywhere between 5 million and 30 million.

Active Reading

11 Identify As you read the text, underline characteristics that make Earth special.

Statistics Table for Earth	
Distance from the sun	1.0 AU
Period of rotation	23 h 56 min
Period of revolution	365.3 days
Tilt of axis	23.45°
Diameter	12,756 km
Density	5.52 g/cm³
Temperature	-89 °C to 58 °C
Surface gravity	100% of Earth's gravity
Number of satellites	1

From space, Earth presents an entirely different scene from that of the other terrestrial planets. Clouds in the atmosphere, blue bodies of water, and green landmasses are all clues to the fact that Earth is a special place.

Earth Is Geologically Active

Earth is the only terrestrial planet whose surface is divided into tectonic plates. These plates move around Earth's surface, which causes the continents to change positions over long periods of time. Tectonic plate motion, together with weathering and erosion, has erased most surface features older than 500 million years.

Humans Have Set Foot on the Moon

Between 1969 and 1972, 12 astronauts landed on the moon. They are the only humans to have set foot on another body in the solar system. They encountered a surface gravity that is only about one-sixth that of Earth. Because of the moon's lower gravity, astronauts could not walk normally. If they did, they would fly up in the air and fall over.

Like Mercury, the moon's surface is heavily cratered. It is estimated that about 500,000 craters larger than 1 km dot the moon. There are large dark areas on the moon's surface. These are plains of solidified lava. There are also light-colored areas. These are the lunar highlands.

The moon rotates about its axis in the same time it orbits Earth. Therefore, it keeps the same side facing Earth. During a lunar day, which is a little more than 27 Earth days, the daytime surface temperature can reach 127 °C. The nighttime surface temperature can fall to −173 °C.

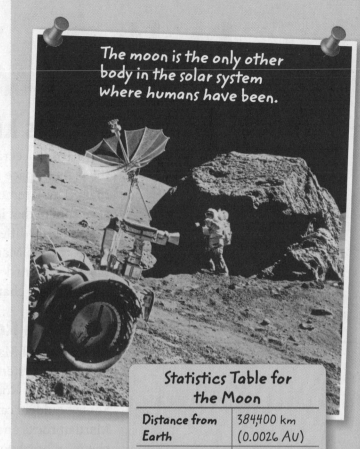

The moon is the only other body in the solar system where humans have been.

Statistics Table for the Moon

Distance from Earth	384,400 km (0.0026 AU)
Period of rotation	27.3 days
Period of revolution	27.3 days
Axial tilt	1.5°
Diameter	3,476 km
Density	3.34 g/cm³
Temperature	−173° C to 127° C
Surface gravity	16.5% of Earth's gravity

Visualize It!

12 Identify In the image, circle any signs of life that you see.

Is It Alive?

© Houghton Mifflin Harcourt Publishing Company • Image Credits: ©U.S. Geological Survey/Science Source/Photo Researchers, Inc

Think Outside the Book

13 Debate Research the surface features of the northern and southern hemispheres of Mars. Decide which hemisphere you would rather explore. With your class, debate the merits of exploring one hemisphere versus the other.

What is known about Mars?

A fleet of spacecraft is now in orbit around Mars (MARZ) studying the planet. Space rovers have also investigated the surface of Mars. These remote explorers have discovered a planet with an atmosphere that is 100 times thinner than Earth's and temperatures that are little different from the inside of a freezer. They have seen landforms on Mars that are larger than any found on Earth. And these unmanned voyagers have photographed surface features on Mars that are characteristic of erosion and deposition by water.

Mars Is a Rocky, Red Planet

The surface of Mars is better known than that of any other planet in the solar system except Earth. It is composed largely of dark volcanic rock. Rocks and boulders litter the surface of Mars. Some boulders can be as large as a house. A powdery dust covers Martian rocks and boulders. This dust is the product of the chemical breakdown of rocks rich in iron minerals. This is what gives the Martian soil its orange-red color.

Statistics Table for Mars

Distance from the sun	1.52 AU
Period of rotation	24 h 37 min
Period of revolution	1.88 y
Tilt of axis	25.3°
Diameter	6,792 km
Density	3.93 g/cm³
Temperature	-140°C to 20°C
Surface gravity	37% of Earth's gravity
Number of satellites	2

Mars's northern polar ice cap is composed of carbon dioxide ice and water ice. Its size varies with the seasons.

Mars Has Interesting Surface Features

The surface of Mars varies from hemisphere to hemisphere. The northern hemisphere appears to have been covered by lava flows. The southern hemisphere is heavily cratered.

Large volcanoes are found on Mars. At 27 km high and 600 km across, Olympus Mons (uh•LIM•puhs MAHNZ) is the largest volcano and mountain in the solar system. Mars also has very deep valleys and canyons. The canyon system Valles Marineris (VAL•less mar•uh•NAIR•iss) runs from west to east along the Martian equator. It is about 4,000 km long, 500 km wide, and up to 10 km deep. It is the largest canyon in the solar system.

Olympus Mons is the largest volcano in the solar system.

Mars Has a Thin Atmosphere

Mars has a very thin atmosphere that is thought to have been thicker in the past. Mars may have gradually lost its atmosphere to the solar wind. Or a body or bodies that collided with Mars may have caused much of the atmosphere to have been blown away.

Unlike Earth, Mars's atmosphere is composed mostly of carbon dioxide. During the Martian winter, temperatures at the planet's poles grow cold enough for carbon dioxide to freeze into a thin coating. During the summer, when temperatures grow warmer, this coating vanishes.

Winds on Mars can blow with enough force to pick up dust particles from the planet's surface. When this happens, giant dust storms can form. At times, these storms cover the entire planet.

Active Reading 14 **Explain** What are two possible reasons why the atmosphere on Mars is so thin?

_____

_____

_____

Hebes Chasma is a 6,000 m–deep depression that is located in the Valles Marineris region.

15 **Compare** Compare and contrast the physical properties of Mars to the physical properties of Earth.

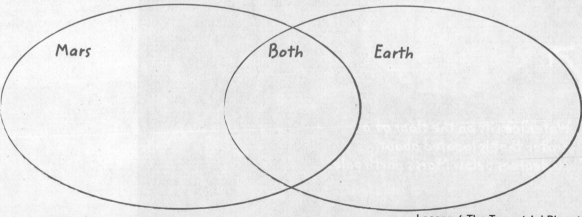

Mars   Both   Earth

Liquid Water Once Flowed on Mars

A number of features on Mars provide evidence that liquid water once flowed on the planet's surface. Many of these features have been struck by asteroids. These asteroid impacts have left behind craters that scientists can use to find the approximate dates of these features. Scientists estimate that many of these features, such as empty river basins, existed on Mars more than 3 billion years ago. Since then, little erosion has taken place that would cause these features to disappear.

In 2000, the *Mars Global Surveyor* took before-and-after images of a valley wall on Mars. Scientists observed the unmistakable trace of a liquid substance that had flowed out of the valley wall and into the valley. Since 2000, many similar features have been seen. The best explanation of these observations is that water is found beneath Mars's surface. At times, this water leaks out onto the Martian surface like spring water on Earth.

This image shows gullies on the wall of a Martian crater. Water that may be stored close to the Martian surface has run downhill into the crater.

Visualize It!

16 Describe How do the features in the image at the right indicate that liquid water once flowed on Mars?

_____

_____

_____

_____

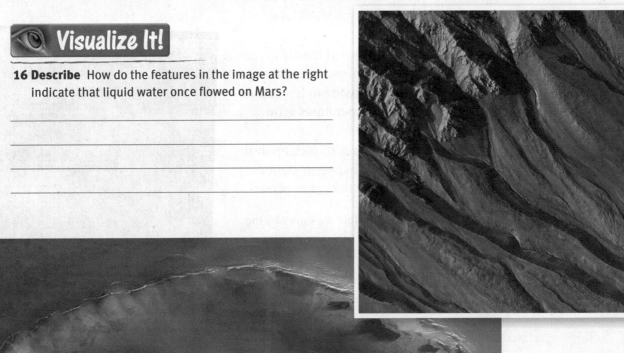

Water ice sits on the floor of a crater that is located about 20 degrees below Mars's north pole.

Roving Mars

The Mars Exploration Rovers *Spirit* and *Opportunity* landed safely on Mars in January 2004. The 185-kg rovers were designed to explore Mars for 90 days. However, in 2009, both rovers were still exploring Mars. They are searching for rocks and soils that indicate that water once flowed on the Martian surface. The rovers are also looking for environments in which life may have existed.

The Martian Surface

Mars's surface is made up mostly of the volcanic rock *basalt,* which is also found on Earth. Boulders of basalt cover the Martian landscape.

Testing the Rovers on Earth

Before leaving Earth, the rovers were tested under conditions that were similar to those that they would encounter on the Martian surface.

Collecting Data on Mars

The Mars rover *Spirit* took this picture of itself collecting data from the Martian surface.

Extend

Inquiry

17 Infer What advantages would a robotic explorer, such as *Spirit* or *Opportunity*, have over a manned mission to Mars?

18 Hypothesize What kind of evidence would the Mars Exploration Rovers be looking for that indicated that water once flowed on Mars?

Visual Summary

To complete this summary, write the answers to the questions on the lines. Then use the key below to check your answers. You can use this page to review the main concepts of the lesson.

Properties of Terrestrial Planets

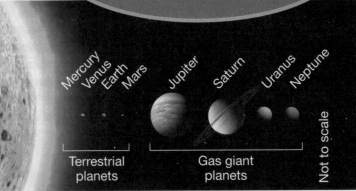

Mercury Venus Earth Mars   Jupiter   Saturn   Uranus Neptune

Terrestrial planets   Gas giant planets   Not to scale

Mercury orbits near the sun.

19 Why do temperatures on Mercury vary so much?

_____

_____

_____

Venus is covered with clouds.

20 Why is Venus's surface temperature so high?

_____

_____

_____

Earth has abundant life.

21 What factors support life on Earth?

_____

_____

_____

Mars is a rocky planet.

22 What makes up the surface of Mars?

_____

_____

_____

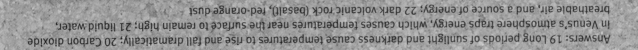

Answers: 19 Long periods of sunlight and darkness cause temperatures to rise and fall dramatically; 20 Carbon dioxide in Venus's atmosphere traps energy, which causes temperatures near the surface to remain high; 21 liquid water, breathable air, and a source of energy; 22 dark volcanic rock (basalt), red-orange dust

23 Compare How are important properties of Mercury, Venus, and Mars different from important properties of Earth?

Lesson Review

Vocabulary

Fill in the blanks with the terms that best complete the following sentences.

1 The _____ are the dense planets nearest the sun.

2 An _____ is equal to the distance between the sun and Earth.

Key Concepts

In the following table, write the name of the correct planet next to the property of that planet.

Properties	Planet
3 Identify Which planet has the highest surface temperature in the solar system?	
4 Identify Which planet has very large dust storms?	
5 Identify Which planet is the most heavily cratered of the terrestrial planets?	
6 Identify Which planet has the highest surface gravity of the terrestrial planets?	

7 Explain What is the difference between prograde rotation and retrograde rotation?

_____

_____

_____

_____

8 Describe What characteristics of Venus's atmosphere make the planet so harsh?

_____

_____

_____

Critical Thinking

Use this table to answer the following questions.

Planet	Period of rotation	Period of revolution
Mercury	58 days 15.5 h	88 days
Venus	243 days (retrograde rotation)	225 days
Earth	23 h 56 min	365.3 days
Mars	24 h 37 min	1.88 y

9 Analyze Which planet rotates most slowly about its axis?

_____

10 Analyze Which planet revolves around the sun in less time than it rotates around its axis?

_____

11 Analyze Which planet revolves around the sun in the shortest amount of time?

_____

12 Explain Why are the temperatures on each of the other terrestrial planets more extreme than the temperatures on Earth?

_____

_____

_____

_____

_____

_____

_____

_____

_____

My Notes

A. Wesley Ward

GEOLOGIST

Geologist Dr. Wesley Ward lives in a desert region of the western United States. The living conditions are sometimes harsh, but the region offers some fascinating places to study. For a geologist like Dr. Ward, who tries to understand the geologic processes on another planet, the desert may be the only place to be.

Dr. Ward was a leading scientist on the Mars Pathfinder mission. The surface of Mars is a lot like the western desert. Dr. Ward helped scientists map the surface of Mars and plan for the Pathfinder's landing. Using data from the Pathfinder, Dr. Ward studied how Martian winds have shaped the planet's landscape. This information will help scientists better understand what conditions are like on the surface of Mars. More importantly, the information will guide scientists in choosing future landings sites. Dr. Ward's work may determine whether human beings can safely land on Mars.

You could say that Dr. Ward's scientific career has hit the big-time. He helped in the making of the Discovery Channel's documentary *Planet Storm*. The program features scientists describing weather conditions on other planets. Dr. Ward and the scientists worked with special effects artists to simulate what these conditions might feel like to astronauts.

The Mars Pathfinder rover **Sojourner** was designed to withstand the fierce Martian dust storms, such as the one shown.

Social Studies Connection

The Pathfinder is not the first attempt scientists have made to explore the surface of Mars. In fact, scientists in different countries have been exploring Mars for over 50 years. Research other missions to Mars and attempts to send rovers to Mars, and present your research in a timeline. Remember to identify where the mission started, what its goals were, and whether it achieved them.

JOB BOARD

Science Writer

What You'll Do: Research and write articles, press releases, reports, and sometimes books about scientific discoveries and issues for a wide range of readers. Science writers who write for a broad audience must work to find the stories behind the science in order to keep readers interested.

Where You Might Work: For a magazine, a newspaper, or a museum, or independently as a freelance writer specializing in science. Some science writers may work for universities, research foundations, government agencies, or non-profit science and health organizations.

Education: A bachelor's degree in a scientific field, with courses in English or writing.

Other Job Requirements: Strong communications skills. Science writers must not only understand science, but must also be able to interview scientists and to write clear, interesting stories.

Telescope Mechanic

What You'll Do: Keep telescopes at large observatories working, climbing heights of up to 30 meters to make sure the telescope's supports are in good shape, which includes welding new components, cleaning, and sweeping.

Where You Might Work: A large observatory or research institution with large telescopes, possibly in the desert.

Education: A high-school diploma with some experience performing maintenance on delicate equipment.

Other Job Requirements. Strong communications skills to consult with other mechanics and the scientists who use the telescopes. Mechanics must be able to weld and to use tools. Mechanics must also have good vision (or wear glasses to correct their vision), and be able to climb up high and carry heavy equipment.

PEOPLE IN SCIENCE NEWS

Anthony Wesley

Witnessing Impact

Anthony Wesley was sitting in his backyard in Australia on July 19, 2009, gazing at Jupiter through his custom-built telescope, when he saw a dark spot or "scar" on the planet (shown). Wesley sent his tip to the National Aeronautics and Space Administration (NASA).

NASA has much more powerful telescopes than a citizen scientist usually does. Scientists at NASA confirmed that a comet had crashed into the planet, leaving a scar. Coincidentally, this crash happened almost exactly 15 years after another comet crashed into Jupiter.

Lesson 5

The Gas Giant Planets

ESSENTIAL QUESTION

What is known about the gas giant planets?

By the end of this lesson, you should be able to describe some of the properties of the gas giant planets and how these properties differ from the physical properties of Earth.

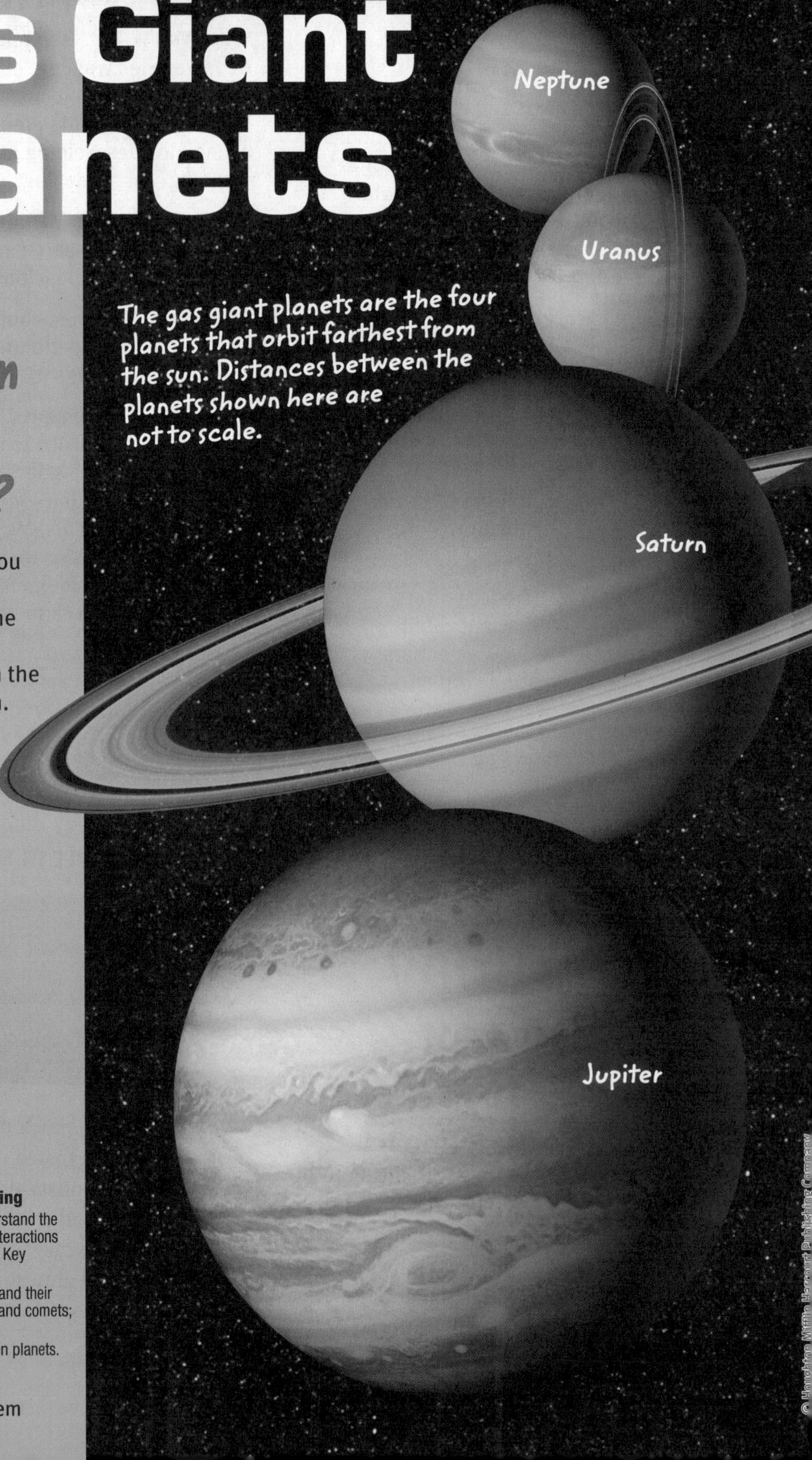
Neptune
Uranus
Saturn
Jupiter

The gas giant planets are the four planets that orbit farthest from the sun. Distances between the planets shown here are not to scale.

Virginia Science Standards of Learning

6.8 The student will investigate and understand the organization of the solar system and the interactions among the various bodies that comprise it. Key concepts include:

6.8.a the sun, moon, Earth, other planets and their moons, dwarf planets, meteors, asteroids, and comets; and

6.8.b relative size of and distance between planets.

Engage Your Brain

1 Predict Circle the term that best completes the following sentences.

Jupiter/Saturn/Uranus is the largest planet in the solar system.

Jupiter/Uranus/Neptune has the strongest winds in the solar system.

Saturn/Uranus/Neptune has the largest ring system of the gas giant planets.

Jupiter/Saturn/Neptune has more moons than any other planet in the solar system.

Jupiter/Uranus/Neptune is tilted on its side as it orbits the Sun.

2 Identify What are the objects that circle Saturn? What do you think they are made of?

_____

_____

_____

Active Reading

3 Apply Many scientific words, such as *gas*, also have everyday meanings. Use context clues to write your own definition for each meaning of the word *gas*.

Example sentence
Vehicles, such as cars, trucks, and buses, use <u>gas</u> as a fuel.

gas:

_____

_____

Example sentence
<u>Gas</u> is one of the three common states of matter.

gas:

_____

_____

_____

Vocabulary Terms

• gas giant
• planetary ring

4 Apply This list contains the key terms you'll learn in this section. As you read, circle the definition of each term.

A Giant Among

Jupiter's high winds circle the planet and cause cloud bands to form. Storms, such as the Great Red Spot shown here, form between the cloud bands.

Ganymede

Callisto

Statistics Table for Jupiter	
Distance from the sun	5.20 AU
Period of rotation	9 h 55 min
Period of revolution	11.86 y
Tilt of axis	3.13°
Diameter	142,984 km
Density	1.33 g/cm³
Mean surface temperature	−150 °C
Surface gravity	253% of Earth's gravity
Number of satellites	63

What is a gas giant planet?

Jupiter, Saturn, Uranus, and Neptune are the gas giant planets. They orbit far from the sun. **Gas giants** have deep, massive gas atmospheres, which are made up mostly of hydrogen and helium. These gases become denser the deeper you travel inside. All of the gas giants are large. Neptune, the smallest gas giant planet, is big enough to hold 60 Earths within its volume. The gas giant planets are cold. Mean surface temperatures range from −150 °C on Jupiter to −220 °C on Neptune.

What is known about Jupiter?

Jupiter (JOO•pih•ter) is the largest planet in the solar system. Its volume can contain more than 900 Earths. Jupiter is also the most massive planet. Its mass is twice that of the other seven planets combined. Jupiter has the highest surface gravity in the solar system at 253% that of Earth. And, although all of the gas giant planets rotate rapidly, Jupiter rotates the fastest of all. Its period of rotation is just under 10 h. Wind speeds on Jupiter are high. They can reach 540 km/h. By contrast, Earth's wind speed record is 372 km/h.

Active Reading

5 Identify As you read the text, underline important physical properties of the planet Jupiter.

Giants!

Europa

Io

Io, Europa, Callisto, and Ganymede are Jupiter's largest moons. All four moons were named for figures in Greek mythology.

Huge Storms Travel Across Jupiter's Surface

Jupiter has some of the strangest weather conditions in the solar system. The winds on Jupiter circle the planet. Clouds are stretched into bands that run from east to west. Storms appear as white or red spots between cloud bands. The best known of these storms is the Great Red Spot. The east–west width of this storm is three times the diameter of Earth. Incredibly, this storm has been observed by astronomers on Earth for the past 350 years.

Jupiter Has the Most Moons

More than 60 moons have been discovered orbiting Jupiter. This is the greatest number of moons to orbit any planet. Jupiter's moons Io (EYE•oh), Europa (yu•ROH•puh), Callisto (kuh•LIS•toh), and Ganymede (GAN•uh•meed) are particularly large. In fact, Ganymede is larger than the planet Mercury.

Jupiter's moon Io is the most volcanically active place in the solar system. There are at least 400 active volcanoes on Io's surface. Jupiter's gravity tugs and pulls on Io. This causes the interior of Io to reach the temperature at which it melts. Lava erupts from Io's volcanoes, which throw tremendous geysers of sulfur compounds into space. Over time, the orbit of Io has become a ring of ejected gases that is visible to the Hubble Space Telescope.

Jupiter's moon Europa has an icy surface. Recent evidence suggests that an ocean of liquid water may lie beneath this surface. Because liquid water is essential for life, some scientists are hopeful that future spacecraft may discover life inside Europa.

6 Apply Io, Europa, Callisto, and Ganymede are known as the *Galilean moons*. The astronomer Galileo discovered these moons using one of the first telescopes. Why do you think that the Galilean moons were the first objects to be discovered with a telescope?

_____

_____

_____

Think Outside the Book

7 Model Select one of the following topics about weather on Jupiter to research: belts and zones; jet streams; storms. Present your findings to the rest of the class in the form of a model. Your model may be handcrafted, or may be an art piece, or may be a computer presentation.

King of the Rings!

What is known about Saturn?

Saturn (SAT•ern) is a near-twin to Jupiter. It is the second-largest gas giant planet and is made mostly of hydrogen and helium. About 800 Earths could fit inside the volume of Saturn. Amazingly, the planet's density is less than that of water.

Saturn Has a Large Ring System

The planetary ring system that circles Saturn's equator is the planet's most spectacular feature. A **planetary ring** is a disk of material that circles a planet and consists of orbiting particles. Saturn's ring system has many individual rings that form complex bands. Between bands are gaps that may be occupied by moons.

Although the rings of Saturn extend nearly 500,000 km in diameter, they are only a few kilometers thick. They consist of trillions of small, icy bodies that are a few millimeters to several hundred meters in size. The rings are mostly pieces left over from the collision of Saturn's moons with comets and asteroids.

Active Reading

8 Identify As you read the text, underline important physical properties about the planet Saturn.

Statistics Table for Saturn

Distance from the sun	9.58 AU
Period of rotation	10 h 39 min
Period of revolution	29.5 y
Tilt of axis	26.73°
Diameter	120,536 km
Density	0.69 g/cm³
Mean surface temperature	−180 °C
Surface gravity	106% of Earth's gravity
Number of satellites	60

Saturn's rings

Saturn's southern aurora

© Houghton Mifflin Harcourt Publishing Company • Image Credits: ©NASA/ESA/Space Telescope Science Institute/Science Source/Photo Researchers, Inc

Saturn's Moon Enceladus Has Water Geysers

In the inner solar system, liquid rock erupts from volcanoes. In some parts of the outer solar system, liquid water erupts from volcanoes. When NASA's *Cassini* spacecraft explored Saturn's moon Enceladus (en•SEL•uh•duhs), it found an icy surface. Scientists believe that Enceladus has a liquid interior beneath this icy surface. Liquid water flows up through cracks in the moon's surface. It either freezes at the surface or forms spectacular water geysers. These geysers are the largest in the solar system.

Saturn's Moon Titan Has a Dense Atmosphere

Titan (TYT'in), the largest moon of Saturn, has an atmosphere that is denser than Earth's. The moon's atmosphere is composed mostly of nitrogen and has traces of compounds such as methane and ethane. Methane clouds form in Titan's atmosphere. From these clouds, methane rain may fall. Unlike Earth, Titan has a crust of ice, which is frozen at a temperature of –180 °C.

In 2005, the *Huygens* (HY•guhnz) Titan probe descended through Titan's atmosphere. It took pictures of a surface with lakes and ponds. The liquid that fills these lakes and ponds is mostly methane.

9 Explain In your own words, write a caption for this illustration of Saturn's moon Enceladus.

_____

_____

_____

Cassini Division in Saturn's ring system

Particles that make up Saturn's ring system

10 Describe Complete this table by writing a description of each structure in Saturn's ring system.

Structure	Description
ring	
gap	
ring particles	

Just Rollin' Along

How is Uranus unique?

Active Reading **11 Identify** As you read the text, underline important physical properties of the planet Uranus.

The atmosphere of Uranus (YUR•uh•nuhs) is composed mostly of hydrogen and helium. However, the atmosphere also contains methane. The methane in Uranus's atmosphere absorbs red light, which gives the planet a blue-green color.

Uranus Is a Tilted World

Uranus's axis of rotation is tilted almost 98°. This means that unlike any other planet in the solar system, Uranus is tilted on its side as it orbits the sun. The planet's 27 moons all orbit Uranus's equator, just like the moons of other planets do. The ring system of Uranus also orbits the equator. Scientists are not sure what event caused Uranus's odd axial tilt. But computer models of the four gas giant planets as they were forming may offer an explanation. The huge gravities of Jupiter and Saturn may have caused the orbits of Uranus and Neptune to change. There may also have been many close encounters between Uranus and Neptune that could have tilted the axis of Uranus.

Statistics Table for Uranus

Distance from the sun	19.2 AU
Period of rotation	17 h 24 min (retrograde)
Period of revolution	84 y
Tilt of axis	97.8°
Diameter	51,118 km
Density	1.27 g/cm³
Mean surface temperature	−210 °C
Surface gravity	79% of Earth's gravity
Number of satellites	27

Houghton Mifflin Harcourt Publishing Company • Image Credits: (bkgd) ©NASA/ESA/STSCI/E.Karkoschka/U.Arizona/Photo Researchers, Inc.

12 Predict Earth has an axial tilt of 23.5°, whereas Uranus has an axial tilt of almost 98°. If Earth had the same axial tilt as Uranus, how would the conditions be different at Earth's North and South Poles?

_____

_____

_____

_____

_____

_____

_____

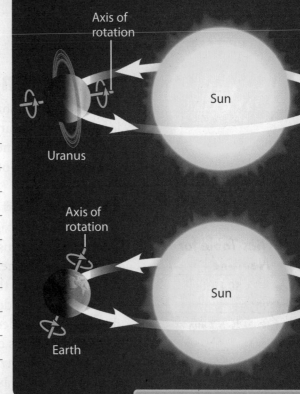

Axis of rotation

Sun

Uranus

Axis of rotation

Sun

Earth

Think Outside the Book

13 Research Astronomers are discovering planets orbiting stars in other solar systems? Find out what kinds of planets astronomers are discovering in these solar systems.

Seasons on Uranus Last 21 Years

It takes Uranus 84 years to make a single revolution around the sun. For about 21 years of that 84-year period, the north pole faces the sun and the south pole is in darkness. About halfway through that 84-year period, the poles are reversed. The south pole faces the sun and the north pole is in darkness for 21 years. So, what are seasons like on Uranus? Except for a small band near the equator, every place on Uranus has winter periods of constant darkness and summer periods of constant daylight. But, during spring and fall, Uranus has periods of both daytime and nighttime just like on Earth.

Uranus's Moon Miranda Is Active

Miranda (muh•RAN•duh) is Uranus's fifth-largest moon. It is about 470 km in diameter. NASA's *Voyager 2* spacecraft visited Miranda in 1989. Data from *Voyager 2* showed that the moon is covered by different types of icy crust. What is the explanation for this patchwork surface? The gravitational forces of Uranus pull on Miranda's interior. This causes material from the moon's interior to rise to its surface. What we see on the surface is evidence of the moon turning itself inside out.

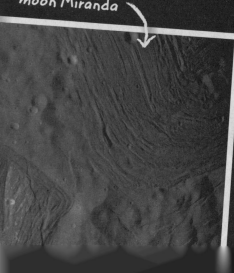

The surface of Uranus's moon Miranda

A Blue, Windy Giant

What is known about Neptune?

Neptune (NEP•toon) is the most distant planet from the sun. It is located 30 times farther from the sun than Earth is. So, sunlight on Neptune is 900 times fainter than sunlight on Earth is. High noon on Neptune may look much like twilight on Earth.

Neptune Is a Blue Ice Giant

Neptune is practically a twin to Uranus. Neptune is almost the same size as Uranus. It also has an atmosphere that is composed of hydrogen and helium, with some methane. The planet's bluish color is caused by the absorption of red light by methane. But because Neptune does not have an atmospheric haze like Uranus does, we can see deeper into the atmosphere. So, Neptune is blue, whereas Uranus is blue-green.

When *Voyager 2* flew by Neptune in 1989, there was a huge, dark area as large as Earth in the planet's atmosphere. This storm, which was located in Neptune's southern hemisphere, was named the *Great Dark Spot*. However, in 1994, the Hubble Space Telescope found no trace of this storm. Meanwhile, other spots that may grow larger with time have been sighted in the atmosphere.

Statistics Table for Neptune	
Distance from the sun	30.1 AU
Period of rotation	16 h 7 min
Period of revolution	164.8 y
Tilt of axis	28.5°
Diameter	49,528 km
Density	1.64 g/cm³
Mean surface temperature	−220 °C
Surface Gravity	112% of Earth's gravity
Number of satellites	13

Great Dark Spot

 **Visualize It!**

14 Predict The wind speeds recorded in Neptune's Great Dark Spot reached 2,000 km/h. Predict what kind of destruction might result on Earth if wind speeds in hurricanes approached 2,000 km/h.

_____

_____

_____

_____

Neptune Has the Strongest Winds

Where does the energy come from that powers winds as fast as 2,000 km/h? Neptune has a warm interior that produces more energy than the planet receives from sunlight. Some scientists believe that Neptune's weather is controlled from inside the planet and not from outside the planet, as is Earth's weather.

Neptune's Moon Triton Has a Different Orbit Than Neptune's Other Moons

Triton (TRYT'in) is the largest moon of Neptune. Unlike the other moons of Neptune, Triton orbits Neptune in the opposite direction from the direction in which Neptune orbits the sun. One explanation for this oddity is that, long ago, there were several large moons that orbited Neptune. These moons came so close together that one moon was ejected. The other moon, Triton, remained behind but began traveling in the opposite direction.

Triton's days are numbered. The moon is slowly spiraling inward toward Neptune. When Triton is a certain distance from Neptune, the planet's gravitational pull will begin pulling Triton apart. Triton will then break into pieces.

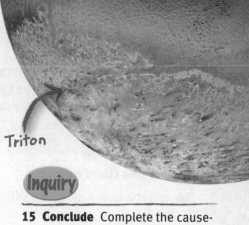

Triton

Inquiry

15 **Conclude** Complete the cause-and-effect chart by answering the question below.

> Triton spirals inward toward Neptune.

↓

> The gravitational pull of Neptune causes Triton to pull apart.

↓

> Triton breaks into pieces.

What do you think will happen next?

_____

_____

_____

_____

A category 5 hurricane on Earth has sustained wind speeds of 250 km/h. Some effects of the winds of a category 5 hurricane can be seen in this image.

Visual Summary

To complete this summary, write the answers to the questions on the lines. Then use the key below to check your answers. You can use this page to review the main concepts of the lesson.

Mercury Venus Earth Mars | Jupiter | Saturn | Uranus Neptune

Terrestrial planets | Gas giant planets

Not to scale

Jupiter has cloud bands.

16 What causes cloud bands to form on Jupiter?

_____

_____

Saturn has a complex ring system.

17 What are Saturn's rings made up of?

_____

_____

Uranus is tilted on its side.

18 What is the tilt of Uranus's axis of rotation?

_____

_____

Neptune is a blue planet.

19 What gives Neptune its bluish color?

_____

_____

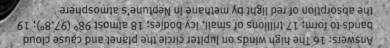

Answers: 16 The high winds on Jupiter circle the planet and cause cloud bands to form; 17 trillions of small, icy bodies; 18 almost 98° (97.8°); 19 the absorption of red light by methane in Neptune's atmosphere

20 Apply Compare the properties of the gas giant planets as a group with properties of Earth.

_____

_____

_____

_____

Lesson Review

Vocabulary

Fill in the blank with the term that best completes the following sentences.

1 A large planet that has a deep, massive atmosphere is called a _____.

2 A _____ is a disk of matter that circles a planet and consists of numerous particles in orbit that range in size from a few millimeters to several hundred meters.

Key Concepts

In the following table, write the name of the correct planet next to the property of that planet.

Properties	Planet
3 Identify Which planet has a density that is less than that of water?	
4 Identify Which planet has the strongest winds in the solar system?	
5 Identify Which planet is tilted on its side as it orbits the sun?	
6 Identify Which planet is the largest planet in the solar system?	

7 Compare How does the composition of Earth's atmosphere differ from the composition of the atmospheres of the gas giant planets?

_____

_____

8 Compare How do the periods of rotation and revolution for the gas giant planets differ from those of Earth?

_____

_____

_____

_____

Critical Thinking

Use this diagram to answer the following questions.

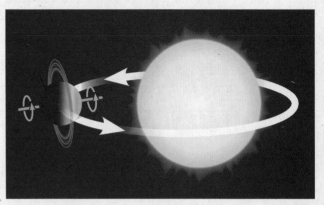

9 Identify Which planet is shown in the diagram? How do you know?

_____

_____

10 Analyze How does the axial tilt of this planet affect its seasons?

_____

_____

_____

_____

11 Analyze Why do you think the wind speeds on the gas giant planets are so much greater than the wind speeds on Earth?

_____

_____

_____

12 Compare List Earth and the gas giant planets in order from the hottest to the coldest planet. How does the temperature of each planet relate to its distance from the sun?

_____

_____

_____

_____

My Notes

Small Bodies in the Solar System

What is found in the solar system besides the sun, planets, and moons?

By the end of this lesson, you should be able to compare and contrast the properties of small bodies in the solar system.

Comet Hale-Bopp was discovered in 1995 and was visible from Earth for 18 months. It is a long-period comet that is thought to take about 2,400 years to orbit the sun.

Virginia Science Standards of Learning

6.1 The student will demonstrate an understanding tscientific reasoning, logic, and the nature of science by planning and conducting investigations in which:

6.1.j current applications are used to reinforce science concepts.

6.8 The student will investigate and understand the organization of the solar system and the interactions among the various bodies that comprise it. Key concepts include:

6.8.a the sun, moon, Earth, other planets and their moons, dwarf planets, meteors, asteroids, and comets.

Engage Your Brain

1 Predict Check T or F to show whether you think each statement is true or false.

T	F	
☐	☐	Pluto is a planet.
☐	☐	The Kuiper Belt is located beyond the orbit of Neptune.
☐	☐	Comets are made of ice, rock, and dust.
☐	☐	All asteroids have the same composition.
☐	☐	Most meteoroids that enter Earth's atmosphere burn up completely.

2 Identify Can you identify the object that is streaking through the sky in the photograph? What do you think makes this object glow?

_____

_____

_____

_____

_____

_____

Active Reading

3 Apply Many scientific words, such as *belt*, also have everyday meanings. Use context clues to write your own definition for each meaning of the word *belt*.

Example sentence
I found a <u>belt</u> to go with my new pants.

belt:

_____

_____

_____

Example sentence
Short-term comets originate in the Kuiper <u>Belt</u>.

belt:

_____

_____

_____

_____

Vocabulary Terms

- **dwarf planet**
- **Kuiper Belt**
- **Kuiper Belt object**
- **comet**
- **Oort cloud**
- **asteroid**
- **meteoroid**
- **meteor**
- **meteorite**

4 Apply As you learn the definition of each vocabulary term in this lesson, create your own definition or sketch to help you remember the meaning of the term.

Bigger is not better

Where are small bodies in the solar system?

Active Reading

5 Identify As you read the text, underline the names of different kinds of small bodies that are found in the solar system.

The sun, planets, and moons are not the only objects in the solar system. Scientists estimate that there are up to a trillion small bodies in the solar system. These bodies lack atmospheres and have weak surface gravity. The largest of the small bodies, the dwarf planets, are found in regions known as the *asteroid belt* and the *Kuiper Belt*. The Kuiper (KAHY•per) Belt is located beyond the orbit of Neptune. Kuiper Belt objects, as you might guess, are located in the Kuiper Belt. Comets, too, are found in the Kuiper Belt. However, comets are also located in the Oort cloud. The Oort (OHRT) cloud is a region that surrounds the solar system and extends almost halfway to the nearest star. Two other types of small bodies, asteroids and meteoroids, are located mostly between the orbits of Venus and Neptune.

Sizes and distances are not to scale.

Mercury   Venus   Earth   Mars   Ceres   Jupiter

What are dwarf planets?

In 2006, astronomers decided that Pluto would no longer be considered a planet. It became the first member of a new group of solar system bodies called *dwarf planets*. Like planets, a **dwarf planet** is a celestial body that orbits the sun and is round because of its own gravity. However, a dwarf planet does not have the mass to have cleared other bodies out of its orbit around the sun.

Five dwarf planets, made of ice and rock, have been identified. Ceres (SIR•eez), located between the orbits of Mars and Jupiter, is about 950 km in diameter and travels at around 18 km/s. Pluto, Eris (IR•is), Haumea (HOW•may•uh), and Makemake (MAH•kay•MAH•kay) are located beyond the orbit of Neptune. They range in size from about 1,500 km (Haumea) to about 2,400 km (Eris). Their orbital periods around the sun range from 250 to 560 years. All travel at speeds of between 3 km/s and 5 km/s.

6 Describe Describe two properties of dwarf planets.

_____

_____

_____

_____

_____

_____

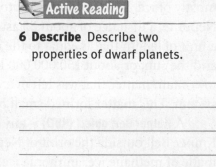

Saturn

Uranus

Neptune

Pluto   Haumea   Makemake   Eris

Visualize It!

7 Analyze Where in the solar system are most of the dwarf planets located?

_____

_____

_____

_____

KBOs

What are Kuiper Belt objects?

The **Kuiper Belt** is a region of the solar system that begins just beyond the orbit of Neptune and contains small bodies made mostly of ice. It extends outward to about twice the orbit of Neptune, a distance of about 55 astronomical units (AU). An AU is a unit of length that is equal to the average distance between Earth and the sun, or about 150,000,000 km. The Kuiper Belt is thought to contain matter that was left over from the formation of the solar system. This matter formed small bodies instead of planets.

A **Kuiper Belt object (KBO)** is any of the minor bodies in the Kuiper Belt outside the orbit of Neptune. Kuiper Belt objects are made of methane ice, ammonia ice, and water ice. They have average orbital speeds of between 1 km/s and 5 km/s. The first Kuiper Belt object was not discovered until 1992. Now, about 1,300 KBOs are known. Scientists estimate that there are at least 70,000 objects in the Kuiper Belt that have diameters larger than 100 km.

Quaoar is a KBO that orbits 43 AU from the sun. It is around 1,260 km in diameter and has one satellite.

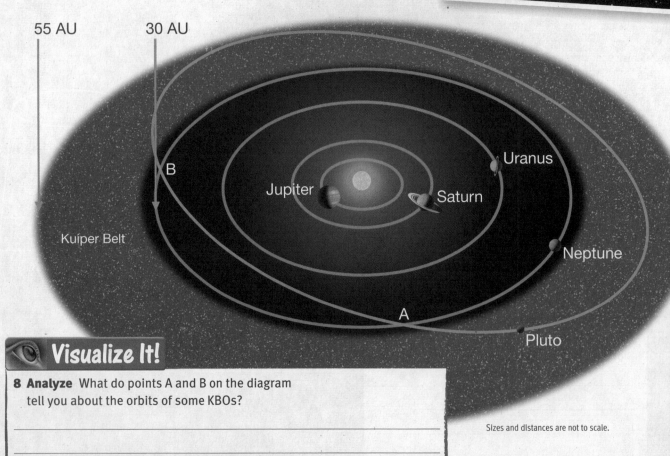

55 AU   30 AU

Uranus

Jupiter   Saturn

B

Kuiper Belt

Neptune

A

Pluto

Sizes and distances are not to scale.

Visualize It!

8 Analyze What do points A and B on the diagram tell you about the orbits of some KBOs?

_____

_____

Pluto: From Planet to KBO

From its discovery in 1930 until 2006, Pluto was considered to be the ninth planet in the solar system. However, beginning in 1992, a new group of small bodies called *Kuiper Belt objects*, or simply KBOs, began to be discovered beyond the orbit of Neptune. Not only are some of the KBOs close to Pluto in size, but some have a similar composition of rock and ice. Astronomers recognized that Pluto was, in fact, a large KBO and not the ninth planet. In 2006, Pluto was redefined as a "dwarf planet" by the International Astronomical Union (IAU).

Charon

Pluto

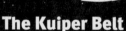

Pluto and Charon

At 2,306 km in diameter, Pluto is the second largest KBO. It is shown in this artist's rendition with Charon (KAIR•uhn), its largest satellite. Many large KBOs have satellites. Some KBOs and their satellites, such as Pluto and Charon, orbit each other.

The Kuiper Belt

The Kuiper Belt is located between 30 AU (the orbit of Neptune) and approximately 55 AU. However, most KBOs have been discovered between 42 and 48 AU, where their orbits are not disturbed by the gravitational attraction of Neptune.

Extend

Inquiry

9 Explain Why is Pluto no longer considered a planet?

10 Research Astronomer Clyde Tombaugh discovered Pluto in 1930. Research why Tombaugh was searching beyond Neptune for "Planet X" and how he discovered Pluto.

11 Debate Research the 2006 IAU decision to redefine Pluto as a "dwarf planet." Combine this research with your research on Pluto. With your classmates, debate whether Pluto should be considered a "dwarf planet" or return to being called the ninth planet in the solar system.

What do we know about comets?

Active Reading **12 Identify** As you read the text, underline the different parts of a comet and their properties.

A **comet** is a small body of ice, rock, and dust that follows a highly elliptical orbit around the sun. As a comet passes close to the sun, it gives off gas and dust in the form of a coma and a tail.

The speed of a comet will vary depending on how far from or how close to the sun it is. Far from the sun, a comet may travel at speeds as low as 0.32 km/s. Close to the sun, a comet may travel as fast as 445 km/s.

Comets Are Made of a Nucleus and a Tail

All comets have a *nucleus* that is composed of ice and rock. Most comet nuclei are between 1 km and 10 km in diameter. If a comet approaches the sun, solar radiation and heating cause the comet's ice to change to gas. A *coma* is a spherical cloud of gas and dust that comes off of the nucleus. The *ion tail* of a comet is gas that has been ionized, or stripped of electrons, by the sun. The solar wind—electrically charged particles expanding away from the sun—pushes the gas away from the comet's head. So, regardless of the direction a comet is traveling, its ion tail points away from the sun. A second tail made of dust and gas curves backward along the comet's orbit. This *dust tail* can be millions of kilometers long.

 **Visualize It!**

13 Identify Use the write-on lines in the diagram to identify the structures of a comet.

Dust tail

 A

 B

 C

Comets Come from the Kuiper Belt and the Oort Cloud

There are two regions of the solar system where comets come from. The first region is the Kuiper Belt, which is where short-period comets originate. The second region is the Oort cloud, which is where long-period comets originate.

Collisions between objects in the Kuiper Belt produce fragments that become comets. These comets are known as *short-period comets*. Short-period comets take less than 200 years to orbit the sun. Therefore, they return to the inner solar system quite frequently, perhaps every few decades or centuries. Short-period comets also have short life spans. Every time a comet passes the sun, it may lose a layer as much as 1 m thick.

Some comets originate in the Oort cloud. The **Oort cloud** is a spherical region that surrounds the solar system and extends almost halfway to the nearest star. Comets can form in the Oort cloud when two objects collide. Comets can also form when an object in the Oort cloud is disturbed by the gravity of a nearby star and is sent into the inner solar system. Comets that originate in the Oort cloud are called *long-period comets*. Long-period comets may take up to hundreds of thousands of years to orbit the sun.

Visualize It! Inquiry

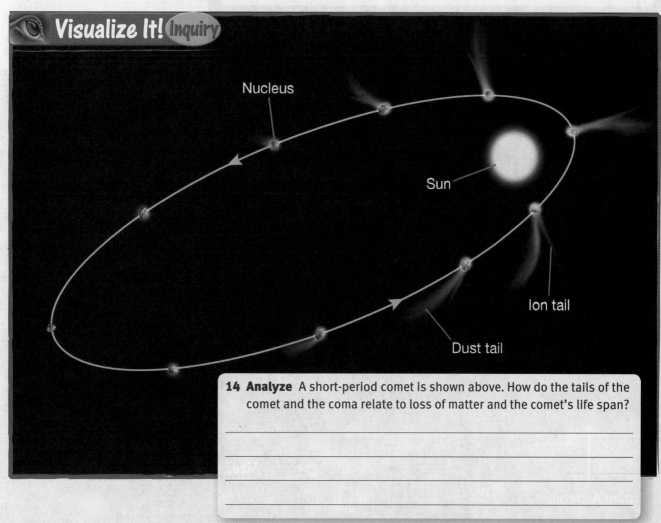

Nucleus

Sun

Ion tail

Dust tail

14 Analyze A short-period comet is shown above. How do the tails of the comet and the coma relate to loss of matter and the comet's life span?

_____

_____

_____

_____

On the rocks

What do we know about asteroids?

15 Identify As you read the text, underline those places in the solar system where asteroids are located.

An **asteroid** is a small, irregularly shaped, rocky object that orbits the sun. Most asteroids are located between the orbits of Mars and Jupiter. This 300 million–km–wide region is known as the *asteroid belt*. The asteroid belt contains hundreds of thousands of asteroids, called *main-belt asteroids*. The largest main-belt asteroid by diameter is Pallas, which has a diameter of 570 km. The smallest asteroid is 4 m in diameter. Groups of asteroids are also located in the orbits of Jupiter and Neptune (called *Trojan asteroids*) and in the Kuiper Belt. Still other asteroids are called *near-Earth asteroids*. Some of these asteroids cross the orbits of Earth and Venus.

Asteroids in the asteroid belt orbit the sun at about 18 km/s and have orbital periods of 3 to 8 years. Although most asteroids rotate around their axis, some tumble end over end through space.

Visualize It!

16 Analyze Where is the asteroid belt located?

_____

_____

_____

_____

_____

_____

Asteroid Belt

Mars

Trojan Asteroids

Sizes and distances are not to scale.

Trojan Asteroids

Jupiter

Asteroids Have Different Compositions

The composition of asteroids varies. Many asteroids have dark surfaces. Scientists think that these asteroids are rich in carbon. Other asteroids are thought to be rocky and to have a core made of iron and nickel. Still other asteroids may have a rocky core surrounded largely by ice. Small, rocky asteroids have perhaps the strangest composition of all. They appear to be piles of rock loosely held together by gravity. Asteroid Itokawa (ee•TOH•kah•wah), shown below, is a rocky asteroid known as a "rubble-pile" asteroid.

Some asteroids contain economic minerals like those mined on Earth. Economic minerals that are found in asteroids include gold, iron, nickel, manganese, cobalt, and platinum. Scientists are now investigating the potential for mining near-Earth asteroids.

Itokawa is a rubble-pile asteroid. Astronomers think that the 500 m—long asteroid may be composed of two asteroids that are joined.

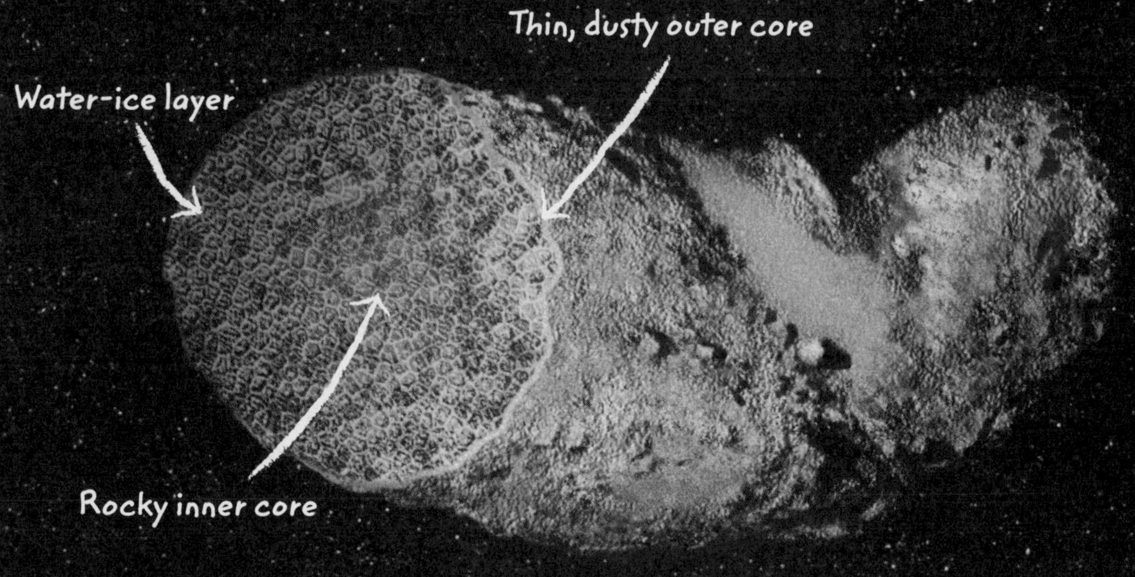

Thin, dusty outer core

Water-ice layer

Rocky inner core

Greetings from Eros!

Think Outside the Book

17 Describe Eros is a near-Earth asteroid that tumbles through space. Imagine that you are the first human to explore Eros. Write a postcard that describes what you found on Eros. Then research the asteroid and find out how close your description came to reality.

Burned Out

What do we know about meteoroids, meteors, and meteorites?

A sand grain- to boulder-sized, rocky body that travels through space is a **meteoroid**. Meteoroids that enter Earth's atmosphere travel at about 52 km/s, as measured by radar on Earth. Friction heats these meteoroids to thousands of degrees Celsius, which causes them to glow. The atmosphere around a meteoroid's path also gets hotter and glows because of friction between the meteoroid and air molecules. A bright streak of light that results when a meteoroid burns up in Earth's atmosphere is called a **meteor**. A **meteorite** is a meteoroid that reaches Earth's surface without burning up.

18 Identify Use the write-on lines below to identify the three objects that are shown.

A A small, rocky body that travels through space is a

_____

B The glowing trail of a body that is burning up in Earth's atmosphere is a _____

C A body that reaches Earth's surface without burning up is a _____

A meteorite 45 m across produced kilometer-wide Barringer Crater in Arizona about 50,000 years ago.

Meteorites Reach Earth

Meteoroids come from the asteroid belt, Mars, the moon, and comets. Most of the meteoroids that enter Earth's atmosphere do not reach Earth's surface. Many meteoroids explode in the upper atmosphere. These explosions are often recorded by military satellites in orbit around Earth. Other meteoroids skip back into space after briefly crossing the upper atmosphere. However, some large meteoroids that enter Earth's lower atmosphere or strike Earth's surface can be destructive. Scientists estimate that a destructive meteorite impact occurs every 300 to 400 years.

© Houghton Mifflin Harcourt Publishing Company • Image Credits: (c) ©Adastra/Taxi/Getty Images; (cr) ©Images of Africa Photobank/Alamy; (bl) ©Jon Arnold Images Ltd/Alamy

Meteorites Have Different Compositions

Meteorites can be divided into three general groups. The first group of meteorites are the stony meteorites. They are the most common form of meteorite. Stony meteorites are made of silicate minerals, just like rocks on Earth. Some stony meteorites also contain small amounts of organic matter. A much smaller group of meteorites are the iron meteorites. Iron meteorites are composed of iron and nickel. The rarest group of meteorites are stony-iron meteorites. Stony-iron meteorites are composed of both silicate minerals and iron and nickel. All three groups of meteorites can originate from asteroids. However, some stony meteorites come from the moon and Mars.

Visualize It!

19 Describe In the boxes below, describe the composition and origin of each group of meteorite. Also, indicate how common each group of meteorite is.

Stony meteorite

_____
_____
_____
_____
_____

Iron meteorite

_____
_____
_____
_____

Stony-iron meteorite

_____
_____
_____
_____
_____

Visual Summary

To complete this summary, answer the questions below. Then use the key below to check your answers. You can use this page to review the main concepts of the lesson.

Small Bodies in the Solar System

Small bodies are found throughout the solar system.

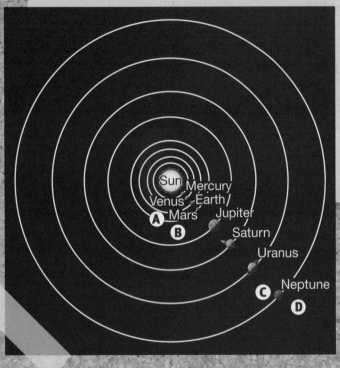

Sun Mercury
Venus Earth
Mars Jupiter
Saturn
Uranus
Neptune

A **B** **C** **D**

Answers: 20 asteroids A, B, C, D; dwarf planets B, D; KBOs C, D; 21 F, F, T

20 Enter the correct letter or letters that indicate a location for each small body in the solar system.

Asteroids	
Dwarf planets	
Kuiper Belt objects	

21 Check true or false to answer the questions below.

T	F	
☐	☐	Comets originate in the asteroid belt and the Kuiper Belt.
☐	☐	Three groups of asteroids are stony, iron, and stony-iron.
☐	☐	Most meteoroids that enter Earth's atmosphere burn up.

22 Compare Make a table in which you compare and contrast comets and asteroids in terms of composition, location in the solar system, and size.

Lesson Review

Vocabulary

Fill in the blank with the term that best completes the following sentences.

1 The _____ is a spherical region that surrounds the solar system and extends almost halfway to the nearest star.

2 A region of the solar system that extends from the orbit of Neptune to about twice the orbit of Neptune is the _____.

3 Most _____ are located between the orbits of Mars and Jupiter.

4 A meteoroid that reaches Earth's surface without burning up is a _____.

Key Concepts

In the following table, write the name of the correct body next to the property of that body.

Property	Body
5 Identify What is a minor body that orbits outside the orbit of Neptune?	
6 Identify What is a small body that follows a highly elliptical orbit around the sun?	
7 Identify What is the largest of the small bodies that are found in the solar system?	
8 Identify What is the glowing trail that results when a meteoroid burns up in Earth's atmosphere?	

Critical Thinking

Use this table to answer the following questions.

Comet	Orbital Period (years)
Borrelly	6.9
Halley	76
Hale-Bopp	2,400
Hyakutake	100,000

9 Apply Which of the comets in the table are short-period comets?

_____

_____

10 Apply Which of the comets in the table most likely originated in the Oort cloud?

_____

_____

11 Infer Why do you think that the speeds of comets increase as they near the sun?

_____

_____

_____

12 Predict Why do you think that some asteroids tumble end over end through space while other asteroids rotate around their axis?

_____

_____

_____

_____

My Notes

Unit 10 · Big Idea ▸ Planets and a variety of other bodies form a system of objects orbiting the sun.

Lesson 1
ESSENTIAL QUESTION
How have people modeled the solar system?

Compare various historical models of the solar system.

Lesson 2
ESSENTIAL QUESTION
Why is gravity important in the solar system?

Explain the role that gravity played in the formation of the solar system and in determining the motion of the planets.

Lesson 3
ESSENTIAL QUESTION
What are the properties of the sun?

Describe the structure and rotation of the sun, energy production and energy transport in the sun, and solar activity on the sun.

Lesson 4
ESSENTIAL QUESTION
What is known about the terrestrial planets?

Describe some of the properties of the terrestrial planets and how the properties of Mercury, Venus, and Mars differ from the properties of Earth.

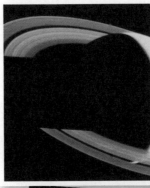

Lesson 5
ESSENTIAL QUESTION
What is known about the gas giant planets?

Describe some of the properties of the gas giant planets and how these properties differ from the physical properties of Earth.

Lesson 6
ESSENTIAL QUESTION
What is found in the solar system besides the sun, planets, and moons?

Compare and contrast the properties of small bodies in the solar system.

Think Outside the Book

2 Synthesize Choose one of these activities to help synthesize what you have learned in this unit.

☐ Using what you learned in lessons 4 and 5, write a short essay explaining where in the solar system besides Earth life could exist.

☐ Using what you learned in lessons 2, 3, and 4, make a poster showing why comets are the fastest-moving bodies in the solar system.

Connect ESSENTIAL QUESTIONS
Lessons 4 and 5

1 Synthesize Explain why the planet Jupiter has more moons than the planet Mars.

_____

_____

_____

_____

Unit 10 Review

Name _____

Vocabulary

Fill in each blank with the term that best completes the following sentences.

1 _____ is the process in which energy is released as the nuclei of small atoms combine to form a larger nucleus.

2 The solar system formed from a _____, which is a rotating cloud of gas and dust that formed into the sun and planets.

3 When an object looks as if the position has shifted when it is viewed from different locations, this is referred to as _____.

4 Earth, Venus, Mars, and Mercury are considered _____, which are highly dense planets nearest the sun.

5 A(n) _____ is a small, rocky object that orbits the sun; many of these objects are located in a band between the orbits of Mars and Jupiter.

Key Concepts

Read each question below, and circle the best answer.

6 This diagram illustrates a historical model of the solar system.

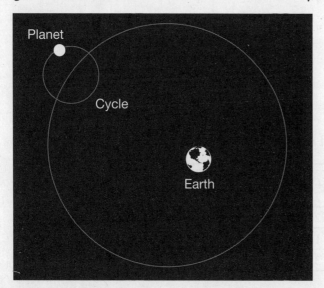

Which type of model is shown?

A geocentric model   **C** Copernican model

B heliocentric model   **D** Aristarchan model

7 Galileo Galilei showed that Earth was not the center of our solar system. By which method did he do this?

   A calculating mathematical models

   B using a telescope to see four moons orbiting Jupiter and the phases of Venus

   C observing the sun

   D assuming that all pre-existing astronomic theories were incorrect

8 The Kuiper Belt, pictured below, is generally thought to contain leftover bits from the formation of the solar system.

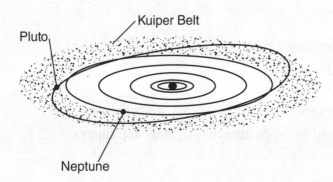

Which of the following describes Kuiper Belt objects?

   A often larger than some planets in the solar system

   B extremely hot

   C minor planet-sized objects that orbit the sun in a flat belt beyond Neptune's orbit

   D 100 AU wide

9 Suppose the comets in the table orbited the sun.

Comet Name	Comet Size (km)	Comet Speed (km/h)
Rasmussen	1	750,000
Zigler	10	2
Schier	5	1.5 million
Brant	3	3,700

Using what you know about comets, which comet is in the closest orbit to the sun?

   A Rasmussen   **C** Schier

   B Zigler   **D** Brant

10 Which of the following is a list of the gas giant planets?

A Jupiter, Saturn, Uranus, and Neptune

B Earth, Mars, and Venus

C Pluto, Saturn, and Jupiter

D Earth, Jupiter, Neptune, and Saturn

11 Below is an illustration of the planet Saturn. Saturn is one of the four gas giant planets.

Saturn

Which of the four statements below is not true about Saturn?

A It travels around the Sun once every 29.5 years.

B It is the only planet with a ring system.

C It is composed mostly of hydrogen and helium gas.

D It has a large number of moons.

12 Earth, Mercury, and Venus are all classified as terrestrial planets. When compared to Earth, which of the following is true of Mercury and Venus?

A Mercury and Venus have a higher surface gravity than Earth.

B Mercury and Venus have a longer period of revolution than Earth.

C Mercury and Venus have slower periods of rotation (longer days) than Earth.

D Mercury and Venus are farther away from the sun than Earth.

13 Which of the following lists accurately relates which terrestrial planets have moons and how many moons they have?

A Mercury and Venus (no moons), Earth (one moon), and Mars (two moons)

B Mercury, Venus, and Earth (one moon each), and Mars (two moons)

C Mercury and Venus (no moons), Earth (two moons), and Mars (two moons)

D Mercury and Venus (no moons), Earth (one moon), and Mars (three moons)

14 Why is nuclear fusion possible in the cores of stars?

A Hydrogen exists only in the cores of stars.

B Hydrogen and helium nuclei require a lot of light to bond together.

C High temperatures and pressures, which are required for fusion to occur, occur in the cores of stars.

D $E = mc^2$ only works in the cores of stars.

15 The sunspot cycle is a period of about 11 years during which the number of sunspots rises and falls. What are sunspots?

A a light area on the sun's corona that is hotter than surrounding areas

B a darker area on the photosphere that is cooler than surrounding areas

C a spot with a weaker magnetic field

D a spot easily seen without a telescope

16 Which describes an effect of centripedal force?

A objects break apart in space

B objects burn at very high temperatures

C objects move in a circular path

D objects move in an elliptical path

17 What does Kepler's first law of planetary motion state?

  A the orbit of a planet around the sun is an ellipse with the sun at one focus

  B the orbit of a planet is dependent on heat

  C the difference between centripedal force and elliptical force

  D the orbital period is infinite

Critical Thinking

Answer the following questions in the space provided.

18 Explain the difference between a meteoroid, a meteor, and a meteorite. Which one would you most likely see on the surface of Earth?

_____

_____

_____

_____

_____

_____

19 Name three characteristics of gas giants that make them different from terrestrial planets.

_____

_____

_____

_____

20 Study the diagrams below.

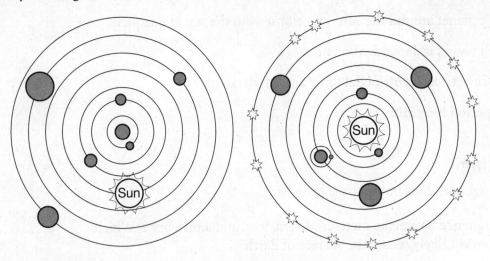

Explain what the two diagrams show. What is significant about them? How were these models developed and by whom? How do the models affect the way we study and think about our solar system?

_____

_____

_____

_____

_____

_____

Connect **ESSENTIAL QUESTIONS**
Lessons 2, 3, 4, 5, and 6

Answer the following question in the space provided.

21 Discuss gravitational force in our universe and how it works. Why is it critical to our universe? Name at least three instances of gravitational forces at work in our solar system.

_____

_____

_____

_____

_____

_____

_____

Exploring Space

Big Idea

People develop and use technology to explore and study space.

What do you think?

Probes send information about the outer solar system back to scientists on Earth. How might humans benefit from space exploration?

Unit 11
Exploring Space

Exploring Space!

The exploration of space began in 1957 with the launch of Sputnik I. Since 1957, humans have walked on the moon, rovers have investigated the surface of Mars, and spacecraft have flown by the most distant planets in the solar system.

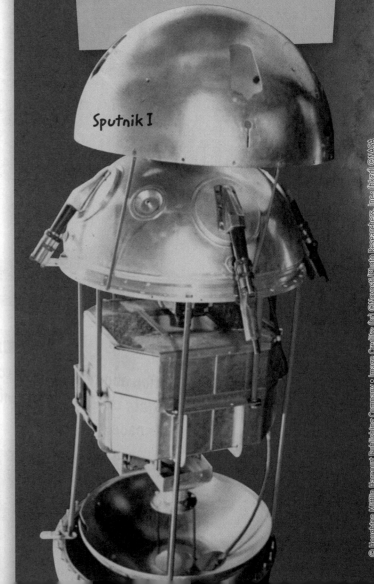

Sputnik I, 1957
On October 4, 1957, the successful launch of the Russian satellite Sputnik I kicked off the race for space.

Sputnik I

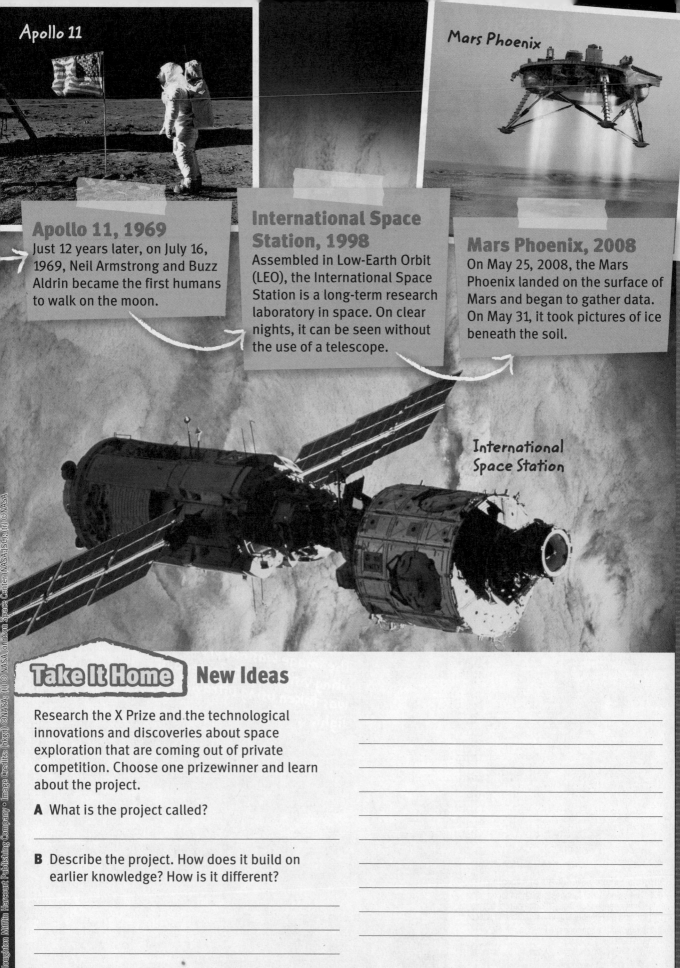

Apollo 11

Mars Phoenix

Apollo 11, 1969
Just 12 years later, on July 16, 1969, Neil Armstrong and Buzz Aldrin became the first humans to walk on the moon.

International Space Station, 1998
Assembled in Low-Earth Orbit (LEO), the International Space Station is a long-term research laboratory in space. On clear nights, it can be seen without the use of a telescope.

Mars Phoenix, 2008
On May 25, 2008, the Mars Phoenix landed on the surface of Mars and began to gather data. On May 31, it took pictures of ice beneath the soil.

International Space Station

Take It Home New Ideas

Research the X Prize and the technological innovations and discoveries about space exploration that are coming out of private competition. Choose one prizewinner and learn about the project.

A What is the project called?

B Describe the project. How does it build on earlier knowledge? How is it different?

Images from Space

ESSENTIAL QUESTION

What can we learn from space images?

By the end of this lesson, you should be able to describe ways of collecting information from space and analyze how different wavelengths of the electromagnetic spectrum provide different information.

This blue object is the sun. The image was not produced using visible light. Instead, it was taken using ultraviolet light.

Virginia Science Standards of Learning

6.1 The student will demonstrate an understanding of scientific reasoning, logic, and the nature of science by planning and conducting investigations in which:

6.1.j current applications are used to reinforce science concepts.

Lesson Labs

Quick Labs
- Using Invisible Light
- A Model of the Universe
- Splitting White Light

S.T.E.M. Lab
- Making a Telescope

 Engage Your Brain

1 Predict Check T or F to show whether you think each statement is true or false.

T	F	
☐	☐	Visible light is a type of electromagnetic radiation.
☐	☐	Artificial satellites can produce images of Earth only.
☐	☐	Earth's atmosphere blocks all ultraviolet radiation from space.
☐	☐	Optical telescopes are used to study objects in the universe.

2 Identify Look at the picture below. Write a caption that explains what the picture shows.

_____
_____
_____
_____
_____
_____

 Active Reading

3 Synthesize You can often define an unknown word if you know the meaning of its word parts. Use the word parts and sentence below to make an educated guess about the meaning of the word *microwave*.

Word part	Meaning
micro-	small
-wave	a movement of up or down or back and forth

Example sentence
Microwaves can be used to heat food.

microwave:

_____
_____

Vocabulary Terms
- **wavelength**
- **electromagnetic spectrum**
- **spectrum**

4 Apply As you learn the definition of each vocabulary term in this lesson, create your own definition or sketch to help you remember the meaning of the term.

What is electromagnetic radiation?

Energy traveling as electromagnetic waves is called *electromagnetic radiation*. Waves can be described by either their wavelength or frequency. **Wavelength** is the distance between two adjacent crests or troughs of a wave. *Frequency* measures the number of waves passing a point per second. Higher-frequency waves have a shorter wavelength. Energy carried by electromagnetic radiation depends on both the wavelength and the amount of radiation at that wavelength. A higher-frequency wave carries higher energy than a lower-frequency wave.

How is electromagnetic radiation classified?

Active Reading 5 **Identify** As you read, underline the name of each part of the electromagnetic spectrum.

There are many different wavelengths and frequencies of electromagnetic radiation. All these wavelengths and frequencies make up what is called the **electromagnetic spectrum**. A **spectrum** is a continuous range of a single feature, in this case wavelength. The form of electromagnetic radiation with the longest-wavelength and the lowest-frequency is radio waves. Radios and televisions receive radio waves. These receivers then produce sound waves. Sound waves are not electromagnetic radiation. Microwaves have shorter wavelengths and higher frequencies than radio waves. The next shorter wavelength radiation is called infrared. Infrared is sometimes called "heat radiation." Visible light has a shorter wavelength than infrared. You see an object when visible light from the object reaches your eyes. Images produced in visible light are the only images we can see without computer enhancement. Even shorter in wavelength is ultraviolet radiation. The shortest wavelengths belong to x-rays and gamma rays.

On the Same

Radio

6 Analyze Write the parts of the electromagnetic spectrum in order from lowest frequency to highest frequency.

_____

_____

_____

_____

_____

_____

_____

Microwave

LOWER ENERGY
LONGER WAVELENGTH

Wavelength?

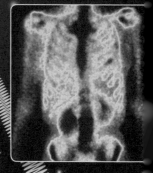

Gamma rays

Infrared

7 Complete Electromagnetic _____ that has a shorter wavelength has a _____ frequency.

Ultraviolet

X-rays

Visible light

**HIGHER ENERGY
SHORTER WAVELENGTH**

The Better to See You With

What are some characteristics of electromagnetic radiation?

Electromagnetic waves can be generated by devices such as cell phones, microwave ovens, and flashlights. Electromagnetic radiation is also generated by heat. Very cool material radiates, or emits energy, mostly as radio waves. Warmer objects may radiate mainly in the infrared. To emit visible light, an object must be hot. Light bulbs are good examples of hot objects that emit light.

Different portions of the electromagnetic spectrum interact differently with matter. Radio waves pass easily through space and the atmosphere. Using special equipment, infrared radiation allows someone to see room-temperature objects, even at night. Microwaves penetrate a small distance into many materials, where they are absorbed. The energy is released as heat. A microwave oven uses this property to cook food. Ultraviolet rays can cause materials to fluoresce (flu•RES), or glow. This property is used for many purposes, from criminal investigation to document protection. For example, documents can be protected against counterfeiting (KOUN•ter•fit•ing) if they use symbols that are detectable only by special lamps. X-rays pass through flesh easily but less easily through bone. Physicians and other doctors can use x-rays to examine the insides of your body.

In small amounts, electromagnetic radiation can be very useful. Large amounts of any type of radiation can cause problems because of the total amount of energy carried. For example, ultraviolet radiation can cause skin cancer. Gamma rays are especially dangerous to living organisms.

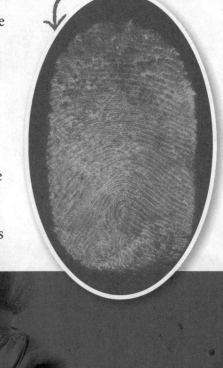

Under an ultraviolet lamp, fingerprints glow.

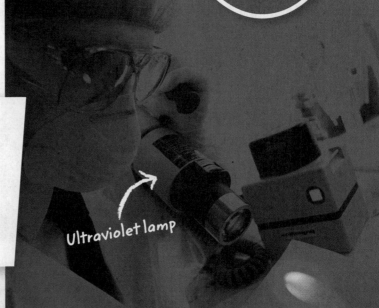

Ultraviolet lamp

Active Reading

8 Identify As you read, underline five ways that people can use electromagnetic radiation.

9 Explain Describe an example of how nonvisible radiation can be used.

_____

_____

_____

_____

Electromagnetic Radiation and Earth's Surface

Radio   Microwave   Infrared   Visible ↓   Ultraviolet   X-ray   Gamma rays

Inquiry

10 Analyze Why are x-ray telescopes and gamma-ray telescopes in space?

_____

_____

_____

_____

What electromagnetic radiation reaches Earth?

If Earth had no atmosphere, energy from the entire electromagnetic spectrum would reach Earth's surface. But not all wavelengths of the electromagnetic spectrum reach Earth's surface, as shown in the illustration above. In the atmosphere, atoms and molecules reflect some of the incoming radiation back into space. Atoms and molecules can also absorb some forms of electromagnetic radiation. For example, water vapor and carbon dioxide molecules absorb much of the infrared and microwave radiation. Most visible light and radio radiation reach Earth's surface.

The higher frequencies of ultraviolet radiation are absorbed by ozone in the atmosphere. Oxygen and nitrogen atoms absorb x-rays and gamma rays. X-rays and gamma rays have high enough energies to damage living tissue and other materials. Fortunately, they are absorbed by molecules in the atmosphere. Therefore, x-rays and gamma rays from space do not reach Earth's surface.

To See or Not to See

How do people detect electromagnetic radiation from objects in space?

Visible light from the sun, moon, planets, and stars can be detected by the human eye or a camera to form an image. Images of objects in space can tell us about their positions and properties. Telescopes are one way to learn about objects in space. They can be placed on mountain tops. Telescopes are also placed in space to collect radiation that does not reach Earth's surface.

All forms of electromagnetic radiation from space can be collected by telescopes. However, special detectors must be used to form images from radiation other than visible light. A radio receiver is used for radio waves. Infrared, x-ray, and gamma-ray detectors are used for those regions of the electromagnetic spectrum.

With Optical Telescopes

Active Reading 11 **Identify** As you read, underline two types of optical telescopes.

Optical telescopes collect visible light with a mirror or a lens. A mirror reflects light, and a lens changes the direction of light rays as they pass through the lens. A telescope that uses a mirror to collect light is called a *reflecting telescope*. A telescope that uses a lens to collect light is a called a *refracting telescope*. The larger the lens or mirror, the more light that can be collected. With more light, the observer can view fainter objects. The light collected is then detected by the eye or other detector, such as a camera.

A reflecting telescope uses a mirror to gather and focus light.

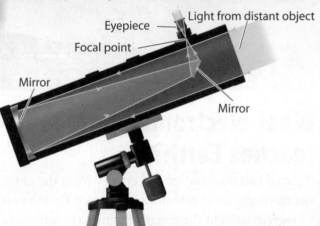

Light from distant object
Eyepiece
Focal point
Mirror
Mirror

A refracting telescope uses a lens to gather and focus light.

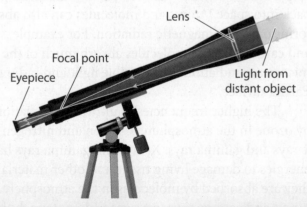

Lens
Focal point
Eyepiece
Light from distant object

The Keck Observatory is on top of Mauna Kea, in Hawaii.

With Non-Optical Telescopes

12 Identify As you read, underline one example of electromagnetic radiation that non-optical telescopes detect.

The first telescopes were used to collect visible light. Today, however, astronomers use telescopes to observe in all parts of the electromagnetic spectrum. Most radio telescopes use metal mirrors to reflect radio waves. Radio waves are reflected onto a radio receiver at the focus. A satellite dish is an example of this kind of radio telescope. Radio waves have long wavelengths. Therefore, many radio telescopes are very large.

Telescopes are often used to produce images. First, the electromagnetic radiation that is collected must reach a detector that is sensitive to that wavelength, just like x-rays that pass through your teeth must reach a material sensitive to x-rays. Then the electromagnetic radiation is collected and processed through a computer to produce an image that we can see.

The computer software also adds color, called *false color*. The addition of false color highlights important details. For example, an image might be colored so that areas emitting low energy are dark and areas emitting high energy are bright. The brightness of an object tells the scientists how much energy that object is producing.

Visualize It!

14 Analyze Compare the mirror in the reflecting telescope with the radio telescope. In what way is a radio telescope like a reflecting telescope?

_____

_____

_____

_____

_____

13 Apply Choose a wavelength from the electromagnetic spectrum other than visible light or x-rays. Imagine that you could look at an image of your hand produced using that wavelength. Then draw a picture of what you think your hand would look like.

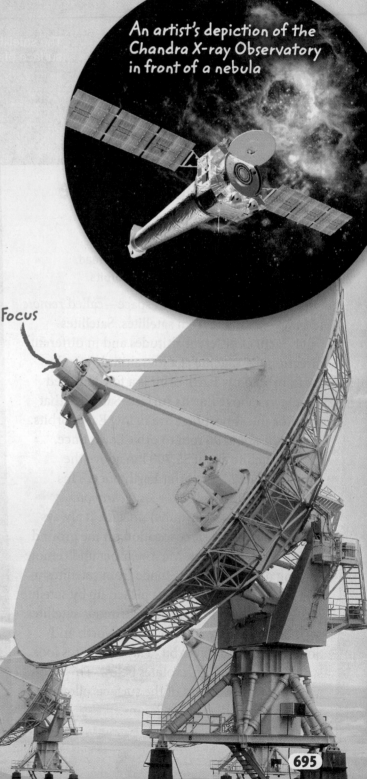

An artist's depiction of the Chandra X-ray Observatory in front of a nebula

Focus

This array of radio telescopes is in New Mexico.

The View from Above

The satellite scans the surface of the Earth.

The satellite transmits the data to a station on the ground.

How can people observe Earth from space?

15 Identify As you read, underline three examples of satellite orbits.

Observations of Earth from space—called *remote sensing*—are made from satellites. Satellites orbit Earth at different altitudes and in different directions. A satellite at a low altitude is in low Earth orbit. Low Earth orbit is a few hundred kilometers above Earth's surface. Satellites that monitor the atmosphere are in low Earth orbits. They take about 90 min to orbit Earth once.

A satellite about 35,700 km above the equator takes 24 h to orbit Earth once. This type of satellite is called a *geosynchronous* (jee•oh•SINGK•kruh•nuhs) *satellite*. It always remains above the same location on the ground as Earth rotates below. Most weather and remote-sensing observations are made from satellites in this orbit. Television signals picked up by satellite dishes also come from geosynchronous satellites.

Some satellites pass over the North and South Poles on every orbit. These satellites look straight down as Earth rotates below. This allows a good look at all areas of the surface, allowing mapping and other observations.

What can you learn about Earth from satellite images?

Images from remote-sensing satellites provide a variety of information. They show evidence of human activity, such as cities. Remote-sensing images of the same place taken on different dates show how things change over time. For example, images of populated areas can show how development has changed over several years, as shown in the two images below of Las Vegas.

The lights seen in images taken at night indicate populated areas and highways. Infrared images can show forests and cleared areas, because trees appear cooler than bare land in infrared images. Images can also show forest fires and can be used to warn people of the danger. Weather satellites provide images of clouds and storms, such as hurricanes. Other images can show features in the atmosphere, such as the aurora and ozone variations.

Think Outside the Book

16 Apply Design your own remote-sensing satellite. Give it a function—what would you like your satellite to monitor? Give your satellite a name.

Visualize It!

17 Analyze Describe one change in urbanization between 1973 and 2006 that you see with these two images.

_____

_____

1973

2006

These false-color images of Las Vegas were produced by a satellite called Landsat. The green represents vegetation, and the lines represent city streets.

© Houghton Mifflin Harcourt Publishing Company • Image Credits: (all) ©Andrew Freeberg(NASA/GSFC)

Seeing Is Believing

What can you learn from space images?

Visible light allows you to see the surfaces of planets and how other objects in space might look. Different types of radiation can be used to produce images to reveal features not visible to the eye. For example, infrared radiation can reveal the temperature of objects. Dust blocks visible light, but some wavelengths of infrared pass through dust, so scientists can see objects normally hidden by dust clouds in space. High-energy objects may be very bright in x-ray or gamma-ray radiation, although difficult to see at longer wavelengths. The four images of the Andromeda galaxy on the right were produced using wavelengths other than visible light, so the colors are all false colors.

Visualize It!

18 Analzye Compare one image of the Andromeda galaxy on the opposite page with the image in visible light on this page.

_____

_____

_____

_____

_____

_____

_____

The Andromeda galaxy in visible light

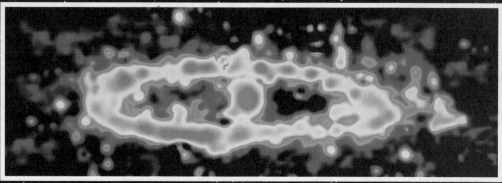

This image of the Andromeda galaxy was produced using radio waves. The reddish-orange color in the center and in the ring represents a source of radio waves. New stars are forming in the ring area.

In this infrared image of the Andromeda galaxy, you can see more detail in the structure of the galaxy. The dark areas within the bright rings are dust. The dust is so thick in some areas that radiation behind the dust is not getting through.

This image of the Andromeda galaxy was produced with a combination of ultraviolet and infrared radiation. The blue areas represent large, young, hot stars. The green areas represent older stars. The bright yellow spot at the very center of the galaxy represents an extremely dense area of old stars.

Visual Summary

To complete this summary, fill in the blanks with the correct word or phrase. Then use the key below to check your answers. You can use this page to review the main concepts of the lesson.

Images from Space

The electromagnetic spectrum is all the wavelengths and frequencies of electromagnetic radiation.

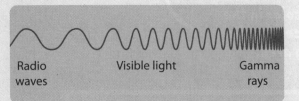

Radio waves   Visible light   Gamma rays

19 Two parts of the electromagnetic spectrum between visible light and gamma rays are

_____

_____

Different types of telescopes are used to detect different ranges of electromagnetic radiation.

20 Optical telescopes detect

_____

Telescopes are available for every portion of the electromagnetic spectrum. Different types of radiation reveal various features not visible to the eye.

21 These two images of Saturn are different because they were made using different wavelengths of

_____

_____

Answers: **19** ultraviolet; x-rays; **20** visible light; **21** electromagnetic radiation

22 Explain Describe how images from space of Earth and other objects are useful.

_____

Lesson Review

Vocabulary

Fill in the blank with the term that best completes the following sentences.

1 The distance between two adjacent crests of a wave is called its _____.

2 The _____ is all the wavelengths of electromagnetic radiation.

3 A _____ is a continuous range of a single feature, such as wavelength.

Key Concepts

4 Explain State why telescopes that detect non-optical radiation are useful for studying objects in space. Give an example.

_____

_____

_____

_____

5 Identify List three examples of telescopes that detect different types of electromagnetic radiation.

_____

_____

_____

6 Explain Describe how wavelength, frequency, and energy are related.

_____

_____

_____

7 Explain Describe one type of electromagnetic radiation that can cause harm to humans.

_____

_____

_____

_____

Critical Thinking

Use this diagram to answer the following questions.

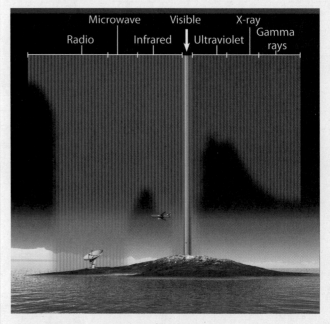

8 Analyze Some infrared radiation reaches Earth, and some does not. Which part does reach Earth—longer wavelength infrared or shorter wavelength infrared?

_____

_____

9 Analyze List two other types of electromagnetic radiation that reach Earth's surface.

_____

_____

10 Apply Describe how remote-sensing satellites can help people stay safe from massive fires.

_____

_____

_____

_____

_____

_____

My Notes

Sandra Faber

ASTRONOMER

What do you do when you send a telescope into space and then find out that it is broken? You call Dr. Sandra Faber, a professor of astronomy at the University of California, Santa Cruz (UCSC). In April 1990, after the *Hubble Space Telescope* went into orbit, scientists found that the images the telescope collected were not turning out as expected. Dr. Faber's team at UCSC was in charge of a device on *Hubble* called the *Wide Field Planetary Camera*. Dr. Faber and her team decided to test the telescope to determine what was wrong.

To perform the test, they centered *Hubble* onto a bright star and took several photos. From those photos, Dr. Faber's team created a model of what was wrong. After reporting the error to NASA and presenting the model they had developed, Dr. Faber and a group of experts began to correct the problem. The group's efforts were a success and put *Hubble* back into operation so that astronomers could continue researching stars and other objects in space.

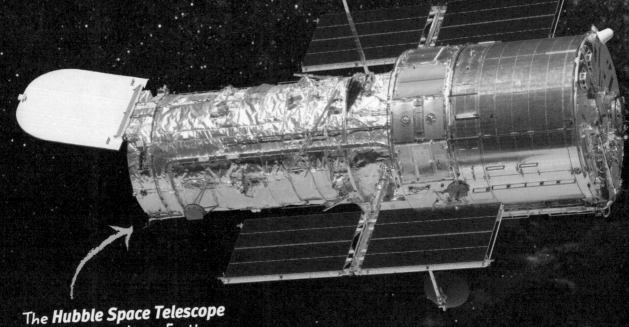

The **Hubble Space Telescope** orbits 569 km above Earth.

Language Arts Connection

Suppose you are a journalist preparing to interview Dr. Sandra Faber. List four questions you would ask her.

JOB BOARD

Astronautical Engineer

What You'll Do: Work on spacecraft that operate outside of Earth's atmosphere, like satellites or space shuttles. Other tasks include planning space missions, determining orbits of spacecraft, and designing rockets and communications systems.

Where You Might Work: Most likely with space agencies. You may also find jobs with aerospace companies or the military.

Education: All engineers must have a four-year college degree in aerospace or astronautical engineering. Many engineers go on to earn a master's degree and a doctorate. Basic engineering classes include algebra, calculus, physics, and computer programming.

Other Job Requirements: You should be able to work well with a team. You should be very careful and exact in your calculations and measurements.

Robotics Technician

What You'll Do: Help engineers build and operate robots, and work with robotic engineers on robotic tools for spacecraft. Use software to solve problems and to test equipment as part of your daily routine.

Where You Might Work: Government space agencies such as NASA, the auto industry, schools, laboratories, and manufacturing plants.

Education: Most technicians complete a two-year technical certificate. Technicians should have a strong interest in math and science. Professional certification is offered to technicians who have at least four years of work experience.

Other Job Requirements: You may also be asked to read blueprints, use microcomputers, and use oscilloscopes.

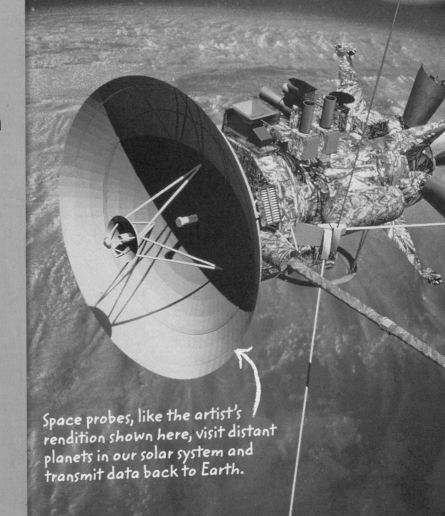

Technology for Space Exploration

ESSENTIAL QUESTION

How do we explore space?

By the end of this lesson, you should be able to analyze the ways people explore space, and assess the role of technology in these efforts.

Space probes, like the artist's rendition shown here, visit distant planets in our solar system and transmit data back to Earth.

Lesson Labs

Quick Labs
• Analyzing Satellite Images
• Design a Spacecraft

S.T.E.M. Lab
• Build a Rocket

Engage Your Brain

1 Predict Check T or F to show whether you think each statement is true or false.

T	F	
☐	☐	Astronauts can travel to distant planets in the solar system.
☐	☐	The space shuttle orbits the moon.
☐	☐	Artificial satellites in space can help you find locations on Earth.
☐	☐	Rovers explore the surfaces of planets and moons.

2 Describe Write your own caption to this photo.

_____

_____

_____

Active Reading

3 Apply Use context clues to write your own definition for the words *analyze* and *transmit*.

Example sentence
Some spacecraft carry technology that can <u>analyze</u> soil and rock samples from objects in space.

analyze:

_____

_____

Example sentence
Satellites <u>transmit</u> data back to Earth.

transmit:

_____

_____

Vocabulary Terms
• space shuttle   • lander
• probe   • rover
• orbiter   • artificial satellite

4 Identify As you read, place a question mark next to any words that you don't understand. When you finish reading the lesson, go back and review the text that you marked. If the information is still confusing, consult a classmate or a teacher.

Beyond the Clouds

How do people travel to space?

On April 12, 1961, Yuri Gagarin became the first human to orbit Earth. Since then, people have continued to travel into space. Large rockets were the first method used to transport humans into space. The space shuttle was developed later and allowed people more time to live and work in space.

With Rockets

To travel away from Earth, large rockets must overcome the pull of Earth's gravity. A *rocket* is a machine that uses gas, often from burning fuel, to escape Earth's gravitational pull. Rockets launch both crewed and uncrewed vehicles into space. During early space missions, the capsules that contained the crews detached from the rockets. The rockets themselves burned up. The capsules "splashed down" in the ocean and were recovered but not reused.

With Space Shuttles

A **space shuttle** was a reusable spacecraft that launched with the aid of rocket boosters and liquid fuel. The shuttle glided to a landing on Earth like an airplane. It carried astronauts and supplies back and forth into orbit around Earth. *Columbia,* the first space shuttle in a fleet of six, was launched in 1981. Until July 21, 2011, more than 100 shuttle missions were completed. Two white, solid rocket boosters (SRBs) helped the space shuttle reach orbit. These boosters detached and were reusable.

Active Reading **5 Explain** What was the purpose of SRBs?

_____

_____

How do people live in space?

People live and work in space on space stations. A *space station* is a long-term crewed spacecraft on which scientific research can be carried out. Currently, the *International Space Station* (ISS) is the only space station in Earth orbit. Six-member crews live aboard the ISS for an average of six months. Because crews live in a constant state of weightlessness, the ISS is the perfect place to study the effects of weightlessness on the human body. Many other scientific experiments are conducted as well. Observations of Earth and earth systems are also made from the ISS.

Booster rockets launched the space shuttle. Following launch, they detached and fell into the ocean. They were retrieved for reuse.

What are some challenges people face in space?

![Active Reading icon] **Active Reading** **6 Identify** As you read, underline challenges humans face when traveling in space.

Astronauts have traveled to the moon, but no human has yet traveled to more distant objects in the solar system. There are many technological challenges to overcome, such as having the fuel necessary for a long return voyage. Other challenges include having sufficient supplies of air, food, and water available for a long journey. Also, the spacecraft must be insulated from the intense cold of space as well as harmful radiation from the sun.

Spacesuits protect astronauts when they work outside a spacecraft. But astronauts still face challenges inside a spacecraft. In space, everything seems weightless. Simple tasks like eating and drinking become difficult. Astronauts must strap themselves to their beds to avoid floating around. The human body experiences problems in a weightless environment. Bones and muscles weaken. So, astronauts must exercise daily to strengthen their bodies.

Visualize It!

Spacesuits protect astronauts from extreme temperatures and from micrometeoroid strikes in space. They provide oxygen to astronauts and remove excess carbon dioxide.

A life support pack supplies oxygen and removes carbon dioxide.

Pressurized suits protect the astronaut from the vacuum of space.

The astronaut is tethered to the shuttle at the waist.

7 Identify What are some technologies humans use to survive outside in space?

_____

_____

_____

_____

_____

_____

The helmet contains communication gear and a protective visor.

The Hubble Space Telescope took this amazing image of Supernova SN1987A in the Large Magellanic Cloud and transmitted the image back to Earth.

Looking Up

What uncrewed technologies do people use to explore space?

Most objects in space are too far away for astronauts to visit. Scientists and engineers have developed uncrewed technologies to gather information about these objects. These technologies include space telescopes, probes, orbiters, landers, and rovers.

Telescopes in Space

Earth's atmosphere distorts light that passes through it. This makes it difficult to obtain clear images of objects in deep space. So some telescopes are placed in Earth orbit to obtain clearer images. Computers in the telescopes gather data and transmit it back to Earth. For example, the *Hubble Space Telescope* is a reflecting telescope that was placed in orbit in 1990. It detects visible light, and ultraviolet and infrared radiation as well. It has greatly expanded our knowledge of the universe.

Other space telescopes collect data using different types of electromagnetic radiation. The *Chandra X-Ray Observatory* and *Compton Gamma-Ray Observatory* were placed in space because Earth's atmosphere blocks most X-rays and gamma rays.

Active Reading **8 Relate** What is one advantage of placing a telescope in space?

_____

_____

_____

Space Probes

A space **probe** is an uncrewed vehicle that carries scientific instruments to distant objects in space. Probes carry a variety of data-collecting instruments, and on-board computers handle data, which are sent back to Earth.

Probes have been especially useful for studying the atmospheres of the gas giant planets. An atmospheric entry probe is dropped from a spacecraft into a planet's atmosphere. These probes relay atmospheric data back to the spacecraft for a short period of time before they are crushed in the planet's atmosphere. Remember, the gas giant planets do not have solid surfaces on which to land, and the pressure within their atmospheres is much greater than the atmospheric pressure on Earth.

Some probes can collect and return materials to Earth. In 2004, NASA's *Stardust* probe collected dust samples as it flew by a comet. The particles were returned to Earth for analysis two years later. It was the first time samples from beyond the moon were brought back to Earth!

The **Mars Pathfinder** lander touched down on Mars in 1997. It found evidence that water once flowed on the surface of the planet.

This artist's rendition shows the encounter of the space probe **Stardust** with Comet Wild 2 in 2004.

Visualize It!

9 Compare How are probes and landers alike? How are they different?

_____

_____

_____

_____

Orbiters

An **orbiter** is an uncrewed spacecraft that is designed to enter into orbit around another object in space. As an orbiter approaches its target, rocket engines are fired to slow down the spacecraft so it can go into orbit. Controllers on Earth can place a spacecraft into orbit around a distant planet or its moons.

Orbiters can study a planet for long periods of time. On-board cameras and other technology are used to monitor atmospheric or surface changes. Instruments are also used to make measurements of temperature and to determine the altitudes of surface features. Orbiters can photograph an entire planet's surface. The data allow scientists to create detailed maps of solar system bodies.

Active Reading **10 Describe** What information can scientists obtain from orbiters?

_____

_____

_____

Landers and Rovers

Orbiters allow astronomers to create detailed maps of planets. They do not touch down on a planet or moon, however. That task is accomplished by landers that are controlled by scientists from Earth. A **lander** is a craft designed to land on the surface of a body in space. Landers have been placed successfully on the moon, Venus, Mars, and on Saturn's moon Titan. Some, such as the *Mars Pathfinder*, have transmitted data for years. The images taken by a lander are more detailed than those taken by an orbiter.

In addition, a lander may carry a rover. A **rover** is a small vehicle that comes out of the lander and explores the surface of a planet or moon beyond the landing site. Both landers and rovers may have mechanical arms for gathering rock, dust, and soil samples.

One of the most successful space missions was the Mars Exploration Rover mission in 2004. During this mission, twin rovers landed on Mars. The rovers, *Spirit* and *Opportunity*, took amazing photos of the surface of Mars. They also found evidence of water below the Martian surface.

Looking Down

How are satellites used to observe Earth?

A satellite is any object in space that orbits another object. An **artificial satellite** is any human-made object placed in orbit around a body in space. Some examples of artificial satellites include remote-sensing satellites, navigation satellites, weather satellites, and communications satellites. Artificial satellites orbit Earth and send data about our planet back to ground stations.

To Study Earth's Features

Scientists use remote-sensing satellites to study Earth. Remote sensing is a way to collect information about something without physically being there. Remote-sensing satellites map and monitor Earth's resources. For example, these satellites identify sources of pollution and monitor crops to track the spread of disease. They also monitor global temperatures, ocean and land heights, and the amount of freshwater ice and sea ice.

Astronauts in the *International Space Station* have photographed volcanoes during different stages of eruption. These photos from space are valuable because scientists can see and study views that are not possible from Earth.

Active Reading

11 **Identify** As you read, underline examples of four different kinds of satellites.

Inquiry

12 **Identify** List two different features on Earth's surface not given as an example here that might be studied from space.

_____

_____

Using satellites, scientists can study images of Earth's features taken from space, such as the eruption of the Gaua volcano in the South Pacific.

To Monitor Changes in Earth Systems

Remote-sensing data provide valuable information on how Earth systems change over time. For example, for more than 30 years, satellites have been observing Arctic sea ice. Images from the European Space Agency's ENVISAT satellite show that a large decline in Arctic sea ice has occurred over the past several years. By analyzing these images, scientists can better determine why the changes are happening.

Images taken by remote-sensing Landsat satellites show changes in the Mississippi River delta over time. When comparing an image taken in 1973 with an image taken in 2003, scientists can see how the delta has changed shape. They can also keep track of changes in the amount of land that is underwater.

To Collect Weather Data

It is difficult to imagine life without reliable weather forecasts. Every day, millions of people make decisions based on information provided by weather satellites. Weather satellites give scientists a big-picture view of Earth's atmosphere. These satellites constantly monitor the atmosphere for events that lead to severe weather conditions. For example, weather satellites are able to provide images of hurricanes. These images help scientists predict the path of the hurricane. People living in the projected pathway can be warned to move to a safer place until the hurricane passes.

Weather satellites also monitor changes in cloud formation and in energy coming from Earth. Information from weather satellites helps airplanes avoid dangerous weather and provides farmers with information that can help them to grow their crops.

Mississippi River

The blue shows the shape of the delta in 1973. The green shows the land surface.

This image shows the shape of the delta in 2003. The black represents the water in the Gulf of Mexico.

Visualize It!

13 Analyze Identify changes in the land surface along the Mississippi River delta using the photos.

_____

_____

_____

_____

Weather satellites monitor the path of Hurricane Igor churning over the Atlantic Ocean in 2010.

For Search and Rescue Operations

The U.S. National Oceanic and Atmospheric Administration (NOAA) has many different satellites. NOAA's environmental satellites carry an instrument package called *SARSAT*. The SARSAT instruments detect distress signals from emergency beacons (BEE•kuhnz). Many ships, airplanes, and individuals on land have emergency beacons. The beacons can be used anywhere in the world, at any time of day. Once the distress signals are received, the satellites relay the signals to a network of ground stations, as shown in the illustration. In the end, the signals go to the U.S. Mission Control Center in Maryland. The Mission Control Center processes the emergency and puts the search and rescue operation into action.

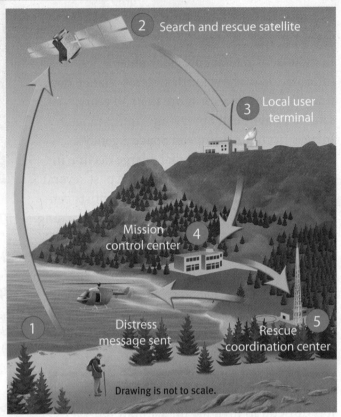

2 Search and rescue satellite

3 Local user terminal

4 Mission control center

1 Distress message sent

5 Rescue coordination center

Drawing is not to scale.

Steps involved in a search and rescue operation

The white areas indicate the most light.

To Provide Composite Images

Data from satellites can be combined to form one image that shows more complete information. The combined image is called a *composite* image. Composite satellite images can give very detailed information about an area's surface features and other features. For example, satellite images can be combined to produce a dramatic image that shows where most of the sources of artificial light are located, as shown here. In this false-color image, data were combined to produce the different colors. A composite image that shows artificial light sources would include images of Earth with no cloud cover.

Think Outside the Book

14 Research Investigate a satellite map that shows surface features for your town or city. What kinds of data does this map contain?

Exploring the Ocean

They may not seem related, but deep-sea exploration and space exploration have something in common. Both use advanced technologies to observe locations that are difficult or dangerous for humans to explore.

Ocean Submersibles

Both marine scientists and space scientists investigate areas most humans will never visit. Ocean submersibles can be crewed or uncrewed.

Black Smokers

Hydrothermal vents are on the ocean floor where the pressure is too great for humans to withstand.

Tube Worms

In the 1970s, scientists aboard a submersible discovered giant tube worms living near an ocean vent. NASA scientists examine the extreme conditions of Mars and other planets for any signs of life.

Extend

Inquiry

15 Identify List two similarities between deep-sea exploration and space exploration.

16 Research and Record List some features of an ocean submersible, for example, *Alvin*. How is the submersible's structure similar to that of spacecraft?

17 Recommend Support more funding for deep-sea exploration by doing one of the following:
- write a letter
- design an ad for a science magazine
- write a script for a radio commercial

For Communication

Communications satellites relay data, including Internet service and some television and radio broadcasts. They are also used to relay long-distance telephone calls. One communications satellite can relay thousands of telephone calls or several television programs at once. Communications satellites are in use continuously.

Communications satellites relay television signals to consumers.

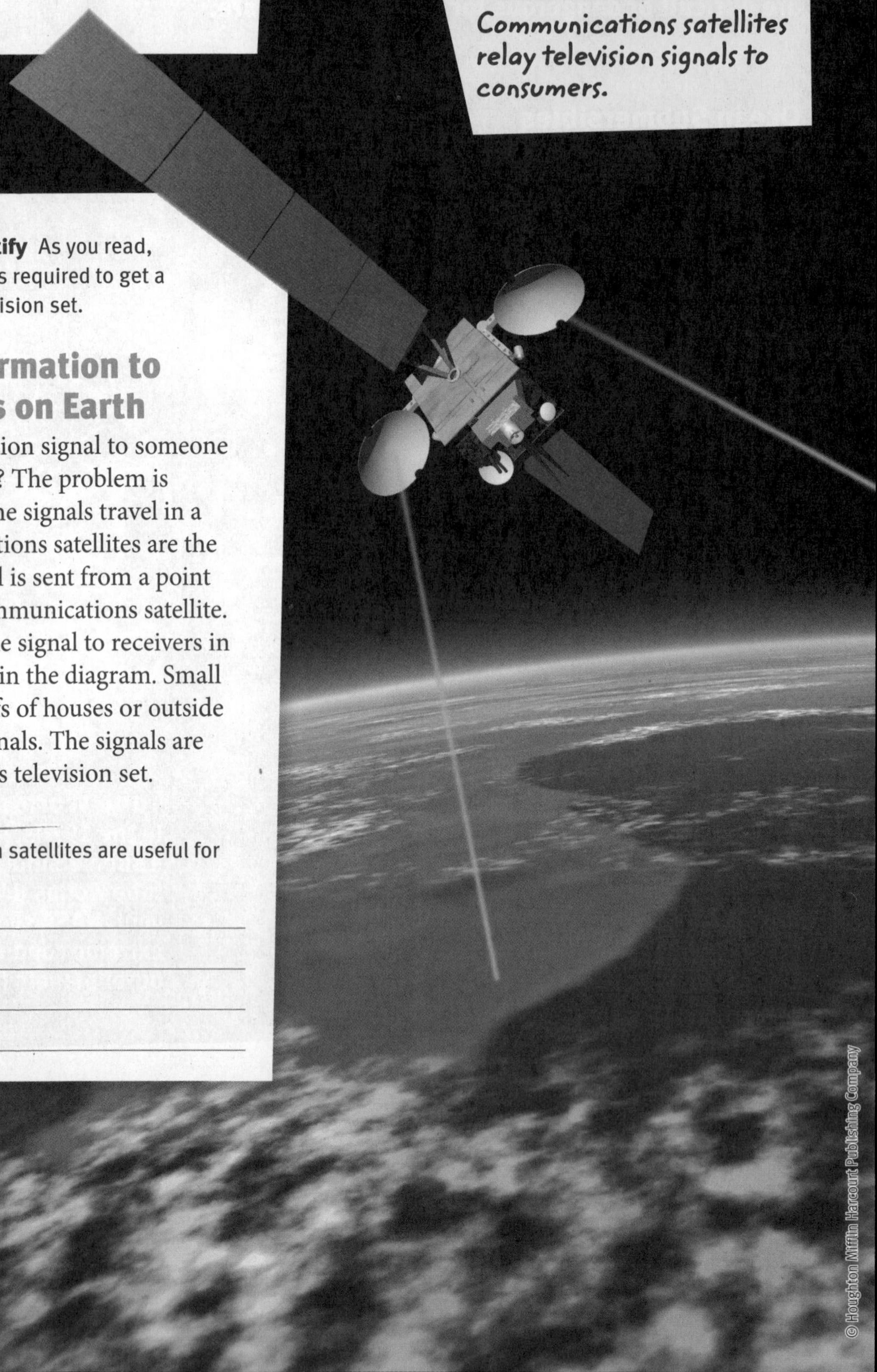

Active Reading **18 Identify** As you read, number the sequence of steps required to get a television signal to your television set.

For Relaying Information to Distant Locations on Earth

How do you send a television signal to someone on the other side of Earth? The problem is that Earth is round, and the signals travel in a straight line. Communications satellites are the answer. A television signal is sent from a point on Earth's surface to a communications satellite. Then the satellite sends the signal to receivers in other locations, as shown in the diagram. Small satellite dishes on the roofs of houses or outside apartments collect the signals. The signals are then sent to the customer's television set.

19 Explain State one reason satellites are useful for communication.

_____

_____

_____

_____

Drawing is not to scale.

20 Apply Write a caption for the image shown here.

_____

_____

_____

_____

For Navigating and Locating

Did you know that satellite technology can actually help keep you from getting lost? The Global Positioning System (GPS) is a network of 24 satellites that orbit Earth. GPS satellites continuously send microwave signals. A GPS receiver receives signals from at least four satellites at one time. Once a GPS receiver on Earth picks up the signals, the technology in the receiver can determine the location of the receiver on Earth's surface. Airplane and boat pilots use GPS for navigation. Many cars now have GPS units that show information on a screen on the dashboard.

GPS satellites send signals that help a receiver calculate its location.

Modern GPS units are small enough to hold in your hand, so you can take them with you and know your location anywhere you go!

Visual Summary

To complete this summary, fill in the blanks with the correct word or phrase. Then, use the key below to check your answers. You can use this page to review the main concepts of the lesson.

Technology for Space Exploration

Humans use crewed technology to travel to and from space.

21 To escape from Earth's gravity, the space shuttle used liquid fuel and

_____

Telescopes in space study different types of electromagnetic radiation.

23 To obtain clearer images, space telescopes orbit above

_____

Artificial satellites provide a wealth of information about Earth.

22 Satellites provide images for military purposes, remote sensing, communications, navigation, and _____

Uncrewed spacecraft can explore distant planets.

24 Examples of uncrewed spacecraft include probes, orbiters, landers, and _____

Answers: 21 solid rocket boosters; 22 weather; 23 Earth's atmosphere; 24 rovers

25 **Provide** Give examples of the kind of information scientists can obtain from each type of uncrewed spacecraft.

Lesson Review

Vocabulary

Circle the term that best completes the following sentences.

1 A *rocket / space shuttle* is a reusable crewed spacecraft.

2 A(n) *lander / orbiter* is a kind of artificial satellite.

3 A(n) *orbiter / rover* often has mechanical arms to gather rock samples.

4 A(n) *orbiter / probe* is more suited to the long-term study of a planet or moon.

5 A *rocket / space shuttle* had detachable capsules that contained the crew.

Key Concepts

6 List Give an example of how satellites are used for communication.

_____

_____

7 Explain Why is most space exploration accomplished with spacecraft that do not have crews on board?

_____

_____

_____

8 Apply How could you benefit from using a GPS unit in your daily life?

_____

_____

_____

9 Explain What is one advantage of using an orbiter to study objects in space?

_____

_____

_____

Critical Thinking

Use the diagram to answer the following questions.

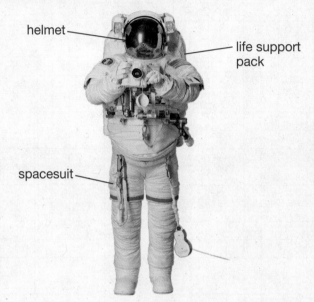

helmet

life support pack

spacesuit

10 Identify Which spacesuit feature provides oxygen to an astronaut?

_____

11 Infer How is the spacesuit designed to protect the astronaut outside of a spacecraft?

_____

_____

_____

12 Infer Why do you think it's important to map a planet's surface before planning a lander mission?

_____

_____

_____

13 Conclude Could a lander be used to study the surface of Saturn? Explain.

_____

_____

_____

My Notes

Testing and Modifying Theories

When scientists develop a theory, they use experiments to investigate the theory. The results of experiments can support or disprove theories. If the results of several experiments do not support a theory, it may be modified.

Tutorial

Read below about the Tomatosphere Project to find out more about how theories are tested and modified. This project exposes tomato seeds to simulated Martian conditions to observe later seed germination.

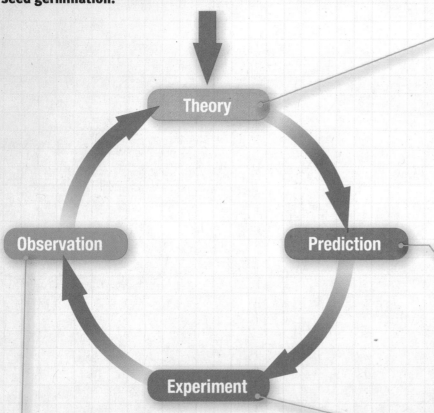

A theory is created/ modified.
Sometimes, two well-supported theories explain a single phenomenon. A theory might be modified based on new data. Scientists can figure out how to supply long-term space missions with food, water, oxygen, and other life-support needs.

A prediction is made.
Predictions are based on prior knowledge. Scientists might predict that if tomato seeds are exposed to Martian conditions, they will still be able to germinate and grow into healthy, fruit-bearing plants.

Observations are made.
Scientists evaluate their observations to see whether or not the results support their hypothesis. If any data disprove the original prediction, scientists may have to modify their theory. The results of the blind studies are gathered and analyzed to see whether exposure to harsh conditions affected the germination of the seeds.

Experiments are done.
Setting up the proper scientific procedure to test the prediction is important. In the Tomatosphere Project, a set of exposed seeds, along with a control group of regular seeds, are planted in thousands of classrooms. At least 20 of each type were planted, to ensure a large enough sample size. The type of seeds were not revealed, as part of a blind study.

You Try It!

Two scientists describe theories that try to explain the motion of galaxies. Use the information provided to answer the questions that follow.

Background

Any objects that have mass, such as Earth and you, exert a gravitational force that pulls them toward each other. An unexpected motion of an object in space, such as a galaxy, could be the result of an unseen object pulling on it. Scientists use electromagnetic radiation, such as visible, infrared, and ultraviolet light, to detect and study visible matter. However, dark matter is a hypothetical material that does not give off electromagnetic radiation that we can detect.

Scientist A

There is more dark matter than visible matter in galaxies. There is just too little visible matter to exert the force that would explain how the galaxies move. The additional force exerted by dark matter would explain the motion we see without having to change our understanding of gravitational force.

Scientist B

We must change our understanding of gravitational force. The farther away from the center of a galaxy you go, the stronger (not weaker) the gravitational force becomes. With this change, the amount of visible matter is enough to explain how the galaxies move. Dark matter is not needed.

1 Predicting Outcomes How would proof that dark matter exists affect each scientist's theory?

_____

_____

_____

_____

2 Predicting Outcomes If experiments fail to detect dark matter, does Scientist A's theory need to be modified? Explain why.

_____

_____

_____

_____

3 Making Inferences What evidence would require both scientists to modify their theories?

_____

_____

_____

_____

Take It Home

Using the Internet, research a scientific theory that has been reproduced in two different experiments. Write a short report that explains how the observations helped develop the theory. How else could this theory could be investigated?

History of Space Exploration

ESSENTIAL QUESTION

What are some milestones of space exploration?

By the end of this lesson, you should understand some of the achievements of space exploration.

In 1993, astronauts walked in space to repair the damaged Hubble Space Telescope.

Virginia Science Standards of Learning

6.8 The student will investigate and understand the organization of the solar system and the interactions among the various bodies that comprise it. Key concepts include:

6.8.i the history and technology of space exploration.

Engage Your Brain

1 Describe Write a word beginning with each letter of the acronym NASA that describes space exploration.

N _____

A _____

S _____

A _____

2 Describe Write your own caption to this photo.

Cape Canaveral, 1961

_____

_____

_____

Active Reading

3 Apply Use context clues to write your own definition for the word *challenge*.

Example sentence
Visiting other planets is a <u>challenge</u> for humans given their great distances from Earth.

challenge:

_____

_____

Vocabulary Term

- **NASA**

4 Identify As you read, place a question mark next to any words that you don't understand. When you finish reading the lesson, go back and review the text that you marked. If the information is still confusing, consult a classmate or a teacher.

How did space exploration begin?

Have you ever looked into the night sky and wondered what exists beyond Earth? If so, you are not alone. People have been curious about space since ancient times. This curiosity and the desire to understand the unknown paved the way for space exploration.

In October of 1957, the Soviet Union launched the first satellite, *Sputnik I*, into low Earth orbit. Though it was a sphere only 585 mm in diameter that contained a 3.5 kg radio transmitter, *Sputnik I* was the first step in space exploration beyond Earth. It was the start of the "Space Age."

The United States clearly understood the advantages of placing technology in space. In response to the Soviet launch of *Sputnik I*, the U.S. launched its first satellite, *Explorer I*, on January 31, 1958. This started what became known as the Space Race between the two nations, which would continue for several decades. In the same year, the National Aeronautics and Space Administration, or **NASA**, was formed. Its purpose was to head up a program of research and development for the "conquest of space."

📖 **Active Reading**

5 Identify As you read, underline the four words that make up the acronym NASA.

6 Infer Why might people continue to pursue space exploration in the future?

_____

_____

_____

_____

1970

1960

1950

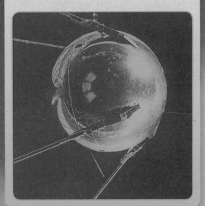

1957: The Space Age began when the Soviet Union launched the first artificial satellite, *Sputnik I*, into low Earth orbit.

1961: The first human to orbit Earth was cosmonaut Yuri A. Gagarin of the Soviet Union, shown below. In the same year, Alan Shepard became the first American in space.

1961–1966: Mission control monitors a Gemini space flight below. During this period, projects Mercury and Gemini focused on launching spacecraft that would prepare for journeys to the moon.

The space shuttle **Atlantis** heads into orbit around Earth.

2010

1998–present: Numerous countries have participated in the construction and use of the *International Space Station*, a long-term research laboratory that orbits Earth.

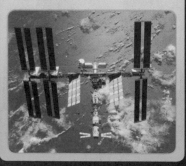

2000

1990

1981: Shuttle flights began in 1981. The space shuttle launched and retrieved satellites from Earth orbit. The space shuttle later flew to the *International Space Station*.

1980

1971: *Salyut 1*, the world's first space station, was launched into orbit by the Soviet Union. Its first crew arrived in the *Soyuz 11* spacecraft and remained on board for 24 days.

1968–1972: Six missions to the moon carried three astronauts each. The first moon landing was *Apollo 11* in 1969. The last moon landing was *Apollo 17* in 1972. A total of 12 astronauts walked on the moon.

Visualize It!

7 Interpret How has space exploration changed over time?

_____

_____

_____

_____

From Earth to the Moon

Alan Shepard prepares for launch in 1961.

Astronauts emerge from the **Gemini 8** capsule after splashdown in 1966.

How have people explored space?

It was not until the 1960s that the first rockets capable of launching space capsules were built and tested. All that was needed to explore space was to place astronauts inside these capsules.

By Using Suborbital Crewed Exploration

Suborbital crewed spacecraft do not orbit Earth because they do not reach the required speed and altitude. So, these flights spend only a very short time in space. The first crewed suborbital spaceflight missions were NASA's Mercury project in 1961. On May 5, 1961, a Redstone rocket launched astronaut Alan B. Shepard, Jr., aboard a capsule called *Freedom 7*. Shepard flew safely for 15 minutes before returning to Earth. The second suborbital flight, which took place on July 21, 1961, was that of astronaut Virgil I. Grissom. Although the capsule sank shortly after splashdown in the Atlantic Ocean, Grissom was rescued safely.

By Using Orbital Crewed Exploration

Orbital crewed spacecraft completely orbit Earth. The first crewed orbital space flight was made on April 12, 1961, by Soviet air force pilot Yuri A. Gagarin (guh•GAR•in) aboard *Vostok 1*. Gagarin orbited Earth for 108 minutes before parachuting safely to Earth. On July 21, 1961, John H. Glenn, Jr., observed Earth from space as he became the first American to orbit Earth. Glenn completed three orbits of Earth in a little less than five hours. On June 16, 1963, cosmonaut Valentina V. Tereshkova became the first woman in space. She orbited Earth 48 times over a three-day period.

Meanwhile, the United States was developing plans for a two-person, crewed Gemini program. Ten crewed Gemini missions would follow. One goal of the Gemini program was to see if astronauts could spend longer periods of time in space. The Soviet Union responded with their own multiperson spaceflights as part of their existing Vostok program. Another milestone took place on March 18, 1965, when Soviet cosmonaut Alexei A. Leonov performed the first walk in space. The first American to walk in space was Edward H. White II on June 3, 1965.

8 Compare How are suborbital and orbital space exploration alike and different?

_____

_____

Valentina Tereshkova of the Soviet Union became the first woman in space in 1963.

By Landing on the Moon

The race to the moon began in the 1960s. On September 12, 1962, President John F. Kennedy committed the United States to "landing a man on the moon and returning him safely to Earth" before the decade ended. The key requirement for a successful moon landing is to travel fast enough to escape Earth's gravity and slow enough to land safely on the moon's surface.

The United States would be the only nation to send astronauts to the moon. Six moon landings took place during the Apollo program of the late 1960s and early 1970s. In 1969, the *Apollo 11* spacecraft took astronauts Neil Armstrong, Edwin "Buzz" Aldrin, and Michael Collins to the moon. While Collins orbited the moon in the lunar spacecraft, Armstrong and Aldrin descended to the moon's surface in the lunar module, named the *Eagle*. The *Eagle* landed in the Sea of Tranquility on July 20, 1969. Millions of people heard Armstrong's breathtaking transmission from the lunar surface, "Tranquility Base here. The *Eagle* has landed." Soon after, Neil Armstrong became the first person to set foot on the moon's surface. Six of the 11 Apollo missions landed on the moon. In total, 12 astronauts walked on the moon.

9 Infer Why was landing on the moon such an important moment in American history?

_____

_____

_____

Visualize It!

10 Interpret What are some requirements for astronauts in order to explore the moon?

_____

_____

_____

_____

Apollo 17 astronauts explored 34 km (21 miles) of the lunar surface in the lunar rover in December of 1972.

Where have people lived and worked in space?

Active Reading 11 **Assess** As you read, underline different uses of space shuttle technology.

As you might imagine, rocket technology is potentially dangerous. Rockets are also expensive, considering that they cannot be reused. Beginning in the 1970s, NASA made plans to build spacecraft that were not only habitable but also reusable.

In Space Shuttles

Space shuttles were crewed space vehicles that lifted off with the aid of rocket boosters and landed like airplanes. Both the space shuttle and its rocket boosters were reusable. Space shuttles orbited Earth while in space. Missions aboard shuttles were an important way to gather data, launch satellites, and transport materials. Space shuttles also docked with the *International Space Station*.

Missions using space shuttles began with the launch of the shuttle *Columbia* in 1981. Until 2011, six shuttles—*Enterprise, Columbia, Challenger, Discovery, Atlantis,* and *Endeavour*—completed a total of more than 100 missions. The *Challenger* and its crew were lost when the shuttle broke apart minutes after liftoff in 1986. An accident also led to the fatal explosion of the *Columbia* in 2003.

Space shuttles carrying supplies have traveled to and docked with the **International Space Station.**

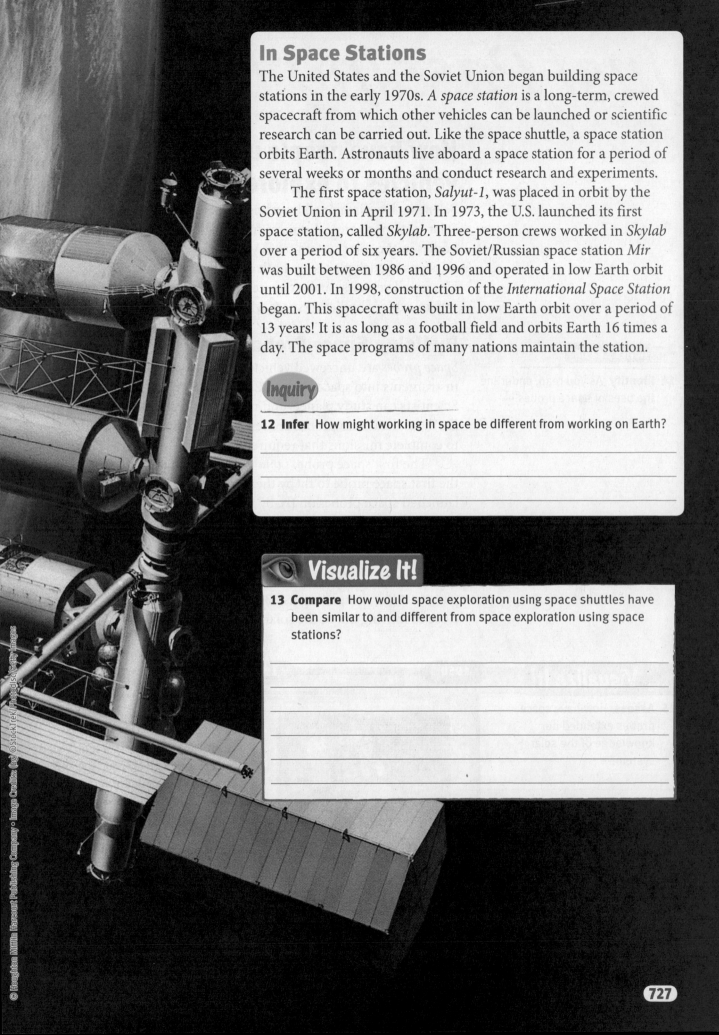

In Space Stations

The United States and the Soviet Union began building space stations in the early 1970s. *A space station* is a long-term, crewed spacecraft from which other vehicles can be launched or scientific research can be carried out. Like the space shuttle, a space station orbits Earth. Astronauts live aboard a space station for a period of several weeks or months and conduct research and experiments.

The first space station, *Salyut-1*, was placed in orbit by the Soviet Union in April 1971. In 1973, the U.S. launched its first space station, called *Skylab*. Three-person crews worked in *Skylab* over a period of six years. The Soviet/Russian space station *Mir* was built between 1986 and 1996 and operated in low Earth orbit until 2001. In 1998, construction of the *International Space Station* began. This spacecraft was built in low Earth orbit over a period of 13 years! It is as long as a football field and orbits Earth 16 times a day. The space programs of many nations maintain the station.

Inquiry

12 Infer How might working in space be different from working on Earth?

_____

_____

_____

Visualize It!

13 Compare How would space exploration using space shuttles have been similar to and different from space exploration using space stations?

_____

_____

_____

_____

_____

_____

Just Passing By

How have people used uncrewed vehicles to explore space?

Scientists have imagined traveling to planets, moons, and even solar systems at great distances from Earth. But reaching other bodies in the solar system takes years or even decades. Crewed missions to such places are both difficult and dangerous. Uncrewed vehicles, such as space probes and orbiters, are a safe way to explore bodies in space without using people.

By Using Space Probes

Space probes are uncrewed vehicles that carry scientific instruments into space beyond Earth's orbit to collect data. Scientists can study planets and moons at great distances from Earth, as data from probes are sent to Earth. Space probes are used to complete missions that require years of travel time in space.

The first space probe, *Luna 1*, was launched in 1959. It was the first space probe to fly by the moon. Since then, scientists have launched space probes on fly-by missions to Mercury and Venus. Some space probes were designed to land on distant planets, such as the landings of *Viking 1* and *Viking 2* on Mars in 1976. Other space probes have been used to explore the far reaches of the solar system. In 1977, *Voyager 2* was launched to explore the gas giant planets. After completing its 33-year mission, the probe is now close to moving out of the solar system and into interstellar space.

🐟 Active Reading

14 Identify As you read, underline the uses of space probes.

👁 Visualize It!

15 Assess How have space probes extended our knowledge of the solar system?

_____

_____

_____

_____

_____

_____

_____

1950　　　　　1960　　　　　1970

In 1962, *Mariner 2* successfully passed within 35,000 km of Venus and returned data from the planet. Here, technicians attach solar panels that powered the probe.

In 1972, *Pioneer 10* was the first space probe to travel through the asteroid belt and make observations of Jupiter.

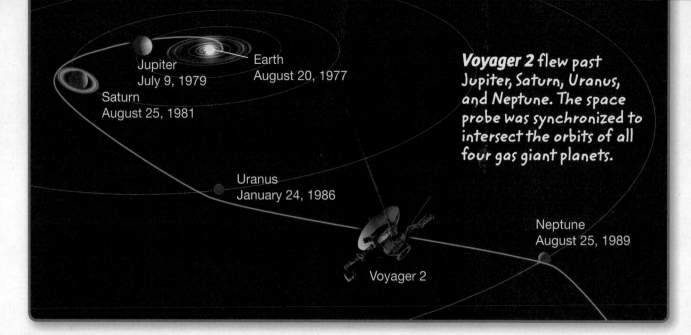

Jupiter
July 9, 1979

Earth
August 20, 1977

Saturn
August 25, 1981

Uranus
January 24, 1986

Voyager 2 flew past Jupiter, Saturn, Uranus, and Neptune. The space probe was synchronized to intersect the orbits of all four gas giant planets.

Neptune
August 25, 1989

Voyager 2

By Using Orbiters

An *orbiter* is a spacecraft that travels to a planet and goes into orbit around it. Several orbiters have explored the planetary features of Mars. The first of these orbiters, *Mars Odyssey* (AHD•ih•see), was launched in 2001. It entered the orbit of Mars after a seven-month journey through space. Two of the missions of the *Mars Odyssey* are to make maps of the Martian surface and to collect data about the chemical makeup of the planet. It was still in service as of 2011.

Launched in 2003, the European Space Agency's *Mars Express* is being used to look for signs of water on Mars. It has also played a role in mapping the surface of Mars and studying the composition of the planet's atmosphere. In 2006, NASA's *Mars Reconnaissance Orbiter* arrived at Mars. It has the most powerful camera ever sent to view another planet. The camera can be used to guide future spacecraft to make precise landings on the Martian surface.

Think Outside the Book

16 **Research** Create a timeline that shows solar-system exploration since 1957. Your timeline should illustrate advances in technology used for space exploration. Share your timeline with the class, and discuss technologies that have made advances in solar-system exploration possible.

1980   1990   2000   2010

Space probe *Galileo* was deployed from the space shuttle *Atlantis* in 1989 to study Jupiter and its moons. It flew by Jupiter in 1995.

In 1997, the *Cassini-Huygens* space probe was launched to study the planet Saturn and its moons, including Enceladus and Titan.

Comet Temple 1 was the target of the *Deep Impact* space probe, which released an impactor into the comet in 2005 to study the composition of its interior.

This photograph from 1958 shows scientists examining the prototype for **Explorer I**, the first United States satellite in space.

© Houghton Mifflin Harcourt Publishing Company • Image Credits: (t) ©Phil Burchman/Archive Photos/Getty Images; (bl) ©Keystone/Getty Images; (br) ©NASA/Science Photo Library

By Using Landers and Rovers

Imagine being able to view a planet's surface from Earth. Robotic exploration on the surface of planets and other bodies in space is done by using landers. A *lander* is designed to land on the surface of a planet and send data back to Earth. A *rover* is a mobile vehicle that is used to physically explore the surface by moving about. The chief advantage of landers and rovers is that they can conduct experiments on soil and rocks. They can also directly record surface conditions, such as temperature and wind flow.

The *Mars Pathfinder*, a lander launched in 1996, placed the Mars rover called *Sojourner* on the planet's surface in 1997. In 2003, NASA sent two more rovers, called *Spirit* and *Opportunity*, to explore Mars. The rovers searched the Martian surface for water and evidence of environments that could possibly support life.

Active Reading

17 List As you read, underline the advantages of using landers and rovers in the exploration of a planet's surface.

Visualize It!

18 Assess How have we learned about Mars from landers and rovers?

_____
_____
_____
_____
_____
_____
_____
_____

1950   1960   1970

In 1962, technicians joined the *Telstar* satellite to a Delta rocket for launch. *Telstar* was the first satellite to transmit TV signals.

Viking 2 landed on Mars in 1976 and took more than 16,000 images of the Martian surface. The lander stopped working in 1978.

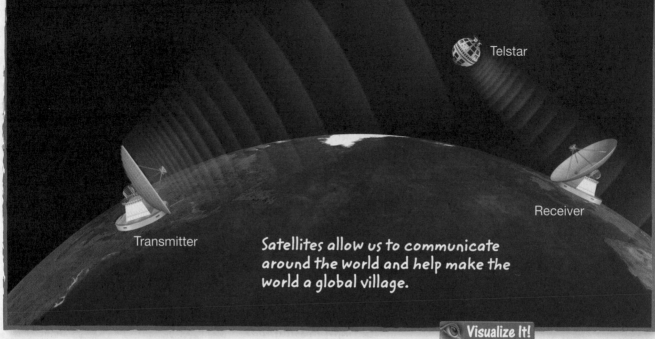

Telstar

Receiver

Transmitter

Satellites allow us to communicate around the world and help make the world a global village.

With Artificial Satellites

When you turn on a TV or a cell phone, a satellite high in the atmosphere often makes this communication possible. An *artificial satellite* is any human-made object placed in orbit around a body in space. Satellites orbit Earth at high speeds. Each satellite has a unique function such as collecting weather data, relaying TV and radio signals, assisting in navigation, and studying Earth's surface.

The *Echo I* satellite was one of the very first communication satellites. It was launched by the United States in 1960. In that same year, the first weather satellite was launched. It carried a video camera to record observations of Earth's atmosphere. A system of orbiting global navigation satellites has been operated by the U.S. since 1978. These satellite systems are used to determine precise locations on Earth. Hundreds of active satellites orbit Earth.

Visualize It!

19 Infer How do satellites transmit data to Earth?

_____

_____

_____

_____

_____

_____

1980   1990   2000   2010

The *Mars Sojourner* lander used an x-ray spectrometer to analyze the Martian surface in 1996.

The *Mars Exploration Rovers Spirit* and *Opportunity* explored opposite sides of the Martian surface in 2004.

NOAA (National Oceanic and Atmospheric Administration) prepared for the launch of a polar orbiter weather satellite in 2009.

Visual Summary

To complete this summary, check the box that indicates true or false. Then, use the key below to check your answers. You can use this page to review the main concepts of the lesson.

History of Space Exploration

Crewed orbital space exploration takes place in a piloted spacecraft that orbits Earth or travels to the moon.

20   T   F   □ □   The first crewed orbital spaceflight mission took place aboard NASA's project Gemini in 1961.

Space probes are uncrewed vehicles that carry scientific instruments into space beyond Earth's orbit to collect data.

21   T   F   □ □   Space probes can travel on the surface of a planet.

A space station is a long-term orbiting crewed spacecraft from which other vehicles can be launched or scientific research can be carried out.

22   T   F   □ □   Space stations are a place where humans can live their daily lives, such as eating, sleeping, and working.

Answers: 20 F; 21 F; 22 T

23 Compare What are some advantages and disadvantages of crewed and uncrewed missions?

Lesson Review

Vocabulary

Fill in the blank with the term that best completes the following sentences.

1 A/An _____ is a human-made object that is placed in orbit around a body in space.

2 _____ is a government agency that runs the space program in the United States.

3 A vehicle that is designed to move about and collect data from the surface of a planet is called a _____

Key Concepts

4 List Identify four ways in which people can directly explore space.

_____

_____

_____

_____

5 Identify What are five ways in which people can explore and study space without physically going there?

_____

_____

_____

_____

_____

6 Summarize Describe three achievements in space exploration that involved the United States.

_____

_____

_____

_____

_____

_____

Critical Thinking

Use the image to answer the following question.

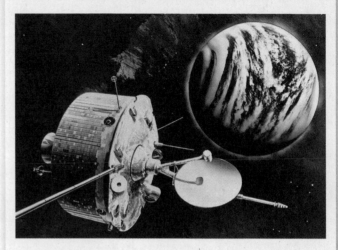

7 Infer Is this an image of an orbiter or a rover? How do you know?

_____

_____

_____

8 Relate How is preparing for a space mission similar to planning for a camping trip? How is it different?

_____

_____

_____

_____

_____

_____

_____

_____

9 Assess What type of technology would you want to use to study the gas giant plants?

_____

_____

_____

_____

_____

My Notes

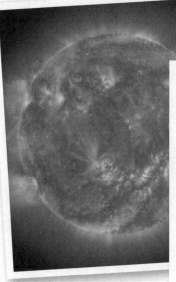

Lesson 1

ESSENTIAL QUESTION
What can we learn from space images?

Describe ways of collecting information from space, and analyze how different wavelengths of the electromagnetic spectrum provide different information.

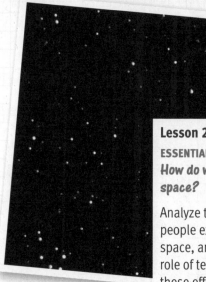

Lesson 2

ESSENTIAL QUESTION
How do we explore space?

Analyze the ways people explore outer space, and assess the role of technology in these efforts.

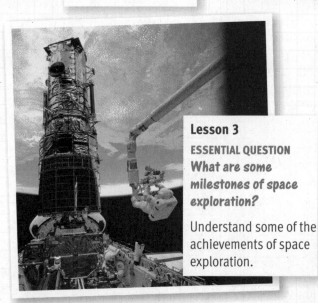

Lesson 3

ESSENTIAL QUESTION
What are some milestones of space exploration?

Understand some of the achievements of space exploration.

Connect ESSENTIAL QUESTIONS
Lessons 1 and 3

1 Synthesize Explain how electromagnetic radiation can be dangerous to humans who are exploring space.

_____

_____

_____

_____

Think Outside the Book

2 Synthesize Choose one of these activities to help synthesize what you have learned in this unit.

☐ Using what you learned in lessons 1 and 2, write a short essay explaining why weather satellites are placed in polar orbits.

☐ Using what you learned in lessons 2 and 3, create a graphic novel to show some of the limitations of human space exploration.

Unit 11 Review

Vocabulary

Fill in each blank with the term that best completes the following sentences.

1 A(n) _____ is any human-made object placed in orbit around a body in space, either with or without a crew.

2 _____ is the United States agency that explores space through crewed and uncrewed missions.

3 The _____ refers to all of the frequencies or wavelengths of electromagnetic radiation.

4 _____ provide information about weather, temperature, land use, and changes on Earth over time.

5 A mobile, uncrewed vehicle that is used to explore the surface of another planet is called a _____.

Key Concepts

Read each question below, and circle the best answer.

6 Satellites in orbit around Earth are used for various purposes. For which one of the following purposes are satellites not used?

A transmitting signals over large distances to remote locations

B monitoring changes in Earth's environment over time

C transporting materials to space stations

D collecting different types of weather data

7 What is the most important reason why astronauts who live on a space station have to exercise every day?

A There is not much else to do, and exercising passes the time.

B It prevents their bones and muscles from weakening.

C Astronauts need to stay in good shape.

D It helps them to sleep better at night.

8 Which one of the following is not an example of technology used in crewed space exploration?

A a space shuttle   **C** a space telescope

B a space station   **D** a rocket

9 Look at the diagram of the electromagnetic spectrum.

The Electromagnetic Spectrum

Wavelength (meters)

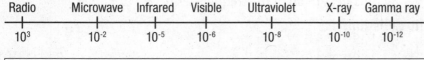
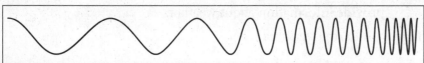

Radio	Microwave	Infrared	Visible	Ultraviolet	X-ray	Gamma ray
10^3	10^{-2}	10^{-5}	10^{-6}	10^{-8}	10^{-10}	10^{-12}

What characteristic determines the different kinds of radiation in the electromagnetic spectrum?

A length of the wave   **C** whether the wave is visible or not

B color   **D** name of the wave

10 Optical telescopes are used to study wavelengths from a certain portion of the electromagnetic spectrum. Which is true of optical telescopes?

A Optical telescopes are used to study objects in space using ultraviolet radiation.

B Optical telescopes are used to receive radio waves from objects in space.

C Optical telescopes are used to study objects in space using infrared radiation.

D Optical telescopes are used to study visible light from objects in space.

11 The chart below lists four waves and their wavelengths.

Wave	Wavelength
Radio	10^3 m
Visible	10^{-6} m
X-ray	10^{-10} m
Gamma ray	10^{-12} m

Which wave will have the highest frequency?

A radio waves   **C** x-rays

B visible waves   **D** gamma rays

12 How are telescopes used in space science?

A Telescopes are used to transmit visible light over long distances.

B Telescopes help in looking at cells.

C Telescopes help to gather data about space for use by astronomers.

D Telescopes are used to communicate over long distances.

Critical Thinking

Answer the following questions in the space provided.

13 Outline a brief history of space exploration, and discuss some problems humans encounter when they explore space.

_____

_____

_____

_____

_____

_____

_____

_____

14 Satellites provide us with various forms of communication.

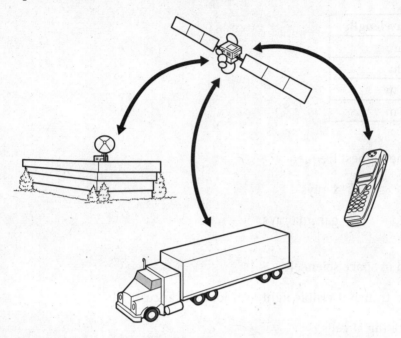

Describe how satellites can aid in communication.

_____

_____

_____

_____

Connect **ESSENTIAL QUESTIONS**
Lessons 1, 2, and 3

Answer the following question in the space provided.

15 Explain the distinction between astronomy and space exploration, and elaborate on the significance of space exploration in our society.

_____

_____

_____

_____

_____

_____

_____

_____

Look It Up!

References

Mineral Properties

Here are five steps to take in mineral identification:

1 Determine the color of the mineral. Is it light-colored, dark-colored, or a specific color?

2 Determine the luster of the mineral. Is it metallic or nonmetallic?

3 Determine the color of any powder left by its streak.

4 Determine the hardness of your mineral. Is it soft, hard, or very hard? Using a glass plate, see if the mineral scratches it.

5 Determine whether your sample has cleavage or any special properties.

TERMS TO KNOW	DEFINITION
adamantine	a nonmetallic luster like that of a diamond
cleavage	how a mineral breaks when subject to stress on a particular plane
luster	the state or quality of shining by reflecting light
streak	the color of a mineral when it is powdered
submetallic	between metallic and nonmetallic in luster
vitreous	glass-like type of luster

Silicate Minerals					
Mineral	Color	Luster	Streak	Hardness	Cleavage and Special Properties
Beryl	deep green, pink, white, bluish green, or yellow	vitreous	white	7.5–8	1 cleavage direction; some varieties fluoresce in ultraviolet light
Chlorite	green	vitreous to pearly	pale green	2–2.5	1 cleavage direction
Garnet	green, red, brown, black	vitreous	white	6.5–7.5	no cleavage
Hornblende	dark green, brown, or black	vitreous	none	5–6	2 cleavage directions
Muscovite	colorless, silvery white, or brown	vitreous or pearly	white	2–2.5	1 cleavage direction
Olivine	olive green, yellow	vitreous	white or none	6.5–7	no cleavage
Orthoclase	colorless, white, pink, or other colors	vitreous	white or none	6	2 cleavage directions
Plagioclase	colorless, white, yellow, pink, green	vitreous	white	6	2 cleavage directions
Quartz	colorless or white; any color when not pure	vitreous or waxy	white or none	7	no cleavage

Nonsilicate Minerals

Mineral	Color	Luster	Streak	Hardness	Cleavage and Special Properties
Native Elements					
Copper	copper-red	metallic	copper-red	2.5–3	no cleavage
Diamond	pale yellow or colorless	adamantine	none	10	4 cleavage directions
Graphite	black to gray	submetallic	black	1–2	1 cleavage direction
Carbonates					
Aragonite	colorless, white, or pale yellow	vitreous	white	3.5–4	2 cleavage directions; reacts with hydrochloric acid
Calcite	colorless or white to tan	vitreous	white	3	3 cleavage directions; reacts with weak acid; double refraction
Halides					
Fluorite	light green, yellow, purple, bluish green, or other colors	vitreous	none	4	4 cleavage directions; some varieties fluoresce
Halite	white	vitreous	white	2.0–2.5	3 cleavage directions
Oxides					
Hematite	reddish brown to black	metallic to earthy	dark red to red-brown	5.6–6.5	no cleavage; magnetic when heated
Magnetite	iron-black	metallic	black	5.5–6.5	no cleavage; magnetic
Sulfates					
Anhydrite	colorless, bluish, or violet	vitreous to pearly	white	3–3.5	3 cleavage directions
Gypsum	white, pink, gray, or colorless	vitreous, pearly, or silky	white	2.0	3 cleavage directions
Sulfides					
Galena	lead-gray	metallic	lead-gray to black	2.5–2.8	3 cleavage directions
Pyrite	brassy yellow	metallic	greenish, brownish, or black	6–6.5	no cleavage

References

Geologic Time Scale

Geologists developed the geologic time scale to represent the 4.6 billion years of Earth's history that have passed since Earth formed. This scale divides Earth's history into blocks of time. The boundaries between these time intervals (shown in millions of years ago, or mya, in the table below), represent major changes in Earth's history. Some boundaries are defined by mass extinctions, major changes in Earth's surface, and/or major changes in Earth's climate.

The four major divisions that encompass the history of life on Earth are Precambrian time, the Paleozoic era, the Mesozoic era, and the Cenozoic era. The largest divisions are eons. **Precambrian time** is made up of the first three eons, over 4 billion years of Earth's history.

The **Paleozoic era** lasted from 542 mya to 251 mya. All major plant groups, except flowering plants, appeared during this era. By the end of the era, reptiles, winged insects, and fishes had also appeared. The largest known mass extinction occurred at the end of this era.

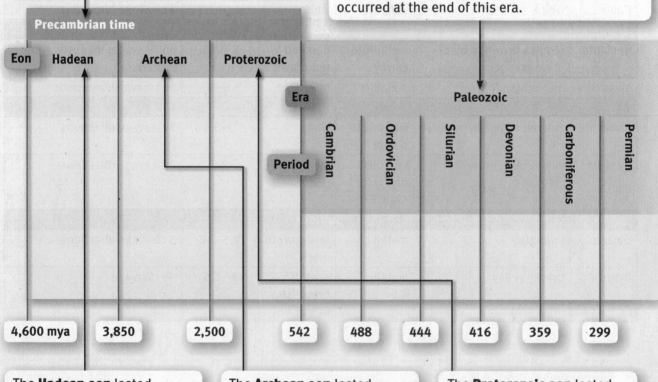

The **Hadean eon** lasted from about 4.6 billion years ago (bya) to 3.85 bya. It is described based on evidence from meteorites and rocks from the moon.

The **Archean eon** lasted from 3.85 bya to 2.5 bya. The earliest rocks from Earth that have been found and dated formed at the start of this eon.

The **Proterozoic eon** lasted from 2.5 bya to 542 mya. The first organisms, which were single-celled organisms, appeared during this eon. These organisms produced so much oxygen that they changed Earth's oceans and Earth's atmosphere.

Divisions of Time

The divisions of time shown here represent major changes in Earth's surface and when life developed and changed significantly on Earth. As new evidence is found, the boundaries of these divisions may shift. The Phanerozoic eon is divided into three eras. The beginning of each of these eras represents a change in the types of organisms that dominated Earth. And each era is commonly characterized by the types of organisms that dominated the era. These eras are divided into periods, and periods are divided into epochs.

The **Mesozoic era** lasted from 251 mya to 65.5 mya. During this era, many kinds of dinosaurs dominated land, and giant lizards swam in the ocean. The first birds, mammals, and flowering plants also appeared during this time. About two-thirds of all land species went extinct at the end of this era.

The **Phanerozoic eon** began 542 mya. We live in this eon.

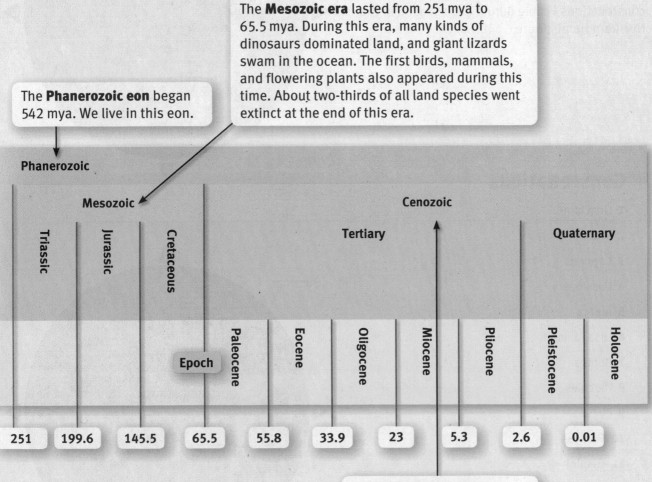

The **Cenozoic era** began 65.5 mya and continues today. Mammals dominate this era. During the Mesozoic era, mammals were small in size but grew much larger during the Cenozoic era. Primates, including humans, appeared during this era.

References

Star Charts for the Northern Hemisphere

A star chart is a map of the stars in the night sky. It shows the names and positions of constellations and major stars. Star charts can be used to identify constellations and even to orient yourself using Polaris, the North Star.

Because Earth moves through space, different constellations are visible at different times of the year. The star charts on these pages show the constellations visible during each season in the Northern Hemisphere.

Spring

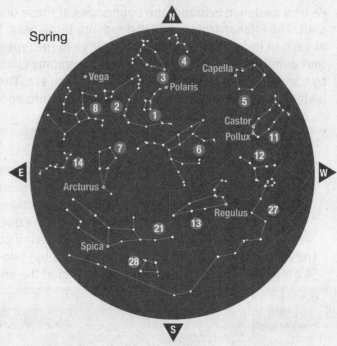

Constellations

1 Ursa Minor
2 Draco
3 Cepheus
4 Cassiopeia
5 Auriga
6 Ursa Major
7 Boötes
8 Hercules
9 Cygnus
10 Perseus
11 Gemini
12 Cancer
13 Leo
14 Serpens
15 Sagitta
16 Pegasus
17 Pisces

Summer

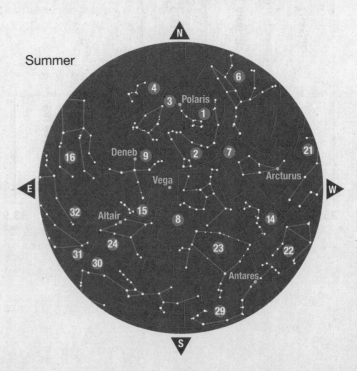

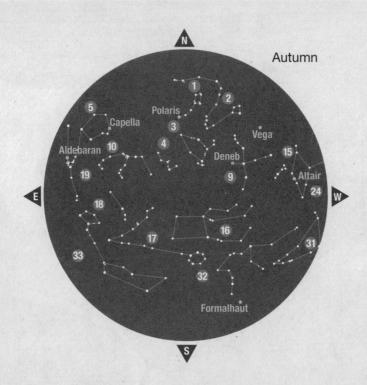

Autumn

Polaris
Capella
Aldebaran
Vega
Deneb
Altair
Formalhaut

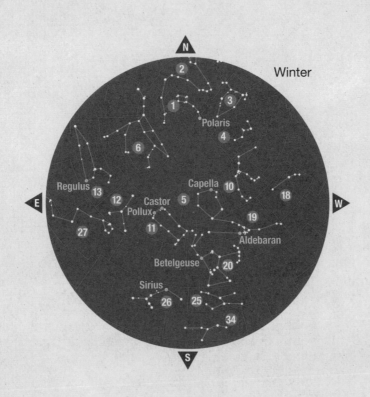

Winter

Polaris
Regulus
Capella
Castor
Pollux
Betelgeuse
Sirius
Aldebaran

Constellations

18 Aries

19 Taurus

20 Orion

21 Virgo

22 Libra

23 Ophiuchus

24 Aquila

25 Lepus

26 Canis Major

27 Hydra

28 Corvus

29 Scorpius

30 Sagittarius

31 Capricornus

32 Aquarius

33 Cetus

34 Columba

World Map

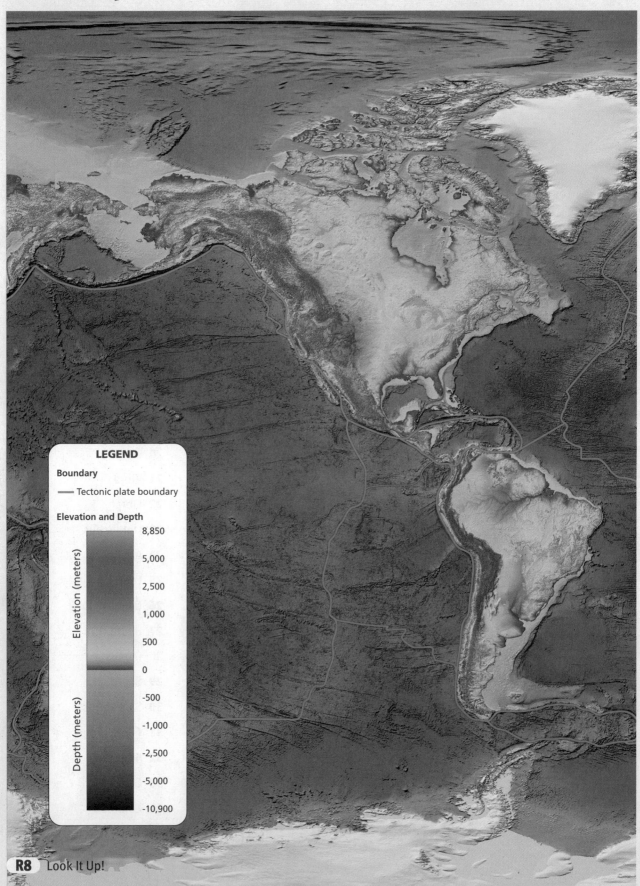

LEGEND

Boundary

—— Tectonic plate boundary

Elevation and Depth

Elevation (meters)

8,850
5,000
2,500
1,000
500
0

Depth (meters)

-500
-1,000
-2,500
-5,000
-10,900

References

Classification of Living Things

Domains and Kingdoms

All organisms belong to one of three domains: Domain Archaea, Domain Bacteria, or Domain Eukarya. Some of the groups within these domains are shown below. (Remember that genus names are italicized.)

Domain Archaea

The organisms in this domain are single-celled prokaryotes, many of which live in extreme environments.

Archaea		
Group	**Example**	**Characteristics**
Methanogens	*Methanococcus*	produce methane gas; can't live in oxygen
Thermophiles	*Sulfolobus*	require sulfur; can't live in oxygen
Halophiles	*Halococcus*	live in very salty environments; most can live in oxygen

Domain Bacteria

Organisms in this domain are single-celled prokaryotes and are found in almost every environment on Earth.

Bacteria		
Group	**Example**	**Characteristics**
Bacilli	*Escherichia*	rod shaped; some bacilli fix nitrogen; some cause disease
Cocci	*Streptococcus*	spherical shaped; some cause disease; can form spores
Spirilla	*Treponema*	spiral shaped; cause diseases such as syphilis and Lyme disease

Domain Eukarya

Organisms in this domain are single-celled or multicellular eukaryotes.

Kingdom Protista Many protists resemble fungi, plants, or animals but are smaller and simpler in structure. Most are single celled.

Protists		
Group	**Example**	**Characteristics**
Sarcodines	*Amoeba*	radiolarians; single-celled consumers
Ciliates	*Paramecium*	single-celled consumers
Flagellates	*Trypanosoma*	single-celled parasites
Sporozoans	*Plasmodium*	single-celled parasites
Euglenas	*Euglena*	single celled; photosynthesize
Diatoms	*Pinnularia*	most are single celled; photosynthesize
Dinoflagellates	*Gymnodinium*	single celled; some photosynthesize
Algae	*Volvox*	single celled or multicellular; photosynthesize
Slime molds	*Physarum*	single celled or multicellular; consumers or decomposers
Water molds	powdery mildew	single celled or multicellular; parasites or decomposers

Kingdom Fungi Most fungi are multicellular. Their cells have thick cell walls. Fungi absorb food from their environment.

Fungi		
Group	**Examples**	**Characteristics**
Zygote fungi	bread mold	spherical zygote produces spores; decomposers
Sac fungi	yeast; morels	saclike spore structure; parasites and decomposers
Club fungi	mushrooms; rusts; smuts	club-shaped spore structure; parasites and decomposers
Lichens	British soldier	a partnership between a fungus and an alga

Kingdom Plantae Plants are multicellular and have cell walls made of cellulose. Plants make their own food through photosynthesis. Plants are classified into divisions instead of phyla.

Plants		
Group	**Examples**	**Characteristics**
Bryophytes	mosses; liverworts	no vascular tissue; reproduce by spores
Club mosses	*Lycopodium;* ground pine	grow in wooded areas; reproduce by spores
Horsetails	rushes	grow in wetland areas; reproduce by spores
Ferns	spleenworts; sensitive fern	large leaves called fronds; reproduce by spores
Conifers	pines; spruces; firs	needlelike leaves; reproduce by seeds made in cones
Cycads	*Zamia*	slow growing; reproduce by seeds made in large cones
Gnetophytes	*Welwitschia*	only three living families; reproduce by seeds
Ginkgoes	*Ginkgo*	only one living species; reproduce by seeds
Angiosperms	all flowering plants	reproduce by seeds made in flowers; fruit

Kingdom Animalia Animals are multicellular. Their cells do not have cell walls. Most animals have specialized tissues and complex organ systems. Animals get food by eating other organisms.

Animals		
Group	**Examples**	**Characteristics**
Sponges	glass sponges	no symmetry or specialized tissues; aquatic
Cnidarians	jellyfish; coral	radial symmetry; aquatic
Flatworms	planaria; tapeworms; flukes	bilateral symmetry; organ systems
Roundworms	*Trichina;* hookworms	bilateral symmetry; organ systems
Annelids	earthworms; leeches	bilateral symmetry; organ systems
Mollusks	snails; octopuses	bilateral symmetry; organ systems
Echinoderms	sea stars; sand dollars	radial symmetry; organ systems
Arthropods	insects; spiders; lobsters	bilateral symmetry; organ systems
Chordates	fish; amphibians; reptiles; birds; mammals	bilateral symmetry; complex organ systems

References

Periodic Table of the Elements

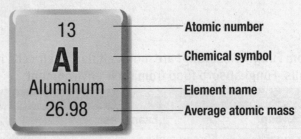

13
Al
Aluminum
26.98

— Atomic number
— Chemical symbol
— Element name
— Average atomic mass

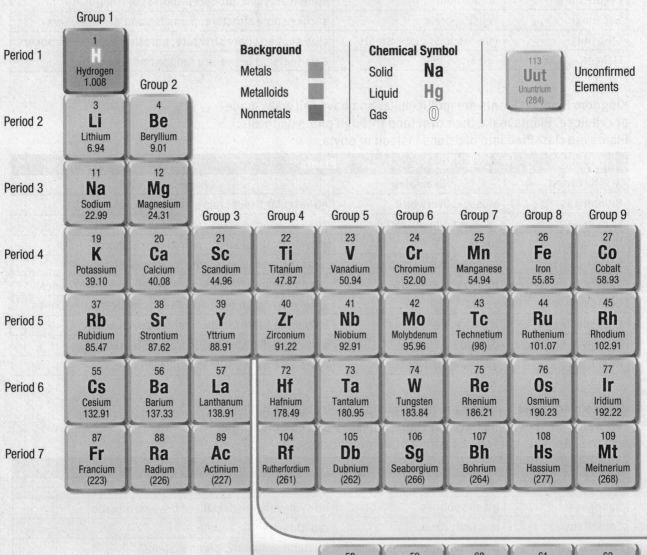

Background	
Metals	
Metalloids	
Nonmetals	

Chemical Symbol	
Solid	**Na**
Liquid	**Hg**
Gas	Ⓞ

113
Uut
Ununtrium
(284)

Unconfirmed Elements

Group 1

Period 1

1
H
Hydrogen
1.008

Group 2

Period 2

3	4
Li	**Be**
Lithium	Beryllium
6.94	9.01

Period 3

11	12
Na	**Mg**
Sodium	Magnesium
22.99	24.31

	Group 3	Group 4	Group 5	Group 6	Group 7	Group 8	Group 9

Period 4

19	20	21	22	23	24	25	26	27
K	**Ca**	**Sc**	**Ti**	**V**	**Cr**	**Mn**	**Fe**	**Co**
Potassium	Calcium	Scandium	Titanium	Vanadium	Chromium	Manganese	Iron	Cobalt
39.10	40.08	44.96	47.87	50.94	52.00	54.94	55.85	58.93

Period 5

37	38	39	40	41	42	43	44	45
Rb	**Sr**	**Y**	**Zr**	**Nb**	**Mo**	**Tc**	**Ru**	**Rh**
Rubidium	Strontium	Yttrium	Zirconium	Niobium	Molybdenum	Technetium	Ruthenium	Rhodium
85.47	87.62	88.91	91.22	92.91	95.96	(98)	101.07	102.91

Period 6

55	56	57	72	73	74	75	76	77
Cs	**Ba**	**La**	**Hf**	**Ta**	**W**	**Re**	**Os**	**Ir**
Cesium	Barium	Lanthanum	Hafnium	Tantalum	Tungsten	Rhenium	Osmium	Iridium
132.91	137.33	138.91	178.49	180.95	183.84	186.21	190.23	192.22

Period 7

87	88	89	104	105	106	107	108	109
Fr	**Ra**	**Ac**	**Rf**	**Db**	**Sg**	**Bh**	**Hs**	**Mt**
Francium	Radium	Actinium	Rutherfordium	Dubnium	Seaborgium	Bohrium	Hassium	Meitnerium
(223)	(226)	(227)	(261)	(262)	(266)	(264)	(277)	(268)

Lanthanides

58	59	60	61	62
Ce	**Pr**	**Nd**	**Pm**	**Sm**
Cerium	Praseodymium	Neodymium	Promethium	Samarium
140.12	140.91	144.24	(145)	150.36

Actinides

90	91	92	93	94
Th	**Pa**	**U**	**Np**	**Pu**
Thorium	Protactinium	Uranium	Neptunium	Plutonium
232.04	231.04	238.03	(237)	(244)

The International Union of Pure and Applied Chemistry (IUPAC) has determined that, because of isotopic variance, the average atomic mass is best represented by a range of values for each of the following elements: hydrogen, lithium, boron, carbon, nitrogen, oxygen, silicon, sulfur, chlorine, and thallium. However, the values in this table are appropriate for everyday calculations.

Group 10	Group 11	Group 12	Group 13	Group 14	Group 15	Group 16	Group 17	Group 18
								2 **He** Helium 4.003
			5 **B** Boron 10.81	6 **C** Carbon 12.01	7 **N** Nitrogen 14.01	8 **O** Oxygen 16.00	9 **F** Fluorine 19.00	10 **Ne** Neon 20.18
			13 **Al** Aluminum 26.98	14 **Si** Silicon 28.09	15 **P** Phosphorus 30.97	16 **S** Sulfur 32.06	17 **Cl** Chlorine 35.45	18 **Ar** Argon 39.95
28 **Ni** Nickel 58.69	29 **Cu** Copper 63.55	30 **Zn** Zinc 65.38	31 **Ga** Gallium 69.72	32 **Ge** Germanium 72.63	33 **As** Arsenic 74.92	34 **Se** Selenium 78.96	35 **Br** Bromine 79.90	36 **Kr** Krypton 83.80
46 **Pd** Palladium 106.42	47 **Ag** Silver 107.87	48 **Cd** Cadmium 112.41	49 **In** Indium 114.82	50 **Sn** Tin 118.71	51 **Sb** Antimony 121.76	52 **Te** Tellurium 127.60	53 **I** Iodine 126.90	54 **Xe** Xenon 131.29
78 **Pt** Platinum 195.08	79 **Au** Gold 196.97	80 **Hg** Mercury 200.59	81 **Tl** Thallium 204.38	82 **Pb** Lead 207.2	83 **Bi** Bismuth 208.98	84 **Po** Polonium (209)	85 **At** Astatine (210)	86 **Rn** Radon (222)
110 **Ds** Darmstadtium (271)	111 **Rg** Roentgenium (272)	112 **Cn** Copernicium (285)	113 **Uut** Ununtrium (284)	114 **Uuq** Ununquadium (289)	115 **Uup** Ununpentium (288)	116 **Uuh** Ununhexium (292)	117 **Uus** Ununseptium (294)	118 **Uuo** Ununoctium (294)

63 **Eu** Europium 151.96	64 **Gd** Gadolinium 157.25	65 **Tb** Terbium 158.93	66 **Dy** Dysprosium 162.50	67 **Ho** Holmium 164.93	68 **Er** Erbium 167.26	69 **Tm** Thulium 168.93	70 **Yb** Ytterbium 173.05	71 **Lu** Lutetium 174.97
95 **Am** Americium (243)	96 **Cm** Curium (247)	97 **Bk** Berkelium (247)	98 **Cf** Californium (251)	99 **Es** Einsteinium (252)	100 **Fm** Fermium (257)	101 **Md** Mendelevium (258)	102 **No** Nobelium (259)	103 **Lr** Lawrencium (262)

References

Physical Science Refresher

Atoms and Elements

Every object in the universe is made of matter. **Matter** is anything that takes up space and has mass. All matter is made of atoms. An **atom** is the smallest particle into which an element can be divided and still be the same element. An **element**, in turn, is a substance that cannot be broken down into simpler substances by chemical means. Each element consists of only one kind of atom. An element may be made of many atoms, but they are all the same kind of atom.

Atomic Structure

Atoms are made of smaller particles called **electrons**, **protons**, and **neutrons**. Electrons have a negative electric charge, protons have a positive charge, and neutrons have no electric charge. Together, protons and neutrons form the **nucleus**, or small dense center, of an atom. Because protons are positively charged and neutrons are neutral, the nucleus has a positive charge. Electrons move within an area around the nucleus called the **electron cloud**. Electrons move so quickly that scientists cannot determine their exact speeds and positions at the same time.

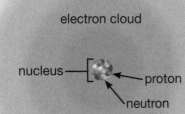

electron cloud

nucleus — proton

neutron

Atomic Number

To help distinguish one element from another, scientists use the atomic numbers of atoms. The **atomic number** is the number of protons in the nucleus of an atom. The atoms of a certain element always have the same number of protons.

When atoms have an equal number of protons and electrons, they are uncharged, or electrically neutral. The atomic number equals the number of electrons in an uncharged atom. The number of neutrons, however, can vary for a given element. Atoms of the same element that have different numbers of neutrons are called **isotopes**.

Periodic Table of the Elements

In the periodic table, each element in the table is in a separate box. And the elements are arranged from left to right in order of increasing atomic number. That is, an uncharged atom of each element has one more electron and one more proton than an uncharged atom of the element to its left. Each horizontal row of the table is called a **period**. Changes in chemical properties of elements across a period correspond to changes in the electron arrangements of their atoms.

Each vertical column of the table is known as a **group.** A group lists elements with similar physical and chemical properties. For this reason, a group is also sometimes called a family. The elements in a group have similar properties because their atoms have the same number of electrons in their outer energy level. For example, the elements helium, neon, argon, krypton, xenon, and radon all have similar properties and are known as the noble gases.

Molecules and Compounds

When two or more elements join chemically, they form a **compound**. A compound is a new substance with properties different from those of the elements that compose it. For example, water, H_2O, is a compound formed when hydrogen (H) and oxygen (O) combine. The smallest complete unit of a compound that has the properties of that compound is called a **molecule**. A chemical formula indicates the elements in a compound. It also indicates the relative number of atoms of each element in the compound. The chemical formula for water is H_2O. So each water molecule consists of two atoms of hydrogen and one atom of oxygen. The subscript number after the symbol for an element shows how many atoms of that element are in a single molecule of the compound.

Chemical Equations

A chemical reaction occurs when a chemical change takes place. A chemical equation describes a chemical reaction using chemical formulas. The equation indicates the substances that react and the substances that are produced. For example, when carbon and oxygen combine, they can form carbon dioxide, shown in the following equation: $C + O_2 \longrightarrow CO_2$

Acids, Bases, and pH

An **ion** is an atom or group of chemically bonded atoms that has an electric charge because it has lost or gained one or more electrons. When an acid, such as hydrochloric acid, HCl, is mixed with water, it separates into ions. An **acid** is a compound that produces hydrogen ions, H^+, in water. The hydrogen ions then combine with a water molecule to form a hydronium ion, H_3O^+. A **base**, on the other hand, is a substance that produces hydroxide ions, OH^-, in water.

To determine whether a solution is acidic or basic, scientists use pH. The **pH** of a solution is a measure of the hydronium ion concentration in a solution. The pH scale ranges from 0 to 14. Acids have a pH that is less than 7. The lower the number, the more acidic the solution. The middle point, pH = 7, is neutral, neither acidic nor basic. Bases have a pH that is greater than 7. The higher the number is, the more basic the solution.

The pH of Some Common Materials

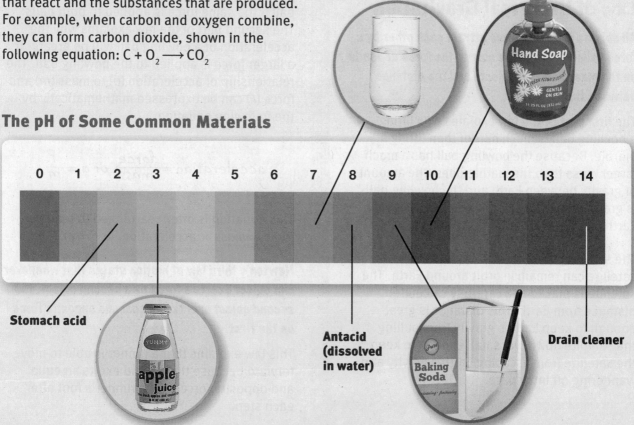

0 1 2 3 4 5 6 7 8 9 10 11 12 13 14

Stomach acid

Antacid (dissolved in water)

Drain cleaner

Hand Soap
GENTLE ON SKIN

apple juice

Baking Soda

References

Physical Laws and Useful Equations

Law of Conservation of Mass

Mass cannot be created or destroyed during ordinary chemical or physical changes.

The total mass in a closed system is always the same no matter how many physical changes or chemical reactions occur.

Law of Conservation of Energy

Energy can be neither created nor destroyed.

The total amount of energy in a closed system is always the same. Energy can be changed from one form to another, but all of the different forms of energy in a system always add up to the same total amount of energy, no matter how many energy conversions occur.

Law of Universal Gravitation

All objects in the universe attract each other by a force called gravity. The size of the force depends on the masses of the objects and the distance between the objects.

The first part of the law explains why lifting a bowling ball is much harder than lifting a marble. Because the bowling ball has a much larger mass than the marble does, the amount of gravity between Earth and the bowling ball is greater than the amount of gravity between Earth and the marble.

The second part of the law explains why a satellite can remain in orbit around Earth. The satellite is placed at a carefully calculated distance from Earth. This distance is great enough to keep Earth's gravity from pulling the satellite down, yet small enough to keep the satellite from escaping Earth's gravity and wandering off into space.

Newton's Laws of Motion

Newton's first law of motion states that an object at rest remains at rest and that an object in motion remains in motion at constant speed and in a straight line unless acted on by an unbalanced force.

The first part of the law explains why a football will remain on a tee until it is kicked off or until a gust of wind blows it off. The second part of the law explains why a bike rider will continue moving forward after the bike comes to an abrupt stop. Gravity and the friction of the sidewalk will eventually stop the rider.

Newton's second law of motion states that the acceleration of an object depends on the mass of the object and the amount of force applied.

The first part of the law explains why the acceleration of a 4 kg bowling ball will be greater than the acceleration of a 6 kg bowling ball if the same force is applied to both balls. The second part of the law explains why the acceleration of a bowling ball will be greater if a larger force is applied to the bowling ball. The relationship of acceleration (a) to mass (m) and force (F) can be expressed mathematically by the following equation:

$$acceleration = \frac{force}{mass}, \text{ or } a = \frac{F}{m}$$

This equation is often rearranged to read $force = mass \times acceleration$, or $F = m \times a$

Newton's third law of motion states that whenever one object exerts a force on a second object, the second object exerts an equal and opposite force on the first.

This law explains that a runner is able to move forward because the ground exerts an equal and opposite force on the runner's foot after each step.

Average Speed

$$\text{average speed} = \frac{\text{total distance}}{\text{total time}}$$

Example:
A bicycle messenger traveled a distance of 136 km in 8 h. What was the messenger's average speed?

$$\frac{136\,km}{8\,h} = 17\,km/h$$

The messenger's average speed was **17 km/h**.

Average Acceleration

$$\text{average acceleration} = \frac{\text{final velocity} - \text{starting velocity}}{\text{time it takes to change velocity}}$$

Example:
Calculate the average acceleration of an Olympic 100 m dash sprinter who reached a velocity of 20 m/s south at the finish line. The race was in a straight line and lasted 10 s.

$$\frac{20\,m/s - 0\,m/s}{10\,s} = 2\,m/s/s$$

The sprinter's average acceleration was **2 m/s/s south**.

Net Force
Forces in the Same Direction

When forces are in the same direction, add the forces together to determine the net force.

Example:
Calculate the net force on a stalled car that is being pushed by two people. One person is pushing with a force of 13 N northwest, and the other person is pushing with a force of 8 N in the same direction.

$$13\,N + 8\,N = 21\,N$$

The net force is **21 N northwest**.

Forces in Opposite Directions

When forces are in opposite directions, subtract the smaller force from the larger force to determine the net force. The net force will be in the direction of the larger force.

Example:
Calculate the net force on a rope that is being pulled on each end. One person is pulling on one end of the rope with a force of 12 N south. Another person is pulling on the opposite end of the rope with a force of 7 N north.

$$12\,N - 7\,N = 5\,N$$

The net force is **5 N south**.

Pressure

Pressure is the force exerted over a given area. The SI unit for pressure is the pascal. Its symbol is Pa.

$$\text{pressure} = \frac{\text{force}}{\text{area}}$$

Example:
Calculate the pressure of the air in a soccer ball if the air exerts a force of 10 N over an area of 0.5 m².

$$\text{pressure} = \frac{10\,N}{0.5\,m^2} = \frac{20\,N}{m^2} = 20\,Pa$$

The pressure of the air inside the soccer ball is **20 Pa**.

Reading and Study Skills

A How-To Manual for Active Reading

This book belongs to you, and you are invited to write in it. In fact, the book won't be complete until you do. Sometimes you'll answer a question or follow directions to mark up the text. Other times you'll write down your own thoughts. And when you're done reading and writing in the book, the book will be ready to help you review what you learned and prepare for tests.

Active Reading Annotations

Before you read, you'll often come upon an Active Reading prompt that asks you to underline certain words or number the steps in a process. Here's an example.

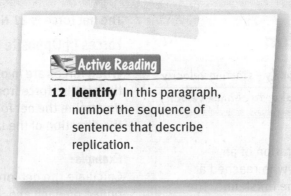

> **Active Reading**
>
> **12 Identify** In this paragraph, number the sequence of sentences that describe replication.

Marking the text this way is called **annotating,** and your marks are called **annotations.** Annotating the text can help you identify important concepts while you read.

There are other ways that you can annotate the text. You can draw an asterisk (*) by vocabulary terms, mark unfamiliar or confusing terms and information with a question mark (?), and mark main ideas with a double underline. And you can even invent your own marks to annotate the text!

Other Annotating Opportunities

Keep your pencil, pen, or highlighter nearby as you read so you can make a note or highlight an important point at any time. Here are a few ideas to get you started.

- Notice the headings in red and blue. The blue headings are questions that point to the main idea of what you're reading. The red headings are answers to the questions in the blue ones. Together these headings outline the content of the lesson. After reading a lesson, you could write your own answers to the questions.

© Houghton Mifflin Harcourt Publishing Company

- Notice the bold-faced words that are highlighted in yellow. They are highlighted so that you can easily find them again on the page where they are defined. As you read or as you review, challenge yourself to write your own sentence using the bold-faced term.

- Make a note in the margin at any time. You might
  - Ask a "What if" question
  - Comment on what you read
  - Make a connection to something you read elsewhere
  - Make a logical conclusion from the text

Use your own language and abbreviations. Invent a code, such as using circles and boxes around words to remind you of their importance or relation to each other. Your annotations will help you remember your questions for class discussions, and when you go back to the lesson later, you may be able to fill in what you didn't understand the first time you read it. Like a scientist in the field or in a lab, you will be recording your questions and observations for analysis later.

Active Reading Questions

After you read, you'll often come upon Active Reading questions that ask you to think about what you've just read. You'll write your answer underneath the question. Here's an example.

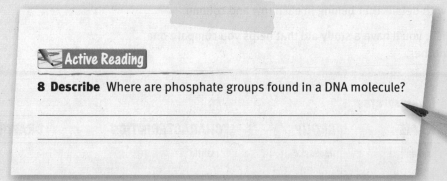

Active Reading

8 Describe Where are phosphate groups found in a DNA molecule?

_____

_____

This type of question helps you sum up what you've just read and pull out the most important ideas from the passage. In this case, the question asks you to **describe** the structure of a DNA molecule that you have just read about. Other times you may be asked to do such things as **apply** a concept, **compare** two concepts, **summarize** a process, or **identify a cause-and-effect** relationship. You'll be strengthening those critical thinking skills that you'll use often in learning about science.

Reading and Study Skills

Using Graphic Organizers to Take Notes

Graphic organizers help you remember information as you read it for the first time and as you study it later. There are dozens of graphic organizers to choose from, so the first trick is to choose the one that's best suited to your purpose. Following are some graphic organizers to use for different purposes.

To remember lots of information	To relate a central idea to subordinate details	To describe a process	To make a comparison
• Arrange data in a Content Frame • Use Combination Notes to describe a concept in words and pictures	• Show relationships with a Mind Map or a Main Idea Web • Sum up relationships among many things with a Concept Map	• Use a Process Diagram to explain a procedure • Show a chain of events and results in a Cause-and-Effect Chart	• Compare two or more closely related things in a Venn Diagram

Content Frame

1 Make a four-column chart.

2 Fill the first column with categories (e.g., snail, ant, earthworm) and the first row with descriptive information (e.g., group, characteristic, appearance).

3 Fill the chart with details that belong in each row and column.

4 When you finish, you'll have a study aid that helps you compare one category to another.

Invertebrates

NAME	GROUP	CHARACTERISTICS	DRAWING
snail	mollusks	mantle	
ant	arthropods	six legs, exoskeleton	
earthworm	segmented worms	segmented body, circulatory and digestive systems	
heartworm	roundworms	digestive system	
sea star	echinoderms	spiny skin, tube feet	
jellyfish	cnidarians	stinging cells	

© Houghton Mifflin Harcourt Publishing Company

Combination Notes

1 Make a two-column chart.

2 Write descriptive words and definitions in the first column.

3 Draw a simple sketch that helps you remember the meaning of the term in the second column.

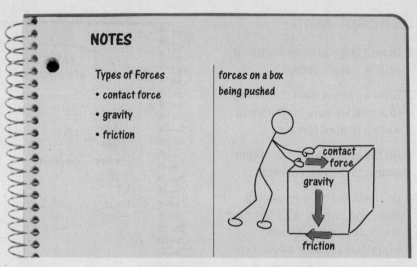

Mind Map

1 Draw an oval, and inside it write a topic to analyze.

2 Draw two or more arms extending from the oval. Each arm represents a main idea about the topic.

3 Draw lines from the arms on which to write details about each of the main ideas.

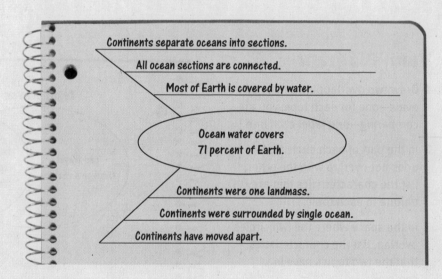

Main Idea Web

1 Make a box, and write a concept you want to remember inside it.

2 Draw boxes around the central box, and label each one with a category of information about the concept (e.g., definition, formula, descriptive details).

3 Fill in the boxes with relevant details as you read.

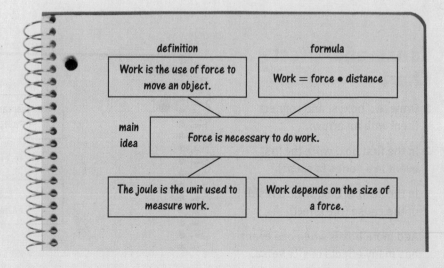

Reading and Study Skills

Concept Map

1 Draw a large oval, and inside it write a major concept.

2 Draw an arrow from the concept to a smaller oval, in which you write a related concept.

3 On the arrow, write a verb that connects the two concepts.

4 Continue in this way, adding ovals and arrows in a branching structure, until you have explained as much as you can about the main concept.

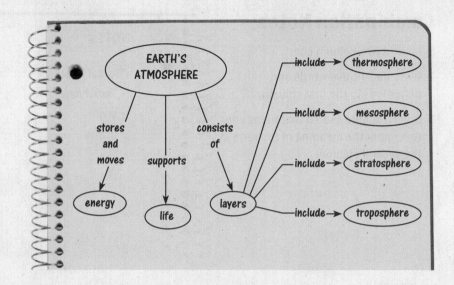

Venn Diagram

1 Draw two overlapping circles or ovals—one for each topic you are comparing—and label each one.

2 In the part of each circle that does not overlap with the other, list the characteristics that are unique to each topic.

3 In the space where the two circles overlap, list the characteristics that the two topics have in common.

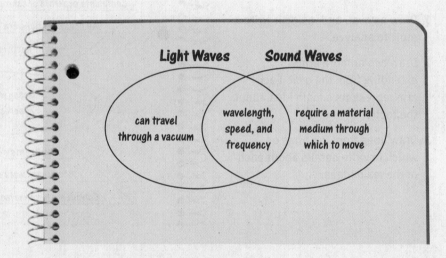

Cause-and-Effect Chart

1 Draw two boxes, and connect them with an arrow.

2 In the first box, write the first event in a series (a cause).

3 In the second box, write a result of the cause (the effect).

4 Add more boxes when one event has many effects or vice versa.

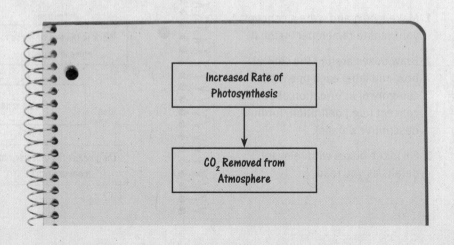

Process Diagram

A process can be a never-ending cycle. As you can see in this technology design process, engineers may backtrack and repeat steps, they may skip steps entirely, or they may repeat the entire process before a usable design is achieved.

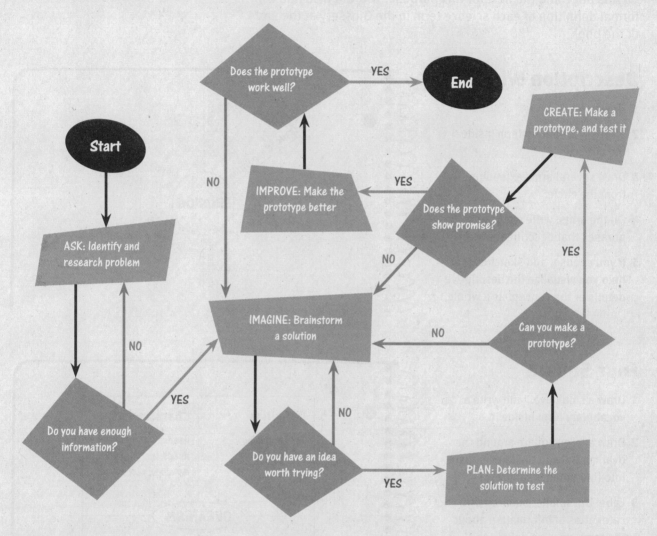

Reading and Study Skills

Using Vocabulary Strategies

Important science terms are highlighted where they are first defined in this book. One way to remember these terms is to take notes and make sketches when you come to them. Use the strategies on this page and the next for this purpose. You will also find a formal definition of each science term in the Glossary at the end of the book.

Description Wheel

1 Draw a small circle.

2 Write a vocabulary term inside the circle.

3 Draw several arms extending from the circle.

4 On the arms, write words and phrases that describe the term.

5 If you choose, add sketches that help you visualize the descriptive details or the concept as a whole.

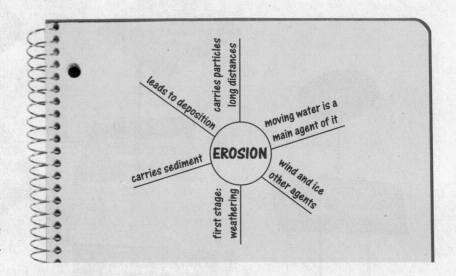

Four Square

1 Draw a small oval, and write a vocabulary term inside it.

2 Draw a large square around the oval, and divide the large square into four smaller squares.

3 Label the smaller squares with categories of information about the term, such as definition, characteristics, examples, non-examples, appearance, and root words.

4 Fill the squares with descriptive words and drawings that will help you remember the overall meaning of the term and its essential details.

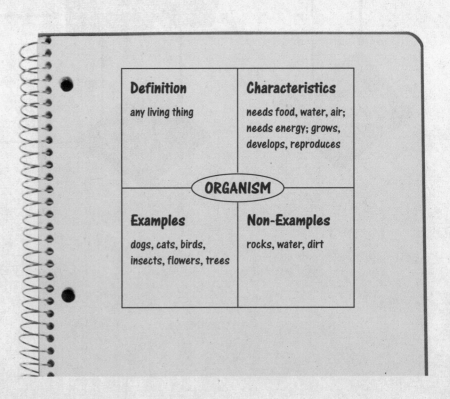

Frame Game

1 Draw a small rectangle, and write a vocabulary term inside it.

2 Draw a larger rectangle around the smaller one. Connect the corners of the larger rectangle to the corners of the smaller one, creating four spaces that frame the word.

3 In each of the four parts of the frame, draw or write details that help define the term. Consider including a definition, essential characteristics, an equation, examples, and a sentence using the term.

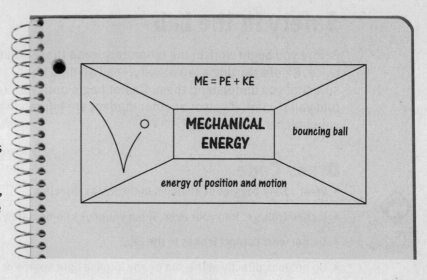

ME = PE + KE

MECHANICAL ENERGY

bouncing ball

energy of position and motion

Magnet Word

1 Draw horseshoe magnet, and write a vocabulary term inside it.

2 Add lines that extend from the sides of the magnet.

3 Brainstorm words and phrases that come to mind when you think about the term.

4 On the lines, write the words and phrases that describe something essential about the term.

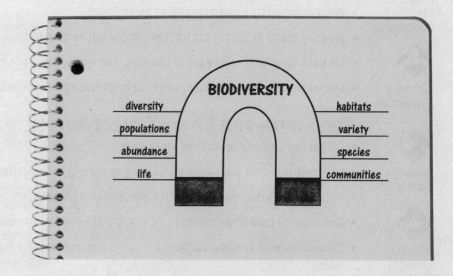

BIODIVERSITY

diversity

populations

abundance

life

habitats

variety

species

communities

Word Triangle

1 Draw a triangle, and add lines to divide it into three parts.

2 Write a term and its definition in the bottom section of the triangle.

3 In the middle section, write a sentence in which the term is used correctly.

4 In the top section, draw a small picture to illustrate the term.

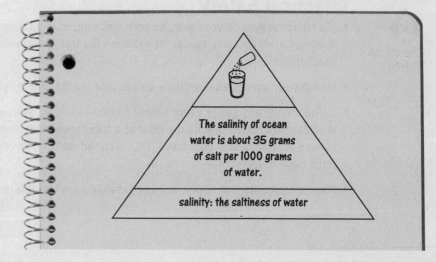

The salinity of ocean water is about 35 grams of salt per 1000 grams of water.

salinity: the saltiness of water

Science Skills

Safety in the Lab

Before you begin work in the laboratory, read these safety rules twice. Before starting a lab activity, read all directions, and make sure that you understand them. Do not begin until your teacher has told you to start. If you or another student are injured in any way, tell your teacher immediately.

Dress Code

Eye Protection

- Wear safety goggles at all times in the lab as directed.
- If chemicals get into your eyes, flush your eyes immediately.
- Do not wear contact lenses in the lab.
- Do not look directly at the sun or any intense light source or laser.

Hand Protection

- Do not cut an object while holding the object in your hand.
- Wear appropriate protective gloves as directed.
- Wear an apron or lab coat at all times in the lab as directed.

Clothing Protection

- Tie back long hair, secure loose clothing, and remove loose jewelry.
- Do not wear open-toed shoes, sandals, or canvas shoes in the lab.

Glassware and Sharp Object Safety

Glassware Safety

- Do not use chipped or cracked glassware.
- Use heat-resistant glassware for heating or storing hot materials.
- Notify your teacher immediately if a piece of glass breaks.

Sharp Objects Safety

- Use extreme care when handling all sharp and pointed instruments.
- Cut objects on a suitable surface, always in a direction away from your body.

Chemical Safety

Chemical Safety

- If a chemical gets on your skin, on your clothing, or in your eyes, rinse it immediately (shower, faucet, or eyewash fountain), and alert your teacher.
- Do not clean up spilled chemicals unless your teacher directs you to do so.
- Do not inhale any gas or vapor unless directed to do so by your teacher. If you are instructed to note the odor of a substance, wave the fumes toward your nose with your hand. This is called wafting. Never put your nose close to the source.
- Handle materials that emit vapors or gases in a well-ventilated area.

Electrical Safety

Electrical Safety

- Do not use equipment with frayed electrical cords or loose plugs.
- Do not use electrical equipment near water or when clothing or hands are wet.
- Hold the plug housing when you plug in or unplug equipment.

Heating and Fire Safety

Heating Safety

- Be aware of any source of flames, sparks, or heat (such as flames, heating coils, or hot plates) before working with any flammable substances.
- Know the location of lab fire extinguishers and fire-safety blankets.
- Know your school's fire-evacuation routes.
- If your clothing catches on fire, walk to the lab shower to put out the fire.
- Never leave a hot plate unattended while it is turned on or while it is cooling.
- Use tongs or appropriate insulated holders when handling heated objects.
- Allow all equipment to cool before storing it.

Wafting

Plant and Animal Safety

Plant Safety

- Do not eat any part of a plant.
- Do not pick any wild plants unless your teacher instructs you to do so.

Animal Safety

- Handle animals only as your teacher directs.
- Treat animals carefully and respectfully.
- Wash your hands thoroughly after handling any plant or animal.

Cleanup

Proper Waste Disposal

- Clean all work surfaces and protective equipment as directed by your teacher.
- Dispose of hazardous materials or sharp objects only as directed by your teacher.

Hygienic Care

- Keep your hands away from your face while you are working on any activity.
- Wash your hands thoroughly before you leave the lab or after any activity.

Science Skills

Designing, Conducting, and Reporting an Experiment

An experiment is an organized procedure to study something under specific conditions. Use the following steps of the scientific method when designing or conducting a controlled experiment.

1 Identify a Research Problem

Every day, you make observations by using your senses to gather information. Careful observations lead to good questions, and good questions can lead you to an experiment. Imagine, for example, that you pass a pond every day on your way to school, and you notice green scum beginning to form on top of it. You wonder what it is and why it seems to be growing. You list your questions, and then you do a little research to find out what is already known. A good place to start a research project is at the library. A library catalog lists all of the resources available to you at that library and often those found elsewhere. Begin your search by using:

- keywords or main topics.
- words similar to, or synonyms of, your keyword.

The types of resources that will be helpful to you will depend on the kind of information you are interested in. And some resources are more reliable for a given topic than others. Some different kinds of useful resources are:

- magazines and journals (or periodicals)—articles on a topic.
- encyclopedias—a good overview of a topic.
- books on specific subjects—details about a topic.
- newspapers—useful for current events.

The Internet can also be a great place to find information. Some of your library's reference materials may even be online. When using the Internet, however, it is especially important to make sure you are using appropriate and reliable sources. Websites of universities and government agencies are usually more accurate and reliable than websites created by individuals or businesses. Decide which sources are relevant and reliable for your topic. If in doubt, check with your teacher.

Take notes as you read through the information in these resources. You will probably come up with many questions and ideas for which you can do more research as needed. Once you feel you have enough information, think about the questions you have on the topic. Then write down the problem that you want to investigate. Your notes might look like those at the top of the next page.

© Houghton Mifflin Harcourt Publishing Company

Research Questions	Research Problem	Library and Internet Resources
• How do algae grow? • How do people measure algae? • What kind of fertilizer would affect the growth of algae? • Can fertilizer and algae be used safely in a lab? How?	How does fertilizer affect the algae in a pond?	Pond fertilization: initiating an algal bloom—from University of California Davis website. Blue-green algae in Wisconsin waters—from the Department of Natural Resources of Wisconsin website.

As you gather information from reliable sources, record details about each source, including author name(s), title, date of publication, and/or web address. Make sure to also note the specific information that you use from each source. Staying organized in this way will be important when you write your report and create a bibliography or works cited list. Recording this information and staying organized will help you credit the appropriate author(s) for the information that you have gathered.

Representing someone else's ideas or work as your own (without giving the original author credit) is known as plagiarism. Plagiarism can be intentional or unintentional. The best way to make sure that you do not commit plagiarism is to always do your own work and to always give credit to others when you use their words or ideas.

Current scientific research is built on scientific research and discoveries that have happened in the past. This means that scientists are constantly learning from each other and combining ideas to learn more about the natural world through investigation. But a good scientist always credits the ideas and research gathered from other people to those people. There are more details about crediting sources and creating a bibliography under step 9.

2 Make a Prediction

A prediction is a statement of what you expect will happen in your experiment. Before making a prediction, you need to decide in a general way what you will do in your procedure. You may state your prediction in an if-then format.

Prediction

If the amount of fertilizer in the pond water is increased, then the amount of algae will also increase.

Science Skills

3 Form a Hypothesis

Many experiments are designed to test a hypothesis. A hypothesis is a tentative explanation for an expected result. You have predicted that additional fertilizer will cause additional algae growth in pond water; your hypothesis should state the connection between fertilizer and algal growth.

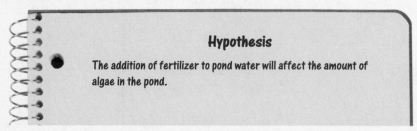

Hypothesis

The addition of fertilizer to pond water will affect the amount of algae in the pond.

4 Identify Variables to Test the Hypothesis

The next step is to design an experiment to test the hypothesis. The experimental results may or may not support the hypothesis. Either way, the information that results from the experiment may be useful for future investigations.

Experimental Group and Control Group

An experiment to determine how two factors are related has a control group and an experimental group. The two groups are the same, except that the investigator changes a single factor in the experimental group and does not change it in the control group.

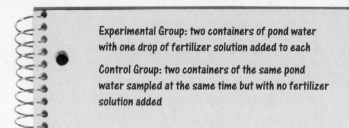

Experimental Group: two containers of pond water with one drop of fertilizer solution added to each

Control Group: two containers of the same pond water sampled at the same time but with no fertilizer solution added

Variables and Constants

In a controlled experiment, a variable is any factor that can change. Constants are all of the variables that are kept the same in both the experimental group and the control group.

The independent variable is the factor that is manipulated or changed in order to test the effect of the change on another variable. The dependent variable is the factor the investigator measures to gather data about the effect.

Independent Variable	Dependent Variable	Constants
Amount of fertilizer in pond water	Growth of algae in the pond water	• Where and when the pond water is obtained • The type of container used • Light and temperature conditions where the water is stored

5 Write a Procedure

Write each step of your procedure. Start each step with a verb, or action word, and keep the steps short. Your procedure should be clear enough for someone else to use as instructions for repeating your experiment.

Procedure

1. Use the masking tape and the marker to label the containers with your initials, the date, and the identifiers "Jar 1 with Fertilizer," "Jar 2 with Fertilizer," "Jar 1 without Fertilizer," and "Jar 2 without Fertilizer."

2. Put on your gloves. Use the large container to obtain a sample of pond water.

3. Divide the water sample equally among the four smaller containers.

4. Use the eyedropper to add one drop of fertilizer solution to the two containers labeled "Jar 1 with Fertilizer" and "Jar 2 with Fertilizer."

5. Cover the containers with clear plastic wrap. Use the scissors to punch ten holes in each of the covers.

6. Place all four containers on a window ledge. Make sure that they all receive the same amount of light.

7. Observe the containers every day for one week.

8. Place a ruler over the opening of the jar and measure the diameter of the largest clump of algae in each container. Record your measurements daily.

Science Skills

6 Experiment and Collect Data

Once you have all of your materials and your procedure has been approved, you can begin to experiment and collect data. Record both quantitative data (measurements) and qualitative data (observations), as shown below.

Algal Growth and Fertilizer

Date and Time	Experimental Group		Control Group		Observations
	Jar 1 with Fertilizer (diameter of algal clump in mm)	Jar 2 with Fertilizer (diameter of algal clump in mm)	Jar 1 without Fertilizer (diameter of algal clump in mm)	Jar 2 without Fertilizer (diameter of algal clump in mm)	
5/3 4:00 p.m.	0	0	0	0	condensation in all containers
5/4 4:00 p.m.	0	3	0	0	tiny green blobs in Jar 2 with fertilizer
5/5 4:15 p.m.	4	5	0	3	green blobs in Jars 1 and 2 with fertilizer and Jar 2 without fertilizer
5/6 4:00 p.m.	5	6	0	4	water light green in Jar 2 with fertilizer
5/7 4:00 p.m.	8	10	0	6	water light green in Jars 1 and 2 with fertilizer and Jar 2 without fertilizer
5/8 3:30 p.m.	10	18	0	6	cover off of Jar 2 with fertilizer
5/9 3:30 p.m.	14	23	0	8	drew sketches of each container

Drawings of Samples Viewed Under Microscope on 5/9 at 100x

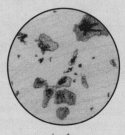
Jar 1 with Fertilizer

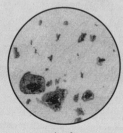
Jar 2 with Fertilizer

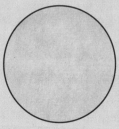
Jar 1 without Fertilizer

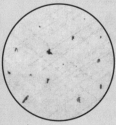
Jar 2 without Fertilizer

7 Analyze Data

After you complete your experiment, you must analyze all of the data you have gathered. Tables, statistics, and graphs are often used in this step to organize and analyze both the qualitative and quantitative data. Sometimes, your qualitative data are best used to help explain the relationships you see in your quantitative data.

Computer graphing software is useful for creating a graph from data you have collected. Most graphing software can make line graphs, pie charts, or bar graphs from data that have been organized in a spreadsheet. Graphs are useful for understanding relationships in the data and for communicating the results of your experiment.

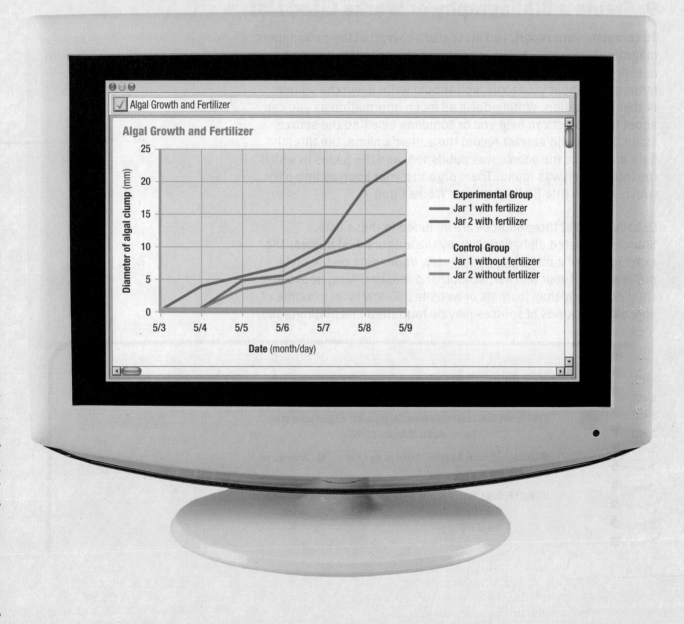

Science Skills

8 Make Conclusions

To draw conclusions from your experiment, first, write your results. Then, compare your results with your hypothesis. Do your results support your hypothesis? What have you learned?

Conclusion

More algae grew in the pond water to which fertilizer had been added than in the pond water to which fertilizer had not been added. My hypothesis was supported. I conclude that it is possible that the growth of algae in ponds can be influenced by the input of fertilizer.

9 Create a Bibliography or Works Cited List

To complete your report, you must also show all of the newspapers, magazines, journals, books, and online sources that you used at every stage of your investigation. Whenever you find useful information about your topic, you should write down the source of that information. Writing down as much information as you can about the subject can help you or someone else find the source again. You should at least record the author's name, the title, the date and where the source was published, and the pages in which the information was found. Then, organize your sources into a list, which you can title Bibliography or Works Cited.

Usually, at least three sources are included in these lists. Sources are listed alphabetically, by the authors' last names. The exact format of a bibliography can vary, depending on the style preferences of your teacher, school, or publisher. Also, books are cited differently than journals or websites. Below is an example of how different kinds of sources may be formatted in a bibliography.

BOOK: Hauschultz, Sara. Freshwater Algae. Brainard, Minnesota: Northwoods Publishing, 2011.

ENCYCLOPEDIA: Lasure, Sedona. "Algae is not all just pond scum." Encyclopedia of Algae. 2009.

JOURNAL: Johnson, Keagan. "Algae as we know it." Sci Journal, vol 64. (September 2010): 201-211.

WEBSITE: Dout, Bill. "Keeping algae scum out of birdbaths." Help Keep Earth Clean. News. January 26, 2011. <www. SaveEarth.org>.

Using a Microscope

Scientists use microscopes to see very small objects that cannot easily be seen with the eye alone. A microscope magnifies the image of an object so that small details may be observed. A microscope that you may use can magnify an object 400 times—the object will appear 400 times larger than its actual size.

Eyepiece Objects are viewed through the eyepiece. The eyepiece contains a lens that commonly magnifies an image 10 times.

Coarse Adjustment This knob is used to focus the image of an object when it is viewed through the low-power lens.

Fine Adjustment This knob is used to focus the image of an object when it is viewed through the high-power lens.

Low-Power Objective Lens This is the smallest lens on the nosepiece. It magnifies images about 10 times.

Arm The arm supports the body above the stage. Always carry a microscope by the arm and base.

Stage Clip The stage clip holds a slide in place on the stage.

Base The base supports the microscope.

Body The body separates the lens in the eyepiece from the objective lenses below.

Nosepiece The nosepiece holds the objective lenses above the stage and rotates so that all lenses may be used.

High-Power Objective Lens This is the largest lens on the nosepiece. It magnifies an image approximately 40 times.

Stage The stage supports the object being viewed.

Diaphragm The diaphragm is used to adjust the amount of light passing through the slide and into an objective lens.

Mirror or Light Source Some microscopes use light that is reflected through the stage by a mirror. Other microscopes have their own light sources.

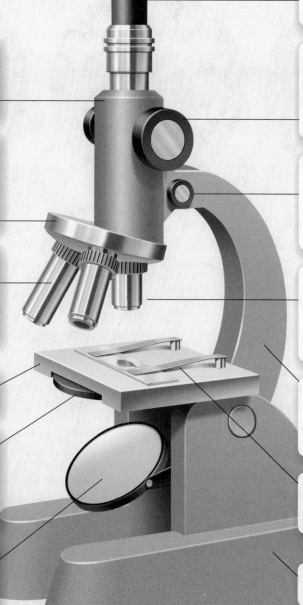

Science Skills

Measuring Accurately

Precision and Accuracy

When you do a scientific investigation, it is important that your methods, observations, and data be both precise and accurate.

Low precision: The darts did not land in a consistent place on the dartboard.

Precision but not accuracy: The darts landed in a consistent place but did not hit the bull's eye.

Precision and accuracy: The darts landed consistently on the bull's eye.

Precision

In science, *precision* is the exactness and consistency of measurements. For example, measurements made with a ruler that has both centimeter and millimeter markings would be more precise than measurements made with a ruler that has only centimeter markings. Another indicator of precision is the care taken to make sure that methods and observations are as exact and consistent as possible. Every time a particular experiment is done, the same procedure should be used. Precision is necessary because experiments are repeated several times and if the procedure changes, the results might change.

Example

Suppose you are measuring temperatures over a two-week period. Your precision will be greater if you measure each temperature at the same place, at the same time of day, and with the same thermometer than if you change any of these factors from one day to the next.

Accuracy

In science, it is possible to be precise but not accurate. *Accuracy* depends on the difference between a measurement and an actual value. The smaller the difference, the more accurate the measurement.

Example

Suppose you look at a stream and estimate that it is about 1 meter wide at a particular place. You decide to check your estimate by measuring the stream with a meter stick, and you determine that the stream is 1.32 meters wide. However, because it is difficult to measure the width of a stream with a meter stick, it turns out that your measurement was not very accurate. The stream is actually 1.14 meters wide. Therefore, even though your estimate of about 1 meter was less precise than your measurement, your estimate was actually more accurate.

Graduated Cylinders

How to Measure the Volume of a Liquid with a Graduated Cylinder

- Be sure that the graduated cylinder is on a flat surface so that your measurement will be accurate.

- When reading the scale on a graduated cylinder, be sure to have your eyes at the level of the surface of the liquid.

- The surface of the liquid will be curved in the graduated cylinder. Read the volume of the liquid at the bottom of the curve, or meniscus (muh•NIHS•kuhs).

- You can use a graduated cylinder to find the volume of a solid object by measuring the increase in a liquid's level after you add the object to the cylinder.

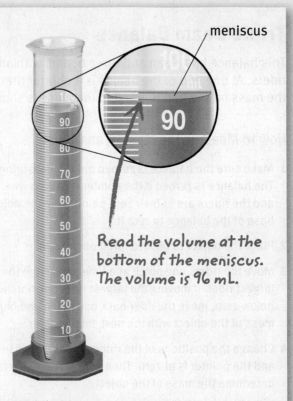

meniscus

Read the volume at the bottom of the meniscus. The volume is 96 mL.

Metric Rulers

How to Measure the Length of a Leaf with a Metric Ruler

1 Lay a ruler flat on top of the leaf so that the 1-centimeter mark lines up with one end. Make sure the ruler and the leaf do not move between the time you line them up and the time you take the measurement.

2 Look straight down on the ruler so that you can see exactly how the marks line up with the other end of the leaf.

3 Estimate the length by which the leaf extends beyond a marking. For example, the leaf below extends about halfway between the 4.2-centimeter and 4.3-centimeter marks, so the apparent measurement is about 4.25 centimeters.

4 Remember to subtract 1 centimeter from your apparent measurement, since you started at the 1-centimeter mark on the ruler and not at the end. The leaf is about 3.25 centimeters long (4.25 cm − 1 cm = 3.25 cm).

Not to scale

Triple Beam Balance

This balance has a pan and three beams with sliding masses, called riders. At one end of the beams is a pointer that indicates whether the mass on the pan is equal to the masses shown on the beams.

How to Measure the Mass of an Object

1 Make sure the balance is zeroed before measuring the mass of an object. The balance is zeroed if the pointer is at zero when nothing is on the pan and the riders are at their zero points. Use the adjustment knob at the base of the balance to zero it.

2 Place the object to be measured on the pan.

3 Move the riders one notch at a time away from the pan. Begin with the largest rider. If moving the largest rider one notch brings the pointer below zero, move the rider back one notch and begin measuring the mass of the object with the next smaller rider.

4 Change the positions of the riders until they balance the mass on the pan and the pointer is at zero. Then add the readings from the three beams to determine the mass of the object.

300 g	position of largest rider
90 g	position of middle rider
+ 3 g	position of smallest rider
393 g	mass of beaker and water

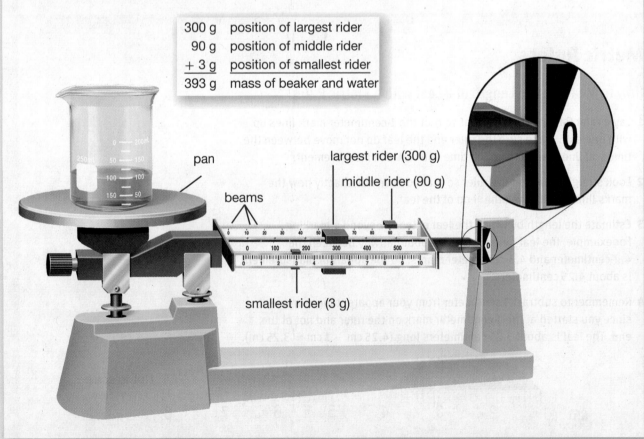

pan

beams

largest rider (300 g)

middle rider (90 g)

smallest rider (3 g)

Electronic Balance

How to Measure the Mass of an Object

1 Be sure the balance is on a flat, stable surface.

2 Zero, or *tare*, the balance using the appropriate key. If you are measuring a specific quantity of a substance using a weigh boat or other container, place the weigh boat or container on the balance pan before zeroing the balance.

3 When the readout on the balance is steady and within a few thousandths of zero grams, place the object to be measured on the balance. If you are measuring out chemicals or other substances, wear gloves and use a clean spatula or similar tool to transfer the substance. Do not reach into containers or touch chemicals with your hands.

4 Record the mass of the object to the nearest milligram (1/1000 of one gram).

Record the mass of an object to the nearest milligram (mg). The mass measured is 5.726 grams.

Spring Scale

Spring scales are tools that measure forces, such as weight, or the gravitational force exerted on an object. A spring scale indicates an object's weight by measuring how far the spring stretches when an object is suspended from it. This type of scale is often used in grocery stores or to measure the weights of large loads of crops or industrial products. Spring scales are useful for measuring the weight of larger objects as well.

How to Measure the Weight of an Object

- Be sure the spring scale is securely suspended and is not touching the ground, wall, or desk. The pointer should be at zero.

- Hang the object to be weighed from the hook at the free end of the spring scale.

- When the object is still—not bouncing, swinging, or otherwise moving—read the object's weight to the nearest 0.5 N.

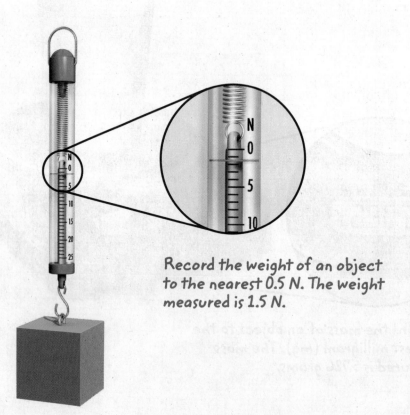

Record the weight of an object to the nearest 0.5 N. The weight measured is 1.5 N.

Thermometer

Many laboratory thermometers are the bulb type shown below. The sensing bulb of the thermometer is filled with a colored liquid (alcohol) that expands as it is heated. When the liquid expands, it moves up the stem of the thermometer through the capillary tube. Thermometers usually measure temperature in degrees Celsius (°C).

How to Measure the Temperature of a Substance

Caution: Do not hold the thermometer in your hand while measuring the temperature of a heated substance. Never use a thermometer to stir a solution. Always consult your teacher regarding proper laboratory techniques and safety rules when using a thermometer.

- Carefully lower the bulb of the thermometer into the substance. The stem of the thermometer may rest against the side of the container, but the bulb should never rest on the bottom. If the thermometer has an adjustable clip for the side of the container, use the clip to suspend the thermometer in the liquid.

- Watch the colored liquid as it rises in the thermometer's capillary tube. When the liquid stops rising, note the whole-degree increment nearest the top of the liquid column.

- If your thermometer is marked in whole degrees, report temperature to the nearest half degree.

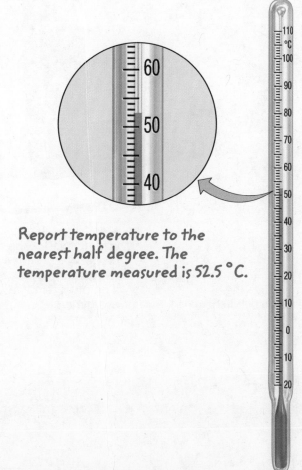

Report temperature to the nearest half degree. The temperature measured is 52.5 °C.

Introduction to Probeware

Probeware is a system of tools that offers a way to measure and analyze various physical properties, such as pressure, pH, temperature, or acceleration. Most probeware systems consist of a sensor, or probe, that is connected to a device such as a computer. As the sensor takes measurements, a computer program records the data. Users can then analyze data using tables, charts, or graphs. Some systems allow you to analyze more than one variable at a time.

Temperature Probe

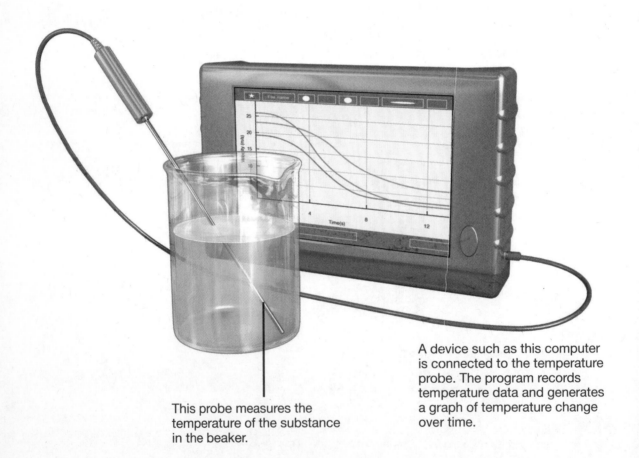

This probe measures the temperature of the substance in the beaker.

A device such as this computer is connected to the temperature probe. The program records temperature data and generates a graph of temperature change over time.

Motion Detector

Use a motion detector to gather information about an object's velocity, position, or acceleration.

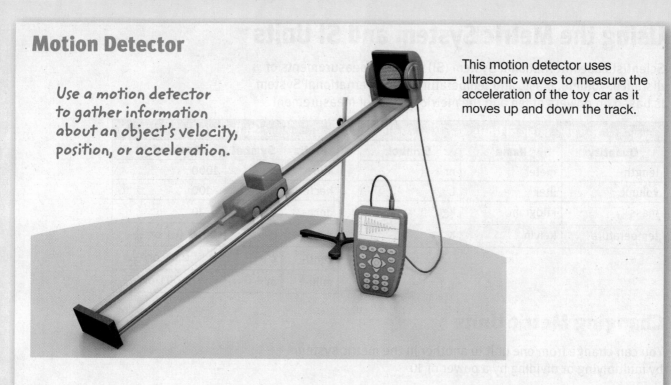

This motion detector uses ultrasonic waves to measure the acceleration of the toy car as it moves up and down the track.

pH Probe

Use a pH probe to determine whether a substance is acidic, neutral, or basic.

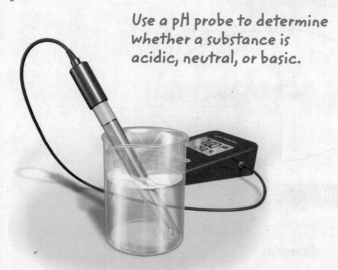
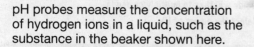

pH probes measure the concentration of hydrogen ions in a liquid, such as the substance in the beaker shown here.

The tip of a pH probe is a thin glass membrane that should not be allowed to dry out. Store pH probes in the appropriate container and solution when you are finished with your investigation.

Caution: Probeware equipment should always be handled carefully. Be sure to follow your teacher's instructions regarding the use and storage of all probeware equipment.

Science Skills

Using the Metric System and SI Units

Scientists use International System (SI) units for measurements of distance, volume, mass, and temperature. The International System is based on powers of ten and the metric system of measurement.

Basic SI Units		
Quantity	**Name**	**Symbol**
length	meter	m
volume	liter	L
mass	kilogram	kg
temperature	kelvin	K

SI Prefixes		
Prefix	**Symbol**	**Power of 10**
kilo-	k	1000
hecto-	h	100
deca-	da	10
deci-	d	0.1 or $\frac{1}{10}$
centi-	c	0.01 or $\frac{1}{100}$
milli-	m	0.001 or $\frac{1}{1000}$

Changing Metric Units

You can change from one unit to another in the metric system by multiplying or dividing by a power of 10

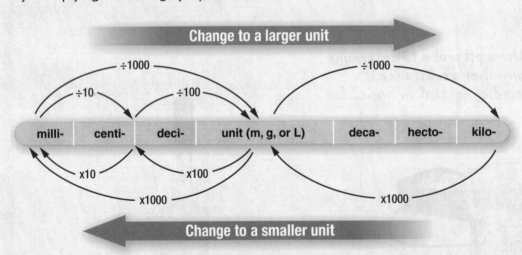

Example

Change 0.64 liters to milliliters.
1 Decide whether to multiply or divide.
2 Select the power of 10.

Change to a smaller unit by multiplying

mL ◄────── x 1000 ────── L

0.64 x 1000 = 640.

ANSWER **0.64 L = 640 mL**

Example

Change 23.6 grams to kilograms.
1 Decide whether to multiply or divide.
2 Select the power of 10.

Change to a larger unit by dividing

g ────── ÷ 1000 ──────► kg

26.3 ÷ 1000 = 0.0263

ANSWER **23.6 g = 0.0236 kg**

Converting Between SI and U.S. Customary Units

Use the chart below when you need to convert between SI units and U.S. customary units

SI Unit	From SI to U.S. Customary			From U.S. Customary to SI		
Length	**When you know**	**multiply by**	**to find**	**When you know**	**multiply by**	**to find**
kilometer (km) = 1000 m	kilometers	0.62	miles	miles	1.61	kilometers
meter (m) = 100 cm	meters	3.28	feet	feet	0.3048	meters
centimeter (cm) = 10 mm	centimeters	0.39	inches	inches	2.54	centimeters
millimeter (mm) = 0.1 cm	millimeters	0.04	inches	inches	25.4	millimeters
Area	**When you know**	**multiply by**	**to find**	**When you know**	**multiply by**	**to find**
square kilometer (km²)	square kilometers	0.39	square miles	square miles	2.59	square kilometers
square meter (m²)	square meters	1.2	square yards	square yards	0.84	square meters
square centimeter (cm²)	square centimeters	0.155	square inches	square inches	6.45	square centimeters
Volume	**When you know**	**multiply by**	**to find**	**When you know**	**multiply by**	**to find**
liter (L) = 1000 mL	liters	1.06	quarts	quarts	0.95	liters
	liters	0.26	gallons	gallons	3.79	liters
	liters	4.23	cups	cups	0.24	liters
	liters	2.12	pints	pints	0.47	liters
milliliter (mL) = 0.001 L	milliliters	0.20	teaspoons	teaspoons	4.93	milliliters
	milliliters	0.07	tablespoons	tablespoons	14.79	milliliters
	milliliters	0.03	fluid ounces	fluid ounces	29.57	milliliters
Mass and Weight	**When you know**	**multiply by**	**to find**	**When you know**	**multiply by**	**to find**
kilogram (kg) = 1000 g	kilograms	2.2	pounds	pounds	0.45	kilograms
gram (g) = 1000 mg	grams	0.035	ounces	ounces	28.35	grams

Temperature Conversions

Even though the kelvin is the SI base unit of temperature, the degree Celsius will be the unit you use most often in your science studies. The formulas below show the relationships between temperatures in degrees Fahrenheit (°F), degrees Celsius (°C), and kelvins (K).

$$°C = \frac{5}{9}\ (°F - 32) \qquad °F = \frac{9}{5}\ °C + 32 \qquad K = °C + 273$$

Examples of Temperature Conversions		
Condition	**Degrees Celsius**	**Degrees Fahrenheit**
Freezing point of water	0	32
Cool day	10	50
Mild day	20	68
Warm day	30	86
Normal body temperature	37	98.6
Very hot day	40	104
Boiling point of water	100	212

Math Refresher

Performing Calculations

Science requires an understanding of many math concepts. The following pages will help you review some important math skills.

Mean

The mean is the sum of all values in a data set divided by the total number of values in the data set. The mean is also called the *average*.

Example

Find the mean of the following set of numbers: 5, 4, 7, and 8.

Step 1   Find the sum.

$$5 + 4 + 7 + 8 = 24$$

Step 2   Divide the sum by the number of numbers in your set. Because there are four numbers in this example, divide the sum by 4.

$$24 \div 4 = 6$$

Answer The average, or mean, is 6.

Median

The median of a data set is the middle value when the values are written in numerical order. If a data set has an even number of values, the median is the mean of the two middle values.

Example

To find the median of a set of measurements, arrange the values in order from least to greatest. The median is the middle value.

13 mm   14 mm   16 mm   21 mm   23 mm

Answer The median is 16 mm.

Mode

The mode of a data set is the value that occurs most often.

Example

To find the mode of a set of measurements, arrange the values in order from least to greatest, and determine the value that occurs most often.

13 mm, 14 mm, 14 mm, 16 mm, 21 mm, 23 mm, 25 mm

Answer The mode is 14 mm.

A data set can have more than one mode or no mode. For example, the following data set has modes of 2 mm and 4 mm:

2 mm   2 mm   3 mm   4 mm   4 mm

The data set below has no mode because no value occurs more often than any other.

2 mm   3 mm   4 mm   5 mm

Ratios

A **ratio** is a comparison between numbers, and it is usually written as a fraction.

Example
Find the ratio of thermometers to students if you have 36 thermometers and 48 students in your class.

Step 1   Write the ratio.

$$\frac{36 \text{ thermometers}}{48 \text{ students}}$$

Step 2   Simplify the fraction to its simplest form.

$$\frac{36}{48} = \frac{36 \div 12}{48 \div 12} = \frac{3}{4}$$

The ratio of thermometers to students is 3 to 4 or 3:4. So there are 3 thermometers for every 4 students.

Proportions

A **proportion** is an equation that states that two ratios are equal.

$$\frac{3}{1} = \frac{12}{4}$$

To solve a proportion, you can use cross-multiplication. If you know three of the quantities in a proportion, you can use cross-multiplication to find the fourth.

Example
Imagine that you are making a scale model of the solar system for your science project. The diameter of Jupiter is 11.2 times the diameter of the Earth. If you are using a plastic-foam ball that has a diameter of 2 cm to represent the Earth, what must the diameter of the ball representing Jupiter be?

$$\frac{11.2}{1} = \frac{x}{2 \text{ cm}}$$

Step 1   Cross-multiply.

$$\frac{11.2}{1} = \frac{x}{2}$$

$$11.2 \times 2 = x \times 1$$

Step 2   Multiply.

$$22.4 = x \times 1$$

$$x = 22.4 \text{ cm}$$

You will need to use a ball that has a diameter of 22.4 cm to represent Jupiter.

Rates

A **rate** is a ratio of two values expressed in different units. A unit rate is a rate with a denominator of 1 unit.

Example
A plant grew 6 centimeters in 2 days. The plant's rate of growth was $\frac{6 \text{ cm}}{2 \text{ days}}$.
To describe the plant's growth in centimeters per day, write a unit rate.

Divide numerator and denominator by 2:

$$\frac{6 \text{ cm}}{2 \text{ days}} = \frac{6 \text{ cm} \div 2}{2 \text{ days} \div 2}$$

Simplify:
$$= \frac{3 \text{ cm}}{1 \text{ day}}$$

Answer The plant's rate of growth is 3 centimeters per day.

Math Refresher

Percent

A **percent** is a ratio of a given number to 100. For example, 85% = 85/100. You can use percent to find part of a whole.

Example
What is 85% of 40?

Step 1   Rewrite the percent as a decimal by moving the decimal point two places to the left.

$$0.85$$

Step 2   Multiply the decimal by the number that you are calculating the percentage of.

$$0.85 \times 40 = 34$$

85% of 40 is 34.

Decimals

To **add** or **subtract decimals,** line up the digits vertically so that the decimal points line up. Then add or subtract the columns from right to left. Carry or borrow numbers as necessary.

Example
Add the following numbers: 3.1415 and 2.96.

Step 1   Line up the digits vertically so that the decimal points line up.

$$\begin{array}{r} 3.1415 \\ + 2.96 \\ \hline \end{array}$$

Step 2   Add the columns from right to left, and carry when necessary.

$$\begin{array}{r} 3.1415 \\ + 2.96 \\ \hline 6.1015 \end{array}$$

The sum is 6.1015.

Fractions

A **fraction** is a ratio of two whole numbers. The top number is the numerator. The bottom number is the denominator. The denominator must not be zero.

Example
Your class has 24 plants. Your teacher instructs you to put 5 plants in a shady spot. What fraction of the plants in your class will you put in a shady spot?

Step 1   In the denominator, write the total number of parts in the whole.

$$\frac{?}{24}$$

Step 2   In the numerator, write the number of parts of the whole that are being considered.

$$\frac{5}{24}$$

So $\frac{5}{24}$ of the plants will be in the shade.

Simplifying Fractions

It is usually best to express a fraction in its simplest form. Expressing a fraction in its simplest form is called **simplifying a fraction**.

Example

Express the fraction $\frac{30}{45}$ in its simplest form.

Step 1   Find the largest whole number that will divide evenly into both the numerator and denominator. This number is called the greatest common factor (GCF).

Factors of the numerator 30:
1, 2, 3, 5, 6, 10, 15, 30

Factors of the denominator 45:
1, 3, 5, 9, 15, 45

Step 2   Divide both the numerator and the denominator by the GCF, which in this case is 15.

$$\frac{30}{45} = \frac{30 \div 15}{45 \div 15} = \frac{2}{3}$$

Thus, $\frac{30}{45}$ written in its simplest form is $\frac{2}{3}$.

Adding and Subtracting Fractions

To **add** or **subtract fractions** that have the same denominator, simply add or subtract the numerators.

Examples

$\frac{3}{5} + \frac{1}{5} = ?$ and $\frac{3}{4} - \frac{1}{4} = ?$

Step 1   Add or subtract the numerators.

$$\frac{3}{5} + \frac{1}{5} = \frac{4}{} \text{ and } \frac{3}{4} - \frac{1}{4} = \frac{2}{}$$

Step 2   Write in the common denominator, which remains the same.

$$\frac{3}{5} + \frac{1}{5} = \frac{4}{5} \text{ and } \frac{3}{4} - \frac{1}{4} = \frac{2}{4}$$

Step 3   If necessary, write the fraction in its simplest form.

$\frac{4}{5}$ cannot be simplified, and $\frac{2}{4} = \frac{1}{2}$.

To **add** or **subtract** fractions that have **different denominators**, first find the least common denominator (LCD).

Examples

$\frac{1}{2} + \frac{1}{6} = ?$ and $\frac{3}{4} - \frac{2}{3} = ?$

Step 1   Write the equivalent fractions that have a common denominator.

$$\frac{3}{6} + \frac{1}{6} = ? \text{ and } \frac{9}{12} - \frac{8}{12} = ?$$

Step 2   Add or subtract the fractions.

$$\frac{3}{6} + \frac{1}{6} = \frac{4}{6} \text{ and } \frac{9}{12} - \frac{8}{12} = \frac{1}{12}$$

Step 3   If necessary, write the fraction in its simplest form.

$\frac{4}{6} = \frac{2}{3}$, and $\frac{1}{12}$ cannot be simplified.

Multiplying Fractions

To **multiply fractions**, multiply the numerators and the denominators together, and then simplify the fraction if necessary.

Example

$\frac{5}{9} \times \frac{7}{10} = ?$

Step 1   Multiply the numerators and denominators.

$$\frac{5}{9} \times \frac{7}{10} = \frac{5 \times 7}{9 \times 10} = \frac{35}{90}$$

Step 2   Simplify the fraction.

$$\frac{35}{90} = \frac{35 \div 5}{90 \div 5} = \frac{7}{18}$$

Math Refresher

Dividing Fractions

To **divide fractions**, first rewrite the divisor (the number you divide by) upside down. This number is called the reciprocal of the divisor. Then multiply and simplify if necessary.

Example

$$\frac{5}{8} \div \frac{3}{2} = ?$$

Step 1   Rewrite the divisor as its reciprocal.

$$\frac{3}{2} \rightarrow \frac{2}{3}$$

Step 2   Multiply the fractions.

$$\frac{5}{8} \times \frac{2}{3} = \frac{5 \times 2}{8 \times 3} = \frac{10}{24}$$

Step 3   Simplify the fraction.

$$\frac{10}{24} = \frac{10 \div 2}{24 \div 2} = \frac{5}{12}$$

Using Significant Figures

The **significant figures** in a decimal are the digits that are warranted by the accuracy of a measuring device.

When you perform a calculation with measurements, the number of significant figures to include in the result depends in part on the number of significant figures in the measurements. When you multiply or divide measurements, your answer should have only as many significant figures as the measurement with the fewest significant figures.

Examples

Using a balance and a graduated cylinder filled with water, you determined that a marble has a mass of 8.0 grams and a volume of 3.5 cubic centimeters. To calculate the density of the marble, divide the mass by the volume.

Write the formula for density: $\text{Density} = \dfrac{\text{mass}}{\text{volume}}$

Substitute measurements: $= \dfrac{8.0 \text{ g}}{3.5 \text{ cm}^3}$

Use a calculator to divide: $\approx 2.285714286 \text{ g/cm}^3$

Answer Because the mass and the volume have two significant figures each, give the density to two significant figures. The marble has a density of 2.3 grams per cubic centimeter.

Using Scientific Notation

Scientific notation is a shorthand way to write very large or very small numbers. For example, 73,500,000,000,000,000,000,000 kg is the mass of the moon. In scientific notation, it is 7.35×10^{22} kg. A value written as a number between 1 and 10, times a power of 10, is in scientific notation.

Examples

You can convert from standard form to scientific notation.

Standard Form	Scientific Notation
720,000	7.2×10^5
5 decimal places left	Exponent is 5.
0.000291	2.91×10^{-4}
4 decimal places right	Exponent is -4.

You can convert from scientific notation to standard form.

Scientific Notation	Standard Form
4.63×10^7	46,300,000
Exponent is 7.	7 decimal places right
1.08×10^{-6}	0.00000108
Exponent is -6.	6 decimal places left

Making and Interpreting Graphs

Circle Graph

A circle graph, or pie chart, shows how each group of data relates to all of the data. Each part of the circle represents a category of the data. The entire circle represents all of the data. For example, a biologist studying a hardwood forest in Wisconsin found that there were five different types of trees. The data table at right summarizes the biologist's findings.

Wisconsin Hardwood Trees	
Type of tree	**Number found**
Oak	600
Maple	750
Beech	300
Birch	1,200
Hickory	150
Total	3,000

How to Make a Circle Graph

1 To make a circle graph of these data, first find the percentage of each type of tree. Divide the number of trees of each type by the total number of trees, and multiply by 100%.

$$\frac{600 \text{ oak}}{3,000 \text{ trees}} \times 100\% = 20\%$$

$$\frac{750 \text{ maple}}{3,000 \text{ trees}} \times 100\% = 25\%$$

$$\frac{300 \text{ beech}}{3,000 \text{ trees}} \times 100\% = 10\%$$

$$\frac{1,200 \text{ birch}}{3,000 \text{ trees}} \times 100\% = 40\%$$

$$\frac{150 \text{ hickory}}{3,000 \text{ trees}} \times 100\% = 5\%$$

2 Now, determine the size of the wedges that make up the graph. Multiply each percentage by 360°. Remember that a circle contains 360°.

$$20\% \times 360° = 72° \qquad 25\% \times 360° = 90°$$

$$10\% \times 360° = 36° \qquad 40\% \times 360° = 144°$$

$$5\% \times 360° = 18°$$

3 Check that the sum of the percentages is 100 and the sum of the degrees is 360.

$$20\% + 25\% + 10\% + 40\% + 5\% = 100\%$$

$$72° + 90° + 36° + 144° + 18° = 360°$$

4 Use a compass to draw a circle, and mark the center of the circle.

5 Then, use a protractor to draw angles of 72°, 90°, 36°, 144°, and 18° in the circle.

6 Finally, label each part of the graph, and choose an appropriate title.

A Community of Wisconsin Hardwood Trees

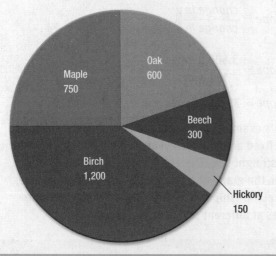

© Houghton Mifflin Harcourt Publishing Company

Math Refresher

Line Graphs

Line graphs are most often used to demonstrate continuous change. For example, Mr. Smith's students analyzed the population records for their hometown, Appleton, between 1910 and 2010. Examine the data at right.

Because the year and the population change, they are the variables. The population is determined by, or dependent on, the year. Therefore, the population is called the **dependent variable,** and the year is called the **independent variable**. Each year and its population make a **data pair**. To prepare a line graph, you must first organize data pairs into a table like the one at right.

Population of Appleton, 1910–2010	
Year	**Population**
1910	1,800
1930	2,500
1950	3,200
1970	3,900
1990	4,600
2010	5,300

How to Make a Line Graph

1 Place the independent variable along the horizontal (x) axis. Place the dependent variable along the vertical (y) axis.

2 Label the x-axis "Year" and the y-axis "Population." Look at your greatest and least values for the population. For the y-axis, determine a scale that will provide enough space to show these values. You must use the same scale for the entire length of the axis. Next, find an appropriate scale for the x-axis.

3 Choose reasonable starting points for each axis.

4 Plot the data pairs as accurately as possible.

5 Choose a title that accurately represents the data.

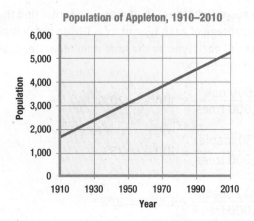
Population of Appleton, 1910–2010

How to Determine Slope

Slope is the ratio of the change in the y-value to the change in the x-value, or "rise over run."

1 Choose two points on the line graph. For example, the population of Appleton in 2010 was 5,300 people. Therefore, you can define point A as (2010, 5,300). In 1910, the population was 1,800 people. You can define point B as (1910, 1,800).

2 Find the change in the y-value.
(y at point A) − (y at point B) =
5,300 people − 1,800 people =
3,500 people

3 Find the change in the x-value.
(x at point A) − (x at point B) =
2010 − 1910 = 100 years

4 Calculate the slope of the graph by dividing the change in y by the change in x.

$$slope = \frac{change\ in\ y}{change\ in\ x}$$

$$slope = \frac{3,500\ people}{100\ years}$$

$$slope = 35\ people\ per\ year$$

In this example, the population in Appleton increased by a fixed amount each year. The graph of these data is a straight line. Therefore, the relationship is **linear**. When the graph of a set of data is not a straight line, the relationship is **nonlinear**. As a result, the slope varies at different points on the graph.

Bar Graphs

Bar graphs can be used to demonstrate change that is not continuous. These graphs can be used to indicate trends when the data cover a long period of time. A meteorologist gathered the precipitation data shown here for Summerville for April 1–15 and used a bar graph to represent the data.

Precipitation in Summerville, April 1–15			
Date	Precipitation (cm)	Date	Precipitation (cm)
April 1	0.5	April 9	0.25
April 2	1.25	April 10	0.0
April 3	0.0	April 11	1.0
April 4	0.0	April 12	0.0
April 5	0.0	April 13	0.25
April 6	0.0	April 14	0.0
April 7	0.0	April 15	6.50
April 8	1.75		

How to Make a Bar Graph

1 Use an appropriate scale and a reasonable starting point for each axis.

2 Label the axes, and plot the data.

3 Choose a title that accurately represents the data.

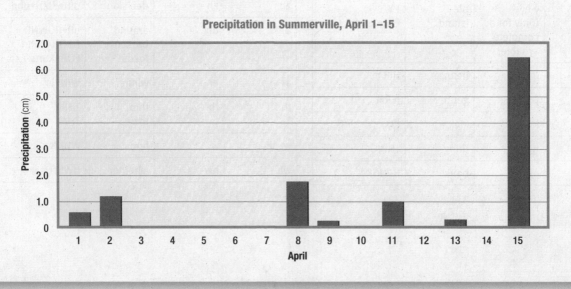

Glossary

Pronunciation Key							
Sound	**Symbol**	**Example**	**Respelling**	**Sound**	**Symbol**	**Example**	**Respelling**
ă	a	pat	PAT	ŏ	ah	bottle	BAHT'l
ā	ay	pay	PAY	ō	oh	toe	TOH
âr	air	care	KAIR	ô	aw	caught	KAWT
ä	ah	father	FAH•ther	ôr	ohr	roar	ROHR
är	ar	argue	AR•gyoo	oi	oy	noisy	NOYZ•ee
ch	ch	chase	CHAYS	o͝o	u	book	BUK
ĕ	e	pet	PET	o͞o	oo	boot	BOOT
ĕ (at end of a syllable)	eh	settee lessee	seh•TEE leh•SEE	ou	ow	pound	POWND
ĕr	ehr	merry	MEHR•ee	s	s	center	SEN•ter
ē	ee	beach	BEECH	sh	sh	cache	CASH
g	g	gas	GAS	ŭ	uh	flood	FLUHD
ĭ	i	pit	PIT	ûr	er	bird	BERD
ĭ (at end of a syllable)	ih	guitar	gih•TAR	z	z	xylophone	ZY•luh•fohn
ī	y eye (only for a complete syllable)	pie island	PY EYE•luhnd	z	z	bags	BAGZ
				zh	zh	decision	dih•SIZH•uhn
				ə	uh	around broken focus	uh•ROWND BROH•kuhn FOH•kuhs
îr	ir	hear	HIR	ər	er	winner	WIN•er
j	j	germ	JERM	th	th	thin they	THIN THAY
k	k	kick	KIK				
ng	ng	thing	THING	w	w	one	WUHN
ngk	ngk	bank	BANGK	wh	hw	whether	HWETH•er

abiotic factor (ay·by·AHT·ik FAK·ter) an environmental factor that is not associated with the activities of living organisms (382)
factor abiótico un factor ambiental que no está asociado con las actividades de los seres vivos

abrasion (uh·BRAY·zhuhn) the process by which rock is reduced in size by the scraping action of other rocks driven by water, wind, and gravity (117)
abrasión proceso por el cual se reduce el tamaño de las rocas debido al efecto de desgaste de otras rocas arrastradas por el agua, el viento o la gravedad

acid precipitation (AS·id prih·sip·ih·TAY·shuhn) rain, sleet, or snow that contains a high concentration of acids (118, 519)
precipitación ácida lluvia, aguanieve o nieve que contiene una alta concentración de ácidos

adhesion (ad·HEE·zhuhn) the attractive force between two bodies of different substances that are in contact with each other (340)
adhesión la fuerza de atracción entre dos cuerpos de diferentes sustancias que están en contacto

air mass (AIR MAS) a large body of air throughout which temperature and moisture content are similar (252)
masa de aire un gran volumen de aire, cuya temperatura y cuyo contenido de humedad son similares en toda su extensión

air pollution (AIR puh·LOO·shuhn) the contamination of the atmosphere by the introduction of pollutants from human and natural sources (517)
contaminación del aire la contaminación de la atmósfera debido a la introducción de contaminantes provenientes de fuentes humanas y naturales

air pressure (AIR PRESH·er) the measure of the force with which air molecules push on a surface (175, 228)
presión del aire la medida de la fuerza con la que las moléculas del aire empujan contra una superficie

air quality (AIR KWAHL·ih·tee) a measure of the pollutants in the air that is used to express how clean or polluted the air is (520)
calidad de aire una medida de los contaminantes presentes en el aire que se usa para expresar el nivel de pureza o contaminación del aire

alluvial fan (uh·LOO·vee·uhl FAN) a fan-shaped mass of material deposited by a stream when the slope of the land decreases sharply (127)
abanico aluvial masa en forma de abanico de materiales depositados por un arroyo cuando la pendiente del terreno disminuye bruscamente

aphelion (uh·FEE·lee·uhn) in the orbit of a planet or other body in the solar system, the point that is farthest from the sun (611)
afelio en la órbita de un planeta u otros cuerpos en el sistema solar, el punto que está más lejos del Sol

aquifer (AH·kwuh·fer) a body of rock or sediment that stores groundwater and allows the flow of groundwater (366)
acuífero un cuerpo rocoso o sedimento que almacena agua subterránea y permite que fluya

artificial satellite (ar·tuh·FISH·uhl SAT·l·yt) any human-made object placed in orbit around a body in space (710)
satélite artificial cualquier objeto hecho por los seres humanos y colocado en órbita alrededor de un cuerpo en el espacio

asteroid (AS·tuh·royd) a small, rocky object that orbits the sun; most asteroids are located in a band between the orbits of Mars and Jupiter (670)
asteroide un objeto pequeño y rocoso que se encuentra en órbita alrededor del Sol; la mayoría de los asteroides se ubican en una banda entre las órbitas de Marte y Júpiter

astronomical unit (as·truh·NAHM·ih·kuhl YOO·nit) the average distance between Earth and the sun; approximately 150 million kilometers (symbol, AU) (636)
unidad astronómica la distancia promedio entre la Tierra y el Sol; aproximadamente 150 millones de kilómetros (símbolo: UA)

atmosphere (AT·muh·sfir) a mixture of gases that surrounds a planet or moon (104, 174, 408)
atmósfera una mezcla de gases que rodea un planeta o una luna

atom (AT·uhm) the smallest unit of an element that maintains the properties of that element (58)
átomo la unidad más pequeña de un elemento que conserva las propiedades de ese elemento

atomic number (uh·TAHM·ik NUM·ber) the number of protons in the nucleus of an atom; the atomic number is the same for all atoms of an element (60)
número atómico el número de protones en el núcleo de un átomo; el número atómico es el mismo para todos los átomos de un elemento

barrier island (BAIR·ee·er EYE·luhnd) a long ridge of sand or narrow island that lies parallel to the shore (132)
isla barrera un largo arrecife de arena o una isla angosta ubicada paralela a la costa

beach (BEECH) an area of the shoreline that is made up of deposited sediment (132)
playa un área de la costa que está formada por sedimento depositado

binary fission (BY·nuh·ree FISH·uhn) a form of asexual reproduction in single-celled organisms by which one cell divides into two cells of the same size (443)
fisión binaria una forma de reproducción asexual de los organismos unicelulares, por medio de la cual la célula se divide en dos células del mismo tamaño

biomass (BY·oh·mas) plant material, manure, or any other organic matter that is used as an energy source (456)
biomasa materia vegetal, estiércol o cualquier otra materia orgánica que se usa como fuente de energía

biosphere (BY·uh·sfir) the part of Earth where life exists; includes all of the living organisms on Earth (105)
biosfera la parte de la Tierra donde existe la vida; comprende todos los seres vivos de la Tierra

centripetal force (sen·TRIP·ih·tl FOHRS) the inward force required to keep a particle or an object moving in a circular path (614)
fuerza centrípeta la fuerza hacia adentro que se requiere para mantener en movimiento una partícula o un objeto en un camino circular

channel (CHAN·uhl) the path that a stream follows (364)
canal el camino que sigue un arroyo

chemical bond (KEM·ih·kuhl BAHND) an interaction that holds atoms or ions together (68)
enlace químico una interacción que mantiene unidos los átomos o los iones

chemical equation (KEM·ih·kuhl ih·KWAY·zhuhn) a representation of a chemical reaction that uses symbols to show the relationship between the reactants and the products (79)
ecuación química una representación de una reacción química que usa símbolos para mostrar la relación entre los reactivos y los productos

chemical formula (KEM·ih·kuhl FOHR·myuh·luh) a combination of chemical symbols and numbers to represent a substance (79)
fórmula química una combinación de símbolos químicos y números que se usan para representar una sustancia

chemical reaction (KEM·ih·kuhl re·AK·shuhn) the process in which atoms are rearranged and chemical bonds are broken and formed to produce a chemical change of a substance (78)
reacción química el proceso por el cual los átomos cambian su disposición y se rompen y forman enlaces químicos de manera que se produce un cambio químico en una sustancia

chemical symbol (KEM·ih·kuhl SIM·buhl) a one-, two-, or three-letter abbreviation of the name of an element (61)
símbolo químico una abreviatura de una, dos o tres letras del nombre de un elemento

chemical weathering (KEM·ih·kuhl WETH·er·ing) the chemical breakdown and decomposition of rocks by natural processes in the environment (118)
desgaste químico la descomposición química que sufren las rocas por procesos naturales del entorno

cirrus cloud (SIR·uhs KLOWD) a feathery cloud that is composed of ice crystals and that has the highest altitude of any cloud in the sky (237)
nube cirro una nube liviana formada por cristales de hielo, la cual tiene la mayor altitud de todas las nubes en el cielo

climate (KLY·mit) the average weather conditions in an area over a long period of time (294)
clima las condiciones promedio del tiempo en un área durante un largo período de tiempo

cloud (KLOWD) a collection of small water droplets or ice crystals suspended in the air, which forms when the air is cooled and condensation occurs (234)
nube un conjunto de pequeñas gotitas de agua o cristales de hielo suspendidos en el aire, que se forma cuando el aire se enfría y ocurre condensación

cohesion (koh·HEE·zhuhn) the force that holds molecules of a single material together (340)
cohesión la fuerza que mantiene unidas a las moléculas de un solo material

comet (KAHM·it) a small body of ice, rock, and cosmic dust that follows an elliptical orbit around the sun and that gives off gas and dust in the form of a tail as it passes close to the sun (668)
cometa un cuerpo pequeño formado por hielo, roca y polvo cósmico que sigue una órbita elíptica alrededor del Sol y que libera gas y polvo, los cuales forman una cola al pasar cerca del Sol

conduction (kuhn·DUHK·shuhn) the transfer of energy as heat through a material (192)
conducción la transferencia de energía en forma de calor a través de un material

conservation (kahn·ser·VAY·shuhn) the wise use of and preservation of natural resources (468, 528)
conservación el uso inteligente y la preservación de los recursos naturales

convection (kuhn·VEK·shuhn) the movement of matter due to differences in density; the transfer of energy due to the movement of matter (190)
convección el movimiento de la materia debido a diferencias en la densidad; la transferencia de energía debido al movimiento de la materia

convection current (kuhn·VEK·shuhn KER·uhnt) any movement of matter that results from differences in density; may be vertical, circular, or cyclical (351)
corriente de convección cualquier movimiento de la materia que se produce como resultado de diferencias en la densidad; puede ser vertical, circular o cíclico

Coriolis effect (kohr·ee·OH·lis ih·FEKT) the curving of the path of a moving object from an otherwise straight path due to Earth's rotation (203, 347)
efecto de Coriolis la desviación de la trayectoria recta que experimentan los objetos en movimiento debido a la rotación de la Tierra

covalent bond (koh·VAY·luhnt BAHND) a bond formed when atoms share one or more pairs of electrons (70)
enlace covalente un enlace formado cuando los átomos comparten uno o más pares de electrones

creep (KREEP) the slow downhill movement of weathered rock material (146)
　arrastre el movimiento lento y descendente de materiales rocosos desgastados

cryosphere (KRY·oh·sfir) those portions of Earth's surface where water occurs in a solid form (103)
　criosfera partes de la superficie de la Tierra donde el agua se encuentra en estado sólido

cumulus cloud (KYOOM·yuh·luhs KLOWD) a low-level, billowy cloud that commonly has a top that resembles cotton balls and a dark bottom (237)
　nube cúmulo una nube esponjada ubicada en un nivel bajo, cuya parte superior normalmente parece una bola de algodón y es obscura en la parte inferior

data (DAY·tuh) information gathered by observation or experimentation that can be used in calculating or reasoning (23)
　datos la información recopilada por medio de la observación o experimentación que puede usarse para hacer cálculos o razonar

day (DAY) the time required for Earth to rotate once on its axis (552)
　día el tiempo que se requiere para que la Tierra rote una vez sobre su eje

deep current (DEEP KER·uhnt) a streamlike movement of ocean water far below the surface (350)
　corriente profunda un movimiento del agua del océano que es similar a una corriente y ocurre debajo de la superficie

deforestation (dee·fohr·ih·STAY·shuhn) the removal of trees and other vegetation from an area (511)
　deforestación la remoción de árboles y demás vegetación de un área

delta (DEL·tuh) a mass of material deposited in a triangular or fan shape at the mouth of a river or stream (127)
　delta un depósito de materiales en forma de triángulo o abanico ubicado en la desembocadura de un río

dependent variable (dih·PEN·duhnt VAIR·ee·uh·buhl) in a scientific investigation, the factor that changes as a result of manipulation of one or more independent variables (23)
　variable dependiente en una investigación científica, el factor que cambia como resultado de la manipulación de una o más variables independientes

deposition (dep·uh·ZISH·uhn) the process in which material is laid down (124)
　sublimación inversa el proceso por medio del cual un material se deposita

desertification (dih·zer·tuh·fih·KAY·shuhn) the process by which human activities or climatic changes make arid or semiarid areas more desertlike (511)
　desertificación el proceso por medio del cual las actividades humanas o los cambios climáticos hacen que un área árida o semiárida se vuelva más parecida a un desierto

dew point (DOO POYNT) at constant pressure and water vapor content, the temperature at which the rate of condensation equals the rate of evaporation (225, 235)
　punto de rocío a presión y contenido de vapor de agua constantes, la temperatura a la que la tasa de condensación es igual a la tasa de evaporación

divide (dih·VYD) the boundary between drainage areas that have streams that flow in opposite directions (365)
　división el límite entre áreas de drenaje que tienen corrientes que fluyen en direcciones opuestas

dune (DOON) a mound of wind-deposited sand that moves as a result of the action of wind (141)
　duna un montículo de arena depositada por el viento que se mueve como resultado de la acción de éste

dwarf planet (DWOHRF PLAN·it) a celestial body that orbits the sun, is round because of its own gravity, but has not cleared its orbital path (665)
　planeta enano un cuerpo celeste que orbita alrededor del Sol, es redondo debido a su propia fuerza de gravedad, pero no ha despejado los alrededores de su trayectoria orbital

Earth system (ERTH SIS·tuhm) all of the nonliving things, living things, and processes that make up the planet Earth, including the solid Earth, the hydrosphere, the atmosphere, and the biosphere (100)
　sistema terrestre todos los seres vivos y no vivos y los procesos que componen el planeta Tierra, incluidas la Tierra sólida, la hidrosfera, la atmósfera y la biosfera

eclipse (ih·KLIPS) an event in which the shadow of one celestial body falls on another (568)
　eclipse un suceso en el que la sombra de un cuerpo celeste cubre otro cuerpo celeste

electromagnetic spectrum (ee·lek·troh·mag·NET·ik SPEK·truhm) all of the frequencies or wavelengths of electromagnetic radiation (690)
　espectro electromagnético todas las frecuencias o longitudes de onda de la radiación electromagnética

electron (ee·LEK·trahn) a subatomic particle that has a negative charge (58)
　electrón una partícula subatómica que tiene carga negativa

element (EL·uh·muhnt) a substance that cannot be separated or broken down into simpler substances by chemical means (60)
　elemento una sustancia que no se puede separar o descomponer en sustancias más simples por medio de métodos químicos

elevation (el·uh·VAY·shuhn) the height of an object above sea level (298)
　elevación la altura de un objeto sobre el nivel del mar

empirical evidence (em·PIR·ih·kuhl EV·ih·duhns) the observations, measurements, and other types of data that people gather and test to support and evaluate scientific explanations (10)
evidencia empírica las observaciones, mediciones y demás tipos de datos que se recopilan y examinan para apoyar y evaluar explicaciones científicas

endothermic reaction (en·doh·THER·mik ree·AK·shuhn) a chemical reaction that requires energy input, usually as heat (82)
reacción endotérmica una reacción química que requiere la entrada de energía, generalmente en forma de calor

energy (EN·er·jee) the capacity to do work (426)
energía la capacidad de realizar un trabajo

energy budget (EN·er·jee BUHJ·it) the net flow of energy into and out of a system (108)
balance energético el flujo neto de energía que entra y sale de un sistema

energy resource (EN·er·jee REE·sohrs) a natural resource that humans use to generate energy (418, 431, 438, 450)
recurso energético un recurso natural que utilizan los humanos para generar energía

energy transformation (EN·er·jee trans·fohr·MAY·shuhn) the process of energy changing from one form into another (428)
transformación de energía el proceso de cambio de un tipo de energía a otro

equinox (EE·kwuh·nahks) the moment when the sun appears to cross the celestial equator (556)
equinoccio el momento en que el Sol parece cruzar el ecuador celeste

erosion (ee·ROH·zhuhn) the process by which wind, water, ice, or gravity transports soil and sediment from one location to another (124)
erosión el proceso por medio del cual el viento, el agua, el hielo o la gravedad transporta tierra y sedimentos de un lugar a otro

estuary (ES·choo·ehr·ee) an area where fresh water from rivers mixes with salt water from the ocean; the part of a river where the tides meet the river current (380)
estuario un área donde el agua dulce de los ríos se mezcla con el agua salada del océano; la parte de un río donde las mareas se encuentran con la corriente del río

eutrophication (yoo·trohf·ih·KAY·shuhn) an increase in the amount of nutrients, such as nitrates, in a marine or aquatic ecosystem (492)
eutrofización un aumento en la cantidad de nutrientes, tales como nitratos, en un ecosistema marino o acuático

exothermic reaction (ek·soh·THER·mik ree·AK·shuhn) a chemical reaction in which energy is released to the surroundings, usually as heat (82)
reacción exotérmica una reacción química en la que se libera energía en el ambiente, generalmente en forma de calor

experiment (ek·SPEHR·uh·muhnt) an organized procedure to study something under controlled conditions (20)
experimento un procedimiento organizado que se lleva a cabo bajo condiciones controladas para estudiar algo

floodplain (FLUHD·playn) an area along a river that forms from sediments deposited when the river overflows its banks (127)
llanura de inundación un área a lo largo de un río formada por sedimentos que se depositan cuando el río se desborda

fog (FAWG) water vapor that has condensed very near the surface of Earth because air close to the ground has cooled (240)
niebla vapor de agua que se ha condensado muy cerca de la superficie de la Tierra debido al enfriamiento del aire próximo al suelo

fossil fuel (FAHS·uhl FYOO·uhl) a nonrenewable energy resource formed from the remains of organisms that lived long ago; examples include oil, coal, and natural gas (415, 438)
combustible fósil un recurso energético no renovable formado a partir de los restos de organismos que vivieron hace mucho tiempo; algunos ejemplos incluyen el petróleo, el carbón y el gas natural

front (FRUHNT) the boundary between air masses of different densities and usually different temperatures (252)
frente el límite entre masas de aire de diferentes densidades y, normalmente, diferentes temperaturas

G

gas giant (GAS JY·uhnt) a planet that has a deep, massive atmosphere, such as Jupiter, Saturn, Uranus, or Neptune (652)
gigante gaseoso un planeta con una atmósfera masiva y profunda, como por ejemplo, Júpiter, Saturno, Urano o Neptuno

geocentric (jee·oh·SEN·trik) describes something that uses Earth as the reference point (598)
geocéntrico término que describe algo que usa a la Tierra como punto de referencia

geosphere (JEE·oh·sfir) the mostly solid, rocky part of Earth; extends from the center of the core to the surface of the crust (101)
geosfera la capa de la Tierra que es principalmente sólida y rocosa; se extiende desde el centro del núcleo hasta la superficie de la corteza terrestre

geothermal energy (jee·oh·THER·muhl EN·er·jee) the energy produced by heat within Earth (457)
energía geotérmica la energía producida por el calor del interior de la Tierra

glacial drift (GLAY·shuhl DRIFT) the rock material carried and deposited by glaciers (142)
deriva glacial el material rocoso que es transportado y depositado por los glaciares

glacier (GLAY·sher) a large mass of ice that exists year-round and moves over land (142)
glaciar una masa grande de hielo que existe durante todo el año y se mueve sobre la tierra

global warming (GLOH·buhl WOHR·ming) a gradual increase in average global temperature (314)
calentamiento global un aumento gradual de la temperatura global promedio

global wind (GLOH·buhl WIND) the movement of air over Earth's surface in patterns that are worldwide (204)
viento global el movimiento del aire sobre la superficie terrestre según patrones globales

gravity (GRAV·ih·tee) a force of attraction between objects that is due to their masses (610)
gravedad una fuerza de atracción entre dos objetos debido a sus masas

greenhouse effect (GREEN·hows ih·FEKT) the warming of the surface and lower atmosphere of Earth that occurs when water vapor, carbon dioxide, and other gases absorb and reradiate thermal energy (178, 312, 516)
efecto invernadero el calentamiento de la superficie y de la parte más baja de la atmósfera, el cual se produce cuando el vapor de agua, el dióxido de carbono y otros gases absorben y vuelven a irradiar la energía térmica

groundwater (GROWND·waw·ter) the water that is beneath Earth's surface (128, 362)
agua subterránea el agua que está debajo de la superficie de la Tierra

H

heat (HEET) the energy transferred between objects that are at different temperatures (186)
calor la transferencia de energía entre objetos que están a temperaturas diferentes

heliocentric (hee·lee·oh·SEN·trik) sun-centered (598)
heliocéntrico centrado en el Sol

humidity (hyoo·MID·ih·tee) the amount of water vapor in the air (225)
humedad la cantidad de vapor de agua que hay en el aire

humus (HYOO·muhs) dark, organic material formed in soil from the decayed remains of plants and animals (153)
humus material orgánico obscuro que se forma en la tierra a partir de restos de plantas y animales en descomposición

hurricane (HER·ih·kayn) a severe storm that develops over tropical oceans and whose strong winds of more than 120 km/h spiral in toward the intensely low-pressure storm center (266)
huracán tormenta severa que se desarrolla sobre océanos tropicales, con vientos fuertes que soplan a más de 120 km/h y que se mueven en espiral hacia el centro de presión extremadamente baja de la tormenta

hydroelectric energy (hy·droh·ee·LEK·trik EN·er·jee) electrical energy produced by the flow of water (453)
energía hidroeléctrica energía eléctrica producida por el flujo del agua

hydrosphere (HY·druh·sfir) the portion of Earth that is water (102)
hidrosfera la porción de la Tierra que es agua

hypothesis (hy·PAHTH·ih·sis) a testable idea or explanation that leads to scientific investigation (22)
hipótesis una idea o explicación que conlleva a la investigación científica y que se puede probar

I

ice age (EYES AYJ) a long period of climatic cooling during which the continents are glaciated repeatedly (311)
edad de hielo un largo período de enfriamiento del clima, durante el cual los continentes se ven repetidamente sometidos a la glaciación

independent variable (in·dih·PEN·duhnt VAIR·ee·uh·buhl) in a scientific investigation, the factor that is deliberately manipulated (23)
variable independiente en una investigación científica, el factor que se manipula deliberadamente

ionic bond (eye·AHN·ik BAHND) the attractive force between oppositely charged ions, which form when electrons are transferred from one atom to another (70)
enlace iónico la fuerza de atracción entre iones con cargas opuestas, que se forman cuando se transfieren electrones de un átomo a otro

jet stream (JET STREEM) a narrow band of strong winds that blow in the upper troposphere (206, 257)
corriente en chorro un cinturón delgado de vientos fuertes que soplan en la parte superior de la troposfera

kinetic energy (kih·NET·ik EN·er·jee) the energy of an object that is due to the object's motion (426)
energía cinética la energía de un objeto debido al movimiento del objeto

Kuiper Belt (KY·per BELT) a region of the solar system that starts just beyond the orbit of Neptune and that contains dwarf planets and other small bodies made mostly of ice (666)
cinturón de Kuiper una región del Sistema Solar que comienza justo después de la órbita de Neptuno y que contiene planetas enanos y otros cuerpos pequeños formados principalmente de hielo

Kuiper belt object (KY·per BELT AHB·jekt) one of the hundreds or thousands of small bodies that orbit the sun in a flat belt beyond Neptune's orbit; also includes dwarf planets located in the Kuiper Belt (666)
objeto del cinturón de Kuiper uno de los cientos o miles de cuerpos pequeños que orbitan alrededor del Sol en un cinturón plano, más allá de la órbita de Neptuno; también incluye los planetas enanos ubicados en el cinturón de Kuiper

land degradation (LAND deg·ruh·DAY·shuhn) the process by which human activity and natural processes damage land to the point that it can no longer support the local ecosystem (510)
degradación del suelo el proceso por el cual la actividad humana y los procesos naturales dañan el suelo de modo que el ecosistema local no puede subsistir

lander (LAN·der) an automated, uncrewed vehicle that is designed to touch down safely on an extraterrestrial body; often carries equipment for exploration of that body (709)
módulo de aterrizaje un vehículo automatizado, no tripulado, diseñado para aterrizar sin peligro en un cuerpo extraterrestre; con frecuencia lleva equipos para explorar ese cuerpo

landslide (LAND·slyd) the sudden movement of rock and soil down a slope (147)
derrumbamiento el movimiento súbito hacia abajo de rocas y suelo por una pendiente

latitude (LAT·ih·tood) the distance north or south from the equator; expressed in degrees (296)
latitud la distancia hacia el norte o hacia el sur del ecuador; se expresa en grados

law (LAW) a descriptive statement or equation that reliably predicts events under certain conditions (8)
ley una ecuación o afirmación descriptiva que predice sucesos de manera confiable en determinadas condiciones

law of conservation of energy (LAW UHV kahn·suhr·VAY·shuhn UHV EN·er·jee) the law that states that energy cannot be created or destroyed but can be changed from one form to another (83)
ley de la conservación de la energía la ley que establece que la energía ni se crea ni se destruye, sólo se transforma de una forma a otra

law of conservation of mass (LAW UHV kahn·suhr·VAY·shuhn UHV MAS) the law that states that mass cannot be created or destroyed in ordinary chemical and physical changes (80)
ley de la conservación de la masa la ley que establece que la masa no se crea ni se destruye por cambios químicos o físicos comunes

lightning (LYT·ning) an electric discharge that takes place between two oppositely charged surfaces, such as between a cloud and the ground, between two clouds, or between two parts of the same cloud (265)
relámpago una descarga eléctrica que ocurre entre dos superficies que tienen carga opuesta, como por ejemplo, entre una nube y el suelo, entre dos nubes o entres dos partes de la misma nube

local wind (LOH·kuhl WIND) the movement of air over short distances; occurs in specific areas as a result of certain geographical features (208)
viento local el movimiento del aire a través de distancias cortas; se produce en áreas específicas como resultado de ciertas características geográficas

loess (LUHS) fine-grained sediments of quartz, feldspar, hornblende, mica, and clay deposited by the wind (141)
loess sedimentos de grano fino de cuarzo, feldespato, hornblenda, mica y arcilla depositados por el viento

lunar phases (LOO·ner FAYZ·iz) the different appearances of the moon from Earth throughout the month (566)
fases lunares la diferente apariencia que tiene la Luna cuando se ve desde la Tierra a lo largo del mes

M

material resource (muh·TIR·ee·uhl REE·sohrs) a natural resource that humans use to make objects or to consume as food and drink (416)
recurso material un recurso natural que utilizan los seres humanos para fabricar objetos o para consumir como alimento o bebida

mesosphere (MEZ·uh·sfir) the layer of the atmosphere between the stratosphere and the thermosphere and in which temperature decreases as altitude increases (176)
mesosfera la capa de la atmósfera que se encuentra entre la estratosfera y la termosfera, en la cual la temperatura disminuye al aumentar la altitud

metallic bond (mih·TAL·ik BAHND) a bond formed by the attraction between positively charged metal ions and the electrons around them (70)
enlace metálico un enlace formado por la atracción entre iones metálicos cargados positivamente y los electrones que los rodean

meteor (MEE·tee·er) a bright streak of light that results when a meteoroid burns up in Earth's atmosphere (672)
meteoro un rayo de luz brillante que se produce cuando un meteoroide se quema en la atmósfera de la Tierra

meteorite (MEE·tee·uh·ryt) a meteoroid that reaches Earth's surface without burning up completely (672)
meteorito un meteoroide que llega a la superficie de la Tierra sin quemarse por completo

meteoroid (MEE·tee·uh·royd) a relatively small, rocky body that travels through space (672)
meteoroide un cuerpo rocoso relativamente pequeño que viaja en el espacio

meteorology (mee·tee·uh·RAHL·uh·jee) the scientific study of Earth's atmosphere, especially in relation to weather and climate (278)
meteorología el estudio científico de la atmósfera de la Tierra, sobre todo en lo que se relaciona al tiempo y al clima

model (MAHD·l) a pattern, plan, representation, or description designed to show the structure or workings of an object, system, or concept (40)
modelo un diseño, plan, representación o descripción cuyo objetivo es mostrar la estructura o funcionamiento de un objeto, sistema o concepto

mudflow (MUHD·floh) the flow of a mass of mud or rock and soil mixed with a large amount of water (147)
flujo de lodo el flujo de una masa de lodo o roca y suelo mezclados con una gran cantidad de agua

N

natural resource (NACH·uh·ruhl REE·sohrs) any natural material that is used by humans, such as water, petroleum, minerals, forests, and animals (414, 466)
recurso natural cualquier material natural que es utilizado por los seres humanos, como agua, petróleo, minerales, bosques y animales

neap tide (NEEP TYD) a tide of minimum range that occurs during the first and third quarters of the moon (581)
marea muerta una marea que tiene un rango mínimo, la cual ocurre durante el primer y el tercer cuartos de la Luna

neutron (NOO·trahn) a subatomic particle that has no charge and that is located in the nucleus of an atom (58)
neutrón una partícula subatómica que no tiene carga y que está ubicada en el núcleo de un átomo

nonpoint-source pollution (nahn·POYNT SOHRS puh·LOO·shuhn) pollution that comes from many sources rather than from a single, specific site (492)
contaminación no puntual contaminación que proviene de muchas fuentes, en lugar de provenir de un solo sitio específico

nonrenewable resource (nahn·rih·NOO·uh·buhl REE·sohrs) a resource that forms at a rate that is much slower than the rate at which the resource is consumed (415, 466)
recurso no renovable un recurso que se forma a una tasa que es mucho más lenta que la tasa a la que se consume

nuclear energy (NOO·klee·er EN·er·jee) the energy released by a fission or fusion reaction; the binding energy of the atomic nucleus (438)
energía nuclear la energía liberada por una reacción de fisión o fusión; la energía de enlace del núcleo atómico

nuclear fusion (NOO·klee·er FYOO·zhuhn) the process by which nuclei of small atoms combine to form a new, more massive nucleus; the process releases energy (626)
fusión nuclear el proceso por medio del cual los núcleos de átomos pequeños se combinan y forman un núcleo nuevo con mayor masa; el proceso libera energía

O

P-Q

observation (ahb·zer·VAY·shuhn) the process of obtaining information by using the senses (21)
observación el proceso de obtener información por medio de los sentidos

ocean current (OH·shuhn KER·uhnt) a movement of ocean water that follows a regular pattern (346)
corriente oceánica un movimiento del agua del océano que sigue un patrón regular

Oort cloud (OHRT KLOWD) a spherical region that surrounds the solar system, that extends from the Kuiper Belt to almost halfway to the nearest star, and that contains billions of comets (669)
nube de Oort una región esférica que rodea al Sistema Solar, que se extiende desde el cinturón de Kuiper hasta la mitad del camino hacia la estrella más cercana y contiene miles de millones de cometas

orbit (OHR·bit) the path that a body follows as it travels around another body in space (610)
órbita la trayectoria que sigue un cuerpo al desplazarse alrededor de otro cuerpo en el espacio

orbiter (OHR·bih·ter) a spacecraft that is designed to orbit a planet, moon, or other body without landing on the body's surface (709)
orbitador una nave espacial diseñada para orbitar alrededor de un planeta, luna u otro cuerpo sin aterrizar sobre la superficie de dicho cuerpo

oxidation (ahk·sih·DAY·shuhn) a chemical reaction in which a material combines with oxygen to form new material; in geology, oxidation is a form of chemical weathering (118)
oxidación una reacción química en la que un material se combina con oxígeno para formar un material nuevo; en geología, la oxidación es una forma de desgaste químico

ozone (OH·zohn) a gas molecule that is made up of three oxygen atoms (409)
ozono una molécula de gas que está formada por tres átomos de oxígeno

ozone layer (OH·zohn LAY·er) the layer of the atmosphere at an altitude of 15 to 40 km in which ozone absorbs ultraviolet solar radiation (178)
capa de ozono la capa de la atmósfera ubicada a una altitud de 15 a 40 km, en la cual el ozono absorbe la radiación solar

parallax (PAIR·uh·laks) an apparent shift in the position of an object when viewed from different locations (598)
paralaje un cambio aparente en la posición de un objeto cuando se ve desde lugares distintos

particulate (par·TIK·yuh·lit) a tiny particle of solid that is suspended in air or water (517)
material particulado una pequeña partícula de material sólido que se encuentra suspendida en el aire o el agua

penumbra (pih·NUHM·bruh) the outer part of a shadow such as the shadow cast by Earth or the moon in which sunlight is only partially blocked (568)
penumbra la parte exterior de la sombra (como la sombra producida por la Tierra o la Luna) en la que la luz solar solamente se encuentra bloqueada parcialmente

perihelion (pehr·ih·HEE·lee·uhn) in the orbit of a planet or other body in the solar system, the point that is closest to the sun (611)
perihelio en la órbita de un planeta u otros cuerpos en el sistema solar, el punto que está más cerca del Sol

photosynthesis (foh·toh·SIN·thih·sis) the process by which plants, algae, and some bacteria use sunlight, carbon dioxide, and water to make food (404)
fotosíntesis el proceso por medio del cual las plantas, las algas y algunas bacterias utilizan la luz solar, el dióxido de carbono y el agua para producir alimento

physical weathering (FIZ·ih·kuhl WETH·er·ing) the mechanical breakdown of rocks into smaller pieces that is caused by natural processes and that does not change the chemical composition of the rock material (114)
desgaste físico el rompimiento mecánico de una roca en pedazos más pequeños que ocurre por procesos naturales y que no modifica la composición química del material rocoso

planetary ring (PLAN·ih·tehr·ee RING) a disk of matter that encircles a planet that consists of numerous particles in orbit, which range in size from dust grains up to objects tens of meters across (654)
anillo planetario un disco de materia que rodea un planeta y está compuesto por numerosas partículas en órbita que pueden ser desde motas de polvo hasta objetos de decenas de metros

planetesimal (plan·ih·TES·uh·muhl) a small body from which a planet originated in the early stages of development of the solar system (617)
planetesimal un cuerpo pequeño a partir del cual se originó un planeta en las primeras etapas de desarrollo del Sistema Solar

point-source pollution (POYNT SOHRS puh·LOO·shuhn) pollution that comes from a specific site (492)
contaminación puntual contaminación que proviene de un lugar específico

polarity (poh·LAIR·ih·tee) a property of a system in which two points have opposite characteristics, such as charges or magnetic poles (338)
  polaridad la propiedad de un sistema en la que dos puntos tienen características opuestas, tales como las cargas o polos magnéticos

potable (POH·tuh·buhl) suitable for drinking (495)
  potable que puede beberse

potential energy (puh·TEN·shuhl EN·er·jee) the energy that an object has because of the position, condition, or chemical composition of the object (426)
  energía potencial la energía que tiene un objeto debido a su posición, condición o composición química

precipitation (prih·sip·ih·TAY·shuhn) any form of water that falls to Earth's surface from the clouds (226)
  precipitación cualquier forma de agua que cae de las nubes a la superficie de la Tierra

probe (PROHB) an uncrewed vehicle that carries scientific instruments into space to collect scientific data (708)
  sonda espacial en exploración espacial, un vehículo sin tripulación que transporta instrumentos científicos al espacio para recopilar información científica

product (PRAHD·uhkt) a substance that forms in a chemical reaction (79)
  producto una sustancia que se forma en una reacción química

prominence (PRAHM·uh·nuhns) a loop of relatively cool, incandescent gas that extends above the photosphere and above the sun's edge as seen from Earth (631)
  protuberancia una espiral de gas incandescente y relativamente frío que, vista desde la Tierra, se extiende por encima de la fotosfera y la superficie del Sol

proton (PROH·tahn) a subatomic particle that has a positive charge and that is located in the nucleus of an atom; the number of protons in the nucleus is the atomic number, which determines the identity of an element (58)
  protón una partícula subatómica que tiene una carga positiva y que está ubicada en el núcleo de un átomo; el número de protones que hay en el núcleo es el número atómico, y éste determina la identidad del elemento

R

radiation (ray·dee·AY·shuhn) the transfer of energy as electromagnetic waves (188)
  radiación la transferencia de energía en forma de ondas electromagnéticas

reactant (ree·AK·tuhnt) a substance that participates in a chemical reaction (79)
  reactivo una sustancia que participa en una reacción química

relative humidity (REL·uh·tiv hyoo·MID·ih·tee) the ratio of the amount of water vapor in the air to the amount of water vapor needed to reach saturation at a given temperature (225)
  humedad relativa la proporción de la cantidad de vapor de agua que hay en el aire respecto a la cantidad de vapor de agua que se necesita para alcanzar la saturación a una temperatura dada

renewable resource (rih·NOO·uh·buhl REE·sohrs) a natural resource that can be replaced at the same rate at which the resource is consumed (415, 466)
  recurso renovable un recurso natural que puede reemplazarse a la misma tasa a la que se consume

reservoir (REZ·er·vwar) an artificial body of water that usually forms behind a dam (497)
  represa una masa artificial de agua que normalmente se forma detrás de una presa

revolution (rev·uh·LOO·shuhn) the motion of a body that travels around another body in space; one complete trip along an orbit (553)
  revolución el movimiento de un cuerpo que viaja alrededor de otro cuerpo en el espacio; un viaje completo a lo largo de una órbita

rockfall (RAHK·fawl) the rapid mass movement of rock down a steep slope or cliff (147)
  desprendimiento de rocas el movimiento rápido y masivo de rocas por una pendiente empinada o un precipicio

rotation (roh·TAY·shuhn) the spin of a body on its axis (552)
  rotación el giro de un cuerpo alrededor de su eje

rover (ROH·ver) a vehicle that is used to explore the surface of an extraterrestrial body (709)
  rover un vehículo que se usa para explorar la superficie de un cuerpo extraterrestre

S

sandbar (SAND·bar) a low ridge of sand deposited along the shore of a lake or sea (132)
  barra de arena un arrecife bajo de arena depositado a lo largo de la orilla de un lago o del mar

satellite (SAT·l·yt) a natural or artificial body that revolves around a celestial body that is greater in mass (564)
  satélite un cuerpo natural o artificial que gira alrededor de un cuerpo celeste que tiene mayor masa

season (SEE·zuhn) a division of the year that is characterized by recurring weather conditions and determined by both Earth's tilt relative to the sun and Earth's position in its orbit around the sun (556)
  estación una de las partes en que se divide el año que se caracteriza por condiciones climáticas recurrentes y que está determinada tanto por la inclinación de la Tierra con relación al Sol como por la posición que ocupa en su órbita alrededor del Sol

shoreline (SHOHR·lyn) the boundary between land and a body of water (129)
orilla el límite entre la tierra y una masa de agua

simulation (sim·yuh·LAY·shuhn) a method that is used to study and analyze the characteristics of an actual or theoretical system (41)
simulación un método que se usa para estudiar y analizar las características de un sistema teórico o real

smog (SMAHG) air pollution that forms when ozone and vehicle exhaust react with sunlight (518)
esmog contaminación del aire que se produce cuando el ozono y sustancias químicas como los gases de los escapes de los vehículos reaccionan con la luz solar

soil (SOYL) a loose mixture of rock fragments, organic material, water, and air that can support the growth of vegetation (152)
suelo una mezcla suelta de fragmentos de roca, material orgánico, agua y aire en la que puede crecer vegetación

soil horizon (SOYL huh·RY·zuhn) each layer of soil within a soil profile (155)
horizonte del suelo una de las capas en que se divide el perfil del suelo; tiene características bien definidas, es relativamente uniforme y se encuentra casi paralela a la superficie terrestre

soil profile (SOYL PROH·fyl) a vertical section of soil that shows the layers, or horizons (155)
perfil del suelo una sección vertical de suelo que muestra las capas u horizontes

solar energy (SOH·ler EN·er·jee) the energy received by Earth from the sun in the form of radiation (454)
energía solar la energía que la Tierra recibe del Sol en forma de radiación

solar flare (SOH·ler FLAIR) an explosive release of energy that comes from the sun and that is associated with magnetic disturbances on the sun's surface (631)
erupción solar una liberación explosiva de energía que proviene del Sol y que se asocia con disturbios magnéticos en la superficie solar

solar nebula (SOH·ler NEB·yuh·luh) a rotating cloud of gas and dust from which the sun and planets formed (615)
nebulosa solar una nube de gas y polvo en rotación a partir de la cual se formaron el Sol y los planetas

solar system (SOH·ler SIS·tuhm) the sun and all of the planets and other bodies that travel around it (598)
Sistema Solar el Sol y todos los planetas y otros cuerpos que se desplazan alrededor de él

solstice (SOHL·stis) the point at which the sun is as far north or as far south of the equator as possible (556)
solsticio el punto en el que el Sol está tan lejos del ecuador como es posible, ya sea hacia el norte o hacia el sur

solvent (SAHL·vuhnt) in a solution, the substance in which the solute dissolves (341)
solvente en una solución, la sustancia en la que se disuelve el soluto

space shuttle (SPAYS SHUHT·l) a reusable space vehicle that takes off like a rocket and lands like an airplane (706)
transbordador espacial un vehículo espacial reutilizable que despega como un cohete y aterriza como un avión

specific heat (spih·SIF·ik HEET) the quantity of heat required to raise a unit mass of homogeneous material 1 K or 1 °C in a specified way, given constant pressure and volume (341)
calor específico la cantidad de calor que se requiere para aumentar una unidad de masa de un material homogéneo 1 K ó 1° C de una manera especificada, dados un volumen y una presión constantes

spectrum (SPEK·truhm) a range of electromagnetic radiation that is ordered by wavelength or frequency, such as the band of colors that is produced when white light passes through a prism (690)
espectro una gama de radiación electromagnética ordenada por longitud de onda o frecuencia, como la banda de colores que se produce cuando la luz blanca pasa a través de un prisma

spring tide (SPRING TYD) a tide of increased range that occurs two times a month, at the new and full moons (580)
marea viva una marea de mayor rango que ocurre dos veces al mes, durante la luna nueva y la luna llena

station model (STAY·shuhn MAHD·l) a pattern of meteorological symbols that represents the weather at a particular observing station and that is recorded on a weather map (282)
estación modelo el modelo de símbolos meteorológicos que representan el tiempo en una estación de observación determinada y que se registra en un mapa meteorológico

stewardship (STOO·erd·ship) the careful and responsible management of a resource (468, 529)
gestión ambiental responsable el manejo cuidadoso y responsable de un recurso

storm surge (STOHRM SERJ) a local rise in sea level near the shore that is caused by strong winds from a storm, such as those from a hurricane (267)
marea de tempestad un levantamiento local del nivel del mar cerca de la costa, el cual es resultado de los fuertes vientos de una tormenta, como por ejemplo, los vientos de un huracán

stratosphere (STRAT·uh·sfir) the layer of the atmosphere that is above the troposphere and in which temperature increases as altitude increases (176)
estratosfera la capa de la atmósfera que se encuentra encima de la troposfera y en la que la temperatura aumenta al aumentar la altitud

stratus cloud (STRAT·tuhs KLOWD) a gray cloud that has a flat, uniform base and that commonly forms at very low altitudes (237)

nube estrato una nube gris que tiene una base plana y uniforme y que comúnmente se forma a altitudes muy bajas

sunspot (SUHN·spaht) a dark area of the photosphere of the sun that is cooler than the surrounding areas and that has a strong magnetic field (630)

mancha solar un área oscura en la fotosfera del Sol que es más fría que las áreas que la rodean y que tiene un campo magnético fuerte

surface current (SER·fuhs KER·uhnt) a horizontal movement of ocean water that is caused by wind and that occurs at or near the ocean's surface (301, 346)

corriente superficial un movimiento horizontal del agua del océano que es producido por el viento y que ocurre en la superficie del océano o cerca de ella

surface water (SER·fuhs WAW·ter) all the bodies of fresh water, salt water, ice, and snow that are found above the ground (362)

agua superficial todas las masas de agua dulce, agua salada, hielo y nieve que se encuentran arriba del suelo

T

temperature (TEM·per·uh·chur) a measure of how hot (or cold) something is; specifically, a measure of the average kinetic energy of the particles in an object (184)

temperatura una medida de qué tan caliente (o frío) está algo; específicamente, una medida de la energía cinética promedio de las partículas de un objeto

terrestrial planet (tuh·RES·tree·uhl PLAN·it) one of the highly dense planets nearest to the sun; Mercury, Venus, Mars, and Earth (636)

planeta terrestre uno de los planetas muy densos que se encuentran más cerca del Sol; Mercurio, Venus, Marte y la Tierra

theory (THEE·uh·ree) a system of ideas that explains many related observations and is supported by a large body of evidence acquired through scientific investigation (9)

teoría un sistema de ideas que explica muchas observaciones relacionadas y que está respaldado por una gran cantidad de pruebas obtenidas mediante la investigación científica

thermal energy (THER·muhl EN·er·jee) the kinetic energy of a substance's atoms (184)

energía térmica la energía cinética de los átomos de una sustancia

thermal expansion (THER·muhl ek·SPAN·shuhn) an increase in the size of a substance in response to an increase in the temperature of the substance (185)

expansión térmica un aumento en el tamaño de una sustancia en respuesta a un aumento en la temperatura de la sustancia

thermal pollution (THER·muhl puh·LOO·shuhn) a temperature increase in a body of water that is caused by human activity and that has a harmful effect on water quality and on the ability of that body of water to support life (492)

contaminación térmica un aumento en la temperatura de una masa de agua, producido por las actividades humanas y que tiene un efecto dañino en la calidad del agua y en la capacidad de esa masa de agua para permitir que se desarrolle la vida

thermosphere (THER·muh·sfir) the uppermost layer of the atmosphere, in which temperature increases as altitude increases (176)

termosfera la capa más alta de la atmósfera, en la cual la temperatura aumenta a medida que la altitud aumenta

thunder (THUHN·der) the sound caused by the rapid expansion of air along an electrical strike (265)

trueno el sonido producido por la expansión rápida del aire a lo largo de una descarga eléctrica

thunderstorm (THUHN·der·stohrm) a usually brief, heavy storm that consists of rain, strong winds, lightning, and thunder (264)

tormenta eléctrica una tormenta fuerte y normalmente breve que consiste en lluvia, vientos fuertes, relámpagos y truenos

tidal range (TYD·l RAYNJ) the difference in levels of ocean water at high tide and low tide (580)

rango de marea la diferencia en los niveles del agua del océano entre la marea alta y la marea baja

tide (TYD) the periodic rise and fall of the water level in the oceans and other large bodies of water (578)

marea el ascenso y descenso periódico del nivel del agua en los océanos y otras masas grandes de agua

topography (tuh·PAHG·ruh·fee) the size and shape of the land surface features of a region, including its relief (298)

topografía el tamaño y la forma de las características de una superficie de terreno, incluyendo su relieve

tornado (tohr·NAY·doh) a destructive, rotating column of air that has very high wind speeds and that may be visible as a funnel-shaped cloud (268)

tornado una columna destructiva de aire en rotación cuyos vientos se mueven a velocidades muy altas y que puede verse como una nube con forma de embudo

tributary (TRIB·yuh·tehr·ee) a stream that flows into a lake or into a larger stream (364)

afluente un arroyo que fluye a un lago o a otro arroyo más grande

troposphere (TROH·puh·sfir) the lowest layer of the atmosphere, in which temperature decreases at a constant rate as altitude increases (176)

troposfera la capa inferior de la atmósfera, en la que la temperatura disminuye a una tasa constante a medida que la altitud aumenta

ultraviolet (uhl·truh·VY·uh·lit) electromagnetic wave frequencies immediately above the visible range (409)
ultravioleta longitudes de onda electromagnéticas inmediatamente adyacentes al color violeta en el espectro visible

umbra (UHM·bruh) a shadow that blocks sunlight, such as the conical section in the shadow of the Earth or the moon (568)
umbra una sombra que bloquea la luz solar, como por ejemplo, la sección cónica en la sombra de la Tierra o la Luna

upwelling (UHP·well·ing) the movement of deep, cold, and nutrient-rich water to the surface (352)
surgencia el movimiento de las aguas profundas, frías y ricas en nutrientes hacia la superficie

urbanization (er·buh·nih·ZAY·shuhn) an increase in the proportion of a population living in urban areas rather than in rural areas (507)
urbanización un aumento de la proporción de población en las áreas urbanas en lugar de en las áreas rurales

visibility (viz·uh·BIL·ih·tee) the distance at which a given standard object can be seen and identified with the unaided eye (229)
visibilidad la distancia a la que un objeto dado es perceptible e identificable para el ojo humano

water pollution (WAW·ter puh·LOO·shuhn) contamination of water by waste matter or other material that is harmful to organisms that are exposed to the water (492)
contaminación del agua contaminación del agua con materiales de desecho u otros materiales que dañan a los organismos que están expuestos al agua

watershed (WAW·ter·shed) the area of land that is drained by a river system (365, 378)
cuenca hidrográfica el área del terreno que es drenada por un sistema de ríos

water table (WAW·ter TAY·buhl) the upper surface of underground water; the upper boundary of the zone of saturation (362)
capa freática el nivel más alto del agua subterránea; el límite superior de la zona de saturación

wavelength (WAYV·lengkth) the distance from any point on a wave to the corresponding point on the next wave (690)
longitud de onda la distancia entre cualquier punto de una onda y el punto correspondiente de la siguiente onda

weather (WETH·er) the short-term state of the atmosphere, including temperature, humidity, precipitation, wind, and visibility (224, 294)
tiempo el estado de la atmósfera a corto plazo que incluye la temperatura, la humedad, la precipitación, el viento y la visibilidad

weather forecasting (WETH·er FOHR·kast·ing) the process of predicting atmospheric conditions by collecting and analyzing atmospheric data (278)
pronóstico del tiempo el proceso de predecir las condiciones atmosféricas reuniendo y analizando datos atmosféricos

weathering (WETH·er·ing) the natural process by which atmospheric and environmental agents, such as wind, rain, and temperature changes, disintegrate and decompose rocks (114)
meteorización el proceso natural por medio del cual los agentes atmosféricos o ambientales, como el viento, la lluvia y los cambios de temperatura, desintegran y descomponen las rocas

wetland (WET·land) an area of land that is periodically underwater or whose soil contains a great deal of moisture (379)
pantano un área de tierra que está periódicamente bajo el agua o cuyo suelo contiene una gran cantidad de humedad

wind (WIND) the movement of air caused by differences in air pressure (202, 228)
viento el movimiento de aire producido por diferencias en la presión barométrica

wind energy (WIND EN·er·jee) the use of the force of moving air to drive an electric generator (452)
energía eólica el uso de la fuerza del aire en movimiento para hacer funcionar un generador eléctrico

Y-Z

year (YIR) the time required for the Earth to orbit once around the sun (553)
año el tiempo que se requiere para que la Tierra le dé la vuelta al Sol una vez

Index

Page numbers for definitions are printed in **boldface** type.
Page numbers for illustrations, maps, and charts are printed in *italics*.

H

hail, 226, *226*
hand-held technology, 715
hanging valley, 143, *143*
HAWT (horizontal-axis wind turbine), 197, *197*
hazardous weather forecast, 287
headland, **129**, *129*, 130, *130*, 131
headwater, 378
health, public, 273
heat, **186**
    specific, **341**
heat exhaustion, 273
    prevention of, 273
    symptoms of, 273
heat radiation, 178, 179, *179*, 690. *See also* infrared radiation.
heat stroke, 273
    prevention of, 273
    symptoms of, 273
Hebes Chasma, *643*
heliocentric, **598**
helium-3, **627**
hemisphere,
    Northern, 554–556, *556*
    Southern, 554–556, *556*
Herschel, Sir William, 595, *595*
high cloud, 238
high-frequency wave, 690
high-pressure system, 254–255
high tide, 579
horizon, soil, 155
horizontal-axis wind turbine (HAWT), 197, *197*
horn (landform), 143, *143*
horse latitude, 205, *205*
How-To Manual for Active Reading, A, R18–R19
Hubble Space Telescope, 702, *702*, 708
humidity, **225**
    relative, 225
humus, **153**, 155, 157
hurricane, **266**, *266*
    damage, 267, *267*
    formation, 266
    safety, 271
Hurricane Hunters, 279, *279*
hydrocarbon, 439
hydroelectric dam, 372–373, *372–373*
hydroelectric energy, **453**, *453*
hydrogen, 80, 81, *81*, 439
hydrogen fuel cell, 421, *421*
hydrogen peroxide, 80
hydrosphere, 100, **102**, *102*, 189, 314
    movement of, 107
hypothesis, **22**, 24

I

ice age, **311**
ice cap, polar, 109
ice erosion, 142–144
ice wedging, 115, *115*. *See also* frost wedging.
independent variable, **23**
industrial, 507
inexhaustible resource, 415
inference, 26
    conclusion and, 27
    prediction and, 27
infrared radiation, 178–179, *179*, 690, 692, 698, *699*
infrared ray, 690, 692, 698
    detector of, 694
input, 244
International Space Station, 687, *687*, 706, 723, 726–727
Internet, 136
Introduction to Probeware, R42–R43
invasive species, 386
Io, 653
ion, 68
ion tail (comet), 668
ionic bond, **70**, *71*
iron, 118
isobar, 283, 245
Itokawa (asteroid), 671, *671*

J

Jackson, Shirley Ann, 74, *74*
jet stream, **206**, *206*, 257, *257*
    polar, 206, *206*
    subtropical, 206, *206*
June solstice, 556, 557
Jupiter,
    moons of, 653
    size of, 652
    statistics, 652
    storms on, 653
    surface of, 653
    temperature of, 652

K

KBO (Kuiper Belt object), 664, **666**, 667, 669
kelp forest, *352*
Kepler, Johannes, 602, *602*, 611
Kepler's laws of planetary motion, 602, 611
    first law, *602*, 611, *611*
    second law, 612, *612*
    third law, 612, *612*
kettle lake, 144, *144*
kinetic energy, 9, 184, *184*, 192, 418, **426**

Kuiper Belt, 664, **666**, 667, 669
Kuiper Belt object (KBO), 664, **666**, 667, 669
Kyoto Protocol, 317, 537

L

laboratory work, 10–11, 20
lahar, 147
Lake Missoula, 145
land, 506
    degradation, 510–511
    importance of, 506
    preservation, 532
    reclamation, 533
    reforestation, 533
    soil and, 508
    soil conservation, 533
    types of land use, 507
    urban sprawl and, 534
land breeze, 208, *208*
land degradation, **510–511**
lander, **709**, 730
landform, 125
    formation of, 126–127, 130, *130*, 144
land resource,
    preservation of, 532, 534
    reforestation, 533
landslide, 147, *147*
Language Arts Connection, 16, 74, 702
La Niña, 310
latitude, **296**
    horse, 205, *205*
law, 8
law of conservation of energy, **83**, 428
law of conservation of mass, **80**
law of universal gravitation, 613
leaching, 155
Leonov, Alexei A., 724
Lesson Review, 15, 33, 45, 65, 73, 87, 111, 121, 135, 149, 161, 181, 195, 211, 231, 243, 261, 275, 289, 305, 321, 343, 357, 371, 391, 411, 423, 435, 447, 459, 475, 501, 513, 525, 539, 559, 571, 585, 605, 621, 633, 647, 661, 675, 701, 717, 733
lichen, 119
life cycle analysis, 460–461
light, visible, 690
lightning, 265, *265*
    safety, 271
lignite, 441
line graph, 37
living system, **100**, 106, 108–109